THE *A. S. W. ROSENBACH FELLOWSHIP*
IN BIBLIOGRAPHY

THE VOICE OF THE OLD FRONTIER

The Voice of the Old Frontier

By

R. W. G. VAIL

Director

THE NEW-YORK HISTORICAL SOCIETY
Rosenbach Fellow in Bibliography

NEW YORK: THOMAS YOSELOFF, INC.

To
Marie, Betty and Bob
Whose Ancestors Lived on the Old Frontier

In 1930 Dr. A. S. W. Rosenbach founded at the University of Pennsylvania a Fellowship in Bibliography. R. W. G. Vail, Director of The New-York Historical Society, former Editor of *Sabin's Dictionary* and President of the Bibliographical Society of America, was the holder of the Fellowship in 1945-46. The present volume contains the three lectures which he delivered at the University in the fall of 1945, supplemented by a bibliographical appendix.

Acknowledgment

BIBLIOGRAPHERS are the jackdaws of scholarship, for they build into their nests the colorful feathers of other birds of more brilliant plumage. But, having completed their nests, they fly away and leave other scholarly birds, who have no taste for bibliographical nest-building, to occupy them and bring forth their broods of historical treatises in the comfortable quarters supplied by the nest-builders.

Credit to other students has been given throughout this bibliography, but I should like to give grateful thanks to a few of the friends who have helped and encouraged me in this undertaking. First, however, I should be remiss if I did not mention some of those who are no longer here to read this acknowledgment of the help they have given through their letters, notes, and published works. They include: G. M. Asher, George Brinley, George Watson Cole, Frank C. Deering, Henry F. De Puy, Wilberforce Eames (above all others), Charles Evans, Charles R. Hildeburn, Leonard L. Mackall and his assistant Azalea Clizbee, Douglas C. McMurtrie, J. T. Medina, Joseph Sabin, Julius F. Sachse, I. N. Phelps Stokes, Peter G. Thomson, and James H. Trumbull.

And to my contemporaries, bibliographers, collectors, and booksellers, I owe a debt of gratitude for information cheerfully supplied and for encouragement in my endeavors. They include Dr. A. S. W. Rosenbach, Randolph G. Adams, John Alden, James T. Babb, Elizabeth Baer, A. C. Bates, Leslie E. Bliss, Julian P. Boyd, Clarence S. Brigham, Ruth Lapham Butler, E. M. Dahlberg, Charles W. David, Charles and Lindley Eberstadt, Joseph Gavit, Frederick R. Goff, Everett D. Graff, Lathrop C. Harper, Thomas J. Holmes, William A. Jackson, Edna L. Jacobsen, Victor Hugo Paltsits, Dorothy Porter, John H. Powell, George A. Schwegmann, Jr., Clifford K. Shipton, Frank T. Siebert, Lewis M. Stark, Thomas W. Streeter, Roland Tree, Henry R. Wagner, Michael J. Walsh, Edna W. Watkins, Oscar Wegelin, George Parker Winship, and Lawrence C. Wroth (last in the alphabet but first in helpfulness).

To the following libraries and their staffs I am also particularly grateful: American Antiquarian Society, Boston Public Library, William L. Clements Library, Connecticut Historical Society, Free Library of Philadelphia, Harvard College Library, Henry E. Huntington Library, Historical Society of Pennsylvania, John Carter Brown Library, Library of Congress (and the Union Catalog), Massachusetts Historical Society, New-York Historical Society, New York Public Library, New York State Library, Newberry Library, Princeton University Library, University of Georgia Library (De Renne Georgia Collection), University of Pennsylvania, University of Virginia, and Yale University Library

Contents

CHAPTER | PAGE

ACKNOWLEDGMENT | vii

INTRODUCTION | xi

1. THE PIONEER'S OWN STORY | 1

2. THE INDIANS' CAPTIVES RELATE THEIR ADVENTURES | 23

3. THE FRONTIER LAND AGENTS OFFER THEIR WARES | 62

CONCLUSION | 80

A BIBLIOGRAPHY OF NORTH AMERICAN FRONTIER LITERATURE | 84

KEY TO LOCATIONS | 84

BIBLIOGRAPHY | 90

INDEX TO THE APPENDIX | 467

Introduction

THE American frontier has always had a fascinating appeal for the historical student, not only because of its wealth of exciting and romantic episode but chiefly because our national character, our distinctive American qualities, were largely developed there. It is to the spirit of the pioneers that we owe our traits of courage, resourcefulness, democratic coöperation, our inquisitiveness and inventive genius, our tolerant humor, our ambition and restless drive, our adaptability, self-reliance, honesty, and fierce love of democracy and personal independence. These traits are, it is true, found on the sea and in our cities, but the frontiersmen came before the merchants or the merchantmen, most of whom, in our early days, were recruited from the back country—from the frontier. If, then, we are to understand the qualities which have made us a great nation, we must know the people and the literature of our frontier.

In planning the approach to this subject there seemed to be two choices, either to give intensive cultivation to a small patch of ground, as Dr. Wroth did so perfectly in the third series of these lectures when he wrote *An American Bookshelf 1755*, or to reap a broader field which seemed to need harvesting but would leave no time for scholarly interpretation. The second alternative was chosen since it seemed to supply a need and since there was not available, except in many scattered sources, a bibliography of the literature of the old frontier. Since it was obviously impossible to include all of our vast frontier literature in a single volume, an attempt was made to include some of the more important or more elusive titles from the beginning of settlement in this country to the year 1800.

The bibliography appended to these lectures will, then, attempt to record a selection of the works written by those living on the frontier of what is now the United States or by agents interested in the promotion of frontier lands, the first editions of which appeared not later than 1800. It will omit voyages and travels by non-residents, military, political, and religious controversial literature which does not also contain accounts of frontier life or which was not closely concerned with the promotion of the sale and settlement of frontier lands. The bibliography omits the Jesuit Relations, Indian treaties, and material on the Spanish Southwest, for which adequate bibliographies already exist. By also omitting Canada and Spanish America it is hoped that our subject may be brought within the covers of a single volume.

By throwing the frontiersmen's own stories, the narratives of Indian captivity, and the promotion literature of the land speculators who opened our frontiers to settlement into a single chronology it is hoped that a broader sweep of the development of the frontier may be gained, in spite of the disadvantage of separating the various editions of the writings of a given author. The index will, however, attempt to repair this defect. Though, with two or three exceptions, books have not been included which were published after 1800, later reprints are · briefly mentioned, generally under the last edition published before that date.

Had it been feasible to visit all of the more than 150 libraries owning the books listed, it would have been possible to obtain fuller or more accurate descriptions. But the location of copies, wherever possible, will permit the student, by the use of the photostat and microfilm, to bring any given book to his desk for a more careful study than could be attempted here. Actual books have been examined whenever possible, facsimiles of titles have been copied when available, and bibliographies have been checked against one another, supplemented by correspondence when necessary, to secure a reasonable amount of accuracy. Later reprints of common books published up to 1800 have been given the briefest of descriptions, but great pains have been taken with little-known rarities, and it is hoped that not a little information has been recorded for the first time. Modern reprints are generally not mentioned since they are almost invariably recorded in Sabin and the other bibliographies cited as authorities.

In one of the old dictionaries the cow was defined as "an animal well known" and so it is with the bibliographies cited in our notes. They too are well known to every librarian and mature student of American history, and copies of them are available in all of our larger American history collections. It has therefore seemed unnecessary to include a bibliography of the reference tools used in our compilation, with which all students in this field are already familiar. I am greatly indebted to Miss Elizabeth Baer's *Seventeenth Century Maryland, a Bibliography*, Baltimore, The John Work Garrett Library, 1949. xxix, 219 p., facsimiles of all titles, 4to, which appeared while the present work was in press.

If this bibliography helps to open a new and fascinating field of study to the beginning specialist in American history, if it gives now and then a new bit of information about a rare or favorite book to the historian, if it gives aid and comfort to the Americana collector and dealer to whom we are all indebted for the gathering of our libraries, the compiler will feel amply repaid for many months of difficult but fascinating research.

1

The Pioneer's Own Story

I F YOU had been traveling up one of the small tributaries of the Watauga River in eastern Tennessee some years ago you might have discovered a venerable beech tree with an ancient inscription carved on it with a hunting knife. As you gaze at it, in imagination you see the whole pageant of our westward-moving pioneer civilization spread out before you, for here in one sentence the voice of the old frontier speaks to you in the words of its greatest son:

"D Boon cilled A BAR on this tree 1760."

Perhaps you light your pipe and sit down with your back to the famous tree. You hear the song of Boone's Creek as it hurries down to join the Watauga, you look out between the tall pines, the rhododendrons, and mountain laurels, and see beyond a vista of the wild and beautiful Blue Ridge Mountains meandering off to the southwest, and you picture the Kentucky blue grass and the valleys of Tennessee just the other side of the highest peaks. This is the land of Boone and Kenton, of Robertson and Sevier, a land of bold adventure, the home of the pioneer.

And as the fragrant smoke curls up from your pipe, your eyes close in retrospect, you see the lean and sturdy Scotch-Irish settlers, driven west from the tidewater by the encroachments of the great plantations, as they make their laborious way on foot, on horseback, or in ox-drawn cart from their old homes in Maryland, North Carolina, or Virginia to the new homes they hope to carve out of the wilderness. You see them toil through the Cumberland Gap or over Braddock's Road all the way to the forks of the Ohio—the Beautiful River. Along the way they are joined by other streams

1

of pioneers coming down the great valleys from Pennsylvania—heavy-set, slow-moving, determined Germans for the most part, Squire Boone and his family among them. And farther north you see many Yankee families, Yorkers and Pennsylvanians moving west by ox team or afoot, until they reach Fort Pitt where they load their wives, children, and dogs, their milk cows and oxen and their scant household gear on to flatboats for the slow but often dangerous journey down the Ohio to their new homes on the Great Kanawha, the Big Sandy, or near the Falls of the Ohio at Louisville.

While you watch the pioneers making their toilsome way over the muddy and rutted mountain roads, you see men of many types among them. There are powerful, wind-tanned men like Boone in their coonskin caps and leather leggings—the explorers, Indian fighters, and fur traders, pushing on ahead of the actual settlers; there are adventurous farmers, millers, blacksmiths, and gunsmiths (the men who made the Kentucky rifles). Rawboned missionaries are among them, eager to save the souls of Indians, frontiersmen, or tough river men; to marry, baptize, or bury their companions, or to preach a campmeeting sermon in an open glade under a sheltering tree. There are runaway slaves and apprentices, redemptioners and fugitives from justice striving to keep one jump ahead of their masters or the law. And there are eager-eyed young men fresh from Yale or Harvard, anxious to found new frontier settlements, to open stores and newspaper offices, sell land, heal the sick, or argue cases in the log courthouses of the county towns.

As you knock out the ashes and prepare to continue your reverie over a second pipeful, you remember that the men who crossed the Alleghenies or floated down the Beautiful River were not the first American pioneers, for pioneering really began at least as early as 1635. We Americans are a restless race, and the grass is always greener in the next field, the land more fertile over the ridge in the distant valley. And so, a few years after the Plymouth and Massachusetts Bay colonies were firmly established, it was but natural that those uneasy souls who are always impatient with established restraints should be willing to brave the frontier in order to insure their greater independence.

So, as you draw contentedly on your pipe under Boone's tree, you watch the men of Massachusetts move westward to the Connecticut Valley to found a new colony on a new frontier. During the last half of the seventeenth century you see them blazing away from the loopholes of their stockaded houses in the Connecticut Valley towns and at Brookfield, Hadley, Deerfield, and Fort Massachusetts, fighting the warriors of King Philip who kill and scalp them when they can and carry away their women and children into captivity. You watch the tide of migration spread in the 1750's into Maine, New Hampshire, and Vermont, and you remember the stories told by the returning captives after months or years among the Indians or with the French in Canada.

Your mind's eye travels through time and space and you see the thrifty Dutch establish their fur-trading posts at Fort Orange and New Amsterdam, you watch their hard-won advantage being wrested from them by the English, and the establishment of the vast manorial system of the Hudson Valley which, with the barrier of the Iroquois farther west and the backward policy of the colonial government, made pioneering difficult. You see the poor Germans from the Palatinate brought into the colony to people the Mohawk and Schoharie valleys at the turn of the eighteenth century, just as Penn had populated his domain from a similar source. Following the Revolution you are amazed at the rapid settlement of Western New York after the Iroquois have been driven from their beautiful Finger Lakes and Genesee Country. The Revolutionary soldiers, fresh from the Sullivan Expedition, return with vivid memories and tall tales of the fertile fields of the Senecas, and so, when these rolling acres are opened for settlement by the land companies in the 1790's, the old soldiers leave their stony and debt-ridden New England farms, and you watch them cross the Hudson and take their families by water up the Mohawk to the site of old Fort Stanwix, across the Wood Creek carry and so to the navigable waters of the Finger Lakes. Here they pause for a while, for the land is good, but after Wayne's defeat of the western Indians at the

Battle of Fallen Timbers in 1794, the west at last is wide open and so they and their restless children push on by ox team and covered wagon, and in later years by canal, lake boat, and train, until a great new empire is born in the northwest.

As you travel in imagination farther south, you find the early settlers of Maryland, Virginia, the Carolinas, and Georgia so preoccupied with the development of their well-watered, level plantation lands, and so hemmed in by the mountains and the Indians, that they do not begin to look with a longing eye to the rugged west much before the eighteenth century; but then you see the common folk being pushed back towards the Appalachians by the slaveholding planters, and you watch the beautiful Shenandoah Valley being settled from Pennsylvania in the first half of the century. Soon after, these Pennsylvanians come crowding into the Piedmont and the Carolina mountains, but are stopped there by the French and Indian War. By about 1759, however, Fort Duquesne and the other French forts are captured and the movement to the west continues, in spite of the royal proclamation of 1763 prohibiting encroachment on the Indian lands. And so, in retrospect, you get back to Daniel Boone and his tree and you wonder whether any of these frontiersmen, often so unlettered and inarticulate, wrote out for us the colorful record of their daily lives in cabin and stockade, of their adventures and achievements in subduing the mighty forests and the savage Indians during the 250 years of their pioneering before the end of the eighteenth century.

The literature of the United States frontier fills many thousands of volumes and so, to put a reasonable limit to our present study, certain types of material mentioned in the introduction have been omitted. This leaves us still with a collection of several hundred titles written by men whose lives touched the frontier, all of which found contemporary publishers not later than 1800. From them we can select only a few titles to suggest the possibilities of further study in this fascinating category and to whet the appetites of those of our collectors who are sensible enough to turn from the overworked fields of English and American first editions to a department of collecting in which the chase is more exciting, the quarry more rewarding and more truly American.

So we will let the pioneer tell his own story. He is generally simple and direct, sometimes boastful, forgetful, or apt to embroider his narrative in order to make a good story of it. But generally his style is plain and honest, while the tale he tells is almost always absorbing and often thrilling. When we read these pioneer narratives, we come to realize how the American qualities of bravery, self-reliance, resourcefulness, and independence were developed on the frontier. We learn why we have certain ideals of democracy, how hard our ancestors fought to win and keep them, and how necessary it is for us to uphold them in our world which, like theirs, is fraught with dangers which threaten our American way of life.

It might be argued that the American frontier began when the first colonists disembarked at Jamestown or set foot on Plymouth Rock, and if so we should certainly want to begin our frontier reading with Thomas Hariot's *Briefe and true report* of Virginia with its incomparable drawings by John White which appeared in 1590, as well as Captain John Smith's *General historie of Virginia* of 1624. We should want to dip into the first account of the exploration and attempted settlement in Maine as James Rosier reported it in his *True relation* of 1605. We might like to read of the baptism and marriage of Pocahontas as Raphe Hamor told of these interesting events in his *True discourse* in 1615, or of the founding of Plymouth in the so-called Mourt *Relation* of 1622, which was based in part on Governor William Bradford's history, otherwise destined to remain unpublished for over two hundred years.

Though most of the seventeenth-century reports of the new settlements were inspired promotion literature and so can be overlooked for the time being, we really ought to examine William Wood's *New England prospect* of 1634 to see how the new colony in Massachusetts was faring and then take up the 1790 edition of John Winthrop's *Journal* and so round out the picture of the founding of the Massachusetts Bay Colony, with Thomas Morton's *New English Canaan* of 1637 included for good measure.

Captain John Underhill's *Newes from America*, 1638, can certainly be included with good conscience since he was one of our first outstanding Indian fighters and so gives us one of our first true frontier narratives of the progress of the Pequot War, just as his friend Church did a little later with King Philip's War. Though, as a writer, Roger Williams is generally thought of as a spirited religious propagandist, he lived on the frontier and knew his local Indians well—so well that he left us some interesting observations on their customs in his *Key into the language of America*, 1643. John Winthrop, too, in his *Declaration of former passages and proceedings betwixt the English and the Narrowgansets*, gave us a brief but important glimpse of Indian affairs in the Plymouth Colony and, at the same time, one of our rarest American imprints since it was printed at Cambridge by Stephen Daye in 1645 and only four copies seem to have survived.

We should, of course, like to find an early pioneer account of New Netherlands, but Father Jogues' description of the colony in 1643 did not appear in print until over two hundred years after its writing. We do have, however, the fascinating narratives of Joannes de Laet, Adriaen van der Donck, and David Pietersz. de Vries to tell us of the founding and early settlement of Dutch New York. Ferdinand Gorgas' *America painted to the life*, 1658-59, gives an account of his unfortunate attempt at establishing a settlement in Maine in the seventeenth century and is excellent pioneer history. Nathaniel Morton's *New England's memorial*, one of the first secular publications of the Cambridge press, in 1669, certainly did report frontier conditions, though its author probably did not wear a coonskin cap or live in the woods.

Daniel Denton's *Brief description of New York*, London, 1670, the first account of that colony in English, is not only of great rarity in perfect condition, but gives a first-hand account of the local flora and fauna and of the Indians as well as of the little village on the tip of Manhattan Island. We do not know that its author ever lived on the frontier, but he certainly described pioneer conditions in a most interesting fashion.

Though the Mathers, William Hubbard, and many others wrote of New England's troubles with the Indians during the last half of the seventeenth century, most of them were armchair strategists and few of them ever dodged an Indian arrow. Thomas Wheeler, however, was a real frontier Indian fighter and, after his return from the relief of Brookfield in 1675, he wrote his detailed and absorbing account of the campaign in his *A thankful remembrance of God's mercy to several persons at Quobaug or Brookfield.* Cambridge, 1676. This simple but thrilling narrative tells how a body of Massachusetts troops under Major Simon Willard went to the rescue of a beleagured blockhouse on the frontier and drove off King Philip's warriors after a pitched battle. He also reports the previous adventures of the besieged settlers, and gives one of the best accounts of Indian methods of making war at that period. The story is a great rarity, and of the six known copies, two are imperfect.

We should like to mention William Penn's two brief accounts of the provinces of Pennsylvania and East Jersey, 1682, but they are really promotion tracts, and Nicholas Bayard's *A narrative of an attempt made by the French of Canada upon the Mohaques country,* New York, 1693, is the work of an armchair strategist and so, in spite of its being unique and of great interest to frontier history, we will not include it here. It is particularly unfortunate that we cannot have on our pioneer shelf Ned Ward's lively and rather naughty *Trip to New England,* 1699, because it is such a sprightly corrective of the familiar picture of long-faced piety recorded by our early ecclesiastics. When he says that "Bishops, bailiffs and bastards, were the three terrible persecutions which chiefly drove our unhappy brethren to seek their fortunes in our forreign colonies," we can better understand some of the more distressing passages in Bradford and Winthrop.

When we come to Charles Wooley's *A two years journal in New-York,* which appeared in London in 1701, we are on a little surer ground, for the author really did live here and left a most interesting account of his stay in the colony during its early years. There were two variant imprints of the first edition, and we know of six copies of one and five of the other. For those who cannot hope for a first edition there are two modern reprints. Tomas Campanius Holm's *Short description of the province of New Sweden,* printed in Swedish in 1702 and available in an English edition of 1834, gives us our best account of the pioneer settlements along the Delaware, and Thomas Nairne's *Letter from South Carolina*, 1710, with reprints in 1718 and 1732, does the same for that colony.

Cadwallader Colden's *History of the five Indian nations*, New York, 1727, and his earlier *Papers relating to the Indian trade*, New York, 1724, are certainly two of the most important titles in the entire field of early pioneer history. Though written by a colonial official who spent most of his time in New York, they record the conditions of the Indian trade of his day as no one else could have written it, for his constant official contact with the New York Indians made him the best-informed man on the subject.

Most of the early tracts on Virginia were promotion literature, but *The present state of Virginia*, London, 1724, by the Reverend Hugh Jones, minister at Jamestown, was written after he had traveled throughout that colony and also in Maryland and North Carolina, and his picture of the life of the times along the frontier is unusually interesting and important.

Samuel Penhallow's *History of the wars of New England with the Eastern Indians*, Boston, 1726, was the best summary of the bloody frontier history of that region from 1703 to 1725 and was written by one who had had an intimate contact with the events he narrates, for he had made a fortune in the Indian and frontier trade out of Portsmouth and had high office in the province. Captain John Lovewell, most inappropriately named, has always seemed a most curious sort of hero, but there is no doubt that he was so considered by his contemporaries. He was the leader of a scalp-hunting expedition which went out to kill as many Indians as possible and reap a rich reward in bounties from the Massachusetts Assembly. Unfortunately for him, he was defeated in a pitched battle and, with several of his force, killed by his intended victims. The Reverend Thomas Symmes immediately prepared a historical sermon on the event which he called *Lovewell lamented* and in which he gave a full account of the campaign. It was printed at Boston in 1725 and proved so popular that it was immediately revised with added details and reprinted as *Historical memoirs of the late fight at Piggwacket.* It was again published at Fryeburg in 1799 and at Portland in 1818, and it is doubtful if more than two or three copies of any of the editions have survived. Though the author was, of course, not in the campaign, he gathered his story from the survivors and so it has the value of a first-hand narrative.

One of the few important autobiographical accounts of New England pioneer life is the *Memoirs* of Captain Roger Clap which first appeared at Boston in 1731 and ran through six other editions. It was written shortly before his death in 1691 and tells of his part in the founding of Dorchester and the defense of Boston. He was a stern Puritan, Captain of the fort in Boston Harbor for twenty-one years, member of the Assembly and the father of fourteen children for whom he wrote out the story of his early hardships on the edge of the wilderness. He hated the divine right of kings and bishops, all Quakers and all Indians, but he loved his wife, his adopted country, and his God.

Major John Mason, like·his famous contemporary in the Plymouth Colony, Miles Standish, had seen service in the Low Countries and was a brave and resourceful professional soldier. When the powerful Pequots made war on the frontier settlements of the Connecticut Valley, Mason left his farm at Windsor and took command of the Connecticut forces and, with the help of Uncas and his Mohegans, surprised and took the Pequot fort at Mystic with great slaughter and wiped out what was left of that once powerful nation at the Great Swamp Fight at Fairfield. On being asked by the General Court of Connecticut to prepare a history of the campaign, he did so, and a copy fell into the hands of Increase Mather who, not knowing its authorship, printed it minus its four prefaces in his *Relation of the troubles which have happened in New England,* 1677. The complete original manuscript was later given by the author's grandson to the Reverend Thomas Prince, who published it at Boston in 1736 under the title: *A brief history of the Pequot War.* It is a simply written but thrilling narrative of the campaign which made the frontier settlements of Connecticut and Massachusetts safe. It is a very rare book and one of the chief ornaments of any New England collection, a splendid example of a frontier narrative written by a frontiersman.

Since William Douglass was a Boston physician rather than a frontiersman, we will merely commend his *A summary, historical and political of the first planting of the British settlements in North America,* Boston, 1749-52, to your attention and pass on to William Stith's *History of the first discovery and settlement of Virginia* which appeared at Williamsburg in 1747. Of course you will say that he too was a city man, a cultured gentleman of the cloth and president of the College of William and Mary. Still, he was close enough to the earliest Virginia frontier to picture it with accuracy, and besides he had access to the official records of the colony and so was fitted to tell the first fifteen years of its story and to leave us a clear account of the founding of Jamestown.

A real frontier clergyman who, in spite of his brief career, had a wide influence on his contemporaries was the Reverend David Brainerd. His journal, first published here in Philadelphia by Bradford in 1746 with the title: *Mirabilia Dei inter Indicos, or the rise and progress of a remarkable work of grace amongst a number of the Indians in . . . New-Jersey and Pennsylvania* was immediately popular. It was reprinted in dozens of editions, generally accompanied by Jonathan Edwards' life of the author, which was also separately published in many editions in complete or abridged form.

We cannot leave this period of Pennsylvania's frontier history without at least a passing reference to the greatest man on that frontier, Conrad Weiser, friend of Indian and frontiersman alike. Though his only writings which seem to have had separate contemporary publication were an election circular in which he urged the citizens to vote against the Quaker policy of not supporting frontier defenses (Philadelphia, 1741), and the *Translation of a German letter* (Philadelphia, 1763), his reports appear in treaties published in 1742 and 1757, and his Pennsylvania to Onondaga journal of 1737 and his Ohio journal of 1748 were published in later years and his autobiography and other journals, used liberally in Wallace's excellent life of Weiser, are still preserved.

Since the original edition and reprints of John Bartram's *Observa-*

tions in his travels from Pensilvania to Lake Ontario, London, 1751,
is familiar to historical students, we need only to remind you of its
importance as an example of frontier writing. Another important
explorer of the back country was the famous Quaker preacher
Thomas Chalkley, who settled in Philadelphia in 1700 and traveled
through most of the colonies, as we know from the *Journal* which
he published in London in 1751.

In order to keep abreast of frontier affairs in New England, we
must consult Samuel Hopkins' *Historical memoirs, relating to the
Housatunnuk Indians* which appeared in Boston in 1753 and was
of enough general interest to be reprinted in abridged form by
Franklin and Hall four years later, with a continuation from the
same press in the form of *An address to the people of New England*
issued along with it. Franklin had already reprinted Reverend
George Whitefield's American *Journals* in 1739 from their earlier
English editions, and of course the famous itinerant had a wide influence on our frontiers although he was not a permanent resident
here. However, Samuel Urlsperger, in his Salzburger colony in
Georgia was a true pioneer, and so we must include his *Nachrichten*
of 1735-52 and his *Americanisches Ackerwerk Gottes,* 1754-67, as
typical of the dozens of German narratives which originated in that
interesting colonial experiment.

One of our greatest pioneers, of course, was George Washington,
and one of the chief ornaments of our frontier library is his famous
Journal, written at the age of twenty-one when he was sent by the
Governor of Virginia to demand the withdrawal of the French from
the Ohio country. The original manuscript in the Public Record
Office is one American treasure which the British government really
ought to return to this country, but failing that we have at least
eight copies of the first Williamsburg, 1754, edition in our great
public and private collections, the distinguished author's own copy
being in the library of Dr. Rosenbach.

Samuel Blodget was a Boston merchant who, at the time of the
Battle of Lake George, was serving as a sutler attached to the
American army and so was in a fine position to write our best eye-
witness account of that important engagement. It was published at

Boston in 1755 to accompany his plan of the battle, and he entitled both the pamphlet and the map *A prospective plan of the battle near Lake George.* Timothy Clement, in the same year, also published at Boston a *Plan of the Battle of Lake George* which is even rarer than the other, if that can be possible. Most of us would be content to own the contemporary English reprint of the Blodget map and pamphlet, but that too is a rarity, so we shall have to be satisfied with its modern English facsimile. To complete the story, we should also have to have Sir William Johnson's *Letter, from the camp at Lake George,* giving the official account of the battle, and Charles Chauncy's *A second letter to a friend; giving a more particular narrative of the defeat of the French army at Lake-George,* Boston, 1755. We should then want the first *Letter to a friend; giving a concise, but just, account of the Ohio-defeat* of General Braddock, also Boston, 1755, or failing that, the *Two letters to a friend* printed together at London the same year. Provost William Smith, of this ancient institution of learning [the University of Pennsylvania], also had something to say on the subject of the Braddock defeat in his *A brief view of the conduct of Pennsylvania, for the year 1755,* published in both London and Paris the following year, which in turn was a sequel to his *A brief state of the Province of Pennsylvania,* London, 1755, in which he paid his disrespects to the Quakers for opposing the defense of the province, and for the way they were unduly influencing the German settlers. And we should also mention the extremely important Lewis Evans map and accompanying treatise of 1755, as well as Dr. John Mitchell's *The contest in America,* London, 1757, to make more complete our chronology of the works which influenced or interpreted the frontier.

Charles Thomson, who was later to be secretary of the Continental Congress, also made an important contribution to our shelf of pioneer books when he published in 1759 his *Enquiry into the causes of the alienation of the Delaware and Shawanese Indians.* This work is of particular interest to us since it prints the first journal of Christian Frederick Post, a man of long frontier experience and a friend of the Indians. He was sent by the Governor of Pennsylvania to the Indians on the Ohio to attempt to win them away from the French interest, and his *Second journal*, London, 1759, records this diplomatic mission.

One unsavory episode of Pennsylvania's frontier history was recorded by Franklin in his *A narrative of the late massacres, in Lancaster County, of a number of Indians, friends of this province, by persons unknown. With some observations on the same*, which he printed in 1764. The history of this affair of the Paxton boys and the voluminous pamphlet war which it inspired is too well known to this audience to call for more than a passing reference.

One of the most picturesque and interesting characters on the frontier was Robert Rogers the Ranger, a great Indian fighter who recorded many details of border warfare in his *Concise account of North America*, London, 1765, and especially in his *Journal*, published the same year. His other journals were not published until many years later, and the record of his courtmartial had to wait for the two volume edition of Kenneth Roberts' *Northwest Passage*, which so attractively depicts the adventures of this old French and Indian War frontiersman.

Provost William Smith made another important contribution to frontier literature in his *An historical account of the expedition against the Ohio Indians in the year 1764* which was printed here the following year and reprinted in London, Dublin, Amsterdam, Paris, and Cincinnati. This narrative of the Bouquet expedition to relieve Fort Pitt from the siege of the Delawares and Shawanese is of particular interest since it tells of the first British military expedition into the territory northwest of the Ohio and the first important victory over the Indians after they were provided with firearms.

Two men of God whose zeal for the conversion and education of the red man and for the saving of pioneer souls are well worth remembering. The first is Charles Beatty, who was the author of a *Journal of a two months tour with a view to promoting religion among the frontier inhabitants of Pennsylvania and the Indians to the westward of the Allegh-geny Mountains*, London, 1768, which gives us our first picture of the life of the Indian towns in southeastern Ohio, a region then far beyond the frontiers. And, though

they were not published at the time, we can hardly omit mention
of the *Journals* of the Reverend Francis Asbury, who visited the
newly settled parts of the country and recorded conditions as he
found them while saving souls for the Methodists. His journals for
1771 to 1778 were printed here in 1792 and the more complete
series, covering the whole period from 1771 to 1815 appeared at
New York in 1821.

In 1770 Philip Pittman, a surveyor who had lived for several
years in the region which he describes, wrote an interesting and informative account of the *Present state of the European settlements
on the Mississippi*. At about the same time another pioneer was recording in his journal his observations of the life of the Delawares
and Shawanese with whom he was laboring as a missionary. He
was the Reverend David Jones, and in *A journal of two visits made
to some nations of Indians on the west side of the river Ohio, in the
years 1772 and 1773*, he tells his adventures. It is interesting that,
on one of his journeys, he had George Rogers Clark as a traveling
companion. Jones was later to serve as chaplain to General Wayne's
army in 1794.

One of the earliest and best-informed authors to write a *History
of the American Indians* was James Adair, a famous Indian trader
and one of the first explorers of the Alleghenies. His book was published in London in 1775 and is still as interesting as when it was
first read by our Revolutionary ancestors, a rare example of the work
of a real frontiersman who was not inarticulate. Another was
Thomas Hutchins, a New Jersey man, who spent practically his
whole life on the frontier and served as assistant engineer of the
Bouquet expedition. His *Topographical description of Virginia,
Pennsylvania, Maryland, and North Carolina* appeared in London
in 1778, was reprinted at Boston in 1787 and in a French edition at
Paris in 1781. Hutchins gives a detailed picture of this important
region during the period of the Revolution, and his book is made
still more valuable by the inclusion of Patrick Kennedy's journal
and some excellent maps. His similar *A historical narrative and
topographical description of Louisiana and West Florida* was published here in 1784.

I should like to have known John Dodge, a patriotic and belligerent Indian trader located at Sandusky who became such a thorn in the flesh of the British along the Lakes during the Revolution that Captain Henry Hamilton, commandant of the fort at Detroit, had him captured and brought to the fort, where he languished in a dungeon for six months. Since the British could prove nothing against him, they finally allowed him to open a store in Detroit where he was robbed and abused by the commandant and later sent to prison in Quebec. He escaped in 1778, made his way to Boston and to the American camp, where his information so impressed General Washington that he sent Dodge to report to Congress on the military situation in the northwest. His story proved so interesting that Bradford induced him to prepare it for publication in 1779 under the title: *A narrative of the capture and treatment of John Dodge, by the English at Detroit.* This lively and pugnacious narrative gives many details of frontier life during the Revolution. We can trace only the Library Company's copy of the first edition, but it was reprinted in London in the same year in Almon's *Remembrancer,* and there were separate editions in Danvers, 1780, and a modern Cedar Rapids edition of 1909.

Sermons are generally not very interesting, but I should like to include on our frontier bookshelf at least one, the Reverend Israel Evans' *A discourse delivered at Easton* before Sullivan's army while it was on the famous expedition of 1779 for the destruction of the Iroquois towns. The old chaplain's patriotic and moving discourse was printed here at Philadelphia and reprinted at Lancaster in that year.

The famous *Letters from an American farmer* by Michel-Guillaume Saint-Jean de Crèvecoeur, London, 1782, were deservedly popular in their day and are still eagerly read by students of eighteenth-century American affairs, but we are also interested in his *Voyage dans la haute Pensylvanie,* Paris [1801], because it deals with the frontier and gives us what is perhaps our best account of the procedure of an Iroquois council. Another American book which had a great influence both here and abroad, as we know from its dozens of editions, is Thomas Jefferson's *Notes on the State of*

Virginia [Paris], 1782. From his comfortable acres at Monticello, Jefferson's enquiring mind reached to the frontier and his modest manual is packed with Indian lore and the general picture of plantation and forest in his native state.

There is another little book about one of the southern states which rivals Jefferson's *Notes* in popularity. It is John Filson's *The discovery, settlement, and present state of Kentucke . . . To which is added an appendix, containing the adventures of Col. Daniel Boon,* Wilmington, 1784. Of course it is the famous Boone narrative which has made this delightful book famous in many editions and translations throughout the years. The courageous and thrilling picture of the discovery and settlement of Kentucky and Tennessee is here told in a few brief pages, each paragraph packed with enough romance to supply the plot for a historical novel. Frequently reprinted in separate pamphlet form, from the excessively rare Norwich, 1786 edition, on down to the present, and included in every history of the pioneers, Boone's brief but significant story is one of the great narratives of the west.

The year 1786 gives us two titles for our bookshelf, and no two volumes could be less alike. One tells of the daily life of a peaceful monastic community, the other a tale of revolution and threatened violence. One is the *Chronicon Ephratense,* printed in German at the famous cloister in 1786 to record their interesting years of old world religious living in a new world frontier setting. The other is the desperate story of Daniel Shays and his rebellion of tax-ridden farmers in western Massachusetts which closed the courts and threatened civil war in 1786, as it was recorded by George R. Minot under the title: *The history of the insurrection in Massachusetts in 1786,* Worcester, 1788. Each in its different way is an important chapter in American economic history. The Ephrata cloister was a pioneering enterprise, and the rebellion drove many a destitute New Englander into the wilderness to the westward in search of newer and better fortunes.

Many a Connecticut Yankee left his stony fields and mortgaged farm when the Ohio Company beckoned in 1787, and floated down the Beautiful River to Marietta and a new home in the Old Northwest. Here the first Fourth of July celebration west of the Allegheny Mountains was held the following year. The proceedings of this holiday gathering, marked by the courageous optimism and patriotic enthusiasm of the frontier, were printed under the title: *An oration delivered at Marietta, July 4, 1788, by the Hon. James M. Varnum . . . speech of his Excellency Arthur St. Clair . . . and proceedings of the inhabitants of the City of Marietta,* Newport, 1788. A year later the enthusiasm for their new home was still undiminished and so the pioneers had another celebration at which Solomon Drowne declaimed with appropriate eloquence *An oration delivered at Marietta, April 7, 1789, in commemoration of the settlement formed by the Ohio Company,* Worcester, 1789.

At about the same time George Henry Loskiel was recording for posterity the forty years' effort of the United Brethren to convert the Delawares and Shawanese. His story was published in German at Barby in 1789 and in English at London in 1794 as *The history of the mission of the United Brethren among the Indians of North America.* His narrative was based on the accounts of David Zeisberger and of Augustus Gottlieb Spangenberg who had already published in German, Barby, 1782, and in English, London, 1788, and Philadelphia, 1789, his own *An account of the manner in which the . . . United Brethren, preach the gospel and carry on their missions among the heathens.*

The Baptists were always popular among the backwoodsmen and their missionaries were active on all the frontiers. Their campmeetings under the trees and baptisms in the icy mountain streams were duly recorded by John Asplund, who trudged from one end of the country to the other to compile his *Annual register of the Baptist denomination,* 1791-92 and his *Universal register,* 1794, both of which are full of pioneer scenes and glimpses of frontier life.

William Bartram, more interested in natural history than in the saving of souls, also covered many a long mile in the Carolinas, Georgia, and the Floridas and published his *Travels* in these states in Philadelphia in 1791. These frontier observations were so popular that they were reprinted not only in London and Dublin but in French, Dutch, and German translations.

The defeat of General St. Clair's army by the western Indians in 1791 brought consternation to the whole country, and especially to the frontier. The tragic story was told in newspapers and pamphlets, but the most interesting of all were the various broadsides which celebrated the event, generally in rugged frontier verse. The most interesting of these was *The Columbian tragedy. Containing a particular and official account of the brave and unfortunate officers and soldiers, who were slain and wounded in the ever-memorable and bloody Indian battle* . . . It was decorated with rows of coffins, one for each of the slain, thirty-nine in the first issue and others added as fuller details came in. This charmingly lugubrious piece includes both prose and verse and was published at Boston in 1791 or 1792. Other funereal broadside poems celebrating the same defeat and massacre appeared at the time, including a *Melancholy account respecting the western army* and Matthew Bunn's *A tragical account of the defeat of Gen. St. Clair by the savages*, Boston [1792], which was also published as *St. Clair's defeat. A poem*, Harrisburg, 1792 and as *Bloody Indian battle, fought at the Miami village . . . A mournful elegy on the occasion*, New-Haven [1798].

One of the most important pioneer narratives of the period during and following the Revolution was John Long's *Voyages and travels of an Indian interpreter and trader*, London, 1791. He fought with the British and Indians during the Revolution and, as trader and explorer, reached parts of the Canadian wilderness which have not even yet been thoroughly explored.

Daniel Gookin's *Historical collections of the Indians in New England* was not published until 1792 when it appeared in the first volume of the Massachusetts Historical Society Collections and in a separate reprint, hence our inclusion of it here. Gookin was a seventeenth-century Massachusetts pioneer who knew the local Indians well and was their friend. His study of their history is one of the important sources, and the original manuscript is still preserved in the F. C. Deering Indian collection.

The greatest of all contemporary encyclopedias of pioneer information of the 1790's was Gilbert Imlay's *Topographical description*, London, 1792, which contained only his own observations, as did the Dublin reprint of the following year. The London edition of 1793 added Filson's *Kentucky* and an index, and in the same year an edition came out in New York, rarer than the rest but less valuable than the London edition of 1797 which is a mine of information since it adds Filson and a total of thirteen rare tracts reprinted in the appendix. This edition has been in constant use since the day of its publication and is still a principal source of information on western geography of the pioneer period. It was published in German in Berlin in 1793.

John Pope's *A tour through the southern and western territories* was printed at Richmond in 1792 and is a very rare volume, only seven copies being known, but it is an important descriptive work covering a part of the country about which very few books of this period have been written. However, Harry Toulmin's *A description of Kentucky* [London], 1792, is, for its specific area, of real importance as a supplement to Pope.

Father Pierre Huet de la Valiniere was a French-Canadian Catholic priest who got himself into hot water with the authorities for siding with the American colonies during the Revolution. He wandered out to the Illinois country in 1786, visited New Orleans, came to Boston, and went several times to Europe, and everywhere he went he had trouble with the authorities, civil, military, and ecclesiastical. At one time during his chequered career he was stationed near Albany, New York, and while there he wrote about his travels and troubles in a long narrative poem in his native language which was published under the following title: *Vraie histoire: ou, simple précis des infortunes* . . . Albany, 1792. Of this engaging work the American Antiquarian Society owns the only copy in the United States, and there are three others in Canada.

The Whiskey Rebellion on the frontiers of Pennsylvania in 1794 had its apologists and historians, including H. H. Brackenridge with his *Incidents of the insurrection*, Philadelphia, 1795, which is a self-defense of one who sympathized with the insurgents, and William Findley, who published his *History of the insurrection* at Philadelphia in 1796.

A rare and little-known work of this period which would be an ornament to any Pennsylvania library is the collection of *Lettres écrites des rives de l'Ohio* by the Marquis Claud François Adrien de Lezay-Marnezia, who dated his book from Fort Pitt and published it in French in Paris in 1801. Its suppression by the French authorities accounts for its scarcity, but we are able to locate half-a-dozen copies.

One very important book which gives more lore of the woods than most of the others is Philip Tome's *Pioneer life; or, thirty years a hunter.* The author was born near Harrisburg in 1782 and was a hunter, trapper, and Indian interpreter in Pennsylvania and western New York. Though published at Buffalo in 1854, the volume records the life of the frontier of the early nineteenth century. It is a very rare book, but if you are a student rather than a collector, there is a modern reprint.

There were a few shady characters on the frontier who got themselves into print and a good many others, like the Girtys, who said little, did much that was evil, and had a good deal written about them by others. Some of the early American rapscallions left a record of their wayward lives other than that kept by the courts, and these autobiographies help us to piece together a complete picture of the times and besides are generally very interesting reading. There was James Dalton, for example, whose *Life and actions* appeared in London in 1730 and who spent some time in New York, Virginia, and the Carolinas. Most of us are familiar with the adventures of Bampfylde-Moore Carew, King of the Gypsies, who was transported to Maryland about 1740 and recorded his American activities in his *Life and adventures* which went through more than thirty editions beginning with 1745. A native American rascal was the notorious Stephen Burroughs, whose *Memoirs* appeared in Hanover, New Hampshire, in 1798 with a second volume in Boston in 1804 and many reprints, the last in 1924 with a preface by Robert Frost.

We might include a pair of British Revolutionary spies in our list. Lieutenant James Moody published his interesting *Narrative* in London in 1782 and the following year, and a New York edition appeared in 1865. The extremely interesting *Journal kept by Mr.*

John Howe, while he was employed as a British spy, during the Revolutionary War was published at Concord, New Hampshire, in 1827. It records his hairbreadth escapes and gives much interesting detail. For good measure he included his later adventures as a smuggler. John Ryer was a rascally Tory who lived at Fordham, New York, and, having killed a deputy sheriff, composed the *Narrative* of his life while he was waiting to be hanged at White Plains, as we may learn from the Danbury edition of 1793 or the chapbook edition without imprint.

The life and adventures of Seth Wyman, embodying the principal events of a life spent in robbery, theft, gambling, passing counterfeit money, etc. was written by himself and printed at Manchester in 1843, but the most charming rogue of the whole lot is Henry Tufts, who wrote *A narrative* of his life and had it published at Dover in 1807. Since the original edition is rare, you may be content to read the New York edition of 1930 called *The autobiography of a criminal* which was edited by Edmund Pearson and slightly expurgated, I regret to say. Tufts' book gives us our best picture of the Revolutionary underworld, thieves' slang and all. He served several enlistments in the American army from which he finally deserted. He stole hearts and horses the whole length of the Atlantic seaboard. He passed counterfeit money, of course, was an itinerant preacher and quack, was nearly hanged for burglary, and escaped from some of the best jails in New England.

We have finished our daydream under Boone's tree on the Watauga, our pipe has burned out and we are ready to resume our journey. We have seen in retrospect our sturdy and resourceful pioneer ancestors as they pushed the Indians and the forests ever westward during the first two centuries of our national growth. We have come to understand a little better the qualities which we have inherited from the men and women of many races who peopled our frontiers, the qualities of bravery, adaptability, ambition, determination, and inventive genius which have made us and which will keep us a great democratic nation. Our people of today may well listen to the voice of the old frontier, for it speaks of courage, honesty, manhood and opportunity and the joys of simple living far from the noise and grime of cities. It tells of hard lives, simple pleasures, and the great happiness which they found in their dearly won independence, which is our heritage to be guarded jealously and defended with bravery and wisdom.

2

The Indians' Captives Relate
Their Adventures

Run fer the Blockhouse, the Injuns are Comin'

AN eminent American littérateur of a few years ago once wrote a hilarious poem in which he brought together for a bull session in Heaven those famous mariners and tellers of tall tales, "Noah an' Jonah an' Cap'n John Smith."* If I had been planning it I should have included Bill Shakespeare in the party or, better still, I should like to have had the Bard and the Captain foregather over a mug of ale in the Mermaid Tavern while they were both still lusty and vigorous. What tales the swashbuckling "Admirall of New England" would have told and what plays with a New World setting might have thrilled the first nighters at the Globe shortly thereafter! Perhaps Prospero would have become an English adventurer, Miranda a Virginia Dare, and Caliban a follower of Powhatan.

It is, indeed, strange that Shakespeare did not make more use of the stories of hardship and adventure, of shipwreck, ambuscade, and captivity which the great explorers and sea rovers of his day were bringing back from the New World. Even if he did not chance to meet any of them personally, their numerous American tall tales were being circulated in the principal European languages while Shakespeare was still working the old mines of Plutarch and Holinshed in search of plots for his histories and tragedies. Perhaps he thought these New World tales were too recent to have the necessary glamour to make them useful as literary material.**

The thrilling adventures of Nuñez Cabeza de Vaca, Hans Staden, and The Gentleman of Elvas were familiar to the people

---

* *Noah an' Jonah an' Cap'n John Smith; a book of humorous verse.* By Don Marquis. New York: Appleton, 1921. x, 157 p., illus.
** See Bibliography, nos. 23, 28 and 35.

23

of Europe in numerous editions and translations in Shakespeare's day, and it is with these three stirring narratives that we begin our long series of stories of captivity among the American Indians which has reached unbroken down to our own time. Only recently we read in the newspapers of the birthday celebration of a New England centenarian who, as a child, had been an Indian captive.

The Greeks had a name for it and they called it *Katharsis;* we might speak of it as "synthetic tragedy." All civilized nations have realized the value of seasoning the joyousness of their recreation with a poem, a play, or a story of the misfortunes and tragedies of others. The Greeks had Aeschylus, we have Eugene O'Neill, but our American ancestors did not believe in play-acting or in the corrupting influence of the novel, so they limited themselves to true tales of horror in the form of deathbed confessions, stories of shipwreck, piracy, plague, and disaster, and of Indian captivity and torture.

It is easy to understand why Indian captivities have been best sellers for the last four hundred years. Most of us have sat up till all hours to get the Count of Monte Cristo or Casanova out of prison or to help our soldiers and nurses escape from Corregidor or from the clutches of the Nazis. Stories of courage, fortitude, hairbreadth escapes, and skill in outwitting the enemy have always appealed to those whose native tongue is English, especially when these adventures are so recent as to be virtually a part of the reader's own experience. Just as World War II is a part of our own life, so King Philip's War, the French and Indian Wars, the Revolution, or the Sioux Wars of the 1860's were part of the lives of those who first read the stories of captivity which were episodes of those campaigns.

The Indian captivities of the sixteenth, seventeenth, and eighteenth centuries which we are considering are far removed from our own experience, but they still have a strong appeal. It certainly is thrilling, in the earliest of these narratives, to watch the clash of the Elizabethan civilization with that of the stone age; to see how courtiers in doublet and hose reacted to their first dramatic meetings with grim-faced warriors in skins and feathers; to watch the expressions on the Indian faces at sight of their first white visitors.

Everything was new and strange and each mode of life had much to learn from the other. There was courage and generosity, cruelty, cunning, and greed on both sides, but the more advanced civilization finally won out, to the satisfaction of the reader, who is generally a product of that civilization. He will not be too complacent, however, if he carefully reads both sides of the story.

It is true that friendly contacts with the Indians added to the comforts of European civilization such luxuries as potato salad, corn licker, Virginia tobacco, and chewing gum, while Benjamin Franklin picked up at various Indian councils a knowledge of the workings of the League of the Iroquois which suggested to him the formation of the United States of America, which in turn suggested the League of Nations and the United Nations.

But most of our knowledge of how to live on an untamed frontier was brought back to the settlements by Indian fighters and captives. From these experiences our ancestors learned that a forest tree was a better protection from an Indian arrow than a steel helmet, and so they developed the Indian method of fighting from cover which so disconcerted the British redcoats and still later the Nips and Nazis. From their Indian captors they also learned the ways of peaceful living in a new world. They remembered the beautiful and poetic native names of the lakes and streams and hills, and passed them on to us; they were taught how to hunt and trap the wild game, how to cure themselves with many new and effective Indian remedies; and they became familiar with such delicacies as fish chowder, succotash, hominy, roast turkey with cranberry sauce, corn on the cob, Indian pudding, and pumpkin pie. But most important of all, the early frontiersmen, hemmed in as they were by the Indian tribes beyond the Appalachians, developed a hardihood, a resourcefulness and a love of liberty which they might not have had were it not for the constant menace of the red men lurking in the neighboring forests. The English, Scotch-Irish, Dutch, German and French settlers became united by the common danger and when war threatened from another quarter, they were strong enough to throw off the British yoke and found a new and united nation.

If we compare the so-called civilized warfare of the Nips and

Nazis with that of the American savages of the colonial and Revolutionary period, we find that the latter really were amateurs in the grim business of cold-blooded slaughter and sadistic inhumanity. It is true that our native Indians often tomahawked their victims, but that was a quick and merciful death while the taking of a scalp was merely their equivalent of winning an iron cross. And we should not forget that in colonial and Revolutionary times we also sometimes paid a bounty for Indian scalps, as everyone knows who is familiar with the story of Hannah Dustin. Only the most valiant of the Indians' foes were reserved for the honor of burning at the stake, with the privilege of showing their courage and fortitude in the face of death. Those who ran the gauntlet were given a fighting chance, and if they reached the safety of the council house at the end of the run for their lives, as did Moses Van Campen, they were treated with consideration and were often honored by adoption into the tribe. Women and children captives, if not killed outright, were not mistreated by the eastern Indians but were either held for ransom or were adopted and used so kindly that they frequently refused to return to white civilization when the opportunity offered, as in the famous cases of Eunice Williams and of Mary Jemison, "the white woman of the Genesee." The latter was carried away from her Pennsylvania home when she was a little girl in 1755 and lived through the Revolution as the wife of a Seneca chief in the Genesee Valley and for many years thereafter. The story of her captivity, which was not published until 1824 and so is too late for our consideration, gives us our best picture of life among the Senecas and of the Revolutionary War from the Indian's point of view. It is deservedly one of the most popular of all Indian captivities and has appeared in thirty-five editions and issues, has had two novels based on it, and the 1942 edition is still in print. There are many Mary Jemisons on the shelves of our libraries and private collections, but the University of Rochester owns all but one issue, and that is to come to it when the present owner's splendid collection is bequeathed to that library to join the Strecker and Vail collections.

The stories of Indian captivity which followed the frontier as it pushed westward were the escape literature of our ancestors. In a day when there was practically no native American fiction, they took the place of our mystery stories and "Westerns." As George Parker Winship points out: "There is nothing in English, or in any other language, that surpasses these narratives of Indian captivities in vividness or in the bare statement of physical suffering and of mental torment."* They were generally written for immediate publication as soon as the captive returned to civilization and so are simple, vivid, direct and, generally, accurate pictures of the exciting and often harrowing adventures of their authors. Many were written by the frontiersmen themselves, while others were ghost-written by their better educated neighbors but based on first-hand accounts dictated by the captives. A modern writer might envy these plain-spoken, untaught authors for the vividness of their narratives, their swift-moving and exciting plots and their sense of suspense and sustained horror, and of course we must always admire them for their courage, fortitude, and resourcefulness. It is not to be wondered at that nearly a thousand editions and issues of these stories of captivity have appeared to enthrall millions of readers from 1542 to the present time. With these Indian tales a native literature began to develop around the American scene, thus leading the way through Cooper and Simms and the Beadle dime novels to the splendid present-day work of such authors as Esther Forbes, Walter D. Edmonds, and Kenneth Roberts.

These delightful narratives are not merely light reading for a winter's evening but are of importance to the historian and biographer, the ethnologist, philologist, the sociologist, the natural scientist, and the medical historian. They have inspired many of our greatest American literary folk and have given a text to many a sermon, some of them preached before the returned captives themselves.

They were even responsible for our first recorded clash of religious faiths, since it was but natural that the zeal of the Canadian priests for the conversion of the protestant captives should cause resentment among their friends back home in New England. Even Eunice, the daughter of the Reverend John Williams, the famous

* *Cambridge History of American Literature.* New York, 1917, I, 6.

Deerfield captive, became a staunch Catholic, married an Indian and refused to return to her father's roof except as an occasional visitor. The first recorded piece of anti-Catholic literature in this country resulted from this priestly proselyting. It was the Reverend François Seguenot's *A letter from a Romish priest in Canada, to one [Mrs. Christina Baker] who was taken captive in her infancy* . . . This attempt of the eager priest to win the former captive to the faith in which he believed was published in Boston in 1729, with a spirited answer by Governor William Burnett, who roundly berated the good father for his endeavor. Though not itself a captivity, it may well be included in our study of the subject and we should not blame the captivity collector for wishing to place on his shelf this elusive tract, of which only eleven copies are recorded.

One feature which most of the captivities have in common is their extreme rarity—hence their popularity among book collectors, whose greatest thrill comes from capturing a unique title which their rivals can hardly hope to acquire. So many of these delightful narratives were printed in small editions at obscure village presses and promptly read to pieces by the captives' friends and neighbors that not a few of them, like the first Mary Rowlandson, are entirely unknown, many others are unique, and scores have survived in only a half-dozen copies. In spite of their elusiveness, the late Frank C. Deering was able to collect some 750 editions of the various captivities. The late Edward E. Ayer found 482 editions of the stories of 237 different captives, now in the Newberry Library, and many others have assembled notable collections, including Field, Brinley, Eames, De Puy, Braeslin, Paullin, Duncan, H. V. Jones, O'Brien, Shea, Manierre, and Littell. There are also many rare captivities in the present-day collections of Messrs. Siebert, Streeter, Frost, Graff, and Dr. Rosenbach, not to mention the dozen great collections in public libraries.

In order to bring our present study within reasonable limits we shall not only have to omit the hundreds of fascinating captivities after 1800 but also those before that date which were published in later years. This leaves us a most interesting group of about seventy-five different narratives, most of which were published during the lives of their heroes and none of them later than the end of the eighteenth century. To cover, even sketchily, this early part of the subject we can, in most cases, mention only the first edition of each title, but shall describe later editions in the bibliography at the end of the volume. Time will not allow us more than a glance at a few of the individual treasures, with brief reference to their importance and rarity, but perhaps even this hurried examination will stimulate the imagination of the student and the enthusiasm of the collector.

Our first group of four sixteenth-century captivities includes one in Texas, one in Florida, one in Brazil, and one in Mexico; one was originally written in Spanish, one in Portuguese, one in German, and one in English. The *Relation* of Alvar Nuñez Cabeza de Vaca, first published in Zamora in 1542 is well known to all students of the early history of Florida. An officer of the ill-fated Narváez expedition sent out from Spain to conquer and settle Florida, he finally found himself among the fifteen survivors who were enslaved by the Indians of Texas in 1528. Two years later he escaped, and after years of traveling from tribe to tribe as a trader and doctor, he arrived in Mexico City in 1536 where he met Cortes and Mendoza, and the following year returned to Spain. His fascinating narrative went through many editions in several languages.

Another survivor of the Narváez expedition was Juan Oritz, a Spaniard of good family, who was captured by the Indians of Florida in 1528 and lived among them for eleven years before he was rescued by Hernando de Soto. His story appears in the *Relaçam verdadeira* of the mysterious Gentleman of Elvas who was the best of the chroniclers of the de Soto expedition to Florida. The first edition was published in Euora in 1557, and it too went through many editions, the finest of all being that published in two volumes by the Florida State Historical Society in 1933. There are three known copies of the original edition, one in the New York Public Library, which also has the first edition of the Cabeza de Vaca relation.

In 1549 a German sailor named Hans Staden sailed from Seville with the expedition of Don Diego de Senabria for the Rio de la Plata, but the ship was later wrecked on the coast of Brazil and Staden was captured by the Tupi Indians, with whom he lived in

constant fear of his life (for they were cannibals) for nine months in
1554 until he was rescued by a French ship. His simple *Warhaftige
Historia,* full of breath-taking suspense, was published in Marburg
in 1557 and quickly ran through numerous editions, the first being
so rare that only five copies are recorded. This is our first full-length
and separately published story of American Indian captivity. Job
Hortop's *The trauailes of an Englishman,* London, 1591, tells the
story of a sailor under Sir John Hawkins in 1567 who was captured
by the Indians north of the Panuco River and taken to Mexico as a
prisoner. His narrative is apparently the first story of the Indian
captivity of an Englishman. These four sixteenth-century narratives
are not only fascinating first-hand stories of adventure but are important to the ethnologist since they give the earliest detailed accounts of the Indians of Texas, Florida, and Brazil.

Let us now glance at the most famous of all stories of Indian captivity, that of Captain John Smith, who was an involuntary guest
for twenty-four days among Powhatan's Indians on the James River
of Virginia in 1607. His rescue by Pocahontas is not mentioned in
the brief account of the adventure which he gives in his *True relation,* London, 1608, but he does devote a paragraph to this romantic
episode in the more elaborate *General historie of Virginia,* London,
1624. Perhaps, in his earlier narrative, he was a little ashamed to
admit that he, a twenty-eight-year-old soldier, generally recognized
as a very tough customer, owed his rescue to an Indian girl of
thirteen. However, by 1624 she had grown up, married John Rolfe,
and was well known at the English court, so he included the episode
in his history and thereby made himself and his heroine forever
famous.

The narratives of the pioneer Catholic priests of New France are
so well known to students of Parkman—the Jesuit Relations, Hennepin, and all the rest—that we need not take time to more than
remind you that many of these devoted missionaries were themselves
captives and have left exciting accounts of their thrilling adventures.
The intelligent observation of the Jesuits, their calm courage and
devotion to their faith, make their narratives live three centuries
after many of them became martyrs among the savage tribes of

New York and the northwest. The Jesuit Relations from 1644 to 1653, conveniently available through the Thwaites translation but exceedingly scarce in their original editions, tell us the stories of the captivities of Fathers Jogues, Bressani, Goupil, du Poncet, Bréboeuf, Chaumont, Lalement, de Nouë, Massé, Daniel, Lalande, Garnier, Chäbanel and others. The relation of 1663-64 also records the hardships of two French soldiers captured by the Mohawks near Three Rivers while they were out hunting, and finally saved from the stake by some friendly Onondagas.

Father Louis Hennepin of the Recollects tells of his own captivity of four months in 1680 among the Sioux near the present city of Minneapolis in his *Description de la Louisiane*, Paris, 1683, and again in his *Nouvelle decouverte*, Utrecht, 1697. These were the most popular early books on New France and our Middle West, as we know from their many translations and editions.

We now come to one of the greatest of all captivities and the third or fourth in popularity if we may judge by its thirty editions and issues. It is our first New England narrative, and only four leaves of the first edition have survived. Here is the title in full:

> The soveraignty & goodness of God, together, with the faithfulness of his promises displayed; being a narrative of the captivity and restauration of Mrs. Mary Rowlandson. Commended by her, to all that desires to know the Lords doings to, and dealings with her. Especially to her dear children and relations. Boston in New-England printed [by Samuel Green, Jr.] for John Ratcliffe, & John Griffin. 1682. [Title within ornamental border].

This made-up title for the lost first edition is based on that of the second edition plus the imprint of the last sermon of the author's husband which was issued with it. Luckily there are extant copies of both the first and second editions of this accompanying sermon. That with the Boston imprint has at the end an erratum for the first edition of the captivity, showing that they were issued together, though each had its own title, pagination, and signature marks. That with the Cambridge imprint has no erratum note, and the second or Cambridge edition of the captivity has the former erratum corrected in the text. The Cambridge editions of both the captivity and the sermon are identical in size, are printed from the same type, and have the same broad, plain black border. From this we may assume that the first edition of the captivity would have the same imprint as the first or Boston edition of the sermon with which it must have been issued. Therefore the first edition of the captivity must have been printed in Boston and not in Cambridge as has generally been assumed. If further proof were needed, we have only to turn to the advertisement of this Boston edition in the first American edition of the *Pilgrim's Progress,* printed in Boston by Samuel Green in 1681, which reads:

> Before long, there will be published . . . the particular circumstances of the captivity, & redemption of Mrs. Mary Rowlandson; and of her children. Being pathetically written, with her own hand.

There are two issues of the second edition of the Rowlandson narrative printed at Cambridge in 1682. In the first it is called the second *addition,* and of this the Boston Public Library has the only copy. The second issue has its title corrected to read *Second edition,* and the British Museum and Huntington Library have copies, the latter lacking the first three leaves. The third edition, printed in London the same year, is not nearly so rare, for there are at least a dozen known copies, eight in public libraries and four in private collections. But of the fourth edition, Boston, 1720, only three copies are recorded, and it might be difficult to find as many as half a dozen of any of the nine other eighteenth-century editions.

Mary Rowlandson was the wife of the minister at Lancaster, Massachusetts, when that frontier town was burned by the Indians on February 10, 1675, and its citizens either killed or carried into captivity. Her sister and brother-in-law were killed in the fight, and Mrs. Rowlandson and her six-year-old daughter wounded, the latter dying a few days later. Her other children were among the captives. She was ransomed on May 2 after a frightful experience with her captors, and her remaining children returned soon after.

Mrs. Rowlandson's story is remarkable as a piece of American literature. Few women of her day were well enough educated to have written it at all, and few of any day could have equalled its dramatic narrative of stark horror. A short paragraph will show the simple yet tragic quality of her writing.

On the tenth of February 1675, came the Indians with great numbers upon Lancaster: Their first coming was about sun-rising; hearing the noise of some guns, we looked out; several houses were burning, and the smoke ascending to Heaven. . . . [And a little later:] Some in our house were fighting for their lives, others wallowing in their blood, the house on fire over our heads, and the bloody heathen ready to knock us on the head, if we stirred out. . . . Thus were we butchered by those merciless heathen, standing amazed, with the blood running down to our heels.

Quentin Stockwell was taken by the Indians at Deerfield in 1677 during King Philip's War and was a captive for about four months. He wrote out his matter-of-fact yet exciting narrative for Increase Mather who included it in his *An essay for the recording of illustrious providences*, Boston, 1684, of which four variant titles are recorded. It was reprinted with a London imprint the same year. The Stockwell narrative was printed again in Richard Blome's *The present state of His Majesties isles and territories in America*, London, 1687, and in at least three modern editions.

We are indebted to that inquisitive old news gatherer, Cotton Mather, for many New England frontier narratives, including the captivities of two heroic women of the seventeenth century. In May 1690 the settlement at Casco, Maine, was wiped out by the Indians. Among the captives was Mrs. Hannah Swarton, who lost her husband in the fight and her eldest son not long after. She had the usual long journey to Quebec and was finally ransomed five years later. Her other children, two sons and a daughter, were also taken by the Indians and, when she wrote out her story for the Reverend Mr. Mather, two of them were still awaiting rescue from Canada.

During a raid on Haverhill, Massachusetts, in 1697, the Indians found Mrs. Hannah Dustan or Dustin, to use the later spelling, in her cabin with her week-old baby and her nurse, Mary Neff, her

husband having managed to reach safety with their seven other
children. After dispatching the baby, the Indians started them on
their strenuous journey through the woods. The two women and
a young boy from Worcester were finally assigned to an Indian
family of two men, three women, and seven children. Just before
dawn, while the Indians slept, Mrs. Dustin and her two companions
dispatched ten of them with their own tomahawks, while a badly
wounded squaw and a small boy escaped. They then scalped their
victims, helped themselves to a canoe, and finally reached civilization, where the General Assembly of Massachusetts paid them the
bounty of fifty pounds for their Indian scalps and admiring friends
loaded them with presents, not the least of which came from the
Governor of Maryland. If you visit Haverhill today you may still
see Hannah with her upraised tomahawk, keeping guard over the
public square.

Mather published these two stories in his *Humiliations follow'd
with deliverances,* Boston, 1697, only two copies of which have survived, one imperfect. The Dustin narrative was reprinted in revised
form in his *Decennium luctuosum,* a history of the Indian wars
from 1688 to 1698, published in Boston in 1699, of which half a
dozen copies are known. Both stories reappeared in his *Magnalia*
in 1702. The story of the burning of York, Maine, and the massacre
or captivity of its people in 1691 appears in Mather's inappropriately
titled: *Fair weather,* Boston, 1692, of which four copies are known
with two variant imprints. He also recorded the burning of Deerfield
and the captivity of Reverend John Williams and his flock, mainly
written by Williams while still a captive, in *Good fetch'd out of evil,*
Boston, 1706, of which four copies have survived, but not one with
its title page.

The Reverend John Williams' own moving story of his captivity
rivals that of Mary Rowlandson in popularity. It went through
seventeen editions in its original form and at least eight editions rewritten and abridged by others. The first edition was called *The
redeemed captive, returning to Zion* and was published in Boston
in 1707 shortly after his return from his two and a half years' captivity in Canada. Both for its historical importance and its rarity,

this is one of the most valuable books in its field. Of the eight known copies, two are imperfect and two in private collections. Of the even rarer second edition, Boston, 1720, there are but three recorded copies, one imperfect. Most of the seven other eighteenth-century editions are rare enough to delight the collector who finds one of them.

For our last seventeenth-century captivity we leave New England and join Jonathan Dickenson, a well-to-do businessman of Jamaica on his voyage with his family to Philadelphia from August 1696 to April of the following year. Shipwrecked on the east coast of Florida, the entire company, including the well-known Quaker preacher Robert Barrow, endured a most harrowing captivity among the Florida Indians, but finally made their way in safety to St. Augustine and eventually to Philadelphia. Dickenson's famous story of their adventures: *God's protecting providence,* was printed here in Philadelphia by Reinier Jansen in 1699 and may have been the first product of his press. It surely would be included among the half-dozen most important stories of Indian captivity and would, of course, rate first in the eyes of a Philadelphia collector—if he could get it. There were eight copies in public libraries, two of them imperfect, of which three cannot now be traced, including two which apparently have disappeared from the Friends Library and Historical Society of Pennsylvania.

This deservedly popular narrative has appeared in twenty-three editions and issues, including one in Dutch and two in German. Benjamin Franklin is supposed to have printed it here in 1735, but if so, no copy has survived. Bradford reprinted it, however, in 1751, and Saur was responsible for the first German edition in 1756. The Cresson family, descended from one of the sailors in the Dickenson party, issued a privately printed edition here in 1868. Though the Historical Society of Pennsylvania apparently no longer has a copy of the first edition, it does own a contemporary copy of the original manuscript which was of great service in the preparation of the handsome and scholarly edition published in 1945 by the Yale University Press.

The popularity of the Indian captivity as a literary form had become so marked by the beginning of the eighteenth century that writers of fiction began to adapt it to their uses, to the confusion of scholars and collectors who have found it difficult, in a number of cases, to distinguish the true from the false coin. Perhaps the first of these novelists to incorporate an Indian captivity into his narrative and at the same time to foist it on the public as a true story of adventure was W. R. Chetwood, who published in London in 1720: *The voyages, dangerous adventures and imminent escapes of Captain Richard Falconer*. For good measure he includes the story of Thomas Randel, another sailor who was supposed to have been an Indian captive in Virginia. This lively yarn went through at least nine editions, all of them English.

The story of Elizabeth Hanson who, with her four children and servant maid, was captured by the Indians near Dover, New Hampshire, in 1725 and redeemed after a year's captivity, was taken down from her own narration by a good Quaker, Samuel Bownas. He had it printed in Philadelphia in 1728 with the title: *God's mercy surmounting man's cruelty*, and again in his own biography, London, 1756. It was very popular, and we can trace some twenty editions of the separate captivity and a dozen of the author's life. There is no record of a perfect copy of the first edition, the only one known lacking its title and last two leaves. However, it contains a contemporary annotation dated 1742 which proves it to be a copy of the first edition, since the second was not published in Philadelphia until 1754.

Perhaps the best written and most interesting captivity in what is now the state of Maine is that of John Gyles, who was captured in 1689 and remained an Indian or French captive for nearly nine years. It was called: *Memoirs of odd adventures, strange deliverances, &c. in the captivity of John Gyles, Esq; commander of the garrison on St. George's River*. It was printed in Boston in 1736 and, as might be expected, there are only half a dozen copies known, two of them imperfect. Perhaps it was unpopular with the author's contemporaries, since he was a military man and did not sprinkle his narrative with biblical quotations, as did most of the other New England captives. Whatever the reason, the story was not reprinted until the Cincinnati edition of 1869. It is sprightly, well written, and is unique among the early narratives in that it uses dialogue.

Avantures du Sr. C. Le Beau, Avocat en Parlement, ou voyage curieux et nouveau parmi les sauvages de l'Amérique Septentrionale, is a little-known work published in Amsterdam in French in 1738. It is probably a true account, dressed up and fictionized, but in any case it gives the author's adventures among the Algonquins and Abenakis in the early part of the eighteenth century and so deserves a place on our shelf of captivities. It contains an interesting map of Canada, a number of attractive Indian plates, and the last half of the second volume tells the story of the author's supposed and probably true captivity.

Another excellent New England captivity which should have been more popular but achieved only two editions is *A narrative of the captivity of Nehemiah How*, published at Boston in 1748 and reprinted at Cleveland in 1904. There are at least four copies each of the two issues of the first edition. How was captured at what is now Putney, Vermont, in 1745, and was a prisoner for three years. His story is brief but absorbing. In it he mentions as fellow captives the Reverend John Norton, of whom we will speak in a moment, and Captain William Pote, whose original manuscript journal is owned by the Newberry Library and was published in 1896.

The Reverend John Norton was chaplain of Fort Massachusetts, near the present Williamstown, and was captured when the fort capitulated to the French and Indians in 1746. His narrative, *The redeemed captive*, appeared in Boston two years later. Of the two issues, some thirteen copies are now known. It was reprinted at Albany in an edition of one hundred copies in 1870. This will always be, both for the historian and the collector, one of the most desirable of captivities, for it is a plain and honest account of stirring and important events and is very rare in good condition.

If we are to include all captivities in the western hemisphere, we must now journey to Patagonia where we find *A narrative of the dangers and distresses: which befel Isaac Morris, and seven more of the crew belonging to the Wager*. This is an account of a thousand-mile journey into the interior, a sixteen months' captivity among the Indians, ransom and enslavement by the Spanish at Buenos Aires, 1741-46. It was published in London in 1751 and reprinted in the *Universal Museum* in 1763. At least four copies are known in this country. Commodore John Byron, grandfather of Lord Byron, was also a victim of the shipwreck of the *Wager*, as he tells us in his *Narrative*, London, 1768, but he escaped without being made captive.

By this time the fur traders and frontier settlers were pushing farther westward, meeting step by step the steady opposition of the French and Indians until the whole Pennsylvania frontier was aflame. There were, of course, many Pennsylvania captives.

The story of Mary Jemison has already been mentioned, but four of these narratives were published almost as soon as the captives returned to their homes and must have been eagerly read by many Philadelphians who knew them. The first is *A narrative of the sufferings and surprising deliverance of William and Elizabeth Fleming* who were captured at the Great Cove in Pennsylvania. Their narrative was printed in Philadelphia "for the benefit of the unhappy sufferers, and sold by them only" in 1756. Only the Sabin-Shea-Deering copy seems to have survived. It was reprinted in 1756 in Philadelphia, Lancaster, New York, and Boston in addition to two issues of a German edition printed by Christopher Saur of Germantown. It is so rare that not more than thirteen copies of all nine editions and issues are known today.

The first captivity in popularity, rivaled only by the Mary Jemison narrative, was that of Peter Williamson which was first published in York, England, in 1757 with a title beginning *French and Indian cruelty; exemplified in the life and various vicissitudes of fortune, of Peter Williamson, a disbanded soldier*. The forty-first edition was published in the author's native Aberdeen in 1885. We can trace but three copies of the first edtion, but most of the others are fairly plentiful, except the unique chapbook edition published as *The travels and surprising adventures of John Thomson*, probably at Falkirk in 1761. The author was stolen from his home as a child, sent to America and sold as a slave in Pennsylvania, where he married, settled on the frontier, was captured by the Indians, escaped, became a soldier, was wounded and again captured at the siege of Oswego and sent to England where he exhibited himself in Indian costume, published two books, was sued for slander by the corporation of Aberdeen, his home town, and thereby had the sale of his books promoted for over a hundred years.

Most of the captives were frontier settlers, but Robert Eastburn was a fur trader and, even more remarkable, a deacon in the Presbyterian church in Philadelphia. But his piety did not spoil his aim, for he shot two Indians with one bullet just before he was captured at Fort Bull near the present city of Rome, New York, while on a trading expedition to Oswego in 1756. He was carried to Canada, thence to England and finally home after nearly two years wandering. His simple, straightforward *Faithful narrative* was published "for the benefit of the author" at Philadelphia in 1758. It was reprinted the same year in Boston and in three later editions. All the editions, including the first two, are fairly common, but it brings a fancy price, nevertheless.

The adventures of two Union County, Pennsylvania, girls who were captured in 1755 and, after a harsh and exciting captivity, escaped to Pittsburgh, proved a nine days' wonder for the people of Philadelphia when their story was published in German and English in 1759, with the title *The narrative of Marie Le Roy and Barbara Leininger, who spent three and one half years as prisoners among the Indians.* Nearly one hundred years later the story of Barbara's sister also appeared as *Regina, the German captive.* Regina was with the Indians for eight years and her story was in print as late as 1919. The original narrative of 1759 gives numerous accounts of Indian torture and many details of aboriginal life. It also includes a long list of other captives whom the girls met during their adventures.

One of the most exciting as well as one of the rarest captivity stories is that of Thomas Brown, who enlisted in Rogers' Rangers in 1756 at the tender age of sixteen. Some months later, just after capturing a party of Frenchmen on Lake Champlain and while on their way back to Fort William Henry, they were attacked by a large party of French and Indians, and Brown was wounded three times and captured. He was taken to Fort Ticonderoga, then to Montreal as an Indian captive, was made to run the gauntlet, was taken to an Indian village on the Mississippi for the winter and back to Montreal with a French trader in the spring. He then escaped, got as far as Crown Point where he was recaptured and returned to Montreal, thence to Albany as an exchanged prisoner. He promptly reënlisted, went on another expedition, was captured once more, taken to Montreal and finally exchanged and returned to his home in 1760 after over three years of the toughest and most exciting frontier fighting. He saw other prisoners tortured to death and burned at the stake, and left a brief but very lively account of his own adventures.

His story is called *A plain narrative of the uncommon sufferings, and remarkable deliverance of Thomas Brown.* Three editions were printed in quick succession in Boston in the year of his return, but it was not reprinted elsewhere until the New York edition of 1908. There are four copies of the first edition, one of which, with the last leaf imperfect, brought $450 at auction in 1916. The imperfect Brinley-Library of Congress copy of the second edition is probably unique, and of the third edition there is a copy in the Newberry Library and an imperfect copy at the American Antiquarian Society, so J. H. Trumbull was almost right when he said in the Brinley catalogue in 1878 that this is "perhaps the rarest of all narratives of Indian captivity."

Our parade of captives now brings us back to Pennsylvania, where we find in the Library Company of Philadelphia the only perfect copy of *A journal of the captivity of Jean Lowry and her children, giving an account of her being taken by the Indians, the 1st of April 1756, from William Mc. Cord's, in Rocky-Spring Settlement in Pennsylvania, with an account of the hardships she suffered.* It was printed in Philadelphia in 1760, and a copy lacking the title and three leaves was sold at auction in 1915.

Now we come to our first story of a Negro captive, which is also the first account of the adventures of any Negro in America. And a lively narrative it is, for it includes shipwreck on the coast of

Florida in 1747, the murder of the rest of the crew by the Indians, the hero's captivity among them, his final ransom and his many adventures in and out of prison in the West Indies and, at last, his return to Boston as cook on the ship which had as passenger his old master General Winslow, who had not seen him for almost thirteen years. It is entitled *A narrative of the uncommon sufferings and surprizing deliverance of Briton Hammon, a Negro man,* and it was printed in Boston in 1760. There is only one edition of this rare little narrative, and the Library of Congress and the New-York Historical Society have the only copies.

Another very rare and perhaps unique captivity tells of the adventures of a Southerner, which is rare, for they generally seem to have kept out of the clutches of the Indians. It is *The horrid cruelty of the Indians, exemplified in the life of Charles Saunders, late of Charles-town, in South Carolina.* It was printed in Birmingham in 1763 and includes an account of the murder of some of his companions and the captivity of Miss York and her venerable father. The title page does not divulge the name of the Indian tribe responsible for all their misery, so we will have to wait until we can visit the Newberry Library and see the unique copy if we want to learn the whole story.

Still another rarity, perhaps more entertaining than reliable, is *The history of the life and sufferings of Henry Grace,* two editions of which were printed for the author at Reading, England, in 1764 and 1765. Of the first edition there seem to be six recorded copies, one in private hands, and of the second, two copies, one in the Ayer collection. The author claims to have been a captive "among the savages in North America" for several years, but he does not tell where or when in his title. A contemporary note in the Deering copy of the second edition, signed by an unidentified "J.P.A.," says: "This Henry Grace, I have seen and believe him to be a worthless dog, and that half his story is false." Like Peter Williamson, Grace returned to his native British Isles where he capitalized on his American adventures, perhaps without too much regard for accuracy.

The most puzzling ghost book in the entire field of Indian cap-

tivities is the *Account of the captivity of William Henry in 1755,
and of his residence among the Senneka Indians six years and seven
months till he made his escape from them.* Printed at Boston, 1766,
170 pp., 4to. There must have been such a book, for extracts from
it, giving a sketch of the author's life and telling two Indian legends,
are reprinted in the *London Chronicle,* June 23, 1768, p. 601, and
June 25, pp. 609-10. The author was an Englishman, educated in
Northamptonshire, who came to America and became a trader
among the Ohio Indians, where he was captured by the Senecas.
The extract from the *Chronicle* is reprinted in the Boston, 1901,
edition of Alexander Henry's *Travels,* pp. vi-xvii but with no information about the mysterious book or its author. We can find no
copy of the book, no reference to it in bibliographies, histories, or
contemporary Boston newspapers, and no account whatever of the
author. The two Seneca myths sound perfectly authentic, however,
and we still hope that some day a copy of the elusive volume will
come to light.

Some unknown English writer of this period who had evidently
read Smith's *Virginia* and *Robinson Crusoe* attempted a novel com-
bining the two which he, or she, called: *The female American; or,
the adventures of Unca Eliza Winkfield. Compiled by herself.* It
appeared in London in 1767, was reprinted at Newburyport about
1800 and again at Vergennes, Vermont, in 1814. Our interest in the
story centers around the captivity of the heroine's father in Virginia
about 1618 and his marriage to the Indian princess who, like
Pocahontas, had saved his life. The main narrative has to do with
the daughter of this romantic match who, being cast away on an
uninhabited island, performs some hocus-pocus worthy of Rider
Haggard, marries her cousin who comes to rescue her, and settles
down to christianize the natives on an adjoining island. The stran-
gest thing about the whole business is that everybody concerned
seems to have the gift of tongues, for whatever native or European
language is spoken, the listeners all understand and speak it. It is a
most amusing little book, full of action, romanticism, stilted English,
and impossible Indian lore. You can read all three editions at the

New York Public Library, but there are only eleven copies of all of the editions in the bibliographies.

And now we come back to Pennsylvania for our first Wyoming Valley adventure. Isaac Hollister of New London was captured, and his father and brother killed, in 1763 near the present town of Newbury. He escaped and was recaptured and sent to the Senecas on the Ohio, from whom he was released nearly four years later through the good offices of Sir William Johnson. On his return to New London in 1767, the local printer published his *A brief narration,* the unique Brinley copy having been sold to the Library of Congress. It was reprinted at Hartford a year or two later (two copies being known) and three times thereafter.

The life, extraordinary adventures, voyages, and surprising escapes of Capt. Neville Frowde, of Cork ♥. . *Written by himself and now first published from his own manuscript* . . . appeared in London in 1773 and was reprinted at Berwick in 1792. We suspect that the author, who was not the hero but Edward Kimber, a novelist of the period, got his inspiration from reading the Isaac Morris narrative of captivity in Patagonia, for this story also includes a shipwreck, a six 'months' sojourn of part of the crew on the coast of South America, capture of the hero by the Indians, his release, arrival at Rio de Janeiro, and final voyage home.

Let us now take from our shelf of captivities a much more substantial volume and one which has been famous for over a century and a half. Jonathan Carver's *Travels through the interior parts of North-America, in the years 1766, 1767, and 1768* are best remembered for the knowledge they give us of the frontiers of Minnesota and Wisconsin and of the Indian tribes of the middlewest. First printed in London in 1778, this book went through at least thirty-five editions in four languages. We are interested in it because of its vivid eye-witness account of the massacre of Fort William Henry in 1757, the author having been one of the English soldiers wounded and captured in that desperate affair. Though he was a prisoner of the French and Indians for only three days and finally escaped to Fort Edward, and though this part of his story fills only seven pages,

it is one of the most spirited accounts of the famous massacre and
so is well worth our notice.

By the beginning of the 1780's we find Revolutionary War narratives sharing the honors with the French and Indian War stories
which had been popular for many years. One of the most interesting
of the frontier heroes of this period was Lieutenant Moses Van
Campen, a militia officer from Northumberland County, Pennsylvania, who was twice an Indian captive. His first adventure,
which he shared with four others, took place in 1780 and lasted only
a few days, but it was lively while it lasted. It was published under
the title: *A narrative of the capture of certain Americans at Westmorland, by savages; and the perilous escape which they effected,
by surprizing specimens of policy and heroism. . . .* It was first
printed at Hartford in 1780 and reprinted at New London in 1784.
Only three copies of the first and one of the second edition have
been located. Van Campen's story, under the title: *A narrative of
the Pennsylvania frontier,* was published both in Washington and
Philadelphia in 1838, and his complete life was later written by his
grandson, J. N. Hubbard. It was called *Sketches of the life and adventures of Moses Van Campen* and appeared at Dansville, New
York, in 1841; Bath, 1841 and 1842 (two issues); and Fillmore,
New York, 1893.

One of the most deservedly popular of all the Revolutionary
frontier narratives is the story of Dr. John Knight and John Slover,
two members of Colonel William Crawford's unfortunate expedition of 1781 against the Wyandot Indians who had been devastat-
ing the Ohio and Pennsylvania frontiers. Though the publisher's
notice of the 1867 edition says that the first edition was printed in
Pittsburgh in 1782, and the late F. C. Deering reported having an
Andover edition of the same year, it has generally been understood
that the narratives were first printed in the Philadelphia *Freeman's
Journal* in 1783 and reprinted there for the first time in the same
year. Dr. Knight's story was written by himself for H. H. Brackenridge, who took down Slover's narrative from his own mouth. He
sent the two narratives to the *Journal* in 1782, and it is doubtful

that they had had a separate publication before they appeared serially in April and May of the following year.

There are two issues of the Philadelphia edition of 1783, the first with the date incorrectly printed 1773. There is but a single copy of the first issue known and two of the second. The pamphlet was reprinted at Andover about 1798 with the addition of the captivity of Mrs. Frances Scott, and at Leominster about 1800. There were at least three later editions, and the stories have appeared in numerous collections. This narrative must have infuriated the frontier since it tells how the popular Colonel Crawford was burned at the stake while the white renegade, Simon Girty, looked on and laughed.

The most famous of all Kentucky narratives—perhaps the greatest of all stories of the frontier—is *The adventures of Col. Daniel Boon.* Whether or not he himself wrote it out in the first place or John Filson took it down at his dictation and added a few flourishes of his own to make it more literary, it is signed with Boone's name as author and it is the greatest single first-hand story of the winning of the west. Originally published as an appendix to Filson's *The discovery, settlement and present state of Kentucke,* Wilmington, 1784, pp. 49-82, it reappeared in the numerous editions of that classic and was reprinted in various separate forms and in many editions from 1786 to 1930, as well as in several almanacs and in virtually every history of the west since its original appearance. The first separate edition, abridged and somewhat rewritten by John Trumbull, was published by him at Norwich in 1786, with the captivity of Mrs. Frances Scott, which took place the previous June, added for good measure. Of this great rarity there seem to be three or four copies, the Eames-Huntington copy, the one sold at Libbie's sale in 1888 and owned in 1943 by Goodspeed, Mr. Streeter's copy, and that in Dr. Rosenbach's collection.

Among his many adventures, Boone tells us how he and John Stewart were captured by the Indians in 1769 while he was on his first exploration of Kentucky and how, a week later, they escaped while their captors slept. He gives an account of the capture of his at Boonesborough in 1776, and of how he and eight men followed their captors and two days later recovered the girls and killed two of the Indians. Boone was captured again in 1778 near the Blue Licks, with his party of twenty-seven men. The latter were turned over to the British at Detroit, but the Indians so greatly admired Boone that they wished to adopt him and so took him to their town at Chelicothe. After being with them some five months Boone discovered that they were about to descend on Boonesborough, so he escaped one day before sunrise, traveled the 160 miles to his home in five days with but one meal during the trip, and got there in time to warn the settlement and help drive off the Indians.

You can never tell where a story of Indian captivity may be lurking. Surely you would not look twice at *A pocket of prose and verse: being a selection from the literary productions of Alexander Kellet, Esq.*, Bath, 1778, but if you turn to the contents you will find "A true relation of the unheard-of sufferings of David Menzies, surgeon, among the Cherokees, and of his surprising deliverance." This volume was reprinted at London as *The mental novelist* in 1783. There are only two copies of the first edition and four of the second.

The English public of the Revolutionary period was eager for stories of Indian adventure, and their hack writers quite willing to supply them. The following yarn, of which the New York Public Library seems to have the only surviving copy, appears to be fictitious and is probably based on the earlier Peter Williamson narrative. Its title tells the whole story: *A full and particular account, of the sufferings of William Gatenby; who is just arrived from America, with a true account of many circumstances relating to this unfortunate war, by which some hundreds of poor families are brought to utter ruin and destruction, to which himself and family have fallen victims. He gives an account of having been attacked by the Indians from the back settlements, who took his wife and child by force away, and killed his two slaves. How he and others pursued them, retook his wife and child, and killed three of the savages.* London, 1784.

The French too had to try their hand at it and so we find *Mis Mac Rea, roman historique, par M. Hilliard-d'Auberteuil.* It purports to have been printed at Philadelphia in 1784, but Sabin suggests that it may have been printed at Brussels. The tragic story of Jane McCrea can hardly be called a captivity since she was murdered almost as soon as captured, but I imagine that no captivity collector would refuse to add this interesting title to his collection if an eighth copy should cross the Atlantic.

Another, probably fictitious, English narrative tells of *The surprizing adventures of John Roach, mariner, of Whitehaven.* The earliest edition was printed at Liverpool in 1785. The hero was supposed to have been captured by Central American Indians in 1770. He escaped and was recaptured a number of times by various tribes, was imprisoned in Nicaragua and finally returned to London by way of Jamaica. Four eighteenth-century editions appeared in the British Isles, and a rewritten and enlarged version in 1810. It became a full-sized book with the hero's name changed to John Rhodes in the New York, 1798, and Newark, 1799, editions, and one episode was reprinted as *The powow* in a rare little 24mo volume printed at Otsego, New York, in 1808.

Every Philadelphia collector and student of our local history is familiar with *A narrative of the captivity and sufferings of Benjamin Gilbert and his family,* written by William Walton, Gilbert's brother-in-law, and published here by Crukshank in 1784. The Gilberts belonged to a prominent Quaker family from Byberry, now a part of this city. In 1780 they were living on the frontier not far from Bethlehem when a Seneca war party swooped down from Niagara, captured their entire household and that of their neighbors the Pearts, a total of fifteen men, women and children. They were carried off to the Indian towns and finally to Canada where they were ransomed after nearly two years of captivity. The story is fascinating reading and of great historical value since, like the Jemison captivity, it records the life of the Senecas during the Revolution and gives the reader a backstage view of the Indian warfare on the frontiers of New York and Pennsylvania. The narrative was reprinted at London in 1785 and 1790, at Doylestown in 1808, at Philadelphia in 1813 and 1848, at Lancaster in 1890, and Cleveland in 1904, the only rare editions being those of 1808 and 1813.

We now come to the simple story of a Negro boy of fourteen who got lost in the forest not far from Charlestown, S. C., where he was captured by an Indian hunter and taken to a Cherokee town in 1769. Through his simple religious faith he escaped burning at the stake, became the friend of the Indians, visited the Creeks and other tribes, and after living most of a year as an Indian returned to his family and finally became a preacher. His story was taken down by Reverend William Aldridge and published at London in 1785 under the title: *A narrative of the Lord's wonderful dealings with John Marrant, a black.* It was such a moving and popular narrative that at least twenty-nine editions appeared in England and America between 1785 and 1838, including one translated into Welsh.

One of the most pitiful stories of "the dark and bloody ground" tells how the Delawares and Mingoes swooped down on a frontier farm on the border of Virginia in 1785, killed the father of the family and the four children and carried off Mrs. Frances Scott, the mother. After some days of captivity she escaped and, after wandering through the mountains for about a month, finally arrived at New Garden, a settlement on the Clinch. Her story was published in the *Connecticut Gazette* in 1786, was included with the Boone narrative printed at Norwich that year, and was reprinted either as the *True and wonderful narrative* or *A remarkable narrative of the captivity and escape of Mrs. Frances Scott* in at least ten New England editions from that date to 1811. This is a captivity of great rarity, not more than two or three copies of any edition being known, and of several editions only a single copy has survived. It was also reprinted in the Philadelphia, 1794, edition of *A narrative of the extraordinary sufferings of Mr. Robert Forbes* and in three later editions, but not in the five earlier editions of this frontier narrative.

Another story which was popular in New England in the late eighteenth century was *A surprising account, of the captivity and escape of Philip M'Donald, and Alexander M'Leod, of Virginia. From the Chickkemogga Indians, and of their great discoveries in the western world. From June 1779, to January 1786, when they returned in health to their friends, after an absence of six years and a half. Written by themselves.* In this probably fanciful story, these two Revolutionary soldiers in the Ohio country were captured with others, saw their friends burned at the stake and expected the same fate for themselves. However, they escaped, crossed the continent to the Pacific, were picked up by a Russian fur-trading expedition, were taken to St. Petersburg, thence to London and home.

No copy of the first edition of this lively bit of early American fiction is known, but a second edition appeared at Bennington in 1786, a third at Pittsfield in 1788, and others at Keene in 1794, Windsor [1795], Haverill, 1796, and Rutland, 1797. We have located three copies of the 1794 edition, two of the second edition of 1786, and one each of the others—a sufficient indication of the rarity of this title in any edition.

The next narrative takes us to West Florida as our scene of action as we examine the only copy of the only recorded captivity published in broadside form. It was picked up in 1937 by the late Matt B. Jones and is now in the John Carter Brown Library. Here is the caption title and imprint: *John Graham's address to the master and worthy family of this house; shewing his sufferings among the Indians in West Florida. Printed in November, 1787. . . .* [Colophon:] *W. Appleton, Printer Darlington* [County of Durham, England].

Life had seemed fair enough to John Graham throughout his ten years of peaceful dealing with the Indians of West Florida. But on a day in 1785 a band with which he was about to do business turned upon his party and wiped it out with gun and hatchet. Graham was carried away and put to torture, but the unpleasant proceedings he describes were interrupted by the arrival of a detachment of British soldiers. For some time thereafter his life was a series of amputations of twisted limbs, of financial losses, shipwrecks, and other disasters which sent him back for refuge to his old home near Durham, and forced him to the practice of virtual mendicancy for the support of his family.*

We now encounter our first captivity in verse form, a fictionized poem with neither surnames nor geographical locations. In it we

* Lawrence C. Wroth in the *Annual Report* of the John Carter Brown Library for 1939, p. 30.

learn how John, returning with his daughter Nelly from nine years
of Indian captivity during and after the Revolution, finds his wife
Phebe married to his old friend Charles who sadly gives her back
to her number one husband. There are sixty pages of not very good
verse, and the title reads: *The returned captive. A poem. Founded
on a late fact.* It was printed at Hudson, New York, in 1787, reprinted at Norwich in 1790 and at Northampton in 1800, with five
known copies of the first edition, two of the second, and two of the
third.

Old Abraham Panther would certainly be surprised if he could
see what fine and fancy prices his little "tupenny" short story is
bringing today. When it was advertised in the *Middlesex Gazette*
in 1787 it was called *An account of a beautiful young lady, who
was taken by the Indians and lived in the woods nine years, and
then was providentially returned to her parent.* Evans surmises that
it was printed by Woodward and Green of Middletown in 1787,
but no copy has turned up in this generation. The anonymous
heroine was supposed to have been born at Albany in 1760, to have
been captured four or five days' journey from her home in 1777
and to have been restored to her father after "seeing no human
being for the space of nine years," which would have ended her
adventure about 1787, the date of the first edition. Who Abraham
Panther, the author, really was no one knows, but he must have
"had something" to have written a best seller which would run
through at least twenty-five editions from the date of the captivity
to 1932. In spite of being pure fiction, this narrative seems to have
a fatal fascination for collectors—and no wonder—for a fourth of
the editions are known only from contemporary advertisements and
it would be almost impossible to find more than three copies of any
of the rest. Printed at obscure village presses in small editions and
distributed by the Yankee peddlers of the time, these tiny pamphlets
of less than a dozen pages were quickly read to pieces, so it is a
wonder that any have survived to grace the catalogues of the booksellers.

An equally popular yarn, this time a mixture of fact and fiction,
was written under the pseudonym of Don Alonso Decalves and

entitled *New travels to the westward, or the unknown parts of America*. It was printed at Boston without date but was advertised as "just published" in the *Boston Gazette* of May 19, 1788. There was also a Norwich edition dated 1788 so we cannot be sure which is the real first. The story tells how a party of fur traders spent nearly fourteen months in a trip up the Mississippi from New Orleans and across the plains and the Rockies to the Pacific Coast in 1786-87, long before the first transcontinental exploring party of which we have an authentic record. This part of the narrative does not ring true, but when they reached the coast the fur traders met a white man named John Vandelure who told them his story of captivity among the local Indians, and that part of the story we are willing to believe, though we are still puzzled to know where Decalves got the story so many years before it appeared in its more legitimate form. There are at least twenty-six known editions of the Decalves story and they are just as rare, interesting, and expensive as the Panther captivity.

The Vandelure captivity appeared, rewritten and greatly expanded, under the title: *A history of the voyages and adventures of John Van Delure*, Montpelier, 1812, and in four other New England editions. Then, to complete the picture, we should mention *A narrative of the voyage taken by Captain James Van Leason*, Philadelphia, 1796, and three later editions, containing the Vandelure captivity as recorded by the sea captain who left him stranded on the Pacific Coast.

Of course one of the greatest of Colonial and Revolutionary heroes was General Israel Putnam who, in the French and Indian War in 1758 as a Major in Rogers' Rangers, was engaged around Fort Ticonderoga. In spite of his skill as a soldier and woodsman he was captured by the Indians, tied to a tree, and a brisk fire was burning around his legs when he was rescued by a French officer. All this we may learn from *An essay on the life of the Honorable Major-General Israel Putnam* by his old friend Colonel David Humphreys which was published at Hartford in 1788 and reprinted ten times. It was also abridged, but still included the captivity story of course, as the *Interesting life and adventures of Gen. Putnam*,

London about 1800, which edition was reprinted with variant titles at least twice.

While at the home of Colonel Schuyler on his way back from his Canadian captivity in 1758, Putnam met another captive, Mrs. Jemima Howe, and so Humphreys tells her story in some detail on pages 74-82 of his biography. But the best-known account of this famous captivity was written by the Reverend Bunker Gay for inclusion in Jeremy Belknap's *History of New Hampshire*, Boston, 1792. The publisher immediately saw that the story was sure to be popular and so reprinted it the same year in a twenty-page pamphlet. It was promptly lifted by Caleb Bingham for use in the dozens of editions of his *American preceptor* from 1794 until after the War of 1812, and then was lifted back from Bingham for a separate edition at Watertown in 1830 and finally became Extra Number 190 of the *Magazine of History* in 1933 in a mangled English version. The story was turned into verse as *The fair captive* by Angela Marco in 1937. The first edition had a long title beginning *A genuine and correct account of the captivity, sufferings & deliverance of Mrs. Jemima Howe, of Hinsdale, in New-Hampshire.* The version of the story reprinted in the *Magazine of History* was entirely rewritten in England, the poor heroine having become in the process the wife of a British officer. It was padded into respectable size by the interpolation of a number of other frontier stories and embellished with a hand-colored and lurid plate by George Cruikshank in which one of the Indians appears to be wearing a Roman helmet. This 1815 London chapbook edition had a title beginning *The affecting history of Mrs. Howe.*

This unfortunate lady, having already had one husband killed and scalped, married again and saw her second husband slain, while she and her seven children were taken captive at the Fort Dummer massacre in 1756. They were carried to Canada and her children were scattered. Colonel Schuyler finally ransomed her, and she recovered her five sons, but the two daughters were forced to take the veil in order to save themselves from their French captors.

A few days after the Wyoming Massacre, a resident of the valley named Luke Swetland was captured by a party of Seneca Indians and carried off to Kendaia near the present village of Romulus in Seneca County, New York, where he remained a prisoner from 1778 to 1779 and was finally rescued by General Sullivan's army during the expedition to subdue the Iroquois Indians. His unhappy narrative gives many details of Indian life as well as one more Revolutionary captivity yarn. It was printed at Hartford in an undated edition which must have appeared after the end of the Revolution but before 1800, probably between 1785 and 1790, and it had a title beginning *A very remarkable narrative of Luke Swetland, who was taken captive four times in the space of fifteen months, in the time of the late contest between Great Britain and America.* Yale has the only known copy of the original edition. It was reprinted at Waterville, N. Y., in enlarged form in 1875, and again, rewritten by Edward Merrifield, a descendant of the hero, at Scranton in 1915.

One of the most famous narratives of Indian captivity in the west is *The remarkable adventures of Jackson Johonnet, of Massachusetts. Who served as a soldier in the western army, in the Massachusetts line, in the expedition under General Harmar, and the unfortunate General St. Clair. Containing an account of his captivity, sufferings and escape from the Kickapoo Indians.* This narrative, if true, is especially important for its first-hand account of the defeat of General St. Clair at the battle of Miami on November 4, 1791, but the story of the author's previous capture and escape from the Indians and his rescue of another prisoner are classics of frontier adventure. The Boston, 1793, edition has sometimes been considered the first, probably because the author came from Massachusetts, but the Providence edition of the same year has this imprint: *Printed at Lexington (Kentucky) 1791. Re-printed at Providence, M,DCC,XCIII.* Though we can trace no copy of the Lexington edition, the news of St. Clair's defeat traveled fast, and the Lexington printer had nearly two months in which to receive and print the story before the end of 1791. That the narrative was written and sent off immediately after the defeat we know, for the author was still with St. Clair at Fort Jefferson when he finished writing. We are certain that none of the seven 1793 editions can be the first since the story was published in Beers' almanac for 1793, printed at Hartford in 1792. We have a record of sixteen separate editions of the story, and it is included in eight of the editions of the Manheim captivity. Mr. Ernest J. Wessen, a careful student of this region, states that there is no announcement of the supposed Lexington edition in the *Kentucky Gazette* for 1791-92. He further maintains that the narrative is, because of errors of fact, completely fraudulent. If this is true, the Beers' almanac edition is probably the first and the narrative an interesting example of historical fiction.

The historically important journal of Captain Thomas Morris, who served under Bradstreet in the Illinois country, tells of his capture by Pontiac while on a mission to various Indian tribes in that region. He several times narrowly escaped death while in Pontiac's camp, but since he was an ambassador from Bradstreet the great chief finally allowed him to proceed on his mission. Having completed it, he rejoined Bradstreet at Detroit, where he wrote out his journal in September 1764. It was printed at London in the author's volume of *Miscellanies in prose and verse*, 1791, and re-printed in Thwaites: *Early western travels* in 1904 and in Extra Number 76 of the *Magazine of History* in 1922. We can trace twelve copies of the first edition.

The most attractive eighteenth-century captivity in novelized form is *The history of Maria Kittle*, by Mrs. Ann Eliza Bleecker, written at Tomhanick, eighteen miles north of Albany, in 1779, in the form of a letter to her half-sister. It was first published in book form in the author's *Posthumous works*, New York, 1793, and was reprinted separately at Hartford in 1797 and again in 1802. It is supposed to be based on the true and pathetic story of Maria Kittle-huyne, but the descriptions, dialogue, and many of the details are from the not too unskilled imagination and pen of the author. Mrs. Bleecker wrote accurately and from experience since her own husband was carried off by the Indians during the Revolution but was recaptured before the marauders reached Canada. The Bur-goyne invasion forced her to flee from her home in 1777, and her youngest daughter died during this sad experience, so she had plenty of first-hand material available when she wrote her story two years later. The narrative tells how Maria Kittle's home near the Hudson was invaded by Indians in 1748 while her husband was gone for help to the near-by village of Schochticook. Her two children and her sister-in-law were murdered, the home rifled and burned, and she and her husband's brother carried to a two years' captivity at Montreal where her husband at last found her. She is supposed to have died in the author's home town the day before the story was written. There are at least sixteen copies of the first edition, eight of the second, and two of the third.

The *Affecting history of the dreadful distresses of Frederick Manheim's family* is an anthology of frontier Indian fighting and captivity, full of pioneer bravery and Indian atrocity. Manheim and his twin daughters were captured on the Mohawk near Johnstown in 1779 during one of the many Indian raids on that region. Since their captors could not decide which was entitled to the two girl captives, they were both tortured to death in horrible fashion. The eight other stories include the captivities of Isaac Stewart, Massy Herbeson, Peter Williamson, and Jackson Johonnet. First printed at Exeter in 1793, with at least three variant imprints, it was reprinted the following year at Philadelphia and in at least six later editions. Several of the narratives found their way into the pages of contemporary almanacs and later collections of frontier tales.

When that lively old Scotsman, Patrick Campbell, was on his *Travels in the interior inhabited parts of North America in the years 1791 and 1792*, Edinburgh, 1793, he ran across a brother Scot named David Ramsay who, in 1772, set up a trading post on the Chaudière River above Port Stanley where he lived with a younger brother. After various hazardous adventures with the Indians, in which he killed several of them he was finally captured and prepared for torture. Though securely tied, he got away, killed eight of his enemies and fled with his brother to Fort Niagara, where he was put into what we might now call "protective custody" by the British, who thus saved his life, for the Indians were clamoring for revenge. He was sent to Montreal for trial, but it was proved that he had killed the Indians in self-defense and so he was released. He wrote out his story for Campbell, who printed it in the old trader's own words. Though the original edition of Campbell's travels is very rare, there are two modern editions, and Ramsay's story appears in the *Publications* of the Buffalo Historical Society.

It is strange that one of the best-written, most detailed, interesting, and historically valuable of all captivities is virtually unknown. Though mentioned by Sabin and Evans, they give no collation and locate no copy. There is, however, a copy at the New-York Historical Society, the title of which begins: *The journal of William Scudder, an officer of the late New-York Line, who was taken captive by the Indians at Fort Stanwix, . . .* [New York?] Printed for the author. MDCCXCIV. Lieutenant Scudder was captured in 1779 and, after many adventures with the Indians, was taken to Montreal and Quebec and was finally released on parole at New York in 1782. The early part of the book tells of his adventures in the various Revolutionary campaigns before his captivity and gives many new details of camp life and the familiar episodes of the war in New York State. He began his journal at Montreal in 1779 and in it tells the daily routine, the rumors, and discouragements of the not too severe captivity of the American officers in prison in Canada. The manuscript was finished in 1784 and so has the merit of contemporary writing and, since it fills 250 pages, it is far more complete than the average captivity story.

For a captivity of almost equal rarity, but very different plot, I would refer you to *A true narrative of the sufferings of Mary Kinnan*, published in Elizabethtown, N. J., in 1795 by Shepard Kollock who, according to the heroine's family, wrote down the story from her dictation. She was captured in Virginia in 1791, taken to Ohio and was with the Indians at the time of St. Clair's defeat and until rescued by her brother at the time of Wayne's victory in 1794. There are two recorded copies of the first edition, two of the second edition, New Haven, 1801, and a like number of the Beers' *Washington Almanac* for 1805 which also contains the story. Five reprints or articles on "Aunt Polly Kinnan" have appeared in other publications. Oscar McMurtry also told her brother's story of the rescue in *A short history of the capture by Indians of Mrs. Mary Kinnan.*

A journal of the adventures of Matthew Bunn is a much more varied and exciting story of the same period. He was an ensign with St. Clair, captured in the Ohio country in 1792, escaped and was recaptured by the renegade George Girty, gave him the slip and surrendered to the British garrison at Detroit the following year. For damning King George and all the royal family he was thrown into jail and sent to Fort Niagara and, to save his hide, joined the Queen's Rangers, escaped, got caught and was given five hundred lashes, escaped again and, after still more adventures along the Niagara frontier, returned to his native Massachusetts in 1795. His story was first printed without date at Providence in 1796 and was reprinted in seven later editions, all but the last two being extremely rare.

Traveling still farther to the northeast, we find *A narrative of the sufferings of James Derkinderen, who was taken prisoner by the Halifax Indians* in 1759. This brief but very interesting journal was "printed verbatim et literatim from the author's manuscript," with all its quaint phraseology and mistakes in spelling, at Philadelphia in 1796. Its two recorded copies speak eloquently of its rarity.

One of the famous New England captivities which was not published until the heroine's old age is *A narrative of the captivity of Mrs. Johnson* which first appeared at Walpole in 1796 and ran through a total of ten editions, three in Scotland and the last at Woodstock, Vermont, in 1926. She was captured at Charlestown, New Hampshire, in 1754, along with her family, gave birth to a daughter while still a captive, and remained in the hands of the Indians and French at Montreal for four years.

The history of Ned Evans by Mrs. Jane West was published in London in 1796 in four volumes, about one hundred pages of the third volume containing the story of the hero's capture by the Cherokees in South Carolina while serving with a British regiment. He was adopted into the tribe and lived with them about eighteen months, when they released him and he returned to Charlestown to learn that the war was over and his regiment had returned to England. Whether this story was founded on an actual experience or not, it was sufficiently interesting to have a second London edition in 1797 and others in Dublin in 1796 and 1805.

Ebenezer Fletcher, a sixteen-year-old fifer in one of the New Hampshire regiments opposed to Burgoyne in 1777, was wounded and captured by the Indians at the battle of Hubbardston. A few weeks later, his wound having partially healed, he managed to escape and, after an exciting series of adventures with wolves and Tories, returned to his regiment and served in the Sullivan expedition against the Iroquois two years later. His *Narrative* appeared at Amherst, New Hampshire, in 1798, went through five other editions, and was said also to have been published in verse. All but the last two editions are exceedingly rare.

Back once more in the early days of the southwest, we find *An account of the remarkable occurrences in the life and travels of Col. James Smith,* who was captured at Fort Duquesne during the Braddock expedition and remained with the Indians from 1755 to 1759. His very full and informative story is one of the great treasures of early Kentucky printing. It appeared at Lexington in 1799 and went through eight editions. The Colonel was an excellent observer of Indian life and wrote another volume of great interest: *A treatise, on the mode and manner of Indian war,* Paris, Kentucky, 1812, which retells his captivity story and gives us one of our first manuals of Indian warfare. It appears to be even rarer than the captivity.

In 1799 a German work appeared at Meissen called *Die wilde Europäerinn oder Geschichte der Frau von Walwille,* with a second edition with a different title in 1809. It purported to tell the story of an Englishwoman who was a captive among the Iroquois from about 1755 to 1759 and wrote her adventures while living at St. John, Newfoundland, in 1778. It is probably fictitious and is certainly rare, for the Deering copy of the second edition is the only one traceable in this country.

Another piece of Indian fiction, also very rare, is the *Narrative of the singular adventures and captivity of Mr. Thomas Barry, among the Monsipi Indians, in the unexplored regions of North America* during the years 1797-99. He was supposed to have been captured while on an Indian trading expedition out of Charleston in 1797 and finally to have escaped with great hardship, accompanied by "an Indian female" who went with him to London, thereby adding a Pocahontas-like heart interest generally lacking in authentic captivity stories. Two editions were printed at Sommers Town, England, in 1800 and 1802 and a third at about the same time at Manchester, published appropriately enough by *A. Swindells*. There are only from one to three copies known of the various editions.

The last book on our captivity shelf is something of a puzzle, for it has generally been considered fictitious because the name of the Indian tribe which captured the hero is unknown to most readers, and some of his adventures seem a little far-fetched. However, the author certainly did live his later life in New England and it is altogether likely that much of the story records his actual captivity. It is called *Memoirs of Charles Dennis Rusoe d'Eres, a native of Canada* and was printed at Exeter in 1800, a neat little book of 176 pages. The story begins with the attack of Montgomery on Quebec and ends with the marriage of the author at Spencer, Massachusetts, in 1794 and his removal to New Hampshire, where he found employment as a blacksmith. His travels took him as far west as Lake Superior and later to Detroit as an interpreter, but he must have learned to draw the long bow from the Indians, for the correct and obvious facts of the narrative are frequently interlarded with episodes which seem entirely fictitious. Though Field considered it "one of the rarest of books relating to the aborigines," there are eleven copies on record and several have been sold at auction or through dealers' catalogues.

Our current newspapers contain many a thrilling narrative of a brave soldier who has been given up for dead but has returned to tell of his hairbreadth escape and miraculous restoration. Our Revolutionary ancestors seldom left a record of their equally exciting adventures, but occasionally one comes to light. Here is a dramatic story from an 1807 newspaper which tells of the return of a Revolutionary Rip Van Winkle, one of General Herkimer's lieutenants at the Battle of Oriskany, who for thirty years had been given up as lost by his sorrowing family but eventually came back, minus his scalp, after a long and distressing captivity.

His name was Petrus Groot, and he was born March 7, 1744, at Crane's Village, a hamlet near Amsterdam on the north side of the Mohawk in Saratoga County. He was a Lieutenant in the Third Tryon County Regiment of militia and was supposed to have been killed at the Battle of Oriskany. The following narrative tells of his return thirty years later and of his second disappearance. Whether he ever reached the shelter of his former home in Amsterdam we do not know. Perhaps, like the other Flying Dutchman, he still wanders the countryside along the Mohawk turnpike, carrying his huge pack. It is curious that both his father and grandfather were carried off by the Indians to Canada before him, the latter at the burning of Schenectady. But we will let his old friend Judge Sanders tell the story as he did in the Albany newspaper one hundred thirty-five years ago.

On Thursday, the 4th inst. about four miles from the city of Schenectady, aside of the Mohawk turnpike, sitting under a tree, I discovered Petrus Groot, who was supposed to have been slain in the Oriskena battle, under General Herkimer, on the 6th of August, in the year 1777. I immediately recognized him, and on conversing with him he confessed himself to be the person I took him to be. I then carried him to the nearest tavern, where I left him to be sent to his children and brothers, from whence, however, he departed before day the next morning, and was seen in Albany on Friday. His mental faculties are much impaired, supposed to have been occasioned by a wound of a tomahawk near the fore part of his head, though he is at most times tolerably rational. His head is bald—the circle or sear of the scalping knife is plainly to be seen on it, and a stab on the side of his neck near his shoulder; has a small scar near his ancle—is a middle sized man, has blue eyes, a long countenance, and stoops much in the shoulder. He speaks English, French, Dutch and Indian; and says he has been last a prisoner among the Indians north of Quebec. Had on an old dark grey coat and old brownish pantaloons—has a large pack with him. He refused to go home, as one of his former neighbors whom he saw would not recognize him, he was fearful his children and brothers would not. He said he would go to the Governor's. Being at times deranged, it is fearful he will stray too far away for his friends to find him. He is of a very respectable family and connexions. Any person who will take him up and bring him to the subscriber, at Schenectady, shall be well compensated for his care and trouble, and will receive the sincere thanks of his children and relatives, and be the means of relieving this poor unfortunate man from his distress, by restoring him to his family and friends.

John Sanders

Schenectady, June 8th, 1807.

N.B. The printers in this and the neighboring states are requested to give the above a few insertions in their respective papers, to aid in restoring a poor sufferer to his children and friends, who has been thirty years a prisoner among the Indians. He is now 63 years of age. He was a lieutenant in the militia at the time he was supposed to be slain.*

Our frontiersmen have trudged the last long mile home from their captivity and their log blockhouses have crumbled into dust, but their memory still lives in the stirring narratives of their sad adventures. Their courage and tenacity moved steadily westward, across the Appalachians, the Plains, and the Rockies until they had carved a mighty nation out of the wilderness and had replaced the stone age with the civilization of today. Great cities have grown at their carrying places and trading posts, and their month-long journeys by blazed trail and canoe are now retraced by air within the hour. Before Pearl Harbor we sometimes wondered if the pioneer virtues had been wiped out by easy living, but we now know that the courage, the resourcefulness, and the hardihood of the old frontiersmen are still strong within us, a vigorous and worthy inheritance from the past which makes it possible for us to face with confidence whatever the future has in store.

* From the Canandaigua, N. Y., *Western Repository*, June 30, 1807, where it was reprinted from the *Albany Gazette* of June 8, 1807, or the next issue thereafter. The author of this appeal was a prominent citizen of Schenectady, a judge, state senator and member of the Council of Appointment. For Groot's genealogy, see *Groot Family, of Albany and Schenectady*. By Jonathan Pearson, in *New York Genealogical and Biographical Record*, January, 1873, pp. 8-12.

3

The Frontier Land Agents
Offer Their Wares

The Grass Is Green in Yonder Field

As you drive along the Roosevelt Highway between the river towns of Wyalusing and Towanda in northern Pennsylvania, you presently find yourself some five hundred feet above the surrounding country with a magnificent view of rolling hills and well-tilled farms spread out before you. At your feet the beautiful Susquehanna curves in a graceful half-circle enclosing a broad, tree-bordered tract of some 2,400 acres. Once more the grass is green in yonder fields, but in the late eighteenth century a thriving village lay there in the bend of the river, a village with handsome houses, taverns, stores and shops, a chapel, a brewery and, if you please, a theatre. To the Americans it was known as Frenchtown, but the inhabitants called it Azilum, for it was to have been the haven of refuge of a lovely queen who never came. They even built a Grande Maison which was to have been the palace of Marie Antoinette and her children. Here, far from the terrors of the French Revolution, a colony of titled refugees lived for a time—a little Paris in the wilderness.

This romantic enterprise was known as the Asylum Company, one of the many land speculations fathered by Robert Morris, and a typical illustration of the gambling in frontier properties which followed the opening of the western country after the Revolution. Let us examine in detail the promotion literature of a few of the more important land companies which flourished between the Revolution and the end of the century, with a brief mention of the earlier material. The old land agents were gamblers in the grand manner and many lost, but it was their vision, enthusiasm, and energy which began the opening of the west. Almost every great

62

name in American Revolutionary history, as well as many from overseas, is to be found on the subscription books of the various land companies, and their speculations stir our imagination for they dealt not in individual farms and building lots, but in hundreds of thousands and often·in millions of acres. Great cities stand today where they built their log taverns and grist mills in the wilderness. Or, since the wheel of fortune did not always turn up a lucky number, the sites of some of their flourishing towns, like Azilum, are known only by the historical markers which tell the sad story of their march to oblivion.

Since in recent years land speculation has flourished in Florida, it seems appropriate that our earliest piece of real estate promotion literature should also have been inspired by an old-world enthusiasm for the same land of flowers, and that the author of this sixteenth-century poem in praise of Florida should himself have been named Flores. This was the first printed encouragement to colonization in what is now the United States, and its four quarto leaves of verse have survived in but a single copy. It was written by Bartolomé de Flores and printed at Seville in 1571 with a title beginning: *Obra nvevamen te compvesta*. It is described and the text reprinted in full in J. T. Medina's *Biblioteca Hispano-Americana* from the unique copy then owned by the author, but now in its permanent home at the John Carter Brown Library in Providence.

Though the seaboard states were founded as havens of refuge from religious persecution, as philanthropic establishments for the amelioration of the condition of the poor, or as homes for unwanted convicts and ne'er-do-wells, most of them were promoted by colonization companies which hoped to reap a rich reward from the discovery of precious minerals, from the fur trade, or from the sale of lands and the formation of settlements in this fascinating, new, and untamed world which their hardy explorers had so recently discovered. In the early seventeenth century the Virginia Company flooded England with its glowing accounts of the new country, using such alluring titles as *Nova Britannia, Virginia richly valued, The new life of Virginia,* and *Good newes from Virginia.*

As early as 1606 Sir Ferdinando Gorges began his active but

none too profitable career as a promoter of the storm-swept coasts
of New England, an adventure which finally ended with the selling
of his interest in Maine to the colony of Massachusetts in 1677.
The Council for New England got under way in 1620 and sent
the *Mayflower* on her famous voyage, and in the following year
the Dutch West India Company was chartered and soon had its
fur-trading posts established at Fort Orange and on Manhattan
Island. The Swedish Australian Company, instituted in 1624, was
soon busy rivaling the Dutch along the Delaware, while the Plymouth colony secured a patent on the Kennebec and began a war of
promotion literature and controversial pamphlets among the rival
claimants to that territory which lasted well into the next century.

Such tracts as White's *Planter's plea* and Captain John Smith's
Advertisements for unexperienced planters of New-England, his
Description of New England and *New Englands trials* and the account of the settlement of Salem contained in *New England's
plantation,* had helped to fan the interest of the adventurous
Puritans, and so the Winthrop fleet sailed away from old England
and the Massachusetts Bay Colony came into being in 1630.

Two years later Lord Baltimore secured his Maryland charter
and founded his new colony as a haven for persecuted Catholics
and, in 1633, issued his first promotion tract: *A declaration of the
Lord Baltimore's plantation in Mary-land, nigh upon Virginia.* This
he followed with *A relation of the successful beginnings of the Lord
Baltimore plantation, A relation of Maryland,* and *A moderate and
safe expedient to remove jealousies and feares,* the latter appearing
in 1646.

Carelessness and an imperfect knowledge of American geography
during the colonization period resulted in overlapping royal grants
and misfortune for some of the adventurers. One of these was Sir
Edmund Plowden, who in 1634 obtained a charter for New Albion,
a vast territory embracing parts of the present states of New Jersey,
Maryland, Delaware, and Pennsylvania as well as Long Island. In
order to promote his wilderness empire he issued, in 1641, *A direction for adventurers with small stock to get two for one* and followed
it seven years later with *A description of the Province of New Albion*

(reprinted in 1650). Most of the same territory having already been granted to the powerful Duke of York, or settled by the Swedes, Sir Edmund found himself without a colony. He died in 1659, but his great-greatgrandson, Francis, continued the vain quest when, in 1784, he sent Charles Varlo to America to sell the land. He issued various promotion pamphlets and broadsides and even advertised Long Island for sale in a tract called *The fairest part of America,* in spite of the fact that it had long ago been sold and settled.

Persecution seems to have attracted the disaffected to Rhode Island without the benefit of promotion literature, and eager settlers were drifting into Connecticut, New Hampshire, Maine, and Vermont in the late sixteen hundreds without the inspiration of land prospectuses. The Dutch were interested in furs rather than farms, and so the West India Company did little to encourage land sales outside of the immediate vicinity of their trading posts on the Hudson. Several Dutchmen and later an Englishman or two did publish interesting descriptions of New Netherland which undoubtedly attracted colonists. Among them were De Laet, van der Donck, De Vries, Denton, and Wooley.

By 1663 Charles II had issued a charter for Carolina to a group of his court favorites, and four years later colonists were being lured in that direction by a promotion pamphlet entitled *A brief description of the Province of Carolina.* This was followed in 1682 by *The present state of Carolina with advice to settlers* and *A letter from South Carolina; giving an account of the soil* which appeared in 1710 with later editions in 1718 and 1732. In spite of these alluring tracts and such others as John Norris's *Profitable advice for rich and poor,* 1712, and *A description of the Golden Islands,* 1720, settlement was slow because of Indian wars, the maladministration of the proprietors, and the greater attractiveness of other colonies.

As a result of the seizure of New Netherlands by the British in 1664, these territories came into the hands of the Duke of York, who promptly turned New Jersey over to Lord Berkeley and Sir George Carteret, who divided their grant into East and West Jersey. Berkeley's share was West Jersey which he sold to John Fenwick and Edward Byllings, from whom the lands passed to William Penn and a group of Quakers who developed them as a haven for persecuted members of their faith. Carteret opened East Jersey and soon had several flourishing settlements of New Englanders. On his death in 1680, a group of Quakers, again headed by Penn, bought the unsold part of the colony and developed it as a place of refuge for the Scotch Covenanters then being driven out of their old home by the British.

The promotion literature of the New Jersey ventures included Penn's *Concessions and agreements,* a constitution for the governing of West Jersey, and George Scot's *The model of the government of the Province of East Jersey in America,* Edinburgh, 1685. In addition to these fundamental documents, there were many other publications issued to attract settlers. The first was John Fenwick's broadside proposals for planting the colony, issued in 1675, a copy of which is in the Historical Society of Pennsylvania. The following year *A further account of New Jersey* appeared and was followed in 1682 by *A brief account of the Province of East Jersey in America.* The next year a tract with practically the same title appeared in Edinburgh for the guidance of Covenanters who might wish to escape to the new world. The founding of Perth Amboy was forecast in the London, 1682, *Proposals by the proprietors of East-Jersey in America for the building of a town on Ambo-Point.* English criticism of the enterprise was answered by *An abstract . . . of . . . testimonys from the inhabitants of New Jersey,* London, 1681. The most interesting and historically valuable of these promotion tracts, both written by actual settlers, were Thomas Budd's *Good order established in Pennsilvania and New Jersey,* 1685, and Gabriel Thomas' *An historical description of the province and country of West New Jersey in America,* 1698.

It would be presumptuous to repeat the magnificent story of the founding of Pennsylvania or even to enumerate the scores of promotion tracts published in several languages between 1681 and the end of the century which were so effective in attracting settlers to the Commonwealth. From Penn's *Some account of the Province of Pennsylvania* and his *Frame of government,* through his later tracts and those by Pastorious, The Free Society of Traders, Frame, Budd, More, Blome, Thomas, and all the rest, the list is impressive and each title a delight to scholar and collector alike.

The charter for Georgia, the youngest of the original thirteen colonies, was secured in 1732 by Oglethorpe and the Earl of Egmont. Their purpose was mainly philanthropic, for they wished to form a colony which could be a refuge for persecuted Protestants and the unfortunate debtors of London. Organized under a trusteeship, the colony was governed for its first twenty-one years by a group of titled or otherwise prominent Englishmen. Though they succeeded in rescuing from their unhappy economic and religious difficulties a great many English, Highland Scotch, Irish, Germans, including many Moravians and German Salzburgers, and a few Jews, the colony did not flourish until the crown took over and appointed a royal governor in 1760.

The promotion literature of Georgia is extensive. The De Renne collection in the University of Georgia Library contains some thirty titles in English and twice that number in German, the latter relating to the Salzburgers. The trustees began their campaign to interest the English people in their philanthropy by publishing *Some account of the designs of the Trustees for Establishing the Colony of Georgia in America,* London, 1732, and followed it with Benjamin Martyn's *A new and accurate account of the provinces of South-Carolina and Georgia,* London, 1732, and his *Reasons for establishing the colony of Georgia,* London, 1733. These were followed by frequent reports and appeals of the trustees and sermons in support of the undertaking.

In 1717 John Law, a Scotch financier, organized the Mississippi Company, later the Company of the Indies, to exploit the resources of Louisiana, then a French colony. His *Full and impartial account of the Company of the Mississippi . . . projected and settled by Mr. Law* was published in London in 1720 and is typical of the flood of promotion literature which he issued in several languages to interest speculators in his scheme. His campaign was highly successful, and thousands of shares of his stock were sold in England, France, Germany, and the Netherlands. When his Mississippi bubble burst, many of his stockholders lost everything they had and his adventure became the most disastrous failure in the history of land speculation.

In the quarter-century preceding the Revolution, numerous land companies were organized to exploit the wilderness beyond the Appalachians, but they were driven back by the Indians, failed to secure their expected grants, or found that their titles were not clear. Among them was the Ohio Company of Virginia, organized in 1748 to exploit the rich Indian trade and to foster settlement west of the Alleghenies. Composed of the leading Virginians of the day, including Washington, it was the spearhead of civilization into the Ohio country. Hoping to secure from the crown a grant of half a million acres in the upper Ohio Valley, they had the territory explored and began to push into the wilderness where they were stopped by the French and Indians and later by the British. Before their grant materialized, the Revolutionary War wiped out their hopes for a new western colony.

The Susquehanna Company, organized in 1753 by a group of prominent Connecticut citizens for the settlement of the Wyoming Valley in Pennsylvania, had a stormy career. It based its claim on the Connecticut charter of 1662, but this claim was fiercely and successfully contested by Pennsylvania. In 1774 Benjamin Trumbull wrote *A plea in vindication of the Connecticut title* and Provost William Smith answered with *An examination of the Connecticut claim.* Barnabas Bidwell took the part of the company with *The Susquehannah title stated and examined,* Catskill, 1796, and the Pennsylvanians countered with *Papers respecting intrusions by Connecticut claimants,* Philadelphia, 1796. Though their early settlements were wiped out by the Indians, and the Yankee-Pennamite wars further disrupted their plans, the company in 1803 finally got clear title to seventeen townships in northeastern Pennsylvania although the territory remained part of Pennsylvania.

At the treaty of Fort Stanwix in 1768 a group of Indian traders and merchants secured an Indian title to a tract south of Pennsylvania and organized the Indiana Company for its exploitation. They failed to get an English grant for the land, and after the

Revolution Virginia successfully blocked their claim. Their spokesman, Samuel Wharton, published several pamphlets in explanation of their rights under the Indian grant and to attract purchasers for their lands. These include the *Case* for the proprietors, probably published in London about 1770, *Facts and observations*, published in London in 1775, *View of the title of Indiana*, Philadelphia, 1775, 1776, and Williamsburg, 1779, and *Plain facts*, Philadelphia, 1781.

This company later merged with others to form the Grand Ohio Company, also known as the Walpole Company and later the Vandalia Company, organized to promote a new colony to contain twenty million acres between the Allegheny Mountains and the Ohio River. Thomas Walpole was the principal promoter and Samuel Wharton the spokesman of this enterprise. In addition to the three titles already mentioned, he wrote a *Statement for the petitioners*, 1771, *Report of the Lords Commissioners . . . on the petition*, 1772, a petition *To the king's most excellent majesty*, 1774, *Considerations on the agreement of the Lords Commissioners*, 1774, and he may have been the author of the anonymous *Advantages of a settlement upon the Ohio in North America*, London, 1763 [i.e., 1773].

The Illinois and Wabash Land Company is of special interest to Philadelphians since William Murray of this city was its founder, and such prominent men as Robert Morris, George Ross, Bernard Gratz, and Silas Deane belonged to it. Organized in 1779 by the consolidation of two earlier companies, it hoped to sell land and promote the Indian trade of the Illinois country. The company finally ended its activities in 1784 when Virginia's western lands were ceded to the national government and private exploitation in that direction was stopped. To promote its interests, the company issued Provost William Smith's *An account of the proceedings of the Illinois and Ouabache Land Companies* in 1796 (reprinted in 1803), and Congress printed their *Memorial* and the report of the House committee, 1797, denying their request that the government confirm their title. They again memorialized Congress in 1810 and 1816 but without favorable action.

After the Revolutionary War and the adoption of the constitution, conditions were greatly improved for the land speculators. The Indians were no longer a serious menace after their defeat by Wayne in 1794, state boundaries and the national currency became fixed, and the land agents could at last give clear titles to their properties. Men of means were eager to recoup their fallen fortunes by land investments, and settlers were streaming west in ever increasing numbers, anxious to buy new homes on the frontier.

General Washington, having retired to Mount Vernon, took up again his old interest in western lands and, in 1784, issued a handbill, now in the New York Public Library, stating that *The subscriber would lease about 30,000 acres of land on the Ohio.* Others were eager to follow his lead.

In 1786 a group of Connecticut Revolutionary War officers headed by General Rufus Putnam and Benjamin Tupper organized the Ohio Company and raised a million dollars through the sale of stock for the purchase of a million and a half acres of land north of the Ohio River. Settlement began at Marietta in 1788 and, though about a third of the land reverted to the government, permanent occupation of the present state of Ohio had begun and one of the most satisfactory of the large-scale land schemes was under way.

The literature of this company began with its *Articles of association,* Worcester, 1786, and New York, 1787, and reports of two meetings of the directors in 1787 and one in 1788 were separately published, followed by the company's *Contract* in 1787 and *Articles of agreement* in 1788. Its most pretentious publication was *An explanation of the map* of the purchase, 1787, which had the distinction of being the first description of Ohio.

A year after the founding of the Ohio Company, Judge John Cleves Symmes of Morristown, New Jersey, and a group of his more influential neighbors negotiated the Miama Purchase, a tract of a million acres on the north side of the Ohio between the Miami and the Little Miami rivers. Settlement began in 1788 and within a year there were three towns in the purchase, including Cincinnati. Like so many others, Symmes had difficulty in making payments to the government and so only secured title to some 311,000 acres, but otherwise the venture was a success. Before removing to the purchase, Symmes published a descriptive pamphlet at Trenton in 1787 addressed *To the respectable public* in which he described his lands and the terms of their purchase and stated that he was reserving for himself only a single township, the site of the present city of Cincinnati. This pamphlet was reprinted the same year and again at Cincinnati in 1796.

In 1787 William Duer and a group of New York speculators contracted for the purchase of nearly five million acres on the Scioto River, northwest of the Ohio Company's purchase. The poet Joel Barlow was selected as their agent and sent to France in 1789 where, with a crooked Englishman inappropriately named Playfair, he organized the Compagnie du Scioto and issued a lying *Prospectus* with a falsified map and another pamphlet of *Avis* which soon brought in numerous purchasers of stock and some five hundred prospective settlers. Playfair ran away with the company's funds, the American owners failed in the panic of 1792, the lands were never paid for, and the poor French investors and settlers were left stranded. Two very interesting pamphlets were printed in Paris in 1790, written as warnings to their countrymen by Frenchmen who had lived on the purchase. One was called *Le Nouveau Mississipi, ou les dangers d'habiter les bords du Scioto,* and the other, *Nouvelles du Scioto, ou relation fidèle du voyage et des infortunes d'un Parisien, qui arrive de ces pays-là où il etait allé pour s'établir.* He feelingly added after the title the phrase: *Vive la France et Paris!* Another Frenchman's *Observations* attacked the company the same year.

When General Sullivan's army went swinging along through the glades and across the ridges on their march to the Indian country in 1779 their keen eyes were watchful, not only for the lurking Iroquois but also for new homes for themselves. As they sat around their campfires on the shores of Canandaigua Lake or on the banks of the Genesee they carefully recorded in their diaries their surprise and joy at finding such rich soil, such thrifty crops of Indian corn and beans and such beautiful rolling country, with lovely lakes and streams, and all within comparatively easy reach of their own stony, unproductive New England farms.

After the Iroquois had been punished for Wyoming and Cherry Valley and had been driven to the protection of the walls of Fort Niagara, with their homes and crops left in ashes, and after peace had been declared, the weary and impoverished soldiers who had been on the Sullivan Expedition went back to their homes fully determined to move to the West and settle in the tax-free, rich, and beautiful Genesee Country. As the discharged Revolutionary soldiers returned from the war they found their farms neglected, their buildings in need of repair, and war taxes swallowing the little they had saved. Very few had received regular pay, and those few found that the depreciated currency given them was of little or no value.

When they gathered of an evening in the public square of Norwalk or in the taproom of the Red Lion Inn at Stockbridge, their conversations very naturally took them back to the Genesee, and those who had seen this wonderful country to the west were often called on to tell of it to their land-hungry neighbors.

During these first years after the war the men of affairs of Philadelphia and Boston, of New York and Lenox were also turning their eyes to these Iroquois lands along the Genesee. They too had lost heavily as a result of the war and were now hoping to rebuild their broken fortunes by speculation in these rich western lands. In order to open the new country for settlement, treaties and agreements were shortly put into effect between the federal government and the Six Nations and between the several states. As a result we find men like Robert Morris and his son Thomas, Oliver Phelps, Nathaniel Gorham, Israel Chapin, Nathaniel Rochester, the Wadsworths, and a host of others actively engaged in buying these lands from the Iroquois and from the states which controlled them and offering them to the Yankee and Pennsylvania farmers. Wealthy merchants in the cities were also induced to buy, while great tracts were sold to rich investors in Holland and England.

In the Phelps and Gorham Purchase of 1788 the proprietors contracted to buy all of Western New York—the Genesee Country—from Massachusetts, subject to the extinguishment of the Indian title. Having secured a third of the tract, they became financially embarrassed and were compelled to allow the rest to revert to Massa-

chusetts. They did not issue a prospectus but did publish, in 1794,
a map of the purchase which was used by their land agents at
Canandaigua and elsewhere; and of course they advertised in the
newspapers.

The unsold part of the Phelps and Gorham Purchase was bought
by Robert Morris who in 1791, issued a prospectus *An account of
the soil, growing timber, and other productions,* printed in London
by his agent, William Temple Franklin, who promptly sold the
entire tract of over a million acres to the English Associates. This
Pulteney Purchase, as it is generally called, was bought by William
Pulteney, William Hornby and Patrick Colquhoun, who placed the
marketing of the tract in the hands of Charles Williamson, a vision-
ary enthusiast whose expense account was apt to outrun his sales.
The last lands were not sold until 1926, the entire undertaking
yielding a fair profit, thanks to the better business methods of
Robert Troup, Williamson's successor as land agent.

Williamson wrote several interesting promotion pamphlets which
were widely distributed and are highly prized by students and collectors today. They include his *Description of the Genesee Country,*
Albany, 1798; same, New York, 1799; *Observations on the proposed state road from Hudson's River . . . to Lake Erie,* New York,
1800 (the road was later built in order to make Williamson's lands
more accessible); *A view of the present situation of the western
parts of the State of New York, called the Genesee Country,* Frede-
rick-Town, 1804; and the same reprinted in three editions as *A
description of the Genesee Country.* A German agent for the company, named William Berczy, had previously translated Morris's
original prospectus, with numerous additions, under the title
Bericht über den Genesee-Distrikt. This appeared in 1791 and
helped the agent round up a small colony of German settlers whom
he later transported to the company's lands, much to Williamson's
embarrassment, for they were totally unsuited to the rigors of
pioneer life.

The third western New York land concern, which eventually
owned and sold most of the territory between Rochester and Buffalo, was the Holland Land Company. In 1792, four Dutch mercan-

tile houses began buying Genesee and Pennsylvania lands and, having added other partners, they perfected their final organization in 1796. They owned a half million acres in Pennsylvania and 1,300,000 acres in western New York, which they handled conservatively through Dutch and American agents until the last acre was sold about 1846.

Their original sales campaign was launched in 1792 by the publication of prospectuses in Dutch and French. The former was written by Pieter Stadnitski, one of the Dutch bankers in the company, and was called *Voorafgaand bericht, wegens eene negotiatie, op landen in America;* the latter, by Captain Benjamin Van Pradelles, had the title *Réflections offertes aux capitalistes de l'Europe.* In 1803 a most interesting little book by the Reverend J. P. L. Bridel, a Swiss minister who had lived for about twenty years in America, was published at Paris in French: *Le pour et le contre ou avis à ceux qui se proposent de passer dans les États-Unis d'Amérique.* A German edition was printed at Basel the following year as *Wie's halt ist, mit dem Reisen nach Amerika.* Both editions contain a most interesting map of the Holland Purchase which was not engraved but set up from separate pieces of type. It is hardly necessary to add that these Holland Company prospectuses are of the greatest rarity.

A group of French aristocrats, dissatisfied with conditions after the French Revolution and filled with zeal for the simple life of the American frontier, organized the Compagnie de New Yorck, generally known as the Castorland Company, in Paris in 1792 with Pierre Chassanis as manager. They contracted for 600,000 acres of land in Jefferson and Lewis counties, New York, and moved into their earthly paradise in 1794. Few of them had ever done a day's work in their lives, but here they were in the bleakest part of New York's northern wilderness, living in log cabins in the snow. Within four years most of these disillusioned Frenchmen had drifted away to find a warmer welcome in the great cities where they eked out a living as dancing masters or teachers of art or music until they became American citizens or found their way back to France.

To promote their enterprise they published in Paris in 1792 an anonymous prospectus, doubtless written by Chassanis, giving a *Description topographique de six cents mille acres de terres dans l'Amérique septentrionale,* to which was added the plan of association of the company. The following year the constitution of the company was printed in Paris, and about 1796 they issued a compilation of *Faits et calculus sur la population de le territoire des États-Unis d'Amérique,* for the information of those about to set out for their new home. The Massachusetts Historical Society owns the original manuscripts of the constitution, names of proprietors, and journal of the company from 1793 to 1796. Rodolphe Tillier, the first resident agent of the company, was removed from office in 1800 and published a *Memoire* justifying his administration [New York? 1800] which he issued in English as a *Translation of a memorial,* Rome, 1800. This was answered in French by Chassanis in a *Réponse au mémoire de Mr. Tillier* which, so far as we know, was the swan song of the Compagnie de New Yorck.

It was the tantalizing custom of these land promoters to issue most of their prospectuses anonymously in order to make them appear the unbiased observations of disinterested bystanders. This unfortunate habit makes it impossible to identify the source of a pamphlet issued in London in 1792 for the exploitation of a tract of eight hundred thousand acres which the author vaguely describes as "lands which are situated on the eastern boundary of Lake Ontario, and on the south side of St. Lawrence River." The prospectus is called *Observations on the present situation of landed property in America,* and it apparently describes one or the other of two tracts, both near neighbors of the Castorland Purchase. From the size of the property it has been assumed that Tract No. 1 of the McComb Purchase was the one described. It seems more probable, however, that the pamphlet was issued to help sell Thomas Boylston's Tract of about the same size which was bounded on the west by Lake Ontario and on the north by St. Lawrence River, while McComb's Purchase was farther east and did not approach the lake.

Returning to the banks of the winding Susquehanna and to the Asylum Company, we find that Robert Morris drew up and published in four folio pages dated 1794 the *Articles of agreement* which were to guide the French émigrés and their backers in handling the affairs of the purchase, while, the following year, the *Plan of association* appeared in a twenty-four page pamphlet. In order to appeal to the distressed French nobility who were seeking a refuge from their republican enemies, an alluring tract on the delights of life in Pennsylvania was published in French and generously addressed *Aux émigrés de toutes les contrées de l'Europe*, Philadelphia, 1794. It was accompanied by a *Plan de vente de trois cent mille acres de terres situées dans les comtés de Northumberland et de Huntingdon dans l'Etat de Pensylvanie, avec observations et notes instructives* which no doubt helped many a royalist to decide in favor of joining his compatriots on the Susquehanna.

In the meantime a quite different enterprise was under way just north of the Pennsylvania border in the state of New York. Two smart Connecticut Yankees, Colonel Jeremiah Halsey and General Andrew Ward, had discovered a gore of land some two miles wide and 245 miles long which, under the original Connecticut charter, they thought the state could claim. It also seems that, at that very moment, the state was building a new State House at Hartford and, its money having run out, the structure stood half-finished with no immediate prospect of its being completed. So the two old Revolutionary soldiers, Yankee fashion, proposed a trade. If the state would deed them the sliver of land, they would finish the State House. Lemuel Hopkins put the case very well in a letter to Oliver Wolcott when he remarked "On the whole, I think that if wild lands with a dubious title, at a vast distance, and covered with Indians will erect our publick buildings, school our children, and expound our Bible we are a most favoured people." So in 1795 the deal went through and the two old Yankees got title to their land and organized the Connecticut Gore Land Company. But trouble began at once. Lawsuits which lasted for years finally decided that Connecticut had no claim to the land and so the title was worthless. But in the interim the company had completed the State House, and the legislature eventually paid them $40,000 for their trouble and disappointment and, in 1808, the Connecticut Gore Land Company went out of business.

The company started its activities in 1795 by publishing its *Brief articles of agreement,* followed the next year by *Supplementary articles of agreement.* While still in the thick of the fight for its title, it issued in 1799 *The Connecticut Gore title, stated and considered, showing the rights of the proprietors.* Three years later it was still fighting and so restated its case in *The rise, progress, and effect of the claim of the Connecticut Gore stated and considered.* But that was the end. It stated and considered no more.

A less amusing but far more important land company was organized the same year as the Gore Company. As a compensation for the lands she had lost in the Wyoming Valley, Connecticut was granted an equal amount of territory west of Pennsylvania along Lake Erie in what is now the state of Ohio. This Western Reserve she sold for $1,200,000 to the Connecticut Land Company which published its *Articles of association* in 1795, followed them the next year with the *Mode of partition of the Western Reserve* and, in 1798, announced in a broadside that the *Lands in New-Connecticut . . . having been surveyed and divided,* were ready to welcome purchasers. They came mainly from New England and (especially after the Erie Canal was built), the population grew rapidly, Cleveland became a great city, and the original name of the region was fittingly preserved in the Western Reserve Historical Society and Western Reserve University.

Seventeen ninety-five was certainly a great year for land companies. One of the most pretentious of all was the North American Land Company, formed in Philadelphia by Robert Morris, John Nicholson, and James Greenleaf with $3,000,000 worth of stock and great hopes of selling six million acres of land in six states. The *Plan of association* was printed in three variant issues in Philadelphia and reprinted in London, and business got under way the following year by the publication in London of the *Plan for the settlement of 552,500 acres of land in the District of Morgan, County of Wilkes, in the State of North Carolina.* But the stock did not sell, and Morris went down with the company and lost his last chance to recoup his fallen fortunes. Still another Philadelphia concern, the Territorial Company, began its activities this year with the expectation of making fortunes for its promoters through the sale of some 310,000 acres of wild lands in the Southwest Territory, now the state of Tennessee, but it, like its greater contemporary, did not progress much beyond its *Plan of association* which Robert Aitken printed in a twenty-one-page pamphlet.

The last and worst of all the wildcat land schemes of 1795 was the fraud of the Yazoo Lands in Georgia. In spite of the counter-claims of the United States, Spain, and the Indians in actual posses-sion, the heavily bribed Georgia legislators passed a law selling a large part of what is now Alabama and Mississippi to four groups of speculators, the Georgia, Georgia-Mississippi, Upper Mississippi, and Tennessee companies. The Georgia-Mississippi Company sold out to a group of northern speculators organized as the New Eng-land Mississippi Land Company. Georgia had no title to these lands and consequently the whole gamble was lost by the thousands of investors, though the resultant litigation continued to drag through the courts until 1814.

The Georgia-Mississippi Company published in 1795 its *Grant* and a *State of facts* concerning the purchase; its successor, the New England Mississippi Land Company issued its *Articles of association* in Boston in 1798; and the Tennessee Company its *Deed of trusts* in 1800. Petitions, recriminations, vindications, and legal opinions were published for years, and the ablest men in the state carried on a pamphlet war attacking the fraud, which seems to have caused a greater stir in Georgia than anything before Sherman's march to the sea.

With all of the ups and downs of fortune which accompanied the land speculation and colonization of this period, it was but natural that a few friendly souls (or disillusioned victims) should undertake to enlighten the people of England and the continent as to the glories (or hazards) of buying American lands. Of course, the most famous and perhaps the most useful of these pamphlets was Frank-lin's *Information for those who would remove to America*, published in 1784, with a German translation in 1786 and other editions in later years. One of the most popular was Thomas Cooper's *Some in-formation respecting America* which appeared in London in 1794 and went through numerous editions, part of it being re-issued as *Thoughts on emigration, in a letter from a gentleman in Philadelphia.*

A man named Hodgkinson published his *Letters on emigration* in 1794, a bitter attack on all things American, which was made up of forged letters purporting to have come from disillusioned English settlers in this country. Another tract written to discourage emigration to America and popular at least to the extent of three editions, was the cleverly titled *Look before you leap; or, a few hints to such as are desirous of emigrating to America,* which appeared in London in 1796. Two years later Thomas Clio Rickman printed his *Emigration to America, candidly considered,* adding his frank opinion and wholesome advice for the guidance of the unwary.

This country must have been a most attractive part of the world when it was new. The wonder of it got hold of the people and filled them with a restless enthusiasm, a constant urge to be getting on to ever newer and brighter scenes. Hope sprang eternal and each new gamble was sure to make a fortune, each unexplored tract of land was more fertile than the last. So our population moved ever westward and our nation grew and prospered.

There still are far horizons and beautiful vistas we have not seen, though the mountains have all been scaled and the prairies fenced and plowed. The atomic age of science and invention has just begun, with many a new trail to be followed, many discoveries to be made, more thrilling than those of Columbus or of Boone. And for all that we still have to do, it is fortunate that we have our American temperament to urge us onward, for now, as always, the grass is green in yonder field.

Conclusion

FROM our listening to the voice of the old frontier we have learned that the pioneer was not always inarticulate, that he wrote simply but forcefully and sometimes vividly and with unconscious dramatic power. He generally told the simple truth without boasting, but was sometimes inclined to draw the long bow in order to make a better story. From what he wrote we have learned how he lived, how accurately and farsightedly he observed his world and his place in it, and we have learned the habits of thought and action and traits of character which were developed in his environment, traits which have meant much in the building of our nation. Through his eyes we have seen a colorful pageant of varied and picturesque personalities performing prosaic, heroic, or heartrending deeds before a backdrop of forests, lakes, mighty rivers, and mountains. We have seen the stubborn retreat of the forests before his ax, and of the Indian, the Frenchman, and the Englishman before his rifle; we have watched him clear his lands, build his mills and factories, his courthouses, schools, and churches until trading posts became great cities and our modern civilization emerged from the wilderness.

We have heard the returned captive tell of his adventures among the Indians and have seen with intense interest the clash of the stone age with the civilization of the seventeenth and eighteenth centuries. We have learned, through the experiences of our ancestors, of the traits of the Indian, his mode of life, his stubborn but futile resistance to the encroachments of the superior civilization. We have learned to prepare his most delicious foods, to use his remedies, and to call our lakes and streams and towns by his poetic and beautiful names.

A study of the promotion literature of the land companies has taught us how important was their role in developing our country, for it was through their efforts that most of our colonies were originally peopled. We have watched the disappointment in the eyes of many an immigrant who found that the new world did not live up to the land agent's rose-tinted specifications; we have seen the tragic despair of many speculators in frontier lands who, through overoptimism or an unfortunate turn of fortune's wheel, found themselves paupers; and we have seen a few fortunes made as well. Though we have learned to be wary of the blandishments of the land agent, most of his customers were satisfied with their rich new lands and their new freedom in a new world, and we have gradually realized that not all the land speculation was a gamble and that without the land companies to stimulate emigration and sales, our country would have been much slower in its settlement and development.

And so we come to the most important part of our volume, its appendix, for if any part of it has permanent scholarly value it will be the 1,300 entries in our bibliography of the frontier literature of the area of the United States from 1542 to 1800 with the locations of thousands of copies in over 150 libraries. No bibliography can ever be complete, and every scholar will find titles missing and will quarrel with the compiler for his deliberate omission of certain works which did not seem to belong. But he must remember that this is a pioneer work in more sense than one, for no other bibliography has attempted to record the more important or more elusive works relative to the early American frontier. So perhaps a few students will be grateful for what he has included rather than censorious for what he has not. It should, at least, prove a handy guide to the more obvious books on the frontier, with a few fascinating side excursions along little-known or unblazed trails.

Appendix

A Bibliography of
North American Frontier Literature,
1542-1800

A selection of works written by those living on the frontier of what is now the United States, stories of Indian captivity within this area and promotion tracts by agents for the sale of frontier lands, the first editions of which appeared not later than 1800.

Key to Locations

The symbols used are those which have become standard through use in the Library of Congress. They are taken from *Symbols used in the Union Catalog of the Library of Congress. Fourth edition. Washington: The Library of Congress. Union Catalog. 1942.* 128 p., 8vo., which see for further explanation and for symbols of other libraries. The following list does not include libraries, private collectors and dealers whose names appear infrequently in the bibliography and are spelled out in full.

An-C-M	Montreal Civic Library, Montreal, Que.
An-C-MS	Bibliothèque St.-Sulpice, Montreal, Que.
AnC-OAr	Public Archives of Canada, Ottawa, Ont.
An-C-T	Toronto Public Library, Toronto, Ont.
An-C-WlvA	Acadia University, Wolfville, N.S.
AU	University of Alabama, University, Ala.
Bib. Nat.	Bibliothèque Nationale, Paris, France
BM	British Museum, London, England
Bodleian	Bodleian Library, Oxford University, England
C	California State Library, Sacramento, Calif.
Cambridge U.	University of Cambridge, England
CaT	See An-C-T
CCP	Pomona College, Claremont, Calif.
CP	Pasadena Public Library, Pasadena, Calif.
CSmH	Henry E. Huntington Library, San Marino, Calif.
Ct	Connecticut State Library, Hartford, Conn.
CtHi	Connecticut Historical Society, Hartford, Conn.
CtHWatk	Watkinson Library, Hartford, Conn.

CtSoP	Pequot Library, Southport, Conn.
CtY	Yale University, New Haven, Conn.
CU-B	University of California, Bancroft Library, Berkeley, Calif.
F.C. Deering	Library of the late Frank C. Deering, Saco, Me.
DFo	Folger Memorial Library, Washington, D.C.
DGU	Georgetown University, Washington, D.C.
DHU	Howard University, Washington, D.C.
DLC	Library of Congress, Washington, D.C.
DNR	U.S. Office of Naval Records and Library, Washington, D.C.
DSG	U.S. Surgeon General's Office (Army Medical Library), Washington, D.C.
FHi	Florida Historical Society, St. Augustine, Fla.
FJ	Jacksonville Free Public Library, Jacksonville, Fla.
FSaHi	St. Augustine Historical Society, St. Augustine, Fla.
FTaSC	Florida State College for Women, Tallahassee, Fla.
GA	Carnegie Library of Atlanta, Atlanta, Ga.
Garrett	The John Work Garrett Library, Baltimore, Md.
GHi	Georgia Historical Society, Savannah, Ga.
Glasgow U.	University of Glasgow, Glasgow, Scotland
GMW	Wesleyan College, Macon, Ga.
GU-De	University of Georgia, De Renne Georgia Library, Athens, Ga.
I	Illinois State Library, Springfield, Ill.
IaU	State University of Iowa, Iowa City, Ia.
ICN	Newberry Library, Chicago, Ill.
ICU	University of Chicago, Chicago, Ill.
IHi	Illinois State Historical Society, Springfield, Ill.
InThE	Emeline Fairbanks Memorial Library, Terre Haute, Ind.
InU	Indiana University, Bloomington, Ind.
IU	University of Illinois Library, Urbana, Ill.
H.V. Jones	Library of the late Herschel V. Jones, sold to the Rosenbach Co., Philadelphia, Pa.
KyLoF	Filson Club, Louisville, Ky.
M-Ar	Massachusetts State Archives, Massachusetts State Library, Boston, Mass.
MA	Amherst College, Amherst, Mass.

MB	Boston Public Library, Boston, Mass.
MBAt	Boston Athenaeum, Boston, Mass.
MBBC	Boston College, Chestnut Hill, Mass.
MBC	Congregational Library, Boston, Mass.
MBHo	Massachusetts Horticultural Society, Boston, Mass.
MdBJ	Johns Hopkins University, Baltimore, Md.
MdBP	Peabody Institute, Baltimore, Md.
MdHi	Maryland Historical Society, Baltimore, Md.
MeB	Bowdoin College, Brunswick, Me.
MH	Harvard University, Cambridge, Mass.
MH-A	Arnold Arboretum, Harvard University, Cambridge, Mass.
MH-BA	Graduate School of Business Administration, Harvard University, Cambridge, Mass.
MHi	Massachusetts Historical Society, Boston, Mass.
MiD-B	Burton Historical Collection, Detroit Public Library, Detroit, Mich.
MiDW	Wayne University, Detroit, Mich.
MiU	University of Michigan, Ann Arbor, Mich.
MiU-C	William L. Clements Library, University of Michigan, Ann Arbor, Mich.
MnHi	Minnesota Historical Society, St. Paul, Minn.
MnU	University of Minnesota, Minneapolis, Minn.
MoSM	Mercantile Library of St. Louis, St. Louis, Mo.
MSaE	Essex Institute, Salem, Mass.
MWA	American Antiquarian Society, Worcester, Mass.
MWH	Holy Cross College, Worcester, Mass.
MWiW	Williams College, Williamstown, Mass.
MWiW-C	Chapin Library, Williams College, Williamstown, Mass.
N	New York State Library, Albany, N.Y.
NB	Brooklyn Public Library, Brooklyn, N.Y.
NBLiHi	Long Island Historical Society, Brooklyn, N.Y.
NBuHi	Buffalo Historical Society, Buffalo, N.Y.
NcD	Duke University, Durham, N.C.
NcWfC	Wake Forest College, Wake Forest, N.C.
NCanHi	Ontario County Historical Society, Canandaigua, N.Y.
NGH	Hobart College, Geneva, N.Y.
Nh	New Hampshire State Library, Concord, N.H.

NhDo	Public Library, Dover, N.H.
NhHi	New Hampshire Historical Society, Concord, N.H.
NHi	New-York Historical Society, New York, N.Y.
NIC	Cornell University, Ithaca, N.Y.
NjHi	New Jersey Historical Society, Newark, N.J.
NjP	Princeton University, Princeton, N.J.
NjPlaSDB	Seventh Day Baptist Historical Society, Plainfield, N.J.
NjR	Rutgers University, New Brunswick, N.J.
NN	New York Public Library, New York, N.Y.
NN-Sc	Schomburg Collection, 135th St. Branch, New York Public Library, New York, N.Y.
NNC	Columbia University, New York, N.Y.
NNH	Hispanic Society, New York, N.Y.
NNP	Pierpont Morgan Library, New York, N.Y.
NNUT	Union Theological Seminary, New York, N.Y.
NNUT-Mc	McAlpin Collection, Union Theological Seminary, New York, N.Y.
NRHi	Rochester Historical Society, Rochester, N.Y.
NRU	University of Rochester, Rochester, N.Y.
NSchU	Union College, Schenectady, N.Y.
NSmB	Smithtown Branch Library, Smithtown Branch, Suffolk County, N.Y.
OCHP	Historical and Philosophical Society of Ohio, Cincinnati, O.
OCl	Cleveland Public Library, Cleveland, O.
OClWHi	Western Reserve Historical Society, Cleveland, O.
OCU	University of Cincinnati, Cincinnati, O.
ODW	Ohio Wesleyan University, Delaware, O.
OFH	Hayes Memorial Library, Fremont, O.
OMC	Marietta College, Marietta, O.
OO	Oberlin College, Oberlin, O.
OU	Ohio State University, Columbus, O.
PBL	Lehigh University, Bethlehem, Pa.
PBM	Moravian College and Theological Seminary, Bethlehem, Pa.
PCDHi	Delaware County Historical Society, Chester, Pa.
PHC	Haverford College, Haverford, Pa.
PHi	Historical Society of Pennsylvania, Philadelphia, Pa.
PMA	Allegheny College, Meadville, Pa.

PP	Free Library of Philadelphia, Philadelphia, Pa.
PPA	Athenaeum of Philadelphia, Philadelphia, Pa.
PPAmP	American Philosophical Society, Philadelphia, Pa.
PPF	Friends Library, 142 N. 16th St., Philadelphia, Pa.
PPFr	Friends Free Library, 5418 Germantown Avenue, Philadelphia, Pa.
PPG	German Society of Pennsylvania, Philadelphia, Pa.
PPiU	University of Pittsburgh, Pittsburgh, Pa.
PPL	Library Company of Philadelphia, Philadelphia, Pa.
PPL-R	Ridgway Branch, Library Company of Philadelphia, Philadelphia, Pa.
PPM	Mercantile Library, Philadelphia, Pa.
PPPrHi	Presbyterian Historical Society, Philadelphia, Pa.
PSC	Swarthmore College, Swarthmore, Pa.
PSC-Hi	Friends' Historical Library, Swarthmore College, Swarthmore, Pa.
PU	University of Pennsylvania, Philadelphia, Pa.
PU-B	Botanical Library, University of Pennsylvania, Philadelphia, Pa.
PU-Mus	University Museum, University of Pennsylvania, Philadelphia, Pa.
Public Record Office	Public Record Office, London, England
RHi	Rhode Island Historical Society, Providence, R.I.
RNHi	Newport Historical Society, Newport, R.I.
A.S.W. Rosenbach	Private Library of Dr. A.S.W. Rosenbach, Philadelphia, Pa.
RP	Providence Public Library, Providence, R.I.
RPA	Providence Athenaeum, Providence, R.I.
RPAt	See RPA
RPB	Brown University Library, Providence, R.I.
RPJCB	John Carter Brown Library, Providence, R.I.
ScC	Charleston Library Society, Charleston, S.C.
ScCoT	Lutheran Theological Southern Seminary Library, Columbia, S.C.
Society of Antiquaries	Society of Antiquaries, London, England
T.W. Streeter	Private Library of Thomas W. Streeter, Morristown, N.J.

TxU	University of Texas, Austin, Tex.
Vi	Virginia State Library, Richmond, Va.
ViU	University of Virginia, Charlottesville, Va.
VtHi	Vermont Historical Society, Montpelier, Vt.
WHi	State Historical Society of Wisconsin, Madison, Wis.

Bibliography

The Voice of the Old Frontier

NUÑEZ CABEZA DE VACA, ALVAR

[Arms of Spain occupying most of page] | La relacion que dio Aluar nu- | ñez cabeça de vaca de lo acaescido enlas Indias | enla armada donde yua por gouernador Pā | philo de narbaez-desde el año de veynte | y siete hasta el año d'treynta y seys | que boluio a Seuilla con tres | de su compañia. | [Colophon, not lined off:] *Fue impresso el presente tratado en la magnifica-noble-y antiquissima-çiudad de Zamora: por los honrrados varones Augustin de paz y Juan Picardo compañeros impressores de libros vezinos dela dicha çiudad. A costa y espensas del virtuoso varon Juan pedro musetti mercader de libros vezino de Medina del campo. Acabose en seys dias del mes de Octubre. Año del nasçimiento d' ñro saluador Jesu Cristo de mil y quinientos y quarenta y dos Años. [1542].* [1]

Title and 66 unnumbered leaves, 4to. H.R. Wagner: *Spanish Southwest*, no. 1. BM (1st signature in facsimile), NN (perfect), RPJCB (1 leaf in facsimile).

The first story of Indian captivity in America and the first account of a journey by Europeans in what is now the United States. Nuñez Cabeza de Vaca was an officer of the ill-fated Narváez expedition, sent out from Spain to conquer and explore Florida, who found himself among the fifteen survivors who were enslaved by the Indians of what is now Texas in 1528. Two years later he escaped and after years of travelling from tribe to tribe as trader and doctor, he arrived in Mexico City in 1536 where he met Cortes and Mendoza and the following year returned to Spain.

. . . . .

[Arms of Spain occupying most of page] | La relacion y comentarios del gouerna | dor Aluar nuñez cabeça de vaca, de lo acaescido en las | dos jornadas que hizo a las Indias. | Con priuilegio. | Esta tassada por los señores del consejo en Ochēta y cinco mr̃s. [Title in red and black] [Colophon:] [Leaf orn.] *Impresso en Valladolid, por Francisco fer-* [leaf orn.] | *nandez de Cordoua. Año de mil y quinien-* | *nientos y cinquenta y cinco años.* [1555]. [2]

Leaves lvi, [2], lvii-clxiiii, 4to. (18.6 x 13 cm.). H.R. Wagner: *Spanish southwest*, no. 1 a; Church 100; new John Carter Brown cat. Bib. Nat., BM,

CCP, CSmH, DLC, ICN, MB, MH, MiU-C, MWA, MWiW-C, NjP, NN, NNH, RPJCB, TxU, ViU, F.C. Deering, H.V. Jones, T.W. Streeter. Second edition. For other editions, see Wagner.

ELVAS, GENTLEMAN OF

Relaçam verdadei | ra dos trabalhos que | ho gouernador | dõ Fernãdo de | souto e cer | tos fidal | gos | portugueses passarom | no descobrimēto da | prouincia da Fro | lida. Agora | nouamēte feita per hũ | fidalgo Deluas. | Foy vista por ho señor inquisidor. | [Colophon:] *Foy impressa esta relaçam do | descoubrimento da Frolida | em casa de Andree de Bur | gos impressor e cauallei | ro da casa do se- | nhor Cardēal | iffante. | acabouse aos dez dias de Febrei- | ro do anno de mil e quinhentos | e cincoenta e sete annos. | na nobre e sempre leal | cidade de Euora. | [1557]* [Title within ornamental border, except last line which is below the border. Colophon on verso of last leaf of text]. [3]

180 folios (i.e., [360] p.), 8vo. (14.2 x 8.8 cm.). BM, NN, Bibliotheca de Ajuda, Portugal.

Title from Sabin 24895 and facsimile edition published by Florida State Historical Society, 1933. For another account of Oritz' adventures, see Garci-lasso de la Vega's *La Florida del Ynca*, Lisbona, 1605; Madrid, 1723, etc.

Includes story of captivity of Juan Oritz who went to Florida with the expedition of Pamfilio de Narváez of 1527-1528 and was a captive until rescued by Hernando de Soto in 1539. He died in 1541.

For other editions and translations, see the Florida State Historical Society edition.

STADEN, HANS

Warhaftige | Historia vnd beschreibung eyner Landt- | schafft der Wilden, Nacketen, Grimmigen Menschfresser | Leuthen, in der Newenwelt America gelegen, vor vnd nach | Christi geburt im Land zu Hessen vnbekant, biss vff dise ij. | nechst vergangene jar, da sie Hans Staden von Hom- | berg auss Hessen durch sein eygne erfarung erkant, | vnd yetzo durch den truck an tag gibt. | Dedicirt dem Durchleuchtigen Hochgebornen herrn, | H. Philipsen Landtgraff zu Hessen, Graff zu Catzen- | elnbogen, Dietz, Ziegenhain vnd Nidda, seinem G. H. | Mit eyner vorrede D. Joh. Dryandri, genant Eych-man, | Ordinarij Professoris Medici zu Marpurgk. | Inhalt des Buchlins volget nach den Vorreden. | *Getruckt zu Marpurg, im jar M.D.LVII.* | [Colophon:] *Zu Marpurg im Kleeblatt, bei | Andres Kolben, vff Fastnacht. 1557.* | [Title in red and black]. [4]

89 unnumbered leaves including woodcuts in the text, folded map of America, 4to. (18.8 x 14.2 cm.). Sabin 90036, new John Carter Brown cat. BM, CSmH, MB, NN, RPJCB.

First edition of one of the earliest of Indian captivities in the New World. Church 105, in a note to the 2d ed., Frankfort, [1557], says: "This is one

of the most important books relating to South America, and deals chiefly
with the Tupi Indians of Brazil. The author was a native of Hesse who
sailed successively in Portuguese and Spanish vessels as a gunner. His first
voyage covers the period from April 29, 1547 to October 8, 1548; the second
from the 4th day after Easter, 1549 to February 20, 1555. During his second
voyage he was taken prisoner by the Tupi people in Brazil and spent nine
months in captivity until rescued by a French vessel."

For 25 other editions in German, Dutch, Flemish, French, Portuguese and
English, see Sabin 90037-90060.

FLORES, BARTOLOMÉ DE

[Cut] | Obra nvevamen | te compvesta, en la | qual se cuĕta, la felice
victoria que Dios por | su infinita bondad y misericordia, fue ser | uido de
dar, al Illustre señor Pedro | Melendez, Almirante y Capitan | de la gouerna-
cion de la mar, | de las Indias, y Adelãtado | de la Florida. | Contra Ivan
Ribao de Na | nacion [sic] Frances. Con otros mil Luteranos, a los | quales
passo à filo de espada, cõ otras curiosi | dades que pone el auctor, de las
viuiendas | de los Indios dela Florida, y sus natu- | rales fayciones. Cõpuesta
en verso | Castellano, por Bartholome de | Flores, natural de Malaga y |
vezino de Cordoua. | [Colophon:] Fue impressa en Seuilla en casa de
Hernando Diaz | impressor de libros, a la calle de la Sierpe. Año de | mil y
quinientos y setenta y vno. | Con licencia del Illustre señor, el Licenciado |
Alonso Caceres de Rueda, Teniente dela Iu | stica de Seuilla y su tierra
por | su Majestad. | [1571].   [5]

4 unnumbered leaves, 4to. RPJCB.

Title from J. T. Medina: Biblioteca Hispano-Americana (1493-1810),
1898,215, where the text is given in full. Described from the only known
copy, with this provenance: Jose Toribio Medina—H.R. Wagner—H.V.
Jones—Rosenbach Company—John Carter Brown Library.

Unique copy of the first printed encouragement to colonization in what
is now the United States. This poem has to do with the Spanish history of
Florida and the natural advantages of the country for prospective settlers.

HARIOT, THOMAS

[Leaf orn.] A briefe and true re- | port of the new found land of Virginia:
of | the commodities there found and to be raysed, as well mar- | chantable,
as others for victuall, building and other necessa- | rie vses for those that are
and shalbe the planters there; and of the na- | ture and manners of the
naturall inhabitants: Discouered by the | English Colony there seated by
Sir Richard Greinuile Knight in the | yeere 1585. which remained vnder
the gouernment of Rafe Lane Esqui- | er, one of her Maiesties Equieres,
during the space of twelue monethes: at | the speciall charge and direction
of the Honourable Sir | Walter Raleigh Knight, Lord Warden of | the
stanneries; who therein hath beene fauou- | red and authorised by her
Maiestie and | her letters patents: | Directed to the aduenturers, fauourers,

| and welwillers of the action, for the inhabi- | ting and planting there: | By Thomas Hariot; seruant to the abouenamed | Sir Walter, a member of the Colony, and | there imployed in discouering. | [device] | *Imprinted at London 1588.*   [6]

24 unnumbered leaves, 4to. (19.5 x 12.5 cm.). Sabin 30377, Church 135. BM, Bodleian, CSmH, MiU-C, NN, University of Leyden.

The second original production in English relating to America.

. . . . .

A briefe and true report | of the new found land of Virginia. | of the commodities and of the nature and man | ners of the naturall inhabitants. Discouered by | the English Colony there seated by Sir Richard | Greinuile Knight in the yeere 1585. Which rema- | ined vnder the gouernment of twelue monethes, | at the speciall charge and direction of the Honou- | rable Sir Walter Raleigh Knight lord Warden | of the stanneries who therein hath beene fauoured | and authorised by her Maiestie | and her letters patents: | This fore booke is made in English | by Thomas Hariot seruant to the abouenamed | Sir Walter, a member of the Colony, and there | imployed in discouering | *Cvm gratia et privilegio Caes. Matis Specialis* | *Francoforti ad Moenvm* | *Typis Ioannis Wecheli, svmtibvs vero Theodori* | *de Bry Anno MDXC.* | *Venales reperivntvr in Officina Sigismvndi Feirabendii.* [Colophon:] *At Franckfort,* | *Imprinted by Ihon We-* | *chel, at Theodore de Bry,* | *owne* | *coast and chardges.* | *MDXC.* [Engraved border, same used in Latin ed., Part I].   [7]

[Title to plates, printed from type:] The trve pictvres | and fashions of | the people in that par- | te of America novv cal- | led Virginia, discowred by Englishmen | sent thither in the years of our Lorde 1585. att the speciall charge and direction of | the Honourable Sir Walter Ralegh Knigt Lord Warden | of the stannaries in the duchies of Corenwal and Oxford who | therein hath bynne fauored and auctorised by her | Maaiestie and her let- | ters patents. | Translated out of Latin into English by | Richard Hacklvit. | Diligentlye collected and draow- | ne by Ihon White who was sent thiter speciallye and for the same pur- | pose by the said Sir Walter Ralegh the year abouesaid | 1585. and also the year 1588. now cutt in copper and first | published by Theodore de Bry att | his wone chardges.

Frontispiece (Adam and Eve), 1 unnumbered leaf and 31 (3-33), [1] pages. *True pictures:* 3 unnumbered leaves, map, and 28 leaves, with 22 numbered (II-XXIII) plates. *Som Picture:* 10 leaves with 5 plates and 3 unnumbered leaves. Folio (32.8 x 23 cm.). Titles and collation from new John Carter Brown catalog. See also Church 204, Sabin 8784. BM (2), Bodleian, CSmH, DFo, DLC, MH, MiU-C, NjP, NN, NSchU, PP, RPJCB, Earl of Crawford, William H. Robinson, Ltd. (1948).

First English edition to reproduce the John White drawings, the first on-the-spot drawings of North American Indians and natural history specimens, the original water color drawings of which are now in the British Museum.

This is Part I of Theodore De Bry's *Great Voyages* and the only part to appear in English. For Latin, French and German editions and modern reprints, see Church, Sabin and John Carter Brown catalog and references to other bibliographies noted in those works.

H[ORTOP], J[OB]

The trauailes of an Englishman. | Containing his svndrie ca- | lamities indured by the space of twentie and odd yeres | in his absence from his natiue countrie; wherein is | truly decyphered the sundrie shapes of wilde | ¶ beasts, birds, fishes, foules, rootes, | plants, &c. | With the description of a man that appeared in the sea: and | also a huge giant brought from China to the | King of Spaine. | No lesse pleasant than approued. | By I. H. | Published with authoritie. | [orn.] | *Imprinted at London for William Wright, and are to be | solde at his shop neere vnto Pauls | Schoole. 1591.*   [8]

16 leaves, 4to. Title from Herschel V. Jones *Adventures in Americana,* 51. BM, Sir R.L. Harmsworth (imp.), H.V. Jones (1928).

Jones *Adventures* says: "Hortop sailed with Sir John Hawkyns in 1567, and was landed north of the Panuco River [at present Tampico, Mexico]. After maltreatment by the Indians, he was taken to Mexico City a prisoner." Apparently the first story of the Indian captivity of an Englishman.

BRERETON, JOHN

A briefe and true relation of the discouerie of the North part of Virginia; being a most pleasant, fruitfull and commodious soile: made this present yeere 1602, by Captaine Bartholomew Gosnold, Captaine Bartholowmew [sic] Gilbert, and diuers other gentlemen their associats, by the permission of the honourable knight, Sir Walter Ralegh, &c. Written by M. Iohn Brereton one of the voyage. Whereunto is annexed a treatise, conteining important inducements for the planting in those parts, and finding a passage that way to the South sea, and China. Written by M. Edward Hayes, a gentleman long since imploied in the like action. *Londini, Impensis Geor. Bishop. 1602.* [Title within wide ornamental border].   [9]

24 p., 8vo. (17.2 x 12.6 cm.). Church 325, New John Carter Brown cat. CSmH, MiU-C, NjP, OClWHi, PP, PU, RPJCB.

First issue of first English publication on the New England coast. Written by one of the first party of English settlers in New England, on Cuttyhunk Island.

. . . . . .

A briefe and true relation . . . and China. With diuers instructions of speciall moment newly added in this second impression. *Londini, Impensis Geor. Bishop. 1602.* [Title within same border as first issue].   [10]

48 p., 8vo. (19 x 12.6 cm.). Church 326, New John Carter Brown cat., Sabin 7730. BM (3 copies, 1 imperfect), CSmH, ICN, MH, NHi, PP, RPJCB.

Second issue, with additions.

ROSIER, JAMES

A | trve relation | of the most prosperous voyage | made this present yeere 1605, | by Captaine George Waymouth, | in the discouery of the land | of Virginia: | Where he discouered 60 miles vp | a most excellent riuer; to- | gether with a most | fertile land. | Written by Iames Rosier: | a gentleman employed | in the voyage. | [printer's ornament] | *Londini* | *Impensis Geor. Bishop.* | *1605.* [Title within heavy ornamental border]. [11]

[39] p., 4to. (14 x 18 cm.). Sabin 73286, Church 331, New JCB cat. BM, CSmH, ICN, MiU-C, NHi, NjP, NN, PP, RPJCB.

First exploration of the coast of Maine, responsible for the attempts of Gorges and Popham to colonize this region. There are five modern reprints.

[SMITH, CAPTAIN JOHN]

A | true re- | lation of such occur- | rences and accidents of noate as | hath hapned in Virginia since the first | planting of that collony, which is now | resident in the South part therof, till | the last returne from | thence. | Written by a gentleman of the said collony, to a worshipfull | friend of his in England. | [Woodcut of ship] | *London* | *Printed for Iohn Tappe, and are to bee solde at the Grey-* | *hound in Paules-Church-yard, by W. W.* | *1608.* [12]

[44] p., 4to. NHi, NN, PP.

The first published account of the Jamestown colony.

There are four issues of the title page, the text being practically identical. The variations occur in the tenth and eleventh lines, as follows:

1. As above.
2. Written by Th. Watson Gent. one of the said collony, to a | worship- full friend of his in England. BM (2), CSmH, NHi.
3. Written by Captaine Smith Coronell of the said collony, to a | wor- shipfull friend of his in England.
   CSmH, H. V. Jones, MB, MiU-C, NN, RPJCB.
4. Written by Captaine Smith one of the said collony, to a | worshipfull friend of his in England. CSmH, NN.

Copies with title pages missing: MH, RPJCB. Another copy NjP.

For further details, see Sabin 82844-82847.

ELVAS, GENTLEMAN OF

Virginia | richly valued, | by the description of the maine land of | Florida, her next neighbour: | out of the foure yeeres continuall trauell and discouerie, | for aboue one thousand miles East and West, of | Don Ferdinando de Soto, and sixe hundred | able men in his companie. | Wherein are truly obserued the riches and fertilitie of those parts, | abounding with things necessarie, pleasant, and profitable | for the life of man: with the natures and dispo- | sitions of the inhabitants. | Written by a Portugall gentleman of Eluas, emploied in | all the action, and translated out of

Portugese | by Richard Haklvyt. | [type orn.] | *At London* | *Printed by Felix* *Kingston* *for* *Matthew* *Lownes,* | *and are to be sold at the signe of the* *Bishops* | *head in Pauls Churchyard.* | *1609.* [13]

[8], 180 p., 4to. (17.2 x 12.6 cm.). Church 337, new John Carter Brown cat., Sabin 24896. BM, Bodleian, CSmH, DLC, ICN, MA, MBAt, MBHo, MH, MiU-C, MWA, N, NHi, NjP, NN, PPL, RPJCB, ViU, A.S.W. Rosenbach.

First translation of *Relacam verdadeira,* above. Published by Hakluyt to encourage interest in Virginia.

This description of the territory south of Virginia is a companion volume to Lescarbot's *Nova Francia,* issued the same year, describing the country north of Virginia. Probably both tracts were issued by the Virginia Company for the encouragement of settlers.

[GRAY, ROBERT]

A | good speed | to Virginia. | Esay 42.4. | He shall not faile nor be discouraged till he haue | set iudgement in the earth, and the iles shall | wait for his law. | [device] | *London* | *Printed by Felix Kyngston for VVilliam* | *Welbie, and are to be sold at his shop at the signe* | *of the Greyhound in* *Pauls Church-* | *yard.* *1609.* [14]

[30] p., 4to. (17.1 x 12.3 cm.). Sabin 27837, Church 336, new John Carter Brown cat. BM, CSmH, DFo, DLC, ICN, MiU-C, MH, NHi, NjP, NN, PP, RPJCB.

Virginia Company promotion tract in form of a sermon.

[JOHNSON, ROBERT]

[Royal arms] | Nova Britannia. | Offring most | excellent fruites by planting in | Virginia. | Exciting all such as be well affected | to further the same. | [medallion vignette between rules] | *London* | *Printed for Samvel* *Macham, and are to be sold at* | *his shop in Pauls Church-yard, at the* | *Signe of the Bul-head.* | *1609.* [15]

18 unnumbered leaves, 4to. (17.7 x 13.3 cm.). Church 338, new John Carter Brown cat., Sabin 36284 and 56098. BM, Bodleian, CSmH (3), DLC (2), ICN, MB, MH, MiU-C, NHi, NjP, NN, RPJCB (3), Vi, ViU.

Church quotes Luther S. Livingston's description of six variants. The NN copy, described above, is perhaps the earliest. No attempt has been made to credit each library with its particular variant.

Reprinted in facsimile by Sabin in 1857.

Not an official publication of the Virginia Company of London.

[LESCARBOT, MARC]

[Printer's orn.] | Nova Francia: | or the | description | of that part of | New France, | which is one continent with | Virginia. | Described in the three late voyages and plantation made by | Monsieur de Monts, Monsieur du Pont-Graué, and | Monsieur de Poutrincourt, into the countries | called by the Frenchmen La Cadie, | lying to the Southwest of | Cape Breton. | Together with an excellent seuerall treatie of all the commodities | of the said countries, and maners of the naturall | inhabitants of the same. | Translated out of French into English by | P.[ierre] E.[rondelle] | [type orn.] | *Londini,* | *Imponsis Georgii Bishop.* | *1609.* [16]

[12], 307 p., 4to. (17.9 x 13.5 cm.). Map: *Figvre de la Terre Nevve* generally found inserted from the French edition. Sabin 40175, Church 341. BM, CSmH, DLC, MH, MHi, NHi, NjP, NN, RPJCB.

A translation of Lescarbot's *Histoire de la Nouuelle France,* Book 2, chapter 31 to end of book 3.

This description of the country north of Virginia is a companion volume to the Gentleman from Elvas' *Virginia richly valued,* issued the same year, describing the country south of Virginia. Probably both tracts were issued by the Virginia Company for the encouragement of settlers.

. . . . .

Another variant identical except for title page which is reset and has the imprint: *London,* | *Printed for Andrew Hebb, and are to be sold at the signe* | *of the Bell in Pauls Church-yard.* [1609]. Sabin 40176, Church 342, new John Carter Brown cat. BM, CSmH, DLC, ICN, MHi, NN, RPJCB. [17]

For other editions and works by Lescarbot, see Sabin, Church and John Carter Brown cat.

Price, Daniel

Savls | prohibition | staide. | Or | the apprehensi- | on, and examination | of Savle. | And the inditement of all that per- | secute Christ with a reproofe | of those that traduce the Honoura- | ble Plantation of | Virginia. | Preached in a sermon commaunded at | Pauls Crosse, vpon Rogation Sunday, be- | ing the 28. of May. | 1609. | By Daniel Price, Chapleine in ordinarie | to the Prince, and Master of Artes | of Exeter Colledge in | Oxford. | *London* | *Printed for Matthew Law, and are to be sold in Pauls* *Church-* | *yard, neere vnto Saint Austines Gate, at the* | *Signe of the Foxe,* *1609.* | [Title within border]. [18]

[46] p., 4to. (17.2 x 13.8 cm.). Sabin 65421, new John Carter Brown cat. DLC, NjP, RPJCB.

Virginia Company promotion sermon.

Symonds, William

Virginia. | [rule] | A | sermon | preached at | White-Chappel, in the | presence of many, Honourable and | Worshipfull, the aduenturers and plan- | ters for Virginia, | 25. April. 1609. | Pvblished for the benefit | and vse of the Colony, planted, | and to bee planted there, and for the ad- | uancement of their Chris- | tian purpose. | By William Symonds, Preacher at Saint | Saviors in Southwarke. | [rule] | [3 lines quoted] | [rule] | *London*

| *Printed by I. Windet, for Eleazar Edgar, and* | *William Welby, and are to be sold in Paules Church-* | *yard at the Signe of the Windmill.* | 1609. | [Title within ruled border].   [19]

[8], 54 p., 4to. (18.2 x 13.9 cm.). Church 344, new John Carter Brown cat. BM, CSmH, DLC, ICN, MB, MWiW-C, NjP, NN, RPJCB.

First Virginia Company promotion sermon.

VIRGINIA COMPANY (of London, 1606-1624)

Considering there is no publicke action, being honest and good in it selfe, and which tendeth to the generall good and benefite of this common-wealth, but that the same is also beneficiall and good in some degree, to euery particular member thereof, we thought it therefore requisite, to impart vnto you . . . how many wayes it hath pleased God to encourage vs to goe on, in that great worke and enterprize of planting colonies of our English nation, in those parts of America, which wee commonly call Virginia, or Noua Britannia; . . . *[London, 1609].*   [20]

Broadside, folio. Title from Sabin 99855. NN, RPJCB.

Sabin, between nos. 99854 and 99888, gives many valuable notes on the Virginia Company of London and includes several blank forms, and titles taken from the Stationers' Register of which there are no known copies. These we have omitted.

.   .   .   .   .

For the planting in Virginia or Nova Britannia. Whereas . . . for the better setling of the Colony and plantation in Virginia, etc. *London, J. Windet. 1609.*   [21]

Broadside, folio. Title from Sabin 99856. BM.

Information as to terms on which laborers are to be accepted as colonists.

CRASHAW, WILLIAM

A | sermon | preached in | London before the right hono- | rable the Lord Lavvarre, Lord Gouer- | nour and Captaine Generall of Virginea, | and others of his Maiesties Counsell for that | kingdome, and the rest of the aduen- | turers in that Plantation. | At the said Lord Generall his | leaue taking of England his natiue countrey, | and departure for Virginea, | Febr. 21. 1609. | By W. Crashaw Bachelar of Diuinitie, | and Preacher at the Temple. | Wherein both the lawfulnesse of that action is | maintained, and the necessity thereof is also demon- | strated, not so much out of the grounds of policie, | as of humanity, equity, and | Christianity. | Taken from his mouth, and published by direction. | [2 lines quoted] | [rule] | *London,* | *Printed for William Welby, and are to be sold* | *in Pauls Church-yard at the signe* | *of the Swan. 1610.*   [22]

[91] p., 4to. (17.5 x 13.5 cm.). Church 345, new John Carter Brown cat. BM, Bodleian CSmH, DLC, MHi, MiU-C, NjP, NN, RPJCB.

Virginia Company promotion sermon.

JOURDAIN, SILVESTER

XVI. | A | discovery | of the Barmv- | das, otherwise | called the Ile of | Divels: | By Sir Thomas Gates, Sir | George Sommers, and Cap- | tayne Newport, with | diuers others. | Set forth for the loue of my coun- | try, and also for the good of the | Plantation in Virginia. | Sil. Iovrdan. | [rule, orn., rule] | *London,* | *Printed by Iohn Windet, and are to be sold by Roger Barnes* | *in S. Dunstanes Church-yard in Fleet-streete, vn-* | *der the Diall.* *1610.*   [23]

[1], 24 p., 4to. A in 2, B-D in 4, the last leaf blank, printed in black letter. The title and pp. [1], [3], 5, 7, 9, 11, 13, 15, 17, 19, 21, 23 have the number XVI printed above the page number, for no apparent reason. 4to. (19 x 13 cm.). Sabin 100460. BM, Bodleian, CSmH, DFo.

This tract, the Virginia Company's *True Declaration,* 1610, and William Strachey's private manuscript account, according to Dr. Joseph Quincy Adams, inspired William Shakespeare to write *The Tempest.* Described from 1940 facsimile edition edited by Dr. Joseph Quincy Adams, Director of the Folger Shakespeare Library. It was reprinted as: *A plaine description of the Barmvdas,* 1613, which see. The author was one of the company of *The Sea-Venture,* flagship of the Virginia Company's fleet which discovered the Bermudas by being wrecked there in 1609. After a year on the island, they built two ships, sailed to Virginia and thence home where they caused great excitement, having been given up for lost.

RICH, ROBERT

Nevves from Virginia. | [orn.] The lost flocke | triumphant. | With the happy arriuall of that famous and | worthy Knight Sr. Thomas Gates: and the well | reputed & valiant Captaine Mr. Chri- | stopher Newporte, and others, | into England. | [orn.] With the maner of their distresse in the | Iland of Deuils (otherwise called Bermoothawes) | where they remayned 42. weekes, & builded | two pynaces, in which they returned | into Virginia. | By R. Rich, Gent. one of the voyage. | [orn.] | *London* | *Printed by Edw: Allde, and are to be solde by Iohn* | *Wright at Christ-Church dore.* *1610.*   [24]

[14] p., 4to. (20.6 x 16.2 cm.). Sabin 70889, Church 346, new John Carter Brown cat. BM, CSmH, Cosin Library, Dublin, NjP, copy offered by Rosenbach Co. in 1946 for $27,800.

Narrative poem. Elder Brewster owned a copy! For reprints, see Sabin.

VIRGINIA COMPANY

By the Counsell of Virginea. | Whereas the good Shippe, called the Her- | cules, is now preparing, and almost in a | readinesse with necessarie prouisions, to | make a supplie to the Lord Gouernour | and the Colonie in Virginea, it is thought | meet (for the auoiding of such vagrant and | vnnecessarie persons as do commonly pro- | fer themselues, being altogether vnser- | uiceable) that none but honest sufficient artificers, as car- | penters, smiths, coopers, fishermen, buckmen, and such | like, shall be entertained into this voyage: of whom so many | as will in due time repaire to the house of Sir Thomas Smith in | Philpot lane, with sufficient testimonie of their skill and good | behauiour, they shall receiue entertainment accordingly. *[London, 1610].*   [25]

Broadside, 4to. (13 x 17.5 cm.). Ornamental initial and text in black letter. Sabin 99857. Society of Antiquaries, NHi (photo).

.   .   .   .   .

A publication by the Counsell of Virginea, touching the plantation there. [Caption title] [Colophon:] *Imprinted at London by Thomas Haveland for William Welby, and are to be sold at his shop in Paul's Churchyard at the signe of the Swanne. 1610.*   [26]

Broadside. Sabin 99858. Society of Antiquaries.

Conditions of the colony and appeal for colonists. Title from Alexander Brown's *Genesis of the United States,* p. 354-356 where it is printed in full.

.   .   .   .   .

[Type orn.] | A | trve and sincere | declaration of the purpose and ends | of the Plantation begun in Virginia, | of the degrees which it hath receiued; and meanes by | which it hath beene aduanced: and the resolution and | conclusion of his Maiesties Councel of that Colo- | ny, for the constant and patient prosecution there- | of, vntill by the mercies of God it shall | retribute a fruitful haruest to the king- | dome of heauen, and this com- | mon-wealth. | Sett forth by the authority of the Go- | uernors and Councellors es- | tablished for that Plantation. | [rule, 2 lines quoted, rule, two lines quoted, rule] | At London. | Printed for I. Stepney, and are to be sold at the signe | of the Crane in Paules Churchyard. | 1610.   [27]

[2], 26 p., 4to. (18.3 x 14.4 cm.). Sabin 99859, Church 347, new John Carter Brown cat. BM, CSmH, DLC, MH, NjP, RPJCB. In the BM, DLC and NjP copies the printer's name is spelled *Stepneth.*

First and most important early account of the colony published by the Virginia Company.

.   .   .   .   .

A | trve decla- | ration of the | estate of the Colonie in | Virginia, | with a confutation of such scan- | dalous reports as haue tended to the dis- | grace of so worthy an enterprise. | Published by aduise and direction of the | Councell of Virginia. | [device] | London, | Printed for William Barret, and are to be sold | at the blacke Beare in Pauls Church-yard. | 1610.   [28]

[2], 68 p., 4to. (17.1 x 12.8 cm.). Sabin 99860, Church 348, new John Carter Brown cat. BM, Bodleian, CSmH, DLC, MBAt, MH, MiU-C, NHi, NjP, NN, PPL, RPJCB.

A plea for the continuation of the colony.

ELVAS, GENTLEMAN OF

The | worthye | and famovs his- | tory, of the travailes, | discouery, & conquest, of that great | continent of Terra Florida, being liuely | paraleld, with that of our now inha- | bited Virginia. | As also | the comodities of the said country, | with diuers excellent and rich mynes, of golde, | siluer, and other mettals, &c. which cannot but | giue vs a great and exceeding hope of our | Virginia, being so neere | of one continent. | Accomplished and effected, by that worthy | Generall and Captaine, Don Ferdinando | de Soto, and six hundreth Spaniards, | his followers. | [rule, orn., rule] | *London* | *Printed for Mathew Lownes,* | *dwelling* | *in Paules Church-yard,* *at the Signe of* | *the Bishops head. 1611.* [29]

[8], 180 p., 4to. (17.9 x 13.8 cm.). Sabin 24897. BM, NN.

Second edition of *Virginia richly valued,* 1609, same sheets with new title page.

For other editions, see nos. 3 and 13 and Sabin 24896.

VIRGINIA COMPANY

[Orn. headband] | By the Counsell of Virginia. | Seeing it hath pleased God, after such hard | successe, . . . | to make a new supply of men, and all | necessarie prouisions, in a fleet of good ships . . . | they shall be entertained for | the voyage, vpon such termes as their qualitie and fitnesse | shall deserue. | *Jmprinted at London for William Welby, 1611.* [30]

Broadside, folio (22.5 x 15 cm.). Ornamental initial and text in black letter. Sabin 99861. Society of Antiquaries, NHi (photo).

[WEST, THOMAS, 3D LORD DE LA WARR]

The | relation of | the Right Honourable the Lord | De-La-Warre, Lord Gouernour | and Captaine Generall of the | colonie, planted in | Virginea. | [type orn. between rules] | *London* | *Printed by William Hall, for* | *William Welbie, dwelling in Pauls Church-* | *yeard at the Signe of the* *Swan.* | *1611.* [31]

[17] p., 4to. (17.2 x 13.5 cm.). Church 349, new John Carter Brown cat., Sabin 102756. BM, CSmH, DLC, ICN, MB, MH, MWiW-C, NjP, NN, PHi, PP, RPJCB.

[JOHNSON, ROBERT]

[Seal of the Council for Virginia] | The | new life | of Virginea: | declaring the | former svccesse and pre- | sent estate of that plantation, being the second | part of Noua Britannia. | Published by the authoritie of his Maiesties | Counsell of Virginea. | *London,* | *Imprinted by Felix Kyngston* *for William Welby, dwelling at the* | *signe of the Swan in Pauls Churchyard.* *1612.* [32]

27 unnumbered leaves, 4to. (18.2 x 13.4 cm.). Church 355, New John

Carter Brown cat., Sabin 53249. BM, Bodleian, CSmH, DLC, ICN, MBAt, MH, MiU-C, MnHi, N, NHi, NjP, NN, PPL, RPJCB, ViU.
Second part of *Noua Britannia*, 1609.
Reprinted in Mass. Hist. Soc. *Coll.*, 2d ser., vol. VIII; and in Force's *Tracts*, vol. 1.

SMITH, CAPTAIN JOHN AND WILLIAM SYMONDS

A map of Virginia. | With a descripti- | on of the covntrey, the | commodities, people, govern- | ment and religion. | Written by Captaine Smith, sometimes Go- | vernour of the countrey. | Wherevnto is annexed the | proceedings of those colonies, since their first | departure from England, with the discourses, | orations, and relations of the salvages, | and the accidents that befell | them in all their iournies | and discoveries. | Taken faithfvlly as they | were written out of the writings of | Doctor Rvessel. Richard Wiefin. | Tho. Stvdley. Will. Phettiplace. | Anas Todkill. Nathaniel Powell. | Ieffra Abot. Richard Pots. | And the relations of divers other diligent observers there | present then, and now many of them in England. | By W.S. | [ornament] | At Oxford, | Printed by Joseph Barnes. 1612. [Title of second part:] The | proceedings of | the English colonie in | Virginia since their first beginning from | England in the yeare of our Lord 1606, | till this present 1612, with all their | accidents that befell them in their | iournies and discoveries. | Also the salvages discourses, orations and relations | of the bordering neighbours, and how they be- | came subject to the English. | Vnfolding even the fundamentall causes from whence haue sprang so many mise- | ries to the vundertakers, and scandals to the businesse: taken faith- | fully as they were written out of the writings of Thomas | Studley the first provant maister, Anas Todkill, Walter | Russell Doctor of Phisicke, Nathaniell Powell, | William Phettyplace, Richard Wjffin, Tho- | mas Abbay, Tho: Hope, Rich: Polts and | the labours of divers other dili- | gent observers, that were | residents in Virginia. | And pervsed and confirmed by diverse now resident in | England that were actors in this business. By W.S. | [ornament] | *At Oxford,* | *Printed by Joseph Barnes. 1612.*   [33]

[8], 39; [4], 110 p., folded map of Virginia, 4to. (17 x 12.7 cm.). BM (2), CSmH, DLC, ICN, MB, MdBP, MH, MiU-C, MWiW-C, N, NjP, NHi, NN (2), NNP, PP, PPiU, RPJCB, ViU.

Four copies (including CSmH, NjP and NN) have inserted a separate printed presentation leaf. The map appears in 10 states, for which see Sabin 82832. See also Baer 1.

VIRGINIA COMPANY

[Seals of the King and Council] | By his Maiesties Counsell of Virginea. | Forasmuch as notwithstanding the late publication of our purpose to make vse of the King his | Maiesties most gratious grant of lotteries, for the aduancement of the Plantation of Virginea, | . . . [text continues, postponing the drawing of the lottery until June] | *London,* | *Imprinted by Felix Kyngston for William Welby, dwelling at the* | *signe of the Swanne in Pauls Churchyard. 1612.* [34]

Broadside, folio (40.5 x 27 cm.). Sabin 99865. RPJCB.

Earliest extant of several broadsides concerned with the lotteries used by the Virginia Company to help pay the expenses of their colony in Virginia.

[JOURDAIN, SILVESTER]

A plaine | description | of the Barmvdas, | now called Sommer | Ilands. | With the manner of their discouerie | anno 1609 by the shipwrack and admirable deliuerance | of Sir Thomas Gates, and Sir George Sommers, wherein | are truly set forth the commodities and profits of | that rich, pleasant, and healthfull | covntrie. | With | an addition, or more ample relation of | diuers other remarkable matters concerning those | ilands since then experienced, lately sent | from thence by one of the colonie now | there resident. | [rule, two lines quoted, rule] | *London,* | *Printed by W. Stansby, for W. Welby.* | *1613.* [35]

[52] p., 4to. (17.2 x 13.5 cm.). Sabin 9759, Church 362, new John Carter Brown cat. BM, CSmH, DFo (2), DLC, NHi, NjP, NN, PPL, RPJCB.

The second edition of *A discovery of the Barmvdas,* 1610, above.

VIRGINIA COMPANY

[Seal of the Council] | By his Maiesties Councell for | Virginia. | Whereas sundrie the aduenturers to Virginia in their zeale | [text continues, announcing the drawing of a lottery on May 10, 1613] | *Imprinted by Felix Kyngston for William Welby, dwelling at the* | *signe of the Swanne in Pauls Churchyard. 1613.* [36]

Broadside, folio. Sabin 99870. Society of Antiquaries. Title from facsimile in John Carter Brown Library: *Three proclamations concerning the lottery for Virginia.* Providence, 1907. Text in black letter with ornamental initial.

WHITAKER, ALEXANDER

Good | newes from | Virginia. | Sent to the Covnsell | and Company of Virginia, resident | in England. | From Alexander Whitaker, the | Minister of Henrico in | Virginia. | Wherein also is a narration | of the present state of that countrey, and | our colonies there. | Perused and published by direction | from that Counsell. | And a preface prefixed of some matters | touching that plantation, very requisite | to be made knowne. | [orn.] | *At London,* | *Imprinted by Felix Kyngston for William* | *Welby, and are to be sold at his shop in* | *Pauls Church-yard at the signe of the* | *Swanne 1613.* [37]

[28], 44 p., 4to. (17.1 x 12.6 cm.). Sabin 103313, Church 364, new John Carter Brown cat. BM, CSmH, DLC, ICN, MiU-C, NjP, NN, PP, PPL, RPJCB (2 copies).

Virginia Company promotion tract by the minister who married Pocahontas and John Rolfe.

HAMOR, RALPH

A trve | discovrse of the | present estate of Vir- | ginia, and the successe of the affaires | there till the 18 of Iune. 1614. | Together. | With a relation of the | seuerall English townes and forts, the assu- | red hopes of that countrie and the peace | concluded with the Indians. | The christening of Powhatans daughter | and her mariage with an English-man. | Written by Raphe Hamor the yon- | ger, late Secretarie in that Colony. | [motto and device] | *Printed at London by Iohn Beale for Wil- | liam Welby dwelling at the signe of the | Swanne in Pauls Church-yard, 1615.*   [38]

[8], 69, [1] p., 4to. (18 x 13.4 cm.). Sabin 30120, Church 365, new John Carter Brown cat. There are 2 issues, the first with 13 lines in the last paragraph of p. 60 and the second with twelve lines less critical of the clergy substituted. BM (2), Bodleian, CSmH (both issues), CtSoP, DLC, ICN (both issues), MB, MH, MHi, MiU-C, N, NHi, NjP (1st issue), NN (both issues), NNC, OClWHi, PP, RPJCB.

Virginia Company promotion tract in which the former Secretary of the colony brings the history down to June 18, 1614 and tells of the baptism of Pocahontas and her wedding to John Rolfe with a letter from the latter telling why he married her.

For other editions, see Sabin and Church.

VIRGINIA COMPANY

A declaration for the certaine time of dravving the great standing lottery. | [Engraved heading showing full length figures of two Indians, the seals of the King and Council and symbols of the lottery] | [text in 3 columns] | *Imprinted at London by Felix Kyngston, for VVilliam VVelby, the 22. of Februarie. 1615.*   [39]

Broadside, folio. Sabin 99872. Society of Antiquaries. Title from facsimile in John Carter Brown Library: *Three proclamations concerning the lottery for Virginia.* Providence, 1907. Two outside columns printed in black letter. The same work prints a facsimile of the royal proclamation suspending the lotteries, 1620.

SMITH, CAPTAIN JOHN

A | description | of New England: | or | the observations, and | discoueries, of Captain Iohn Smith (Admirall | of that country) in the North of America, in the year | of our Lord 1614: with the successe of sixe ships, | that went the next yeare 1615; and the | accidents befell him among the | French men of warre: | with the proofe of the present benefit this | countrey affoords: whither this present yeare, | 1616, eight voluntary ships are gone | to make further tryall. | [ornament] | *At London | Printed by Humfrey Lownes, for*

Robert Clerke; and | are to be sould at his house called the Lodge, | in Chancery lane, ouer against Lin- | colnes Inne. 1616. [Colophon:] *At London printed the 18. of Iune, in | the yeere of our Lord 1616.*   [40]

[16], 61, [2] p., map of New England, 4to. (18.1 x 12.7 cm.). BM (3, 2 imperfect), CSmH, DLC, ICN, MB (2), MH, MiU-C, MWiW-C, NHi, NN, PP, PPL, RHi, RPJCB.

The first book to have the name New England on its title page and the principal emigrant guide of the Pilgrims.

There are nine states of the map of New England, for which see Sabin 82819 and Church 369.

There are at least four copies (including BM, DLC and MB) including a preliminary leaf of explanation not included in the collation.

For modern reprints, Washington, 1837 and Boston, 1865, see Sabin 82820 and 82821.

VIRGINIA COMPANY

[Type orn.] | By His Maiesties | Counseil for Virginia. | [rule] | A briefe de | claration of | the present state of things in Virginia, and | of a diuision to be now made, of some part | of those lands in our actuall possession, as well | to all such as haue aduentured their | monyes, as also to those that | are planters there. [Caption title] *[London, 1616].*   [41]

8 p., 4to. (16.8 x 13 cm.). Sabin 99873, new John Carter Brown cat. BM, CSmH, RPJCB.

. . . . .

By his Maiesties Councell for Virginia. Whereas vpon the returne of Sir Thomas Dale, knight, (Marshall of Virginia) the Treasurer, Councell, and Company of the same, haue beene thoroughly informed and assured of the good estate of that Colony . . . [Emigrants wanted. Samuel Argall made governor, etc.] *[London, 1617?].*   [42]

Broadside, folio. Title from Sabin 99874. CSmH.

[BONOEIL, JOHN]

Observa | tions to be | followed, for the | making of fit roomes, to keepe | silk-wormes in: | as also, | for the best manner of | planting of mulbery trees, to | feed them. | Pvblished by avthority | for the benefit of the noble plantation | in Virginia. | [device] | At London, | Imprinted by Felix Kyngston. 1620.   [43]

28 p., 4to. (17.1 x 13.1 cm.). Sabin 99883, Church 382 A, new John Carter Brown cat. Bodleian, CSmH, MH, RPJCB.

The Virginia Company, deluded by the belief that silk could be produced in America, published several tracts for the encouragement of that industry among its colonists, of which this is the first.

SMITH, CAPTAIN JOHN

New | Englands | trials. | Declaring the successe of 26. ships | employed
thither within these sixe yeares: | with the benefit of that countrey by sea
and | land: and how to build threescore sayle | of good ships, to make a
little | Navie Royall. | Written by Captaine | Iohn Smith. | [ornament] |
London, | *Printed by William Iones.* |*1620.*   [44]

[20] p. 4to. BM, BODLEIAN, CSmH, ICN.

New England colonization tract. *Trials* does not mean tribulations, but
attempts at colonization.

Each of the known copies has a different heading for the presentation
address.

For full description, see Sabin 82833, and, for the Cambridge, 1873
reprint, 82834.

VIRGINIA COMPANY

A | declaration | of the state of | the Colonie and affaires | in Virginia: |
with | the names of the aduenturors, | and summes aduentured in | that
action. | [rule] | By His Maiesties Counseil for | Virginia. 22. Iunij. 1620.
| [rule] | [Royal seal] | *London:* | *Printed by T.S. 1620.*   [45]

[4], 11 (verso blank), 8; 30, blank leaf; 4 p., 4to. (16.8 x 13 cm.). Sabin
99877, new John Carter Brown cat. RPJCB.

First ed., first issue.

.   .   .   .   .

With collation: [4], 11 (verso seal of the Council); 8; 30, blank leaf; 4;
39. Sabin 99878, new John Carter Brown cat. MWiW-C, RPJCB, W. M.
Hill.   [46]

First edition, second issue.

.   .   .   .   .

[4], 11 (verso seal of the Council); 16, 30, blank leaf; 4; 39. Sabin
99879, Church 381, new John Carter Brown cat. BM, Bodleian, CSmH,
MH, NN, PHi, RPJCB.   [47]

First edition, third issue.

.   .   .   .   .

With *Colony* for *Colonie* in title and printer's name spelled out: *Thomas
Snodham.*   [48]

[2], 92 p., 4to. (17 x 12.6 cm.). Sabin 99880, new John Carter Brown
cat. BM, Bodleian, Cambridge U., DLC, NHi, NjP, NN, RPJCB.

Second edition, first issue.

.   .   .   .   .

[2], 97 p. Sabin 99881, Church 382. CSmH, MiU-C, NN.   [49]

Second edition, second issue.

For contents of various issues, see Sabin.

. . . . .

A note of the ship- | ping, men, and provisions, sent | to Virginia, by the Treasurer and | Company, in the yeere 1619. [Caption title] *[London, 1620].*   [50]

[3] p., folio (27.5 x 16 cm.). Sabin 99882. NN.

[SPARKE, MICHAEL]

Greevovs | grones | for the poore. | Done by a well-willer, who wisheth, that the | poore of England might be so proui- | ded for, as none should neede to go a begging | within this realme. | The poore afflicted are, | So that they perish fast: | If now no order taken be, | Then ruine comes at last. | [device] | *London | Printed for Michaell Sparke.* | 1621.   [51]

[5], 22, [1] p., 4to. Sabin 88961, Church 387. CSmH, ICN, MiU-C.

Dedicated to the Virginia Company and issued in their interest.

VIRGINIA COMPANY

[Type orn.] | A note of the ship- | ping, men, and provisions, sent | and prouided for Virginia, by the Right Hono- | rable, the Earle of Sovthampton, and the Company, | this yeare, 1620. | [Caption title] *[London, 1621].*   [52]

[3] p., folio (24 x 17.5 cm.). BM, Public Record Office, Society of Antiquaries.

BONOEIL, JOHN

His Maiesties | graciovs letter to the | Earle of Sovth-hampton, | Treasurer, and to the Councell and Company of | Virginia heere: commanding the present setting vp | of silke works, and planting of vines in Virginia. | And the letter of the Treasurer, Councell, and Company, to | the Gouernour and Councell of State there, for the strict exe- | cution of his Maiesties royall commands herein. | Also a treatise of the art of making silke: | or, | Directions for the making of lodgings, and the breeding, nourishing, | and ordering of silkewormes, and for the planting of mulbery | trees, and all other things belonging to the silke art. | Together with instructions how to plant and dresse vines, and | to make wine, and how to dry raisins, figs, and other fruits, | and to set oliues, oranges, lemons, pomegranates, | almonds, and many other fruits, &c. | And in the end, a conclusion, with sundry profitable | remonstrances to the colonies. | Set foorth for the benefit of the two renowned and most | hopefull sisters, Virginia, and the Summer-Ilands. | [rule] | By Iohn Bonoeil Frenchman, seruant in these imployments | to his most excellent Maiesty of Great Brittaine, | France, Ireland, Virginia, and the Summer-Ilands. | [rule] | Published by authority. | [rule] | *London Printed by Felix Kyngston. 1622.*   [53]

[12], 88 p., illus., 4to. (17 x 13.2 cm.). Sabin 99886, Church 389, new John Carter Brown cat. BM, CSmH, ICN, MBAt, MH, NjP, NN, PHi, RPJCB.

A Virginia Company silk promotion tract.

B[ROOKE], C[HRISTOPHER]

A | poem | on | the late mas- | sacre in Virginia. | VVith particular mention of those men | of note that suffered in that disaster. | [rule] | Written by C. B. Gent. | [rule] | [Royal seal and seal of Virignia Company] | [rule] | *Imprinted at London by G. Eld, for Robert Mylbourne, and are to be | sold at his shop, at the great South doore of Pauls. 1622.*   [54]

[23] p., 4to. Sabin 100510. Public Record Office, Rosenbach Company (1946).

One of the first books of English poetry about America. Dedicated to the Virginia Company and published as part of their promotion program.

Herschel V. Jones *Adventures in Americana* 86 with title reproduced. The Jones copy purchased by the Rosenbach Company by whom it was offered in their 1946 catalog, no. 134 at $32,500. and again at same price in their 1947 catalog, no. 113.

For another poem on the same subject, see: *Good newes from Virginia,* [1624].

COPLAND, PATRICK

[Type orns.] | A declaration how the monies (viz. | seuenty pound eight shillings sixe | pence) were disposed, which was gathered | (by M. Patrick Copland, preacher in the Roy- | all Iames) at the Cape of good hope, (towards the | building of a free schoole in Virginia) of the Gen- | tlemen and marriners in the said ship: a list of whose | names are vnder specified, for Gods glory, their comfort, | and the incouragement of others to the furthering of the | same, or the like pious worke. | [Caption title] [Colophon:] *Imprinted at London by F. K. 1622.*   [55]

7 p., 4to. (19.5 x 15.5 cm.). Sabin 99884, Church 392. CSmH, Public Record Office.

Copland was chaplain of the *James* and the school was located at Charles City, Virginia. For this gift he was made a free brother of the Virginia Company.

. . . . .

Virginia's God be thanked, | or | a sermon of | thanksgiving | for the happie | successe of the affayres in | Virginia this last | yeare. | Preached by Patrick Copland at | Bow-Church in Cheapside, before the Honorable | Virginia Company, on Thursday, the 18. | of Aprill 1622. And now published by | the commandment of the said hono- | rable Company. | Hereunto are adjoyned some epistles, | written first in Latine (and now Englished) in | the East Indies by Peter Pope, an Indian youth, | borne in the bay of Bengala, who was first taught | and converted by the said P. C. And after bap- | tized by Master Iohn Wood, Dr in Divinitie, | in a famous assembly before the Right | Worshipfull, the East India Company, | at S. Denis in Fan-Church streete | in London, December 22, | 1616. | [rule] | *London* | *Printed by I. D. for William Sheffard and Iohn Bellamie,* | *and are to be* *sold at his shop at the two Grey-* | *hounds in Corne-hill, neere the Royall* | *Exchange. 1622.* | [Title within double ruled border). [56]

[12], 36 p., 4to. (17.8 x 13.3 cm.). Sabin 16691, Church 390, new John Carter Brown cat. BM, Bodleian, CSmH, CtSoP, ICN, MH, MSaE, NjP, NN, RPJCB.

Virginia Company promotion sermon. Contains what is probably the first account of what is now North Carolina.

COUNCIL FOR NEW ENGLAND

A briefe relation | of the | discovery | and plantation | of | New England: | and | of svndry accidents | therein occvrring, from | the yeere of our Lord M.DC.VII. to this | present M.DC.XXII. | Together with the state thereof as now it standeth; | the generall forme of gouernment intended; and the | diuision of the whole territorie into coun- | ties, baronries, &c. | [orn.] | *London,* | *Printed by John Haviland, and are to be* | *sold by William Bladen,* | *M.DC.XXII.* [57]

[36] p., 4to. (17.3 x 13 cm.). Sabin 52619, Church 394, Stokes VI:259, new John Carter Brown cat. BM, CSmH, ICN, MiU, MiU-C, MWiW-C, NHi, NN, OClWHi, PP, PPL, RPJCB.

One of the earliest and most important of early Massachusetts accounts and the first account in English of the Dutch on Manhattan Island.

For other editions, see Sabin and Stokes.

[CUSHMAN, ROBERT]

A | sermon | preached at | Plimmoth in | Nevv-England | December 9. 1621. | in an assemblie of his | Maiesties faithfull | subiects, there | inhabit- ing. | VVherein is shevved | the danger of selfe-loue, and the | sweetnesse of true friendship. | Together | vvith a preface, | shewing the state of the country, | and condition of the | savages. | [3 lines quoted] | Written in the yeare 1621. | [rule] | *London* | *Printed by I. D. for Iohn Bellamie,* | *and are to be sold at his shop at the two Gray-* | *hounds in Corne-hill, neere the Royall* | *Exchange. 1622.* | [Title within double ruled border]. [58]

[8], 19 p., 4to. (30.1 x 23.6 cm.). Church 391, new John Carter Brown cat. Bodleian, CSmH, CtY, ICN, RPJCB.

First printed New England sermon and one of the earliest accounts of the New England Indians.

DONNE, JOHN

A | sermon | vpon the VIII. verse | of the I. Chap- | ter of the Acts | of the Apostles. | Preach'd | to the Honourable Company of the | Virginian Plantation. | 13°. Nouemb. 1622. | By | Iohn Donne Deane of St. | Pauls, London. | *London.* | *Printed by A. Mat:* | *for Thomas Iones* | *and are to be sold at his shop in the Strand, at the* | *blacke Rauen, neere vnto Saint* | *Clements Church.* | *1622.*   [59]

[4], 49, [1] p., 4to. (18.7 x 13.9 cm.). Sabin 20601, new John Carter Brown cat. BM, Cambridge U., CSmH, DFo, DLC, ICN, MH, MHi, NjP, NN, RPJCB.

Virginia Company promotion sermon. There were varying issues of this edition. Reprinted for the same printer, 1624. Church 401, new John Carter Brown cat. CSmH, DFo, MBAt, NN, RPJCB. Reprinted in his: *Five sermons vpon speciall occasions.* London, 1626.

[MOURT (OR MORTON), GEORGE, ED.]

A | relation or | iournall of the beginning and proceedings | of the English plantation setled at Plimoth in New | England, by certaine English aduentur- ers both | merchants and others. | With their difficult passage, their safe ariuall, their | ioyfull building of, and comfortable planting them- | selues in the now well defended towne | of New Plimoth. | As also a relation of fovre | seuerall discoueries since made by some of the | same English planters there resident. | I. In a iourney to Pvckanokick the habitation of the Indians grea- | test King Massasoyt: as also their message, the answer and enter- tainment | they had of him. | II. In a voyage made by ten of them to the Kingdome of Nawset, to seeke | a boy that had lost himselfe in the woods: with such accidents as befell them | in that voyage. | III. In their iourney to the Kingdome of Namaschet, in defence of their | greatest King Massasoyt, against the Narrohiggonsets, and to reuenge the | supposed death of their interpreter Tisquantum. | IIII. Their voyage to the Massachusets, and their entertainment there. | With an answer to all such obiections as are any way made | against the lawfulnesse of English plantations | in those parts. | [Type orn.] | *London,* | *Printed for Iohn Bellamie, and are to be sold at his* | *shop at the two* | *Greyhounds in Cornhill neere the Royall Exchange. 1622.*
                                                                            [60]

[12], 72 p., 4to. (17.3 x 13 cm.). Church 393, new John Carter Brown cat., Sabin 51198. BM, CSmH, CtSoP, DFo, DLC, ICN, MB, MH, MiU-C, MWiW-C, NN (both issues), PP, PPL, PPL-R, RHi, RPJCB, ViU.

There are two issues of the first page of text.

This narrative, probably written by William Bradford and Edward Winslow, gives the earliest account of the voyage of the Mayflower, text of the Mayflower Compact, settlement of Plymouth and adventures of Miles Standish. For reprints, see Sabin.

SMITH, CAPTAIN JOHN

New Englands | trials. | Declaring the successe of 80 ships | employed thither within these eight yeares; | and the benefit of that countrey by sea | and land. | With the present estate of that happie plan- | tation, begun but by 60 weake men | in the yeare 1620. | And how to build a fleete of good shippes | to make a little Nauie Royall. | Written by Captaine Iohn Smith, sometimes Go- | uernour of Virginia, and Admirall | of New England. | The second edition. | [ornament] | *London,* | *Printed by William Iones.* | *1622.* [61]

[32] p., 4to. (17.2 x 12.5 cm.). BM (2), Bodleian, CSmH, ICN, NN, PPL, RPJCB.

For full description, see Sabin 82835. For Washington, 1837, Cambridge, [1867], and other reprints, see Sabin 82836-82837.

VIRGINIA COMPANY

The inconveniences | that have happened to some per- | sons which have transported themselves | from England to Virginia, without prouisions neces- | sary to sustaine themselues, hath | greatly hindred the progresse of that noble plantation: For preuention of the like disorders | hereafter, that no man suffer, either through ignorance or misinformation; it is thought re- | quisite to publish this short declaration: wherein is contained a particular of such neces- | saries, as either priuate families or single persons shall haue cause to furnish themselves with, for their better | support at their first landing in Virginia; whereby also greater numbers may receiue in part, | directions how to provide themselues. | [rule] | [List, in two columns, with prices, of clothing, food, weapons, tools and household implements] | [rule] | *Imprinted at London by Felix Kyngston. 1622.* [62]

Broadside, folio. Sabin 99887. BM, CSmH, NN, RPJCB, Society of Antiquaries.

. . . . .

[Type orn.] | A note of the shipping, men, and prouisions sent and | prouided for Virginia, by the Right Honorable Henry | Earle of South- hampton, and the Company, and other pri- | uate aduenturers, in the yeere 1621. &c. | [Caption title] *[London, 1622?].* [[63]

4 p., folio (27 x 16.5 cm.). Sabin 99888. CSmH, NN, Society of Antiquaries.

. . . . .

Mo[u]rning Virginia. *[London. Henry Gosson. 1622].* [64]

Sabin 100489. Known only from the entry by Gosson at Stationers' Hall, July 10, 1622.

This, like *A poem on the late massacre in Virginia,* was published to commemorate the Great Massacre of April, 1622 when all of the Virginia settlements, except Jamestown which had been warned by a friendly Indian, were wiped out and several hundred killed by the Indians under the leadership of Opechancanough, brother and successor of Powhatan.

WASSENAER, NICHOLAAS VAN, AND BAREND LAMPE

Historisch Verhael | alder ghedenck-weerdichste geschiedenissē, | die hier en daer in Europa, als in Duijtsch-lant, Vranck-rijck, | Enghelant, Spaengien, Hungarijen, Polen, Seven-berghen, Walla- | chien, Moldavien, Turckijen, en Neder-lant, van den beginne | des jaers 1621: tot den Herfst toe, voorgevallen sijn. | door Doct. Claes Wassenaer. | 1622. | t'Amsterdam | Bij Jan Evertss Cloppenburg op't Water. | 1622. [Colophon:] t'Amsterdam, | Ghedruckt ten huyse van Ian Evertsen Cloppenburgh. | [Engraved title with vignette] *[1622-1635]*.   [65]

21 parts in 5 vols., 4to. (18.8 x 14.8 cm.). Sabin 102039, Asher 330, New John Carter Brown cat., Stokes VI:264. BM, CSmH, DLC, NHi, NN, RPJCB.

A semi-annual chronicle covering the years 1621 to 1635, parts 18 to 21 being by Lampe, published from 1622 to 1635, the titles varying. Part 12, folios 37-38, contains the earliest printed account of the settlement of Manhattan Island in 1626. Later parts contain unique information of outstanding importance for the early history of New Netherland.

"Historical account of the most memorable events which have occurred here and there in Europe . . . from the beginning of the year 1621, to the Autumn. By Dr. Claes Wassenaer. 1622"

[WATERHOUSE, EDWARD]

A | declaration | of | the state of the | colony and affaires in Virginia. | With | a relation of the barba- | rous massacre in the time of peace and league, | treacherously executed by the natiue infidels | vpon the English, the 22 of March last. | Together with the names of those that were then massacred; | that their lawfull heyres, by this notice giuen, may take order | for the inheriting of their lands and estates in | Virginia. | And | a treatise annexed, | written by that learned mathematician Mr. Henry | Briggs, of the Northwest passage to the South Sea | through the continent of Virginia, and | by Fretum Hudson. | Also a commemoration of such worthy bene- | factors as haue con- | tributed their Christian charitie towards the aduance- | ment of the colony. | And a note of the charges of necessary prouisions fit for euery man that | intends to goe to Virginia. | [rule] | Published by authoritie. | [rule] | Imprinted at London by G. Eld, for Robert Mylbourne, and are to be | sold at his shop, at the great South doore of Pauls. 1622.   [66]

[7], 54 p., folded broadside, 4to. (17.1 x 12.9 cm.). Sabin 99885, Church 396, new John Carter Brown cat. BM, CSmH, DLC, ICN, MH, MWiW-C, NHi, NjP, NN, PPL-R, PU, RPJCB (2).

The broadside, previously issued as a separate: *The inconveniences | that have happened to some per- | sons . . . 1622*, is inserted before p. 1.

A Virginia Company promotion tract.

[Type orn.] | Good newes from Virginia, | Sent from Iames his Towne this present moneth of March, 1623 by a | gentleman in that country. To the tune of, *All those that be good fellows.* | [cut of ship, type orn., cut of soldier] | [text in double column, black letter, with type ornaments between the columns and at foot of page] | [text continued on second page facing first page, type orns. between the columns] | [Colophon:] *Printed at London for Iohn Trundle. [1624].*   [67]

Broadside, folio (38.5 x 30.5 cm.), folded to form two pages of text facing each other (verso blank). Twenty-two eight line stanzas. Sabin 100478. Public Record Office. Another copy owned by William H. Robinson, Ltd., London, 1948.

Ballad celebrating the recovery of the Jamestown colony from the massacre of 1622 when 347 colonists were killed by the Indians. Earliest known example of printed verse by an American resident. For another poem on the same subject, but not by an American resident, see under Christopher Brooke. For still another poem on the Jamestown colony, see under Richard Rich.

Description from photostat of P. R. O. copy and from text and facsimile reproduction in William H. Robinson, Ltd. cat. 77, 1948, no. 98, offered at $11,000.

The Public Record Office copy was reproduced in Mass. Hist. Soc. Photostat Americana second series, 1936, no. 105, with copies in 15 leading libraries.

SMITH, CAPTAIN JOHN

The | generall historie | of | Virginia, New-England, and the Summer | Isles: with the names of the adventurers, | planters, and governours from their | first beginning. Ano: 1584. to this | present 1624. | With the procedings of those severall colonies | and the accidents that befell them in all their | journeys and discoveries. | Also the maps and descriptions of all those | countryes, their commodities, people, | government, customes, and religion | yet knowne. | Divided into sixe bookes. | By Captaine Iohn Smith sometymes Governour | in those countryes & Admirall. | of New-England. | London. | Printed by I.D. and | I.H. for Michael | Sparkes. | 1624.   [68]

Engraved title, [12], 96, 105-248 p., 4 folded maps, folio.

There are eight issues of the title page, the text being practically identical but with variations in the maps and portraits:

1. Engraved title of 1624 with portrait of Charles as Prince.
2. Large paper copies with engraved title of 1624.
3. Type-printed title of 1625, preceded by engraved title of 1624.
4. Engraved title of 1626 with portrait of Charles as King.
5. Engraved title of 1627.
6. Engraved title of 1631.

7. Earlier engraved title of 1632 with altered imprint.
8. Later engraved title of 1632 with portrait of King Charles re-engraved.

Maps: Ould Virginia, Virginia, Summer Ils, New England, several variant issues of each. Portraits inserted in some copies: Duchess of Richmond (two engravings) and Pocahontas, variant issues of each.

For full descriptions and locations of the various editions, see Sabin 82823-82830 and Baer 7, 9, 11, 13, 17, 19.

W[INSLOW], E[DWARD]

Good | newes | from New-England: | or | a true relation of things very re- | markable at the plantation of Plimoth | in New-England. | Shewing the wondrous providence and good- | nes of God, in their preservation and continuance, | being delivered from many apparent | deaths and dangers. | Together with a relation of such religious and | civill lawes and customes, as are in practise amongst | the Indians, adjoyning to them at this day. As also | what commodities are there to be raysed for the | maintenance of that and other planta- | tions in the said country. | [rule] | Written by E. W. who hath borne a part in the | fore-named troubles, and there liued since | their first arrivall. | [rule] | *London* | *Printed by I.D. for William Bladen and Iohn Bellamie, and* | *are to be sold at their shops, at the Bible in Pauls-Church-* | *yard, and at the three Golden Lyons in Corn-hill,* | *neere the Royall Exchange. 1624.*   [69]

[8], 67 (misnumbered 59) p., 4to. (19.1 x 14.3 cm.). Church 403-404, new John Carter Brown cat., Sabin 104795. BM, CSmH (both issues), CtSoP, CtY, ICN, MB (1st), MHi (2d), MiU-C (2d), NN (1st), PPL (1st), RPJCB (1st with title and added leaf of 2d inserted). No attempt made to identify ownership of the two issues of all copies.

. . . . .

Same title with upper rule removed from title and following inserted above lower rule: *Wherevnto is added by him a briefe relation of a credible* | *intelligence of the present estate of Virginia.*   [69A]

[8], 69 (misnumbered 59) p., 4to. (19.1 x 14.3 cm.).

A continuation of Mourt's Relation from Dec. 11, 1621-Sept. 10, 1623. For reprints, see Sabin.

LAET, JOANNES DE

Nieuvve Wereldt | Ofte | Beschrijvinghe | van | West-Indien, | Wt veelderhande Schriften ende Aen-teeckeninghen | van verscheyden Natien by een versamelt | Door | Ioannes de Laet, | Ende met | Noodighe | Kaerten ende Tafels voorsien. | [printer's device] | *Tot Leyden,* | *In de Druckerye van Isaack Elzevier.* | *Anno 1625. Met Privilegie der Ho. Mo. Heeren Staten Generael, voor 12. Iaren.*   [70]

[24], 510, [16] p., 10 folded Spanish-American maps, folio (33.8 x 22.6

cm.). Sabin 38554, Asher 1, new John Carter Brown cat. NHi, NN, RPJCB, etc.

"The New World, or the description of the West Indies from several manuscripts and notes of several nations, collected by Joannes de Laet, and provided with the necessary maps and tables." Chapters 7-11, p. 100-109, description of New Netherland.

First edition. For 2d ed., see: *Beschrijvinghe van West-Indien*, 1630.

LEVETT, CHRISTOPHER

A | voyage | into Nevv | England | begun in 1623. and ended | in 1624. | Performed by Christopher Levett, | his Maiesties Woodward of Somerset-shire, and | one of the Councell of New-England. | Yorkes [cut of ship] Bonauen- | ture. | *Printed at London, by William Iones,* | *and are to be sold by Edward Brewster, at the signe* | *of the Bible in Paules Church yard,* | *1628.* [71]

[6], 38 p., 4to. (17.2 x 12.6 cm.). Sabin 40751, new John Carter Brown cat. BM, CSmH, NHi, PP, RPJCB.

Levett travelled the New England coast from Cape Ann to Maine and gives a valuable account of his life with the Indians.

[HIGGINSON, FRANCIS]

New-Englands | plantation. | Or, | a short and trve | description of the | commodities and | discommodities | of that countrey. | [rule] | Written by a reuerend Diuine now | there resident. | [rule] | [woodcut arms] | [rule] | *London,* | *Printed by T.C. for Michael Sparke,* | *dwelling at the Signe of* *the Blew Bible in* | *Greene Arbor in the little Old Bailey.* | *1630.* [72]

[22] p., 4to. (19 x 14 cm.). Church 416, Sabin 31739, new John Carter Brown cat.

First edition. The Pilgrim Colony from July to September, 1629.

. . . . .

New-Englands | plantation. | Or, | a short and trve | description of the | commodities and | discommodities | of that countrey. | Written by Mr. Higgeson, a reuerand Diuine | now there resident. | Whereunto is added a letter, sent by Mr. Graues | an Enginere, out of New-England, | The second edition enlarged. | *London,* | *Printed by T. and R. Cotes. for Michael Sparke, dwelling* | *at the Signe of the Blue Bible in Greene-* | *Arbor. 1630.* [73]

[28] p., 4to. Brinley 312.

. . . . .

New-Englands | plantation. Or, | a short and trve | description of the | commodities and | discommodities | of that countrey. | Written by Mr. Higgeson, a reuerend Diuine | now there resident. | Whereunto is added

a letter, sent by Mr. Graues | an Enginere, out of New-England, | The third edition enlarged. | *London,* | *Printed by T. and R. Cotes. for Michael Sparke, dwelling* | *at the Signe of the Blue Bible in Greene-* | *Arbor. 1630.*
[74]
[26] p., 4to. (17.4 x 12.9 cm.). Sabin 31740, new John Carter Brown cat.

Locations of the three editions, not all identified as to edition: CSmH (1st), DLC (3d), ICN, MB, MH (3d), MHi, MiU-C, MWiW-C, NHi (1st), NN (all 3), OU, PPL (1st), RPJCB (1st, 3d).

LAET, JOANNES DE

Beschrijvinghe | van | West-Indien | door | Ioannes de Laet. | Tweede druck: | In ontallijcke plaetsen ver- | betert, vermeerdert, met eenige | nieuwe Caerten, beelden van | verscheyden dieren ende | planten verciert. | *Tot Leyden, bij de Elzeviers. A°. 1630.* | [Engraved title within ornamental border]. [75]
[28], 622, [18] p., 14 folded maps, folio. (31.4 x 19.5 cm.). Sabin 38555, Asher 2, new John Carter Brown cat. MB, RPJCB, etc.

Second edition, revised and enlarged. For 1st ed., see: *Nieuvve Wereldt,* 1625. RPJCB has two copies with variant title on first map, one in Dutch as in 1st ed., the other in Latin as in third edition.

[PHILLIPS, GEORGE ?]

The | humble | reqvest of | his Maiesties | loyall subjects, the Governour | and the Company late gone for | Nevv-England; | to the rest of their brethren, in and of the | Church of England. | For the obtaining of their prayers, | and the removall of suspitions, and mis- | constructions of their intentions. | [rule, orn., rule] | *London,* | *Printed for Iohn Bellamie. 1630.*
[76]
[2], 10 p., 4to. (18.2 x 13.5 cm.). Sabin 104846, new John Carter Brown cat. Bodleian, CSmH, MB, RPJCB.

Dated and signed: From Yarmouth aboord the Arabella April 7. 1630. Io: Winthrope Gov., Rich: Saltonstall, Charles Fines, Isaac Iohnson, Tho: Dudley, George Philipps, William Coddington, &c. &c.

Attributed with convincing proof to Rev. George Phillips, the only clergyman on the flagship, *Arabella,* of the Winthrop fleet, by H. W. Foot in Mass. Hist. Soc. Proceedings, vol. 63, 1931, p. 193-227. Has also been attributed to Governor John Winthrop, merely because he was the first to sign it, and to John White on the strength of a dubious statement made 50 years after the signing of the document, for which see note in Sabin, which also records several reprints.

This first official statement of The Company of the Massachusetts Bay is generally called *The Puritans' Farewell to England.* It states their principles and reasons for emigrating to New England.

SMITH, CAPTAIN JOHN

The | true travels, | adventvres, | and | observations | of | Captaine Iohn Smith, | in Europe, Asia, Affrica, and America, from Anno | Domini 1593. to 1629. | His accidents and sea-fights in the Straights; his service | and stratagems of warre in Hungaria, Transilvania, Wallachia, and | Moldavia, against the Turks, and Tartars; and his three single combats | betwixt the Christian armie and the Turkes. | After how he was taken prisoner by the Turks, sold for a slave, sent into | Tartaria; his description of the Tartars, their strange manners and customes of | religions, diets, buildings, warres, feasts, ceremonies, and | living; how hee slew the Bashaw of Nalbrits in Cambia, | and escaped from the Turkes and Tartars. | Together with a continuation of his generall history of Virginia, | Summer-Iles, New England, and their proceedings, since 1624. to this | present 1629; as also of the new plantations of the great | river of the Amazons, the iles of St. Christopher, Mevis, | and Barbados in the West Indies. | All written by actuall authours, whose names | you shall finde along the history. | *London,* | *Printed by J. H. for Thomas Slater, and are to bee | sold at the Blew Bible in Greene Arbour. 1630.* [77]

[12], 60 p., folded plate, folio (28.3 x 18.7 cm.). BM (2), CSmH (2), CtSoP, DLC, ICN, MB, NjP, NN (4), PPL, RPJCB, etc.

Smith's coat of arms appears on the verso of the title of most copies, though in some it is missing and in others it appears on a separate leaf facing the title. The folded plate, showing Smith's various adventures, appears in two states, for which see Sabin 82851. For textual variations and later reprints, see Sabin 82851 and 82852.

VAUGHAN, SIR WILLIAM

The Newlanders | cvre. | Aswell of those violent sicknesses | which distemper most minds in these | latter dayes: as also by a cheape and | newfound dyet, to preserue the | body sound and free from all diseases, | vntill the last date of life, through | extreamity of age. | . . . | Published for the weale of Great Brittaine, | By Sir William Vaughan, Knight. | . . . | *Imprinted at London by N.O. for F. Constable, and are to be sold at his shop in Pauls Church | at the signe of the Craine. 1630.* [78]

[16], 143 p., 8vo. (14.5 x 9 cm.). Sabin 98694, S.T.C. 24619, new John Carter Brown cat. BM, CSmH, DFo, Garrett, MH, RPJCB, Henry Stevens Son & Stiles (1948). See also Baer 10, 12, 15, 16.

First medical treatise written in America on specific diseases. The author's promotion tracts are omitted since they deal with Newfoundland and not the present territory of the United States. Contains an autobiographical preface and a section on an epidemic of scurvy in Lord Baltimore's colony.

WEST-INDISCHE COMPAGNIE

Vryheden | By de Vergaderinghe van | de Negenthiene vande Geoctroyeerde | West-Indische Compagnie vergunt aen allen | den ghenen, die

eenighe Colonien in Nieu- | Nederlandt sullen planten. | In het licht
ghegheven | Om bekent te maken wat Profijten ende Voordeelen | aldaer
in Nieu-Nederlandt, voor de Coloniers ende der | selver Patroonen ende
Meesters, midtsgaders de | Participanten, die de Colonien aldaer | planten,
zijn becomen. | [engraving] | t'Amstelredam, | Voor Marten Iansz Brandt
Boeckvercooper | woonende by | de nieuwe Kerck | in de Gereformeerde
Catechismus, Anno 1630.   [79]
   [15] p., 4to. (19.4 x 14.6 cm.). Sabin 102920, Asher 331, Stokes IV:77,
new John Carter Brown cat. CSmH, MiU-C, NjP, RPJCB.

.   .   .   .   .   .

   Except that Nieu of Nieu-Nederlandt in the title is spelled Nieuw and,
in the imprint, a period follows Catechismus instead of a comma. CSmH,
DLC, NHi.   [79A]

.   .   .   .   .   .

   Same, except that Voor in the imprint is replaced by By. NN.   [79B]
   "The charter of privileges and exemptions granted by the assembly of
the Nineteen, in the name of the authorized West India Company, to all
who may plant a colony in New Netherland. Published with a view to make
known what profits and advantages are to be obtained in that country by
colonists and their masters and patrons." This, the earliest separate publication relating to New Netherland, was the foundation of the system of
patroonships and is most important in other respects for the history of the
province.—Stokes.

(WHITE, JOHN]

   The | planters | plea. | Or | the grovnds of plan- | tations examined, | and
vsuall objections answered. | Together with a manifestation of the causes
mooving | such as have lately vndertaken a plantation in | Nevv-England:
| For the satisfaction of those that question | the lawfulnesse of the action. |
[rule] | 2 Thes. 5. 21. | Prove all things, and holde fast that which is good.
| [type orn.] | London, | Printed by William Iones. | 1630.   [80]
   [4], 84 p., 4to. (19 x 13.5 cm.). Sabin 103396, Church 418, new John
Carter Brown cat. BM, CSmH, CtSoP, DLC, ICN, MB, MBAt, MHi,
MiU-C, MWA, NHi, NN, PHi, RPJCB.
   Promotion tract by a founder of the Massachusetts Bay Colony who, how-
ever, never lived there but secured his information from actual settlers.
   For modern reprints, see Sabin 103397.

SMITH, CAPTAIN JOHN

   Advertisements | for the unexperienced planters of | New-England, or
any where. | Or, | the path-way to experience to erect a | plantation. | With
the yearely proceedings of this country in fishing | and planting, since the

yeare 1614. to the yeare 1630. | and their present estate. | Also how to prevent the greatest inconveniences, by their | proceedings in Virginia, and other plantations, | by approved examples. | With the countries armes, a description of the coast, | harbours, habitations, land-markes, latitude and | longitude: with the map, allowed by our Royall | King Charles. | By Captaine Iohn Smith, sometimes Governour of | Virginia, and Admirall of New-England. | *London,* | *Printed by Iohn Haviland, and are to be sold by* | *Robert Milbourne, at the Grey-hound* | *in Pauls Church-yard. 1631.* [81]

[8], 40 p., map of New England, 4to. (17.8 x 14 cm.). BM (2), CSmH, CtY, DLC, ICN, MH, MiU-C, MWiW-C, PP, RPJCB.

There are at least nine states of the map of New England. Portrait of King Charles inserted in two copies, that of the Prince of Orange in one.

For fuller details, see Sabin 82815.

For Dutch translations, Leyden, 1706 and [1706], see Sabin 82817-82818.

For modern reprints, see Sabin 82815 note and 82816.

WEST-INDISCHE COMPAGNIE

Vryheden ende Exemptien | voor de Patroonen, Meesters ofte Particulie- | ren, die op Nieu-Nederlandt eenighe Colonien | ende Vee sullen planten geconsidereert ten dienst | van de Generale West-Indische Compagnie in | Nieu-Nederlandt, ende het voordeel van de Pa- | troonen, Meesters ende Particulieren. | [Caption title] [Colophon:] *t'Amstelredam,* | [rule] | *Gedruckt by Theunis Jacobsz. Anno 1631.* [82]

[11] p., 4to. (18.5 x 12.5 cm.). Sabin 102921.

Title from Mass. Hist. Soc. photostat of a copy privately owned in Holland, 1927.

Charter of privileges and exemptions published for the encouragement of colonists in New Netherland.

. . . . . .

West-Indische Compagnie. | Articulen, | met | Approbatie vande Ho: | Mog: | Heeren Staten Generael der Vereenichde Nederlan- | den, pro- visioneelijc baraemt by Bewinthebberen van | de Generale Geoctroyeerde West-Indische Compa- | gnie, ter Vergaderinge vande Negenthiene, over het | open ende vry stellen vanden Handel ende Negotie op | de Stadt Olinda de Parnambuco, ende Custen van Brasil. | Hier zijn achter by ghedruckt | De Vryheden van Nieu-Nederlant. | [woodcut of ship] | *t'Amstelredam,* | *Gedruckt voor Marten Iansz. Brants Boeck-verkooper by de Nieuwe Kerck,* | *inde Gereformeerde Catechismus, Anno 1631.* [Colo- phon:] *t'Amstelredam,* | *Gedruckt by Theuni, Jacobsz. Anno 1631.* [83]

[23] p., 4to. (18.2 x 14.1 cm.). Sabin 102924, Asher 332, new John Carter Brown cat. BM, MiU-C, RPJCB.

Earlier editions, for which see Sabin, do not contain the privileges for New Netherland.

"Articles of the West India Company, with the approbation of their High Mightinesses the States General of the United Netherlands, provisionally laid down by the Governors of the said Company in the assembly of the Nineteen, on the opening and freeing of the trade to the city of Olinda de Pernambuco, and to the coasts of Brazil. To which is appendid: The Privileges of New Netherland."

LAET, JOANNES DE

Novvs Orbis | seu | Descriptionis | Indiae Occidentalis | Libri XVIII. | Authore | Ioanne de Laet Antverp. | Novis Tabulis Geographicis et variis | Animantium, Plantarum Fructuumque | Iconibus illustrati. | Cvm Privilegio. | *Lvgd. Batav. apud Elzevirios. A°. 1633.* | [Engraved title within ornamental border].   [84]

[32], 690 [i.e., 622], [18] p., 14 folded maps, illus. in text, folio (34.5 x 22 cm.). Sabin 38557, Asher 3, new John Carter Brown cat. MBAt, MH, NHi, NN, RPJCB, etc.

"The New World or description of the West Indies, in 18 books, by John de Laet of Antwerp, ornamented with new maps and various engravings of animals, plants and fruits." Chapters 7-12, p. 101-110, description of New Netherland.

Third (first Latin) edition.

[USSELINX, WILLEM]

Argonautica Gvstaviana; Das ist: Nothwendige NachRicht von der Newen Seefahrt vnd Kauffhandlung . . . *Gedruckt zu Franckfurt am Mayne, bey Caspar Rödteln, Im Iahr Christi 1633. Mense Junio. Mit der Cron Schweden Freyheit.*   [85]

[20], 56, 51 p., folio. Sabin 98187. CSmH, DLC, MH, NN, PHi, RPJCB.

The largest and most important publication of the founder of the Dutch and Swedish West India Companies and probably the first piece of American promotion literature in German. It had considerable influence in beginning the German and Swedish migration to Pennsylvania and Delaware. For his other publications, see Sabin 98186-98216.

[WHITE, ANDREW?]

A declaration of the Lord Baltimore's plantation in Mary-land, nigh upon Virginia: Manifesting the nature, quality, condition, and rich utilities it contayneth. [Caption title] [Dated at end of p. 7:] February, 10. anno 1633. *[London? 1633].*   [85A]

8 p., small 4to. Sabin 103351. Archives of the Roman Catholic Archdiocese of Westminster, London.

Reprinted, with introduction by Lawrence C. Wroth, in an edition of 100 copies, Baltimore, 1929.

Title from Lawrence C. Wroth's *Maryland colonization tracts*, in *Essays offered to Herbert Putnam*, New Haven, 1929, p. 539-555, which see for Lord Baltimore's later promotion tracts.

The first Maryland promotion tract, and the only known copy.

. . . . . .

A | relation | of | the successefull beginnings of the Lord | Baltemore's plantation in | Mary-land. | Being an extract of certaine letters written from | thence, by some of the Aduenturers, to their | friends in England. | To which is added, | The conditions of plantation propounded by his Lord- | ship for the second voyage intended this present | yeere, 1634. | [orn.] | Anno. Dom. 1634. *[London? 1634].*   [86]

[2], 14 p., 4to. (18.1 x 13.8 cm.). Sabin 45316, new John Carter Brown cat., Baer 21. BM, DGU, RPJCB.

The second Maryland promotion tract. Revised as: *A relation of Maryland,* 1635. Reprinted in 1865.

WOOD, WILLIAM

Nevv | Englands | prospect. | A true, lively, and experimen- | tall description of that part of America, | commonly called Nevv England: | discovering the state of that coun- | trie, both as it stands to our new-come | English planters; and to the old | native inhabitants. | Laying downe that which may both enrich the | knowledge of the mind-travelling reader, | or benefit the future voyager. | [rule] | By William Wood. | [rule] | [type orn.] | [rule] | *Printed at London by Tho.* Cotes, *for Iohn Bellamie, and are to be sold* | *at his shop, at the three Golden Lyons in Corn-hill, neere the* | Royall *Exchange. 1634.*   [87]

[8], 98, [5] pp., folded map, 4to. (18.1 x 13.8 cm.). Sabin 105074, Church 427, new John Carter Brown cat. BM, CSmH, CtSoP, MB, MH, MHi, MWiW, N, NN, PHi, PP, RPJCB.

Map: *The south part of New-England, as it is planted this yeare, 1634.* First detailed map of the region.

Earliest topographical account of the Massachusetts Colony by a resident of four years.

[CALVERT, CECIL, BARON BALTIMORE]

A | relation | of | Maryland; | together, | VVith [in a bracket:] A map of the countrey, | The conditions of plantation, | His Majesties Charter to the | Lord Baltimore, translated | into English. [end of bracket] | These bookes are to bee had, at Master William | Peasley Esq; his house, on the back-side of Dru- | ry-Lane, neere the Cock-pit Playhouse; or in | his absence, at Master Iohn Morgans house in | high Holbourne, over against the Dol-

phin, | London. | [rule] *[London:] September the 8. Anno Dom. 1635.* |
[rule].   [88]

[2], 56, 25 [i.e. 23], [1] p., folded map, 4to. (17 x 12.8 cm.). Sabin
45314, Church 432, new John Carter Brown cat., Baer 22. BM, CSmH,
DLC, Garrett, ICN, MdHi (lacks map and 2 leaves), MiU-C, MH (lacks
map), N, NHi, NIC, NN, RPJCB (lacks map).

Folded map of Maryland: *Noua Terrae-Mariae tabula* | [signed:] *T. Cecill
sculp.* (29.2 x 39.1 cm.).

Lord Baltimore's second promotion tract, revised.

WOOD, WILLIAM

New Englands prospect. . . . [etc., as in 1st ed., 1634] *London . . . 1635.*
                                                                                 [89]

[8], 83, [5] p., folded map (same as 1st ed. but dated 1635), 4to. (19.2 x
13.6 cm.). Sabin 105075, Church 433, new John Carter Brown cat. BM,
CSmH, DLC, ICN, MB, MH, MHi, MSaE, MWA, MWiW, NHi, NN,
RPJCB.

Same text as 1st ed., with errata corrected.

MORTON, THOMAS

New English Canaan | or | New Canaan. | Containing an abstract of
New England, | composed in three bookes. | The first booke setting forth
the originall of the natives, their | manners and customes, together with
their tractable nature and | love towards the English. | The second booke
setting forth the naturall indowments of the | country, and what staple
commodities it | yealdeth. | The third book setting forth, what people are
planted there, | their prosperity, what remarkable accidents have happened
since the first | planting of it, together with their tenents and practise | of
their church. | Written by Thomas Morton of Cliffords Inne gent, upon
tenne | yeares knowledge and experiment of the | country. | [type ornament]
| *Printed at Amsterdam,* | *by Jacob Frederick Stam.* | *In the yeare 1637.* [90]

188, [3] p., 4to. (15 x 20 cm.). CtY, DLC, ICN, MB, MH, MiU-C,
MWA, MWiW-C, N, NHi, NjP, NN, PPL, RPJCB.

Reprinted in Force Tracts vol. 2, no. 5.

The S.P.G. Library, London, has a copy with the imprint: *Printed for
Charles Greene, and are to be sold in Paul's Church-Yard [n.d.].*

The most entertaining book on the early Plymouth and Massachusetts
colonies. Valuable for natural history and Indians but an amusing and in-
accurate satire on social life for which the author was banished from New
England.

[VINCENT, PHILIP]

A | true relation of | the late battell fought | in New England, between |
the English, and the | salvages: | VVith the present state of | things there.

| London, | Printed by M.P. for Nathanael Butter, | and Iohn Bellamie. 1637. [91]

[14], 11-23, [1] p., 4to. (17 x 12.4 cm.). Sabin 99760-99762, new John Carter Brown cat. BM, CSmH, NN, RPJCB.

There are three issues, alike as to imprint, date and collation but differing in typographical errors for which see Sabin.

Though not in New England at the time, the author probably secured his information from some one who took part in the campaign.

UNDERHILL, CAPTAIN JOHN

Nevves from | America; | or, | a new and experi- | mentall discoverie of | New England; | containing, | a trve relation of their | war-like proceedings these two yeares last | past, with a figure of the Indian fort, | or palizado. | [first column:] Also a discovery of these | places, that as yet have | very few or no inhabi- | tants which would yeeld | speciall accommodation | to such as will plant | there, [bracket] | Viz. | [bracket] [second column:] Queena-poick. | Agu-wom. | Hudsons River. | Long Island. | Nahanticut. | Martins Vinyard. | Pequet. | Naransett Bay. | Elizabeth Islands. | Puscataway. | Casko with about a hun- | dred islands neere to | Casko. | [rule] | By Cap-taine Iohn Underhill, a Commander | in the warres there. | [rule] | London, | Printed by J.D. for Peter Cole, and are to be sold at the signe | of the Glove in Corne-hill neere the | Royall Exchange. 1638. [92]

[2], 44 p., folded plan, 4to. (18 x 13.2 cm.). Sabin 97733, Church 441, new John Carter Brown cat. BM, CSmH (plan in facsim.), DLC, ICN, MB, MH, NHi, NjP, NN, PP, PPL, RPJCB.

Folded plan: *The figure of the Indians' fort or palizado in | New Eng-land | and the maner of the destroying | it by Captayne Vnderhill | and Captayne Mason | [signed in lower left corner:] R H. 34 x 27.5 cm.*

Only contemporary printed account of the Pequot War by a participant and the first extensive account in English of the territory now New York, for which see Stokes VI, 264. For reprints, see Sabin.

[VINCENT, PHILIP]

A | true | relation of | the late battell fought | in New England, be-tween | the English, and the Pequet | Salvages: | In which was slaine and taken pri- | soners about 700 of the Salvages, | and those which escaped, had their | heads cut off by the Mohocks: | VVith the present state of | things there. | London, | Printed by M.P. for Nathaniel Butter, | and Iohn Bellamie. 1638. [93]

[14], 11-23, [1] p., 4to. (18.1 x 13.7 cm.). Sabin 99763-99765, Church 442, new John Carter Brown cat. CSmH (2), ICN, MB (2), NN, PPL, RPJCB (2).

The sheets of the 1637 edition with a new title page. There are three issues, alike as to imprint, date and collation but differing in typographical errors for which see Sabin.

.   .   .   .   .

A trve | relation | of | the late battell fought in New- | England, between the English and the | Pequet Salvages. | In which were slaine and taken prisoners | about 700. of the Salvages, and those which | escaped, had their heads cut off by | the Mohocks: | With the present state of things | there. | London, | Printed by Thomas Harper, for Nathanael Butter, | and Iohn Bellamie, 1638. [Title within ornamental border.]   [94]

[22] p., 8vo. (17.4 x 12.9 cm.). Sabin 99766, Church 443, new John Carter Brown cat. BM, CSmH, MH, NN, PPAmP, RPJCB.

Second edition, completely reset.

WOOD, WILLIAM

New | Englands | prospect. | . . . [etc., as in 1st ed., 1634] London, | Printed by Iohn Dawson, and are to be sold by Iohn Bellamy | at his shop, at the three Golden Lyons in Corne- | hill, neere the Royall Exchange, | 1639.   [95]

[8], 83, [5] p., map (same as 1st ed. but dated 1639), 4to. (18.5 x 13.9 cm.). Sabin 105076, Church 444, new John Carter Brown cat. BM, CSmH, ICN, MBAt, MH, MHi, NHi, NN, PPL, RPJCB.

Same as 1st ed. but reset.

LAET, JOANNES DE

L'Histoire | dv | Nouveau Monde | ou | Description | des Indes | Occidentales, | Contenant dix-huict Liures, | Par le Sieur Iean de Laet, d'Anuers; | Enrichi de nouuelles tables geographiques & figures des | animaux, plantes & fruicts. | [printer's device] | A Leyde, | Chez Bonauenture & Abraham Elseuiers, Imprimeurs | ordinaires de l'Vniuersité. | [rule] | CIↃ IↃCXL. | [Title in red and black].   [96]

[28], 632, [12] p., 14 folded maps, illus. in text, folio (35 x 22 cm.). Sabin 38558, Asher 4, new John Carter Brown cat. NHi, NN, RPJCB, etc.

Fourth (first French) edition. Book III, chapters 7-12, p. 74-82 describe New Netherland, with additional material not in 1st ed.

EVELIN OR EVELYN, JOHN

A | direction | for adventvrers | with small stock to get two for one, | and good land freely: | and for gentlemen, and all servants, labourers, and | artificers to live plentifully. | And the true description of the healthiest, pleasantest, and richest | plantation of new Albion, in North Virginia, proved by thirteen witnesses. | Together with, | a letter from Master Robert Evelin, that lived there many | yeares, shewing the particularities, and excellency thereof. | With a briefe of the charge of victuall, and necessaries, to transpors [sic] | and buy stocke for each planter, or labourer, there to get his | master 50 l. per annum, or more in twelvetrades, and | at 10. l. charges onely a man. | [rule, orn., rule] | *[London?] Printed in the yeare, 1641.*   [97]

[8] p., 4to. (17.5 x 14 cm.). Sabin 63312, Church 451, Baer 23. CSmH.

Reprinted in Beauchamp Plantagenet's *A description of the Province of New Albion*, 1648. Evelin's letter was addressed to Lady Plowden.

New Albion, granted to Sir Edmund Plowden and associates in 1634, included parts of New York, Long Island, New Jersey, Pennsylvania and Delaware. This grant was rendered ineffective by King Charles II's grant to his brother, the Duke of York, in 1664, but Plowden's heirs sold a third of the grant to Charles Varlo just before the Revolution and he tried, unsuccessfully, to lay claim to the land in 1784. See under Varlo.

Nevv | Englands | first fruits; | in respect. | First of the [bracket] Conversion of some, | Conviction of divers, | Preparation of sundry [bracket] of the Indians. | 2. Of the progresse of learning, in the Colledge at | Cambridge in Massacusets Bay. | With | divers other speciall matters concerning that countrey. | Published by the instant request of sundry friends, who desire | to be satisfied in these points by many New-England men | who are here present, and were eye or eare- | witnesses of the same. | [3 lines quoted, orn., rule] | *London,* | *Printed by R.O. and G.D. for Henry Overton, and are to be* | *sold at his shop in Popes-head-Alley. 1643.*   [98]

[2], 26, [1] p., 4to. (18.7 x 14 cm.). Sabin 52758, Church 458, new John Carter Brown cat. BM, CSmH, ICN, MB, MBC, MHi, NHi, NN, PP, PPL, RPJCB, N.E. Hist. Gen. Soc.

First of the series of 11 tracts published in the interest of the Corporation for the Propagation of the Gospel among the Indians of New England, generally known as the Eliot Indian Tracts. Earliest attempts to convert and civilize the New England Indians and first account of Harvard College in print.

VAN RENSSELAER, KILIAEN

Insinuatie, Protestatie, ende Presentatie van weghen | den Patroon van de Colonie van Rensselaers-wijck. | [Caption title] [Signed at end:] . . . achtsten September 1643. In Amsterdam, | Was onderteeckent | Kiliaen van Rensselaer. | *[Amsterdam, 1643].*   [99]

Broadside, folio. (32.3 x 22.6 cm.). Sabin 98544.

Described from Mass. Hist. Soc. photostat of a privately owned copy, 1922.

. . . . . .

Redres | van de | Abuysen ende Faulten in de | Colonie van Rensselaers-wijck. | [cut of a ship] | t'Amsterdam. | [rule] | *Gedruckt by Thunis Iacobsz, Woonende in de Wolve-* | *straet, in de Histozie van Josephus, Anno 1643.*   [100]

[16] p., 4to. (18.3 x 12.6 cm.). Sabin 98545.

Described from Mass. Hist. Soc. photostat of a privately owned copy, no. 205, 1928.

Signed at end: "In Amsterdam desen vijfden September. 1643. | Onderstont | Kiliaen van Rensselaer, Patroon van | de Colonie van Rensselaerswijck."

. . . . .

Waerschovwinge, | Verboth, ende Toe-latinghe, weghens de Colonie van | Rensselaers-wyck. | [Caption title] [Colophon:] *t'Amsterdam, Gedruckt by Theunis Jacobsz. inde Historie van Iosephus. | [1643].* [101]

Broadside, folio. (38.4 x 27 cm.). Sabin 98546.

Described from Mass. Hist. Soc. photostat of a privately owned copy, 1922.

Dated at end of text: "Amsterdam desen 2 September, 1643."

Promotion literature for Rensselaerswyck, now Albany, New York and surrounding country, the only one of the early Dutch patroonships to succeed. The ring and seal of the first Patroon were recently given to the New-York Historical Society by Kiliaen van Rensselaer V, a member of the Society's board of trustees.

WILLIAMS, ROGER

A key into the | language | of | America: | or, | an help to the language of the natives | in that part of America, called | New-England. | Together, with briefe observations of the cu- | stomes, manners and worships, &c of the | aforesaid natives, in peace and warre, | in life and death. | On all which are added spirituall observations, | generall and particular by the authour, of | chiefe and special use (upon all occasions,) to | all the English inhabiting those parts; | yet pleasant and profitable to | the view of all men: | By Roger Williams | of Providence in New-England. | *London,* | *Printed by Gregory Dexter, 1643.* [102]

[16], 197 [i.e. 205], [3] p., 8vo. (14.9 x 9 cm.). Sabin 104339, Church 460, new John Carter Brown cat. BM, CSmH, MB, MH, MHi, MiU-C, MWA, NN, PHi, RPJCB.

The first book by the author, first book on the Indian linguistics of New England and one of the first descriptions of the manners and customs of those Indians, written by one intimately associated with them. For reprints, see Sabin.

LAET, JOANNES DE

Historie | ofte | Iaerlijck Verhael | van de | Verrichtinghen der Geoctroyeerde | West-Indische Compagnie, | Zedert haer Begin, tot het eynde van't jaer | sesthien-hondert ses-en-dertich; | Begrepen in Derthien Boecken, | Ende met verscheyden koperen Platen verciert: | Beschreven door | Ioannes de Laet | Bewint-hebber der selver Compagnie. | [printer's device] | *Tot*

Leyden, | [rule] | *By Bonaventuer ende Abraham Elsevier, Anno 1644.* | *Met Privilegie.* | [Title in red and black]. [103]

[32], 544, 31, [12] p., 13 folded plates and maps, folio (31.7 x 20.1 cm.). Sabin 38556, Asher 22, new John Carter Brown cat. NHi, RPJCB, etc.

"History or yearly narrative of the proceedings of the privileged West India Company, from its creation to the end of 1636; comprised in 13 books, and ornamented with several copper plates. Described by Joannes de Laet, one of the Directors of that Company." Includes information on New Netherland.

MEGAPOLENSIS, JOHANNES, JR. (i.e., John of Meklenburg)

Een kort Ontwerp, | vande | Mahakvase Indianen | haer Landt, tale, statuere, | dracht, Godes-dienst | ende magistrature. | Aldus beschreven ende nu kor- | telijck den 26. Augusti 1644. Opge- | sonden uyt nieuwe Neder-Lant. | Door Johannem Megapolensem | Juniorem, Predicant | aldaar | mitsgaders een kort verhael | van het leven ende statuere der | Staponjers, in Brasiel. | [device] | *t'Alckmaer,* | *By Ysbrant Jansz. van Houten, Boeck-* | *verkooper ende Stadts-Drucker, inde* | *Lange-Straet, inde Druck-Pars.* *[1644?].* [104]

[32] p., 8vo. Title from J.C. Pilling: *Bibliography of the Iroquoian languages,* 1888, p. 119, which describes the only known copy at the University of Ghent.

The Brazilian narrative begins on p. [21] with a separate title page.

Reprinted in: *Beschrijvinghe van Virginia, Nieuw Nederlandt, Nieuw Engelandt,* . . . *t'Amsterdam, By Joost Hartgers* . . . *1651,* p. 42-49, the volume containing the first published view of New Amsterdam. An imperfect translation appears in E. Hazard: *Historical collections,* vol. 1, Phil., 1792, p. 517-526; and in an improved translation as: "A short sketch of the Mohawk Indians in New Netherland, their land, stature, dress, manners, and magistrates, written in the year 1644, by Johannes Megapolensis, junior, minister there. . . . with an introduction and notes by John Romeyn Broadhead," in New York Hist. Soc. Coll., 2d ser., vol. 3, part 1, New York, 1857, p. 137-160. This interesting and important narrative was written by the first Protestant missionary to the North American Indians.

When Father Isaac Jogues, the Jesuit missionary to the Indians, was rescued from the Mohawks by the Dutch, he was befriended by Megapolensis at Rensselaerwyck in 1643 and left an excellent description of his first captivity (before his later return to the Mohawks and martyrdom) and one of the earliest accounts of New Netherland, for which, see his: *Narrative of a captivity among the Mohawk Indians, and a description of New Netherland in 1642-3, and other papers. New York, 1856* and same, *1857.* Sabin 36142; *Novum Belgium, description de Nieuw Netherland et notice sur René Goupil. New York, 1862.* Sabin 36143; and the same translated: *Novum Belgium: an account of New Netherland in 1643-4. New York, 1862.* Sabin 36144.

WINTHROP, JOHN

A | declaration of former | passages and proceedings betwixt the English | and the Narrowgansets, with their confederates, Wherein | the grounds and justice of the ensuing warre are opened | and cleared. | Published, by order of the Commissioners for the united Colonies: | At Boston the 11 of the sixth month | 1645. | *[Cambridge: Printed by Stephen Daye. 1645].*   [105]

7 p., 4to. (19 x 14 cm.). Sabin 104844, Evans 17. CSmH, MHi, NN, RPJCB.

Caption title. Signed: "Jo: Winthrop President, in the name of all the Commissioners."

Reproduced from Winthrop's own copy in Mass. Hist. Soc. Photostat Americana, 2d ser., 1936, no. 2. Reprinted in Hazard's Hist. Coll. and in Records of the Colony of New Plymouth, IX:50.

[CALVERT, CECIL, BARON BALTIMORE]

A moderate and safe expedient to remove jealousies and feares, of any danger, or prejudice to this state, by the Roman Catholicks of this Kingdome, and to mitigate the censure of too much severity towards them. With a great advantage of honour and profit to this state and nation. [orn.] *[London?] Printed in the year of our Lord, 1646.*   [106]

16 p., small 4to. Willard A. Baldwin, Garrett, Law Society of London, NNUT-Mc, RPJCB, Stonyhurst College (imp.).

Title from Lawrence C. Wroth's *Maryland colonization tracts,* in *Essays offered to Herbert Putnam,* New Haven, 1929, p. 539-555; Baer 27.

WINSLOW, EDWARD,

Hypocrisie unmasked: | by | a true relation of the proceedings of the | Governour and Company of the Massachusets against | Samvel Gorton (and his accomplices) a notorious | disturber of the peace and quiet of the severall governments | wherein he lived: With the grounds and reasons thereof, exa- | mined and allowed by their Generall Court holden at Boston in | New-England in November last, 1646. | Together with a particular answer to the manifold slan- | ders, and abominable falsehoods which are contained in a book | written by the said Gorton, and entituled, Simplicities defence | against seven-headed policy, &c. | Discovering | to the view of all whose eyes are open, his manifold | blasphemies; as also the dangerous agreement which he and his | accomplices made with ambitious and treacherous Indians, who | at the same time were deeply engaged in a desperate conspiracy | to cut off all the rest of the English in the other plantations. | VVhereunto is added a briefe narration (occasioned by | certain aspersions) of the true grounds or cause of the first plan- | ting of New-England; the president of their churches in the | way and worship of God; their communion with the Reformed | Churches; and their practise towards those that dissent from | them in matters of religion and church-government. | [rule] | By Edw. Winslow. | [rule] | [3 lines quoted] | [rule] | Published by authority. | [rule] | *London,*

Printed by Rich. Cotes for John Bellamy at the three Golden | Lions in Cornhill, neare the Royall Exchange, 1646. | [Title within fleur-de-lis border]. [107]

[8], 103 p., 4to. (17.5 x 13.3 cm.). Sabin 104796, Church 477. BM, Bodleian, CSmH, CtY, DLC, ICN, MB, MiU-C, NHi, NN, RPJCB.

Though primarily a religious controversial tract, this work is included because of its importance as a source book on the founding of New England and the life of the Pilgrims in Holland before coming to America. It was written as an answer to Samuel Gorton's *Simplicities defence against seven-headed policy. London, 1646.* Church 475. Winslow was answered by John Child's *New-Englands Jonas cast up at London. London, 1647,* Sabin 12705, Church 478, to which Winslow replied with *New-Englands salamander, discovered. London, 1647.* Sabin 104797. The Child tract is of special interest since it was the first publication to reprint the Freeman's Oath, the first piece of North American printing, now lost. The sheets of *Hypocrisie unmasked* were reissued with a new title page: *The danger of tolerating levellers. London, 1649.* For modern reprints of these tracts, see Church and Sabin.

[SHEPARD, THOMAS?]

The | day-breaking, | if not | the sun-rising | of the | Gospell | with the | Indians in New-England. | [rule, 6 lines quoted, rule] | *London, | Printed by Rich. Cotes, for Fulk Clifton, and are to bee | sold at his shop under Saint Margarets Church on | New-fish-street Hill, 1647. |* [Title within border of type ornaments]. [108]

[2], 25 p., 4to. (17.8 x 13.2 cm.). Sabin 80207, Church 482, new John Carter Brown cat. BM, Bodleian, CSmH, CtHWatk, CtSoP, DLC, ICN, MB, MH, MHi, MWA, NHi, NN, PHi, RPJCB.

Second of the Eliot Indian Tracts. Good account of the life of the Indians.

John Wilson is suggested as possible author by S.A. Green in Mass. Hist. Soc. Proceed., vol. 26, 1890-91, p. 392-395.

Good news from | Nevv-England: | with | an exact relation of the first plan- | ting that countrey: A description of the | profits accruing by the worke. | Together with a briefe, but true | discovery of their order both in Church | and Common-wealth, and maintenance al- | lowed the painfull labourers in that vineyard | of the Lord. | With | The names of the severall towns, | and who be preachers to them. | *London; | Printed by Matthew Simmons, | 1648. |* [Title within border]. [109]

[2], 25, [1] p., 4to. (17.3 x 12.9 cm.). New John Carter Brown cat. RPJCB.

A poem.

[PLANTAGENET, BEAUCHAMP, *Pseud. of Sir Edmund Plowden?*]

A | description | of | the province of | New Albion. | And a direction for adventurers with small | stock to get two for one, and good land freely: | and for gentlemen, and all servants, labourers, and | artificers to live plentifully. | And a former description re-printed of the heal- | thiest, pleasantest, and richest plantation of New Albion in | North Virginia, proved by thirteen witnesses. | Together with | a letter from Master Robert Evelin, that lived there | many years, shewing the particularities, and excellency | thereof. | With a briefe of the charge of victuall, and necessaries, to | transport and buy stock for each planter, or labourer, | there to get his master 50 l. per annum, or more in twelve | trades, and at 10 l. charges onely a man. | [rule] | *[London:] Printed in the year 1648.*   [110]

32 p., 4to. (17.9 x 13.4 cm.). Sabin 19724 and 63310, Church 488, new John Carter Brown cat., Baer 28. BM, CSmH, Garrett, ICN, MH, MiU-C, MWiW-C, NN, PPL, RPJCB.

Promotion literature for New Albion, a tract comprising part of New York, Long Island, New Jersey, Pennsylvania and Delaware, granted by Lord Strafford, then Viceroy of Ireland, to Sir Edmund Plowden or Ploeyden in 1634. The above tract may have been written by Plowden or by Robert Evelin, author of *A direction for adventurers,* here reprinted from the separate edition of 1641. Completely unreliable. The mention of a settlement on Manhattan Island in 1613 has no foundation in fact, for which see Stokes VI: 263.

SHEPARD, THOMAS

The | clear sun-shine of the Gospel | breaking forth | upon the | Indians | in | Nevv-England. | Or, | An historicall narration of Gods | wonderfull workings upon sundry of the | Indians, both chief governors and common-people, | in bringing them to a willing and desired submission to | the ordinances of the Gospel; and framing their | hearts to an earnest inquirie after the knowledge | of God the Father, and of Jesus Christ | the Saviour of the world. | [rule] | By Mr. Thomas Shepard Minister of the Gospel of | Jesus Christ at Cambridge in New-England. | [rule, 7 lines quoted, rule] | *London, Printed by R. Cotes for John Bellamy at the three golden | Lions in Cornhill near the Royall Exchange, 1648.* | [Title within border of type ornaments].   [111]

[14], 38 p., 4to. (17.4 x 13.2 cm.). Sabin 80205, Church 489, new John Carter Brown cat. CSmH, MB, MH, MWA, NHi, NN, RPJCB, etc.

Third of the Eliot Indian Tracts. Includes Eliot's account of his missionary journeys among the Indians.

Breeden-Raedt | aende | Vereenichde Nederlandsche | Provintien. | Gelreland. | Holland. | Zeeland. | Wtrecht. | Vriesland. | Over-Yssel. | Groeningen. | Gemaeckt ende gestelt uyt diverse ware en waerachtige | memorien Door I.A.G.W.C. | *Tot Antwerpen,* | *Ghedruct by Francoys van Duynen, Boeckverkooper by* | *de Beurs in Erasmus 1649.*   [112]

45 p., 4to. (19.1 x 14.5 cm.). Asher 334, new John Carter Brown cat., Stokes VI:259. CSmH, CtY, DLC, MiU-C, MWiW-C, N, NjP, NN (2 variants), PHi, RPJCB, ViU.

This "Homely advice to the United Netherland Provinces . . . Made up and composed from divers true and faithful documents, by J.A. G.W.C." was the first separate publication on New Netherland. It is anonymous but has been incorrectly attributed to Isaac Allerton and to Cornelis Melyn. The two NN variants differ only in the allignment of the titles. Stokes thinks that the initials G.W.C. following those of the author may refer to Geoctroyeerde West-Indische Compagnie, used to show the author's supposed official connection to the West India Company. For translations, see Sabin and Stokes.

BULLOCK, WILLIAM

Virginia | impartially examined, and left | to publick view, to be considered by all judi- | cious and honest men. | Under which title, is compre- | hended the degrees from 34 to 39, wherein | lyes the rich and healthfull countries of Roanock, | the now plantations of Virginia | and Mary-land. | Looke not upon this booke, as | those that are set out by private men, for private | ends; for being read, you'l find, the publick | good is the authors onely aime. | For this piece is no other then the adventurers | or planters faithfull steward, disposing the ad- | venture for the best advantage, advising | people of all degrees, from the highest | master, to the meanest servant, | how suddenly to raise their | fortunes. | Puruse the table, and you shall finde the | way plainely layd downe. | By William Bvllock, Gent. | 19 April, 1649. Imprimatur, Hen: Whaley. | *London: Printed by John Hammond, and are to be sold at his house | over-against S. Andrews Church in Holborne. 1649.*
[113]

[12], 66 p., 4to. (18.6 x 14 cm.). Sabin 9145, Church 490, new John Carter Brown cat., Baer 29. BM, CSmH, CtY, DLC, Garrett, ICN, MB, MdHi, MH, MiU-C, MWiW-C, N, NHi, NjP, NN, NNP, RPJCB, Vi, ViU.

ELIOT, JOHN, AND THOMAS MAYHEW

The | glorious progress | of the | Gospel, | amongst the | Indians in New England. | Manifested | by three letters, under the hand of that fa- | mous instrument of the Lord Mr. John Eliot, | and another from Mr. Thomas Mayhew jun: both Preachers of | the Word, as well to the English as Indians in New-England. | Wherein | the riches of Gods grace in the effectuall calling of | many of them is cleared up: as also a manifestation of the hungring | desires of many people in sundry parts of that country, after the | more full revelation of the Gospel of Jesus Christ, to the | exceeding consolation of every Christian reader. | Together, | with an appendix to the foregoing letters, hol- | ding forth conjectures, observations, and applications. | By I.D. Minister of the Gospell. | [rule] | *Published by Edward Winslow* | [rule] | [4 lines quoted] | *London, Printed for Hannah Allen in Popes-head-Alley. 1649.* | [Title within border of type ornaments].
[114]

[8], 28 p., 4to. (17.5 x 13.3 cm.). Sabin 22152, Church 497, new John

Carter Brown cat. BM, CSmH, DLC, MB, MHi, MiU-C, NHi, NN, RPJCB.

Fourth of the Eliot Indian Tracts.

A perfect description of | Virginia: | being, | a full and true relation of the present state | of the plantation, their health, peace, and plenty: the number | of people, with their abundance of cattell, fowl, fish, &c. with severall | sorts of rich and good commodities, which may there be had, either | naturally, or by art and labour. Which we are fain to | procure from Spain, France, Denmark, Swedeland, Germany, | Poland, yea, from the East-Indies. There | having been nothing related to the | true estate of this planta- | tion these 25 years. | Being sent from Virginia, at the request of a gentleman of worthy note, | who desired to know the true state of Virginia as it now stands. | Also, | a narration of the countrey, within a few | dayes journey of Virginia, West and by South, where people come | to trade: being related to the Governour, Sir William Berckley, | who is to go himselfe to discover it with 30 horse, and 50 foot, | and other things needfull for his enterprize. | With the manner how the Emperor Nichotawance | came to Sir William Berckley, attended with five petty kings, | to doe homage, and bring tribute to King Charles. With his | solemne protestation, that the sun and moon should lose | their lights, before he (or his people in that country) | should prove disloyall, but ever to keepe faith | and allegiance to King Charles. | [orn.] | *London, Prind for Richard Wodenoth, at the Star under Peters | Church in Cornhill. 1649.*   [115]

[4], 19 p., 4to. (18 x 13 cm.). Sabin 60918, Church 496, new John Carter Brown cat., Baer 30. BM, CSmH, CtY, DLC, Garrett, ICN, MA, MBAt, MH, MiU-C, MWiW-C, NHi, NjP, NN, PPL, RPJCB, Vi, ViU.

For reprints see Sabin.

WINSLOW, EDWARD

The | dangers of tolerating | levellers | in a civill state: | or, | An historicall narration of the dange- | rous pernicious practices and opinions, where- | with Samvel Gorton and his | levelling accomplices so much disturbed and mo- | lested the severall plantations in New-England; | (Parallel to the positions and proceedings of the present | levellers in Old-England.) | wherein their severall errors dangerous and | very destructive to the peace both of Church and State, | their cariage and reviling language against Magistracy | and all civill power, and their blasphemous speeches | against the holy things of God: | together, | with the course that was there taken for suppressing them, | are fully set forth; | with a satisfactory answer to their complaints made | to the Parliament: | By Edw. Winslow of Plymouth in New-England. | *London, Printed by Rich Cotes for John Bellamy at the three Golden | Lions in Corn-hill, neare the Royall Exchange, 1649.*   [116]

[4], 103 p., 4to. (17.5 x 13.3 cm.). Sabin 104794. BM, MB, NN, RPJCB.

A reissue of the sheets of *Hypocrisie unmasked*, 1646, with a new title page and the dedication replaced with a table of contents.

DONCK, ADRIAEN VAN DER

Vertoogh | van | Nieu-Neder-Land. | Weghens de Gheleghentheydt, | Vruchtbaerheydt, en Sobe- | ren Staet desselfs. | [orn.] | *In's Graven-Hage,* | [rule] | *Ghedruckt by Michiel Stael, Bouck-verkooper woonende* | *op't Buyten-Hof, tegen-over de Gevange-Poort, 1650.*   [117]

49 p., 4to. (17.8 x 13.7 cm.). Sabin 20595, Church 499, Asher 5, new John Carter Brown cat., Stokes VI:260. BM, CSmH, DLC, ICN, MiU-C, MWiW-C, N, NHi, NN, RPJCB.

This "Account of New-Netherland, its situation, fertility and the miserable state thereof" is the most important historical work on the colony up to that time. See also his *Beschrijvinge van Nieuvv-Nederlant, 1655.*

For translations, see Sabin 20596-20597. The author came to New Amsterdam in 1642, was sheriff of Rensselaerwyck and owned an estate near the present Yonkers.

[PLANTAGENET, BEAUCHAMP, *Pseud. of Sir Edmund Plowden?*]

A | description | of the | Province | of | New Albion. | And a direction for adventurers | with small stock to get two for one, and good land freely. | And for gentlemen, and all servants, labourers, | and artificers, to live plentifully. | And a former description re-printed of the healthiest, plea- | santest, and richest plantation of Nevv Albion in | North Virginia, proved by thirteen witnesses. | Together with | a letter from Master Robert Evelin, that lived | there many yeers, shewing the particularities, and ex- | cellency thereof. | With a brief of the charge of victual, and necessaries, to trans- | port and buy stock for each planter, or labourer, there to get | his master fifty pounds per annum, or more, in twelve trades, | and at ten pounds charges onely a man. | [rule] | *London,* | *Printed by James Moxon, in the yeer MDCL.*   [118]

[8], [24] [misnumbered 32] p. Numbers 17-24 omitted in pagination, 4to. (19.5 x 14.5 cm.). Sabin 63311, Church 504, Baer 31. CSmH, DLC.

See note to first edition, 1648, no. 110.

[Row of type ornaments] | A treatise of New | England | Published in Anno Dom. 1637. | [rule] | And now reprinted. | [rule] | [Caption title] *[London?* Not later than *1650].*   [119]

16 p., 4to. (18 x 12.7 cm.). Sabin 96741. MH. Photostat at NHi.

No copy of original edition of this interesting promotion tract is known, unless it is summarized from Thomas Morton's *New English Canaan,* 1637. It includes an early account of New Netherland.

WILLIAMS, EDWARD

Virgo Triumphans: | or, | Virginia | richly and truly valued; more especi- | ally the South part thereof: viz. | The fertile Carolana, and no lesse excel- | lent Isle of Roanoak, of Latitude from | 31 to 37 Degr. relating the meanes of | raising infinite profits to the Adventu- | rers and Planters: | Humbly presented as the Auspice of a beginning Yeare, | To the Parliament of England, | And Councell of State. | [rule] | By Edvvard Williams, Gent. | [rule, cut of two deer, rule] | *London, Printed by Thomas Harper, for John Stephenson,* | *and are to be sold at his Shop on Ludgate-Hill, at the Signe* | *of the Sunne, 1650.*   [120]

[14], 47, [8] p., 4to. (19 x 14 cm.). Sabin 104193, Church 509, new John Carter Brown cat. BM, CSmH, DLC, ICN, MBAt, MH, NHi, NN, PPL, RPJCB, Vi.

Author states that "the whole substance of it . . . was communicated to me by . . . Mr. John Farrer." Farrer's annotated copy with ms. map used in 3d ed. is in NN. This copy has only the title and "To the reader" leaves as preliminary leaves and may be an early issue before the other preliminary leaves were added.

First edition, reprinted as:

.   .   .   .   .

Virginia: more especially the South part thereof, richly and truly valued: viz. the fertile Carolana, and no less excellent Isle of Roanoak, of Latitude from 31. to 37. Degr. relating to the meanes of raysing infinite profits to the Adventurers and Planters. The second edition, with addition of The Discovery of Silkworms, with their benefit. And implanting of mulberry trees. Also the dressing of vines, for the rich trade of making wines in Virginia. Together with the making of the saw-mill, very usefull in Virginia, for cutting of timber and clapboard to build withall, and its conversion to many as profitable uses. By E.W. gent. *London, Printed by T.H. for John Stephenson, at the Signe of the Sun below Ludgate. 1650.*   [121]

2 parts in one volume, [12], 47, [8]; [6], 75, [3] p., including illus., 4to. Sabin 104190. BM, CSmH, DLC, MH, MiU-C, NHi, NjP, NN, PHi, Vi.

The second part is the author's *Virginia's discovery of silk vvormes,* below. Main text of the first part is identical with that of 1st ed. above.

Reissued as parts 3-4 of *Copy of a petition from the Governor and Company of the Sommer Islands,* 1651. Sabin 100450. For modern reprints, see Sabin.

.   .   .   .   .

Virginia's | discovery of | silke-vvormes, | with their benefit. | And | the implanting of mulberry trees. | Also | the dressing and keeping of vines, for the rich trade | of making wines there. | Together with | the making of the saw-mill, very usefull in Virginia, | for cutting of timber and clapboard, to build with- | all, and its conversion to other as profitable uses. | [cut of two deer, rule] | *London,* | *Printed by T.H. for John Stephenson, at the Signe of* | *the Sun, below Ludgate, 1650.*   [122]

[6], 75, [3] p., including illus., 4to. (17.3 x 12.9 cm.). Sabin 104192, Church 508, new John Carter Brown cat. BM, CSmH (early issue with

errors in pagination not in other copies), CtSoP, DLC, ICN, MH, MiU-C, NHi, NN, PHi, RPJCB.

Issued as a separate as well as part of *Virginia . . . richly and truly valued*, above.

BLAND, EDWARD, AND OTHERS

The | discovery | of | Nevv Brittaine. | Began August 27. Anno Dom. 1650. | By [bracket] Edward Bland, Merchant. | Abraham Woode, Captaine. | Sackford Brewster, | Elias Pennant, | [bracket around the last two names] Gentlemen. | From Fort Henry, at the head of Appa- | mattuck River in Virginia, to the Fals | of Blandina, first river in New Brit- | taine, which runneth West, being | 120. mile South-west, between 35. | & 37. degrees, (a pleasant country,) | of temperate ayre, and fertile soyle. | [rule] | *London,* | *Printed by Thomas Harper for John Stephenson, at the* | *Sun below Ludgate.* M.DC.LI.   [123]

[8], 16 p., folded map of Virginia, Maryland, etc., and plate, 4to. (16.4 x 11 cm.). Sabin 52518, Church 511, new John Carter Brown cat., Baer 33. BM, CSmH, DLC, MiU-C, NHi, PBL, RPJCB.

Front. plate of *Indian wheat* [i.e., corn] and *Indian jay.*

WHITFIELD, HENRY

The light appearing more and more to- | wards the perfect day. | Or, | A farther discovery of the present state | of the Indians | in | New-England, | concerning the progresse of the Gospel | amongst them. | Manifested by letters from such as preacht | to them there. | [rule] | Published by Henry Whitfeld, late Pastor to the | Chuch [sic] of Christ at Gilford in New-England, who | came late thence. | [rule, 3 lines quoted, rule] | *London,* | *Printed by T.R. & E.M. for John Bartlet, and are to be* | *sold at the Gilt Cup, neer St. Austins gate in Pauls* | *Church-yard. 1651.* | [Title within border of type ornaments].   [124]

[8], 46 p., 4to. (17.4 x 13 cm.). Sabin 103688-103689, Church 514, new John Carter Brown cat. BM, CSmH (1st), CtSoP, CtY (2d), DLC (1st), ICN, MB (2d), MBAt, MH (1st), MiU-C (1st), MWA (1st), NBLiHi, NHi (1st), NN (both), PHi (1st), RPJCB (1st).

Variant title: [11 lines] | *Published by H. Whitfeld, late Pastor to the Church* | *of Christ at Gilford in New-England, who came* | *late thence.* | [6 lines]. The two variants are indicated as 1st or 2d, above, but there is no proof as to which is earlier. The Church catalog says: "The First Issue has the word 'church' spelled 'chuch' on the title page. This error was corrected in many copies." However, Sabin failed to find this correction in any copy examined.

Fifth of the Eliot Indian Tracts. Edited by Whitfield from five letters of Eliot describing his Indian town of Natick, founded 1650, and one of Thomas Mayhew.

WILLIAMS, EDWARD

Virginia in America, richly valued: more especially the Southerne parts. With the tendure of the vine, and silkeworme, making wines and silks there: and framing of saw-mills, to cut timber for building. Shewing also divers other means of raysing infinite profits to Adventurers and Planters. Together with a compleat map of the country, from 35. to 41. Degrees of Latitude discovered, and the West Sea. *London, Printed for John Stephenson . . . M.DC.LI.*   [125]

No copy located. Sabin 104191 copies title from Huth Catalogue, vol. 5, p. 1595, where it is stated that the copy of the second edition described there has the above title page inserted. In the Sabin note, Col. Lawrence Martin describes four issues of Farrer's *Mapp of Virginia discovered to ye falls* . . . 1651, which was used in this edition and also in Edward Bland's *The discovery of Nevv Brittaine*, 1651, same publisher. Baer 35.

WOODNOTH, ARTHUR

A short | collection | of the | most remarkable passages | from the originall to the dissolution | of the | Virginia | Company. | [rule, orn., rule] | *London, | Printed by Richard Cotes for Edward Husband, at the | Golden Dragon in Fleetstreet, 1651.* | [Title within border of fleurs-de-lis].   [126]

[4], 20 p., 4to. (17.1 x 12.6 cm.). Church 515, new John Carter Brown cat. BM, CSmH, CtSoP, DLC, ICN, NN, PHi, RPJCB.

Written about 1645 by the former Deputy Governor of the Somers Island Company.

WHITFIELD, HENRY

Strength | ovt of | VVeaknesse; | Or a glorious | manifestation | of the further progresse of the | Gospel among the Indians in | New-England. | Held forth in sundry letters from | divers ministers and others to the | Corporation established by Parliament for | promoting the Gospel among the heathen in | New-England: and to particular members there- | of since the last treatise to that effect, former- | ly set forth by Mr. Henry whitfield, late Pastor of Gil- | ford in Nevv-England. | Published by the aforesaid Corporation. | [4 lines] | *London, Printed by M. Simmons for John Blague | and Samuel Howes, and are to be sold at their | shops in Popes-Head-Alley.* 1652. [Title within border of type ornaments].   [127]

[12], 33, [1] p., 4to. (18.4 x 14 cm.). Sabin 92797, Church 519, new John Carter Brown cat. PHi, RPJCB.

For the many confusing variations of this and the following editions, see Sabin 92797-92800.

Sixth of the Eliot Indian Tracts.

. . . . .

Strength ovt of | weaknesse; | Or a glorious | manifestation | of the further progresse of | the Gospel among the Indians | in Nevv-England. |

Held forth in sundry letters | from divers ministers and others to the | Corporation established by Parliament for | promoting the Gospel among the hea- | then in New-England; and to particular | members thereof since the last trea- | tise to that effect, pu[b]lished by | Mr Henry Whitfield late Pastor | of Gilford in New-England. | [4 lines] | *London;* | *Printed by M. Simmons for John Blague and* | *Samuel Howes, and are to be sold at their* | *shop in Popes-Head-Alley. 1652.* [Title within border of type ornaments].
[128]

[15], verso blank, 40 p., 4to. DLC, MB, MH, MHi, MWA, NN, NNUT, PHi, RPJCB.

. . . .

Strengtn | ovt of | weaknesse; | or a glorious | manifestation | of the further progresse of | the Gospel among the Indians | in Nevv-England. | Held forth in sundry letters | from divers ministers and others to the | Corporation established by Parliament for | promoting the Gospel among the hea- | then in New-England; and to particular | members thereof since the last trea- | tise to that effect, formerly set | forth by Mr Henry Whitfield | late Pastor of Gilford in | New-England. | Published by the aforesaid Corporation. | [4 lines] | *London;* | *Printed by M. Simmons for John Blague and* | *Samuel Howes, and are to be sold at their* | *shop in Popes-Head-Alley. 1652.* [129]

[15], verso blank, 40 p., 4to. CSmH, DLC, MB, MWA, NN (3), PHi, RPJCB (4).

. . . .

Strength out of weakness. | Or a glorious | manifestation | of the further progresse of the | Gospel | amongst | the Indians | in | New-England. | Held forth in sundry letters | from divers ministers and others to the | Corporation established by Parliament for | promoting the Gospel among the hea- | then in New-England; and to particular | members thereof since the last trea- | tise to that effect, formerly set | forth by Mr Henry Whitfield | late Pastor of Gilford in | New-England. | Published by the aforesaid Corporation. | [3 lines] | *London, Printed by M. Simmons for John Blague* | *and Samuel Howes, and are to be sold at their* | *shop in Popes Head Alley. 1652.* [130]

[15], verso blank, 40 p., 4to. CtY, DLC (2), MB, MH, NHi (2), NN, RPJCB (2).

For 1657 edition see under his: *Banners of grace and love.*

ELIOT, JOHN, AND THOMAS MAYHEW

Tears of repentance: | Or, A further | narrative of the progress of the Gospel | amongst the | Indians | in | New-England: | Setting forth, not only their present state | and condition, but sundry confessions of sin | by diverse of the said Indians, wrought upon | by the saving power of the Gospel; Together | with the manifestation of their faith and hope | in Jesus

Christ, and the work of grace upon | their hearts. | Related by Mr. Eliot and Mr. Mayhew, two faithful laborers | in that work of the Lord. | Published by the Corporation for propagating the Gospel there, for the | satisfaction and comfort of such as wish well thereunto. | [rule, two lines quoted, rule] | *London: Printed by Peter Cole in Leaden Hall, and are to [be] sold at | his shop, at the Sign of the Printing-Press in Cornhil, | near the Royal Exchange. 1653.* | [Title within border of type ornaments].   [131]

[36], 47 p., 4to. (17.6 x 13.8 cm.). Sabin 22166, Church 527, new John Carter Brown cat. BM, CSmH (1st), CtY, DLC, ICN, MB, MH, MWA, NHi, NN, PHi, RPJCB (2d and 3d).

There are three issues of last page: 1. *Finis* same size as text; 2. *Finis* same size. as text, with list of books added; 3. *Finis* in larger type between two type-ornament rules.

Seventh of the Eliot Indian Tracts.

[JOHNSON, EDWARD]

A | history | of | New-England. | From the English planting in the yeere | 1628. untill the yeere 1652. | Declaring the form of their government, | civill, military, and ecclesiastique. Their wars with | the Indians, their troubles with the Gortonists, | and other heretiques. Their manner of gathering | of churches, the commodities of the country, | and description of the principall towns | and havens, with the great encou- | ragements to increase trade | betwixt them and old | England. | With the names of all their governours, magistrates, | and eminent ministers. | [rule, 6 lines quoted, rule] | *London, | Printed for Nath: Brooke at the Angel | in Corn-hill. 1654.*
                                                                              [132]

[4], 236, [4] p., 4to. (18.9 x 13.3 cm.). Sabin 36202, Church 532, new John Carter Brown cat. BM, CSmH, CtSoP, DLC, ICN, MB, MBAt, MiU-C, MWA, NHi, NN, RPB, RPJCB.

Earliest general account of Massachusetts, better known as *Wonder-working Providence.* The unsold remainder was bound up with Sir Ferdinando Gorges' *America painted to the life,* 1659, with a new title page giving Gorges as author.

For modern reprints, see Sabin.

DONCK, ADRIAEN VAN DER

Beschryvinge | van | Nieuvv-Nederlant | (Ghelijck het tegenwoordigh in Staet is) | Begrijpende de Nature, Aert, gelegentheyt en vrucht- | baerheyt van het selve Lant; mitsgaders de proffijtelijcke en- | de gewenste toevallen, die aldaer tot onderhout der Menschen, (soo | uyt haer selven als van buyten ingebracht) gevonden worden. | Als Mede | De maniere en onghemeyne eygenschappen | vande Wilden ofte Naturellen vanden Lande. | Ende | Een bysonder verhael vanden wonderlijcken Aert | ende het Weesen der Bevers, | Daer Noch By Gevoeght is | Een Discours over de gelegentheyt van Nieuw

Nederlandt, | tusschen een Nederlandts Patriot, ende een | Nieuw
Nederlander. | Beschreven door | Adriaen vander Donck, | Beyder Rechten
Doctoor, die teghenwoor- | digh noch in Nieuw Nederlant is. | [wdct. arms
of New Netherland] | *t'Aemsteldam,* | [rule] | *By Evert Nieuwenhof, Boeck-
verkooper, woonende op't* | *Ruslandt in't Schrijf-boeck, Anno 1655.*   [133]

[8], 100, [3] p., plate in text, 4to. (18.6 x 15.1 cm.). Sabin 20593,
Stokes VI:260, Church 535, Asher 7, new John Carter Brown cat. BM,
CtHWatk, DLC, ICN, MB, NBLiHi, NHi, NjP, NN, PBL, RPJCB.

Plate on p. 9: *t' Fort nieuw Amsterdam op de Manhatans,* same as in:
Beschryvinghe van Virginia, 1651.

Another issue with slight variations noted in their cat., at RPJCB. This
"Description of New Netherland (such as it now is), comprehending the
nature, character, situation and fruitfulness of the said lands; together with
the profitable and fortunate accidents there to be found for the support of
man (whether natives or foreigners.) As also the manners and uncommon
qualities of the savages or aborigines of the land. And a particular account
of the·wonderful nature and habits of the beaver; to which is also added a
discourse on the situation of New Netherland, between a Netherlands
patriot and a New Netherlander. Described by Adriaen van der Donck,
Doctor of Laws, who is still in New Netherland" is especially valuable for
its first-hand account of the local Indians. For translations, see Sabin.

ELIOT, JOHN

A late and further | manifestation | of the | progress of the Gospel |
amongst the | Indians | in | New-England. | Declaring their constant love
and zeal to | the truth: With a readinesse to give | accompt of their faith
and hope; as of | their desires in Church commu- | nion to be partakers of |
the ordinances of | Christ. | Being a narrative of the examinations of the
Indians, about | their knowledge in religion, by the elders of the churches.
| Related by Mr John Eliot. | [rule] | Published by the Corporation, estab-
lished by | act of Parliament, for Propagating the Gospel there. | [rule, 2
lines quoted, rule] | *London: Printed by M.S. 1655.* | [Title within border
of type ornaments].   [134]

[8], 23 p., 4to. (17.7 x 13.1 cm.). Sabin 22162, Church 536, new John
Carter Brown cat. BM, Bodleian, CSmH, DLC, MB, MH, MWA, NN,
PHi, RPJCB.

Eighth of the Eliot Indian Tracts.

VRIES, DAVID PIETERSZ. DE

Korte historiael, | ende | Journaels aenteyckeninge, | Van verscheyden
Voyagiens in de vier | deelen des Wereldts-Ronde, als Europa, | Africa,
Asia, ende Amerika gedaen, | Door D. | David Pietersz. | de Vries, Artillerij-
Meester vande Ed: M: | Heeren Gecommitteerde Raden van Staten van
West- | Vrieslandt ende 't Noorder-quartier. | Waerin verhaelt werd wat

Batailjeshy te Water | gedaen heeft: Yder Landtschap zijn Gedierte, Gevogelt, | wat soozte van Vissen, ende wat wilde Menschen naer 't leven | geconterfaeyt, ende van de Bosschen ende Kavieren | met haer Vzuchten. | [cut] | *t'Hoorn*, | [rule] | *Voor David Pietersz. de Vries, Artillerij-Meester van't Noorder-* | *quartier. Tot Alckmaer, by Symon Cornelisz. Brekegeest, Anno 1655.*   [135]

[8], 190, [2] p., copperplate port and illus. in text, 4to. (19.6 x 15 cm.). Sabin 100852, Church 547, new John Carter Brown cat., Stokes VI:257. CSmH, MiU-C, NHi, NIC, NN (2), NNC, RPJCB.

Author was the first historian of New Netherland and lived there 1632-1644. For later editions and translations, see authorities cited above.

DONCK, ADRIAEN VAN DER

Beschrijvinge | van | Nieuvv-Nederlant, | . . . | En hier achter by gevoeght | Het Voordeeligh Reglement vande Ed. Hoog. Achtbare | Heeren de Heeren Burgermeesteren deser Stede, | betreffende de saken van Nieuw Nederlandt. | Den tweeden Druck. | Met een pertinent Kaertje van 't zelve Landt verçiert, | en van veel druck-fouten gesuyvert. | [woodcut] | *t'Amsteldam,* | *By Evert Nieuwenhof, Boeck-verkooper* | *woonende op* | *'t Ruslandt* | *in't Schrijf-boeck* | *Anno 1656.* | *Met Privilegie voor 15 Jaren.*
[136]

[8], 100, [4], Conditien [8] p., map, 4to. (19.6 x 15.5 cm.). Sabin 20594, Asher 8, new John Carter Brown cat. which see for variations from 1st ed., Stokes VI:260. BM, DLC, MH, MiU-C, MWiW-C, N, NHi, NN, PBL, RPJCB (2 eds. of *Conditien*), ViU.

The *Conditien* at end has separate title page, same printer, [8] p. Another edition at RPJCB has the imprint: *t'Amsterdam,* | *By Jan Banning, Ordinaris Drucker* | *deser Stede, in't jaer 1656.* [14] p., (17.6 x 14 cm.).

The plate of the 1st ed. is replaced with an engraving of part of N.J. Visscher's map and view of New Amsterdam, reengraved and signed by *E. Nieuwenhoff.*

This "Description of New Netherland . . . And to this is appended: The advantageous regulations of the Most Worshipful the Burgomasters of this city, regarding the affairs of New Netherland. The second edition, ornamented with a pertinent map of that land, and cleared of many printing faults," has added the regulations of the Burgomasters for immigration into New Netherland and was obviously intended to be used by the Dutch West India Company for promotion purposes.

GOOKIN, DANIEL

To all persons whom these may concern, in the several | townes, and plantations of the United Colonies | in New-England. | Dated this 25 of March 1656. | *[n.p., 1656].*   [137]

Broadside, 4to. Sabin 95886, Ford: Mass. bdsds, 14. Bodleian, RPJCB.

A hand bill stating that the Lord Protector has authorized Daniel Gookin of Cambridge to invite colonists to remove from New England to Jamaica. See F.W. Gookin: *Daniel Gookin, 1612-1687, Assistant and Major General of the Massachusetts Bay Colony.* Chicago, 1912, including a facsimile of the above.

See also his: *Historical collections of the Indians of New England,* 1792.

HAMMOND, JOHN

Leah and Rachel, | or, | the two fruitfull sisters | Virginia, | and | Maryland | Their present condition, im- | partially stated and related. | With | a removall of such imputations as are scandalously | cast on those countries, whereby many deceived | souls, chose rather to beg, steal, rot in prison, | and come to shamefull deaths, then to better their being | by going thither, wherein is plenty of all things | necessary for humane subsistence. | [rule] | By John Hammond. | [rule] | [3 lines from Ecclesiastes] | [rule] | *London, Printed by T. Mabb, and are | to be sold by Nich. Bourn, neere the Royall | Exchange, 1656.* [137A]

[6], 32 p., 4to. (18.7 x 13.7 cm.). Sabin 30102, Church 548, new John Carter Brown cat., Baer 46. BM, CSmH, MH, MWiW-C, PPL, RPJCB.

A lively promotion tract upholding Lord Baltimore and condemning the Puritans.

New-Haven's | settling in | New-England. | And some | lawes | for | government: | published for the use of that Colony. | [rule] | Though some of the orders intended for | present convenience, may probably | be hereafter altered, and as | need requireth other | lawes added. | [rule] | *London: | Printed by M.S. for Livewell Chapman, at the | Crowne in Popes-head-Alley. | 1656.* [138]

[2], 81 p., 4to. Sabin 53017 (title incorrectly transcribed). MBAt, MWA, NN.

Earliest book on the New Haven Colony. Five or six copies known.

WEST-INDISCHE COMPAGNIE

Conditien, | die door de Heeren Bvrgermeesteren | der Stadt Amstelredam, volgens't gemaeckte | Accoordt met de West-Indische Compagnie, | ende d' Approbatie van hare Hog. Mog. de | Heeren Staten Generael der Ver- | eenighde Nederlanden, daer op gevolght, ge- | presenteert werden aen alle de gene, die als | Coloniers na Nieuw-Nederlandt willen ver- | trecken, &c. | [woodcut] | *t'Amsterdam, | By Jan Banning, Ordinaris Drucker | deser Stede, in't jaer 1656.* [139]

[14] p., 4to. (17.6 x 14 cm.). Sabin 102887, Asher 337, new John Carter Brown cat. BM, DLC, NN, RPJCB.

. . . . . .

t'Amsterdam, By de Weduwe van Jan Banning . . . 1659. DLC. [140]

This "Conditions offered by the Burgomasters of the city of Amsterdam, according to the agreements with the West India Company, and with the approbation of their High Mightinesses the States General of the United Netherlands, to all those who will go as colonists to New Netherland, etc." shows the considerable changes in the conditions since their first publication. For details of these changes, see Asher.

WHITFIELD, HENRY

The | banners | of grace and love | displayed | in the farther conversion of the Indians | in New-England: | held forth in sundry letters from divers ministers to | the Corporation established by Parliament, for promoting | the Gospel amongst the heathen in New-England; | and farther attested by | Edm. Callamy | Simon Ashe | VVill. Spurstow | Lazarus Seaman | George Griffith | Phil. Nye | VVilliam Bridge | Henry Whitfield | Joseph Carryll | Ralph Venning. | *London,* | *Printed by W. Godbid, for Edw. Farnham, and are to* | *be sold at his shop in Popeshead-Alley,* | *M. DC. LVII.*   [141]

[15], verso blank, 40 p., 4to. Sabin 3213 and note following 92800. Bodleian, MH.

A reissue of the 1652 sheets of *Strength out of weakness.*

ELIOT, JOHN

A further accompt | of the progresse of the | Gospel | amongst the Indians | in | New-England | and | of the means used effectually to advance the same. | Set forth | in certaine letters sent from thence declaring a | purpose of printing the Scriptures in the | Indian tongue into which they are already | translated. | With which letters are likewise sent an epi- | tome of some exhortations delivered by the In- | dians at a fast, as testimonies of their obedi- | ence to the Gospell. | As also some helps directing the Indians how to | improve naturall reason unto the knowledge | of the true God. | [rule] | *London, Printed by M. Simmons for the Corpo-* | *ration of New-England,* *1659.* | [Title within border of type ornaments].   [142]

[11], 35 [1] p., 4to. (17.3 x 13.3 cm.). Sabín 22149, Church 556, new John Carter Brown cat. BM, Bodleian, CSmH, CtHWatk, DLC, ICN, MB, MH, NHi, NN, RPJCB.

Second title at p. [22]: *Some* | *helps* | *for the* | *Indians* | [etc., 10 lines] | *by Abraham Peirson.* | *Examined and approved by Thomas Stanton Interpre-* | *ter Generall . . .* | [etc., 2 lines] | *London,* | *Printed by M. Simmons, 1659.* [Reprint of first signature of first book in the language of the Indians of Connecticut, printed at Cambridge, 1658, copies at BM (spurious title page) and NN].

Ninth of the Eliot Indian Tracts.

GORGES, FERDINANDO

America | painted to the life. | The true | history | of | the Spaniards proceedings in the conquests of the | Indians, and of their civil wars among them- | selves, from Columbus his first discovery, | to these later times. | As also, | of the original undertakings of the advancement of | plantations into those parts; | With a perfect relation of our English discoveries, shewing | their beginning, progress and continuance, from the year | 1628. to 1658. Declaring the forms of their govern- | ment, policies, religions, maners, customs, military disci- | pline, wars with the Indians, the commodities of their | countries, a description of their towns and havens, | the increase of their trading, with the names of | their governors and magistrates. | More especially, an absolute narrative of the North | parts of America, and of the discoveries and | plantations of our English in | Virginia, New-England, and Berbadoes. | [rule] | Published by Ferdinando Gorges, Esq; | [rule] | A work now at last exposed for the publick good, to stir up the heroick and | active spirits of these times, to benefit their countrey, and eternize | their names by such honorable attempts. | For the readers clearer understanding of the countreys, they are lively | described in a compleat and exquisite map. | [rule, one line quoted, rule] | *London, Printed for Nath Brook at the Angel in Cornhil. 1659.* | [Title in red and black within double ruled border]. [6], 51 p., port., map. [second title:] A | briefe narration | of the | originall undertakings | of the | advancement | of | plantations | into the parts of | America. | Especially, | shewing the begining, progress | and continuance of that of | New-England. | [rule] | Written by the right Worshipfull, Sir Ferdinando Gorges | Knight and Governour of the fort and island of | Plymouth in Devonshire. | [rule] | *London: | Printed by E. Brudenell, for Nath. Brook at the | Angell in Corn hill. 1658.* [2], 57 p. [third title:] America | painted to the life. | A | true history of the originall undertakings of the advancement | of plantations into those parts, with a perfect relation of | our English discoveries, shewing their beginning, progress, and | continuance, from the year, 1628. to 1658. declaring the forms of | their government, policies, religions, manners, customes, military | discipline, warres with the Indians, the commodities of their | countries, a description of their townes, and havens, the increase | of their trading with the names of their governours and magistrates. | More | especially an absolute narrative of the North parts of America, and | of the discoveries and plantations of our English in | New-England. | [rule] | Written by Sir Ferdinando Gorges Knight | and Governour of the fort and Island of Plimouth in | Devonshire, one of the first and chiefest pro- | moters of those plantations. | [rule] | Publisht since his decease, by his Grand-child Ferdinando Gorges Esquire, | who hath much enlarged it and added severall accurate descripti- | ons of his owne. | [rule] | A work now at last exposed for the publick good, to stir up the heroick and active spirits | of these times, to benefit their country, and eternize their names | by such honourable attempts. | [rule] | For the readers clearer understanding of the country's they are lively described in a | compleat and exquisite map. | [one line quoted] | [rule] | *London; Printed by E. Brudenell, for·Nathaniel Brook dwelling at | the Angel in Corn-hill. 1658.* [4], 236 p. [fourth title:] America | painted to the life. | The | history | of the | Spaniards proceedings in America, their con- | quests of the Indians, and of their | civil wars among themselves. | From | Columbus his first discovery, to these | later times. | [rule] | By | Ferdinando Gorges, Esq; | [rule, one line quoted, rule, orn., rule] | *London, Printed by T.J. for Nath. Brook at the Angel* | *in Cornhil. 1659.*   [143]

[4], 52, table, 10 leaves, 4to. (18 x 13.5 cm.). Sabin 28020, Church 559, new John Carter Brown cat., Baer 50. BM, CSmH, CtY, Garrett, ICN, MB, MBAt, MH, MHi, MiU-C, MWA, N, NHi, NjP, NN, NNP, PBL, PP, RPJCB.

Edited by Ferdinando Gorges, grandson of the author. The third title is not by Gorges but consists of the unsold sheets of Edward Johnson's *History of New England, or wonder working providence,* 1654, impudently inserted in this volume by the publisher. There is a folded copperplate frontispiece of an Indian, a folded map of America and, in some copies, a plate of the Spanish cruelties from Las Casas. See Church and John Carter Brown cat.

This work is important for its account of the settlement of Maine, 1628-1658, where the author had a large patent. He quarrelled with the Massachusetts Bay colonists whom he considered squatters on his land.

STEENDAM, JACOB

Klacht van Nieuw-Amsterdam, | in Nieuw-Nederlandt, | tot | Haar Moeder: | Van haar begin, wasdom en tegenwoor- | digen stand. | [Colophon:] *t'Amsterdam,* | *By Pieter Dirchsz. Boeteman, Boeck-drucker, op de Engelantiers-gracht. 1659.*   [144]

Broadside, folio (36.2 x 25.2 cm.). Sabin 91167, new John Carter Brown cat. RPJCB.

An allegorical poem about New Amsterdam by the first Dutch poet of New York.

For English translation, see Sabin notes.

ELIOT, JOHN

A further account of the progress | of the | Gospel | amongst the Indians | in New England: | being | A relation of the confessions made | by several Indians (in the pre- | sence of the elders and mem- | bers of several churches) in or- | der to their admission into | church-fellowship. | Sent over to the Corporation for Propagating the Gospel of | Jesus Christ amongst the Indians in New England at Lon- | don, by Mr John Eliot one of the laborers in the Word | amongst them. | *London,* | *Printed by John Macock.* *1660.*   [145]

[8], 76, [1] p. 4to. (17.1 x 12.7 cm.). Sabin 22151, new John Carter Brown cat. RPJCB, etc.

Tenth of the Eliot Indian Tracts.

STEENDAM, JACOB

't Lof | Van | Nuw-Nederland. | Daar in, kort, en grondig word ange- | wesen d'uytmuntende hoedanigheden, die het | heeft in de suyverheyt des Luchts, vruchtbaar- | heyt des Aardrijks, voort-teling des Vees, | overvloed des Wilds, en Visschen: met | de wel-gelegentheyt tot Schip- | vaard, en Koophandel. | Door | Jacob Steen-Dam | *t'Amsterdam,* | *Voor Jacobus van der Fuyk: Boekver-* | *kooper in de stil-steech Anno 1661.* | [Colophon:] *t'Amsterdam,* | *Gedrukt by Pieter Dircksz. Boeteman,* | *op de Engelantiers-gracht. 1661.* [146]

[12] p., 4to. (19 x 14.4 cm.). Sabin 91168. NN, RPJCB.

For English translation, see Sabin note.

Poem about New Netherland by the first Dutch poet of New York.

[BERKELEY, SIR WILLIAM]

A | discourse | and view of | Virginia. | *[London? 1662–3?]* [147]

12 p., 4to. Sabin 4889 and 100459, Baer 59. BM, CSmH, Garrett, NjP, A.S.W. Rosenbach.

Kort Verhael | van Nieuw- | Nederlants | Gelegentheit, Deughden, | Natuerlijke Voorrechten, en by- | zondere bequaemheidt ter bevolkingh: | Mitsgaders eenige | Requesten, Vertoogen, Deductien, enz. ten dien einden | door | eenige Liefhebbers ten verscheide tijden omtrent 't laetst | van't Jaer 1661. gepresenteert aen de A.A. Heeren Bur- | germeesteren dezer Stede, of der zelver E. E. Hee- | ren Gecommitteerde, enz. | Ziet breeder achter de Voor-Reden den Korten Inhout, mitsga- | ders de Waerschouwingh aen de Boek-verkoopers, staende | Hier vervolgens op d'ander-of tegen-zijde. | [orn.] | *[Amsterdam:] Gedruckt in't Jaer 1662.* [148]

[8], 84 p., 4to. (19.8 x 15.2 cm.). Sabin 38253, Church 575, Asher 13, Stokes VI:261, new John Carter Brown cat. BM, CSmH, NHi, NN, RPJCB.

Written by a Mennonite under the initials H.V.Z.M. and others. It is a colonization tract, a plea for help, a description of the country, especially along the Delaware River, account of the Indians and a statement of the Dutch title to New Netherland. The title in English: "A short account of New-Netherland's situation, virtues, natural, privileges and peculiar fitness for population. Together with some requests, representations, deductions, etc., presented for that purpose by some amateurs at different times about the end of the year 1661, to the Burgomasters of this city or to their Deputies, etc. See more at full the brief contents, at the end of the preface, together with the warning to the booksellers, standing hereafter on the other side or reverse." (Quoted from Asher). Reissued from same sheets with new title: *Zeekere Vrye-Voorslagen,* 1663.

PLOCKHOY, PIETER CORNELISZOON

Kort en klaer ontwerp | dienende tot | Een orderling Accoordt, | om | Den arbeyd, onrust en moeye- | lyckheyt, van Alderley-handwerkst- | lieyden te verlichten | door | Een onderlinge Compagnie ofte | Volck-planting (onder de protectie vande H: Mo: | Heeren Staten Generael der vereenigde Nederlan- | den; en byzonder onder het gunstig gesag van de | Achtbare Magistraten der Stad Amstelre- | dam aen de Zuyt-revier in Nieu-ne- | der-land of te rechten; Bestaende in | Land bouwers | Zee-vaerende Personen, | Alderhande noodige Ambachts-luyden, en Meesters | van goede konsten en weten- schappen. | Steunende op de voorvechters van hare Acht- | baerheden (als hierna volgt) tot dien zynde verleent. | t'Samen gestelt | Door Pieter Cornelisz. Plockhoy van Zierckzee, voor hem selven en andere | Lief-hebbers van Nieu-neder-land. | *t'Amsterdam gedruckt by Otto Barentsz. Smient,* *Anno 1662.* [149]

[16] p., 4to. Sabin 63425, Asher 339. CSmH.

"A short and concise plan, intended as a mutual agreement for lessening the labor and difficulty of all kinds of artisans, by a common company or colony (under the protection of their High Mightinesses the States General of the United Netherlands, and especially under the favorable authority of the Worshipful Magistracy of the city of Amsterdam) to be founded on South River in New Netherland; consisting of husbandmen, miners, work- men of all necessary trades, and masters of necessary arts and sciences. Confiding in the privileges granted to the said Right Worshipful to that end, (so as here will be found). Composed by Cornelius Plockhoy of Zierkzee, for himself and other lovers of New-Netherland."

Plockhoy's cooperative colony of 24 families on the Horekill in the present state of Delaware was destroyed by the English in 1664. For his other writings, see BM and DLC catalogues.

Zeekere | Vrye-Voorlagen, en | Versoeken, | tot Bevorderingh | van een bestandige, voor Hollandt hooghnutte, en | niet min verheerlijkende Vrye Volx | Uitzetting, | tot | Verbreiding, of Voortplanting van des zelfs Vryen | Staet, in't ongemeen gezont van Climaet, en zeer vrucht- | baar, mitsgaders Rivier-en Visch-rijck | Nieuw-Nederlandt. | [. . . 10 lines] | Het eerste Deel. | *t'Amsterdam,* | *Gedrukt voor den Autheur, en men vindtze te koop* *by* | *Jan Rieuwertsz. in Dirk-van-Assen-en by Pieter Arentsz.* | *inde Beurs-* *steeg. 1663.* [150]

[8], 84 p., 4to. (19.1 x 15.3 cm.). Old John Carter Brown cat. 926, new ditto, Stokes VI:261. RPJCB.

"Certain free proposals and petitions for the promotion of a permanent beginning of a free people highly useful for Holland, and not glorified in spreading or propagating the free state itself, in the uncommon healthiness of the climate, and very fruitful and abounding in rivers and fish, New Netherland.—Also, with a succinct account of the situation, virtues, natural advantages, and especial fitness for population of the same New Netherland. All at the desire of several wealthy admirers of a free people's plantation, to the comfort and riddance of all Holland's necessities, upon real and the very best grounds of free state government, free from all frauds, assumed military constraint and ambitious schemes, and proposed for a trial. The first [and only] part." A reissue of the sheets with new title page and vesrso, of *Kort Verhael van Nieuw-Nederlants,* 1662, which see.

HILTON, WILLIAM

A | relation | of | a discovery lately made on the coast of | Florida, | (From lat. 31. to 33 deg. 45 min. North-lat.) | By William Hilton Commander, and | Commissioner with Capt. Anthony Long, | and Peter Fabian, in the Ship Adventure, which | set sayl from Spikes Bay, Aug. 10. 1663. and was | set forth by several gentlemen and mer | -chants of the Island of Barbadoes. | Giving an account of the nature and tempera | -ture of the soyl, the manners and disposition | of the natives, and whatsoever else is | remarkable therein. | Together with | proposals made by the Commissioners | of the Lords Proprietors, to all such per | -sons as shall become the first setlers on the | rivers, harbors, and creeks there. | *London,* | *Printed by J. C.* *for Simon Miller at the Star neer the* | *West-end of St. Pauls, 1664.* [151]

[4], 34, [2] p., 4to. (17.7 x 13.8 cm.) Church 586, New John Carter Brown cat., Sabin 31919. BM (4 copies, 1 imperfect), CSmH, DLC, MH, NN, PP, RPJCB.

Earliest piece of Carolina promotion literature. The NN copy has the imprint: *London, Printed by J.C. for Richard Moon, Book-seller in Bristol, 1664.*

NICOLLS, RICHARD, FIRST ENGLISH GOVERNOR OF NEW YORK

[Row of type ornaments] | The | conditions for New-Planters | In the territories of His Royal Highnes | the | Duke of York | [Caption title] . . . | The lands which I intend shall be first Planted, are there [pen corrected to *these,* i.e., *those*] upon the West side of | Hudsons-River, at, or adjoyning to the Sopes, . . . [Esopus, now Kingston, N.Y. and adjoining territory] . . . [Signed:] R. Nicolls. *[Boston: Marmaduke Johnson? May, 1665].* [152]

Broadside, folio (30 x 20.5 cm.). Sabin 53619, Evans 98, Ford: Mass. Bdsds. 28. DLC, MHi, NHi.

The Ebenezer Hazard—Peter Force—Library of Congress copy (with a small piece missing from the right side removing one word) has this manuscript note in the autograph of Governor Nicolls in the lower left margin: "The Governour hath purchast all the Sopes land, wch now is ready for planters to put the plough into [,] it being cleere ground." And below this, a note in the same hand: "This was printed at Boston in May 1665."

The Fitz John Winthrop (Governor of Connecticut)—R.C. Winthrop— B.R. Winthrop—New-York Historical Society copy (with hole the size of a quarter at left center, repaired in pen facsimile from MHi copy), endorsed on back in autograph of Governor Winthrop: "Col. Richard Nicolls conditions for new planters."

The Massachusetts Historical Society copy. See Mass. Hist. Soc. 2 Proceedings IX:423.

Another copy (lacking row of type ornaments above title) was reproduced in a facsimile at NHi, present location of original unknown.

Bibliographers have credited the printing of this item to Samuel Green of Cambridge since his was the only press officially printing in the American colonies between 1649 and 1675 when John Foster set up his press in Boston. However, Governor Nicolls' manuscript note on the Library of Congress copy of this broadside definitely says that "This was printed at Boston in May 1665" and Mr. George Parker Winship points out that Marmaduke Johnson, originally with the Cambridge press, had returned from London to Boston in May, 1665 with a new printing outfit of his own, ready to set up a press in Boston but that the Massachusetts Legislature promptly forbade him to print in Boston. He then returned to Cambridge where he printed alone, 1665-1668, alone and with Green, 1669-1672 and again alone from 1673 to 1674. It may well be that Johnson printed, either openly or surreptitiously, in Boston for a few weeks in 1665 before (or after) he had been forbidden to print there and before he returned to Cambridge in the same year. At any rate, Nicolls *says* that his broadside was printed at Boston and Marmaduke Johnson was the only printer there at the time. If this contention is true, the date of Boston's first printing must be moved back ten years, for John Foster, generally credited as Boston's first printer, did not begin until he printed Increase Mather's *The wicked mans portion* in 1675. This broadside may, then, be the only recorded example of Boston's first printer.

It is also probable that Green, the official printer of the colony, at Cambridge, would have been reluctant to print a broadside which would tend to attract settlers away from New England and for the printing of which he would probably be criticized.

The liberal terms of the purchase, based on the Duke's Laws, established liberty of conscience, the right to make local laws and to choose local civil and military officers.

See *Minutes of the Executive Council of the Province of New York,* I:245, for: "The names of those that Coll. Nicolls p[ro]mised lands to at Esopus being now [1668] there;" same, 289: A register, 1670, "of all the lands granted by ye authority of his R: H. lyeing within the Precincts of Kingston;" and same, 241-309, for collateral documents.

ALSOP, GEORGE

A | character | of the Province of | Mary-land, | Wherein is described in four distinct | parts, (Viz.) | I. The scituation, and plenty of the Province. | II. The laws, customs, and natural demea- | nor of the inhabitant. | III. The worst and best usage of a Mary- | land servant, opened in view. | IV. The traffique, and vendable commodities | of the countrey. | Also | A small treatise on the wilde and | naked Indians (or Susquehanokes) | of Mary-Land, their customs, man- | ners, absurdities, & religion. | Together with a collection of histo- | rical letters. | [rule] | By George Alsop. | [rule] | *London,*

Printed by T.J. for Peter Dring, | at the sign of the Sun in the Poultrey: 1666. | [Title within fleur-de-lis border]. [153]

[xxii], 118, [3] p., port., folded map, 8vo. (12.7 x 7.9 cm.). Sabin 963, Church 594, new John Carter Brown cat., Baer 60. BM, CSmH, DLC, ICN, MH, MHi, MiU-C, MWiW-C, NN (lacks port.), PHi, RPJCB.

Portrait of the author and folded map of Maryland: *A land-skip of the | Province of | Mary land | or the | Lord Baltimors | Plantation neere | Virginia | By Geo: Alsop Gent:* (11.9 x 16.3 cm.).

For reprints, see Church, John Carter Brown notes and Baer.

A brief description | of | the Province | of | Carolina | on the coasts of Florida. | And | more perticularly of a new-plantation | begun by the English at Cape-Feare, | on that river now by them called Charles-River, | the 29th of May. 1664. | Wherein is set forth | the healthfulness of the air; the fertility of | the earth, and waters; and the great pleasure and | profit will accrue to those that shall go thither to enjoy | the same. | Also, | directions and advice to such as shall go thither whether | on their own accompts, or to serve under another. | Together with | a most accurate map of the whole Province. | [rule] | London, Printed for Robert Horne in the first Court of Gresham- | Colledge neer Bishopsgate-street. 1666. [154]

[4], 10, [2] p., folded map. (18 x 13.3 cm.). Church 595, New John Carter Brown cat., Sabin 10961. BM (2 copies), CSmH, DLC (lacks map), ICN, MiU-C, N, NHi, NjP, NN, RPJCB, ViU.

First printed description of Carolina and, with Hilton's *Relation,* the earliest promotion tract of the colony.

MORTON, NATHANIEL

New-Englands | memoriall: | or, | a brief relation of the most memorable and remarkable | passages of the providence of God, manifested to the | planters | of | New-England in America; | with special reference to the first colony thereof, called | New-Plimouth. | As also a nomination of divers of the most eminent instruments | deceased, both of Church and Commonwealth, improved in the | first beginning and after-progress of sundry of the respective | jurisdictions in those parts; in reference unto sundry | exemplary passages of their lives, and | the time of their death. | [rule] | Published for the use and benefit of present and future generations, | By Nathaniel Morton, | Secretary to the Court for the Jurisdiction of New-Plimouth. | [rule, 6 lines quoted, rule] | Cambridge: | Printed by S.G. and M.J. for John Usher of Boston. 1669. | [Title within double ruled border]. [155]

[12], 198, [10] p., 4to. (17 x 13.8 cm.). Sabin 51012, Evans 144, Church 606, new John Carter Brown cat. BM (2), CSmH, Ct, CtSoP, CtY, DLC, ICN, MB (imperfect), MH, MHi, MiU-C, MSaE, MWA (imperfect), MWiW, MWiW-C (John Evelyn's copy), NBLiHi, NHi, NN, PPL, RPAt, RPJCB.

The voyage of the Mayflower and the history of the Plymouth Colony,

1620-1646, by the nephew of Governor William Bradford, based on his journal and that of Edward Winslow. One of the great books of New England history.

SHRIGLEY, NATHANIEL

A true | relation | of | Virginia | and | Mary-Land; | with the commodities therein, which in | part the author saw; the rest he had from know- | ing and credible persons in the Moneths of February, | March, April and May: | By Nathaniel Shrigley, Anno. 1669. | Published by allowance. | *London,* | *Printed by Tho. Milbourn for Thomas Hodson Book-binder,* | *living the next door to the Signe of the Blew-Boar in* | *Redcross Street.* *[1669].*   [156]

[2], 5 p., 4to. (17.2 x 12.4 cm.). Baer 64. BM, CSmH, Garrett (*Hudson* for *Hodson* in imprint), NN, PPL, PU, RPJCB.

A first hand account of the Chesapeake region.

DENTON, DANIEL

A | brief description | of | New-York: | formerly called | New-Netherlands. | With the places thereunto adjoyning. | Together with the | manner of its scituation, fertility of the soyle, | healthfulness of the climate, and the | commodities thence produced. | Also | some directions and advice to such as shall go | thither: an account of what commodities they shall | take with them; the profit and pleasure that | may accrew to them thereby. | Likewise | a brief relation of the customs of the | Indians there. | [rule] | By Daniel Denton. | [rule] | *London,* | *Printed for John Hancock, at the first shop in Popes-Head-Alley in* | *Cornhil at the three Bibles, and William Bradley at the three Bibles* | *in the Minories. 1670.*   [157]

[vi], 21 p., 4to. (20.5 x 15.5 cm.). Starred copies have perfect title pages: BM (2), *CSmH, DLC, ICN, MH, MIU-C, MWiW-C, *N, NBLiHi, *NjP, *NN (2, 1 perfect), *NNC, NHi, NNP, NSmB, RPJCB (2), ViU, John Garrett, will eventually go to MdBJ.

The first English book on New York. Since the title page was longer than the text, part or all of the imprint has been cut off by careless binders in all but five copies. The first preliminary leaf is blank. In some copies the word *likewise* in the title has a space between the first two letters.

Reprints: Hist. Soc. of Pa. *Proceedings,* No. 1, 1845, and as a separate; ([William] Gowans' Bibliotheca Americana No. 1), with introduction and notes by Gabriel Furman New York, 1845; with introduction by Felix Neumann, Cleveland, 1902; with bibliographical note recording all known copies by Victor Hugo Paltsits. New York, 1937. (Facsimile Text Society Pub. 40).

Provenance. Only first copy is uncut. Only first five copies have perfect title pages. This record based on notes of Dr. V.H. Paltsits, with additions.

1. John F. McCoy, Charles H. Kalbfleisch, Robert Hoe Jr., Herman LeRoy Edgar, Grenville Kane, Princeton University Library.
2. Columbia University Library. Bought at auction in a pamphlet volume for $10.00 prior to 1897 when its identity was first discovered.
3. Lord Ashburton, Henry C. Nattali, Dodd, Mead & Co., E. Dwight Church, Henry E. Huntington Library and Museum.
4. Col. Thomas Aspinwall, S.L.M. Barlow, Brayton Ives, Dodd, Mead & Co., Frederick R. Halsey, Henry E. Huntington Library and Museum (duplicate sale), G.A. Baker & Co., W.D. Breaker, Mrs. W.D. Breaker, New York State Library.
5. Earl of Sheffield, Dodd & Livingston, Henry F. DePuy, Lathrop C. Harper, George F. Baker, Jr., New York Public Library.
6. British Museum.
7. British Museum.
8. John Carter Brown Library, 1866.
9. John Carter Brown Library, 1846.
10. Gabriel Furman, James Lenox (1846), Lenox Library, New York Public Library.
11. Harvard College Library since 1830.
12. Long Island Historical Society since 1889.
13. Rufus King, New York Historical Society.
14. British Museum triplicate, Lathrop C. Harper, Chapin Collection of Williams College Library.
15. William Menzies, Library of Congress since 1875.
16. Edward E. Ayer, Newberry Library.
17. Edward N. Crane, Theodore N. Vail, Lathrop C. Harper, William L. Clements Library of University of Michigan.
18. Theodore Irwin, Pierpont Morgan Library.
19. Sotheby auction 1901, Henry Stevens Son & Stiles, Francis P. Harper, Bangs & Co. auction 1903, Oscar Wegelin, R.H. Handley, R.H. Handley Collection deposited at Smithtown Branch Public Library, Smithtown Branch, Suffolk Co., N.Y.
20. George Brinley, Ogden Goelet, Lathrop C. Harper, John W. Garrett, The John W. Garrett Library of The Johns Hopkins University.
21. Bernard Quaritch 1929, Lathrop C. Harper, Tracy W. McGregor 1930, The Tracy W. McGregor Library of The University of Virginia.

ELIOT, JOHN

A brief | narrative | of the | progress of the Gospel amongst | the Indians in New-England, in | the year 1670. | Given in | by the Reverend Mr. John Elliot, | Minister of the Gospel there, | [etc., 6 lines] | *London,* | *Printed for John Allen, formerly living in Little Britain at* | *the Rising-Sun, and now in Wentworth street near Bell-* | *Lane, 1671.*   [158]

11 p., 4to. (17.4 x 13.1 cm.). Sabin 22142, new John Carter Brown cat. RPJCB, etc.

Eleventh and last of the Eliot Indian Tracts. For account of their printing, see George Parker Winship's *The Eliot Indian Tracts*, in: *Bibliographical Essays. A Tribute to Wilberforce Eames*, 1924, p. 179-192. For fuller details and reprints, see Sabin, Church and Pilling's Algonquian Languages.

STEENDAM, JACOB

Zeede-sangen | voor de | Batavische- | Jonkheyt: | behelsende | verscheyden bedenkelijke, en stichtelijke | stoffen: op bekende, en vermake- | lijke Sangtoonen gepast: | door | Jacob Steen-dam. | . . . | *Batavia,* | *by Pieter Walberger: Boek-* | *drukker en Letter-gieter, der E. Oost-* | *Indise Comp:* *wonende in de Prince-* | *straet, in de Batavische Mercurius.* | *[1671].*   [159]

[8], 110 p., 8vo. Sabin 91169. Photostat of the Ogden Goelet copy in NHi.

Includes poems on life in New Amsterdam. For translations of Steendam's poems, see Sabin note.

JOSSELYN, JOHN

New-Englands | rarities | discovered: | in | birds, beasts, fishes, serpents, | and plants of that country. | Together with | the physical and chyrurgical remedies | wherewith the natives constantly use to | cure their distempers, wounds, | and sores. | Also | A perfect description of an Indian squa, | in all her bravery; with a poem not | improperly conferr'd upon her. | Lastly | A chronological table | of the most remarkable passages in that | country amongst the English. | [rule] | Illustrated with cuts. | [rule] | By John Josselyn, Gent. | [rule] | *London, Printed for G. Widdowes at the* | *Green Dragon in St. Pauls Church yard, 1672.* | [Title within double ruled border].
[160]

[4], 114, [2] p., plate and illus., 8vo. (14 x 8.5 cm.). Sabin 36674, Church 618, old John Carter Brown cat. 1080. BM, CSmH, MB, MH, MHi, NjP, NN, RPJCB.

The earliest work on the natural history and Indian remedies of New England.

LEDERER, JOHN

The | discoveries | of | John Lederer, | in three several marches from | Virginia, | to the west of | Carolina, | and other parts of the continent: | begun in March 1669, and ended in September 1670. | Together with | a general map of the whole territory | which he traversed. | Collected and translated out of Latine from his Discourse | and Writings, | By Sir William Talbot Baronet. | [2 lines quoted from Virgil] | *London, Printed by J.C.* *for Samuel Heyrick, at Grays-* | *Inne-gate in Holborn. 1672.*   [161]

[viii], 27 p., folded map, 4to. (18.6 x 14.3 cm.). Baer 72. BM, CSmH, DLC, ICN, MH, NHi, NjP, NN, NIC, PPL, RPJCB, ViU, etc.

Folded map of Carolina inscribed: *A map of the whole territory traversed by Iohn Lederer in his three marches.* Signed in lower left corner: *Cross sculpsit.* (16 x 20.5 cm.).

The author was a German doctor, sent out by Governor Berkeley of Virginia, and was probably the first person to reach the crest of the Appalachians and see the Valley of Virginia. A book of great historical and ethnological value in spite of inaccuracies.

Reprinted with an introduction by H.A. Rattermann, Cincinnati, 1879; Rochester, 1902; and in Alvord and Bidgood: *The first explorations of the Trans-Allegheny regions by the Virginians.* Cleveland, 1912, p. 131-171.

JOSSELYN, JOHN

An | account | of two | voyages | to | New-England. | Wherein you have the setting out of a ship, | with the charges; the prices of all necessaries for | furnishing a planter and his family at his first com- | ing; a description of the countrey, natives and | creatures, with their merchantil and physical use; | the government of the countrey as it is now pos- | sessed by the English, &c. A large chronological ta- | ble of the most remarkable passages, from the first dis- | covering of the Continent of America, to the year | 1673. | [rule] | By John Josselyn Gent. | [rule, 7 lines quoted, rule] | *London, Printed for Giles Widdows, at the Green Dragon | in St. Paul's-Church-yard.* 1674. | [Title within double ruled border].   [162]

[8], 279, 3 p., 8vo. (14.5 x 9.5 cm.). Sabin 36672, Church 627, old John Carter Brown cat. 1104, Baer 76. BM, CSmH, Garrett, MBAt, MHi, NHi, NjP, NN, RPJCB, etc.

Original observations based on a residence in New England in 1638-1639 and 1663-1671.

A brief and true | narration | of the late | wars | risen in | New-England: | Occasioned by the quarrelsome disposition, | and perfidious carriage | of the | barbarous, savage and heathenish | natives | there. | *London: Printed for J.S. 1675.*   [163]

8 p., 4to. Sabin 52616, old John Carter Brown cat. 1134. NN, RPJCB.

This is the first of 11 quarto King Philip's War tracts.

FENWICK, JOHN

[No title. Text begins:] Friends, These are to satisfie you, . . . that we shall no doubt find, but that New Cesarea or New Jersey, which is the place which I did purchase: together with the government thereof, is a healthy, pleasant, and plentiful country: . . . and the character given thereof, by John Ogilby in his America, which I herewith send. . . . dated this 8th of the 1st month, 1675. *[n.p., 1675].*   [164]

1 leaf, folio. Sabin 24081. PHi.

.   .   .   .   .

A testimony against John Fenwick, concerning his proceeding about New-

Cesaria, or New-Jersey, in the Province of America: Also John Fenwick's letter of condemnation sent to Friends; upon their testifying against his Proceedings. *[n.p., ca. 1675].* [165]

1 leaf, folio. Sabin 24082.

JOSSELYN, JOHN

An account of two voyages to New-England. [etc., as in 1st ed., 1674] Second edition. *London, Printed for Giles Widdows, at the Green Dragon in St. Paul's-Church-yard. 1675.* [166]

Same imprint, collation and size as first edition. Sabin 36672, Baer 79. MH, etc.

. . . . .

New-Englands rarities discovered: [etc., as in 1st ed., 1672] The second addition [sic]. *London, Printed for G. Widdowes at the Green Dragon in St. Pauls Church yard, 1675.* [167]

Same imprint, collation and size as first edition. Old John Carter Brown cat. 1123. RPJCB, etc.

The | present state | of | NEW-ENGLAND, | with respect to the | Indian VVar. | Wherein is an account of the true reason thereof, | (as far as can be judged by men.) | Together with most of the remarkable passages that have hap- | pened from the 20th of June, till the 10th of November, 1675. | [rule] | Faithfully composed by a Merchant of Boston, and communicated | to his friend in London. | [rule] | Licensed Decemb. 13. 1675. Roger L'Estrange. | [rule] | [royal arms] | [rule] | *London,* | *Printed for Dorman Newman, at the Kings-Arms in the Poultry, and at the* | *Ship and Anchor at the Bridg-foot on Southwark side. 1675.* [168]

19 p., folio (29 x 18 cm.). Sabin 65324, Church 636, old John Carter Brown cat. 1133. CSmH, DLC, ICN, MBAt, MiU-C, NjP, NN, RPJCB.

. . . . .

Second edition reset with *New-England* in title printed with upper and lower case type instead of solid caps as in first edition. Some copies have imprint date changed with a pen to read *1676.* Same imprint, date and collation. CtSoP, DLC, MH, NjP, NN. [169]

This is the first of the five folio King Philip's War tracts.

[WHARTON, EDWARD]

New-England's | present | sufferings, | under | their cruel neighbouring | Indians. | Represented | in two letters, lately written | from Boston to London. | [double rule] | *London, Printed [by B. Clark] in the year 1675.* [170]

[2, recto misnumbered 1], 4-7, [1] p., 4to. (18 x 13.5 cm.). Sabin 103100,

Church 639-640, old John Carter Brown cat. 1138. CSmH (both issues), NN (2d issue), RPJCB (1st issue).

Second issue, same imprint and date, 8 p., 4to. with numerous textual variations, for which see Church.

By a New England Quaker, gloating over the retribution visited by the Indians on his enemies the Puritan tyrants for their cruelty towards the Friends. Suppressed by the London Quakers and their printer, B. Clark, reprimanded for printing it.

This is the second of 11 quarto King Philip's War tracts.

A continuation | of the state of | New-England; | being a farther account of the | Indian Warr, | and of the engagement betwixt the joynt forces | of the United English Collonies and the Indians, on the | 19th. of December 1675. With the true number of the | slain and wounded, and the transactions of the English | army since the said fight. With all other passages that | have there hapned from the 10th. of November, 1675. to the | 8th. of February 167⅝. | Together with an account of the intended rebellion | of the Negroes in the Barbadoes. | [rule] | Licensed March 27. 1676. Henry Oldenburg. | [rule, royal arms, rule] | *London, Printed by T.M. for Dorman Newman, at the Kings Armes in | the Poultry, 1676.*   [171]

20 p., folio (29.5 x 18.5 cm.). Sabin 52623, Church 645, old John Carter Brown cat. 1153. CSmH, CtSoP, DLC, ICN, MBAt, MiU-C, NjP, NN, RPJCB. The uncut CtSoP copy has 3 line errata slip pasted at end.

This is the second of the five folio King Philip's War tracts.

A farther brief and true | narration | of the late | wars | risen in | New-England, | occasioned by the quarrel- | some disposition and perfidious | carriage of the barbarous and sa- | vage Indian natives there. | With an account of the fight, | the 19th of December last, 1675. | [rule] | London, February 17th, 167⅝. | Licensed, | Henry Oldenburg. | [rule] | *London, Printed by J.D. for M.K. and are to be sold | by the booksellers, 1676.*   [172]

12 p., 4to. (17.9 x 13.4 cm.). Sabin 52638. NN (the S.L.M. Barlow copy no. 1234).

Includes a letter of Edward Rawson to the inhabitants of the Colony of Massachusetts, dated at Boston, December 7, 1675, p. 6-8. This is the seventh of 11 quarto King Philip's War tracts.

[HARTSHORNE, RICHARD, AND OTHERS]

A | further account | of | New Jersey. | In an abstract of | letters | lately writ from thence, | by several inhabitants there resident. | [rule, orn., rule] | *Printed in the year 1676.*   [173]

[2], 13 p., 4to. (21 x 15.5 cm.). Church 649. BM, CSmH, NjN, NN, PPL, RPJCB.

Six letters written by Quaker settlers to friends in England. The first of a series of at least nine promotion tracts and broadsides published by the Scottish proprietors of East New Jersey.

MATHER, INCREASE

A | brief history | of the | warr | with the Indians in | Nevv-England, | (From June 24, 1675. when the first English-man was mur- | dered by the Indians, to August 12. 1676. when Philip, alias | Metacomet, the principal author and beginner | of the warr, was slain.) | Wherein the grounds, begin- ning, and progress of the warr, | is summarily expressed. | Together with a serious exhortation | to the inhabitants of that land, | [rule]. | By Increase Mather, Teacher of a church of | Christ, in Boston in New-England. | [rule] | [8 lines quoted] | [rule] | *Boston, Printed and sold by John Foster over* | *against the Sign of the Dove. 1676.* [Title within double ruled border].

[174]

[6], 51, [8]; [4], 26 p., 4to. (18.5 x 14 cm.). Holmes: *Increase Mather* 16A, Sabin 46640, Church 642. CSmH, DLC (imp.), Glasgow U., MB (imp.), MH, MHi, MWA, MWiW-C, NHi, NN, NNP, PPL, RPJCB, ViU (2).

Both the *History* and *Exhortation* were issued separately as well as together.

. . . . .

A brief | history | of the | war | with the | Indians | in | New-England. | From June 24. 1675. (when the first Englishman was murder- | ed by the Indians) to August 12. 1676. when Philip, | alias Metacomet, the principal author and | beginner of the war, was slain. | Wherein the grounds, begin- ning, and progress of the war, is summarily | expressed. Together with a serious Exhortation to the | inhabitants of that land. | [rule] | By Increase Mather, Teacher of a church of | Christ, in Boston in New-England. | [rule] | [7 lines quoted] | [rule] | *London, Printed for Richard Chiswell, at the* *Rose and Crown in St. Pauls* | *Church-Yard, according to the original copy* *printed* | *in New-England. 1676.* | [Title within ruled border]   [175]

[8], 51, [1], 8 p., 4to. (21.3 x 15.8 cm.). Holmes *Increase Mather* 16B, Sabin 46641, Church 643. Copies in most large libraries. List in Mather.

This is the third of 11 quarto King Philip's War tracts.

A | new and further narrative | of the state of | New-England, | being, | a continued account of the bloudy | Indian-War, | from March till August, 1676. | Giving a perfect relation of the several devasta- | tions, engage- ments, and transactions there; as also the | great successes lately obtained against the barbarous In- | dians, the reducing of King Philip, and the killing of | one of the queens, &c. | Together with a catalogue of the losses in the whole, sustain- | ed on either side, since the said war began, as near as can be collected. | [rule] | Licensed October 13. Roger L'Estrange. | [rule, royal arms, rule] | *London, Printed by J.B. for Dorman Newman at the* *Kings Arms* | *in the Poultry, 1676.*   [176]

[2], 14 p., folio. (28.5 x 17 cm.). Sabin 52445, Church 646, old John Carter Brown cat. 1154. CSmH, CtSoP, DLC, ICN, MB, MH (no royal arms on title), MiU-C, NjP, NN (2 copies each with a different coat of arms on title), RPJCB.

There are three issues of the title page, one with no royal arms on title (MH), and others with different cuts used for the royal arms (NN has both).

This is the third of the five folio King Philip's War tracts.

News from | New-England, | being | a true and last account of the present bloody wars | carried on betwixt the infidels, natives, and the | English Christians, and converted Indians of | New-England, declaring the many dreadful | battles fought betwixt them: as also the many | towns and villages burnt by the merciless hea- | thens. And also the true number of all the Chri- | stians slain since the beginning of that war, as it | was sent over by a Factor of New-England to a | Merchant in London. | [rule] | Licensed by Roger L'Estrange. | [rule] | *London,* | *Printed for J. Coniers at the Sign of the Black-Raven* | *in Duck-Lane, 1676.* [177]

[2], 6 p., 4to. (17 x 13 cm.). Sabin 55060-55061, Church 647, old John Carter Brown cat. 1151. BM (2d ed), CSmH (1st ed), ICN (1st ed), NN (1st ed), RPJCB (1st and 2d eds).

The second edition differs from the first only in that the license on title reads: *Licensed Aug. 1. Roger L'Estrange;* and a new paragraph has been added at end of last page, beginning: *There has been a treaty.* For reprints, see Sabin 55062-55063.

This is the fourth of 11 quarto King Philip's War tracts.

[PENN, WILLIAM]

The description of the Province of West-Jersey, in America: as also proposals to such who desire to have any propriety therein. *[n.p., ca. 1676].*
[178]

1 leaf, folio. Sabin 59692.

[TOMPSON, BENJAMIN]

New Englands crisis. | Or a brief | narrative, | of New-Englands lamentable | estate at present, compar'd with the for- | mer (but few) years of | prosperity. | Occasioned by many unheard of cruel- | tyes practised upon the persons and estates | of its united colonyes, without respect of | sex, age or quality of persons, by the | barbarous heathen thereof. | Poetically described. | By a well wisher to his | countrey. | *Boston,* | *Printed and sold by John Foster, over against* | *the Sign of the Dove. 1676.* [179]

31 p., 8vo. Sabin 96155, Evans 225. CSmH, MBAt (lacking title).

For reprints, see Sabin.

Though an 8 vo., this is included as the fifth of 11 quarto King Philip's War tracts, since the following tract supplements it. It is signed on p. 29:

B. *Tompson.* All of his poems are reprinted in H. J. Hall's *Benjamin Thompson . . . first native-born poet of America,* 1924.

. . . . .

New Englands tears for her present miseries: or, A late and true relation of the calamities of New-England since April last past. With an account of the battel between the English and Indians upon Seaconk Plain: and of the Indians burning and destroying of Marlbury, Rehoboth, Chelmsford, Sudbury, and Providence. With the death of Antononies the Grand Indian Sachem; And a relation of a fortification begun by women upon Boston Neck. Together with an elegy on the death of John Winthrop Esq; late Governour of Connecticott, and Fellow of the Royal Society. Written by an inhabitant of Boston in New England to his friend in London. With allowance. *London Printed for N.S. 1676.*   [180]

[2], 14 p., 4to. Sabin 96156. RPJCB.

This is the sixth of 11 quarto King Philip's War tracts.

A | true account | of the most | considerable occurrences | that have hapned in the | Warre | between the | English and the Indians | in | New-England, | from the fifth of May, 1676, to the fourth | of August last; as also of the successes it hath | pleased God to give the English against them: | as it hath been communicated by letters to a friend in London. | [rule] The most exact account yet printed. | [rule] | [six lines quoted] | [rule] Licensed, October 11. 1676. | Roger L'Estrange. | [rule] | *London,* | *Printed for Benjamin Billingsley at the Printing-Press in Cornhill, 1676.*   [181]

[2], 10 (misnumbered 6) p., folio. (28.5 x 17 cm.). Sabin 97085, Church 648, old John Carter Brown cat. 1155. BM, CSmH, CtSoP, DLC, ICN, MB, MH, MiU-C, NjP, NN, RPJCB.

This is the fourth of the five folio King Philip's War tracts.

WHEELER, THOMAS

A thankfull | remembrance | of Gods mercy | to several persons at Quabaug or | Brookfield: | partly in a collection of providences about them, | and gracious appearances for them: and partly in a | sermon preached by Mr. Edward Bulkley, | Pastor of the Church of Christ at Concord, upon a | day of thanksgiving, kept by divers for their wonder- | full deliverance there. | Published by Capt. Thomas VVheeler. | . . . | *Cambridge,* | *Printed and sold by Samuel Green 1676.*   [182]

[6], 14 (misnumbered 10), 32 p., 4to. Sabin 103200, Evans 226. CtY, DLC (imp.), MHi, MWA (imp.), NN, RPJCB.

This is the eighth of 11 quarto King Philip's War tracts. It tells the thrilling story of the siege and defense of Brookfield, Mass., July 28-Aug. 21, 1675, and of the relief of the garrison and defeat of the Indians by a body of troops from Boston under the command of Major Simon Willard. For reprints, see Sabin. See also Nathan Fiske's *Remarkable providences,* 1776.

FENWICK, JOHN

The true state of the case between John Fenwick, Esq. and John Edridg and Edmund Warner, concerning Mr. Fenwick's Ten Parts of his land in New West Jersey, in America. *[London] 1677.*   [183]

9 p., 12mo. PHi.

Reprinted, 1765.

HUBBARD, WILLIAM

A | narrative | of the troubles with the | Indians | in New-England, from the first planting thereof in the | year 1607. to this present year 1677. But chiefly of the late | troubles in the two last years, 1675. and 1676. | To which is added a discourse about the warre with the | Pequods | in the year 1637. | [rule] | By W. Hubbard, Minister of Ipswich. | [rule, 6 lines quoted, rule, 6 lines quoted, rule] | Published by authority. | [rule] | *Boston;* | *Printed by John Foster, in the year 1677.* | [Title within double ruled border].   [184]

[14], 132, [8], 7-12, 88 p., map, 4to. (19.7 x 14.3 cm.). Sabin 33445, Church 650, Evans 231. BM, CSmH, CtY, ICN, MB, MH, MHi, MiU-C, MWA, MWiW-C, NHi, NIC, NN, PHi, PP, PPL, RPJCB, ViU, etc. Randolph G Adams (see below) locates 51 copies of which 23 are perfect.

The title of the famous "White Hills" folded map begins: *A map of* | *New-England.* | *Being the first that ever was here cut* . . . and was engraved by John Foster, the printer. For a detailed study of the first American and English editions of the tract, their issues and their maps, see Randolph G. Adam's paper: *William Hubbard's "Narrative," 1677,* in the Bibliographical Society of America *Papers,* vol. 33, 1939, p. 25-39.

This is the ninth of 11 quarto King Philip's War tracts and the most famous of them all.

.   .   .   .   .

The | present state | of | New-England. | Being a | narrative | of the troubles with the | Indians | in | New-England, from the first planting | thereof in the year 1607, to this present year 1677: | but chiefly of the late troubles in the two last | years 1675, and 1676. | To which is added a discourse about the war | with the Pequods in the year 1637. | [rule] | By W. Hubbard Minister of Ipswich. | [rule] | [Three lines quoted] | [rule] | *London:* | *Printed for Tho. Parkhurst at the Bible and Three Crowns in* *Cheapside,* | *near Mercers-Chappel, and at the Bible on London-Bridg.* *1677.* | [Title within double ruled border].   [185]

[14], 131, [13], 88 p., map, 4to. (19.4 x 14.6 cm.). Sabin 33446, Church 651. Copies in most large libraries. Randolph G. Adams (see below) locates 50 copies of which 38 are perfect.

The title of the "Wine Hills" folded map begins: *A map of* | *New-Eng-*

land . . . For a detailed study of text and map, see paper by Randolph G. Adams cited under first edition.

MATHER, INCREASE

A relation | of the troubles which have hapned in | New-England, | by reason of the Indians there. | From the year 1614. to the year 1675. | [rule] | Wherein the frequent conspiracyes of the Indians to cutt off the | English, and the wonderfull providence of God, in disappointing | their devices, is declared. | Together with an historical discourse concerning the | prevalency of prayer; shewing that New Englands | late deliverance from the rage of the heathen is an eminent | answer to prayer. | [rule] | By Increase Mather | Teacher of a Church in Boston in New-England. | [rule] | [six lines quoted] | [rule] | [three lines quoted] | [double rule] | Boston, | Printed and sold by John Foster. 1677. | [Title within double ruled border] [Variant title:] A relation | of the troubles which have hapned in | New-England, | by reason of the Indians there. | From the year 1614. to the year 1675. | Wherein the frequent conspiracyes of the Indians to cutt off the | English, and the wonderfull providence of God, in | disappointing their devices, is declared. | Together with an historical discourse concerning the prevalency of | prayer | shewing that New Englands late deliverance from the rage of the | heathen is an eminent answer to prayer. | [rule] | By Increase Mather | Teacher of a Church in Boston in New-England. | [rule, 6 lines quoted, rule, 3 lines quoted, rule] | *Boston;* | *Printed and sold by John Foster. 1677.* | [Title within double ruled border].   [186]

[6], 76; An historical discourse, [6], 19 p., 4to. (18.5 x 14 cm.). Sabin 46726-46727, Church 654, Holmes: Increase Mather 110 A. The *Historical discourse*, bound with but not a part of the *Relation*, Sabin 46692. Evans 238. Bodleian, CSmH (2d state of title), DLC (2d), Glasgow U. (1st state of title), ICN, MB (1st), MHi (1st), MWiW-C (2d), NN (2d), RPJCB (imp.), ViU. (4 copies, one 1st, three 2d).

Includes earliest use of Major John Mason's narrative of the Pequot War later published in 1736, which see. The *Relation*, edited by Samuel G. Drake, was reprinted in 1864.

This is the tenth of 11 quarto King Philip's War tracts.

More nevvs | from Virginia, | being | a true and full relation | of all occurrences in that countrey, | since the death of Nath. Bacon | with | an account | of thirteen persons that have been | tryed and executed for their rebel- | lion there. | *[London:] Printed for W. Harris in the year 1677.*
                                                                                          [187]
[2], 1-3, 6-7 p., 4to. Sabin 100488. L.C. Harper (1935).

See *Strange news from Virginia.*

Strange news | from | Virginia; | being a full and true | account | of the | life and death | of | Nathanael Bacon Esquire, | who was the only cause and original of all the late | troubles in that country. | With a full relation of all the accidents which have | happened in the late war there between the | Christians and Indians. | [rule] | *London,* | *Printed for William Harris, next door to the Turn-* | *Stile without Moor-gate. 1677.* [188]

8 p., 4 to. (19 x 14.5 cm.). Church 657A, Sabin 92716. CSmH, MH, MiU-C, NN, RPJCB.

Sketch of Bacon's life, defending his sobriety, but gives facts of his rebellion from Governor Berkeley's point of view.

The | Warr | in | New-England | visibly ended. | King Philip that barbarous Indian now be- | headed, and most of his bloudy adherents sub- mitted to | mercy, the rest fled far up into the countrey, which | hath given the inhabitants encouragement to prepare for their | settlement. | Being a true and perfect account brought in by Caleb More | Master of a vessel newly arrived from Rhode-Island. | And published for general satisfaction. | [rule] | Licensed November 4. Roger L'Estrange. | [rule, royal arms, rule] | *London, Printed by J.B. for Dorman Newman at the Kings-arms* | *in the Poultry, 1677.* [189]

[2], 2 p., folio. (27 x 17.5 cm.). Sabin 101454, Church 652, old John Carter Brown cat. 1170. BM, CSmH, ICN, MiU-C, NjP, NN, RPJCB.

There are two variant imprints, those at ICN, MiU-C and RPJCB read- ing: *London, Printed by J.B. for Francis Smith at the Elephant and Castle in Cornhill. 1677.*

The tract is signed *R.H.* and is supposed to be by Richard Hutchinson.

This is the fifth of the five folio King Philip's War tracts.

King Philip's war club is exhibited in the Indian Museum, Wayside Museums, Harvard, Mass.

BRADSTREET, SIMON, AND OTHERS

An advertisement. Whereas, the lands of Narragansett, and Niantick Countryes, and parts adjacent . . . Dated, Boston, July 30, 1678, and signed by Simon Bradstreet, John Saffin and Elisha Hutchinson. *[Boston? 1678].* [190]

Broadside. Title from W.C. Ford's *Massachusetts Broadsides,* 64. Public Record Office, London.

A very early piece of New England promotion literature.

STODDARD, ANTHONY, AND OTHERS

Report of the Trustees, appointed to receive contributions for the ransom of the captives taken by the Indians at Hatfield, Sept. 19. 1677. *[Boston: Printed by John Foster. August, 1678].* [191]

Broadside, folio. Title from Evans 257 who fails to locate a copy, but probably same as:

. . . . .

[Colony seal] | At a | Council | Held at Boston the 22d. of August 1678.
[Boston: Printed by John Foster, 1678].   [192]

Broadside. Title from W.C. Ford's *Massachusetts Broadsides*, 68. MHi.

An accounting for money raised for the redemption and provision of
captives taken by the Indians at Hatfield, September 19, 1677, and carried
to Canada.

SELLER, JOHN

A description of New-England. | Published by John Seller. | [Caption
title] *[London, 1680?].*   [193]

4 p., folded map, folio. (46 x 28 cm.). Sabin 79026, Phillips Atlases,
Stokes II:157. MH (text and map), map (1st state) DLC, (2d state, in
Seller's *Atlas Maritimus, or Sea-Atlas*, London, 1765) DLC, MB, RPJCB,
etc.

Important folded map: *A mapp | of New England | by | John Seller
Hydrographer | to the King | And are to be sold at his | shop at the
Hermitage in Wapping | and by Iohn Hills | in Exchange Alley in Cornhill
| London | (53.5 x 44 cm.).* Includes territory from Hudson River to Cape
Cod and from Long Island to Casco Bay. First state of map (DLC) does not
have dedication and coat of arms filled in. Second state with both complete,
reproduced in Stokes II, pl. C52.

An | abstract, | or | abbreviation | of some few of the | many (later and
former) | testimonys | from the | inhabitants | of | New-Jersey, | and other
| eminent persons. | Who have wrote particularly concerning | that place. |
[double rule] | London, Printed by Thomas Milbourn, in the year, 1681.
[Title within double ruled border].   [194]

32 p., 4to. (21 x 15.5 cm.). Church 669, Baer 97. BM, CSmH, Garrett,
RPJCB, A.S.W. Rosenbach.

One of the Scottish Proprietors' Tracts.

PENN, WILLIAM

Some | account | of the | Province | of | Pennsilvania | in | America;
lately granted under the great seal | of | England | to | William Penn, &c. |
Together with priviledges and powers neces- | sary to the well-governing
thereof. | Made publick for the information of such as are or may be | dis-
posed to transport themselves or servants | into those parts. | [rule] | London:
Printed, and sold by Benjamin Clark | Bookseller in George-Yard Lombard-
street, 1681.   [195]

[2], 10 p., folio (31 x 19.5 cm.). Church 671, Sabin 59733. BM, CSmH,
ICN, MH, MiU-C, MWiW-C, NN, PHi, PP, RPJCB, ViU.

Penn's first account of his colony. Same, translated as:

• • • • •

Een Kort Bericht | van de Provintie ofte Landschap | Penn-Sylvania |
genaemt, leggende in | America; | . . . | *Tot Rotterdam,* | *Gedrukt by Pieter
van Wynbrugge, Boek-Drukker in de* | *Leeuwe-straat, in de Wereld Vol-
Druk. Anno 1681.*   [196]

24 p., 4to. Sabin 59710. First Dutch translation. Same, translated as:

• • • • •

Eine | Nachricht | wegen der Landschaft | Pennsilvania | in | America:
| . . . | *In Amsterdam, gedruckt bey Christoff Cunraden, im Jahr 1681.*
                                                                                                 [197]

31 p., 4to. Sabin 59719. PHi. First German account of Pennsylvania.
Reprinted in *Leipzig, 1683.*

• • • • •

A brief account of the | Province of Pennsylvania, | lately granted by
the | King, | under the Great | Seal of England, | to | William Penn | and
his | heirs and assigns. | [Caption title] [Colophon:] *London,* | *Printed for
Benjamin Clark in George-yard in Lombard-* | *street. 1681.*   [198]

8 p., folded map, folio. (30.5 x 18.5 cm.). Church 670. CSmH (text
only), DLC (map only), MH, PHi.

First edition. On p. 8: "There is likewise printed a Map of Pennsylvania,
together with a description at the end of it; and some proposals." Though
we have not found the description and proposals, DLC has the map:

A map of | some of the south and east bounds | of Pennsylvania | in
America. | being partly inhabited. | *Sold by John Thornton at the Signe
of England* | *Scotland and Ireland in the Minories, and by* | *John Seller at
his shop in Popeshead* | *Alley in Cornhill London.* | *[ca. 1680]* (52.5 x
43.5 cm.). For his *Present state of West Jersey,* 1681, see Baer 98.

• • • • •

Kurtze Nachricht | von der Americanischen Landschafft Pennsilvania. |
[Caption title] [1681?].   [199]

Title from facsimile in *Pennsylvania-German Society Proceedings,* VII,
1896, p. 216 from a copy at PHi. There were also Dutch and French
editions of *A brief account,* according to Sachse.

A[SH], T[HOMAS]

Carolina; | or a | description | of the present state of that | country, | and
| the natural excellencies thereof; viz. The | healthfulness of the air,
pleasantness of the place, | advantage and usefulness of those rich commo- |
dities there plentifully abounding, which much | encrease and flourish by
the industry of the plan | -ters that daily enlarge that colony. | Published
by T. A. Gent. | Clerk on board His Majesties Ship the Richmond, which
was | sent out in the year 1680, with particular instructions to | enquire

into the state of that country, by His Majesties | special command, and return'd this present year, 1682. | *London, Printed for W.C., and to be sold by Mrs. Grover in Pelican | Court in Little Britain, 1682.*   [200]

[2], 40 p., 4to. (23 x 15 cm.). Title from Sabin 2172, Church 673. CSmH, DLC, MB, MH, MiU, MiU-C, MWiW-C, N, NjP, PP, PPM, RPJCB, ViU.

Promotion literature of the Lords Proprietors of Carolina.
There are several modern reprints.

A brief account of the Province of East-Jersey in America. Published by the present proprietors, for information of all such persons who are or may be inclined to setle themselves, families, and servants in that country. *London. Printed for Benjamin Clark, in George-Yard in Lombard-Street, Bookseller. M.DCLXXXII.*   [201]

[2], 6 p., 4to. Old John Carter Brown cat. 1237, Sabin 53078. DLC, RPJCB.

List of proprietors, which appears on title of second issue below, is on separate slip pasted at end of text.

A brief | account | of the | Province | of | East-Jersey | in | America. | Published | by the present proprietors thereof, | viz, | [first column:] William Penn, | Robert West, | Thomas Rudyard, | Samuel Groome, | Thomas Hart, | Richard Mew, | [two brackets] | [second column:] Thomas Wilcox, | Ambrose Rigg, | John Heywood, | Hugh Hartshorne, | Clement Plumsted, | Thomas Cooper, | [two brackets] | [third column:] Who intend to | take in twelve | more to make | the number of | proprietors | twenty four. | [end of third column] | For information of all such persons who are | or may be inclined to setle themselves, fa- | milies, and servants in that country. | [rule] | *London,* | *Printed for Benjamin Clark in George-Yard in Lombard-* | *street, Bookseller, MDCLXXXII.* [Title within double ruled border].   [202]

[2], 6 p., 4to. (20 x 15 cm.). Church 674 A. BM, CSmH, NN, RPJCB.
Reprinted in Smith's History of New Jersey.
One of the Scottish Proprietors' Tracts.

CAROLINA, LORDS PROPRIETORS OF

A true | description | of | Carolina. | [Caption title] [Colophon:] *London, Printed for Joel Gascoin at the Plat near Wapping old Stairs, and R[obert Greene] | at the Rose and Crown in Budg-Row. | [1682].*   [203]

[4] p., folded map, 4to. (19.5 x 15 cm.). Sabin 97115. DLC (map), RPJCB (text).

Map: To the | Right Honorable | Will. Earle of Craven, | Pallatine and the rest of ye | true and absolute Lords and | Proprietors, of the Province of | Carolina. | This map is humbly dedicated | by Ioel Gascoyne. | [rule] | A new map | of the Country of | Carolina. | With it's rivers, harbors, planta- | tions, and other accomodations. | don from the latest surveighs | and best information. by order | of the Lords Proprietors. | [rule] | Sold by Ioel Gascoyne at the Signe of | the Plat nere Wapping old Stayres. | And by Robert Greene at the Rose and | Crowne in ye middle of Budge Row. | London. | [1682] (58 x 49 cm.). Coastline from *St. Augustin* to *C*[ape] *Henry* and west to the *Apalatian Mountaines.* Inset map: *A particular map | for the going into | Ashly and Cooper | River,* showing *Charles Towne, Old Charles towne* and numerous plantations.

Described from photostat copy at NHi, NN.

Has same advertisement at end, for Nathan Sumers's stump pulling machine, as in: *The present state of Carolina,* 1682.

F., R.

The | present state | of | Carolina | with | advice to the setlers. | [rule] By R.F. | [rule, orn., rule] | *London,* | *Printed by John Bringhurst, at the Sign of the | Book in Grace-Church-Street, 1682.* | [Title within border of type ornaments].   [204]

36 p., 4to. (21 x 15 cm.). Sabin 23586 and 87919. CSmH, NHi, NN.

Mass. Hist. Soc. Photostat Americana, no. 143, 1925.

Promotion literature of the Lords Proprietors of [South] Carolina.

Has same advertisement at end, for Nathan Sumers's stump pulling machine, as in: *A true description of Carolina,* [1682].

Free Society of Traders in Pennsylvania

The | articles, | settlement and offices | of the Free | Society | of | Traders | in | Pennsilvania: | agreed upon by divers | merchants | and others for the better | improvement and government | of | trade | in that | Province. | [rule] | *London,* | *Printed for Benjamin Clark in George-Yard in Lombard-street,* | *Printer to the Society of Pennsilvania, MDCLXXXII.* | [Title within double ruled border].   [205]

[5], 1-[10] p., folio (31 x 20 cm.). Sabin 59897. MWiW-C, N, NHi, NN, PHi, ViU.

Preface signed by Nicholas More, James Claypoole and Philip Ford. See also William Penn: *A letter . . . to the committee of the Free Society of Traders,* 1683.

[Penn, William]

A brief account of the Province of Pennsilvania lately granted by the King, under the Great Seal of England, to William Penn, and his heirs and assigns. *London: . . . Benjamin Clark . . . 1682.*   [206]

8 p., 4to. Title from Sabin 59680. DLC.

. . . . .

A brief account of the Province of Pennsilvania in America, lately |
granted under the Great Seal of England to William Penn, &c. *[n.p., 1682?]*
                                                                    [207]
[2] p., folio (31 x 19.5 cm.). Sabin 59681. MH, NHi.

. . . . . .

The frame of the | government | of the | Province of Pennsilvania | in |
America: | together with certain | laws | agreed upon in England | by the |
Governour | and | divers free-men of the aforesaid | Province. | To be further
explained and confirmed there by the first | Provincial Council and General
Assembly that shall | be held, if they see meet. | [rule] | *[London:] Printed
[by William Bradford (later of Philadelphia and New York) at the press of
his master, Andrew Sowle, at the Crooked-Billet in Holloway-Lane in
Shoreditch] in the year MDCLXXXII.*   [208]
[4], 11 p., folio. (30.1 x 18.1 cm.). Sabin 59696, Church 676. BM,
CSmH, DLC, MH, NHi, PHi (William Penn's own copy with his bookplate), RPJCB.

. . . . . .

Plantation work | the | work | of this | generation. | Written in true-love
| to all such as are weightily inclined | to transplant themselves and fami- |
lies to any of the English plantati- | ons in | America. | The | most material
doubts and objections against it | being removed, they may more cheerfully
pro- | ceed to the glory and renown of the God of | the whole earth, who in
all undertakings is to | be looked unto, praised and feared for ever. | [rule] |
[one line quoted] | [rule] | *London, Printed for Benjamin Clark in George-
Yard in | Lombard-street, 1682.*   [209]
[2], 18 p., 4to. (20 cm.). Sabin 63318. DLC, PHi, PPF, RPJCB.

Title from facsimile in *Pennsylvania-German Society Proceedings,* VII,
1896, p. 217.

For proof of authorship, see *William Penn in America,* 1888, p. 55-56.

Since it is signed *W.L.,* Sabin attributed it to William Loddington and
DLC adopts this attribution. It has also been attributed to George Fox. However, it contains "An abstract of some passages out of divers letters from America relating to Pennsylvania" and most of these letters were addressed to William Penn. Whether or not Penn wrote the tract, it was obviously written
to promote his lands.

Proposals by the proprietors of East-Jersey in America; for the building of
a town on Ambo-Point, and for the disposition of lands in that Province. And
also for encouragement of artificers and labourers that shall transport themselves thither out of England, Scotland and Ireland. *London. Printed for
Benjamin Clark, in George-Yard in Lombard Street. MDCLXXXII.*   [210]
[2], 6 p., 4to. Old John Carter Brown cat. 1238. RPJCB.

The beginnings of Perth Amboy, N.J.
One of the Scottish Proprietors' Tracts.

ROWLANDSON, MARY

The soveraignty & goodness of God, together, with the faithfulness of his promises displayed; being a narrative of the captivity and restauration of Mrs. Mary Rowlandson. Commended by her, to all that desire to know the Lord's doings to, and dealings with her. Especially to her dear children and relations. *Boston in New-England Printed [by Samuel Green Jr.] for John Ratcliffe, & John Griffin. 1682.* | [Title within border of type ornaments] [Second title:] The | possibility of God's for- | saking a people, | that have been visibly near & dear to him; | together, | with the misery of a people thus forsaken, | set forth in a | sermon, | preached at Weathersfield, Nov. 21. 1678. | Being a day of fast and hu- | miliation. | By Mr. Joseph Rowlandson Pastor of the | Church of Christ there. Being | also his last sermon. | [4 lines quoted] | *Boston in New-England* | *Printed [by Samuel Green Jr.]* *for John Ratcliffe & John Griffin.* | *1682.* | [Title within border of type ornaments]. [211]

vi, 73; [6], 22 p., small 4to. Evans 330-331, Sabin 73577 (Sermon only). Four leaves only of the Narrative are known, two each at CtHi and MHi; Sermon at MB.

First edition of the first published New England Indian captivity, of which no copy is known to exist, except for four leaves of an unidentified seventeenth century edition, two at CtHi and two at MHi, which are doubtless of this edition. In both cases these sheets had been used as end papers for Samuel Willard's *Covenant-keeping,* Boston, 1682. MB has a copy of the accompanying sermon. Title in part from Evans 331, based on that of the 2d ed. and imprint from the Sermon of the 1st ed.

Advertised as follows in the 1st American edition of Bunyan's *Pilgrim's Progress. Boston: Samuel Green [Jr.], 1681.* CSmH, MB (imp.), MWA (imp.): "Before long, there will be published two Sermons . . . As also the particular circumstances of the Captivity, & Redemption of Mrs. Mary Rowlandson; and of her children. Being pathetically written, with her own Hand."

At the end of p. 22 of the second title (the sermon) is the following: "ERRATA. In the Preface to Mrs. Rowlandson's Narrative Page 1, Line 3, for *Thursday* read *Tuesday*." This note proves that the two titles were issued together, presumably with the Sermon last in the volume. Each title was probably also issued separately. Since no copy of the 1st. ed. of the Narrative containing the first page of the preface with the incorrect reading *Thursday* has survived, we cannot verify the presence of the erratum on that page, but since the correction was made in the second edition in which the reading is *Tuesday*, it is obvious that the above copy of the Sermon was originally issued with the lost 1st ed. of the Narrative. And since the 1st ed. of the Sermon has the Boston imprint and the border of type ornaments, it is reasonable to believe that the 1st ed. of the Narrative had the same imprint and border. The copy of the 2d ed. of the Narrative in MB is now bound with the 1st ed. of the Sermon and they are both the Prince copies. Though it is possible that Samuel Green Sr. used a surplus stock of his son's 1st ed. of the Sermon with his own 2d ed. of the Narrative, it is not probable, for the two Prince copies of Narrative and Sermon were separately listed in the Prince Library catalog of 1870 and had separate call numbers, and furthermore, they were in a library binding put on them between 1870 and 1889 when Dr. Eames described them in Sabin 73577-73578 as being then bound together. It is therefore evident that these particular copies were probably issued as separates and were not originally bound together. The 1st ed. of the Sermon was reproduced in Mass. Hist. Soc. Photostat Americana, 2d ser., Dec., 1937, no. 48.

* * * * *

The | Soveraignty & Goodness | of | God, | Together, | With the Faithfulness of His Promises | Displayed; | Being a | Narrative | Of the Captivity and Restoration of | Mrs. Mary Rowlandson. | Commended by her, to all that desires to | know the Lords doings to, and | dealings with Her. | Especially to her dear Children and Relations, | [rule] | The second Addition [sic] Corrected and amended. | [rule] | Written by Her own Hand for Her private Use, and now | made Publick at the earnest Desire of some Friends, | and for the benefit of the Afflicted. | [rule, 3 lines quoted, rule] | *Cambridge,* | *Printed by Samuel Green [Sr.], 1682.* | [Title within heavy plain border] [Second title as in 1st ed. with imprint as above. Title within heavy plain border].   [212]

[6], 73; [6], 22 p., small 4to. Sabin 73578, Evans 332. MB (Narrative only).

Second edition, first issue with *Addition* in first title instead of *Edition.*

* * * * *

Second issue with *Edition* correctly used in first title and with the first half of the book reset. BM (Narrative only), CSmH (lacks first three leaves [title and preface]) of Narrative and right-hand half of title of Sermon. Sabin and Evans describe the Narrative only. The Narrative was reproduced in Mass. Hist. Soc. Photostat Americana, 2d ser., Dec., 1937, no. 47, from the John Cotton-Thomas Prince-MB copy.   [213]

In the Cambridge as well as the Boston editions, the Narrative and Sermon were probably issued together (as well as separately) for they have the same type, ornaments, borders and imprints. The erratum in the preface of the Narrative has been corrected to read *Tuesday* and so there is no errata note at the end of the Sermon. Also, the 1st English ed. of 1682 has the correction and lacks the errata note, showing that it was reprinted from a copy of the 2d. American ed. Also, the 1st English ed, reprints the Sermon as well as the Narrative, showing that the copy used by the English printer had the Narrative and Sermon issued together. Since signature A of both the Narrative and Sermon of the Cambridge edition, and the Sermon of the Boston edition, are complete without a general title page, it is probable that none was issued with the first two American editions. Therefore it is probable that both the Boston and Cambridge editions were originally issued without general title pages and that both the Narrative and Sermon were also issued separately in both editions.

. . . . . .

A true | history | of the | captivity & restoration | of | Mrs. Mary Rowlandson, | a minister's wife in New-England. | Wherein is set forth, the cruel and inhumane | usage she underwent amongst the heathens, for | eleven weeks time: and her deliverance from | them. | Written by her own hand, for her private vse: and now made | publick at the earnest desire of some friends, for the benefit | of the afflicted. | Whereunto is annexed, | a sermon of the possibility of God's forsaking a peo- | ple that have been near and dear to him. | Preached by Mr. Joseph Rowlandson, husband to the said Mrs. Rowlandson: | it being his last sermon. | *Printed first at New-England: And Re-printed at London, and sold | by Joseph Poole, at the Blue Bowl in the Long-Walk, by Christs- | Church Hospital. 1682.* | [Title within fleur-de-lis border]. [214]

[6], 46 p., 4to. Sabin 73579. CSmH, CtHWatk, CtY, F.C. Deering, ICN, Lancaster Town Library, MWiW-C, NN, PP, RPJCB, A.S.W. Rosenbach, T.W. Streeter, etc.

Mrs. Mary White Rowlandson, the wife of Rev. Joseph Rowlandson, pastor of the church at Lancaster, Massachusetts, was captured, with others, at the attack on that town, February 20, 1676, by the Wampanoag Indians and their allies led by King Philip. Her husband was in Boston at the time with two neighbors trying to secure military protection for the town. She and her youngest child were wounded and the child died soon after. She was with the Indians eleven weeks and five days when she was redeemed by John Hoar (ancestor of Senator Hoar) at Redemption Rock in Princeton, Massachusetts, May 2, 1676, for the value of twenty pounds. In her various "removes" she was taken as far west as the Connecticut River. Two of her other children, captured at the same time, were redeemed shortly after their mother. Her narrative gives the names of several other captives. Her narrative was the first story of Indian captivity published in New England and the first in North America with the exception of those in Florida in the fifteen hundreds. Her beautiful English oak chest, brought to America about 1638 by her father, John White, is owned by the Lancaster Town Library which also has the largest collection of the various editions of her narrative.

W., J.

A | letter | from | New-England | concerning their | customs, manners, | and | religion. | [rule] | Written upon occasion of a report about a | Quo

Warranto | brought against that | Government. | [double rule] | *London,* | *Printed for Randolph Taylor near Stationers Hall, 1682.*   [215]

[2], 9 p., folio (28.9 x 18.2 cm.). Sabin 52641, Church 674. Bodleian, CSmH, ICN, MWA, NN, RPJCB.

Reprinted with Edward Ward's *Trip to New-England,* in Club of Colonial Reprints Pub. 2, with introduction and notes by George Parker Winship, Providence, 1905.

Has to do with the Quo Warranto proceedings to annul the Massachusetts charter but of great importance for its gossiping, satirical picture of the knavery of the not-so-Puritans.

[WILSON, SAMUEL]

An | account | of the | Province | of | Carolina | in | America. | Together with | an abstract of the patent, | and several other necessary and useful par- | ticulars, to such as have thoughts of tran- | sporting themselves thither. | Published for their information. | [rule] | *London:* | *Printed by* | *G. Larkin for Francis Smith, at the Elephant* | *and Castle in Cornhil. 1682.* | [Title within double ruled border].   [216]

27 p., map, 4to. (21 x 15.5 cm.). Sabin 104685, Church 677, 678, old John Carter Brown cat. 1261. There are three issues: 1st. has pp. 10, 11, 14, 15, 25, 26 and 27 wrongly numbered; 2d. only 25, 26 and 27 are wrongly numbered; 3d. all pages correctly numbered. There are also errors in spelling in 1st issue corrected later. BM, CSmH (1st, 2d), CtHWatk, DLC, MB, MBAt, MH, MiU-C, NHi (2d), NjP (1st, 3d), NN (3d), PHi, PPL, RPJCB.

The map: *A new description of Carolina by order of the Lords Proprietors* is not in all copies. The author was secretary of the Proprietors.

.   .   .   .   .

Second edition identical with 3d issue of 1st ed. except that last three lines of title above the imprint read: *sporting themselves thither. Published for their* | *information.* | *The second edition corrected.* | And the word *elephant* in the imprint is spelled *elephan.* BM, CSmH, NHi, NN.   [217]

Advertisement | concerning | East-New-Jersey | [Caption title] [At end:] *Edinburgh, Printed by John Reid, Anno Dom. 1683.*   [217A]

Broadside, folio (29.5 x 18 cm.). RPJCB.

One of the Scottish Proprietors' Tracts.

A | brief account of the | Province | of | East: New: Jarsey | in America: | published by the | Scots Proprietors | having interest there. | For the information of such, as may have a desire to transport them- | selves, or their families thither. | Wherein | the nature and advantage of, and interest in

a forraign plantation | to this country is demonstrated. | [type orn.] | [rule] |
Edinburgh, | *Printed by John Reid, Anno Dom. 1683.*   [218]
  15 p., 4to. (18 x 14.5 cm.). Church 683, Sabin 53079, Baer 107. BM,
CSmH, ICN, NN, RPJCB.
  Reprinted in *Historical Magazine,* 2d ser., vol. 1, from which 25 separates
were printed.
  One of the Scottish Proprietors' Tracts.

[CRAFFORD, JOHN]

  A new and most | exact account | of the fertile and famous colony of |
Carolina (On the continent of America) | whose latitude is from 36 Deg.
of North Latitude, to 29 Deg. | Together with a | maritine [sic] account of
its rivers, barrs, soundings and harbours; | also of the natives, their religion,
traffick and commodities. | Likewise the advantages accrewing to all adven-
turers by the cu- | stoms of the countrey; Being the most healthful and
fertile | of His Majesties territories on the said continent of | America. | As
also an account of the islands of Bermudas, the harbours, situa- | tion, people,
commodities, &c, belonging to the said islands; | the whole being a com-
pendious account of a voyage made (by | an ingenious person) for a full
discovery of the above-said places. | Begun in October 82, and finished this
present year, 1683. | *Dublin, Printed for Nathan Tarrant at the Kings-Arms
in Corn-Market. 1683.*   [219]
  7 p., 4to. Sabin 17334.
  At end of last page: "Taken by John Crafford, who was Super cargo of
the good Ship the James of Erwin, burthen about 50 Tuns."

FORD, PHILIP

  A vindication of William Penn, | Proprietary of Pensilvania, from the
late aspersions | spread abroad on purpose to defame him. With | an abstract
of several of his letters since his | departure from England. | [Caption title]
[Signed at end:] Philip Ford, London, 12th, 12th month, 1682-3. | *[London,
1683].*   [220]
  Title from facsimile in *Pennsylvania-German Society Proceedings,* VII,
1896, p. 218, from a copy at PHi. Baer 106B. Garrett, PHi.

•   •   •   •   •

  (I) | [rule] | A vindication of William Penn, Proprietary of Pennsilva- |
nia, from the late aspersions spread abroad on purpose to | defame him. |
[Caption title] [colophon:] *London. Printed for Benjamin Clark in George-
Yard in Lombard-street, 1683.*   [221]
  2 p., folio. (32 x 20 cm.). Sabin 25067, Church 679, Baer 106A. BM,
CSmH, DLC, Friends Libraries in London, Garrett, MH.
  "This leaf was published to contradict the reports, which were circulated
after Penn had sailed for America, that he had died on reaching here, and

that he had closed his career professing faith in the Church of Rome. It contains abstracts of the first letters written by Penn from America [in November and December, 1682]"—Note by Cole in Church catalog.

HENNEPIN, LOUIS

Description | de la | Louisiane, | nouvellement decouverte | au Sud' Oüest de la Nouvelle France, | par ordre du Roy. | Avec la Carte du Pays: Les Mocurs | & la Maniere de vivre | des Sauvages. | Dediée a Sa Majesté | Par le R. P. Louis Hennepin | Missionnaire Recollet & | Notaire Apostolique. | [Monogram of Amable Auroy] | *A Paris,* | *Chez la Veuve Sebastien Huré,* | *ruë* | *Saint Jacques, à l'Image S. Jerôme,* | *près S. Severin.* | M. DC. LXXXIII. | *Avec Privilege dv Roy.*   [222]

[2], [8], [2], 312, 107 p., folded map, 12 mo. Copies in most large libraries.

Map: Carte | de la | Nouuelle France | et de la | Louisiane | Nouuelle-ment decouuerte | dediée | Au Roy | l'An 1683. | Par le Reuerend Pere | Louis Hennepin | Missionaire Recollect | et Notaire Apostolique. | inue. et fecit N. Guerard. Roussel scripsit. (48.2 x 29.2 cm.).

Title from Victor Hugo Paltsits: *Bibliography of the works of Father Louis Hennepin.* Chicago, 1903, which see for later editions and translations.

Includes an account of Hennepin's four months captivity among the Sioux near the present city of Minneapolis in 1680.

[LOCKHART, GEORGE]

A further account of | East-New-Jersey | by a | letter | write [sic] to one of the | proprietors | thereof, by a countrey-man, who has a great plantation there. | Together | with the description of the said province, as it is in | Ogilbies Atlas, Printed | in the year, 1671. | *Edinburgh, Printed by John Reid, Anno Dom. 1683.*   [223]

7 p., 4to. RPJCB.

For description, see John Carter Brown Library Annual Report for 1941.

Reproduced in Massachusetts Historical Society photostat series, 133, 1941. Photo copy also in NjP.

The letter from George Lockhart to Robert Barkley, dated London, June 2, 1683, is on p. 3-4.

One of the Scottish Proprietors' Tracts.

PASKELL, THOMAS

(I) | [double rule] | An abstract of a | letter | from | Thomas Paskell | of | Pennsilvania | to his friend J. J. of Chippenham. | [Caption title] [Colophon:] *London, Printed by John Bringhurst, at the Sign of the Book* | *in Grace-Church-Street. 1683.*   [224]

2 p., folio (29.2 x 18.4 cm.). Sabin 58991, Church 684. BM, CSmH, ICN, RPJCB.

Signed at end: *Thomas Paskell* and dated: *Pensilvania, the last of January, 1682-3.* An interesting account of life in the new colony of Pennsylvania.

There were two Dutch editions, the second in 1684, according to J.F. Sachse.

PENN, WILLIAM

A | letter | from | William Penn | Proprietary and Governour of | Pennsylvania | in America, | to the | committee | of the | Free Society of Traders | of that Province, residing in London. | Containing | a general description of the said Province, its soil, air, water, seasons and produce, | both natural and artificial, and the good encrease thereof. | Of the natives or aborigines, their language, customs and manners, diet, houses or wig- | wams, liberality, easie way of living, physick, burial, religion, sacrifices and cantico, | festivals, government, and their order in council upon treaties for | land, &c. their justice upon evil doers. | Of the first planters, the Dutch, &c. and the present condition and settlement of the | said Province, and courts of justice, &c. | To which is added, an account of the City of | Philadelphia | newly laid out. | Its scituation between two navigable rivers, Delaware and Skulkill. | With a | portraiture or plat-form thereof, | wherein the purchasers lots are distinguished by certain numbers inserted, directing | to a catalogue of the said purchasers names | and the prosperous and advantagious settlements of the Society aforesaid, within | the said city and country, &c. | [rule] | *Printed and sold by Andrew Sowle, at the Crooked-Billet in Holloway-Lane in | Shoreditch, and at several stationers in London,* 1683. [Title within double ruled border]. [225]

10, [4], p., folded map, folio, (31 x 20 cm.). Church 685, 686, 687; Sabin 59712. BM (3, eds. unknown), CSmH (1st, 3d, 4th), DLC (1st, 2d), ICN (1st), MB (1st, 2d), MiU-C (1st), MWiW-C (3d), NHi (1st, 3d), NN (3d, 4th), PHC (1st), PHi (1st), PP (1st), PU (1st), RPJCB (1st), ViU (2d). Some copies lack the last 4 pages.

For identification of the four variants, see Church. Folded plan: *A portraiture of the city | of | Philadelphia | . . . appears in two states.*

The first description of Philadelphia.

Advertisement, | To all trades-men, husbandmen, servants and others who are willing to transport themselves unto | the Province of New-East-Jersey in America, a great part of which belongs to Scots-men, | proprietors thereof. [caption title] Whereas several noblemen, gentlemen, and others, who . . . are interested and concerned in the Province, do intend (God willing) to send several ships thither, in May, June, and July ensuing, 1684. from Leith, Montross, Aberdeen and Glasgow . . . *[Edinburgh?, 1684].* [226]

Broadside, folio. NN.
One of the Scottish Proprietors' Tracts.

[CAROLINA, LORDS PROPRIETORS OF]

Carolina | described more fully then heretofore. | Being an impartial | collection | made from the several relations of that place in | print, since its first planting (by the English,) and | before, under the denomination of Florida, from | diverse letters from those that have transpor- | ted themselves (from this Kingdom of Ireland.) | And the reasons of those that have been in | that country several years together. | [rule] | whereunto is added the charter, with the | fundamental constitutions | of that Province. | [rule] | With sundry necessary observations made thereon; use- | full to all that have a disposition to transport them- | selves to that place; with the account of what ship- | ing bound thither from this Kingdom, this present | Summer. 1684. | And the charges of transporting of persons and goods. | [rule] | *Dublin, Printed 1684.* | [Title within ruled border].   [227]

56 p. (paging irregular), 4to. (19.3 x 14.6 cm.). Sabin 10963, Church 688. CSmH, MWiW-C, NN.

MATHER, INCREASE

An | essay | for the recording of | illustrious | providences, | wherein an account is given of | many remarkable and very me- | morable events, which have hap- | pened in this last age; | especially in | New-England. | [rule] | By Increase Mather, | Teacher of a church at Boston in | New-England. | [rule] | [6 lines quoted] | [rule] | *Boston in New-England* | *Printed by Samuel Green for Joseph Browning,* | *and are to be sold at his shop at the corner of* | *the Prison Lane. 1684.* | [Title within ornamental border].   [228]

[22], 372, [8] p., 8vo. (13 x 9 cm.). Holmes *Increase Mather* 52A-D, Sabin 46678-46680, Church 690-691. BM (3d, 2 copies), Bodleian (2d, 3d.), C (3d), CSmH (2d, 3d, 4th), CtY (lacks title), DLC (1st, 3d), Glasgow U. (1st), ICN (3d), MB (1st, 2 copies, one lacking title), MBAt (2d?), MH (1st, 2 copies, 2d, imp., 3d), MHi (2d), MWA (3d, 2 copies, 1 imp.), MWiW-C (2d), NN (3d), RPJCB (3d), J. H. Scheide (2d, imp.), ViU (3d, 2 copies, 1 imp.).

The text of this first edition is the same in all copies but there are four title pages, two American and two English, both cancels and probably printed in London: 1st., as above; 2d. has title reset without border and with last line reading: *the Prison-Lane next the Town-House, 1684.;* 3d. reset with the imprint: *Printed at Boston in New-England, and are to |* *be sold by George Calvert at the Sign of the | Half-moon in Pauls Church-* *yard, London, 1684.,* title within double ruled border; 4th. title reset with last two lines reading: *be sold by Tho. Parkhurst at the Bible and Three |* *Crowns in Cheapside near Mercers Chappel. 1687.*

This collection of remarkable happenings is particularly interesting for its witchcraft and the first printing of Quentin Stockwell's own account of his captivity among the Wachusett Indians during King Philip's War, 1677-1678, p. 39-57. Reprinted in Richard Blome: *The present state of his Majesties isles and territories in America* . . . *London, 1687,* with a French translation, *Amsterdam, 1688* and *1715* and a German translation, *Leipzig, 1697,* for which see Sabin 5969-5971. Also three recent American editions of the separate Stockwell captivity and two modern reprints of Mather's *Essay* as: *Remarkable providences, London 1856* and *1890,* for which see Holmes.

PASTORIUS, FRANCIS DANIEL

Copia eines, von einem Sohn an seine Eltern aus America, abgelassenen Brieffes, | sub dato Philadelphia, den 7. Martii 1684. | Liebwerthester Herr Vatter und Frau Mutter! | [Caption title] *[n.p., 1684].*   [229]

Broadside. Title from facsimile in *Pennsylvania-German Society Proceedings,* IX, 1899, p. 133, of a copy in an unidentified library in Zurich, Switzerland.

.   .   .   .   .

I | [ornamental headband] | Sichere Nachricht auss America, wegen der Landschafft | Pennsylvania, von einem dorthin gereissten Teutschen, | de dato Philadelphia, den 7. Martii 1684. [Caption title] [Frankfort? 1684].

[229A]

Title from facsimile of first page in *Pennsylvania-German Society Proceedings,* IX, 1899, p. 132, of a copy in an unidentified library in Zurich, Switzerland. The number of pages is not given but the first page is numbered I and there is a catchword, showing that the letter occupies two or more pages. The letter is translated in the following pages 133-151. This interesting description of conditions in the new German colony in Pennsylvania is a report in the form of a letter to the Frankfort Land Company which had sent over many of the first German settlers. This letter and also that to Pastorius' parents, above, is also translated in J. F. Sachse's *Letters from Germantown, 1683-1684.* Lübeck and Philadelphia, 1903.

[PENN, WILLIAM]

Information and direction | to | such persons as are inclined | to | America, | more | especially those related to the Province | of | Pennsylvania. | [Caption title] *[London, ca. 1684].*   [230]

4 p., double column, folio (30.7 x 19.5 cm.). Title from Sabin 59707. NHi, PHi.

States terms for the sale of Penn's lands and describes the best type of house to be built on them.

. . . . .

Missive | van | William Penn, | Eygenaar en Gouverneur van | Pennsyl-
vania, | in America. | . . . | *Amsterdam,* | *Gedruckt voor Jacob Claus, Boekver-
kooper in de Prince-straat, 1684.*   [231]
23 p., plan of Philadelphia, 4to. Title from Sabin 59716, which gives full
title. DLC.
Dutch edition of the preceding title.
Same from Dutch into German as *Beschreibung . . . [Hamburg],* 1684.
[2], 32 p., 4to. Baer 108. Garrett, NN, PHi, RPJCB.

. . . . .

With variant Dutch title, same imprint and date.   [232]
28 p., plan of Philadelphia, 4to. Title from Baer 109. Sabin 59717 and
old John Carter Brown cat. 1293 give abbreviated title. CtY, Garrett, ICN,
NjP, NN, RPJCB.

A French translation of most of this letter appears, with six other papers on
Pennsylvania in:

. . . . .

Recüeil | de | diverses | pieces, | concernant | la | Pensylvanie. | *A la Haye,*
| *Chez Abraham Troyel,* | *Marchand Libraire, dans la Grand Sale* | *de la
Cour, M.DCLXXXIV.*   [233]
118 p., 12mo. (12.5 x 7.5 cm.). Sabin 60445, Church 692, old John
Carter Brown cat. 1294, Baer 110. BM (imperfect), CSmH, DLC, ICN,
N, RPJCB.
There was also a German edition.

[TRYON, THOMAS]

The country-man's companion: or, a new method of ordering horses &
sheep so as to preserve them both from diseases and causalties, . . . By Philo-
theos Physiologus, the author of the Way to Health, . . . *London, Printed
and sold by Andrew Sowle, at the Crooked-Billet in Holloway-Court in
Holloway-Lane, near Shoreditch. [1684?].*   [234]
[8], 173, [3] p., 8vo. Sabin 97285. BM, DLC, NN, RPJCB.
Sabin notes editions with the imprints: *Printed for T. Malthus at the Sun
in the Poultrey. 1684;* and: *Sold by R. Taylor, near Stationers Hall. 1693.*
P. 100 to the end was reprinted as: *The planter's speech,* below.

. . . . .

The planter's | speech | to his | neighbors & country-men | of | Pennsyl-
vania, | East & West-Jersey, | and to all such as have transported | themselves
into new-colonies for the | sake of a quiet retired life | to which is added, |
the complaints of our | supra-inferior-inhabitants. | *London:* | *Printed and
sold by Andrew Sowle* | *in Shoreditch, 1684.*   [235]

17, 14-73, [3] p., 8vo. (13.5 x 8 cm.). Sabin 97288, Church 693. CSmH.

Printed from the same setting of type as pages 100 and following of the previous title, with a new title page and with the signature marks and pagination changed. Title and introduction reprinted in Proud's *History of Pennsylvania*, vol. 1, 1797, p. 226-227.

[WERTMULLER, JORIS, AND CORNELIUS BOM]

Twee Missiven | geschreven uyt Pensilvania, | d'Eene door een Hollander, woonachtig in | Philadelfia, | d'Ander door een Switser, woonachtig in | German Town | dat is Hoogduytse Stadt. | Van den 16 en 26 Maert 1684. Nieuwe Stijl. | . . . | *Tot Rotterdam, by Pieter van Alphen. Anno 1684.* [236]

2 leaves, 4to. Sabin 60746. DLC (incomplete, lacking the letter from Philadelphia).

Two letters written from Pennsylvania, one by a Dutchman resident in Philadelphia, the other by a Swiss dwelling in Germantown. The letter from Germantown, dated March 16, 1684, is signed by Joris Wertmuller, and is reprinted in S.W. Pennypacker's *Settlement of Germantown*, 1894, p. 100-102, Same in *Pennsylvania-German Society Proceedings*, IX 1898, p. 152-159; and in his *Hendrick Pannebecker*, 1894, p. 27-31. DLC. The other letter, by Cornelius Bom, a cake baker, October 12, 1684, is also in *Hendrick Pannebecker*, p. 32-39. These are the first published letters by German settlers of Pennsylvania.

An | advertisement | concerning the Province of | East-New-Jersey | in | America. | [rule] | Published for the information of such as are desirous to be con- | cerned therein, or to transport themselves thereto. | [rule] | *Edinburgh,* | *Printed by John Reid, Anno Dom. 1685.* [237]

[2], 22 p., 4to. (18.5 x 13.5 cm.). Church 695. CSmH, Garrett, MH, NN, RPJCB.

Baer 117 identifies four variants.

One of the Scottish Proprietors' Tracts.

BOM, CORNELIUS

Missive van | Cornelis Bom, | geschreven uit de Stadt | Philadelphia. | In de Provintie van | Pennsylvania, | leggende op d'Oostzyde van de | Znyd [Zuyd] Revier van Nieuw Nederland. | Verhalende de groote Voortgank | van de selve Provintie. | Waer by komt | de Getuygenis van | Jacob Telner. | van Amsterdam. | [orn.] | *Tot Rotterdam gedrukt, by Pieter van | Wijn-brugge, in de Leeuweststraet. 1685.* [238]

Title from *Pennsylvania-German Society Proceedings*, VII, 1896, p. 178, 225. PBM, PHi.

By a Dutch baker in Philadelphia. See also under Joris Wertmuller, 1684. Translation in *Pennsylvania-German Society Proceedings*, IX, 1898, p. 154-162.

Pennsylvania German promotion tract.

BUDD, THOMAS

Good order established in Pennsylvania & New-Jersey in America, Being a true account of the country; with its produce and commodities there made. And the great improvements that may be made by means of publick storehouses for hemp, flax and linnen-cloth; also, the advantages of a publick-school, the profits of a publick-bank, and the probability of its arising, if those directions here laid down are followed. With the advantages of publick granaries. Likewise, several other things needful to be understood by those that are or do intend to be concerned in planting in the said countries. All which is laid down very plain, in this small treatise; it being easie to be understood by any ordinary capacity. To which the reader is referred for his further satisfaction. By Thomas Budd. *[Philadelphia:] Printed [by William Bradford] in the year 1685.* [239]

39, [1] p., 4to. (19.7 x 15.6 cm.). Church 694, Old John Carter Brown cat. 943, Sabin 8952, Evans 386. BM, CSmH (Brinley-Lenox-Church copy), DLC, ICN, MiU-C, NHi, NN, PHi, PP, PPF, PPL, RPJCB.

Second title printed in Philadelphia by William Bradford.

[PENN, WILLIAM]

A | further account | of the Province of | Pennsylvania | and its | improvements. | For the satisfaction of those that are adventurers, and | enclined to be so. | [Caption title] *[London, 1685].* [240]

20 p., 4to. (18.5 x 14.5 cm.). Sabin 59701, Church 696, Old John Carter Brown cat. 1320, Baer 118. CSmH, DLC, MiU-C, NHi, NNP, PHi, PPiU, RPJCB, ViU.

Signed by William Penn and dated. Slip of errata pasted on p. 20.

. . . . .

A further account of the Province | of Pennsylvania, and its improvements. | For the satisfaction of those that are adventurers, and | inclined to be so. | [Caption title] *[London, 1685].* [241]

16 p., 4to. Old John Carter Brown cat. 1321, Baer 118. NN, PHi, RPJCB.

. . . . .

Tweede | Bericht ofte Relaas | Van | William Penn, Eygenaar en Gouverneur van de Provintie van | Pennsylvania, | in America. | Behelsende een korte Beschrijvinge van den | tegenwoordige toestand en gelegentheid | van die Colonie. | Mitsgaders, een aanwijsinge op wat voor Conditien, die gene die | onmachtig zijn, om haar selven te konnen transporteeren, daar- | heenen souden konnen worden gebracht, met voordeel tot de gene, die | daer Penningen toe souden verschieten. | Uyt het Engels overgeset. | t'Amsterdam, | By Jacob Claus, Boekverkoper in de Prince-straat. | [1685]. [242]

20 p., 4to. Sabin 59738, old John Carter Brown cat. 1322, Baer 119. BM, ICN, MWiW-C, PHi, RPJCB.

Dutch translation of 241.

Scot, George

The | model | of the | government | of the | Province | of | East-New-Jersey | in | America; | and encouragements for such as designs | to be concerned there. | Published for information of such as are de- | sirous to be interested in that place. | *Edinburgh,* | *Printed by John Reid, and sold be* [sic] | *Alexander Ogston Stationer in the* | *Parliament Closs. Anno* | *Dom. 1685.* [243]

[8], 272 p., 12mo. (14 x 8.5 cm.). Church 697, Sabin 78186, Baer 120. *1st issue:* Garrett, ICN, N, NHi, NjHi, NjP, NN, PHi, RPJCB. *2d issue:* BM, CSmH, ICN, MH, MiU-C, NjHi, NN, ViU. One of the issues in DLC, MdBP.

NjP imprint ends *Reid.* Two issues of pp. 37-38, for which see note in Church.

Reprinted in W. A. Whitehead: *East Jersey under the proprietory governments.* N.Y., 1846, and *Newark, 1875.* Foundation stone of New Jersey history.

Amsterdam, Holland, Burgomasters of

Conditien, Die doore de Heeren Burgomeesteren der Stadt Amsterdam; volgens 't gamaeete Accoort met de West Indische Companie, . . . *Amsterdam: Evert Nieuwenhof. 1686.* [244]

4 leaves, 4to. Sabin 15186.

. . . . .

Amsterdam, 1659. Sabin 55281. DLC. [245]

For 1656 editions, see under Donck.

Conditions offered . . . to all those who will go as colonists to New Netherland.

Nouvelle | relation | de la Caroline | par | Un Gentil-homme François arrivé, | depuis deux mois, de ce nou- | veau pais. | Où il parle de la route qu'il faut tenir, | pour y aller le plus surement, & | de l'etat où il a trouve cette | nouvelle contrée. | [printer's device] | *A la Haye* | [rule] | *Chez Meyndert Uytweft* | *Marchand Libraire de Meurant* | *dans le Gortstraet.* | *[1686].*
[246]

36 p., 12mo. (13 x 7 cm.). MH, RPJCB.

Described from Mass. Hist. Soc, Photostat Americana, 2d ser., 1936, no 54.

See John Carter Brown Library annual report, 1928, p. 14.

[Penn, William]

Information | and | direction | to | such persons as are inclined | to | America, | more especially | those related to the Province | of | Pensilvania. [double rule] | *Re-printed in the year,* | *1686.*   [247]

8 p., 4to. (20 x 13 cm.). Church 698. CSmH.

. . . . .

Instruction très-exacte pour ceux qui ont desein de se transporter en Amerique, et principalement pour ceux qui sont déja interessés dans la Province de Pennsylvanie. *[n.p.]* 1686.   [248]

24mo. Title from Sabin 102226. BM.

Same in French.

. . . . .

Nader Informatie en Bericht voor die gene die genegen zijn, om zich na America te begeeven, en in de Provincie van Pensylvania geinteresseerd zijn, of zich daar zoeken neder te zetten. Met een Vooreden . . . nooit voor dezen in druk geweest: maar nu eerst uytgegeven door Robert Webb. *t'Amsterdam, By Jacob Claus, Boekverkoper in de Prinse-straat, 1686.*   [249]

8, 11 p., 4to. Title from Sabin 102227, old John Carter Brown cat. 1332. BM, PHi, RPJCB.

Same in Dutch. The old John Carter Brown catalog, which gives the title in full, enters this edition under Robert Webb, author of the preface. For modern reprints, see Sabin.

. . . . .

Nader Informatie of Onderrechtinge voor de gene die | genegen zijn om na America te gaan, en | wel voornamentlijk voor die geene die in de Provin- | tie van Pensylvania geintresseert zijn. | [Caption title] *[Amsterdam? 1686].*   [250]

Same in Dutch. Title from facsimile in *Pennsylvania-German Society Proceedings,* VII, 1896, p. 214. RPJCB.

Plan pour former un Establisse- | ment en Caroline. | [Caption title] [Colophon:] *A la Haye.* | *Chez Meindert Uytwerf, Marchand* | *Libraire dans l'Acterum. l'An 1686.*   [251]

15 p., double column, 4to. (19.5 x 15 cm.). RPJCB.

Title from Mass. Hist. Soc. Photostat Americana, 2d. ser., 1936, no. 15.

[Blome, Richard]

The | present | state | of His Majesties | isles and territories | in | America, | viz. | Jamaica, Barbadoes, | S. Christophers, Mevis, | Antego, S. Vincent, | Dominica, New-Jersey, | Pensilvania, Monserat, [bracket] | [bracket] Anguilla, Bermudas, | Carolina, Virginia, | New-England, Tobago. | New-

Found-Land. | Mary-Land, New-York. | With new maps of every place. | Together with | astronomical tables, | which will serve as a constant diary or calendar, | for the use of the English inhabitants in those | islands; for the year 1686, to 1700. | Also a table by which, at any time of the day or night here in | England, you may know what hour it is in any of those parts. | And how to make sun-dials fitting for all those places. | [rule] | Licens'd, July 20. 1686. Roger L'Estrange. | [rule] | *London:* | *Printed by H. Clark, for Dorman Newman, at the* | *Kings-Arms in the Poultrey, 1687.* | [Title within double ruled border]. [252]

[8], 262, [35] p., port., pl., 7 maps, 8vo. Title from Sabin 5972, Ayer supp. 19, Baer 124. Two issues. Copies in most large libraries.

Important for its promotion of European emigration to America and for its reprint of the captivity of Quentin Stockwell, p. 221-232.

. . . . .

In French: *L'Amerique angloise . . . Amsterdam,* 1688. [253]

[4], 331 p., 7 maps, 12mo. Sabin 5969, Baer 126. Copies in most large libraries.

. . . . .

In French: *Description des isles et terres . . . Amsterdam,* 1715. Sabin 5970. MH. [254]

. . . . .

In German: *Englischem America . . . Leipzig,* 1697. Sabin 5971. [255]

[DURAND, OR DURANS, OF DAUPHINÉ, fl. 1685-7]

Voyages | d'un | Francois, | exilé pour la | religion, | avec | une description de la | Virgine & Marilan | dans | L'Amerique. | [orn.] | *A la Haye,* | *Imprimé pour l'Autheur, 1687.* [256]

140 p., 12mo. (13 x 7.5 cm.). Sabin 100837. DLC, RPJCB.

Propositions pour la Virgine, signed at end: "Londres ce 30. May 1687, de la part des Proprietaires Nich: Hayward.", p. 137-140. Inducements to settlers.

For other editions and translations, see Sabin.

Described from Mass. Hist. Soc. photostat edition from DLC copy, 1925.

MORE, NICHOLAS

A | letter | from | Doctor More, | with | passages out of several letters | from persons of good credit, | relating to the state of improvement of | the Province of | Pennsylvania. | Published to prevent false reports. | *[London]* *Printed in the year 1687.* [257]

11 p., 4to. Old John Carter Brown cat. 1339. RPJCB, A.S.W. Rosenbach.

Preface by William Penn in whose interest the tract was published.
Reprinted in Penna. Mag. of Hist. and Biog., IV, p. 445-455.

MATHER, COTTON

The present state of New-England. | [rule] | Considered in a | discourse |
on the necessities and advantages of a | public spirit | in every man; |
especially, at such a time as this. | Made at the lecture in Boston | 20. d. I. m.
1690. | Upon the news of an invasion by bloody | Indians and French-men,
begun | upon us. | [rule] | By Cotton Mather. | [rule] | [2 lines quoted] |
[rule] | *Boston | Printed by Samuel Green. 1690.*   [258]
     [2], 52 p., 8vo. (14.5 x 9 cm.). Holmes: Cotton Mather 304. CSmH,
CtY, DLC (imp.), MH, MHi, MWA, NN, RPJCB, ViU.
     A brave and patriotic pioneer sermon in time of danger.

PASTORIUS, FRANCIS DANIEL

Vier Kleine | doch ungemeine | und sehr Nützliche | Tractätlein | [etc., 15
lines] | durch | Franciscum Danielem | Pastoriun. J.U.L. | aus der | in Pen-
sylvania neulichst von-mir in | Grund angelegten, und nun mit gutem | suc-
cess aufgehenden Stadt: | *Germanopoli | Anno Christi M.DC.XC.*   [259]
     Title from facsimile of title page in J. F. Sachse's *Falckner's Curieuse
Nachricht von Pensylvania.* Philadelphia, 1905, p. 20.
     Though a religious tract, it tended to interest the German protestants in
the safe haven of Pennsylvania.

[PENN, WILLIAM]

Some | proposals | for a second settlement in the | Province of Pennsyl-
vania. | [Caption title] [Colophon:] *[London:] Printed and sold by Andrew
Sowle, at the Crooked-Billet in Holoway-Lane, Shoreditch, 1690.*   [260]
     Broadside, folio (34 cm.). Sabin 59735. DLC.

.   .   .   .   .

The | frame | of the | government | of the Province of | Pennsylvania | in
America. | [rule, orn., rule] | *[London:] Printed and sold by Andrew Sowle
at | the Crooked-Billet in Holloway-Lane in | Shoreditch, 1691.*   [261]
     8vo. Sabin 59697. Title from facsimile in *Pennsylvania-German Society
Proceedings,* VII 1896, p. 233, from a copy in PHi.

.   .   .   .   .

Some | letters | and an | abstract of letters | from | Pennsylvania, | con-
taining | the state and improvement of that | province. | Published to prevent
mis-reports. | *[London:] Printed, and sold by Andrew Sow[l]e, at the
Crooked-Billot [sic] in Hollo- | way-Lane, in Shoreditch, 1691.*   [262]

12 p., 4to. Sabin 60621, old John Carter Brown cat. 1423. RPJCB.
A William Penn promotion tract.

FRAME, RICHARD

A short | description | of | Pennsilvania, | Or, a relation what things are
known, | enjoyed, and like to be discovered in | in [sic] the said Province. |
Presented as a token of good will to, the | [people] of England. | [rule] | By
Richard Frame. | [rule] | *Printed and sold by William Bradford in | Phila-
delphia, 1692.*   [263]

8 p., 4to. (17.5 x 12 cm.). Sabin 25421, Hildeburn 38, Evans 594. PPFr,
PPiU, PPL (1st leaf mutilated).

A delightful pioneer description of Pennsylvania in verse. Reprinted by
S. J. Hamilton, with an introduction by Horatio Gates Jones, in an edition of
118 copies in 1867.

Described from a photostat made by Mass. Hist. Soc. in 1926 of the
mutilated copy in PPL.

MATHER, COTTON

Fair weather. | [row of type orns.] | or | considerations | to dispel | the
clouds, & allay the storms, | of | discontent: | in a | discourse | which with |
an entertaining variety, both of ar- | gument and history, layes open, the |
nature and evil of that per- | nicious vice, and offers diverse | antidotes against
it; | [rule] | By Cotton Mather. | [rule] | Whereto there is prefixed a cata-
logue of | sins against all the commancments, whereof | all that would make
thorough work of repen- | tance, especially at this day when the God of |
Heaven so loudly calls for it, shou'd make | their serious and sensible con-
fessions before | the Lord; with an humble and fervent ad- | dress unto this
whole people, there-about. | [rule] | *Boston, Printed by Bartholomew Green,
and | John Allen, for Benjamin Harris at the | London Coffee House. 1692.*
                                                                                     [264]

[2], 93, [1] p., 12mo. (12.2 x 6.3 cm.). Sabin 46313, Evans 560, Holmes:
Cotton Mather bibliog. 118. CtY (Buttolph imprint), M. B. Jones copy
(Buttolph imprint), present location unknown, MHi (Buttolph imprint),
MWA (Harris imprint), lacks last leaf.

Variant imprint has name of *Nicholas Buttolph* in place of *Benjamin
Harris.*

Holmes corrects previous bibliographers, showing that this work is dated
1692 instead of 1691 and that there was probably no 1694 edition.

Important for its account of the assault on York, Maine by the Eastern
Indians and their murder of Rev. Shubael Dummer, 50 others killed and 100
captured on January 25, 1692, n.s.

Reprinted in *Decennium Luctuosum*, 1699, and in the *Magnalia*, 1702.

PASTORIUS, MELCHIOR ADAM, AND FRANCIS DANIEL PASTORIUS

Kurtze | Beschreibung | des H. R. Reichs Stadt | Windsheim | . . . | durch | Melchiorem Adamum Pastorium, | ältern Burgemeistern und Ober-Rich- | tern in besagter Stadt. | *Gedruckt zu Nürnberg | bey Christian Sigsmund Froberg.* | *Im Jahr Christi 1692.*   [265]

[2], 148, 32 p., 8vo. (15.7 x 8.9 cm.). Baer 145. PHi.

Title from *Pennsylvania German Society Proceed.,* VII, 1897, p. 187.

This historical sketch of his native town, by the father of Francis Daniel Pastorius, includes as an appendix the first extended German account of the settlement of Pennsylvania, which the son sent to his parents in Germany in 1686. It has the caption title:

Francisci Danielis Pastorii | Sommerhusano-Franci. | Kurtze Geographische Beschreibung | der letztmahls erfundenen | Americanischen Landschafft | Pensylvania, | Mit angehenckten einigen notablen Bege- | benheiten und Bericht-Schreiben an dessen Hrn. | Vattern, Patrioten und gute Freunde.

Later enlarged as: *Umständige Geographische Beschreibung,* 1700.

BAYARD, NICHOLAS AND CHARLES LODOWICK

A | narrative | of an attempt made by the | French of Canada | upon the | Mohaques Country | being Indians under the protection of their Majesties | government of New-York. | To which is added, | 1. An account of the present state and strength of Canada, given by two | Dutch-men, who have been prisoners there, and now made their escape, | 2. The examination of a French prisoner | 3. His Excellency Benjamin Fletcher's speech to the Indians. | 4. The answer of the five Nations of the Mohaques to his Excellency. | 5. Proposals made by the four chief sachems of the five Nations, to his Ex- | cellency, | and his Excellency's reply thereto. | 6. An address from the corporation of Albany to his Excellency, returning thanks | for his Ex- | cellency's early assistance for their relief, &c. | [Caption title on p. 1] [Colo- | phon at end of p. 14:] *Printed and sold by William Bradford, Anno 1693.*

[266]

14 p., folio, (28 x 18 cm.). Eames 14, Hasse 1, Evans 632, Sabin 4035. Unique copy in Public Record Office, London.

Early account of Indian warfare in the Mohawk Valley, telling how the Canadian French and Indians captured and burned three Mohawk castles, were attacked by the local militia and Mohawks and withdrew on the arrival of reenforcements from New York under Governor Benjamin Fletcher. Also brief narrative of the captivity and escape of Cornelius Claese van den Bergh and Andries Casparus, captured the previous year by the Canadian Indians and escaped from the French. The 14th known example of Bradford's New York printing.

Facsimile edition reprinted with introduction and notes by Adelaide R. Hasse. New York: Dodd, Mead & Company, 1903. [7], 14 p., large 4to., in an edition of 25 copies on Japan vellum at $10.00 and 500 copies on laid paper at $4.00.

Reprinted as Second series, No. 38 of Mass. Hist. Soc. Photostat Americana, 1937.

. . . . .

A journal of the late actions of the French at Canada. With the manner of their being repuls'd, by His Excellency, Benjamin Fletcher, their Majesties Governour of New-York. Impartially related by Coll. Nicholas Reyard [Bayard], and Lieutenant Coll. Charles Lodowick, who attended His Excellency, during the whole expedition. To which is added, I. An account of the present state and strength of Canada, given by two Dutch men, who have been a long time prisoners there, and now made their escape. II. The examination of a French prisoner. III. His Excellency Benjamin Fletcher's speech to the Indians. IV. An address from the corporation of Albany, to His Excellency, returning thanks for His Excellency's early assistance for their relief. Licensed, Sept. 11th 1693. Edward Cooke. *London, Printed for Richard Baldwin, in Warwick-Lane, 1693.* [267]

[iv], 22 p., 4to., Sabin 4035. BM, CSmH, MH, MWiW-C, NjP, NN, RPJCB.

English edition of the above. Reprinted for Joseph Sabin, *New York, 1868.* [4], 55 p., 4to. Sabin 4036.

Mather, Cotton

The short history of New-England. | [rule] | A | recapitulation | of | wonderful passages | which have occurr'd, | first in the protections, and | then in the afflictions, of | New-England. | With a | representation | of certain matters calling for the | singular attention of that country. | Made at Boston-lecture, in the audience | of the Great and General Assembly | of the Province of the Massachu- | sett-Bay, June 7. 1694. | [rule] | By Cotton Mather. | [rule, 4 lines quoted, rule] | *Boston. Printed by B. Green, for | Samuel Phillips, at the Brick Shop, at | the West End of the Exchange, 1694.* | [Title within ruled border]. [268]

67, [1] p., 8vo. (12.7 x 7 cm.). Sabin 46509, Evans 700, Holmes: Cotton Mather bibliog. 354. MWA, RPJCB.

Describes the Indian encroachments on the frontiers and deplores the tendency of young people pioneering beyond the frontier, going "out from the institutions of God, swarming into new settlements, where they and their untaught families are like to perish for lack of vision." A description of the unsettled times in the new settlements, due to political and religious contriversies and the threat of invasion by the French and Indians from Canada.

Mayhew, Matthew

A brief | narrative | of | the success which the Gospel | hath had, among the | Indians, | of | Martha's Vineyard (and the places adjacent) | in New-

England. | With | some remarkable curiosities, concerning the | numbers, the customes, and the present cir- | cumstances of the Indians on that Island. | Further explaning [sic] and confirming the ac- | count given of those matters, by Mr. Cotton | Mather in the Life of the Renowned | Mr. John Eliot. | By Matthew Mayhew. | Whereto is added, | An account concerning the present state of | Christianity among the Indians, in | other parts of New-England: expressed | in the letters of several worthy persons, | best acquainted there-withall. | *Boston in N.E. Printed by Bartholomew Green, | Sold by Michael Perry under the Exchange. 1694.*   [269]

    55 p., 8vo. Sabin 47151, Evans 701. MHi.

    Reprinted in England the following year, as: *The conquests and triumphs of grace . . . London, 1695.* Sabin 47152. RPJCB, ViU.

    Continued by Experience Mayhew's: *A discourse shewing that God dealeth with men as with reasonable creatures. . . . from . . . 1694. to 1720 . . . Boston, 1720.* MB, MHi, NHi, for which, with other similar titles by this author, see Sabin 47123-47125.

[SCOTTOW, JOSHUA]

    A | narrative | of the planting of the Massachusets | Colony | Anno. 1628. With the Lords signal | presence the first thirty | years. | Also a caution from New-Englands apostle, | the great | Cotton, | how to escape the calamity, which might | befall them or their posterity, | and confirmed by the evangel-ist | Norton | with prognosticks from the famous | Dr. Owen. | Concerning the fate of these churches, and animadversions | upon the anger of God, in sending of evil angels | among us. | [rule] | Published by Old Planters, the authors of the Old | Mens Tears. | [rule] | [7 lines quoted] | [rule] | *Boston Printed and sold by Benjamin Harris, at the | sign of the Bible over against the Blew-Anchor. 1694.*   [270]

    [4], 75, [1] p., 8vo. Evans 709, old John Carter Brown cat. 1472. MHi, RPJCB.

    The author was a strict Puritan merchant of Boston.

[SEELIG, JOHANN GOTTFRIED]

    Copia | eines Send-Schreibens auss | der neuen Welt, betreffend | die Erzehlung einer gefährlichen | Schifffarth, und glücklichen Anländung etlicher | Christlichen Reisegefehrten, welche zu dem En- | de diese Wall-fahrt angetretten, den Glau- | ben an Jesum Christum allda auss- | zubreiten | Tob. XII. 8. | Der Könige und Fürsten Rath und Heimlichkeiten | soll man verschweigen, aber Gottes Werck soll | man herrlich preisen und offenbaren. | [rule] | *[Halle or Frankfort?] Gedruckt im Jahr 1695.*   [271]

    12 p., 4to. Sabin 16673. DLC, PHi.

    Title from facsimile in *Pennsylvania-German Society Proceedings,* VII, 1896, p. 238, from a copy in PHi.

For author, see above reference, p. 189. Seelig's letter was written from *Germandon* in Pennsylvania, August 7, 1694, to A.H. Francke, giving an account of the voyage and later situation of the German Pietists who left Germany for Pennsylvania two years earlier under the leadership of Johann Kelpius. Translated by Dr. Oswald Seidensticker in Penna. Mag. of Hist. and Biog., XI, p. 430 and following.

[MATHER, COTTON]

Great examples of judgment and mercy, or several relations of terrible & barbarous things endured by many English captives, in the hands of the Eastern Indians: whereto is added A Narrative of Hannah Swarton, containing a great many wonderful passages, relating to her captivity & deliverance. *Printed for & sold by Joseph Wheeler, at his shop at the head of the Dock in Boston, Price stitch'd 8d. [1696?]*   [272]

72 p., 16mo. Evans 793, Holmes: Cotton Mather bibliog. vol. 1, p. 452.

Title from *Tully's Almanack for 1697* for a work projected but never published, according to Mr. Holmes. Much of the material, including the Hannah Swarton captivity, was published in *Humiliations*, 1697, which see.

[SCOTTOW, JOSHUA, EDITOR ?]

Massachusetts | or | the first planters of New-England, | the end and manner of their coming thi- | ther, and abode there: in several | epistles | [17 lines quoted] | *Boston in New-England, Printed by B. Green, and | J. Allen. Sold by Richard Wilkins, at his shop | near the Old-Meeting-House. 1696.*
                                                                        [273]

[2], 56 p., 8vo. (14.5 x 9 cm.). Sabin 78431-3, Evans 773, Church 761. CSmH, CtSoP, ICN, MB, MBAt, MH, MHi, MWA, NHi, NN, NNC, RPJCB.

There are three variant title pages: 1. As above, with *thi-* | *ther* divided and 17 lines of quotation on title; 2. with *thither* undivided and 17 lines of quotation; 3. with *thi-* | *ther* divided and 13 lines of quotation, for which see Sabin.

Important for inclusion of long letter of Thomas Dudley, Deputy-Governor of the Colony of Massachusetts Bay, covering the period from the Summer of 1630 to March, 1631, the best contemporary account of the beginning of the colony; and first reprint of the *Humble request* of 1630. See Sabin and Church for contents and long notes on the importance of the volume and a record of reprints.

HENNEPIN, LOUIS

Nouvelle | Decouverte | d'un tres grand | Pays | Situé dans l'Amerique, | entre | Le Nouveau Mexique, | et | La Mer Glaciale, | Avec les Cartes, & les Figures necessaires, & de plus | l'Histoire Naturelle & Morale, & les avan-

tages, | qu'on en peut tirer par l'établissement des Colonies. | Le tout dedie |
à | Sa Majesté Britannique. | Guillaume III. | Par le | R. P. Louis Hennepin,
| Missionaire Recollect & Notaire Apostolique. | *A Utrecht,* | *Chez Guillaume
Broedelet,* | *Marchand Libraire. MDCXCVII.*   [274]

Engraved title and [2], [23], [26], [19], 312, 10 p. with star 313 inserted,
313-506 p., 2 plates, 2 maps, 12mo. Copies in most large libraries.

Plates: First published view of Niagara Falls; the Buffalo.

Maps: Carte | d'un tres grand | Pays | entre le | Nouveau Mexique | et la |
Mer Glaciale | Dediée a | Guiliaume IIIe. | Roy de la Grand Brettagne | Par
le R. P. | Louis de Hennepin | Mission: Recol: et Not: Apost: | Chez G.
Broedelet | a Utreght | J. V. Vianen del. et fecit. | (52 x 43 cm.).; Carte |
d'un tres grand Pais | Nouvellement découvert | dans | l'Amerique Septen-
trionale | entre le | Nouveau Mexique et la | Mer Glaciale | avec le Cours
du Grand Fleuve | Meschasipi | Dediée a Guiliaume IIIe | Roy de la Grand
Brettagne | Par le R. P. | Louis de Hennepin | Mission: Recoll: et Not:
Apost: | Chez G. Broedelet | a Utreght. | (44.3 x 37.5 cm.).

Title from Victor Hugo Paltsits: *Bibliography of the works of Father Louis
Hennepin.* Chicago, 1903, which see for later editions and translations.

Includes Hennepin's captivity among the Sioux in 1680.

[MATHER, COTTON]

Humiliations follow'd with deliverances. | [rule] | A brief discourse | on
the matter and method, | of that | humiliation | which would be | an hopeful
symptom of our deliverance | from calamity. | Accompanied and accommo-
dated | with | a narrative, | of a notable deliverance lately | received by some
| English captives, | from the hands of cruel Indians. | And some improve-
ment of that narrative. | Whereto is added | A narrative of Hannah Swarton,
containing | a great many wonderful passages, relating to | her captivity and
deliverance. | [rule] | *Boston in N.E. Printed by B. Green, & J. Allen,* | *for
Samuel Phillips at the Brick Shop. 1697.*   [275]

72 p., 12mo. (12.5 x 6.9 cm.). Sabin 46363, Holmes: Cotton Mather
bibliog. 178. CSmH, DLC (imperfect).

A narrative of a notable deliverance from captivity, p. 41-47, is the famous
story of the captivity and escape of Hannah Dustan of Haverhill, Mass. It
was reprinted, with additions, in his: *Decennium Luctuosum,* 1699 which
was reprinted in his *Magnalia,* 1702. *A narrative of Hannah Swarton,* p. 52-
72, was also reprinted in the *Magnalia,* 1702. Also separately reprinted; rewritten, probably by Christopher C. Dean by whom it was copyrighted, as:
Hannah Swanton [sic], | *the Casco Captive:* | *or the* | *Catholic Religion in
Canada,* | *and its* | *influence on the Indians in Maine.* | *Written for the
Massachusetts Sabbath School Society, and revised* | *by the Committee of
Publication* | *Boston:* | *Massachusetts Sabbath School Society,* | *Depository
No. 13 Cornhill* | 1837. 63 p., 16mo. Sabin 94022. NN. Same, Second
edition, 1839. 60 p. Sabin 94022. NHi, NN. Same, Third edition, [n.d.].

72 p., including front., illus., plate. DLC. "What is here presented . . . is taken chiefly from the Rev. Cotton Mather's *Magnalia* . . ." Hannah Swarton (or Swanton) was captured in May, 1690 in the attack on Falmouth, Maine by the French and Indians. Taken to Canada with her four children, she was sent out in February, 1691, to beg food from the French settlers and was by them taken to Quebec and ransomed by the Intendent in whose house she remained as a servant until November, 1695 when she was returned to Boston with other captives.

The story of Hannah Dustan (Duston or Dustin) was rewritten as: *Heroism | of | Hannah Duston, | together with | the Indian wars of New England. | By | Robert B. Caverly. | . . . | Boston: B.B. Russell & Co. Publishers. | 1874.* 407 p., 13 pl., 12mo. Ayer 44. Same, 1875. 408 p., 14 pl. Ayer 45. Same enlarged as: *History of the Indian wars of New England. Boston: J.H. Earle, 1882.* 2 vols., plates.

Haverhill, Massachusetts was burned March 15, 1697 by a band of Abnaki Indians, 27 women and children being killed. Hannah Dustin, her nurse Mary Neff and a young boy captured from Worcester in 1695, "Samuel Lennarson" [i.e., Samuel Leonard's son], while captives, tomahawked their guard of 12 Indians, one squaw escaping, scalped them, escaped in a canoe, reached Boston and collected the bounty on the Indian scalps. They were the heroes of the hour. It is probable that Mather, who prints her narrative in quotation marks, had it from her pastor, Rev. Benjamin Rolfe, minister of Haverhill. Her week-old baby was killed but her husband, with their seven other children, escaped.

SEWALL, SAMUEL

Phaenomena quaedam | Apocalyptica | ad aspectum Novis Orbis configurata. | Or, some few lines towards a description of the New | Heaven | as it makes to those who stand upon the | New Earth | [rule] | By Samuel Sewall sometime Fellow of Harvard Colledge at | Cambridge in New-England. | [rule, 7 lines quoted, rule, 4 lines quoted, rule] | *Massachuset; | Boston, Printed by Bartholomew Green, and John Allen, | and are to be sold by Richard Wilkins, 1697.* | [Title within double ruled border]. [276]

[8], 60 p., 4to. (21.6 x 15 cm.). Sabin 79443, Evans 813, Church 769. BM, Bodleian, CSmH, DLC, MB, MWA, NHi, NN, RPJCB.

In spite of its formidable title, one of the best sources for the pioneer period of New England history. Sewall's most important work, next to his *Diaries*, published in 1878-1879.

HENNEPIN, LOUIS

Nouveau | Voyage | d'un Pais plus grand que | l'Europe | Avec les reflections des entreprises du Sieur | de la Salle, sur les Mines de St. Barbe, &c. | Enrichi de la Carte, de figures expressives, des moeurs | & manieres de vivre des Sauvages du Nord, | & du Sud, de la prise de Quebec Ville Capital- | le de la Nouvelle France, par les Anglois, & des | avantages qu'on peut retirer du chemin recourci | de la Chine & du Japon, par le moien de tant | de Vastes Contrées, & de Nouvelles Colonies. | Avec approbation & dedié à sa Majesté | Guillaume III. | Roy de la grande | Bretagne | par le | R. P. Louis Hennepin, | Missionaire Recollect & Notaire Apostolique. | *A Utrecht,* | *Chez Antoine Schouten,* | *Marchand Libraire. 1698.* | [Title in red and black].

[277]

[2], [20], [38], [10], 389 p., 4 plates, folded map, 8vo. Copies in most large libraries. The William III dedication copy in NjP.

Plates, engraved and designed by I. van Vianen: *Avantures mal heureuses du Sieur de la Salle; Le Sieur de la Salle mal-heureusemet* [sic] *assasiné; Cruautéz in-oüies des sauvages Iroquois; Prise de Quebeek* [sic] *par les Anglois.*

Map: Carte | d'un nouueau | Monde, | entre le nouueau | Mexique, | et la mer Glacialle | Novellement decouvert par le | R. P. Louis de Hennepin | Missionaire Recolleet [sic] natif d'Aht. | en Hainaut | dediée a sa Majesté | Britanique, le Roy | Guilaume Troisieme. (46.5 x 29 cm.). Engraved by *Gasp: Bouttats.*

Another and very rare issue with imprint: *Utrecht, Chez Ernestus Voskuyl,* | *Imprimeur, 1698.* CSmH. Title from Victor Hugo Paltsits: *Bibliography of the works of Father Louis Hennepin.* Chicago, 1903, which see for later editions and translations.

.   .   .   .   .

A | new Discovery | of a | Vast Country in America, | Extending above Four Thousand Miles, | between | New France and New Mexico. | With a | Description of the Great Lakes, Cata- | racts, Rivers, Plants, and Animals: | Also, The Manners, Customs, and Languages, of the | several Native Indians; | And the Advantages of | Commerce with those different Nations. | With a | Continuation: | Giving an Account of the | Attempts of the Sieur De la Salle upon the | Mines of St. Barbe &c. The taking of | Quebec by the English; With the advantages | of a Shorter Cut to China and Japan. | Both Parts Illustrated with Maps and Figures, | and Dedicated to His Majesty K. William. | By L. Hennepin, now Resident in Holland. | To which is added, Several New Discoveries in North- | America, not publish'd in the French Edition. | *London: Printed for M. Bentley, J. Tonson, H. Bon-* | *wick,* *T. Goodwin, and S. Manship. 1698.* [The "Bon" edition].   [278]

Engraved title and [2], [8], [4], [8], 299; [2], [9], [1], [16], [4], 178; [2], 303-355 p., 6 plates and 2 folded maps, 8vo. Copies in most large libraries.

Plates: View of Niagara Falls; Buffalo; *The unfortunate Adventures of the Sieur de la Salle; The Sieur de la Salle unhappily assassinated; Vnheard of Crueltys of the Iroquois; Taking of Quebec by the English.*

Maps: *A Map of a Large Country Newly Discovered in the Northern America* (43 x 37 cm.); *A Map of A New World* (44.3 x 27 cm.).

. . . . .

Reset, *London, Printed for M. Bentley, J. Tonson, | H. Bonwick, T. Good-win, and S. Manship. 1698.* | [The "Ton" edition].   [279]

Engraved frontispiece and [2], [8], [4], [8], 243; [2], [8], [15], [7], 184; 185-228 p., 6 plates and 2 maps, 3vo. Copies in most large libraries.

Plates: Same subjects as in previous edition but with those in part two reversed and better engraved.

Maps: Same as in previous edition.

Title from Victor Hugo Paltsits: *Bibliography of the works of Father Louis Hennepin.* Chicago, 1903, which see for details of collation and for later editions.

THOMAS, GABRIEL

A historical and geographical account | of the | Province and country | of | Pensilvania; | and of | West-New-Jersey | in | America. | The richness of the soil, the sweetness of the situation, | the wholesomness of the air, the navigable rivers, and | others, the prodigious encrease of corn, the flourishing | condition of the city of Philadelphia, with the stately | buildings, and other improvements there. The strange | creatures, as birds, beasts, fishes, and fowls, with the | several sorts of minerals, purging waters, and stones, | lately discovered. The natives, aborogmes [sic], their lan- | guage, religion, laws, and customs; the first planters, | the Dutch, Sweeds, and English, with the number of | its inhabitants; as also a touch upon George Keith's | new religion, in his second change since he left the | Quakers. | [rule] | With a map of both countries. | [rule] | By Gabriel Thomas, | who resided there about fifteen years. | | [rule] | *London, Printed for, and sold by A. Baldwin, at | the Oxon Arms in Warwick-Lane, 1698.*   [280]

[8], 55, [1], [11], 34 p., folded map, 8 vo. (17.5 x 10 cm.). Church 778, Sabin 95395, Baer 188. Copies in most large libraries.

The second part has a separate title page. Folded map: *Pennsylvania and West Jersey.*

A German translation, omitting the part on West Jersey, appeared as: *Continuatio der Beschreibung der Landschafft Pensylvaniae . . . Franckfurt und Leipzig,* 1702, for which see Sabin 95394. BM, CSmH, CtY, NN, PHi, RPJCB. For modern reprints, see Sabin 95396 and Baer 188.

DICKENSON, JONATHAN

God's protecting Providence man's surest help and defence in the times of the greatest difficulty and most imminent danger; evidenced in the re-markable | deliverance of divers persons, from the devouring waves of the sea, amongst which they suffered shipwrack. And also from the more cruelly devouring jawes of the inhumane canibals of Florida. Faithfully related by one of the persons concerned therein; Jonathan Dickenson. [four lines quoted from the Psalms] *Printed in Philadelphia by Reinier Jansen. 1699.*   [281]

[12], 96 p., 8vo. (18 x 13.3 cm.). Sabin 20014, Ayer 64, Evans 863, Hildeburn 69, Church 779. CSmH (Church 779, described as "The Brinley copy." Since the perfect Brinley copy 3390 was sold to Lenox, as recorded in the Church catalog, and Brinley's imperfect second copy 3391 lacked last three leaves of preface, had final leaf of text slightly imperfect, with a two page document signed by the author inserted, each leaf inlaid, bound in dark green levant morocco, it cannot be the present Church-CSmH copy which is perfect); Friends Reference Library, London; Friends Library, Philadelphia (In their printed catalogs of 1831 and 1853, in a pamphlet volume which, however, is now missing); ICN (Ayer 64, bought from the dealer, George H. Richmond, and formerly in Marshall C. Lefferts library, with his bookplate, who probably secured it from the Charles H. Kalbfleisch library); MH (Gift of Harvard's former President, James Walker, with first two leaves imperfect and supplied in photostat); NN (Brinley 3390 to James Lenox, from which the MHi photostat reprint was made); PHi (Brayton Ives copy, bought at his sale, 1891, lot 273 for $380. by Charles R. Hildeburn, but now missing); PPL (P.E. du Simitière copy, bought at his sale in 1785. Title repaired, last leaf missing).

First edition and probably the first title printed by Reinier Jansen. A contemporary MS, differing somewhat from the printed text, is in PHi, from the Hoffman sale, lot 1295. Mass. Hist. Soc. Photostat Americana, 2d ser., 89, 1939.

Jonathan Dickenson, a thirty-three year old Quaker merchant from Jamaica, with his wife and six-months-old son, a well-known elderly Quaker missionary named Robert Barrow, and some twenty-odd other passengers, mariners and slaves and an Indian girl named, of all things, *Venus,* set out from Port Royal in the barkentine *Reformation* on August 23, 1696, bound for Philadelphia. While off the east coast of Florida, they ran into a storm and were presently wrecked near Jupiter Island, about twenty miles north of the present site of West Palm Beach. They managed to get safely ashore but were promptly seized by a fierce tribe of Indians who stripped them of their clothes (they were tormented by insects) and other possessions. The Indians, though hostile, made no effort to kill or enslave the pitiful casta-ways but allowed them to make their way, on foot or in native canoes, up the coast some two hundred miles to St. Augustine. Here they eventually arrived in a starving condition and were befriended by the Spaniards who sent them on to Charleston, South Carolina. A few weeks later they reached Philadelphia and the journal ends with the death of Robert Barrow.

[MATHER, COTTON]

Decennium Luctuosum. | [rule] | An | history | of | remarkable occur-rences, | in the long | war, | which | New-England hath had with the | Indian salvages, | from the year, 1688. | to the year, 1698. | Faithfully composed and improved. | [rule, one line quoted, rule] | *Boston in New-England.* | *Printed by B. Green, and J. Allen, for Samuel Phillips,* | *at the Brick Shop near the Old-Meeting-House. 1699.* | [Title within ruled border]. [282]

254, [2] p., 8vo. (12.5 x 7.8 cm.). Sabin 46280, Evans 873, Holmes: Cotton Mather bibliog. 84 A. Bodleian, F. C. Deering, MB (imperfect), MBAt, MWA (imperfect), ViU.

The appended sermon has a separate title: *Observable things . . . at* p. 199.

Reprinted in the *Magnalia,* 1702, 1820, 1853, and in C.H. Lincoln: *Narratives of the Indian Wars (Original Narratives of Early American History),* 1913.

The narrative of the captivity of Hannah Dustan is here reprinted, revised, from his *Humiliations,* 1697.

[WARD, EDWARD]

A | trip | to | New-England. | With a | character | of the | country and people, | both | English and Indians. | [rule, orn., rule] | *London, Printed in the year, 1699.* | [Title within double ruled border]. [283]

16 p., folio. (28.2 x 19 cm.). Sabin 101286, Church 788. CSmH, CtY, DLC, ICN, MB, MH, MHi, MiU-C, NN, RPJCB.

A satirical, racy and scurrilous tract on the men and women of New England. The author, a London tavern keeper, wit and pamphleteer, often pilloried for his scurrility, banished from old to New England and back again, gives us a most amusing picture of the not-so-Puritans which aroused their ire and that of their descendants. Though not to be taken too literally, his picture of life in New England shows a side of the Puritan character not generally dwelt on in the histories of that region written by their clergymen. Whether you believe it or not, it is delightful reading.

The following note is taken from Sabin: The sheets of the work were reissued, with other remainders of Ward's pamphlets, as no. 8 in "A Collection of the Writings . . . of Mr. Edward Ward," London, 1701. MHi. It was reprinted in various issues of the collected writings of Ward, being included in "Writings of the Author of the London Spy," London, 1704, and London, 1706. MH. Reproduced in reduced facsimile in "Five Travel Scripts commonly attributed to Edward Ward," New York, 1933. Reprinted (together with "A Letter from New-England," by J. W., 1782) with an introduction and notes by G. P. Winship, in the latter's "Boston in 1682 and 1699," Providence, 1905. (Club of Colonial Reprints, Pub. 2). 100 copies printed.

DICKENSON, JONATHAN

God's protecting Providence, . . . evidenced in the remarkable deliverance of Robert Barrow, with divers other persons, . . . *Printed in Philadelphia: Re-printed in London, and sold by T. Sowle, in White-Hart-Court in Gracious-street, 1700.* [284]

[10], 89 p., 8vo. (16.2 x 9.9 cm.). Sabin 20015, Ayer 65. Copies in most large libraries.

. . . . . .

Second issue, same title reset.   [285]
[10], 85, book list [8] p., 8vo. (18.2 x 10.5 cm.). Ayer supp. 43. Copies in most large libraries.

NEW YORK PROVINCE, HOUSE OF REPRESENTATIVES

Some queries sent up to his Excellency the Earl of Bellomont, by the House of Representatives of the Province of New-York, the 31th [sic] July, 1700, concerning his Excellency's proposition to them of building a fort for the defense of the Five Nations of Indians. . . . *William Bradford . . . New York. 1700.*   [286]

2 p., folio. Sabin 86720. Public Record Office.

The existence of this unique New York frontier item and Bradford imprint was first reported by Adelaide Hasse in the New York Public Library Bulletin, vol. 7, 1903, p. 61. To protect the frontier and the fur trade from the encroachments of the French in Canada, it was urged that a fort be built to protect the Iroquois Indians who were friendly with New York and whose friendship and furs were a necessary part of the Colony's economy.

PASTORIUS, FRANCIS DANIEL

Umständige Geogra- | phische | Beschreibung | der zu allerletzt erfundenen | Provintz | Pennsylva- | niae, | in denen End-Gräntzen | Americae | in der West-Welt gelegen, | Durch | Franciscum Danielem | Pastorium, | J.V. Lic. und Friedens-Richtern] daselbsten. | Worbey angehencket sind eini- | ge notable Begebenheiten, und | Bericht-Schreiben an dessen Herrn | Vattern | Melchiorem Adamum Pasto- | rium, | und andere gute Freunde. | *Franckfurt und Leipzig, | Zufinden bey Andreas Otto. 1700.*   [287]

[12], 140 p., 8vo. (16 x 9.5 cm.). Sabin 59028, Baer 208. BM, CtY, DLC, Garrett, ICN, MHi, NIC, NN (2 variants), PHi, PPG, PPL, RPJCB.

Described from Mass. Hist. Soc. Photostat Americana, 2d ser., 1936, no. 27. For modern reprints see Baer 208.

Did much to stimulate German emigration to Pennsylvania.

DICKENSON, JONATHAN

God's protecting Providence . . . [as in 1700 ed.] *1701.*   [288]

Same collation as 1700 ed., title and text reset. 8vo. (15.5 x 9.5 cm.). PHi.

An 8 p. summary, apparently from the 1700 or 1701 London edition, appears in various editions of: *God's mercies in the great deep, recorded in several wonderful and amazing accounts of sailors.* London, [ca. 1703];

same, 4th ed., London, 1734; same, as: *God's wonders . . . Fourth edition.*
London, 1741. NHi; same, Gravesend, 1803. Sabin 27629; same, as: *God's
mercies* . . . Newburyport: Thomas and Whipple . . . W. Allen, printer,
1805. Titles, except as indicated, from 1945 ed. of Dickenson.

W[OLLEY], C[HARLES]

A two years | journal | in | New-York: | and part of its | territories | in
| America. | [rule] | By C.W. A.M. | [rule] | *London,* | *Printed for John
Wyat, at the Rose in* | *St. Paul's Church-Yard: and Eben Tracy,* | *at the
three Bibles on London-Bridge.* | M DCCI. | [Title within double ruled
border]. [289]

[8], 104 p. (pp. 97-104 misnumbered), 8vo. (14 x 8.5 cm.). Sabin
104994, Church 800-801. BM, CSmH, ICN, N, NHi, RPJCB.

. . . . .

With imprint: *London,* | *Printed for Dickenson Boys in Lowth,* | *and George
Barton in Boston, MDCCI.* BM, CSmH, MB, NN, PP. [290]

By a Church of England clergyman who lived in New York, 1678-1680.
Interesting description of New York and the local Indians.

The Henry F. De Puy copy of the 1st issue had several typographical
errors in sheet C, all noted in Church, which were corrected in other copies
of this and the 2d issue. The title of the 2d issue is pasted on a stub of the
cancelled 1st issue title.

For reprints, see Sabin.

CAMPANIUS HOLM, TOMAS

Kort beskrifning | om | Provincien | Nya Swerige | uti | America, | som
nu förtjden af the Engelske kallas | Pensylvania. | Aflärde och trowärdige
mäns skriften och berättelser ihopaletad och sammanskrefwen, samt med
äthskillige figurer | utzirad af | Thomas Campanius Holm. | *Stockholm
Tryckt uti Kongl. Boktr. hvs Sal. Wantijfs* | *Antiamed egen bekostnad, af
J. H. Werner ahr MDCCII.* [291]

Engraved and printed title, [18], 190, [2] p., maps, plates, 4to. Sabin
10202. DLC, ICN, MiU-C, MWA, MWiW-C, NjP, NN, PBL, PHi, PPA,
PPiU, PPL-R, PU, RPJCB, ViU.

The author, never in America, wrote his narrative from his grandfather's
notes, verbal accounts of his father and from the manuscripts of Peter
Lindstrom, an engineer.

An English translation by Peter S. Du Ponceau was published in Historical Society of Pennsylvania Memoirs, vol. 3, part 1, 1834 and as a
separate. A partial translation also appears in New York Historical Society
Collections, vol. 2, 1814.

See also C.D. Arfwedson's *A brief history of the Colony of New Sweden,* translated from the original Swedish edition, Upsala, 1825, in *Pennsylvania German Society Proceedings*, vol. XVIII, 1909.

FALCKNER, DANIEL

Curieuse Nachricht | von | Pensylvania | in | Norden-America | Welche, | auf Begehren guter Freunde, | Uber vorgelegte 103. Fra- | gen, ven seiner Abreiss aus Teutsch- | land nach obigem Lande Anno 1700. | ertheilet, und nun Anno 1702 in den Druck | gegeben worden. | Von Daniel Falknern, Professore, | Burgern und Pilgrim allda. | [rule] | *Franckfurt und Leipzig*, | *Zu finden bey Andreas Otto, Buchhändlern.* | *Im Jahr Christi 1702.* [292]

iv, 58 p., 12mo. Sabin 23739. PHi, PPL.

Curious tidings from Pennsylvania in Northern America which, at solicitation of good friends, regarding 103 propounded questions, upon his departure from Germany to the above country, anno 1700, were imparted, and now, anno 1702, are given in print, by Daniel Falckner, Professor [of religion], Citizen and Pilgrim in that place.

The first of numerous editions of the book which did more than any other to stimulate the great German emigration to Pennsylvania. A promotion tract of the Franckfort Land Company.

Reprinted, with Pastorius: *Umstandige Geographische Beschreibung* and a translation of Gabriel Thomas: *Account*, as: *Continuatio* | *der* | *Beschreibung der Landschafft* | *Pensylvaniae* | ... *Franckfurt und Leipzig*, ... 1702.

For an English translation, see J.F.Sachse's: *Falckner's Curieuse Nachricht von Pensylvania*. Philadelphia, 1905. (Reprinted from Pennsylvania-German Society Proceedings, vol. 14).

[FALCKNER, JUSTUS]

Abdruck | eines Schreibens | an | Tit. Herrn | D. Henr. Muhlen, | aus Germanton, in der Ameri- | canischen Province Pensylvania, sonst No- | va Suecia, den ersten Augusti, im Jahr | unsers-Heyls eintausend siebenhundert | und eins, | den Zustand der Kirchen | in America betreffend. | *[n.p.]* MDCCII.   [293]

Title from *Pennsylvania-German Society Proceedings*, VII, 1896, p. 252, from photographic copy in PHi of original in University of Rostock Library.

An account of the religious condition of the Pennsylvania Germans in 1700-1701 by Justus Falckner, brother of Daniel Falckner, whom he accompanied to America.

MATHER, COTTON

Magnalia Christi Americana: | or, the | ecclesiastical history | of | New-England, | from | its first planting in the year 1620. unto the year | of our Lord, 1698. | [rule] | In seven books. | [rule] | [contents in 22 lines] | [rule] | By the Reverend and Learned Cotton Mather, M.A. | and Pastor of the North Church in Boston, New-England. | [rule] | *London:* | *Printed for*

Thomas Parkhurst, at the Bible and Three | Crowns in Cheapside. MDCCII.
| [Title within double ruled border]. [294]

[28]; [2], 38; [2], 75, [1]; [2], 238; [2], [omitting p. 1-124] 125-222; [2], 3-100; [2], 88, [2]; [2], 3-118, [4] p., folded map of New England and New York, folio. Large paper copies (38 x 23.5 cm.), small paper copies (31 x 20.3 cm.). Sabin 46392, Holmes: Cotton Mather bibliog. 213 A. Copies in most large libraries. Following copies are either large paper or have the errata, as indicated: BM (l.p.), MBC (l.p.), the late M.B. Jones, present location unknown (errata), MHi (2 l.p.), NIC (l.p.), NjP (l.p.), NN (l.p.), RPJCB (l.p.), Dr. A.S.W. Rosenbach (errata), ViU (l.p. and 2 with errata).

"Errata. In some copies there is inserted, at the end usually, an errata sheet of two leaves printed as two pages on one side of the sheet, containing corrections grouped in books. This sheet was doubtless compiled by Cotton Mather after bound copies of the *Magnalia* came to his hand. It was printed in Boston and added to some few copies. No copies of the errata were published with the *Magnalia* originally. Nor were the corrections of these errata embodied in the text of either of the reprints."—Holmes.

Reprinted, *Hartford, 1820.* 2 vols., 8vo.; *Hartford, 1853-1855.* 2 vols., ports., with introduction, memoir and index. For full details, see Dr. Thomas J. Holmes's scholarly bibliography of Mather which devotes p. 573-596 to this great work.

In addition to frequent incidental references to other Indian captives, this work reprints, from his: *Humiliations follow'd with deliverances,* 1697: *A narrative of Hannah Swarton, containing wonderful passages, relating to her captivity and her deliverance,* Book VI, p. 10-14; and: *A notable exploit; wherein, Dux Faemina Facti* [the captivity and escape of Hannah Dustan and her companions], Book VI, p. 90-91.

PASTORIUS, FRANCIS DANIEL, GABRIEL THOMAS AND DANIEL FALCKNER

Continuatio | der | Beschreibung der Landschafft | Pensylvaniae | an denen End-Gräntzen | Americae. | Uber vorige des Herrn Pastorii | Relationes. | In sich haltend: | Die Situation, und Fruchtbarkeit des | Erdbodens. Die Schiffreiche und andere | Flüsse. Die Anzahl derer bisshero gebauten Städte. | Die seltsame Creaturen an Thieren, Vögeln und Fischen. | Die Mineralien und Edelgesteine. Deren eingebohrnen wil- | den Völcker Sprachen, Religion und Gebräuche. Und | die ersten Christlichen Pflantzer und Anbauer |dieses Landes. | Beschrieben von | Gabriel Thomas | 15. Jährigen Inwohner dieses | Landes. | Welchem Tractaetlein noch beygefüget sind: | Des Hn. Daniel Falckners | Burgers und Pilgrims in Pensylvania 193. | Beantwortungen uff vorgelegte Fragen von | guten Freunden. | [rule] | *Franckfurt und Leipzig,* | *Zu finden bey Andreas Otto, Buchhaendlern.* | *Im Jahr Christi 1702.* [295]

[4], 40, [6], 58 p., folded map, 8vo. Sabin 95394. BM, CSmH, CtY, NN, PHi, RPJCB. Title from facsimile in *Pennsylvania-German Society*

Proceedings, VII, 1896, p. 255, from an original in PHi, lacking last line of imprint.

Promotion literature of the Frankfort Land Company. For earlier editions, see under the three authors. The first part of this tract is a continuation of Pastorius' *Umständige Geographische Beschreibung*, 1700. The second part, with separate title page and collation is Daniel Falckner's *Curieuse Nachricht*, 1702.

PASTORIUS, FRANCIS DANIEL

Umständige Geographische Beschreibung . . . Pennsylvaniae . . . [etc. as in 1st ed., 1700] *Zufinden bey Andreas Otto. 1704.*   [296]

[12], 140 p., 8vo. Sabin 59028. PHi.

Same as 1st ed. but reset. Title from E.F. Robacker's *Pennsylvania German literature*, 1943.

[BEVERLEY, ROBERT]

The | history | and | present state | of | Virginia, | in four parts. | I. The history of the first settlement | of Virginia, and the government there- | of, to the present time. | II. The natural productions and conveni- | encies of the country, suited to trade | and improvement. | III. The native Indians, their religion, laws, | and customs, in war and peace. | IV. The present state of the country, as to | the polity of the government, and the | improvements of the land. | [rule] | By a native and inhabitant of the place. | [rule] | *London:* | *Printed for R. Parker, at the Unicorn, under the Piazza's | of the Royal-Exchange. MDCCV.* [Title within double ruled border].   [297]

[12], 104, 40, 64, 83, folded sheet after p. 50, tables and errata pp. 16, [4], engraved title and 14 plates, 8vo. (23 x 19 cm.). BM, DLC, MB, MBAt, MH, MHi, NjP, NN, PHi, RPJCB, etc.

Engravings by S. Gribelin after White's drawings in De Bry's Latin edition of Hariot's *Admiranda narratio.*

The first comprehensive history of Virginia, written by a native and intended as promotion literature. A valuable first hand account of conditions, written by a self consciously American observer of nature, the Indians, political and social life.

[WILLIAMS, JOHN]

[Good fetch'd out of evil: a collection of memorables relating to our captives. *Boston, Printed by B. Green, 1706.].*   [298]

[2], 46 p., 12mo. (14.3 x 9.2 cm.). Holmes: Bibliography of Cotton Mather 150 A, Sabin 104260, Evans 1257. MB (lacks title leaf and lower half of A2), MH (lacks title leaf and B12); Pocumtuck Valley Mem. Ass'n (lacks title leaf and others), ViU (lacks title leaf, lower half of A2 and B12).

Contents: Rev. John Williams: *Pastoral letter, Chateauriche* [Canada],

May 28. 1706. [while still a captive]; *Some instructions, written by Mr. John Williams, for his little son, when the child was in danger of taking in the Popish poisons* [36 four-line verses]; *A poem, written by a captive damsel* . . . [signed at end:] *Decemb. 23d. 1703., Mary French; Astonishing deliverances* . . . [from Indian captivity, ending with:] *A copy of a letter sent unto one of the ministers in Boston,* [dated Sept. 18, 1703 and signed:] *William Clap.*

Reprinted 1783, which see.

The popularity of this most interesting work is shown from the fact that a thousand copies were sold the first week but of the four known copies, not one has a title page and all have other imperfections. It was edited by Cotton Mather.

ARCHDALE, JOHN

A new | description | of that | fertile and pleasant province | of | Carolina: | with a | brief account | of its | discovery, settling, | and the | government | thereof to this time. | With several remarkable passages of Divine | Providence during my time. | [rule] | By John Archdale: Late | Governour of the same. | [rule] | *London:* | *Printed for John Wyat, at the Rose in St. Paul's* | *Church-Yard. 1707.*   [299]

[8], 32 p., 4to. (21.8 x 16.3 cm.). Sabin 1902, Church 828. BM, CSmH, DLC, ICN, MBAt, MH, MHi, NjP, NN, RPJCB.

The new province of Carolina prospered under Governor Archdale who came in 1685, became popular and introduced the cultivation of rice.

BEVERLEY, ROBERT

Histoire | de la | Virginie, | contenant | I. L'histoire du premier etablissement dans la Vir- | ginie, & de son gouvernement jusques à présent. | II. Les productions naturelles & les commoditez | du pais, avant que es Anglois y negociassent, & | l'ameliorassent. III. La religion, les loix, & | les coutumes des Indiens naturels, tant dans la | guerre, que dans la paix. IV. L'etat présent du | pais, tant a l'égsrd de la police, que de l'ame- | lioration du pais. | Par un auteur natif & habitant du pais. | Traduite de l'Anglois, | enrichie de figures. | [monogram] | *A Amsterdam,* | *Chez Thomas Lombrail, Marchand* | *Libraire dans le Beurs-straat.* | [rule] | *M D CC VII.* [Title in red and black].   [300]

[6], 432, [16] p., engraved title, 14 plates and folded table, 12mo. (16 x 9.5 cm.). In most large libraries.

. . . . . .

Title abbreviated, *A Amsterdam,* | *Chez Claude Jordan, Libraire, vis-à-vis du* | *Lombart, proche la Ville de Lion.* | *MDCCXII.*   [301]

Same collation. Same sheets with new title page. In most large libraries.

. . . . .

Same title as Lombrail ed., *Imprimé à Orleans, & se vend | a Paris, Chez, Pierre Ribou, proche les Au- | gustins, a la descente du Pont-neuf, | à l'Image Saint Loüis.* | [rule] | *M. DCCVII.* | *Avec aprobation, & privilege du Roy.*
[302]
[7], 416, [18] p., engraved title, 14 plates and folded table, 12mo. (16 x 9 cm.).

Pirated from Lombrail ed. of same year, with plates copied in reverse. In most large libraries.

. . . . .

Amsterdam: J. F. Bernard, 1718. Sabin considers this a doubtful entry. No copy located.   [303]

Dickenson, Jonathan

Ongelukkige schipbreuk en yslyke reystogt, van etlyke Engelschen, in | den Jaare 1696 van Jamaika in West-Indiën, na Pensylvania t'scheep gegaan, en in de Golf van Florida gestrand, alwaar zy onder de menscheneeters vervielen, en byna ongelooflyke wederwaerdigheden uytstonden. In't Engelsch beschreeven door Jonathan Dickenson, eenen van de reyzigers. En daaruyt vertaald door W. Sewel. . . . *Te Leyden, by Pieter van der Aa, Boekverkooper. Met. privilegie. [1707].*   [304]
100, [7] p., 3 folded plates, map, 8vo. (16.9 x 10.3 cm.). Sabin 20017, Ayer 74. Has prologue and index. Copies in most large libraries.

. . . . .

Same Dutch translation reprinted in Pieter van der Aa: *Naaukerige Versameling . . . 1707,* vol. 2, with plates and map but without prologue and index; and in De Jansoon van der Aa: *De Aanmerkenswaardigste en Alomberoemde Zee-en Landreisen. Hague,* 1706-1727, vol. 6, part 24. Copies in most large libraries.   [305]

[Mather, Cotton]

Frontiers well-defended. | [rule] | An | essay, | to direct the | frontiers | of a | countrey exposed unto the incur- | sions of a barbarous enemy, | how to behave themselves in their | uneasy station? | [rule] | Containing admonitions of piety, | propos'd by the compassion of | some friends unto their welfare, | to be lodg'd in the families of | our frontier plantations. | [rule] | *Boston, in N.E. Printed by T. Green,* | 1707. | [Title within ruled border].
[306]
50, [2]; *The Fall of Babylon,* 20 p., 12mo. (12 x 6 cm.). Sabin 46332, Evans 1311, Holmes: Cotton Mather bibliog. 138. CtY, MHi, MWA.

The Fall of Babylon, a catechism, issued as part of the above, with caption title only, last 20 p. Same issued separately with title in an edition of "some hundreds" of copies for distribution in Maryland to offset the Catholis influence on the pioneers. *Frontiers well-defended* was intended as a guide to settlers on the northern and western frontiers of New England who might be captured by the French and Indians and carried to Canada where they would be under the influence of the Catholic priests, a possibility which greatly worried the New England clergy and with reason for not a few of the captives turned Catholic.

. . . . .

A | memorial | of the present deplorable state of | New-England, | with the many disadvantages it lyes under, | by the male-administration of their | present Governour, | Joseph Dudley, Esq. | and his son Paul, &c. | Together with | the several affidavits of people of worth, | relating to several of the said Governour's mer- | cenary and illegal proceedings, but particularly his | private treacherous correspondence with Her Ma- | jesty's enemies the French and Indians. | To which is added, a faithful, but melancholy account | of several barbarities lately committed upon Her Majesty's sub- | jects, by the said French and Indians, in the East and West parts | of New-England. | [rule] | Faithfully digested from the several original letters, pa- | pers, and MSS. by Philopolites. | [rule] | *[London:] Printed [by Benjamin Harris] in the year, MDCCVII. and sold by S. Phillips | N. Buttolph, and B. Elliot. Booksellers in Boston. | [1707].*   [307]

[4], 41, [1] p., 4to. (15 x 10.2 cm.). Holmes: Cotton Mather bibliog. 230 A. BM, Bodleian, Ct, Public Record Office, ViU.

Though mainly concerned with the corruption of Governor Joseph Dudley, this work is of interest to us for the separate section at the end which has the caption title: *An account of several barbarities lately committed by the Indians in New-England; intermix'd with some memorable providences.*, p. 31-41. This includes *a letter from a captive at Port-Royal*, dated Sept. 18. 1703, and signed *W.C.*, p. 38-40 and gives the first published account of the captivity of Mrs. Hannah (Heath) Bradley of Haverhill, twice a captive, 1697 and 1703 who met the squaw wounded by Hannah Dustan, the only adult of the party of Indians who escaped her attack, as described by Mather in his *Humiliations*, 1697. She is also mentioned in Emma L. Coleman's *New England captives carried to Canada*, 1925, vol. 1, p. 346-347.

WILLIAMS, JOHN

The redeemed captive, returning | to Zion. | [rule] | A faithful history | of | remarkable occurrences, | in the | captivity | and the | deliverance | of | Mr. John Williams; | minister of the Gospel, in Deerfield, | who, in the desolation which befel that | plantation, by an incursion of the French | & Indians, was by them carried away, | with his family, and his neighbourhood, | unto Canada. | Whereto there is annexed a sermon | preached by him, upon his return, at | the lecture in Boston, Decemb. 5. 1706. | On those words, Luk. 8. 39. Return to thine | own house, and shew how great things

God | hath done unto thee. | [rule] | *Boston in N.E. Printed by B. Green, for | Samuel Phillips, at the Brick Shop 1707.* | [Title within double ruled border].   [308]

[6], 104 p., 8vo. (14.9 x 9.5 cm.). Sabin 104264, Evans 1340. BM, F.C. Deering, ICN, H.V. Jones-Rosenbach Co.-W. M. Elkins-PP (1st 2 leaves and p. 5-6 in facsim.), MH, MHi, MWA (title in facs.), RPJCB, T.W. Streeter.

On verso of title: *Imprimatur,* | *J. Dudley.*

The sermon has a separate title page at p. [88]: *Reports of Divine kindness:* . . . [same imprint].

First edition of one of the two most famous New England stories of Indian captivity, the other being that of Mary Rowlandson.

Deerfield was attacked February 29, 1703 | 4 (O.S.) and some 112 people captured, and many killed. Reverend John Williams, pastor of the church, a native of Roxbury and graduate of Harvard, had been the minister there for many years. His two youngest children were killed and his wife was tomahawked on the way to Canada. The rest of his family was carried to Canada where his daughter Eunice remained, turned Catholic, married an Indian and returned years later, with her children, to visit her relatives. In spite of his antagonism to the priests and their beliefs, he was well treated. He lived at Chateau Riche, below Quebec, until exchanged and sent to Boston where he arrived November 21, 1706. He resumed his ministry at Deerfield and died in 1729 at the age of 66. See notes to 1795 edition.

[KOCHERTHAL, JOSHUA VON]

Aussführlich | und | umständlicher Bericht | von der berühmten Landschafft | Carolina, | in dem | Engelländischen America | gelegen. | An Tag gegeben | von | Kocherthalern. | Zweyter Druck. | [orn.] | *Franckfurt am Mayn,* | *Zu finden bey Georg Heinrich Oehrling,* |*Anno* 1709.   [309]

Title from PHi copy in *Pennsylvania-German Society Proceedings,* VIII, 1897, p. 32, which also gives a synopsis of the tract. The author brought a German colony to America in December, 1709, the beginning of the Palatinate emigration to New York where Kocherthal's followers founded Newburg on the Hudson, named for Neuburg, Germany.

The first edition of this tract appeared in 1706. For an answer, attempting to discourage emigration to America, see under Anton Wilhelm Boehme, 1711, no. 314.

.   .   .   .   .

4. Druck, mit Anhängen, zweyer Engelischen gethanen Beschreibung, und eines auff der Reyse dahin begriffenen Hochteutschen auss Londen Benachrichtigung, nebst einer Land-carte von Carolina vermehrt. *Franckfurt am Mäyn, Zu finden bey Georg Heinrich Oehrling, Anno 1709.*   [310]

80 p., folded map, 8vo. (16.5 x 9.5 cm.). DLC.

The first appendix translates the portion relating to South Carolina from Richard Blome's *Present state,* 1686, probably using the German edition: *Englischem America,* 1697.

LAWSON, JOHN

A new | voyage | to | Carolina; | containing the | exact description and natural history | of that | country: | together with the present state thereof. | And | a journal | of a thousand miles, travel'd thro' several | nations of Indians. | Giving a particular account of their customs, | manners, &c. | [rule] | By John Lawson, Gent. Surveyor- | General of North-Carolina. | [rule] | *London:* | *Printed in the year 1709.*   [311]

[6], 258, [1] p., map, plate, 4to. Sabin 39451-39453. NjP, NN, etc.

First published in Stevens's *Collection of voyages,* vol. 1, with separates on large paper.

The four kings of Canada. Being a succinct account of the four Indian princes lately arrived from North America. With a particular description of their country, their strange and remarkable religion, feasts, marriages, burials, remedies for their sick, costumes, manners, constitution, habits, sports, war, peace, hunting, fishing, utensils belonging to the savages with other extraordinary things worthy observations, as to the natural or curious productions, beauty, or fertility of that part of the world. *London: Printed and sold by John Baker, at the Black Boy in Paternoster Row 1710*   [312]

47 p., 12mo. Old John Carter Brown cat. 136. An-C-OAr, CSmH, ICN, MiU-C, Nat'l Library of Scotland, NHi, RPJCB, H.M. Sage.

In 1709 Colonel Peter Schuyler of Albany, New York, took five Iroquois chiefs to England (one died en route): "King" Hendrick and John of the Wolf Clan, Brant ("Old Smoke," grandfather of Chief Joseph Brant) of the Bear Clan, all Mohawks, and Etaw Caume of the Turtle Clan, a River Indian. They met the Queen and court and were made much of. A considerable literature grew up around them, of which the above is the best known title since it was published in a modern facsimile. For this literature, see Freda F. Waldon's *Queen Anne and "The Four Kings of Canada," a bibliography of contemporary sources,* in *Canadian Historical Review,* September, 1935, p. 266-275. Their portraits were frequently painted and engraved, for which see R.W.G. Vail's *Portraits of "The Four Kings of Canada," A bibliographical footnote,* in *To Doctor R. Essays here collected and published in honor of the seventieth birthday of Dr. A.S.W. Rosenbach July 22, 1946. Philadelphia 1946,* p. 218-226, 2 plates.

[NAIRNE, THOMAS]

A | letter | from | South Carolina; | giving an | account | of the | soil, air, product, trade, govern- | ment, laws, religion, people, mili- | tary strength,

&c. of that Province; | Together with the manner and necessary | charges of settling a plantation | there, and the annual profit it will produce, | Written by a Swiss Gentleman, to his friend at Bern. | *London,* | *Printed for* A. Baldwin, *near the Oxford-* | *Arms in Warwick-lane. 1710.* [313]

63 p., 8vo. Sabin 87859. DLC, MiU-C, N, NjP, RPJCB.

Later editions, 1718 and 1732.

[BOEHME, ANTON WILHELM]

Das verlangte, nicht erlangte Canaan | bey den Luft-Gräbern; | oder | Ausführliche Beschreibung | von der unglücklichen Reise derer jungsthin aus Teutschland nach dem | Engelländischen in America gelegenen | Carolina und Pensylvanien | wallenden Pilgrim, absonderlich dem einseitigen übelgegründeten | Kochenthalerlschen Bericht | wohlbedächtig intgegen gesetzt | [etc., 11 lines and row of type ornaments] | *Franckfurt und Leipzig, MDCCXI.* [314]

[16], 127 p., 8vo. (19 cm.). Sabin 98990. BM, CSmH, DLC, MH, NN.

Title from facsimile from a copy owned by S.W. Pennypacker (in 1896), reproduced in *Pennsylvania-German Society Proceedings,* VII, 1896, p. 389, accompanied by a translation of chapter 6, telling of the life of the Palatinates during their temporary stay in England before coming to New York, p. 388-405. Same title in facsimile, in same *Proceedings,* vol. VIII, 1897, p. 48, with an English translation on the following page: "The Canaan, sought for, but not found, by those who till the air; or a full description of the unhappy voyage of the Pilgrims who recently went from German to the English possessions in Carolina and Pennsylvania; especially directed against the one-sided and unfounded report of Kocherthal. I. An answer to some questions on this subject, with an introduction by Moritz Wilhelm Hoen. II. Admonitions to the Germans who have already journeyed thither, by Anton Wilhelm Boehme. III. The Sermon on the Mount, and prayers, to be used by them, on the way. IV. Dissuasion against forsaking Germany by the English Crown. V. Short account of their misfortunes. VI. Another account. VII. An extract from the sermon of John Trebecco, delivered in London to the emigrants. All bound together out of love for truth, and patriotic motives. Frankfort and Leipzig, 1711."

Each part has its own pagination, showing that it was issued separately as well as in collected form with the inclusive title as above. This tract was written as a reply to Joshua Kocherthal's *Aussführlich und umständlicher Bericht,* 1709, no. 309.

.   .   .   .   .

Das verlangte, nicht erlangte Canaan [etc., as in 1st ed., 1711] *Hamburg: Wierng. 1712.* [315]

384, [2] p., 8vo. Title from Sabin 32377 who does not locate a copy.

LAWSON, JOHN

Allerneueste Beschreibung der Provintz Carolina in West-Indien. . . . Aus dem Englischen übersetzt durch M. Vischer. *Hamburg, . . . Thomas von Wierings Erben . . . Anno 1712.* [316]

[14], 365, [3] p., map and plate, 12mo. De Renne I:4. DLC, GU-De, MH, NjP, NN (imperfect), RPJCB.

German edition of: *A new voyage to Carolina,* 1709, no. 311.

[NORRIS, JOHN]

Profitable | advice | for rich and poor. | In a | dialogue, or discourse | between | James Freeman, a Carolina Planter, | and | Simon Question, a West-Country Farmer, | containing | a description, | or true relation | of | South Carolina, | an | English Plantation, or Colony, in America: | with | propositions for the advantageous set- | tlement of people, in general, but espe- | cially the laborious poor, in that fruit- | ful, pleasant, and profitable country, | for its inhabitants. | Entered in the Hall-Book, according to law. | *London, Printed by J. How, in Grace-Church-street* | *1712; and sold in parcels by Robert Davis,* | *Bookseller, in Bridgewater, Somersetshire, and by in* | *with gilt forrels, Price 1 s. 6 d.* [317]

110, [2] p., 12mo. Sabin 55502. DLC, RPJCB.

The author, a native of Somersetshire, England, had settled in Charleston, South Carolina.

[CROZAT, ANTHONY]

A | letter | to a | member | of the P - - - - - - - - t | of | G - - - t-B - - - - - n, | occasion'd by the | priviledge granted by the | French kings | to | Mr. Crozat. | [rule] | *London: | Printed for J. Baker, at the Black-Boy in Pater-* | *Noster-Row, 1713. (Price 6d.).* [318]

44 p., 12mo. (17.1 x 11.1 cm.). RPJCB.

Crozat had an exclusive French trading monopoly in Louisiana for fifteen years but gave it up after the first five years. He was made manager of the first French settlement on the Gulf Coast in 1712.

LAWSON, JOHN

The | history | of | Carolina; | containing the | exact description and natural history | of that | country: | . . . | *London: Printed for W. Taylor at the Ship, and J. Baker at the Black-* | *Boy, in Pater-noster-Row. 1714.* [319]

[6], 258, [1] p., map, plate, 4to. Sabin 39451-39453.

Second edition of: *A new voyage to Carolina,* 1709.

[MATHER, COTTON]

Duodecennium Luctuosum. | [rule] | The history of a long | war | with

Indian salvages, | and their directors and abettors; | from the year, 1702. to
the year, 1714. | Comprised in a | short essay, to declare the voice of the |
glorious God, in the various occurrences | of that war, which have been
thought mat- | ters of more special observation. | A recapitulation made in the
audience, | of His Excellency the Governour, | and the General Assembly of
the | Massachusett Province; at Boston, | 30 d. VII. m. 1714. | [rule, 2 lines
quoted, rule] | *Boston: Printed by B. Green, for Samuel Gerrish,* | *at his shop
on the North-side of the T. House. 1714.* | [Title within double ruled
border].   [320]

[2], 30 p., 8vo. (12.4 x 7.5 cm.). Sabin 46289, Evans 1688, Holmes:
Cotton Mather bibliog. 96. CSmH, F.C. Deering, MB, MBAt, MHi, MWA,
NN, RPJCB.

An account of the Indian attacks on Deerfield and Haverhill, with a general narrative of the Indian war then in progress, with many references to the
captives carried off to Canada.

[CHURCH, THOMAS]

Entertaining passages | relating to | Philip's War | which | began in the
month of June, 1675. | As also of | expeditions | more lately made | against
the common enemy, and Indian rebels, | in the eastern parts of New-
England: | with | some account of the Divine Providence | towards | Benj.
Church Esqr; | [rule] | By T. C. | [rule] | *Boston: Printed by B. Green, in
the year 1716.* [Title within double ruled border].   [321]

[2], ii, 120 p., 4to. (19.2 x 13.5 cm.). Evans 1800, Sabin 12996, Church
862. CSmH, DLC, ICN, MB, MH, MHi, MSaE, RPJCB.

Compiled by Thomas Church from notes of his father, Colonel Benjamin
Church, an important officer in the King Philip's War. The most popular
history of that war. For modern editions, see Sabin 12976-7, 12998.

This is the last of 11 quarto King Philip's War tracts, included because
its material is contemporary.

MONTGOMERY, ROBERT

A | discourse | concerning the design'd | establishment | of a new | colony
| to the | South of Carolina, | in the | most delightful country of the | uni-
verse. | [rule] | By Sir Robert Mountgomery, Baronet. | [rule] | [orn.] | [rule]
| *London:* | *Printed in the year.* 1717. | [Title within double ruled border].
                                                                              [322]

[2], 30, 3 p., folded plate, 8vo. (19.2 x 12.3 cm.). Sabin 51194, Church
866, De Renne I:6, old John Carter Brown cat. 224. BM, DLC, GU-De,
ICN, MBAt, MH, NN, RPJCB.

Folded plan with inscription on either side of a coat of arms: *A plan repre-
senting the form of setling the districts,* | *or county divisions in the Margra-
vate of Azilia.* | (31.6 x 30.3 cm.).

Refers to Sir Robert Montgomery's grant of the land between the rivers

Altamaha and Savannah, now part of Georgia. His promotion scheme failed. See also his *A description of the Golden Islands,* 1720.

. . . . .

Proposal | for | raising a stock, and settling a new | colony in Azilia, &c. | [Caption title] *[n.p., 1717?].*   [323]
4 p., double column, 4to. RPJCB.

LAWSON, JOHN

The history of Carolina; . . . [as in 2d ed., 1714] *London: Printed for T. Warner . . . 1718.*   [324]
[6], 258, [1] p., map, plate, 4to. Sabin 39451-39453. MBAt, MH.
Third edition of *A new voyage to Carolina,* 1709. Reprinted at Raleigh, 1860.

[NAIRNE, THOMAS]

A | letter | from | South Carolina; | giving an | account | of the | soil, air, product, trade, government, | laws, religion, people, military | strength, &c. of that Province. | Together, | with the manner and necessary charges of | settling a plantation there, | and the annual profit it will produce. | Written by a Swiss Gentleman, to his friend at Bern. | The second edition. | *London,* | *Printed for R. Smith, at the Bible, under the | Royal Exchange, 1718. (Price 6d.).*   [325]
56 p., 8vo. Sabin 87860. DLC, MH, MiU-C, NHi, NN, RPJCB.
For 1st ed., see 1710, for 3d ed., see 1732.

[CHETWOOD, W. R.]

The | voyages, | dangerous | adventures | and imminent | escapes | of | Captain Richard Falconer: | containing | the laws, customs, and manners of the | Indians in America; his shipwrecks; his marry- | ing an Indian wife; his narrow escape from the | Island of Dominico, &c. | Intermix'd with | the voyages and adventures of | Thomas Randel, of Cork, pilot; with | his ship- wreck in the Baltick, being the only man | that escap'd: his being taken by the Indians of | Virginia, &c: | Written by himself, now alive. | *London,* | *Printed for W. Chetwood . . .* [4 lines] *1720.*   [326]
[2], [vii]-viii, 72, 136, 179 p., engraved front, 8vo. (19.5 x 11.2 cm.). Title from Ayer 93 and Sabin 23723. F.C. Deering, DLC, ICN, MBBC, MH, MWA, PPM, RPJCB.
Indian captivity, probably fictitious.

DICKENSON, JONATHAN

God's protecting Providence, . . . The third edition. *Printed in Philadel-*

phia: Re-printed in London, and sold by the assigns of J. Sowle, at the Bible in George-Yard, Lombard Street, 1720. [327]

[10], 94, [12] p., 8vo. (17 x 10.8 cm.). Sabin 20015, Ayer 66. Copies in most large libraries.

[LAW, JOHN]

A | full and impartial | account | of the | Company | of | Mississipi, | otherwise call'd the | French East-India-Company, | projected and settled by Mr. Law. | Wherein the nature of that establishment and the | almost incredible advantages thereby accruing to the | French King, and a great number of his subjects, are | clearly explain'd and made out. With an account of | the establishment of the Bank of Paris, by the said | Mr. Law. To which are added, A description of | the country of Mississipi, and a relation of the | first discovery of it: In two letters from a gentleman | to his friend. | [rule] | In French and English. | [rule] | *London:* | *Printed for R. Francklin, at the Sun in Fleetstreet,* | *W. Lewis in Covent-Garden, J. Roberts in* | *Warwick-Lane, J. Graves in St. James's-Street, and* | *J. Stagg in Westminster-Hall.* MDCCXX. *Price 1 s.* [328]

[4], 79, [1] p., 8vo. (20.5 x 12.5 cm.). Sabin 26144. DLC, MH, MHi, MiU-C, RPJCB, etc.

John Law's "Mississippi Bubble," a scheme for exploiting the resources of the Mississippi Valley and Louisiana, organized as the Compagnie de l'Occident, the Mississippi Company and, later, the Company of the Indies, 1718-1720 (when the bubble burst), to 1731, resulted in many investors becoming impoverished and in the publication of a large pamphlet literature written by the promoters and victims in England, Holland and France in 1720, for which see Winsor 5:75-78. Since nothing came of the project, its literature is omitted here save for its principal English-French promotion tract, above, and the most amusing satire on the scheme, a large volume of prose, verse, copper plates and caricatures, humorous and, some of them, very broad:

Het groote Tafereel | der Dwaasheid, | vertoonende de opkomst, voortgang en ondergang der Actie, | Bubbel en Windnegotie, in Vrankryk, Engeland, en | de Nederlanden . . . *[Amsterdam]* 1720. 25, 52, 31, 8, 9, p., port. and 73 plates, folio. Sabin 28932. DLC, MWA, NN, etc.

"This great theatre of folly, representing the origin, progress and downfall of the South Sea Bubble in France, England and Holland . . ."

[MONTGOMERY, ROBERT?]

An account of the foundation and establishment of a design now on foot for a settlement on the Golden Islands to the South of Port Royal, in Carolina. By authority of a Royal Charter. *London. 1720.* [329]

8 p., 4to. Title from Sabin 10955 who locates no copy.

. . . . .

A | description | of the | Golden Islands, | with an account of the under- | taking now on foot for making a set- | tlement there: | Explaining, | 1st, The nature of that design, in general | 2dly, The measures already taken: And, | 3dly, Those intended to be taken hereafter. | [double rule] | *London:* | *Printed and sold by J. Morphew near Sta-* | *tioners-Hall. 1720. Price six-* | *pence.* | [Title within double ruled border]. [330]

45 p., 8vo. (18.3 x 11.2 cm.). Sabin 19719, De Renne I:6; old John Carter Brown cat. DLC, GU-De, MH, RPJCB.

These islands, off the Georgia coast, are St. Simon's, Sapolo, St. Catherine's and Ossabaw and were part of Sir Robert Montgomery's grant of land between the rivers Altamaha and Savannah which he called the Margravate of Azilia. See his *A discourse,* 1717.

ROWLANDSON, MARY

The | soveraignty and goodness of | God, | together with the faithfulness of his | promises displayed: | being a | narrative | of the captivity and restauration of | Mrs. Mary Rowlandson. | Commended by her, to all that desire to | know the Lords doings to, & dealings | with her; especially to her dear chil- | dren and relations. | [rule] | Written by her own hand, for her private use, | and now made publick at the earnest desire of | some friends, and for the benefit of the afflicted. | [rule] | The second edition. | Carefully corrected, and purged from abundance | of errors which escaped in the former impression. | [rule] | *Boston:* | *Printed by T. Fleet, for Samuel* | *Phillips, at* | *the Three Bibles and Crown in King-* | *Street, 1720.* | [Title within border of type ornaments]. [331]

80 p., 8vo. (15 cm.). Sabin 73580, Evans 2173. BM, DLC, Lancaster Town Library.

WILLIAMS, JOHN

The redeemed captive returning to Zion. A faithful history of remarkable occurrences, in the captivity and the deliverance of Mr. John Williams, Minister of the Gospel, in Deerfield, who, in the desolation which befel that plantation, by an incursion of the French and Indians, was by them carried away, with his family, and his neighbourhood, unto Canada. The second edition. *Boston: Printed by T. Fleet, for Samuel Phillips, at the Three Bibles and Crown in King-Street. 1720.* [332]

[6], 98 p., 8vo. Sabin 104263, Evans 2197. F.C. Deering, NN, H.V. Jones-Rosenbach Co. (title and dedication in facsimile).

The sermon is omitted in this edition.

GEORGIA, PROPOSED NEW ENGLAND PROVINCE OF

A | Memorial, | Humbly shewing the past and present state of the land | lying waste and un-inhabited between Nova-Scotia, and | the Province of

Main in New-England in America. | [Caption title] *[London?, ca. 1721* or a year or two earlier]. [333]

2, [2] p., folio (30.5 x 18 cm.). Sabin 47634, Hildeburn 170. MB, PPL. Hildeburn, for no apparent reason, assigns the printing to Andrew Bradford of Phila.

Memorial, p. 1-2, blank [3], docketed caption [4].

. . . . .

An abstract | of the scheme of government so far as it | relates to the grantees in trust, for settling the land | lying between Nova-Scotia and the Province of Maine | in New-England, in America. | [Caption title] *[London?, ca. 1721* or a year or two earlier]. [334]

[4] p., folio (30.5 x 20.5 cm.). MB.

Abstract, p. [1-3], docketed caption [4].

. . . . .

Doctor [Charles] Pinfold's state of the case of the Petitioner's, for | settling His Majesties waste land, lying between Nova Scotia, and the Province | of Main in New-England, in America. | [Caption title] *[London?, 1721].* [335]

3, [1] p., folio (30 x 23 cm.). MB.

State, p. 1-3, docketed caption [4]. Signed and dated at end of text on p. 3: *Charles Pinfold. Doctors Commons. March 17. 1721.* Followed by Ms note: "This case was written for the Rt Honble the Lord Viscount Townsend by his order."

Scheme to found a colony between the Kennebec and St. Croix rivers to be called Georgia, to be settled by soldiers and refugees for the purpose of raising naval stores and improving England's defenses. The scheme was promoted by Thomas Coram, a London merchant. For the history of this abortive land scheme, see Robert E. Moody's: *Three documents concerning a proposal to establish a province of Georgia in New England,* in *New England Quarterly,* March, 1941, p. 113-120.

MORTON, NATHANIEL

New-England's | memorial; | or, | a brief relation of the most memorable and | remarkable passages of the providence of | God, manifested to the | planters | of | New-England in America: | with special reference to the first colony | thereof, called | New-Plimouth | . . . | Published for the use and benefit of | present and future generations. | By Nathaniel Morton, | Secretary to the Court for the Juris- | diction of New-Plimouth. | [6 lines quoted] | *Boston, Reprinted for Nicholas Boone, at the Sign of the | Bible in Cornhill. 1721.* [Variant imprint:] *Boston, Reprinted for Daniel Henchman, at the corner | shop over against the Brick-Meeting-House. 1721.* [Title within double ruled border]. [336]

[10], 248, [1] p., 16mo. (15.2 x 9.5 cm.). Sabin 51013, Evans 2266, 2267. DLC, MB, MH, MWA, NB, NjP, NHi, NN, RPJCB.

[BEVERLEY, ROBERT]

The history and present state of Virginia, in four parts. [etc., as in 1st ed., 1705] The second edition revis'd and enlarg'd by the author. *London: Printed for F. Fayram and J. Clarke at the Royal Exchange, and T. Bickerton in Pater-Noster-Row*, 1722. [337]

[8], 284, [24], advs. [4] p., engraved title and 14 plates as in 1st English ed., 8vo. (18.5 x 11.5 cm.). Copies in most large libraries.

Some copies have the imprint: *London: Printed for B. and S. Tooke in Fleetstreet; F. Fayram and J. Clarke at the Royal-Exchange, and T. Bickerton in Pater-Noster-Row, 1722.* NjP, etc.

Original dedication omitted, entirely new preface and many additions and suppressions of critical comments on contemporaries. Therefore, original text is much more interesting.

. . . . .

Same title, By Robert Beverly [sic] . . . Reprinted from the author's second revised edition, London, 1722. With an introduction by Charles Campbell, author of the "Colonial history of Virginia." *Richmond, Va.: J.W. Randolph*, 1855. [338]

xx, 264 p., 8vo. Copies in most large libraries.

. . . . .

The history and present state of Virginia. By Robert Beverley. Edited with an introduction by Louis B. Wright. Published for The Institute of Early American History and Culture at Williamsburg, Virginia by *The University of North Carolina Press Chapel Hill,* 1947. [339]

xxxv, 366 p., facsimiles of original engraved title page and 14 plates, 8vo. (23.5 x 15.5 cm.).

Text of the first edition with principal changes in the second edition, an important introduction and notes. The first of a series of historical publications of the Institute.

COXE, DANIEL

A | description | of the English Province of | Carolana, | by the Spaniards call'd | Florida, | and by the French | La Louisiane. | As also of the great and famous river | Meschacebe or Missisipi, | the five vast navigable lakes of fresh | water, and the parts adjacent. | Together | with an account of the commodities of the | growth and production of the said Province. | And a preface containing some considera- | tions on the consequences of the French | making settlements there. | [rule] | By Daniel Coxe, Esq; | [rule, one line quoted, rule] | *London;* | *Printed for B. Cowse, at the Rose and Crown in* | *St. Paul's Church-Yard. M DCC XXII.* [340]

[54], 122 p., folded map, 8vo. (19.3 x 11.7 cm.). Sabin 17279, Church 886. BM, CSmH, DLC, ICN, MBAt, MH, NjP, NN, RPJCB.

Folded map of the southeastern part of North America: *A map of* | *Carolana* | *and of the River* | *Meschacebe* | *&c.* | with an insert: *A map of* | *the mouth of the* | *River* | *Meschacebe.* (42.4 x 54.5 cm.).

Promotion tract for the Province of Carolana (Georgia, the Floridas, Alabama, Mississippi and Louisiana). The author's father claimed this territory as proprietor under the English crown, in spite of the French claim to much of it. The author lived there fourteen years and explored much of the territory he claimed. The first account of Louisiana in English.

[CHETWOOD, W. R.]

The voyages, dangerous adventures and imminent escapes of Captain Richard Falconer: . . . The second edition corrected. *London: Printed for J. Marshal . . . MDCCXXIV.* [341]

[6], 224, [6] p., front., 12mo. (17.3 x 10 cm.). Ayer supp. 31, Sabin 23723. F. C. Deering, ICN.

COLDEN, CADWALLADER

Papers | relating to | an act of the Assembly | of the | Province of New-York, | for encouragement of the Indian trade, &c. and | for prohibiting the selling of Indian goods to the French, | viz. of Canada. | I. A petition of the merchants of London to His Majesty, | against the said act. | II. His Majesty's order in Council, referring the said | petition to the Lords Commissioners for Trade & Plantation. | III. Extract of the minutes of the said Lords, con- | cerning some allegations of the merchants before them. | IV. the report of the said Lords to His Majesty on the | merchants petition, and other allegations. | V. The report of the Committee of Council of the | Province of New-York, in answer to the said petition. | VI. A memorial concerning the furr-trade of New-York, | by C. Colden, Esq; | With a map. | [rule] | Published by authority. | [rule] | *Printed and sold by William Bradford in the City of New-York, 1724.* [342]

[2], 24 p., folded map, folio. (29.5 x 18.5 cm.). Sabin 14272, Evans 2512, Stokes VI, p. 259-260. British War Office, Public Record Office, NHi (map imperfect), NN (perfect Brinley 3384), PHi, PP, PPAmP.

Folded map: *A map of the countrey of the Five Nations* | *belonging to the Province of New York and of* | *the lakes near which the nations of Far Indians* | *live with part of Canada taken from the map of the* | *Louisiane done by Mr. De Lisle in 1718.* (35.5 x 22 cm.). Map used without change as a separate and also in Colden's *History of the Five Nations,* 1727; but greatly improved and issued as a separate in 1735 (See Stokes for date). ICN, NHi, NN.

The first important study of the Iroquois Indians and of the colonial trade with them.

Jones, Hugh

The | present state | of | Virginia. | Giving | a particular and short account of the In- | dian, English, and Negroe inhabitants of that | colony. Shewing their religion, manners, government, | trade, way of living, &c. with a description of | the country. | From whence is inferred a short view of | Maryland and North Carolina. | To which are added, | schemes and propositions for the better promotion of | learning, religion, inventions, manufactures, and trade in | Virginia, and the other plantations. | For the information of the curious, and for the service of such | as are engaged in the propagation of the Gospel and advancement | of learning, and for the use of all persons concerned in the | Virginia trade and plantation. | [rule, 3 lines quoted, rule] | By Hvgh Jones, A.M. Chaplain to | the Honourable Assembly, and lately Minister of | James-Town, &c. in Virginia. | [rule] | *London:* | *Printed for J. Clarke, at the Bible under the Royal-* | *Exchange. M DCC XXIV.* [343]

[4], viii, 151, [1] p., 8vo. (18.7 x 11.5 cm.). Sabin 36511, Church 890. Copies in most large libraries, a second issue at MWiW-C.

An accurate descriptive and promotional history by a professor at the College of William and Mary.

Purry, Jean Pierre

Memoire | presenté à Sa Gr. | Mylord Duc de Newcastle, | Chambellan de S.M. le Roi George, &c. | Secretaire d'Etat: | Sur l'état present de la Caroline & sur les moyens | de l'ameliorer; | Par Jean Pierre Purry, de Neufchâtel de Suisse. | [Caption title] [Colophon:] *Imprimé à Londres, chez G. Bowyer, & se trouve chez Paul Vaileant, dans le Strand.* | *MDCCXXIV.* [344]

11 p., 4to. Sabin 66725. DLC, RPJCB.

. . . . . .

A memorial presented to . . . the Duke of Newcastle . . . concerning the present state of Carolina, and the means of improving it. *[London: Printed by G. Bowyer for Paul Vaileant, in the Strand? 1724?].* [345]

4to. Title from BM cat. BM.

Reprinted as: *Memorial presented,* 1880. Sabin 66726.

For his later tracts, see under 1731 and 1732.

Symmes, Thomas

Lovewell lamented. | [rule] | Or, a | sermon | occasion'd by the fall | of the brave | Capt. John Lovewell | and several of his | valiant company, | in the late | heroic action | at Piggwacket. | Pronounc'd at Bradford, May 16 1725 | By Thomas Symmes, V.D.M. | [rule, 2 lines quoted, rule] | *Boston in New-*

England: | *Printed by B. Green Junr. for S. Gerrish,* | *near the Brick Meeting House in Cornhill.* | *1725.* | [Title within double ruled border].   [346]

[4], xii, 32 p., 8vo. (17.5 x 11 cm.). Sabin 94107, Evans 2705. CSmH, DLC, MB, MH, MHi, MSaE, MWA, MWiW-C, NN, PP.

Lovewell, engaged in a retaliatory expedition against the Indians who had been harrying the Maine settlements, fought a battle at Piggwacket (Fryeburg, Maine) on May 9, 1725 in which the leader and about a third of his men were killed.

A historical preface to the sermon tells the story of the battle.

.   .   .   .   .

Historical memoirs | of the late fight at | Piggwacket, | with a | sermon | occasion'd by the fall of the brave | Capt John Lovewell | and several of his valiant company, | in the late | heroic action there. | Pronounc'd at Bradford, May, 16. 1725. | [rule] | By Thomas Symmes, V.D.M. | [rule] | The second edition corrected. | [rule, 2 lines quoted, rule] | *Boston in New England:* | *Printed by B. Green Jun. for S. Gerrish, near the* | *Brick Meeting-House in* | *Cornhill. 1725.* | [Title within double ruled border].   [347]

[4], xii, 32 p., 8vo. (16.7 x 10.6 cm.). Sabin 94108, Church 897, Evans 2706. CSmH, MB, MBAt, MH, MHi, MSaE, MWA, NN, RPJCB.

.   .   .   .   .

The Voluntier's March; being a full and true account [of] the bloody fight which happen'd between Capt. Lovewell's Company, and the Indians at Pigwoket. An excellent new song. *[Boston: J. Franklin, 1725].*   [348]

Title from an advertisement in the *New-England Courant,* May 31, 1725. Sabin 100759, George Lyman Kittredge: *The ballad of Lovewell's Fight,* in *Bibliographical essays, a tribute to Wilberforce Eames,* 1924, p. 93-120, where James Franklin, the printer, is suggested as the probable author. Reprinted in Farmer and Moore's *Collections, historical and miscellaneous,* February, 1824. For the best known contemporary account of the battle, see nos. 346 and 347.

[CHETWOOD, W.R.]

The voyages, dangerous adventures and imminent escapes of Captain Richard Falconer . . . *[n.p.]* 1726. DNL, PHC.   [349]

COXE, DANIEL

A description of the English Province of Carolana [. . . as in 1st ed., 1722] The second edition. *London: Printed for Edward Symon, against the Royal Exchange in Cornhill.* 1726.   [350]

[56], 122 p., folded map, 8vo. BM.

Sheets of 1st ed. with new title page.

PENHALLOW, SAMUEL

The | history | of the | wars of New-England, | with the Eastern Indians. | Or, a | narrative | of their continued perfidy and cruelty, | from the 10th of August, 1703. | To the peace renewed 13th of July, 1713. | And from the 25th of July, 1722. | To their submission 15th December, 1725. | Which was ratified August 5th 1726. | [rule] | By Samuel Penhallow, Esqr. | [rule, 2 lines quoted, rule] | *Boston:* | *Printed by T. Fleet, for S. Gerrish at the lower* | *end of Cornhill, and D. Henchman over-against* | *the Brick Meeting-House in Cornhill, 1726.* | [Title within double ruled border].   [351]

[2], iv, [2], 134, [1] p., 8vo. (16.2 x 9.6 cm.). Sabin 59654, Church 904, Evans 2796. BM, CSmH, DLC, ICN, MB, MBAt, MH, MHi, MWA, MWiW-C, NHi, NN, PPL, RPJCB, ViU.

The author came from England to Portsmouth, N.H. in 1686 and lived in that province until his death in 1726. He was Chief Justice of the province and wrote this excellent history, to a considerable extent, from first-hand knowledge. For reprints, see Evans.

[COLDEN, CADWALLADER]

The | history | of the | Five Indian Nations | depending on the Province | of | New-York | in America. | [rule, type orn., rule] | *Printed and sold by William Bradford in* | *New-York, 1727.*   [352]

[2], xvii, [1], 119 p., 8vo. (15.5 x 10 cm.). Evans 2849, Sabin 14270, Church 905, Stokes VI, 259-260. BM, CSmH, ICN, MWiW-C, NHi (2 copies, 1 in original binding), NN, PHi, PP, PPL-R, PU-MUS, RHi, RPJCB, ViU.

The first history of the Iroquois Indians. See L.C. Wroth's *American bookshelf, 1755.* Philadelphia, 1934. Page 73 is without page number in one of the copies at NHi. On the page preceding the text there is an advertisement for the map issued with Colden's *Papers relating to the Indian trade* in 1724 which was being sold as a separate, without change, in 1727 and is sometimes (according to Stokes) found bound up with the present volume, though the map is not part of the volume. The map was reissued as a separate, with many changes and additions, in 1735, copies of this later and rarer issue being at ICN, NHi and NN.

COXE, DANIEL

A description of the English Province of Carolana [. . . as in 1st ed., 1722] *London: Printed for Edward Symon, against the Royal Exchange in Cornhill. 1727*   [353]

[56], 122 p., folded map, 8vo. Sabin 17280. BM.

Sheets of 1st ed. with new title page.

[ALLEN, MRS. I.]

A short narrative | of the claim, title and right of the heirs of the Honourable | Samuel Allen, Esq; deceased, to the Province of New-Hampshire | in New-England: Transmitted from a Gentlewoman in London, | to her friend in New-England. | [Caption title] *[Boston, 1728].*   [354]

13 p., small folio, (19 x 14.5 cm.). Sabin 864, Evans 3106. MHi, MWA, RPJCB.

The covering letter transmitting the claim is signed *I.A.* The tract recites the claim of the grandson, not yet of age, of Col. Samuel Allen, former Governor and Commander in Chief of that part of New Hampshire "from three miles north of Merrimack." Since the title says that the claim was transmitted by a gentlewoman of London and since the letter is signed *I.A.*, it is reasonable to assume that the letter was written by the mother of the minor grandson and heir. The verso of p. 11 is blank, followed by a *Postscript* on p. 13.

Described from Mass. Hist. Soc. Photostat Americana, 2d ser., 1936, no. 93.

HANSON, ELIZABETH

God's mercy surmounting man's cruelty, exemplified in the captivity and redemption of Elizabeth Hanson, wife of John Hanson, of Knoxmarsh at Keacheachy, in Dover township, who was taken captive with her children and maid-servant, by the Indians in New-England, in the year 1724. In which are inserted, sundry remarkable preservations, deliverances, and marks of the care and kindness of Providence over her and her children, worthy to be remembered. The substance of which was taken from her own mouth, and now published for a general service. *To be sold by Samuel Keimer in Philadelphia; and by W. Heurtin goldsmith in New-York, 1728.*   [355]

40 p., 12mo. (16 cm.). CSmH (lacks title and pp. 37-40).

Title from advertisement in *Pennsylvania Gazette,* Dec. 24, 1728 which was copied by Hildeburn 327 which was, in turn, copied by Evans 2996, both without collation or location. Field 645* supplied an incorrect title, wrongly dated 1724, copied by Sabin 30263.

The only known copy of this first edition lacks title and pages 37-40 but is identified as the first edition by the contemporary inscription on p. 9: *Thomas Persall's Book lent to R. B. 1742, ye 6 month.* written 12 years before the publication of the second edition. This copy first appeared in Merwin-Clayton auction of two private libraries, Dec. 5, 1911, lot 260, where it was sold to Wilberforce Eames for $22.00 who sold it with his imprint collection to the Henry E. Huntington Library.

There are two versions of the text of this narrative, both based on the same original manuscript. The English editions follow one version and the American editions the other. The English text seems the simpler and more

natural while the American seems to be the same text worked over and
"improved." An attempt was made to give it a more polished style. No
American edition attributes the work to Rev. Samuel Bownas who nowhere
assumes its authorship, though the first English edition, published seven
years after his death, states that it was "taken in substance from her own
mouth, by Samuel Bownas." He says in his autobiography, published three
years after his death, (*An account of the life* . . . London, 1756), p. 147
"From thence I went to visit the widow Hanson, who had been taken into
captivity by the Indians, an account of which I took from her own mouth,
being in substance as followeth," and then he tells in his own words the brief
story of her captivity, devoting to it but a single page, at the end of which
he says: "After my return to Europe [he was in Ireland in 1740] I saw at
Dublin a relation of this extraordinary affair in a printed narrative, which
was brought over by a friend from America." The only known printed
narrative of the captivity available in 1740 was the Philadelphia, 1728 first
edition but Bownas does not claim its authorship but seems to have heard
of its existence for the first time in Dublin. His statement certainly does not
sound as though he considered himself the author of it. We know from his
own account that he visited Mrs. Hanson during his visit to America in
1726-1727 but he gives in a single page the account he wrote out at that
time.

Both versions of the complete narrative are written in the first person,
presumably by, or at least, dictated by Mrs. Hanson herself and the American
edition is signed at the end: *E.H.* A note at the end of the first English
edition, after stating: "The substance of the foregoing account was taken
from her own mouth by Samuel Bownas," goes on to say: "And in the
seventh month, called September, 1741, Samuel Hopwood was with her,
and received the relation much to the same purpose." And no doubt many
other people went to see the famous captive and some of them no doubt
wrote out what she told them. It seems odd that the English editions always
say that the *substance* of the published narrative was taken down by Bownas
from the captive's dictation. Does this mean that he made a few notes and
then embroidered the tale to suit himself? Or did some one else use his notes
in writing up the complete story, putting it into the first person, as though
it were written by the captive herself? If some one else wrote the narrative,
Bownas would naturally be surprized to find an American printed edition
when he visited Dublin. If he had written it, even if it had been published
without his knowledge, he certainly would have commented on it in his
autobiography and, if he did write it, why did not the American publisher
attribute it to him as the English publisher did after his death? He was a
famous Quaker preacher, both in the British Isles and in America, so one
would think that the American publisher would have used his name to help
sell the book if he was really the author or ghost writer, but no American
edition mentions him in any way. Certainly, when he saw the published
American edition he did not claim it as his own and no one thought to
attach his name to it until after his death. It all looks very peculiar and

certainly there is a reasonable doubt, based on Bownas' own statements, that he ever wrote the text as published in the extended version. Evidently two ghost writers, one English and one American, worked over copies of the original narrative for publication in the two countries. Who they were we do not know. The English text is so simply told in homely language of the period that it would almost seem that the captive had written it herself, which is borne out by the fact that the story is in the first person and the American edition has her initials at the end as author. The Library of Congress catalogs the story under Elizabeth Hanson as author and not under the name of Bownas who never claimed that he wrote it and was surprised when he first saw it in print.

Elizabeth Hanson was taken captive by the Indians with her four children and a maidservant at Kachecky, August 27, 1724, and was redeemed by her husband the following year, being absent from her home twelve months and six days. Apparently she was taken by Indians from Maine or New Brunswick for she was taken to Port Royal where her husband found her. Three of the children and the maid were ransomed with Mrs. Hanson but the eldest daughter was not given up and afterward married a Frenchman.

[Seguenot, Father François, of Montreal]

A | letter | from a | Romish Priest | in Canada, | to one [Mrs. Christina Baker] who was taken captive in | her infancy, and instructed in the | Romish faith, but some time | ago returned to this her native | country. | With an answer thereto, | by a person to whom it was | communicated [Governor William Burnett, of Massachusetts]. | *Boston: Printed for D. Henchman, at | the Corner Shop over against the Brick Meeting- | House in Corn-hill. MDCCXXIX.*   [356]

[2], ii, 26 p., 8vo. Sabin 78904, Evans 3216. BM, CSmH, DGU, DLC, ICN, MBAt, MH, MHi, MWA, NHi, RPJCB.

Many Indian captives carried to Canada were converted to Catholicism, notably Eunice Williams, daughter of Rev. John Williams, which, of course, raised the ire of their Congregational relatives back in New England.

Dalton, James

Life and actions of James Dalton, a noted street robber, . . . with account of his running away with the ship when he was first transported, and like-ways the tricks he played in New York, the Bermudas, Virginia, Carolina, and other parts of America, taken from his own mouth while in Newgate. *[London, 1730].*   [357]

8vo. Sabin 18351. BM.

The British Museum has another life of Dalton, London, 1720, which, however, does not appear to contain his American adventures.

Rare early account of the life of a criminal in America.

CLAP, ROGER

Memoirs | of | Capt. Roger Clap. | Relating some of God's remarkable | providences to him, in bringing | him into New-England; and some | of the straits and afflictions, the | good people met with here in | their beginnings. | And | instructing, counselling, directing | and commanding his children and | childrens children, and household, | to serve the Lord in their gene- | rations to the latest posterity. | [rule] | Heb. xi.4. - - - He being dead, yet speaketh. | [double rule] | *Boston in New-England:* | *Printed by B. Green, 1731.* [Title within double ruled border].   [358]

[4], ii, 34, 10 p., 8vo. (15.5 x 9.5 cm.). Evans 3403, Sabin 13206, Church 913. CSmH, MB, MBC, MH, MHi, NHi, NN, PPL-R, RPJCB.

One of the best accounts of pioneer life in Massachusetts. Clap came to New England in 1630, was Captain of Boston Castle, 1665-1686, and died in 1691.

PURRY, JEAN PIERRE

Description abregee de l'etat present de la Caroline Meridionale. *Neufchâtel. 1731?*   [359]

8vo. Sabin 66723.

Sabin took the title from a footnote in [Benjamin Martyn:] *New and accurate account of the Provinces of South Carolina and Georgia,* 1732. Martyn says: "About two years ago [1731], Captain Purry, a Swiss gentleman, wrote an authentic account of that country [South Carolina] in French, which was printed at Neufchâtel in Switzerland: and to shew that he believed himself when he gave a beautiful description of South Carolina, he has gone to settle there with six hundred of his countrymen." Purry was the founder of Purrysburg, Beaufort County, South Carolina.

. . . . .

A description of the Province of South Carolina, drawn up at Charles Town, in September, 1731. Translated from Mr. Purry's original treatise, in French, and published in the Gentleman's Magazine, for August, September, and October, 1732. *Washington City: Printed by Peter Force. 1837.*   [360]

16 p., 8vo.

Force's Tracts, II, no. 11. Signed by Purry and three others. Also reprinted in Carroll's *Historical collections of South Carolina,* II:121-140, with "Proposals by Mr. Peter Purry, of Neufchâtel, for encouragement of such Swiss Protestants as should agree to accompany him to Carolina, to settle a new colony." Rich, quoted by Sabin, thinks that the original of the tract translated in the Gentleman's magazine could not have been printed before 1732 which tends to prove that the *Description abregee,* 1731? is a different work. We have been unable to trace copies of this 1731 tract, but see his *Mémoire,* 1724. For the second edition, see under 1732.

[BEISSEL, JOHANN CONRAD, AND OTHERS]

Vorspiel | der | Neuen-Welt. | Welches sich in der letzten Abendröthe | als ein paradisischer Lichtes-glantz | unter den Kindern Gottes | hervor gethan. | In | Liebes, Lobes, Leidens, Krafft | und Erfahrungs liedern abgebildet, die | gedrückte, gebückte und Creutz- | tragende Kirche auf Erden. | Und wie inzwischen sich | Die obere und Triumphirende Kirche | als eine Paradiesische vorkost her- | vor thut und offenbahret. | Und daneben, als | Ernstliche und zuruffende wächterstimmen | an alle annoch zerstreuete Kinder Gottes, das sie | sich sammlen und bereit machen auf den | baldigen; Ja bald herein brechen- | den Hockzeit-Tag der braut | des Lamms. | *Zu Philadelphia: Gedruckt bey Benjamin | Francklin, in der Marck-Strass. MDCCXXXII.*   [361]

200 p., 8vo. Evans 3503, Hildeburn 452. PHi.

Promotion tract for Beissel's Ephrata Community, near Lancaster, Pennsylvania, a religious retreat for Seventh Day Baptists which flourished as such until about 1800 and still exists, though all but two of the original buildings have disappeared. See their *Chronicon Ephratanese;* Oswald Seidensticker's *Ephrata, eine Amerikanische Klostergeschichte;* and J.F. Sachse's *The German Sectarians of Pennsylvania,* Vol. I-II.

[NAIRNE, THOMAS]

A | letter | from | South Carolina; | giving an | account | of the | soil, air, product, trade, govern- | ment, laws, religion, people, | military strength, &c. | of that | Province; | Together with the manner and necessary | charges of setling a plantation | there, and the annual profit it will produce. | Written by a Swiss Gentleman, to his friend at Bern. | The second [i.e., third] edition. | *London: | Printed for J. Clarke at the Bible under the | Royal-Exchange. 1732. Price 1 s.*   [362]

63, [1] p., 8vo. Sabin 87861. DLC, MH, NHi, NN, RPJCB, ScC.

Earlier editions, 1710 and 1718.

[MARTYN, BENJAMIN]

A | new and accurate account | of the | Provinces | of | South-Carolina | and | Georgia: | with many curious and useful observati- | ons on the trade, navigation and planta | -tions of Great-Britain, compared with her | most powerful maritime neighbours in an- | tient and modern times. | *London: | Printed for J. Worrall at the Bible and | Dove in Bell-Yard near Lincoln's-Inn; and sold | by J. Roberts near the Oxford-Arms in | Warwick-Lane. 1732. | (Price one shilling).*   [363]

[4], 76 p., 8vo. (19.5 x 12 cm.). Sabin 56847, De Renne I:31. DLC, GU-De, MBAt, MH, MiU-C, NHi, RPJCB, ViU.

First ed., 1st issue. Second issue published in 1733.

Frequently attributed to James Edward Oglethorpe but for more probable attribution to Martyn, see *Bibliographical essays, a tribute to Wilberforce Eames*, 1924, p. 289-291.

· · · · ·

Select | tracts | relating to | colonies. | Consisting of | [first column:] I. An essay on plantati- | ons. By Sir Francis | Bacon Lord Chan- | cellor of England. | II. Some passages taken | out of the History of | Florence, &c. | III. A treatise. By John | [double vertical rule, second column:] De Witt Pensioner | of Holland. | IV. The benefit of plan- | tations or colonies. | By William Penn. | V. A discourse concer- | ning plantations. By | Sir Josiah Child. | [rule, orn., rule] | *London,* | *Printed for J. Roberts at the Oxford-Arms in | Warwick-Lane.* | *[1732].*   [364]

[8], 40 p., 8vo. (21 x 14 cm.). Sabin 78992, De Renne I:36. GU-De, NHi, NN.

The treatise ascribed to John De Witt was almost certainly written by Pieter de la Court, according to De Renne. It was probably prepared by Benjamin Martyn for the promotion of James Edward Oglethorpe's Georgia colony.

· · · · ·

[Ornament] | Some account of the designs of the | Trustees for establishing the Colony | of Georgia in America. | [Caption title] *[London, 1732?]*   [365]

4 p., folio (36.3 x 19 cm.). Sabin 27109 and 86573. De Renne I:18. BM, GU-De, RPJCB.

The BM and RPJCB copies have the lower half of p. 4 blank, the GU-De copy has this space occupied by an untitled map of South Carolina, Georgia and Florida, for a discussion of which see De Renne and V.W. Crane's *The promotion literature of Georgia*, in *Bibliographical essays, a tribute to Wilberforce Eames*, 1924, p. 287-288. There is a second issue with the map, and with head and tail pieces by John Pine.

· · · · ·

London, 1732. Sabin 86574. BM, RPJCB.   [366]

[PURRY, JEAN PIERRE]

Description abregee | de l'etat présent de la | Caroline | Meridionale, | nouvelle edition, | avec des | eclaircissemens | les | actes | des | concessions | faites à ce sujet a l'auteur, tant pour luy que pour | ceux qui voudront prendre parti avec luy. | Et enfin une | instruction | qui contient les | conditions, sous lesquelles on pourra l'accompagner. | *A Neufchatel.* | [rule] | *Se vend chez le Sr. Jacob Boyve à Neufchatel;* | *et chez le Sr. Secretaire Du Bois à St. Sulpy.* | *[1732].*   [367]

36 p., 4to. (23.7 x 18.3 cm.). De Renne I:32. GU-De.

The main text was "faite à Charlestoun au Moi de Septembre 1731." At end: "Instruction pour ceux qui auroient dessein d'accompagner le soussigné Jean Pierre Purry en Caroline."

Georgia, | oder: | kurtze Nachricht | von dem | Christlichen Vorhaben | der | Königlich-Englischen Herren Commissarien | zu Aufrichtung der neuen Colonie Georgia in Süd- | Carolina in America, | wie auch | der in London sich befindenden Societaet, | so von Fortpflantzung der Erkäntniss Christi | den Namen hat, | Dreyhundert Protestantische | Emigranten | nach ermeldtem Georgia aufzunehmen, | Ingleichem | von | den guten Conditionen | dieser Aufnahme, | und denen | Bereits gemachten schönen Anstalten, solche, so aus ihrem | Vaterlande um der Religion willen Friedens-Schlussmässig ausgehen, | und sich nach Georgia frenwillig zu gehen gehöriger Orten | angeben, | dahin sicher zu bringen, | unter | Königl. Gross-Britannischer Majestät | Allerhöchst und Hohen Genehmhaltung, | auch auf Verlangen | Hoch-ermeldten Königlichen Herren Commissarien | und der Hoch-Löblichen Societaet, | dem Druck überlassen. | [double rule] | *Franckfurt, Anno 1733.*   [368]

[8] p., folio, (32 x 19.5 cm.). PHi, RPJCB.

Title from Mass. Hist. Soc. Photostat Americana 2d ser., 1936, no. 65.

[MARTYN, BENJAMIN]

A | new and accurate account | of the | Provinces | of | South-Carolina | and | Georgia: | [. . . as in 1st ed., 1732] | 1733. | (Price one shilling). [369]

[4], 76 p., 8vo. (19.3 x 11.6 cm.). Sabin 87900, De Renne I:47. DLC, GU-De, MWiW-C, NN.

First ed., 2d issue. Identical with 1st issue, 1732, except for date on title. Reprinted in Ga. Hist. Soc. Coll., I, 1840, p. 42-78.

.   .   .   .   .

Reasons | for establishing the | Colony of Georgia, | with regard to the | trade of Great Britain, | the | increase of our people, and the employment and | support it will afford to great numbers of our own poor, | as well as foreign persecuted Protestants. | With some account of the country, and the design | of the Trustees. | [rule, 3 lines quoted, rule] | *London:* | *Printed for W. Meadows, at the Angel in Cornhill. MDCCXXXIII.*   [370]

39 p., map and plate. small folio (25.4 x 19 cm.). Sabin 45002, De Renne I:44. DLC, FTaSC, GU-De, MHi, MWA, MWiW-C, NjP (2d issue), NHi, PP, PPL, PPL-R, RPJCB (2 issues), U. It is not certain which issue is owned by these libraries.

Map without caption showing South Carolina, Georgia and Florida.

Plate without caption showing men felling trees, building house, with settlement laid out in distance, signed: *T. Pine Inv. et Sculpt.*

. . . . . .

With addition of a Postscript, p. 41-48. De Renne I:45. GU-De, MHi (lacks plate), MWA, NHi, RPJCB. [371]

. . . . . .

Same title, By Benjamin Martyn, Esq; | [rule, 3 lines quoted, rule] | The second edition. | [rule] | [same imprint, date]. Same collation and size. Sabin 45003, De Renne I:45. GU-De, MH, NcD, RPJCB. [372]

SMITH, SAMUEL

A | sermon | preach'd before the | Trustees for Establishing the Colony of | Georgia in America, | and before the | Associates of the late Rev. Dr. Thomas Bray, | for Converting the Negroes in the British Plantations, | and for other good Purposes. | At their | first yearly-meeting, | in the | Parish Church of St. Augustin, | on Tuesday February 23, 1730-31. | [rule] | By Samuel Smith, L.L.B. Lecturer | of St. Alban's, Wood-Street. | [rule] | Publish'd at the desire of the Trustees and Associates. | [rule] | To which is annexed | some account of the designs both of the Trustees | and Associates. | [rule] | *London: Printed by J. March, and sold by Messieurs Mount and Page, on | Tower-Hill. MDCCXXXIII.* | [Title within double ruled border]. [373]

42 p., folded map, 4to. (19.9 x 16.7 cm.). De Renne I:47. GU-De.

Folded map: Untitled map of South Carolina, Georgia and Florida (13.3 x 18.7 cm.). Second state of the map which appeared first in Benjamin Martyn's *Some account,* 1732.

First of the series of promotion sermons for the Trustees for Establishing the Colony of Georgia, continued, with a few breaks, until 1750.

[CHETWOOD, W.R.]

The voyages, dangerous adventures and imminent escapes of Captain Richard Falconer . . . Third edition. *London, 1734.* [374]

. . . . . .

Fourth edition. *London: J. Marshall, 1734.* [375]
Sabin 23723. DLC, IU, MiU, NN, OFH.

DICKENSON, JONATHAN

God's protecting Providence . . . *London, for A. Betteforth and C. Hitch at the Red Lion . . . 1734.* [376]
Not seen. F.C. Deering.

HALES, STEPHEN

A | sermon | preached before the | Trustees | for Establishing the | Colony

of Georgia, . . . | . . . | on Thursday, March 21. 1734. | . . . | *London,* |
Printed for T. Woodward, at the Half-Moon, between the two | Temple-
Gates, in Fleet-Street. MDCCXXXIV.   [377]

    62, [2] p., 4to. (21.5 x 16 cm.). De Renne I:50. GU-De.

Kurtze Relation aus denen vom 5.9. und 12. Nov. 1734. Engelland
erhaltenen, theils geschreibenen theils gedruckten Briefen von dem in
Gravesend und London angelangten, aus 57. Köpffen bestehenden und nach
Georgien in West-Indien gehenden zweyten Transport Saltzburgischer
Emigranten, als Gross-Britannischer Colonisten, woraus zu ersehen ist, mit
was vor einer ungemeinen Liebe dieser Transport von der Englischen Nation
aufgenommen worden, und mit was vor einer gantz besondern Sorgfalt die
Herren von der Societaet sich dieser Leuthe so geist-als leiblicher Wohlfahrt
sich befohlenan seyn lassen. *[n.p., 1734].*   [378]

    [8] p., 4to. De Renne I:51. GU-De.

    The beginning of the Saltzburger migration to Georgia.

Neue Nachricht | alter und neuer | merckwürdig-keiten | enthaltende |
ein vertrautes Gespräch | und sicher Briefe | von der | Landschafft Carolina
| und übrigen | Englischen Pflantz-Städten | in America. | *Zu finden zu* |
Zürich, Bern, Basel, Schaffhausen, und St. Gallen, | *in den Bericht-Häuseren*
| *gegen Ende des Jahrs 1734.*   [379]

    79, [1] p., 8vo. Sabin 87899. DLC.

New York Province

    At a council held at Fort-George in New-York | on the 5th of November,
1734. | Present | His Excellency William Cosby, Esq; Captain General and
Go | -vernour in Chief of the Province of New York. | . . . Whereas several
large tracts of good and profitable land within the Province of New-York,
in North-America, do still remain uncultivated and unimproved . . . [terms
for the granting of said lands] [at end:] Signed by order of his Excellency
in Council, | Fred. Morris, D. Cl. Conc. | [rule] | *Printed and sold by*
William Bradford in New-York, 1734.   [380]

    3 p., folio. (26.5 x 18 cm.). NHi.

    Reprinted in Donald Campbell's *The Case of Lieutenant Donald Camp-*
bell, [1767?], p. 11-13. BM, NHi.

Der nunmehro in dem Neuen Welt vergnügt und ohne Heimwehe
lebende Schweitzer, oder Beschreibung des gegenwärtigen Zustands der
Königlichen Englischen Provinz Carolina. *Bern. 1734.*   [381]

    46 p., 8vo. Sabin 10975.

RECK, GEORG PHILIPP FRIEDRICH, BARON VON,
   AND JOHANN MARTIN BOLZIUS

An | extract | of the | journals | of | Mr. Commissary Von Reck, | who
conducted the first transport of | Saltzburgers to Georgia: | and of the |
Reverend Mr. Bolzius, | one of their ministers. | Giving an account of their
voyage | to, and happy settlement in | that Province. | [rule] | Published by
the direction of | the Society for Promoting | Christian Knowledge. |
[double rule] | *London:* | *Printed by M. Downing, in Bartholomew Close.* |
[rule] | *M.DCC.XXXIV.*   [382]

   [4], 72 p., 8vo. (16.8 x 10.2 cm.). Church 917, De Renne I:52. BM,
CSmH, GU-De, MH, NN, RPJCB.

   Account of the voyage and settlement of the first colony of Saltzburgers
at Ebenezer in what is now Effingham County, Georgia, January 8 - May 13,
1733-4, arriving at Charlestown, March 7th. This is the only one of the
numerous journals of the Saltzburger migration to appear in English. For
the complete series in German, see under Samuel Urlsperger, 1735, no. 389.

RUNDLE, THOMAS

A | sermon | preached at | St. George's Church | Hanover Square, | on
Sunday February 17, 1733-4. | To recommend the charity for establishing
the | new Colony of Georgia. | By T. Rundle, LL.D. Prebendary of |
Durham. | Published at the request of the Right Honourable the | Lord
Viscount Tyrconnel, the Honourable | Colonel Whitworth, Churchwardens,
| and several of the parishioners. | *London:* | *Printed for T. Woodward,
at the Half-Moon between* | *the two Temple Gates, Fleet-street; and
J. Brindley,* | *in New Bond-street. MDCCXXXIV.*   [383]

   24 p., 4to. (21 x 17.1 cm.). De Renne I:52. GU-De, RPJCB.

WALDO, SAMUEL

   Samuel Waldo of Boston, Merchant, intending with all possible expedition to settle two towns of forty families each, on a tract of land, to which
his title is indisputable, lying on the western side of a navigable river known
by the name of St. George's River . . . *[Boston. 1734].*   [384]

   Broadside, 4to. Sabin 101003, Ford 654. DLC.

   Signed and dated at foot: Samuel Waldo. Boston 3d March, 1734.

   Advertisement. [of 3700 acres of land in New Jersey to be sold by John
Sikes in the rights of Joseph Helby] *[Philadelphia: Printed by B. Franklin.
1735].*   [385]

   Broadside, folio. Evans 3862. PHi.

DICKENSON, JONATHAN

God's protecting Providence man's surest help and defense, in times of the greatest difficulty and most imminent danger; evidenced in the remarkable deliverance of divers persons, from the devouring waves of the sea, amongst which they suffered shipwreck; and also from the more cruelly devouring jaws of the inhumane canibals of Florida. Faithfully rerated [sic] by one of the persons concerned therein, Jonathan Dickenson. [quotation from the Psalms] The second edition. *Printed and sold by B. Franklin in Market-Street, Philadelphia. Price one shilling and six pence. [1735].*   [386]

No copy known. Title from *Pennsylvania Gazette,* April 1, 1736, where it is advertised as *Just published.* Joseph Smith: *Friends books,* Sabin 20015, Evans 3896, Hildeburn 507.

A new voyage to Georgia. | By a young gentleman. | Giving an account of his travels to South Carolina, | and part of North Carolina. | To which is added, | a curious account of the Indians, | by an honourable person. | And a poem to James Oglethorpe, Esq. | on his arrival | from Georgia. | *London: J. Wilford. 1735*   [387]

62 p., 8vo. Sabin 27079. NN.

For second issue, see under 1737, no. 399.

A short account of the first settlement of the Provinces of Virginia, Maryland, New-York, New-Jersey, and Pennsylvania, by the English. To which is annexed a map of Maryland, according to the bounds mentioned in the charter, and also of the adjacent country, anno 1630. *London: Printed in the year MDCCXXXV.*   [388]

22 p., folded map, 4to. DLC, MH, MWA.

Title of the map: *A map of Virginia according to Captain John Smith's map published anno 1606. Also of the adjacent country called by the Dutch Niew Nederlant. Anno 1630. By John Senex. 1735.*

Reprinted by the American Geographical Society in 1922.

URLSPERGER, SAMUEL

Der ausführlichen Nachrichten von der Königlich-Gross-Britannischen Colonie Saltzburgischer Emigranten in America. Erster [-Dritter] Theil. . . . Herausgegeben von Samuel Urlsperger . . . *Halle, in Verlegung des Wäysenhauses,* M DCC XXXXI [i.e. *1735 - MDCCLII*].   [389]

19 parts in 3 vols., port., maps and plans, all folded., 4to. Sabin 98133, De Renne I:57-68. DLC, GU-De, MH, NN, RPJCB.

The parts originally published separately, 1735-1752 and reissued in 3 vols., dated 1741, 1746 and 1752. For full collation, see Sabin, De Renne and DLC cat. which also list reprints of some of the parts. Continued as *Americanisches Ackerwerk Gottes,* 1754-1767, no. 470.

History of the short lived German Salzburger settlements at Ebenezer and elsewhere in Georgia which flourished for about 30 years.

WALDO, SAMUEL

Boston, May 22d. 1735. | Whereas since my return from St. George's River in the eastern parts of this | Province, where I have been . . . *[Boston, 1735].*   [390]

Broadside. Sabin 101005, copied from Ford 660 who locates no copy.

GYLES, JOHN

Memoirs | of | odd adventures, | strange deliverances, &c. | in the captivity of | John Gyles, Esq; | Commander of the garrison on St. George's River. | [rule] | Written by himself. | [rule, 8 lines quoted, double rule] | *Boston, in N.E.* | *Printed and sold by S. Kneeland and T. Green, in Queenstreet,* | *over against the Prison. MDCCXXXVI.*   [391]

[4], 40, [4] p., 4to. (20.3 x 14.5 cm.). Sabin 27370 and 29387, Evans 4021, Ayer 106. F.C. Deering, ICN, MB, MH (imp.), MHi (imp.), RPJCB.

The author's own copy, with his annotations and corrections designed for a new edition presumably never published, containing the autograph of his daughter *Mary Gyles Her Book 1736*, bought Aug. 28, 1934 by Matt B. Jones and sold through Goodspeed's Bookshop to F.C. Deering in 1937 for $1,000. The Rev. Jeremy Belknap copy in the Boston Public Library has this MS note: "Said to be *really* written & embellished by Joseph Seccombe, Chaplain of the Garrison at St. George's [Thomaston, Maine], afterwards minister of Kingston in N. Hampshire."

Mass. Hist. Soc. Photostat Americana, 2d ser., 1936, no. 7. Reprinted with notes by S.G. Drake, Cincinnati, 1869. Copies in most large libraries.

John Gyles (ca. 1678-1755) was captured by the Indians at the attack on Pemaquid on August 2, 1689 with his mother, brother and sisters. The women were ransomed after several years of captivity. He was held by the Indians for six years, sold to a Frenchman on the St. Johns River with whom he lived three years when he was released in 1698 and returned to Boston on an English ship.

MASON, JOHN

A | brief history | of the | Pequot War: | especially | of the memorable taking of their fort at | Mistick in Connecticut | in | 1637. | [rule] | Written by | Major John Mason, | a principal actor therein, as then chief Captain and Com- | mander of Connecticut forces. | [rule] | With an introduction and some explanatory notes | by the Reverend | Mr. Thomas Prince. | [rule, 9 lines quoted, double rule] | *Boston: Printed & sold by S. Kneeland &* *T. Green* | *in Queen-street, 1736.*   [392]

[2], vi, x, 22 p., 8vo. (18.4 x 12.2 cm.). Sabin 45454, Evans 4033, Church 924. CSmH, CtHi, CtSoP, DLC, ICN, MB, MBAt, MWiW-C, NHi, NjP, NN, PP, RPJCB.

The best contemporary account of the war. Written by one of the leaders of the campaign, for the General Court of Connecticut and sent by Allyn, Secretary of the Colony, to Rev. Increase Mather shortly after Mason's death. Mather, thinking that it had been written by Allyn, credited him with its authorship and used the narrative in his *A relation of the troubles* . . . , 1677, which see. Mason's grandson, who owned the original manuscript, placed it in the hands of Rev. Thomas Prince for editing and publication. It was reprinted in the *Case of the Governor and Company of Connecticut and Mohegan Indians.* London, 1769, and in separate editions in 1869 and 1897, as well as in Mass. Hist. Soc. Coll., 2d ser., vol. 8.

URLSPERGER, SAMUEL

Send-Schreiben an die Evangelische Gemeinde der zu Eben Etzer [sic] in America niedergelassenen Saltzburgischen Emigranten von Conrad Schnellers . . . Abgelassen von Samuel Urlspurger . . . *[Augsburg?] Gedruckt bey Johann Jacob Lotter, und zu haben in dem Evangelischen Armenhaus allhier. [1736].*   [393]

22 p., 8vo. Sabin 98137. RPJCB.

Dated at end: *Augspurg, am Sonntage Septuag. 1736.*

One of the Saltzburger Georgia promotion tracts.

· · · · ·

Zuverläsziges Sendschreiben von den geist-und leiblichen Umständen der Saltzburgischen Emigranten, die in America niedergelassen haben, wie sich solche bis den 1sten September 1735. befunden, und von denen Herren Predigern in Eben Ezer und einigen Saltzburgen selbst nach Teutschland überschrieben worden, herausgegeben von Samuel Urlsperger . . . *Halle, in Verlegung des Wäysenhauses, 1736.*   [394]

14 p., 4to. Sabin 98138, De Renne I:69. DLC, GU-De, MH, NN, RPJCB.

One of the Saltzburger Georgia promotion tracts.

WALDO, SAMUEL

A defence of the title of the late John Leverett Esq; to a tract of land in the eastern parts of the Province of the Massachusetts Bay, commonly called Muscongus Lands, lying upon St. George's, Muscongus and Penobscott Rivers. By Mr. Samuel Waldo of Boston, Merchant, one of the Associates and Proprietors of those lands. *[Boston] Printed in the year, 1736.*   [395]

41 p., folio. Sabin 101001, Evans 4098. BM, DLC, MB, MBAt, MH, MHi, MWA, RPJCB.

Relates to the grant by the Plymouth Council in 1629 to John Beauchamp and Thomas Leverett, of about 1000 square miles between the rivers Muscongus and Penobscot. It was first called the Lincolnshire, or Muscongus

Patent, and later the Waldo Patent, from General Samuel Waldo, who purchased the land.

That the controversy continued in later years is evident from three Massachusetts Commonwealth broadsides (Ford 2425, 2825 and 2846): "Resolve confirming a grant of land of thirty miles square, to the | heirs of Brigadier Waldo, on certain conditions, July 4, 1785. "MHi, MWA, NN; "Resolve appointing commissioners, to settle differences with residents on the | Waldo Claim, &c. March 9, 1797. Printed by Young & Minns, Printers to the State." MHi; "Whereas the Legislature of this Commonwealth by a resolve passed on the ninth | day of March last, appointed Nathan Dane, . . ." [on lands of Samuel Waldo and Henry Knox] [1797]. MHi.

For Waldo's connection with the grant, see Maine Hist. Soc. Collections, ser. I, vol. 6, 1859, p. 319-332.

WATTS, GEORGE

A | sermon | preached before the | Trustees | for Establishing the | Colony of Georgia . . . | March 18. 1735. | . . . | London: | Printed by M. Downing, in Bartholomew-Close near | West-Smithfield. M.DCC.XXXVI.   [396]

27 p., 4to. (21.9 x 16.6 cm.). De Renne I:70. GU-De, RPJCB.

[WESLEY, SAMUEL?]

Georgia, | a poem. | Tomo Chachi, | an ode. | A copy of verses on Mr. Oglethorpe's | second voyage to Georgia. | [rule, 2 lines quoted, rule, orn., double rule] | London: | Printed: And sold by J. Roberts in Warwick-Lane. | [rule] | M DCC XXXVI. | (Price one shilling.) | [Title within double ruled border].   [397]

19 p., folio. (34.8 x 22.3 cm.). Sabin 27047, DeRanne vol. 1, p. 68. GU-De.

The first poem is anonymous, that on Tomo Chachi is by Rev. Thomas Fitzgerald (1695?-1752), according to DeRenne.

"The Reverend Samuel Wesley has been credited with the poems . . . : *Georgia, a Poem. . . .*"—V.W. Crane: *The promotion literature of Georgia*, in *Bibliographical essays, a tribute to Wilberforce Eames*, 1924, p. 293.

Neu-Gefundenes Eden. Oder ausführlicher Bericht von Süd und Nord Carolina, Pensilphania, Mary Land & Virginia. Entworffen durch zwey in dise Provintzen gemachten Reisen, Reiss-Journal, und ville Brieffen, dadurch der gegenwärtige Zustand dieser Länderen warhafftig entdecket und dem Nebenmenschen zu gutem an Tag gelegt wird. Samt beygefügtem Anhang, oder Freye Unterweisung zu dem verlohrnen, nun aber wieder gefundenen Lapide Philosophorum, dadurch man bald zur Vergnügung und wahrer Reichthum gelangen kan. *In Truck verfertiget durch Befelch der Helvetischen Societät. 1737.*   [398]

[16], 288 p., map, 12mo. Sabin 52362. RPJCB.

This new-found Eden, or a detailed account of South and North Carolina, Pennsylvania, Maryland, and Virginia is a result of two journeys made through these provinces, and includes considerable correspondence which bears on the condition of the country, contains also full information concerning its resources, evidently intended to promote emigration. Description and note from Sabin.

A new | voyage | to | Georgia. | By a | young gentleman. | Giving an account of his travels | to South Carolina, and part of | North Carolina. | To which is added, | A curious account of the Indians. | By an honourable person. | And | A poem to James Oglethorpe, Esq; on his | arrival from Georgia. | [rule] | The second edition. | [rule] | London: | Printed for J. Wilford, at the Three | Flower de Luces, behind the Chapter- | House, in St. Paul's Church-Yard. 1737. | (Price one shilling.).   [399]
[2], 62 p., 8vo. (19.1 x 11.5 cm.). Sabin 27079, De Renne I:71. DLC, GU-De, MBAt, NN.

Though called second edition on title, De Renne calls it a second issue of the first edition since it is merely the first issue with a new title page.

WARREN, ROBERT

Industry and diligence in our callings earnestly recommended: | in a | sermon | preached before the | . . . Trustees | for Establishing the | Colony of Georgia . . . | . . . March 17, 1736-7. | . . . | London: | Printed for W. Meadows, at the Angel in Cornhill. M.DCC.XXXVII.   [400]
16 p., 4to. (22 x 16.7 cm.). De Renne I:73. GU-De, RPJCB.

BEARCROFT, PHILIP

A | sermon | preached before the | . . . Trustees | for Establishing the | Colony of Georgia . . . March 16, 1737-8. | . . . | London: | Printed by John Willis, at the Angel-and-Bible in Tower-Street; and sold by | T. Woodward at the Half-Moon in Fleet-Street, M.DCC.XXXVIII. (Price six-pence.).
[401]
[2], 22, [1] p., 4to. (21.9 x 17.3 cm.). De Renne I:73. GU-De.

LE BEAU, C[LAUDE]

Avantures du Sr. C. Le Beau, Avocat en Parlement, ou Voyage Curieux et Nouveau parmi les Sauvages de l'Amérique Septentrionale. Dans le quel on trouvera une description du Canada, avec une relation très particulière des anciennes coutumes, moeurs & façons de vivre des barbares qui l'habitent & de la manière dont ils se comportent aujourd'hui. Ouvrage enrichi d'une carte & des figures necessaires. Amsterdam: Herman Uytwerf. MDCCXXX-VIII.   [402]
2 vols., [14], 370, [6]; [2], 430, [6] p., 6 plates, folded map, 12mo. Sabin

39582. BM, CSmH, IHi, MBAt, MdBP, MH, MiU-C, MnHi, MWA, NHi, NN, PPL, PPL-R, RPJCB.

The author's personal experiences among the Iroquois, Hurons, Algonquins, etc.

NEW YORK PROVINCE

Encouragement given for people to remove and | settle in the Province of New-York in | America. [Caption title] [Promise to grant˙Lauchlin Campbell 30,000 acres of land "at the Wood-Creek" north of Saratoga, New York, and lands to 30 families "already landed here" and to "all Protestants that incline to come and settle in this Colony"] [Colophon:] *Printed by William Bradford, Printer to the King's most excellent | Majesty | for the Province of New-York, 1738.* [403]

Broadside, folio. (29.5 x 17 cm.). NHi.

Reprinted in Donald Campbell's *The case of Lieutenant Donald Campbell* [1767?], p. 13-14. BM, NHi.

BERRIMAN, WILLIAM

A | sermon | preach'd before the | . . . Trustees | for Establishing the | Colony of Georgia . . . | March 15, 1738-9. | . . . | *London, | Printed for John Carter, at the Blackamore's Head opposite to | the Royal Exchange in Cornhill. M.DCC.XXXIX.* [404]

24 p., 4to. (22.2 x 17.1 cm.). De Renne I:76. GU-De, RPJCB.

CROWE, WILLIAM

The duty of public spirit | recommended in a | sermon | preach'd before the | . . . Trustees | for Establishing the | Colony of Georgia . . . | . . . March 20, 1739-40. | . . . | *London: | Printed for John Clarke, at the Bible under the | Royal Exchange in Cornhill. M.DCC.XL.* [405]

23, [1] p., 4to. (21.7 x 16.4 cm.). De Renne I:82. GU-De, RPJCB.

KLEINKNECHT, CONRAD DANIEL

Conrad Daniel Kleinknechts, Ulm. Pastor. Leipheim. Zuverlässige Nachricht, von der, durch das Blut des erwürgten Lammes theurerkaufen Schwarzen Schaaf-und Lämer-Heerde, oder von den neubekehrten Malabarischen Christen in Ost-Indien auf der Königl. Dänischen Küsten Coromandel &c. in einem aufrichtigen Send-Schreiben und dessen Fortsetzung an einem Christlichen Politicum: darinnen von Anfang dieses Millions-Wercks und dessen Wachsthum bis auf unsere Zeiten, hinlängliche ertheilet wird: welches als ein Kurzer Auszug der sämtlichen in Halle bisher gedruckten Ost-Indischen Berichten seyn mag. Deme noch beygefügt: Nachrichten von den Englis. Colonisten Georgiens zu Eben-Ezer in America; wie auch dem Bekehrungs-Werck unter den Juden, Muhammedanern,

Türcken und andern Völckern, &c. *Augspurg: Gedruckt und zu finden bey*
Johann Jacob Lotters sel. Erben. 1740.   [406]
[36], [3]-216, 2 blank leaves, [16], 376, [56] p., front., 16mo. De Renne
I:85. GU-De.
A Salzburger Georgia promotion tract.

BATEMAN, EDMUND

A | sermon | preached before the | . . . Trustees | for establishing the |
Colony of Georgia . . . | . . . March 19, 1740-1, | . . . | London: | Printed
for John and Henry Pemberton, at the Golden | Buck in Fleet-Street.
M.DCC.XLI | (Price six-pence.).   [407]
[2], 21, [1] p., 8vo. (22.2 x 17.1 cm.). De Renne I:89. GU-De.

[CHRISTIE, THOMAS]

A | description | of | Georgia, | by a gentleman who has resided there
upwards | of seven years, and was one of the first | settlers. | [rule, orn.,
rule] | *London: Printed for C. Corbett. MDCCXLI.*   [408]
8 p., folio. Sabin 27037, John Carter Brown Report, 1943-4, p. 36-37.
MH, RPJCB.
Reprinted in Force's Tracts, II, no. 12.

COXE, DANIEL

A description of the English Province of Carolana. . . . *[London:] Printed*
for and sold by Oliver Payne, at Horace's Head in Pope's-Head Alley,
Cornhill, opposite the Royal Exchange, 1741.   [409]
[54], 122 p., folded map, 8vo. Sabin 17281. BM, DLC, MB, MH, etc.

.   .   .   .   .

Issued with two other works and a general title page as: *A collection of*
voyages and travels, in three parts. . . . [Same imprint and date].   [410]
[6], 142; viii, 86; [54], 122 p., 2 maps, 8vo. Sabin 17278. BM.
In spite of the longer title, the text is the same as that of the 1st ed., 1722.
Reprinted, St. Louis, 1840, and in B.F. French: *Historical collections of*
Louisiana, vol. 2, 1850, p. 221-276.

[MARTYN, BENJAMIN]

An | account | shewing the progress of the | Colony of Georgia | in |
America | from its | first establishment. | [rule, orn., rule] | London: | Printed
in the year M.DCC.XLI.   [411]
[2], 71 p., folio (31.3 x 19.5 cm.). Sabin 45000, De Renne I:90.
GU-De, etc.

Signed: *By order of the Trustees, Benj. Martyn, Secretary.*
For reprints, see Sabin, De Renne. See 418.

.   .   .   .   .

An | impartial enquiry | into the | state and utility | of the | Province of
Georgia. | [behive orn.] | *London:* | *Printed for W. Meadows, at the Angel
in Cornhill.* | *MDCCXLI.* | *(Price one shilling and six-pence.)*   [412]
[4], 104 p., 8vo. (21 x 13 cm.). Sabin 45001, De Renne I:94. GU-De,
MBAt, MH, NHi (2 issues), PP, RPJCB, etc.

Copy without final line of title giving price, NHi. Verso of half title
contains adv. for 2d ed. of Martyn's *Reasons for establishing the Colony
of Georgia.*

TAILFER, PATRICK, AND OTHERS

A | true and historical | narrative | of the colony of | Georgia, | in America,
| from the first settlement thereof until | this present period: | containing |
the most authentick facts, matters and | transactions therein. | Together with
| His Majesty's charter, representations of the | people, letters, &c. | and | a
dedication to His Excellency General | Oglethorpe. | [rule] | By [bracket]
Pat. Tailfer, M.D. | Hugh Anderson, M.A. | Da. Douglas, and others, |
land-holders in Georgia, at present in Charles-Town in | South-Carolina. |
[rule] | [six lines of Latin quoted] | [rule] | *Charles-Town, South-Carolina:*
| *Printed by P. Timothy, for the authors, 1741.*   [413]
[2], xxiv, 176 p., 8vo. Sabin 94215-94218, Evans 4816, De Renne I:95.
DLC, GU-De, NN, RPJCB.

.   .   .   .   .

Same title with variant punctuation and imprint date in Roman:
M.DCC.XLI.   [414]
xviii, 78, 87-118 p., 8vo. CSmH, DLC, GU-De, M, MB, MBAt, MiU-C,
MWA, NHi, NIC, NN, RPJCB.

.   .   .   .   .

Same title with variant punctuation and imprint: *Printed for P. Timothy,
in Charles-Town, South-Carolina;* | *and sold by J. Crokatt, in Fleet-street,
London.* | *[1741].*   [415]
[2], xvi, 112 p., 8vo. BM, BODLEIAN, GU-De, M, MH, NHi, NN,
RPJCB.

Reprinted in Force Tracts, I, 1836 and as a separate by Force, 1835, in
Ga. Hist. Soc. Coll., 2, 1842, and in American Colonial Tracts, I, no. 4,
1897.

The 2d and 3d eds., according to De Renne cat., probably printed in
London.

An attack on Oglethorpe's colonization literature. Sabin 94215-94218.

WEISER, CONRAD

Ein Wohl-gemeindter und Ernstlicher Rath an unsere Lands-Leute, die Teutschen. *[Philadelphia: Benjamin Franklin. 1741].*   [416]

[2] p., folio. Sabin 102508. PHi.

Signed and dated: *Conrad Weiser. 20. Sept. 1741.* "An election circular. Conrad Weiser, then living in Tulpehocken, advises his countrymen, not to vote for the Quakers who opposed the levying of taxes for all kinds of warfare, even defensive, but for the Government candidates. He calls attention to the dangers threatening from a league of the French in Canada and on the Ohio with the Indians."—Seidensticker.

GEORGIA, TRUSTEES FOR ESTABLISHING THE COLONY OF, IN AMERICA

Resolutions of the Trustees for Establishing the Colony of Georgia in America, in Common Council assembled [8 March 1741 | 2], relating to the grants and tenure of lands within the said Colony. *[London, 1742].*   [417]

4 p., folio. Sabin 27104.

[MARTYN, BENJAMIN]

An | account, | shewing the progress of the | Colony of Georgia | in | America | from it's [sic] | first establishment. | Published per order of the Honourable the Trustees. | *London: Printed in the year M,DCC,XLI. | Maryland: Reprinted and sold by Jonas Green, | at his Printing-Office in Annapolis.* 1742.   [418]

[2], [i]-iii, [iv], 68 p., small folio (29.1 x 19.4 cm.). Sabin 45000, Evans 4961, Wroth: *History of printing in Colonial Maryland,* 106. DLC, MdHi (2 copies, 1 lacking appendices 4-11), NN (imperfect).

An answer to *A true and historical narrative of the Colony of Georgia in America. Charleston, S.C.: Peter Timothy, 1741.*

For reprints, see Wroth, from whom the above description is taken.

[STEPHENS, THOMAS]

The hard | case | of the | distressed people of Georgia. | [Caption title] *[London, 1742].*   [419]

4 p., folio. (37 x 24.8 cm.). De Renne I:105. GU-De.

Dated and signed: "London, April 26th, 1742. Thomas Stephens, Agent for the people of Georgia." [i.e., Talifer and the other malcontents]. The following title was evidently issued to accompany the above:

.   .   .   .   .

An account shewing what money has been received by the Trustees for the use of the Colony of Georgia. *[London, 1742?].*   [420]

[2] p. folio broadsheet (42.1 x 53 cm.). Sabin 27008, De Renne I:102. GU-De.

Another attack on the policies of Oglethorpe by the agent of the malcontents.

STEPHENS, WILLIAM

A | journal | of the | proceedings | in | Georgia, | beginning | October 20, 1737. | [rule] | By William Stephens, Esq. | [rule] | To which is added, | A state of that Province, | as attested upon oath | in the | Court of Savannah, | November 10, 1740. | [rule] | Vol. I. [II.] | [rule] | London: | Printed for W. Meadows, at the Angel in Cornhill. | MDCCXLII. [Title of vol. 3:] A | journal | of the | proceedings | in | Georgia, | beginning | October 20, 1737. | [rule] | By William Stephens, Esy. | [rule] | Vol. III. | [rule] | *London: | Printed for W. Meadows, at the Angel in Cornhill.* | MDCCXLII. [421]

3 vols., 8vo. (19 x 12.3 cm.) (Detailed collation in De Renne). Sabin 91313, De Renne I:105. Complete sets: Advocates' Library, Edinburgh, GHi, GU-De, RPJCB.

Covers the period from October 20, 1737 to October 28, 1741.

70 copies printed, all but 30 of vol. 3 burned with the printing office. Part of Vol. III was reprinted separately as:

. . . . .

Journal | received | February 4, 1741. | By the | Trustees | for Establishing the | Colony of Georgia, | in | America, | from | William Stephens, Esq. | Secretary for the affairs of the Trust | within the said Colony. | Commencing | September 12, 1741. | and ending | October 28 following. | [rule] | *London: | Printed for W. Meadows, at the Angel in Cornhill.* | MDCCXLII. [422]

[44] p., 8vo. (19.1 x 12 cm.). De Renne I:107. GU-De.

Reset text same as *Journal,* vol. III, p. 348-391. Only 100 copies printed.

. . . . .

A | state | of the | Province of Georgia, | attested upon oath | in the | Court of Savannah, | November 10, 1740. | *London: | Printed for W. Meadows, at the Angel in Cornhill.* | MDCCXLII. [423]

[4], 32 p., 8vo. (21.7 x 13.4 cm.). De Renne I:108, Sabin 27113. CSmH, CtY, DLC, GU-De, MB, MBAt, MH, MiU-C, MWA, NHi, NjP, NN, RPJCB. The NjP copy has 36 numbered pages.

Promotion tract in answer to the malcontent Patrick Tailfer and his associates (413-415). Written by the loyal Secretary of the colony. For an answer by his son, London agent of the malcontents, see no. 426.

Reprinted from the appendix of vol. 2 of Stephens: *A journal of the proceedings in Georgia,* London, 1742, 3 vols., 8vo. De Renne I: 105.

Reprinted in Force Tracts, I, 1836 and elsewhere, for which see Sabin 91315-91316. See also Sabin 91305-91307, 91313-91314 and 94215, and the De Renne Georgia catalog.

[EGMONT, JOHN PERCEVAL, SECOND EARL OF]

Faction detected by the evidence of facts. [12 lines quoted] *Dublin: Printed for G. Faulkner, in Essex-Street. MDCCXLIII.*   [424]

[2], 170, [4] p., 8vo. De Renne I:110. GU-De.

A defense of the Oglethorpe administration of Georgia and an answer to Thomas Stephens: *Brief account,* 1743.

KING, JAMES

A | sermon | preached before the | . . . Trustees | for establishing the | Colony of Georgia . . . | . . . March 17, 1742-3. | . . . | *London:* | *Printed for John Clarke, under the Royal-Exchange.* | *M.DCC.XLIII.*   [425]

22 p., 4to. (22.2 x 16.9 cm.). De Renne I:110. GU-De.

[STEPHENS, THOMAS]

A | brief account | of the | causes | that have retarded the | progress | of the | Colony of Georgia, | in | America; | attested upon oath. | Being | a proper contrast | to | A State of the Province of | Georgia. | Attested upon oath; | and some other misrepresentations on the | same subject. | [double rule] | *London:* | *Printed in the year M.DCC.XLIII.*   [426]

[4], 24, 101 p., 8vo. (20 x 12.2 cm.). De Renne I:113. GU-De, RPJCB.

See [William Stephens]: *A state of the province of Georgia,* 1742; and Patrick Tailfer: *A true and historical narrative of the colony of Georgia,* 1741.

Written by the London agent of the malcontents who opposed the administration of Oglethorpe, in answer to the above tract no. 423 by his father, Secretary to the colony.

BRUCE, LEWIS

The happiness of man the glory of God. | [rule] | A | sermon | preached before the | . . . Trustees | for establishing the | Colony of Georgia . . . | . . . March 15, 1743, | . . . | *London:* | *Printed by Daniel Browne, in Crane-Court, Fleet-Street.* | [rule] | *M DCC XLIV.*   [427]

[2], 53, [1] p., 4to. (22.2 x 17 cm.). De Renne I:116. GU-De, RPJCB.

MOORE, FRANCIS

A | voyage | to | Georgia. | Begun in the year 1735. | Containing, | An account of the settling the town of | Frederica, in the Southern part of the | Province; and a description of the soil, | air, birds, beasts, trees, rivers, | islands, &c. | With | The rules and orders made by the Honour- | able the Trustees for that Settle- | ment; including the allowances of provisions, |

cloathing, and other necessaries to the families | and servants which went thither. | Also | A description of the town and county of Savannah, | in the Northern part of the Province, the manner of | dividing and granting the lands, and the improve- | ments there: With an account of the air, soil, | rivers, and islands in that part. | [rule] | By Francis Moore, author of Travels into the | Inland Parts of Africa. | [double rule] | *London:* | *Printed for Jacob Robinson in Ludgate-Street, 1744.*   [428]

[2], 108, [2] p., 8vo. (18.7 x 12 cm.). Sabin 50352, De Renne I:117. GU-De.

The | present state | of the | country and inhabitants, Europeans and | Indians, | of | Louisiana, | on the north continent of America. | By an officer at New Orleans to his friend at Paris. | Containing | the garrisons, forts and forces, price of | all manner of provisions and liquors, &c. also | an account of their drunken lewd lives, which | lead them to excesses of debauchery and vil- | lany. | To which are added. | letters from the Governor of that Province on | the trade of the French and English with the natives: also | proposals to them to put an end to their traffick with the | English. Annual presents to the savages; a list of the | country goods, and those proper to be sent there, &c. | Translated from the French originals, taken in the Golden | Lyon prize, Rasteaux, Master, by the Hon. Capt. Aylmer, | Commander of His Majesty's Ship the Portmahon, and by | him sent to the Admiralty Office. | *London:* | *Printed for J. Millan, near Whitehall. 1744.* | *(Price one shilling).*   [429]

55 p., 8vo. (19 cm.). Sabin 42283, old John Carter Brown cat. 773. DLC, RPJCB, etc.

Includes Alabama, the Mississippi Valley, Ohio Valley and the Illinois country to Canada. Sabin mentions a second edition of the same date.

CAREW, BAMPFYLDE-MOORE

The | life and adventures | of | Bampfylde-Moore Carew, | the noted | Devonshire stroller and dog-stealer; | as related by himself, during his passage to the | plantations in America. | Containing, | a great variety of remarkable transactions in a va- | grant course of life, which he followed for the | space of thirty years and upwards. | [rule, orn., rule] | *Exon: Printed by the Farleys, for Joseph | Drew, Bookseller, opposite Castle-Lane, 1745.* | *(Price two shillings.).*   [430]

[2], 152, 145-152 [i.e., 160] p., small 4to. (19.9 x 12.7 cm.). Sabin 27615. ViU.

First edition, first issue, with page numbers 145-152 repeated. In second issue, the pagination is corrected and pages 161-164 added.

The Tracy W. McGregor-ViU copy belonged to the author and has a manuscript note in his hand at the foot of p. 49: "This is surely the dam [word crossed out] most damned book that was ever read I say that should not say it being the author."

Pasted on the second fly leaf facing the title is an engraved portrait of: *Mr. Bampfylde Moore Carew | King of the Beggars* showing a bust portrait with a book in the subject's right hand, the title reading: *The | laws | of the | Beggars.* The portrait measures 13.7 x 9 cm. and was probably taken from a later and smaller edition.

.   .   .   .   .   .

The life and adventures of Bampfylde-Moore Carew, the noted Devonshire stroller and dog-stealer, as related by himself, during his passage to the plantations in America: Containing, a great variety of remarkable transactions in a vagrant course of life, which he followed for the space of thirty years and upwards. *Exon, Printed by the Farleys, for Joseph Drew, bookseller, opposite Castle-lane, 1745.*   [431]

[2], v, 164 p., 8vo. (20 cm.). Sabin 27615. NcWfC.

1st ed., 2d issue, with pagination corrected and pages 161-164 added. Has *stroller* correctly spelled in title. In an earlier varient (no copy located) it is spelled *stroler.* There are 10 variant titles representing more than 30 editions of this colonial underworld best seller in the Union Catalog at DLC.

This story of the adventures of the "King of the Gypsies" in America is one of the few eighteenth century American criminal autobiographies and is a delightful bit of social and criminal history of the times. Sabin, quoting Stevens, says of him: "Carew was born in Devonshire, was tried at Exeter about 1739 or 1740, and banished to Maryland, where he went at the cost of the public. He gives an amusing account of the country, and his adventures in Maryland, Virginia, New Jersey, New York and Connecticut, till he embarked at New London for England. His accounts of how he bamboozled and bled Whitfield, Thomas Penn, Governor Thomas, and many others of good repute, are amusing, true or not." This son of a clergyman was the most skillful and entertaining panhandler of his day in America and his narrative gives details of how he fooled his victims, including prominent men of Philadelphia and New York City. He was born in 1693 and lived to the good old age of about 77 years.

BRAINERD, DAVID

Mirabilia Dei inter Indicos, or the rise and progress of a remarkable work of grace amongst a number of the Indians in the Provinces of New-Jersey and Pennsylvania, justly represented in a journal kept by order of the Honourable Society (in Scotland) for Propagating Christian Knowledge. With some general remarks. Published by the Rev. & worthy correspondents of the said Society. With a preface by them. *Philadelphia: Printed and sold by William Bradford in Second-street. [1746].*   [432]

viii, 253 p., 8vo. Sabin 7340, Evans 5748. Copies in most large libraries.

Author's copy with his MSS corrections owned in Philadelphia. Sabin says some copies were printed on finer paper than others.

There are many later editions in America and England, some of them abridged and generally accompanying Jonathan Edwards: *An account of the life of the late Reverend Mr. David Brainerd . . . Boston, 1749,* and later editions, one in Dutch, *Utrecht, 1756.* Sabin 21929.

[MARTYN, BENJAMIN]

Neueste und richtigste | Nachricht | von der Landschaft | Georgia | in dem | Engelländischen Amerika. | Worinnen enthalten: | 1. Die Original-Berichte, welche die Königlichen | Commissarien über die Beschaffenheit dieser | Landschaft eingeschicket haben. | 2. Ein zuverlässiger Bericht derer vornehmsten Pri- | vilegien, Freyheiten und Wohlthaten, so alle | diejenigen zu geniessen haben, die sich in dieser | fruchtbaren Provinz häusslich niederlassen; Nebst | einem Unterricht für selbige zu ihrer Dahinreise. | Durchaus mit Anmerkungen | die der Uebersetzer bey seinem vieljährigen Aufenthalt | in Amerika augestellet hat, begleitet | von | J.[ohann] M.[atthias] K.[ramer] | [double rule] | *Göttingen | Aus der Universitäts Buchdruckerei. | Verlegts Johann Peter Schmid, 1746.* | [Title in red and black].   [433]

88 p., 8vo. (18.8 x 11 cm.). Sabin 56848, De Renne I: 120. GU-De, NHi.

Sabin enters under Oglethorpe, De Renne under Kramer, the translator, but it is a translation of Benjamin Martyn's *A new and accurate account,* 1732 and 1733.

RIDLEY, GLOCESTER

A | sermon | preached before the | . . . Trustees | for establishing the | Colony of Georgia . . . | . . . March 20, 1745-6. | . . . | *London: | Printed for John Clarke, under the Royal Exchange Cornhill.* | M DCC XLVI.   [434]

[2], 21, [1] p., 4to. (22 x 17.1 cm.). De Renne I: 120. GU-De.

COLDEN, CADWALLADER

The history of the Five Indian Nations depending on the Province of New-York in America. . . . *London: T. Osborne, MDCCXLVII.*   [435]

xvi, [4], 90, iv, 91-204, 283 p., folded map, 8vo. Sabin 14273. Copies in most large libraries.

Text of first edition altered by the English editor, with Colden's *Papers relating to the Indian trade* (with its map reengraved and other illustrative documents added.

STITH, WILLIAM

The | history | of the | first discovery | and | settlement | of | Virginia: |

being | an essay towards a general | history of this colony. | By William
Stith, A.M. | Rector of Henrico Parish, and one of the Governors of | William and Mary College. | . . . | *Williamsburg:* | *Printed by William Parks,*
M,DCC,XLVII.   [436]

viii, 256, 247-331, v, 34 p., 8vo. Sabin 91860, Evans 6071, Church 963.
Copies in most large libraries.

There were two issues of this first edition, the first with p. 104 and 323
misnumbered 410 and 223 and numerous other variations, and the second
with the errors corrected. The second issue is collated: viii, 304, 295-331,
v, 34. For other variations, see long note in Sabin. Both issues are printed
both on fine and on poor paper, signature X of both being on poor paper.

The first history of Virginia, covering the period up to 1624 and based
on original manuscript sources, many now lost, largely those collected by his
uncle, Sir John Randolph. His printed sources included Smith, Hariot and
Purchas. The same sheets were reissued in London in 1753. Reprinted New
York, 1865, for which see Sabin 91862.

How, NEHEMIAH

A | narrative | of the captivity | of | Nehemiah How, | who was taken
by the Indians at the Great- | Meadow Fort above Fort-Dummer, where he
was | an inhabitant, October 11th 1745. | Giving an account of what he
met with in his | travelling to Canada, and while he was in prison | there.
| Together with an account of Mr. How's death | at Canada. | [rule, 7 lines
quoted, rule] | *Boston: N.E.* | *Printed and sold opposite to the Prison in*
Queen- | *Street. 1748.*   [437]

23 p., small 4to. (15.8 x 11.4 cm.). H.V. Jones *Adventures in Americana*
164. F.C. Deering, MB, MWA, PP.

First edition, first issue with obituary of How on p. 23 and without list
of subscribers. The H.V. Jones-Rosenbach Co.-W.M. Elkins copy is at PP.

. . . . .

22, [2] p., small 4to. Sabin 33220, Evans 6162, Ayer 136. ICN, MBAt,
NHi, NN.   [438]

First edition, second issue, completely reset with obituary on p. 22 and
with two unnumbered pages of subscribers added at end.

Reprinted in S.G. Drake's *Indian captivities,* 1839, etc. Reprinted, as a
separate, edited by V.H. Paltsits, Cleveland, 1904.

Nehemiah How was captured at Great Meadow Fort, now Putney,
Vermont, Oct. 11 (old style), 1745 by a party of St. Francis Abenakis.
They attacked the fort but were repulsed. How was taken to Crown Point,
down Lake Champlain to Chambly, thence to Quebec where the French
put him in prison with other captives including Rev. John Norton and
William Pote, both of whom left accounts of their adventures. How's narrative is especially valuable for its record of the many other Indian captives

and of the life of the prison. He died in the prison on May 25, 1747. Historically, his is one of the most valuable of all Indian captivities.

NORTON, JOHN

The redeemed captive. | Being a | narrative | of the taken [sic] and carrying into captivity | the Reverend | Mr. John Norton, | when Fort-Massachusetts surrendered to a large body | of French and Indians, August 20th 1746. | With a particular account of the defence made before the | surrender of that fort, with the articles of capitula- | tion &c. | Together with an account, both entertaining and affecting, | of what Mr. Norton met with, and took notice of, | in his travelling to, and while in captivity at Canada, | and 'till his arrival at Boston, on August 16. 1747. | [rule] | Written by himself. | [rule] | [10 lines quoted] | [rule] | *Boston: Printed & sold [by Gamaliel Rogers and Daniel Fowle] opposite the Prison. 1748.*   [439]

40 p., 8vo. (16.7 x 10.2 cm.). Sabin 55891, Evans 6211, Church 965, Ayer 215. CSmH, CtY (title imp.), DLC, F.C. Deering, ICN (1st issue, imp.), MB, MBC (now missing), MH, MHi, MWA, MWiW-C, PP (1st issue), F.T. Siebert.

There were two issues, the first with *taken* for *taking* in fourth line of title and other variations noted by Ayer, the second with *taking* in title and other variations.

Norton was the Chaplain at Fort Massachysetts, between the present towns of Williamstown and North Adams and was captured by the French and Indians with the rest of the garrison and taken to the prison at Quebec where he found Nehemiah How (see his *Narrative,* 1748) and other captives including William Pote whose original *Journal* is owned by ICN and was printed at New York in 1896. (Ayer 225-226). Norton's simple, honest and brave narrative is one of the best of the captivities.

The Norton narrative was reprinted as the appendix to S.G. Drake: *Particular history of the five years' French and Indian War. Albany,* 1870 and, from the same type as a separate (100 copies printed) with the title: *Narrative of the capture and burning of Fort Massachusetts by the French and Indians, in the time of the war of 1744-1749, and the captivity of all those stationed there, to the number of thirty persons. Written at the time by one of the captives, the Rev. Mr. John Norton, Chaplain of the fort. Now first published with notes, by Samuel G. Drake. Albany: Printed for S.G. Drake of Boston, by Joel Munsell. 1870.* 51 p., 4to. It was again reprinted, with an introduction and notes by Victor Hugo Paltsits, in an edition of 267 copies, at Cleveland in 1904.

THORESBY, RALPH

The excellency and advantage of doing good: | Represented in a | sermon | preached before the | . . . Trustees | for Establishing the | Colony of Georgia, . . . | . . . March 17, 1747-8. | . . . | *London:* | *Printed for*

W. Meadows, next John's Coffee-House in Cornhill. | *MDCCXLVIII.* | (*Price 6d.*).   [440]

[2], [5]-21, [1] p., 4to. (22 x 17.3 cm.). De Renne I:124. GU-De.

CHALKLEY, THOMAS

A | collection | of the | works | of | Thomas Chalkley. | In two parts. | . . . *Philadelphia: Printed by B. Franklin, and D. Hall.* | *MDCCXLIX.* [441]

[2], v-xiii, [4], 590 p., 8vo. Evans 6297, Hildeburn 1121. NjP, PHi.

Second title: A | journal, | or, | historical account, | of the | life, travels, and Christian experiences, | of that | antient, faithful servant of Jesus Christ, | Thomas Chalkley; | who departed this life in the Island of | Tortola, the fourth day of the ninth | month, 1741. | . . . *Philadelphia:* | *Printed by B. Franklin, and D. Hall,* | *MDCCXLIX.*

Third title: The | works | of | Thomas Chalkley. | Part II. | Containing | his epistles, and other writings. | [same imprint and date].

[DOUGLASS, WILLIAM]

A summary, historical and political, of the first planting, progressive improvements, and present state of the British settlements in North America. Containing . . . Vol. 1. [one line quoted] *Boston, New-England: Printed and sold by Rogers and Fowle in Queen-Street. MDCCXLIX.*   [442]

[2], iii, [3], 568 p., 8vo. Evans 6307, Sabin 20726, Stokes VI:261. Copies in most large libraries.

Issued in 36 parts, 1747-1749. For a scholarly appraisal of this work, see Lawrence C. Wroth: *An American bookshelf 1755.* (Publications of the Rosenbach Fellowship in Bibliography, no. III), Philadelphia, 1934, p. 87-91. Continued in 1752, no. 455.

HARVEST, GEORGE

A | sermon | preached before the | . . . Trustees | for Establishing the | Colony of Georgia . . . | . . . March 16, 1748-9. | . . . | *London:* | *Printed for W. Meadows, at the Angel in Cornhill; and M. Cooper* | *at the Globe in Pater-Noster-Row. 1749.*   [443]

[4], [3]-22 p., 4to. (21.9 x 16.7 cm.). De Renne I:127. GU-De.

COLDEN, CADWALLADER

The history of the Five Indian Nations depending on the Province of New-York in America . . . The second edition. *London: John Whitson, Lockyer Davis and John Ward. MDCCL.*   [444]

xvi, [4], 90, iv, 91-204, 283 p., folded map, 8vo. Sabin 14274. Copies in most large libraries.

The 1747 edition with a new title page.

DOOLITTLE, THOMAS

A short | narrative | of mischief done by the | French and Indian enemy, | on the | western frontiers | of the Province of the | Massachusetts-Bay; | from the beginning of the French War, | proclaimed by the King of France | March 15th 1743,4; and by the King | of Great Britain March 29th | 1744, to August 2d 1748. | Drawn up by the Reverend Mr. Doolittle of North- | field in the County of Hampshire; and found among | his manuscripts after his death. | And at the desire of some, is now published, with some small | additions, to render it more perfect. | [rule] | *Boston:* | *Printed and sold by* | *S. Kneeland, in Queenstreet.* | [rule] | *MDCCL.* [445]

[2], 22 p., 8vo. (17.5 x 10 cm.). Sabin 20613, Evans 6488. NN, PPL.

A day-by-day account of Indian attacks, captivities, etc. in Western Massachusetts.

FRANCKLIN, THOMAS

A | sermon | preached before the | . . . Trustees | for Establishing the | Colony of Georgia . . . | . . . March 16, 1749-50. | . . . | *London: Printed* | *for R. Francklin, in Russel-street, Covent-Garden.* | [rule] | *MDCCL.*
[446]

20 p., 4to. (22 x 17 cm.). De Renne I: 129. GU-De.

[PROPRIETORS OF BRUNSWICK TOWNSHIP, MAINE]

Advertisement, Whereas the Plymouth Proprietors (so called) have im- powered John North, Lieut. of Pemaquid Fort, and Samuel Goodwin [to survey land at the eastern parts of the Province, and defending title] *[Boston, 1750].* [447]

Broadside. Title from Ford 907. MHi, MWA.

First of a series of broadsides and pamphlets in the contest between the Plymouth Company (The Kennebeck Purchase) and the Proprietors of Brunswick Township, Maine, over title to that territory.

BARD, JOHN

A | letter | to the | proprietors | of the | Great-Nine-Partners-Tract. | On | The subject of Jacob Reigner & Company's patented | land, to the North- ward of the Fish Creek, | in Dutchess County; which the said proprietors have | of late years included in their patent, and still claim. | [rule] | By John Bard. | One of the assigns of said Jacob Reigner & Company. | [rule, orn., rule] | *New-York:* | *Printed and sold by J. Parker, at the New Printing-* | *Office, in Beaver-Street, 1751.* [448]

22+ p., map, 8vo. (19 cm.). Church 976. CSmH.

Apparently one leaf, p. 23-24 was cancelled in the only surviving copy, for the words *Now, Gentlemen* at the end of the last line of page 22 have been crossed out with ink but the catchword *if* at the foot of the page remains. Following p. 22, a sheet containing the plan and appendix, on thinner paper, has been inserted; plan with title: *The | Great Nine Partners Tract* (recto blank), *Appendix*, [2] p.

By Dr. John Bard, leading colonial physician of New York and first President of the New York Medical Society.

Bartram, John

Observations, | on the | inhabitants, climate, soil, rivers, productions, | animals, and other matters worthy of notice. | Made by | Mr. John Bartram, | in his travels from | Pensilvania | to | Onondago, Oswego and the Lake Ontario, | in Canada. | To which is annex'd, a curious account of the | cataracts at Niagara. | By Mr. Peter Kalm, | a Swedish gentleman who travelled there. | [orn.] | *London: | Printed for J. Whiston and B. White, in | Fleet-Street, 1751. | (Price one shilling and six-pence.)*   [449]

[2], 94 p., plate, folded plan, 8vo. (22 x 15 cm.). Sabin 3868, Church 977. Copies in most large libraries.

Frontispiece folded plan of the town of Oswego and plate containing a plan and view (the first published) of an Iroquois Long House.

Dr. Cole, in the Church catalog, says: "This is a very reliable work by two of the most eminent observers and naturalists of their day." Bartram went to Onondaga, the central council fire of the Iroquois, with Conrad Weiser, to study the botany of the country. Kalm's account is the first scientific description of Niagara Falls in English. For the importance of this work, see L.C. Wroth's *American bookshelf, 1755.* Philadelphia, 1934.

Chalkley, Thomas

A collection of the works of that antient, faithful servant of Jesus Christ, Thomas Chalkley . . . The second edition. *London: Luke Hind. 1751.*   [450]

ix, 580 p., 8vo. Title from Sabin 11747. Many later editions.

.   .   .   .   .

A journal or historical account of the life, travels and Christian experiences of that antient, faithful servant of Jesus Christ, Thomas Chalkley . . . The second edition. *London: Luke Hind. 1751.*   [451]

ix, 326 p., 8vo. Title from Sabin 11749. Many later editions.

Thomas Chalkley came to America in 1700, settled in Philadelphia and travelled and preached in the colonies from New England to North Carolina. His journal contains a first hand account of frontier conditions.

Dickenson, Jonathan

God's protecting Providence, . . . evidenced, in the remarkable deliverance of Robert Barrow, with divers other persons, . . . The fourth edition. . . . *Philadelphia: Printed and sold by William Bradford, at the sign of the Bible, in Second-Street. M,DCC,LI.*   [452]

[2], [6], 80 p., 8vo. Sabin 20015, Hildeburn 1212, Evans 6658. DLC, FJ, FSaHi, NN, PHC, PPFr, PPL, PSC-Hi.

MORRIS, ISAAC

A | narrative | of the | dangers and distresses | which befel | Isaac Morris, | and | seven more of the crew, | belonging to | the Wager store-ship, | which attended | Commodore Anson, | in his voyage to the South Sea: | containing | an account of their adventures, | after they were left by Bulkeley and Cummins, | on an uninhabited part of Patagonia, in South America; | where they remained about fifteen months, 'till they were | seized by a party of Indians, and carried above a thousand | miles into the Indian country, with whom they resided up- | wards of sixteen months: after which they were carried to | Buenos-Ayres, and ransomed by the Governor, who sent | them on board the Asia, a Spanish man of war, and con- | fined them there above thirteen months; when the Asia | sailed for Europe. | Interspersed with | a description of the manners and | customs of the Indians in that part of the | world, particularly their manner of taking the wild | horses in hunting, as seen by the author himself. | The whole | serving as a supplement to Mr. Bulkeley's Journal, | Campbell's Narrative, and Ld. Anson's Voyage. | [rule] | By I. Morris, late midshipman of the Wager. | [rule] | *London:* | *Printed for S. Birt, at the Bible and Ball, in Ave-mary-* | *Lane; and sold by A. Tozer, bookseller, in Exeter.* | *[1751].*   [453]

87 p., 8vo. (19.5 x 12.5 cm.). Sabin 50834. CSmH, DNR, MH, NHi, NjP, RPJCB.

A captivity among the Indians of Patagonia for sixteen months, then with the Spanish at Buenos-Aires, 1741-1746. Reprinted at Dublin the following year.

PROPRIETORS OF BRUNSWICK TOWNSHIP, MAINE

Advertisement. | At a meeting of the Proprietors of the Township of Brunswick in the County of York . . . on May 15th 1751; the following vote was passed. | Whereas in order to open the eyes of people, and to undeceive those persons that have been unwarily led to | take up under the Plymouth Company's Claim, to lands in Kenebeck River . . . *[Boston. 1751].*   [454]

Broadside. Title from Ford 931. MHi, MSaE.

Part of the contest between the Plymouth Company (Kennebeck Purchase) and the Proprietors of Brunswick Township, Maine, over title to that territory.

[DOUGLASS, WILLIAM]

A summary, historical and political, of the first planting, progressive improvements, and present state of the British settlements in North-America. . . . Vol. II, Part 1. [3 lines quoted] *Boston: Printed and sold by Daniel Fowle in Queen-street; where may be had the first volume bound or*

*stitch'd. Also some odd numbers to compleat imperfect setts. 1751. [i.e.,
1752].*   [455]

[4], 416 p., 8vo. Evans 6663, Sabin 20726, Stokes VI:261. Copies in
most large libraries. Vol. 2 of the MHi copy has a new title page dated 1753
and new pages 417-440 added from Salmon's *Geographical and historical
grammar, London, 1757.*

Issued in 26 parts, 1750-1752, the inside front cover of the last part
recording the author's death in October, 1752. Reprinted with maps, *London,
1755* and *1760,* for which see Sabin 20727 and 20728, corrected by Wroth,
p. 176-177.

Volume I was published in 1749, no. 442.

LE BEAU, C[LAUDE]

Geschichte des Herrn C. Le Beau, oder merckwürdige und neue Reise
zu denen Wilden des Nordlichen Theils von America. Worinnen man eine
Beschreibung von Canada, nebst einem gantz besondern Bericht von denen
alten Gebräuchen, Sitten, und Lebens-Arten dererjenigen Wilden, die
darinnen wohnen, antrifft. Aus dem Frantzösischen übersetzt von W. E.
Burkhard Roslern. *Erfurt: Joh. David Jungnicol. 1752.*   [456]

2 vols., plates and map, 12mo. Sabin 39583. RPJCB.

.   .   .   .   .

Zweyte Auflage, 1756. BM.   [457]

.   .   .   .   .

Des Hern. Claudii Le Beau, Parlements-Advocaten zu Paris, Neue Reise
unter die Wilden in Nord-America; . . . übersetzt von Johann Bernhard
Nack. *Frankfurt: . . . Gebrüdern von Duren. 1752.*   [457A]

2 vols., [4], 415; [2], 504 p., 3 plates, 8 vo. Sabin 39584.

.   .   .   .   .

Leipzig, 1752. IU, NN.   [458]

Translations of his: *Avantures . . . Amsterdam, 1738,* which see.

MORRIS, ISAAC

A narrative of the dangers and distresses which befel Isaac Morris . . . [as
in 1st ed., 1751] *Dublin: 1752.*   [459]

8vo. Title from L.C. Harper cat. 168, 1945, no. 1103. $45.00. CSmH,
NNH.

Reprinted in *Universal Museum,* vol. 2, 1763.

HOPKINS, SAMUEL

Historical memoirs, | relating to the | Housatunnuk Indians: | or, | An

account of the methods used, and pains | taken, for the propagation of the Gospel | among that heathenish-tribe, and the suc- | cess thereof, under the ministry of the late | Reverend Mr. John Sergeant: | together, | with the character of that eminent worthy missionary; and an | address to the people of this country, representing the very | great importance of attaching the Indians to their interest, | not only by treating them justly and kindly, but by using | proper endeavours to settle Christianity among them. | [rule] | By Samuel Hopkins, A.M. | [rule, 3 lines quoted, rule] | *Boston: N.E.* | *Printed and sold by S. Kneeland, in Queen-Street, opposite* | *to the Prison.* 1753.
[460]

[2], iv, 182 p., small 4to. (20 x 14 cm.). Sabin 32945, Evans 7023, Church 986. Copies in most large libraries.

One of the best accounts of the work of a frontier missionary to the Indians. Sergeant worked among the Housatonic or Stockbridge Indians of Western Massachusetts, 1734-1749. The author, minister at Housatunnuk or Great Barrington, Mass. from 1743 to 1769 and later at Newport, R.I., was the founder of the sect of Hopkinsonians. This work was partially reprinted and continued in his *An address to the people of New England,* 1757; and abridged as: *An abridgement of Mr. Hopkin's historical memoirs,* 1757.

PLYMOUTH COMPANY (The Kennebeck Purchase)

Remarks | on the plan and extracts of deeds lately publish- | ed by the proprietors of the township of Bruns- | wick. (as they term themselves) agreeable to their | vote of January 4th 1753. | N.B. By virtue of these deeds, the Plymouth Company, on one | part, and Sir Byby Lake and others, in opposition to them, | claim certain tracts of land, lying upon the River Kennebeck, | at the Eastward. | [Caption title] *[Boston, 1753].* [461]

8, 4 p., 4to. (24 x 18.7 cm.). Evans 7098, Sabin 69482. CtHWatk, MHi, NHi, NN, RPJCB.

PROPRIETORS OF BRUNSWICK TOWNSHIP, MAINE

An | answer | to | the remarks of the Plymouth Company, | or (as they call themselves) the Proprietors of the | Kennebeck Purchase from the late Colony of | New-Plymouth, published by virtue of their | vote of 31st of January last; on the plan and | extracts of deeds published by the Proprietors | of the Township of Brunswick. | Agreeable to their vote of the 4th of January immediately | preceeding. | Wherein, | the many trifling cavils against said plan and extracts are | answered, many aspersions cast on them wiped off: and | their entire consistency with each other fully shewn. | And also the boundaries of the Plymouth Company's tract | upon Kennebeck-River are at large set forth and ascertain'd. | *Boston: in N.E. Printed in the year* MDCCLIII. [462]

34 p., 4to. Sabin 63498, Evans 6976. MBAt, MiU-C, MWA, NN, RPJCB.

PLYMOUTH COMPANY

A | defence | of the remarks | of the | Plymouth Company, | on the plan and extracts of deeds published by | the Proprietors (as they term themselves) of the | Township of Brunswick. | Being | a reply to their Answer to said Remarks, lately published, | according to their vote of March 28. 1753. | [rule, orn., rule] | *Boston: N.E.* | *Printed in the year MDCCLIII.*   [463]

[2], 50 p., 4to. (23.5 x 18 cm.). Evans 6988, Sabin 19252. CtHWatk, CtY, MH, MWA, NHi, NN, RPJCB.

.   .   .   .   .

2d issue with folded map. RPJCB.   [464]

Map: *A true copy of an ancient | plan of E. Hutchinson's Esqr. & from Jose Heath | in 1719 . . . 1752.*

STITH, WILLIAM

The | history | of the | first discovery | and | settlement | of | Virginia. | By William Stith, A.M. | President of the College of William and Mary | in Virginia. | . . . | Virginia, Printed: | *London, Reprinted for S. Birt | in Ave-Mary-Lane.* | *M.DCC.LIII.*   [465]

Collation as in the two issues of the 1747 edition. Sabin 91861, Evans 7125. First issue: CSmH, DLC; second issue: CtY, MH, NN, NNC, RPJCB.

Reissues, with new title pages, of the two issues of the original Williamsburg, 1747 edition, which see. See Sabin 91860-91861.

CHALKLEY, THOMAS

A | collection | of the | works | of | Thomas Chalkley. | In two volumes. | . . . | Vol. I. [II.] | The second edition. | *Philadelphia:* | *Printed and sold by James Chattin,* | *in Church-Alley.* 1754.   [466]

[4], viii, 325; iv, 244, vii p., 8vo. Sabin 11746, Evans 7166, Hildeburn 1351. BM, NN, PHi.

HANSON, ELIZABETH

God's mercy surmounting man's cruelty, exemplified in the captivity and redemption of Elizabeth Hanson . . . [etc., as in 1st ed., 1728] The second edition. *Philadelphia: Printed and sold by James Chattin, in Church-Alley.* 1754.   [467]

23, [1] p., 12mo. (14.8 x 9 cm.). Evans 7160, Sabin 30264. PHi.

The captive's home is spelled *Kecheachy* on title.

[KIMBER, EDWARD]

The history of the life and adventures of Mr. Anderson, containing his strange varieties of fortune in Europe and America. Compiled from his own papers. [motto] *London, Printed for W. Owen, 1754.* [468]

[2], 288 p., 12mo. (17 cm.). Sabin 1380. DLC, MdBP, MiU-C, RPJCB.

For evidence of authorship, see F.G. Black: *Edward Kimber, in Harvard Studies and Notes in Philology and Literature,* vol. 17, 1935, p. 27-42.

A novel of travel, adventure and Indian captivity in America.

．　．　．　．　．

Dublin: Richard James, 1754. [469]

154 p., 12mo. Title from BM cat. BM.

URLSPERGER, SAMUEL

Americanisches Ackerwerk Gottes; oder zuverlässige Nachrichten, den Zustand der americanisch englischen und von salzburgischen Emigranten erbauten Pflanzstadt Ebenezer in Georgien betreffend . . . Erstes [-Viertes] Stück herausgegeben von Samuel Urlsperger . . . *Augsburg, MDCCLIIII [-MDCCLXVII].* [470]

5 vols., front. port., 4to. Sabin 98131, De Renne I:131-133. DLC, GU-De, MH, NN, RPJCB.

A continuation of his *Ausführliche Nachrichten,* 1735, no 389.

For full collations, see Sabin and De Renne.

WASHINGTON, GEORGE

The | journal | of | Major George Washington, | sent by the | Hon. Robert Dinwiddie, Esq; | His Majesty's Lieutenand-Governor, and | Commander in Chief of Virginia, | to the | Commandant | of the | French forces | on | Ohio. | To which are added, the | Governor's letter, | and a translation of the | French officer's answer. | [double rule] | *Williamsburg: | Printed by William Hunter. 1754.* [471]

28 p., 8vo. (20 x 12.5 cm.). Sabin 101710, Church 998. BM, CSmH, ICN, NN (Brinley 4189), PHi, RPJCB, A.S.W. Rosenbach (George Washington's own copy with his autograph), J.H. Scheide (Hartford-White-Jones).

The original manuscript is in the Public Record Office, London. Major Washington, aged 22, was sent to demand the withdrawal of the French at Fort Le Boeuf, to report on their forces and to treat with the Indians. It is a volume of great historical importance, a beautiful imprint and an item of great rarity and sentimental interest. This, Washington's first published work, covers the period from October, 1753 to January, 1754.

For later editions see Church 998, Sabin 41650, 51661, 101710.

．　．　．　．　．

The | journal | of | Major George Washington, | sent by the | Hon. Robert Dinwiddie, Esq; | His Majesty's Lieutenant-Governor, and | Commander in

Chief of Virginia, | to the | Commandant of the French forces | on | Ohio |
To which are added, the | Governor's letter: | and a | translation of the
French officer's answer. | With | a new map of the country as far as the |
Mississippi. | [double rule] | *Williamsburgh Printed,* | *London, Reprinted*
for T. Jefferys, the corner | *of St. Martin's Lane.* | [rule] | *MDCCLIV.* |
(Price one shilling.)   [472]

32 p., folded map, 8vo. (18.7 x 12 cm.). Sabin 101710, Church 999. BM,
CSmlI, DLC, MB, MBAt, MH, MiU-C, NHi, NIC, NjP, NN, RPJCB,
WHi.

Folded map: Map | of the Western parts | of the Colony of | Virginia, | as
far as the | Mississipi. (23.4 x 35.5 cm.). The several states of the map are
described by Sabin which also records numerous reprints of the journal.

BLODGET, SAMUEL

A | prospective-plan | of the | battle near Lake George, | on the | eighth
day of September, 1755. | With an | explanation thereof; | containing | a full,
tho' short, history of that important affair. | By Samuel Blodget, | occasionally
at the camp, when the battle was fought. | *Boston; New-England:* | *Printed*
by Richard Draper, for the author. | *MDCCLV.*   [473]

[2], 5 p., text in double columns, folded plan, 4to.

The folded plan, engraved by Thomas Johnston of Boston, measures 44 x
34.5 cm. and has the title: *A prospective plan of the battle fought near Lake*
George on the 8th of September 1755, between 2000 English with 250
Mohawks under the command of General Johnson and 2500 French and
Indians under the command of General Dieskau in which the English were
victorious, captivating the French general with a number of his men, killing
700 and putting the rest to flight. [signed:] S. Blodget del. Thos. Johnston
Sculp. There are two issues of the plan, the first without trees around Fort
Edward.

This first historical print engraved in North America and best eye-witness
account of the famous battle was written and the plan drawn by Samuel
Blodget, a sutler attached to the British army under General (later Sir)
William Johnson. Sabin 5955, Evans 7363, Brinley 209 and 8073-4, Stokes
and Haskell p. 32-33, Stauffer 1501, Green: *Ten facsim. reprod.* 33-35,
Wroth and Adams: *Amer. wdcts.* 18. BM (plan, lacking title); George
Brinley 209-Ogden Goelet-Goodspeed's Book Shop-Henry Stevens, Son &
Stiles, 1943 (pam. and plan 1st issue); DLC (pam.); MH (pam. and plan
1st issue); MHi (pam. and plan 2d issue); MWA (plan 1st issue); MWiW
(pam. and plan (Chapin)); N (pam.); NHi (plan 1st issue); NN (pam.
and plan 1st issue); PPAmP (pam.); PP (pam. and plan 1st issue); PU
(pam.); RPJCB (pam. and plan 1st issue).

Plan reproduced in Mas. Hist. Soc. Proceed., 2d ser., 5, 1890, p. 416; and
in Samuel A. Green: *Ten fac-simile reproductions relating to New England.*
Boston, 1902.

Both pamphlet and plan were reprinted in London by Thomas Jefferys in 1756, the plan being very inaccurately copied and its parts rearranged. Copies in many of the larger libraries. This edition of the plan was reproduced in the *Documentary history of New York* and elsewhere. Both plan and pamphlet were reprinted in facsimile, with an introduction, by Henry Stevens, Son and Stiles of London in 1911.

An even rarer contemporary plan of the battlefield, issued without accompanying text, was: *To His Excellency William Shirley Esqr: Capt. General & Govr. in Chief . . . of ye Massachusetts Bay . . . this plan of Hudsons Rivr from Albany to . . . Crown Point . . . ye land defended on ye 8th of Sept. last . . . & sundry particulars respecting ye late engagement . . . by your most devoted humble servt. Timo. Clement Survr. Haverl. Feb. 10: 1756* [signed:] *Engraved & printed by Thomas Johnston Boston New-England April 1756.* 69.5 x 44 cm. MWA, MWiW, NHi, RPJCB. (First two fine, last two poor copies).

Evans 7390, wrongly titled and dated 1755. Fielding 763. Winsor: *Nar. and crit. hist. Amer.*, V, p. 586 (redrawing of copy now at NHi). Wroth and Adams: *Amer. wdcts and engravings*, 1670-1800. Prov., 1946, 19.

For another account of the battle, see under Charles Chauncy, no. 477.

[CHAUNCY, CHARLES]

A letter to a friend, giving a concise, but just, account, according to the advices hitherto received, of the Ohio-defeat; and pointing out also the many good ends, this inglorious event is naturally adapted to promote: or, shewing wherein it is fitted to advance the interest of all the American British colonies, To which is added, some general account of the New-England forces, with what they have already done, counter-balancing the above loss. *Boston: N.E. Printed and sold by Edes and Gill, at their Printing-Office next to the Prison in Queen-Street, M,DCC,LV.* [474]

[15] p., 4to. Evans 7381, Sabin 12320. BM, DLC, MB, MBAt, MH, MHi, MiU-C, MWA, MWiW-C, NHi, NN, RPJCB, ViU.

. . . . . .

Bristol [Eng.]: *Re-printed by Edward Ward on the Tolzey. 1755* [475]
[4], 30 p., 8vo. (22.3 x 14 cm.). Sabin 12320. ICN, MWA, NHi, NN, PHi, RPJCB.

. . . . . .

Boston, New-England, printed; | *London reprinted:* | *And sold by J. Noon, at the White-Hart, Cheapside,* | *near the Poultry, 1755.* [476]
28 p., 8vo. Sabin 12320. MWA.

One of the best contemporary accounts of the Braddock defeat, but with a New England bias.

. . . . . .

A second letter to a friend, giving a more particular narrative of the defeat of the French army at Lake-George, by the New-England troops, than has yet been published, representing also the vast importance of this conquest to the American-British colonies. To which is added, such an account of what the New-England governments have done, to carry into effect their design against Crown-Point, as will shew the necessity of their being help'd by Great-Britain, in point of money. *Boston, N.E.: Printed and sold by Edes and Gill, at their Printing-Office, next to the Prison in Queen-Street, MDCCLV.* [477]

16 p., 4to. Evans 7382, Sabin 12328. DLC, ICN, MB, MH (imp.) MHi, MWiW-C, RPJCB, ViU.

One of the two contemporary accounts of the Battle of Lake George. For the other, see under Samuel Blodget, no. 473.

. . . . .

Two letters to a friend, on the present critical conjuncture of affairs in North America; particularly on the vast importance of the victory gained by the New-England militia under the command of General Johnston [Sir William Johnson], at Lake-George. Being the most genuine account of this action yet published. *Boston printed: London Re-printed, for T. Jefferys, at the corner of St. Martin's Lane, in the Strand. MDCCLV.* [478]

[2], 54 p., 8vo. Sabin 97569. BM, DLC, MBAt, N, RPJCB.

A reprint of the two letters above.

COLDEN, CADWALLADER

The history of the Five Indian Nations depending on the Province of New-York in America. . . . The third edition. *London: Lockyer Davis. M DCC LV.* [479]

xii, [iv], 260; [4], 251, [4] p., map, 8vo. Sabin 14275. Copies in most large libraries.

. . . . .

Reprint of first edition, with introduction and notes by John Gilmary Shea. *New York: T.H. Merrill. 1866.* [480]

xl, [2], xvii, [1], 141 p., port and map, 8vo. Sabin 14271. Copies in most large libraries.

100 small paper and 25 large paper copies printed. For other recent editions, see DLC catalog.

EVANS, LEWIS

Geographical, historical, | political, philosophical and mechanical | essays. | The first, containing | an | analysis | of a General Map of the | Middle British Colonies | in | America; | and of the country of the Confederate

Indians: | a description of the face of the country; | the boundaries of the Confederates; | and the | maritime and inland navigations of the several rivers | and lakes contained therein. | By Lewis Evans. | *Philadelphia:* | *Printed by B. Franklin, and D. Hall. MDCCLV.* [481]

iv, 32 p., folded map, small folio (27.8 x 21 cm.). Sabin 23175, Evans 7411, Hildeburn 1412, W.J. Campbell: Franklin imprints, 1918, p. 125. Copies in most large libraries, some without the map.

. . . . .

With addition to imprint: *And sold by R. and J. Dodsley, in Pall-Mall, London.* [482]

. . . . .

Added above the imprint: *The second edition.* [483]

. . . . .

2d ed., with addition to the imprint: *And sold by J. and R. Dodsley, in Pall-Mall, London.* [484]

A general map of the | Middle British Colonies, in America; | Viz Virginia, Màriland, Dèlaware, Pensilvania, | New-Jersey, New-York, Connecticut, and Rhode Island: | Of Aquanishuonigy, the Country of the Confederate Indians; | Comprehending Aquanishuonîgy proper, their place of residence, | Ohio and Tiiuxsoxrúntie their deer-hunting countries, | Couxsaxráge and Skaniadaráde, their beaver-hunting countries; | Of the lakes Erie, Ontário and Champlain, | And of part of New-France: | Wherein is also shewn the antient and present seats of the | Indian nations. | By Lewis Evans. 1755. | [at left of cartouch:] Engraved by Jas Turner in Philadelphia. | [In lower right corner:] Published according to Act of Parliament, by Lewis Evans, June 23. 1755. and | sold by R. Dodsley, in Pall-Mall, London, & by the Author in Philadelphia. (66 x 49 cm.).

For this, the most important map of the American colonies, see: H.N. Stevens: *Lewis Evans his map,* 3d ed., London, 1924; L.C. Wroth: *An American bookshelf, 1755,* Phil., 1934; L.C. Wroth and M.W. Adams: *American woodcuts and engravings,* no. 17; L.H. Gipson: *Lewis Evans;* Stauffer 3331.

The map was reissued with improvements in Thomas Pownall's *Topographical description,* London, 1776, without the extension and, again, with the extension. For the various reissues and piracies of Evans' maps, see Stevens.

HAZARD, SAMUEL

Scheme for the settlement of a new colony to the westward of Pennsylvania, for the enlargement of his Majesty's dominions in America, for the further promotion of the Christian religion among the Indian natives, and for the more effectual securing them in his Majesty's alliance. | [Caption title] *[n.p., May, 1755]*.   [485]

Broadsheet, folio. (33 x 20.3 cm.). Title from L.C. Wroth's *American bookshelf, 1755.* Philadelphia, 1934, p. 172, where it was described for the first time. Ct.

Text includes a petition to the Governor, Council and Representatives of the Colony of Connecticut, May 8, 1755.

. . . . . .

Scheme for the settlement [. . . as above] [Caption title] *[n.p., July, 1755]*   [486]

Broadsheet, folio. (36.8 x 21.6 cm.). Title from Wroth, as above. Ct (2 copies). Photostats of both broadsheets at RPJCB.

Text includes a petition to the King. Dated at Philadelphia, July 24th, 1755.

"Hazard's proposal was to occupy a tract west of Pennsylvania belonging by charter right to the colony of Connecticut, and on May 8, 1755 he personally petitioned the Connecticut Assembly to release to him its claim to the lands he intended to settle, saying, among many other things, that he had already engaged 3,508 settlers."—Wroth. Though the Assembly granted his petition, it was never confirmed by the crown and the scheme was abandoned, though unsuccessfully resubmitted by his son, Ebenezer Hazard, in 1774.

JOHNSON, WILLIAM

Camp at Lake George, | Sept. 9. 1755. | To the Governours of the several Colonies who raised the Troops | on the present Expedition, | Gentlemen, | . . . | I am, most respectfully, | Gentlemen, | your most Obedient Servant, | Wm. Johnson. | *[n.p., 1755]*.   [487]

3 p., folio. (31 x 19 cm.). MHi.

. . . . . .

Camp at Lake George, | Sept. 9. 1755. | To the GOVERNOURS of the several Colonies who raised the Troops | on the present Expedition. | Gentlemen, | . . . | I am, Gentlemen, | most respectfully | your most Obedient Servant, | Wm. Johnson. | *[n.p., 1755]*.   [488]

3 p., folio. (29.5 x 19 cm.). RPJCB.

. . . . . .

Camp on Lake George, Sept. 9. 1755. | To the Governors of the several Colonies who raised | the Troops on the present Expedition. | Gentlemen, | . . . | I am, most respectfully, Gentlemen, | Your Most Obedient Servant, | Wm. Johnson. | [Followed by a 10 line postscript dated at *Newport, Sept. 20. 1755* telling of the French losses, the death of Hendrick, the Mohawk Sachem, and the approach of reenforcements]. *[n.p., 1755]*.   [489]

3 p., folio. (31.5 x 19 cm.). RPJCB.

. . . . . .

[Letter dated] Camp at Lake George, Sept. 9, 1755. To the Governours of the several Colonies who raised the Troops on the present Expedition . . . [giving an Account of the Action of the preceding Day]. *[n.p., 1755]*.

[490]

3 p., folio. Sabin 36338, Evans 7441. Neither distinguishes the different editions. DLC, MH, MHi (3), MWA, MWiW (2), NHi (MS copy and 3 variant photostats), RPJCB (2), ViU.

Major General William Johnson's report of the Battle of Lake George, Sept. 8, 1755, written the following day. As a reward for his success in the campaign he was made Sir William Johnson.

[SMITH, PROVOST WILLIAM]

A brief | history | of the rise and progress of the | charitable scheme, | carrying on by a | society of noblemen and gentlemen | in | London, | for the relief and instruction of poor Ger- | mans, and their descendants, settled in Penn- | sylvania, and the adjacent British colonies in | North-America. | Published by order of the gentlemen appointed Trustees-General, | for the management of the said charitable scheme. | *Philadelphia:* | *Printed by* *B. Franklin, and D. Hall.* | *MDCCLV.* [491]

[2], 18 p., 4to. Sabin 84588. NHi, PHi, PPL, RPJCB.

A promotion scheme to attract German emigration to Pennsylvania and to keep it from the French settlements on the Ohio. There were 800 copies of the English edition, 1,000 of the German edition (below) and 500 of a combined English and German edition.

. . . . . .

Eine | kurtze Nachricht, | von der Christlichen und | liebreichen Anstalt, | welche zum besten und zur Unterweis- | sung der armen Teutschen, und ihrer Nach- | kommen in Pennsylvanien, und anderen | daran gräntzenden Englischen Provinzien in | Nord-America errichtet worden ist. | Herausgegeben auf Befehl derer, zu Ausführung dieser | Sache, bestimmten Herren General Trustees. | *Philadelphia, Gedruckt durch* *Anton Armbrüster, in der* | *Dritten-Strass, 1755.* [492]

16 p., 4to. Sabin 84625. PHi.

A German translation of the above.

. . . . . .

A brief | state | of the | Province | of | Pennsylvania, | in which | the conduct of their Assemblies for several | years past is impartially examined, and the | true cause of the continual encroachments of | the French displayed, more especially the secret | design of their late unwarrantable invasion | and settlement upon the River Ohio. | To which is annexed, | an easy plan for restoring quiet in the public mea- | sures of that Province, and defeating the ambitious | views of the French in time to come. | In a letter from a gentleman who | has resided many years in Pennsylvania | to his friend in London. | *London:* | *Printed for R. Griffiths, at the Dunciad, in Pater-* | *Noster-Row. 1755.*   [493]

[2], 45 p., 8vo. Sabin 84589. CSmH, MB, MH, MWA, NN, PHi, RPJCB.

An attack on the Quakers for their policy in the Assembly of refusing support to plans for the defense of the Province, and accusing them of influencing the ignorant German vote by improper means. See L.C. Wroth's *An American bookshelf, 1755,* Phil., 1934, for a discussion of the significance of this work.

. . . . .

The second edition, same imprint, date and collation. Sabin 84590. CSmH, DLC, MWA, NN, RPJCB, WHi.   [494]

. . . . .

Dublin: | *Re-printed by Richard James, Bookseller in* | *Dame-Street.* | *MDCCLV.*   [495]

47, [1] p., 8vo. Sabin 84591. CSmH, DLC.

BOWNAS, SAMUEL

An account of the life, travels, and Christian experiences of the work of the ministry of Samuel Bownas. *London: Printed and sold by Luke Hinde, at the Bible in George-Yard, Lombard-Street, 1756.*   [496]

viii, 3-198, [2] p., 8vo. (20.1 x 12.3 cm.). Sabin 7097. F.C. Deering, DLC, IaU, ICN, MH, MiU-C, NHi, PHC, PPL, PSC-Hi, RPJCB.

His travels covered most of our frontiers. Brief account of the captivity of Elizabeth Hanson, p. 147-148. For fuller account, see under her name.

DICKENSON, JONATHAN

Die Göttliche Beschützung ist der Menschen gewisseste Hülffe und Beschirmung zu allen Zeiten, auch in den grössesten Nöthen und Gefahren. Aus Erfahrung gelernet. Bey einer merckwürdigen Geschichte da verschiedene Personen aus der grosen Wassers gefahr errettet worden, in dem sie nicht nur Schiffbruch erlitten sondern auch aus den noch grausamern Rachen der unmenschlichen Canibalen oder Menschen-fressern in Florida sind befreyet worden. Getreulich aufgezeignet von einem welcher selbst persöhnlich dabey gewesen, nehmlich von Jonathan Dickinson. [five lines quoted from the Psalms] Die 4te edition. Zu Philadelphia gedruckt und nun zum ersten mal in Teutsch heraus gegeben. *Germanton. Gedruckt und zu haben bey Christoph Saur 1756.*   [497]

32 [i.e., 98] p., 16mo. Evans 7646, Hildeburn 1462. DLC, NN.

. . . . .

Translation, . . . zum zweyten mal in Deutsch heraus gegeben. *Germanton.
Gedruckt und zu haben bey Christoph Saur 1756.* [498]

98 p., 16mo. MdBP, MWA.

Second issue with final pagination corrected and with *zweyten* in place of
ersten in title. One of the issues also in PHi, PPL-R.

EVANS, LEWIS

Geographical, historical, | political, philosophical and mechanical | essays.
| Number II. Containing, | A | letter | representing, the impropriety of
sending forces to Virginia: | The importance of taking Fort Frontenac; |
and that the preservation of Oswego was owing to General Shirley's | pro-
ceeding thither. | And containing objections to those parts of Evans's General
Map and | Analysis, which relate to the French title to the country, on the |
North-West side of St. | Laurence River, between Fort Frontenac | and
Montreal. &c. | Published in the New-York Mercury, No. 178, Jan. 5.
1756. | With an | answer, | to so much thereof as concerns the public; | and
the several articles set in a just light. | By Lewis Evans. | *Philadelphia:* |
*Printed [by B. Franklin and D. Hall] for the Author; and sold by him in
Arch-Street:* | *and at New-York by G. Noel, Bookseller near Counts's Market.* ·
| *MDCCLVI.* [499]

42, [1] p., 4to. (20 x 12.5 cm.). Sabin 23176, Evans 7652, Hildeburn
1463, W.J. Campbell: *Franklin imprints,* 1918, p. 130, L.C. Wroth: *An
American bookshelf, 1755,* 1934. NN, PHi, PU, RPJCB, etc.

. . . . .

London: | *Printed for R. and J. Dodsley in Pall-Mall.* | *MDCCLVI.*
[500]

35 p., 4to. (25 x 18.5 cm.). Sabin 23176. NHi, etc.

FLEMING, WILLIAM AND ELIZABETH

A narrative of the sufferings and surprising deliverance of William and
Elizabeth Fleming, who were taken captive by Capt. Jacob, commander of
the Indians, who lately made an excursion on the inhabitants of the Great-
Cove, near Conecochieg, in Pennsylvania, as related by themselves. *Philadelphia: Printed for the benefit of the unhappy sufferers, and sold by them
only. [1756].* [501]

28 p., 12mo. Sabin 24708, Evans 7658, Hildeburn 1467. F.C. Deering.

Probably the first edition, though priority of all 1756 editions is uncertain.
Probably the Brinley 5548 copy sold to "Stuart" for $17.00 and later sold at
the Joseph B. Shea sale, Part I, American Art-Anderson sale 4353, Dec. 1,

1937, no. 189, which copy was bought by F.C. Deering, from which catalogue the above title is taken.

.   .   .   .   .

A | narrative | of the | sufferings, | and | surprizing deliverance | of | William and Elizabeth Fleming, | who were taken captive by Capt. Jacob, com- | mander of the Indians, who lately made an | excursion on the inhabitants of the Great- | Cove, near Conecochieg, in Pennsylvania, as | related by themselves. | [two lines quoted] | *Philadelphia:* | *Printed by* *James Chattin, for the benefit of* | *the unhappy sufferers. 1756.* | *Price 6d.*
[502]

28 p., 8vo. (15.7 x 9.5 cm.). NN (lacking p. 25-28).

.   .   .   .   .

A narrative of the sufferings and surprising deliverance of William and Elizabeth Fleming, who were taken captives by Captain Jacobs, in a late excursion by him and the Indians under his command, on the inhabitants of the Great-Cove, near Conecochieg, in Pennsylvania, as related by themselves. The second [Chattin?] edition. *Philadelphia: James Chattin. 1756.*
[503]

Title from Hildeburn 1466 who gives no collation nor location. Evans 7659, ditto.

.   .   .   .   .

A narrative of the sufferings and surprising deliverance of William and Elizabeth Fleming, who were taken captive by . . . the Indians . . . as related by themselves. *Lancaster: William Dunlap. 1756.*   [504]

Title from Hildeburn 1465 who took his title from an advertisement and so gives no collation or location. Evans 7659, ditto.

.   .   .   .   .

A full and authentic narrative of the sufferings and surprising deliverances of William and Elizabeth Fleming, who were taken captive by Captain Jacob, commander of the Indians, who lately made an excursion on the inhabitants of the Great-Cove, near Conecochieg, in Pennsylvania, as related by themselves. [one line quoted] *New York: Printed and sold by* *J. Parker and and W. Weyman, in Beaver-Street. 1756*   [505]

Title from Evans 7661 who evidently copied an advertisement on copyright entry, for he gives no collation or location.

.   .   .   .   .

A narrative of the sufferings and surprizing deliverances of William and Elizabeth Fleming, who were taken captive by Capt. Jacob, commander of the Indians, who lately made the incursions on the frontiers of Pennsylvania, as related by themselves. [one line quoted] A narrative necessary to be read by all who are going in the expedition, as well as every British subject. Wherein it fully appears, that the barbarities of the Indians is owing to the French, and chiefly their priests. *Boston; New-England, Printed and sold by Green & Russell, at their Printing Office, near the Custom-House, and next to the Writing-School in Queen-Street. 1756.* [506]

20 p., 8vo. (20.5 cm.). Sabin 24708, Evans 7662. DLC (imperfect), MBAt, MHi, MWA.

. . . . . .

Eine | Erzehlung | von den | Trübsalen | und der | wunderbahren Befreyung | so geschehen an | William Flemming | und dessen | Weib Elisabeth | welche bey dem verwichenen Einfall | der Indianer über die Einwohner im | grossen Wald (Grät Grov) bey Can- | nagodschick in Pensilvanien sind | gefangen genommen worden. | Nach ihrer eigenen Aussage. | . . . | . . . | *Zu Läncester gedruckt von W. Duglas | und ins Teutsche übersetzt, und gedruckt zu | Germanton bey Christoph Saur 1756. | Auch zu haben bey David Däschler zu Philad.* [507]

28, [1] p., 16mo. (16.2 x 9.7 cm.). Title from Ayer supp. 57, Hildeburn 1468, Evans 7663. ICN, PHi.

. . . . . .

Another issue with collation: 29, [1] p. MWA, PHi, PPiU. [508]

. . . . . .

2d ed. [1756?]. PPL-R. and Harry C. Marder whose copy was issued with the fourth edition, in German, of the Jonathan Dickenson captivity, which see. [509]

For a later reprint of this German edition, *Frankfurt und Leipzig,* see under the Jonathan Dickenson captivity, 1774.

The first notice of the captivity of the Flemings appeared in the *Pennsylvania Gazette,* published in Philadelphia by Franklin and Hall, November 13, 1755.

This brief but detailed and vivid narrative is told by William and Elizabeth Fleming, each part of the narrative being given in the words of the captive. William Fleming was born in Scotland and two years and four months before the story was written, at the age of twenty, he came to America and was, at first, a frontier peddler. He then secured two pieces of frontier Pennsylvania land on which he lived successively. About a year before the story opens, he married Elizabeth, an Irish girl of 24 and settled on "Licken Creek" about the first of the preceding June. Two months later he moved to his other property on "Conalloway Creek." On November 1st, 1755 he was captured near his home by Captain Jacob and one of his warriors, belonging to a party of 50 Delawares and Shawnese Indians from Fort Duquesne. His wife Elizabeth was also captured, their home looted and burned. Of the neighboring Hicks family, Fleming saw one of the boys tomahawked and scalped, one other was killed and five captured. That night the Flemings escaped but became separated in the dark. However, each made his way back to the settlement in safety, after several hair-breadth escapes from roving Indians. The narrative includes the brief story of another frontiersman, recently escaped, who came to warn the settlement.

This number has been cancelled.   [510]

MITTELBERGER, GOTTLIEB

Gottlieb Mittelberger's | Reise | nach | Pennsylvanien | im Jahr 1750. | Und | Rükreise nach Teutschland | im Jahr 1754. | Enthaltend | nicht nur eine Beschreibung des Landes | nach seinem gegenwärtigen Zustande, son- | dern auch eine ausführliche Nachricht von den | unglükseligen und betrübten Umständen der meisten | Teutschen, die in dieses Land gezogen sind, | und dahin ziehen. | *Stuttgard:* | *Gedrukt bey Gottlieb Frederich Zenisch. 1756.*   [511]

[8], 120 p., 12mo. Sabin 49761. DLC, MH.

. . . . .

Frankfurth und Leipzig, | *1756.*   [512]

[8], 120 p., 12mo. (17.5 x 12 cm.). NHi.

The author was a schoolmaster and organist in New Providence, Philadelphia County, Pennsylvania, for three years and gives an interesting account of the early German colonists.

POWNALL, THOMAS

Proposals for securing the friendship of the Five Nations. *New-York: Printed and sold, by J. Parker and W. Weyman, at the New-Printing-Office in Beaver-street. 1756.*   [513]

14 p., table, 8vo. Evans 7767. PPL.

. . . . .

Considerations | towards a | general plan of measures | for the | English Provinces. | Laid before the Board of Commissioners at Albany, | by Mr. Pownall. | *New-York printed,* | *Edinburgh reprinted, and sold by* | Mess. *Hamilton & Balfour,* | [rule] | *M,DCC,LVI.*   [514]

19 p., 12mo. (15.2 x 9.3 cm.). DLC, NHi.

Pownall's advice, for fortifying the frontiers and making friends with the Iroquois, was followed by the British government and the resulting policy had much to do with the downfall of France in North America.

[SMITH, PROVOST WILLIAM]

A brief | state | of the | Province | of | Pennsylvania, | . . . [as in 1st ed., 1755] The third edition. | *London:* | *Printed for R. Griffiths in Pater-noster-Row. 1756*   [515]

47 p., 8vo. Sabin 84592. CSmH, DLC, MBAt, MH, MHi, NHi, NN, PP, PU, RPJCB.

Reprinted in New York, 1865. Sabin 84593.

For an answer to this tract, see [Joseph Galloway's] *A true and impartial state of the Province of Pennsylvania,* Sabin 60742. For importance of the tract and identity of author, and for the historical value of the *Brief state,* see L.C. Wroth's *An American bookshelf, 1755.* Philadelphia, 1934.

. . . . .

A | brief view | of the conduct of | Pennsylvania, | for the year 1755; | so far as it affected the general service of the | British colonies, particularly the expedition | under the late General Braddock. | With an account of the shocking inhumanities. | committed by incursions of the Indians upon the | Province in October and November; which occasioned | a body of the inhabitants to come down, while the | Assembly were sitting, and to insist upon an imme- | diate suspension of all disputes, and the passage of | a law for the defence of the country. | Interspers'd with several interesting anecdotes and original | papers, relating to the politics and principles of | the people called Quakers: Being a sequel to | a late well-known pamphlet, | intitled, | A brief state of Pennsylvania. | In a second letter to a friend in London. | . . . | *London: Printed for R. Griffiths in Pater-noster Row; and sold | by Mr. Bradford in Philadelphia. 1756.* | *(Price one-shilling and six-pence.).* [516]

88 p., 8vo. Sabin 84594. CSmH, DLC, MBAt, MH, NN, PHi, PP, RPJCB, WHi.

See L.C. Wroth's *An American bookshelf, 1755.* Philadelphia, 1934, for a discussion of the significance of this work.

A French abridgement appears on p. 21-78 of: *État présent de la Pensilvanie, Paris, 1756.* Sabin 19370.

HOPKINS, SAMUEL

An | abridgment | of | Mr. Hopkins's | historical memoirs, | relating to the | Housatunnuk, or Stockbridge Indians: | or, | A brief account of the methods used, and | pains taken, for civilizing and propagating the | Gospel among that heathenish tribe, | and the success thereof, under the ministry of | the late Rev. Mr. John Sergeant. | *Philadelphia:* | *Printed and sold by B. Franklin, and D. Hall.* | *M,DCC,LVII.* [517]

40 p., 8vo. Evans 7916, Sabin 32947, Hildeburn 1531. MB, PHi, etc.

Includes a letter by Conrad Weiser on Indian affairs.

For complete 1st ed., see his *Historical memoirs, 1753;* for a continuation, see:

. . . . .

An | address | to the | people of New-England. | Representing | the very great importance of attaching the | Indians to their interest; not only by | treating them justly and kindly; but by using pro- | per endeavours to settle Christianity among them. | By Samuel Hopkins, A.M. | Pastor of a church in Springfield. | [4 lines quoted] | Printed in Boston, 1753. Being a con- clusion to the | Historical Memoirs relating to the Housatunnuk In- | dians: with an account of the methods used for the | propagation of the Gospel amongst the said Indians, by | the late reverend Mr. John Sergeant. | Now recommended to the serious consideration of the inhabi- | tants of Penn- sylvania, and the other colonies. | *Philadelphia:* | *Reprinted by B. Franklin, and D. Hall. 1757.*   [518]

27 p., 8vo. (17.5 x 9.3 cm.). Sabin 32946, Evans 7917, Hildeburn 1532. NN, PHi, etc.

[JOHNSON, WILLIAM]

Relaçaõ | de huma batalha, succedida no campo de Lake | Giorge na America Septentrional, entre as | tropas Inglezas commandadas pelo Coronel | Guilhelmo, e as Francezas das quaes era | commandante o General Baraõ Dieskau, aos | 30. de Junho do prezente anno de 1757. | Traduzida no idioma Portuguez. | Extrahida de huma carta escrita pelo mesmo | Coronel, logo despois do successo, ao General | Wensvort, Governador da nova Hamsphire, | e mandada inclusa em outra escrita em Post- | maute Capital da mesma Provincia. | [orn.] | *Lisboa:* | *Anno M.DCC.LVII.* | *Com todas as licenças necessarias.*   [519]

7 p., 4to. (19 x 13.3 cm.). Old John Carter Brown cat. 1157. DLC, MH, MiU, MWiW-C, NHi, RPJCB.

Portuguese translation of Major General William Johnson's report of the Battle of Lake George, Sept. 8, 1755. One of a curious series of at least ten tracts on the French and Indian War published in Portuguese in Lisbon between 1755 and 1758, originals of part of the series being in MB, NN, RPJCB and elsewhere with photostat copies in NHi and other libraries. Two of these give accounts of the Braddock Expedition: *Relaçam verdadeira da tomada das praças que na America fizeraõ os Francezes aos Inglezes . . . Lisbon: D. Rodrigues, 1755.* 4to. Reprinted in Mass. Hist. Soc. Photostat Series 119; and *Noticia certa, e manifesto publico da Grande Batalha qui tiverao os Francezes e Inglezes, junto as Ribeiras do Ohio em 9 de Julho de 1755, com a noticia individual de todas as accoens obradas nesta expedicao. Morte do celebre General Braddock, e de outros officiaes e soldados . . . Lisboa, D. Rodrigues, 1755.* 8 p., 4to. NHi.

[MITCHELL, JOHN]

The | contest | in | America | between | Great Britain and France, | with | its consequences and importance; | giving an account of the | views and designs of the French, | with the interests of Great Britain, and | the situation of the British and French | colonies, in all parts of America: | in which | a proper barrier between the two | nations in North America is pointed out, |

with a method to prosecute the war, | so as to obtain that necessary security
for our | colonies. | By an impartial hand. | . . . | *London: A. Millar.
M,DCC,LVII.* [520]

[2], xlix, [1], 17-244 p., 8vo. Sabin 49693, Thomson 838. DLC, MB,
MH, MiU-C, MWA, MWiW-C, NcWfC, NN, PMA, PPL-R, RPJCB.

Dr. John Mitchell, physician, botanist and geographer, a resident of
Virginia, had an unusual knowledge of American geography and of the
activities of the French on the lakes, in Ohio and West Virginia.

WILLIAMSON, PETER

French and Indian cruelty; | exemplified in the | life | and various
vicissitudes of fortune, of | Peter Williamson, | a disbanded soldier. | Con-
taining | a particular account of the manners, customs, and dress, of the |
savages; of their scalping, burning, and other barbarities, com- | mitted on the
English, in North-America, during his re- | sidence among them. Being at
eight years of age, stolen from | his parents and sent to Pensylvania, where
he was sold as a | slave. Afterwards married and settled as a planter, 'till the |
Indians destroy'd his house and everything he had, and carried | him off a
captive; from whom, after several months captivity, | he made his escape,
and serv'd as a volunteer and soldier in many | expeditions against them. |
Comprehending in the whole, | a summary of the transactions of the several
provinces | of Pensylvania (including Philadelphia), New-York, | New-
England, New-Jersey, &c. &c. From the com- | mencement of the war in
these parts; particularly, those rela- | tive to the intended attack on Crown
Point and Niagara. | And an accurate and succinct detail of the operations
of the | French and English forces, at the siege of Oswego, | where the author
was wounded and taken prisoner; and | being afterwards sent to England,
was, on his arrival at Ply- | mouth, discharg'd as incapable of further service.
| Written by himself. | *York:* | *Printed for the author, by N. Nickson,*
1757. | . . . | . . . [521]

iv, 103 p., 8vo. (19.3 x 11.2 cm.). Sabin 104467, Ayer 315. BM, ICN,
PPiU.

Reprinted as "Authentic instances of French and Indian cruelty . . ." in
The Grand Magazine of Magazines, vol. 1, July-December, 1758. MWA, etc.

First edition of the most popular of all Indian captivities.

Peter Williamson was born near Aberdeen, Scotland in 1730. At the age
of eight he was kidnapped and taken to Philadelphia, sold for sixteen pounds
to a Scotchman named Hugh Wilson who had undergone the same experience when a child. Wilson was kind to him, sent him to school for five
winters and when he died, left Williamson two hundred pounds in cash and
one hundred and twenty pounds more in property, Williamson then being
about 17 years old. After seven years he married and his father-in-law gave
him a farm in Berks County near the Forks of the Delaware. There, on
October 2, 1754, he was captured by Indians, probably Shawnese or Dela-

wares, his buildings burned, and he was taken to their village, Alamingo. His wife, being away from home, was not captured. After spending the Winter with the Indians, they took him on an expedition to the white settlements, he escaped en route and arrived at the house of his father-in-law in January, 1755, finding that his wife had died two months before.

He then joined the army and was sent to Boston and from there to Oswego. When that place was captured by the French, he was wounded, captured and taken to Montreal and sent, with other prisoners, to England, reaching Plymouth November 6, 1756. He made a living from his writings, from exhibiting himself in Indian costume, and by operating a coffee room in Edinburgh. He died in 1799.

EASTBURN, ROBERT

A faithful | narrative, | of | the many dangers and sufferings, as well as | wonderful deliverances of Robert East- | burn, during his late captivity among the | Indians: Together with some remarks | upon the country of Canada, and the | religion, and policy of its inhabitants; the | whole inter-mixed with devout reflections. | [rule] | By Robert Eastburn. | [rule] | Published at the earnest request of many | friends, for the benefit of the author. | [rule] | With a recommendatory preface, by the | Rev. Gilbert Tennent. | [rule, 6 lines quoted, rule] | *Philadelphia:* | *Printed by William Dunlap.* 1758.   [522]

45, [1] p., 12mo. (20.2 x 13.2 cm.). Sabin 21664, Evans 8116, Ayer 88, Church 1024. CSmH, F.C. Deering, DLC, ICN, MH, MHi, MWA, NHi, ODW, PHi, PP, PPL, PPL-R, RPJCB, F.T. Siebert.

Eastburn was captured at Fort Williams, near the present city of Rome, N.Y., March 27, 1756, cruelly treated by French and Indians in Canada, escaped from Montreal, reached Quebec where he was befriended and sent to England, thence to Boston and home to Philadelphia after an absence of 20 months. His son, also a captive in Canada, returned with him. They were better treated by the French in Quebec than by their own people either in Old or New England.

.   .   .   .   .

A faithful | narrative | of | the many dangers and sufferings, as well as wonder- | ful and surprizing deliverances of Robert East- | burn, during his late captivity among the Indians: | Together with some remarks upon the country of | Canada, and the religion and policy of its inha- | bitants; the whole intermixed with devout reflections. | By Robert Eastburn. | Published at the earnest request of many | persons, for the benefit of the public. | With a recommendatory preface by the | Rev. Gilbert Tennent. | [6 lines quoted] | *Philadelphia: Printed.* | *Boston; Re-printed and sold by Green & Russell,* | *opposite the Probate-Office in Queen-street.* 1758.   [523]

[4], 34, [1] p., 8vo. (18.4 x 12.4 cm.). Sabin 21664, Evans 8117. CtY, DLC, MB, MHi, MWA, NN, PHi, PPL, RPJCB.

Reprinted Cleveland, 1904 and in Ashbel Green's *Memoirs of Rev. Joseph Eastburn*, Phil., 1828; same, Hartford, 1843. Excerpts in English *Annual Register*, 1758 and *Court Miscellany*, 1766.

MAYLEM, JOHN

Gallic | perfidy: | A Poem. | [rule] | By John Maylem [bracket] Philo-Bellum. | [rule, cut of Indian with bow and arrow, thick-thin rule] | *Boston: New-England:* | *Printed and sold by Benjamin Mecom, at The New* | *Printing-Office, July 13. 1758.—Where may* | *be had that noted little book, called Father Abra-* | *ham's Speech.* [524]

15 p., small 8vo. (18 x 11.5 cm.). Title from Wilberforce Eames' *The Antigua press and Benjamin Mecom*. Worcester, 1929, Evans 8194, Wegelin's *American poetry*, 269. F.C. Deering, MBAt, MHi, MWA, NN.

A narrative poem of 198 lines, describing the attack and capture of Fort William Henry on Lake George, by the French and Indians under General Montcalm, in August, 1757; the taking captive of the author by the Indians, and their cruelty to the prisoners; and finally of the author's redemption at Montreal.

The author also wrote: *The conquest of Louisbourg*. Boston, 1758 and Newport, 1775. See L.C. Wroth's *American bookshelf*, 1755. *Philadelphia*, 1934, p. 107.

WILLIAMS, JOHN

The redeemed captive, returning to Zion. A faithful history of remarkable occurrences, in the captivity and deliverance, of Mr. John Williams; Minister of the Gospel in Deerfield, who, in the desolation which befel that plantation, by an incursion of the French and Indians, was by them carried away, with his family, and his neighbourhood, unto Canada. Drawn up by himself. Whereto there is annexed a sermon preached by him, upon his return, at the lecture in Boston, December 5. 1706. . . . The third edition. As also an appendix: Containing an account of those taken captive at Deerfield, February 29. 1703,4. of those kill'd after they went out of town, those who returned, and of those still absent from their native country; of those who were slain at that time in or near the town; and of the mischief done by the enemy in Deerfield, from the beginning of its settlement to the death of the Rev. Mr. Williams, in 1729. With a conclusion to the whole. By the Rev. Mr. [Stephen] Williams of Springfield, and the Rev. Mr. [Thomas] Prince of Boston. *Boston: Printed and sold by S. Kneeland, opposite the Probate-Office in Queen-street. 1758.* [525]

[4], iv, 104 p., 8vo. Sabin 104264, Evans 8285, Ayer.308. BM, CSmH, DLC, F.C. Deering, ICN, MB, MBAt, NN, RPJCB.

The sermon has a separate title page.

WILLIAMSON, PETER

French and Indian cruelty; | exemplified in the | life | and various
vicissitudes of fortune, of | Peter Williamson, | [. . . etc., as in 1st ed., 1757] |
(The second edition, with corrections and amendments.) | York: | *Printed
and sold by J. Jackson, in Peter-gate; and by | all the booksellers in town,
1758. | Price one shilling.*   [526]
     iv, 104 p., 8vo. (20.5 x 11.6 cm.). Sabin 104468, Ayer 316. CSmH,
DLC, ICN, NHi, NN, NRU, OFH, RPJCB.

. . . . .

French and Indian cruelty; | exemplified in the | life | and various
vicissitudes of fortune, of | Peter Williamson, | [. . . etc., as in 1st ed.,
1757] | Also, a curious discourse on kidnapping, with proper directions for
trades- | men and others, to avoid slavery, when transported from their native
country. | Together with a description of the most convenient roads for the
British forces | to invade Canada in three divisions, and make themselves
masters of it the | next campaign, 1759. | Dedicated to the Rt. Hon. William
Pitt, Esq; | written by himself. | The third edition, with considerable im-
provements. | *Glasgow: | Printed by J. Bryce and D. Paterson, | for the
benefit of the unfortunate author. 1758. | (Price one shilling).*   [526A]
     iv, 112 p., 8vo. (18.1 x 11.4 cm.). Sabin 104469, Ayer 317. An-C-T,
BM, CSmH, F.C. Deering, ICN, MB, PHi, WHi.

. . . . .

Some | considerations | on | the present state of affairs. | Wherein | the
defenceless situation of Great-Britain, is | pointed out, and an easy rational
and just scheme | for it's security, at this dangerous crisis; proposed, | in a
militia, formed on an equal plan, | that can neither be oppressive to the
poor, nor of- | fensive to the rich, as practised by some of his | Majesty's
colonies abroad; | interspersed | with an account of the first settlement of the
Province of | Pensylvania, the origin of the quarrel, between some | of the
traders there, and the Indians; and an im- | partial representation of the
debates betwixt the Governor | and Assembly, in relation to that quarrel. |
Likewise | a short description of the air, soil, produce, &c. of the | several
colonies on the Continent of North-America. | The whole concluded | with
a summary detail of the education, manners, and | religion of the Indians, not
heretofore mention'd. | [rule] | Written by Peter Williamson, author | of
the French and Indian Cruelty. | [rule, 8 lines quoted, rule] | *York: Printed
for the Author, and sold by | all the booksellers in town, 1758.*   [527]
     iv, 56 p., 8vo. (20.5 x 12 cm.). Sabin 104488. BM, CSmH, MH, NHi,
NN.

ACRELIUS, ISRAEL

Beskrifning om de Swenska Församlingars Forna och Närwarande
Tilstånd, uti det så kallade Nya Swerige, sedan Nya Nederland, men nu

för tiden Pensylvanien, samt nästliggande orter wid Alfwen [sic] De la Ware, Wäst-Yersey och New-Castle County, uti Norra America; utgifwen af Israel Acrelius . . . *Stockholm, Tryckt hos Harberg & Hesselberg, 1759.* [528]

[20], 533, [1] p., 4to. (19.5 x 16 cm.). Sabin 133. DLC, MiU-C, NHi, etc.

A history of New Sweden; or, the settlements on the River Delaware, by the provost of the Swedish churches in America, 1749-1756. A first hand account of the civil and ecclesiastical history of the Swedish settlements. A translation was published by the Historical Society of Pennsylvania in 1874; a partial translation in New York Hist. Soc. Coll., 2d ser., 1841, vol. I, p. 401-448; and in Old South Leaflets, General Series, vol. 4, 1898.

BOWNAS, SAMUEL

An account of the life, travels, and Christian experiences of . . . [Title as in 1st ed., 1756] *London printed, Philadelphia, Re-printed, by William Dunlap, at the Newest Printing Office, in Market-Street,1759.* [529]

[2], viii, 242 p., 8vo. (17.5 x 12 cm.). Sabin 7097. BM, CtHWatk, DLC, MH, MWA, N, NHi, NN, PHC, PHi, PPM, PSC-Hi.

This edition mentions Elizabeth Hanson but does not tell the story of her captivity.

. . . . . .

The journals of the lives and travels of Samuel Bownas, and John Richardson. *London printed: Philadelphia, Reprinted, and sold by William Dunlap, at the Newest Printing-Office, in Market-Street, 1759.* [530]

[2], viii, 242; vi, 220 p., 8vo. Each part has separate title. Sabin 71024, Evans 8308. BM, CtHWatk, DLC, NN, PHi.

DICKENSON, JONATHAN

God's protecting Providence, . . . [etc., as in 1720 ed.] The fourth edition. *London: Printed and sold by Luke Hinde, at the Bible in George-yard, Lombard-street, 1759.* [531]

[14], 126 p., 12mo. (15.7 x 9.2 cm.). Copies in most large libraries.

LE ROY, MARIE

Die | Erzehlungen | von | Maria le Roy | und | Barbara Leininger, | welche vierthalb Jahr unter den In- | dianern gefangen gewesen, und am 6ten May | in dieser Stadt glücklich angekommen. | Aus ihrem eignen Munde niedergeschrieben und | zum Druck befördert. | [rule] | *Philadelphia gedruckt und zu haben in der teut-* | *schen Buchdruckerey das Stück vor* *6 Pentz.* | *M,DCCLIX.* [532]

14 p., 8vo. (18.7 x 12.4 cm.). Evans 8347. PHi. Same in English:

. . . . .

The | narrative | of | Marie Le Roy | and | Barbara Leininger, | who spent
three and one half years as prisoners | among the Indians, and arrived
safely | in the city on the sixth of May. | Written and printed as dictated by
them. | *Philadelphia:* | *Printed and for sale in the German Printing Office.* |
Sixpence per copy. | *MDCCLIX.* | *[Harrisburg, 1878].*   [533]

In Pennsylvania Archives, 2d ser., vol. 7, 1878, p. 401-412; same, reprint,
vol. 7, 1891, p. 427-438. Ayer supp. 88. Translations also in Lebanon
County Hist. Soc. Pubs., vol. 3, 1905; Pennsylvania Mag. of Hist. and
Biog., vol. 29, October, 1905, p. 407-420.

The German Printing Office was conducted by Benjamin Franklin, with
Anthony Armbrüster as compositor until some time in 1759 when it was
continued by Peter Miller and Ludwig Weiss, the work still being done by
Armbrüster. It is therefore not certain whether this is a Franklin or a Miller
and Weiss imprint.

Marie Le Roy was the daughter of Jean Jacques Le Roy who came to
Pennsylvania from Rotterdam Nov. 22, 1752. In 1755 the family lived on
Penn Creek near Shamokin (near the present Selinsgrove, Pa.) when their
house was attacked on Oct. 16, 1755, Marie and one of her brothers
captured, and her father killed. The Indians also killed their neighbor,
Leininger, and one son and captured his daughters Barbara, aged twelve,
and Regina, aged nine. These two sisters were separated, Barbara remaining
with the Le Roy girl. On March 16, 1759 they escaped with Owen Gibson
and David Breckenridge and reached Pittsburgh, then in the hands of the
English. Their interesting story contains important frontier history and lists
the names and residences of over forty other captives.

Regina Leininger, whose later adventures do not appear in the Le Roy
book, was taken to Ohio where she lived as a captive until the Bouquet
expedition released the captives and she, with others, was taken to Carlisle,
Pennsylvania, where her mother identified her through the girl's remembering a hymn which her mother had taught her when she was little. She was
nine years old when captured and lived for nine years with the Indians.
She became known as "Regina the German captive" and it was supposed
that her name was Hartman until she was identified as the lost Leininger
girl by Dr. Heilman. For her story, see the following:

Rev. H.M. Muhlenberg: *Halische Nachrichten,* vol. II, p. 445-493, 1029,
in which he tells of securing her story from Regina in 1765; also his *Journals,*
1942, 1945, 2 vols.; R. Weiser: *Regina: the German captive.* Baltimore,
1856. MWA; same, 3d ed., Baltimore, 1860. NHi; same, Phil., 1893, illus.
(Scott and O'Shaughnessy sale 30, 1917, no. 156); same, Phil., 1919. (J.B.
Shea library, part I, American Art-Anderson Galleries sale 4353, Dec. 2,
1937, no. 275). Based on recollections of the author's grandmother, Mrs.
Esther Weiser (1734-1820), daughter-in-law of Conrad Weiser, who knew
Regina and her mother; H.M.M. Richards: *Lebanon County in the French
and Indian War. Paper read before the Lebanon County Historical Society,*

April 21, 1901. . . . Regina the German captive, Part I. The location, by Captain H.M.M. Richards. Part II. The story, by S.P. Heilman . . . , in Lebanon Co. Hist. Soc. *Papers,* vol. 2, 1902, p. 55-97; *Regina the German captive* (reprint of part of preceding), [Lebanon, Pa., 1902], p. 81-97; same, [Lebanon, Pa., 1904], [2], 81-97 p., 8vo. NN, OClWHi; S.P. Heilman's *A final word as to Regina, the German captive,* paper read before the Lebanon County Hist. Soc., Aug. 18, 1905, and appendices. [Lebanon? 1905]. [2], 202-251 p., illus., 8vo. (Separate from Lebanon Co. Hist. Soc. *Historical Papers and Addresses,* vol. III, p. 200-251). Identifies the Regina Hartman of the earlier narratives as the Regina Leininger of the Le Roy narrative, a translation of which appears at p. 235-248. DLC, NN; *Regina the German captive,* and *The narrative of Barbara Leininger,* by H.M.M. Richards, in the Pennsylvania German Society *Proceedings,* vol. 15, 1906, p. 78-126.

POST, CHRISTIAN FREDERICK

The | second journal | of | Christian Frederick Post, | on a message from the | Governor of Pensilvania | to the | Indians on the Ohio. | [type orn.] | London: | Printed for J. Wilkie, at the Bible and Sun, in | St. Paul's Church-Yard. | MDCCLIX.   [534]

67 p., 8vo. Sabin 64453. DLC, MB, MH, MiU-C, MWiW-C, NHi, PPL-R, RPJCB.

Account of an attempt to separate the Indians from the French interest, written by a German with long experience among the Indians by whom he was held in great respect. For an appreciation of this and the first journal of this devoted Moravian missionary, see L.C. Wroth's *American bookshelf, 1755.* Philadelphia, 1934.

For his first journal, see under Charles Thomson, no. 535.

Title from facsimile in Maggs Bros. cat. 769, 1947, no. 1211, £ 45.

[THOMSON, CHARLES]

An enquiry into the causes of the alienation of the Delaware and Shawanese Indians from the British interest, and into the measures taken for recovering their friendship. Extracted from the public treaties, and other authentic papers relating to the transactions of the government of Pensilvania and the said Indians, for near forty years; and explained by a map of the country. Together with the remarkable journal of Christian Frederic Post, by whose negotiations, among the Indians on the Ohio, they were withdrawn from the interest of the French, who thereupon abandoned the fort and country. With notes by the editor explaining sundry Indian customs, &c. Written in Pensylvania. *London, Printed for J. Wilkie, at the Bible, in St. Paul's Churchyard. MDCCLIX.*   [535]

184 p., frontispiece folded map, 8vo. (22.5 x 10.6 cm.). Sabin 95562, Church 1029, Thomson 1145. CSmH, DLC, MB, MdBP, MH, MiU-C, NHi, NjP, NN, PHi, PPL, PU, RPJCB, WHi.

Important frontier Indian narrative by Charles Thomson, later Secretary of the Continental Congress. Includes the important first journal of Christian Frederic Post. For his second journal, see no. 534. Reprinted, Philadelphia, 1867. For the importance of this work, see L.C. Wroth's *An American Bookshelf, 1755.* Philadelphia, 1934.

Folded map: *A map of the Province of* | *Pennsylvania.* | *intended chiefly to illustrate the account of the several* | *Indian purchases* | *made by the Proprietaries of the said Province* | . . . | *T. Jefferys sculp.* (19 x 25.3 cm.). RPJCB has John Penn's copy with his MS notes.

WILLIAMSON, PETER

French and Indian cruelty: | exemplified in the | life, | and various vicissitudes of fortune, of | Peter Williamson. | [. . . etc., as in 1st ed., 1757] | Also, a curious discourse on kidnapping. | Written by himself. | The fourth edition, with considerable improvements. | *London:* | *Printed for the unfortunate author,* | *and sold by R. Griffiths, opposite* | *Somerset-House, in the Strand.* 1759. | . . .   [536]

120 p., front. port., 8vo. (19.1 x 10.8 cm.). Sabin 104470, Ayer 318. BM, DLC, F.C. Deering, ICN, MH, MWA, NN, RPJCB.

Frontispiece: Mr. Peter Williamson in the dress of a Delaware Indian.

"Mr. Peter Williamson . . . being come to London, where he exhibits himself in Indian dress, displaying and explaining their method of fighting . . ."—*The Grand Magazine,* London, June, 1759.

BROWN, THOMAS

A plain narrativ[e] of the uncommon sufferings and remarkable deliverance of Thomas Brown, of Charlestown, in New-England; who returned to his father's house the beginning of Jan. 1760, after having been absent three years and about eight months: containing an ·account of the engagement between a party of English, commanded by Maj. [Robert] Rogers, and a party of French and Indians, in Jan. 1757; in which Capt. Spikeman was killed; and the author of this narrative having received three wounds (one thro' his body) he was left for dead on the field of battle:—how he was taken captive by the Indians, and carried to Canada, and from thence to the Mississippi; where he lived about a year, and was again sent to Canada, during all which time he was not only in constant peril of his own life; but had the mortification of being an eye-witness of divers tortures and shocking cruelties, that were practiced by the Indians on several English prisoners;— one of whom he saw burnt to death, another tied to a tree and his entrails drawn out, &c &c. *Boston: Printed and sold by Fowle and Draper, at their printing office in Marlborough Street. 1760.*   [537]

27 p., 8vo. (17.5 cm.). Evans 8557. ICN, MHi, MiU, NjP (last leaf imperfect), OCl, NN (photostat).

. . . . .

The second edition. Same imprint and date. [Price 8 coppers.]   [538]
27 p., 17.5 cm. Sabin 63223. Evans 8558. DLC (Brinley 469).

. . . . .

The third edition. Same imprint and date.   [539]
24 p., 12mo. (16.7 x 11 cm.). Ayer 37. ICN. MWA (lacks first 2 leaves, last leaf imperfect).

. . . . .

Reprinted from second edition, in *Magazine of History,* Extra no. 4, 1908.
[540]
One of the most exciting as well as one of the rarest captivity stories is that of Thomas Brown who enlisted in Rogers' Rangers in 1756 at the age of 16. Some months later, just after capturing a party of Frenchmen on Lake Champlain and while on their way back to Fort William Henry, they were attacked by a large party of French and Indians, Brown was wounded three times and captured. He was taken to Fort Ticonderoga, then to Montreal as an Indian captive, was made to run the gauntlet, was taken to an Indian village on the Mississippi for the winter and back to Montreal with a French trader in the Spring. He then escaped, got as far as Crown Point where he was recaptured and returned to Montreal, thence to Albany as an exchange prisoner. He promptly reenlisted, went on another expedition, was captured once more, taken to Montreal and finally exchanged and returned to his home in 1760 after over three years of the toughest and most exciting frontier fighting. He saw other prisoners tortured and burned at the stake and left a brief but very lively account of his adventures.

HAMMON, BRITON
    A | narrative | of the | uncommon sufferings, | and | surprizing deliverance | of | Briton Hammon, | a Negro man, . . . servant to | General Winslow, | of Marshfield, in New-England; | who returned to Boston, after having | been absent almost thirteen years. | Containing | an account of the many hardships he underwent from | the time he left his master's house, in the year 1747, | to the time of his return to Boston.—How he was | cast away in the capes of Florida; . . . the horrid cru- | elty and inhuman barbarity of the Indians in murder- | ing the whole ship's crew; . . . the manner of his being | carry'd by them into captivity. Also, an account of | his being confined four years and seven months | in a close dungeon, and the remarkable manner in | which he met with his good old master in London; who | returned to New-England, a passenger, in the same ship. | [rule] | *Boston, Printed and sold by Green & Russell,* | *in Queen-Street. 1760.*   [541]
    14 p., 16mo. (18 cm.). Sabin 51836, Evans 8611. DLC, NHi.

The earliest of two stories of the captivity of a Negro among the Indians, the other being the narrative of John Marrant, no. 730.

HANSON, ELIZABETH

An account of the captivity of Elizabeth Hanson, now or late of Kachecky, in New-England: who, with four of her children and servant-maid, was taken captive by the Indians, and carried into Canada. Setting forth the various remarkable occurrences, sore trials, and wonderful deliverances which befel them after their departure, to the time of their redemption. Taken in substance from her own mouth, by Samuel Bownas. *London: Printed and sold by Samuel Clark, in Bread-Street, near Cheapside. MDCCLX.*   [542]

[2], 28, [1] p., 8vo. (18.5 x 12 cm.). DLC, F.C. Deering, ICN, MBAt, MWiW-C, NhHi, N, NN, RPJCB.

Most copies lack the final leaf of advertisement.

. . . . .

The second edition, same imprint, *M DCC LX.*   [543]

[2], 28, [1] p., 8vo. Sabin 30265, Church 1031. CMC, CSmH, DLC, ICN, MWiW-C, NHi, PHi, RPJCB.

In some copies the advertisement leaf follows the title but it is at end in NHi copy.

LOWRY, JEAN

A | journal | of the captivity of | Jean Lowry | and her | children, | giving an account of her being taken by the | Indians, the 1st of April 1756, from | William Mc. Cord's, | in Rocky-Spring Settlement in | Pennsylvania, | with an account of the hardship she suffered, &c. | *Philadelphia:* | *Printed by William Bradford, at | the corner of Front and Market-Streets. 1760.*   [544]

31 p., 8vo. Evans 8642, Hildeburn 1683. PPL-R.

A copy, lacking title and three leaves, sold in Scott and O'Shaughnessy sale 8, 1915, no. 242.

WILLIAMSON, PETER

A brief account of the war in N. America: shewing, the principal causes of our former miscarriages: as also, the necessity and advantage of keeping Canada, and the maintaining a friendly correspondence with the Indians. To which is added, a description of the natives,—their manner of living, &c. . . . By Peter Williamson, formerly a planter in the Back Settlements of Pensylvania. *Edinburgh: Printed for the author, and sold by R. Griffiths, in the Strand, London . . . [1760].*   [545]

[2], 38 p., 8vo. Sabin 104465. MB.

Signed and dated: Peter Williamson. Edin. Feb. 8, 1760.

BOWNAS, SAMUEL

An account of the life, travels, and Christian experiences of . . . [Title as in 1st ed., 1756] The second edition. *London: Printed and sold by Luke Hind, at the Bible in George-yard, Lombard-street. 1761.* [546]

iii [i.e., viii], 198 p., 8vo. (21.2 x 13.3 cm.). Sabin 7097. ICN, NHi, NN, PSC, PSC-Hi, RPJCB, Vi.

PLYMOUTH COMPANY

Advertisement. | The Proprietors of the Kennebeck Purchase from the late | Colony of New-Plymouth, hereby inform the publick, that | besides the twelve townships . . . Dated, Boston, 20th February, 1761. *[Boston, 1761].* [547]

Broadside. Title from Ford 1233. MWA.

Part of the contest between the Plymouth Company (Kennebeck Purchase) and the Proprietors of Brunswick Township, Maine, over title to that territory.

[WILLIAMSON, PETER]

Memorial for poor Peter Williamson, late of the Province of Pennsylvania in North America, planter, now residenter in Edinburgh, pursuer, against, Alexander Cushnie, late Dean-of-Guild and Procurator Fiscal of the Borough-Court of Aberdeen, and others, defenders. With an abstract of the proof. [By Andrew Crosbie] [Caption title] *[Edinburgh, July 27th, 1761].* [548]

18 p., 4to. RPJCB.

Title from RPJCB Annual Report, 1943-4, p. 57 and from catalog of W.H. Duncan sale, Swann auction 63, 1943, no. 311.

· · · · ·

The | travels | and | surprising adventures of John Thomson, | who was taken, and carried to America, | and sold for a slave there:—How he was | taken captive by the savages:—With an | account of his happy delivery, after four | months slavery, and his return to Scotland. | [large woodcut of soldier on horse] | Entered according to order. *[Falkirk? 1761?].* [549]

12 p., small 8vo. F.C. Deering.

Copy offered for ten pounds by Museum Book Store, London, cat. 88, 1923, no. 798; same copy in American Art Galleries auction, January 30, 1925, no. 114 with title reproduced. Probably this copy bought by Mr. Deering.

A barefaced plagiarism of the Peter Williamson narrative.

WILLIAMSON, PETER

French and Indian cruelty; exemplified in the life and various vicissitudes of fortune of Peter Williamson; who was carried off from Aberdeen in his infancy, and sold as a slave in Pensylvania. Containing the history of the author's adventures in N. America; his captivity among the Indians, and manner of his escape; the customs, dress, &c. of the savages; military operations in that quarter; with a description of the British settlements, &c. &c. To which is added, an account of the proceedings of the magistrates of Aberdeen against him on his return to Scotland; a brief history of his process against them before the Court of Session, and a short dissertation on kidnapping. The fifth edition, with large improvements. *Edinburgh: Printed for the author, and sold by him at his shop in the Parliament House.* MDCCLXII. [550]

vi, 120, 119-147 p., front. port. and folded map, 12mo. (17 x 9.9 cm.). Sabin 104471, Ayer supp. 139. BM, DLC, ICN, ICU, NN, NRU (lacks port. and map).

Hanson, Elizabeth

An abstract of an account of the captivity of the wife and children of John Hanson. [Abridged from the London, 1760 edition, in:] The British Mars, containing several schemes and inventions to be practised on land and sea against the enemies of Great Britain. By Joseph Robson, Engineer. *[London:] Printed for the author; and sold by William Flexney, near Grays-inn Gates, Holborn. MDCCLXIII.* [551]

p. 200-210 of the above work, 8vo. (22 x 13.5 cm.). Sabin 72260. NHi, NN.

A second part of this work was published in 1764.

Plymouth Company

Advertisement. The Proprietors of the Kennebeck Purchase from the late Colony of New-Plymouth [in regard to townships and land on Kennebeck River] Dated, May 18, 1763, and signed, David Jeffries, Proprietors Clerk. *[Boston, 1763].* [552]

Broadside. Title from Ford 1294. MWA, PHi.

Apparently the last round in the contest between the Plymouth Company (Kennebeck Purchase) and the Proprietors of Brunswick Township, Maine, over the title to that territory.

Saunders, Charles

The | horrid cruelty | of the | Indians, | exemplified in the life of | Charles Saunders, | late of | Charles-town, in South Carolina. | Giving | an accurate and concise account of his | captivity and unheard of sufferings a- | mong the Indians, the bloody death of | his unfortunate companions, the murder | of young Mr. York, the captivity and | release of Miss York, and her venera- | ble father; with other wonderful inci- | dents, never before publish'd. | Written and sold by the author. | *Birmingham:* | *Printed by T. Warren jun . . .* | *. . . 1763.* [553]

20 p., 8vo. (14.8 x 8.6 cm.). Ayer 245. ICN.

The ICN copy ends with p. 16.

WEISER, CONRAD

Translation | of a | German letter, | wrote by | Conrad Weiser, Esq; | Interpreter, on Indian Affairs, for the | Province of Pennsylvania. | [Caption title] *[Philadelphia, 1763].* [554]

7 p., 8vo. (19 cm.). Title from copy at PPL. PHi, PPL (2).

Written in 1746 and first published in Samuel Hopkins' *Abridgement,* 1757.

Contains material on the Onondagas not found elsewhere. He had gone to them to obtain their permission for the erection of a trading house "on the waters of the Ohio or on Lake Erie." He took his son along to learn the Indian language and customs. For the account by one of his travelling companions, see John Bartram's *Observations,* 1751.

He also wrote a brief historical sketch of the Six Nations, which appears in the preface of *The treaty held with the Indians of the Six Nations at Philadelphia, in July 1742. To which is prefix'd an account of the first Confederacy of the Six Nations, their present tributaries, dependents, and allies. London: Re-printed and sold by T. Sowle Raylton and Luke Hinde, at the Bible in George-Yard, Lombard-Street. (Price six-pence.)* [ca. 1747].

xii, 37, [1] p., 8vo. (19.5 x 12.5 cm.). De Puy 19. ICN, MH, NHi, PHi, RPJCB, WHi.

For other writings of Weiser, published after 1800, see note to Sabin 102508.

[CHETWOOD, W. R.]

The voyages, dangerous adventures and imminent escapes of Captain Richard Falconer . . . Fifth edition. *London: G. Keith, 1764.* [555]

Ayer 94, Sabin 23723. ICN, OCU.

[FRANKLIN, BENJAMIN]

A | narrative | of the late | massacres, | in | Lancaster County, | of a | number of Indians, | friends of this Province, | by persons unknown. | With some observations on the same. | [rule, orn., double rule] | *[Philadelphia:] Printed [by Anthony Armbruster] in the year M,DCC,LXIV.* [556]

31 p., 8vo. (20 x 11.5 cm.). Sabin 25557, Evans 9667, Hildeburn 1992. CtHWatk, CtY, DLC, MB, MHi, MiU-C, NHi, NN, PHC, PHi, PPL-R, RPJCB.

The most famous of the many Paxton Boys tracts. The menace of the Pontiac conspiracy filled the Pennsylvania frontier with fear and hysterical hate of all Indians. As a result, some 50 Scotch-Irish settlers, called the Paxton Boys, massacred 22 innocent and friendly Indian men, women and children at Conestoga near Lancaster in 1763, causing political repercussions which spread throughout the state and resulted in the publication of many pamphlets. See B.J. Wallace's *Insurrection of the Paxton Boys,* 1860, Evans under 1764. Most of these tracts in NHi, PHi.

GRACE, HENRY

The | history | of the | life and sufferings | of | Henry Grace, | of | Basingstoke in the County of Southampton. | Being a narrative | of the hardships he underwent during several years | captivity among the savages in North | America, and of the cruelties they practise to | their unhappy prisoners. | In which is introduced | an account of the several customs and manners of the | different nations of Indians; as well as a compendious | description of the soil, produce and various animals of | those parts. | [rule] | Written by himself. | [double rule] | *Printed for the author:* | *and sold at his house in Basingstoke, and at the Printing-* | *Office in Reading [England].* *M DCC LXIV.* | *(Price one shilling.).*   [557]

56 p., 8vo. (20.2 x 12 cm.). Sabin 28184, Ayer 109. DLC, ICN, MH, NN, NNM, F. T. Siebert.

The author claims to have been a captive "among the savages in North America" for several years but his title page does not tell where or when. Like Peter Williamson, Grace returned to his native British Isles where he capitalized on his American adventures, perhaps without too much regard for accuracy.

[GRONDEL, JEAN-PHILIPPE GOUJON DE]

Lettre | d'un | officier | de la Louisiane | a M *** | Commissaire | de la Marine a *** | [orn.] | *A la Nouvelle Orleans.* | [thick-thin rule] | *M. DCC. LXIV.*   [558]

45 leaves, 12mo. (16 x 9.3 cm.). Herschel V. Jones catalog: *Adventures in Americana,* 1928, 176; Wilberforce Eames: *Americana collection of Herschel V. Jones,* 1938, 516. Herschel V. Jones—Rosenbach Co.

Really printed in Holland and so *not* the earliest known New Orleans imprint. See Villiers du Terrage: *Les dernières années de la Louisiane Française,* p. 329.

WOOD, WILLIAM

New-England's prospect. Being a true, lively, and experimental description of that part of America, commonly called New-England: discovering the state of that country, both as it stands to our new-come English planters; and to the old native inhabitants. And laying down that which may both enrich the knowledge of the mind-travelling reader, or benefit the future voyager. The third [fourth] edition. By William Wood. London, Printed in

1639. *Boston, New-England, Re-printed, by Thomas and John Fleet, in Cornhill; and Green and Russell, in Queen-Street, 1764.* [559]

[2], xviii, 128 p., 8vo. Sabin 105077, Evans 9884. Copies in most large libraries.

For modern reprints, see Sabin.

[FENWICK, JOHN]

The | true state | of the | case | between | John Fenwick, Esq; | and | John Edridge & Edmund Warner, | concerning | Mr. Fenwick's Ten Parts of his | Land in West-New-Jersey, | in America. | *London, Printed in the year 1677. And | Philadelphia, Re-printed by Andrew Steuart, for | John Hart, MDCCLXV.* [560]

8 p., 8vo. Sabin 24083, Evans 9970, Hildeburn 2176. PHi.

For first edition, see under 1677.

GRACE, HENRY

The | history | of the | life and sufferings | of | Henry Grace, | of | Basingstoke in the County of Southampton. | Being a narrative | of the hardships he underwent during several years | captivity among the | savages in North America, | and of the cruelties they practise to their unhappy | prisoners. | In which is introduced | an account of the several customs and manners of the | different nations of Indians; as well as a compendious | description of the soil, produce and various animals of | those parts. | Written by himself. | The second edition. | *Printed for the author: | and sold at his house in Basingstoke, and at the Printing- | Office in Reading [England]. M DCC LXV. | (Price one shilling).* [561]

56 p., 8vo. (20.1 x 12 cm.). Ayer supp. 61. F.C. Deering, ICN.

Note in a contemporary hand in the Joseph B. Shea—F.C. Deering copy: "This Henry Grace, I have seen—And believe him to be a worthless Dog, & that half this story is false. J.P.A."

ROGERS, ROBERT

A concise | account | of | North America: | containing | a description of the several British Colonies | on that Continent, including the Islands of | Newfoundland, Cape Breton, &c. | As to | their situation, extent, climate, soil, produce, rise, | government, religion, present boundaries, and | the number of inhabitants supposed to be in each. | Also of | the interior, or Westerly parts of the country, upon the | Rivers St. Laurence, the Mississipi, Christino, and | the Great Lakes. | To which is subjoined, | an account of the several nations and tribes of Indians | residing in those parts, as to their customs, manners, go- | vernment, numbers, &c. | Containing many useful and entertaining facts, never before | treated of. | [rule] | By Major Robert Rogers. | [rule] | *London: | Printed for the author, | and sold by J. Millan, Bookseller, near Whitehall. | MDCCLXV.* [562]

vii, [1], 264 p., 8vo. (20 x 12.5 cm.). Sabin 72723. Copies in most large libraries.

The projected second part was never published, though the separately published *Journals* are sometimes bound to match the *Concise account* with the bindings lettered I and II, as in the NHi copy.

Particularly valuable for the description of the Indians and the then little known western part of the country.

. . . . . .

Journals | of | Major Robert Rogers: | Containing | an account of the several excursions he made | under the generals who commanded upon | the continent of North America, during | the late war. | From which may be collected | the most material circumstances of every cam- | paign upon that continent, from the commence- | ment to the conclusion of the war. | [rule, orn., double rule] | *London: | Printed for the Author, | and sold by J. Millan, Bookseller, near Whitehall. | MDCCLXV.*   [563]

viii, 236, [1], [2] p., 8vo. (21 x 13 cm.). Sabin 72725. Copies in most large libraries.

Covers the years 1755-1760. The projected second part was never published, though the separately published: *A concise account* is sometimes bound to match the *Journals* with the bindings lettered I and II, as in the NHi copy.

A plain and honest account, which however does not slight the author's own importance, of frontier campaigning during the French and Indian War, written by the famous commander of "Rogers' Rangers," the hero of Kenneth Roberts: *Northwest Passage.*

[SMITH, PROVOST WILLIAM]

An | historical account | of the | expedition | against the | Ohio Indians, in the year 1764. | Under the command of | Henry Bouquet, Esq; | Colonel of Foot, and now Brigadier General in America. | Including | his transactions with the Indians, relative to the delivery of their prisoners, | and the preliminaries of peace. | With an | introductory account | of the preceeding campaign, and battle at Bushy-Run. | To which are annexed | milirary papers, | containing | reflections on the war with the savages; a method of forming frontier settle- | ments; some account of the Indian country, with a list of nations, fight- | ing men, towns, distances and different routs. | The whole illustrated with a map and copper-plates. | Published from authentic documents, by a lover of his country. | *Philadelphia: | Printed and sold by William Bradford, at the London | Coffee-House, the corner of Market and Front-streets. M.DCC.LXV.*   [564]

[2], xiii, 71 p., folded map and 2 folded plates. Sabin 84616, Evans 10167. CSmH, DLC, NN, PHi, PPL, PU, RPJCB.

For historical importance, see Sabin note and L.C. Wroth's *An American bookshelf, 1755*, Phil., 1934.

TIMBERLAKE, HENRY

The | memoirs | of | Lieut. Henry Timberlake, | (Who accompanied the Three Cherokee Indians to England | in the year 1762) | containing | whatever he observed remarkable, or worthy of public | notice, during his travels to and from that nation; | wherein the country, government, genius, and cus- | toms of the inhabitants, are authentically described. | Also | the principal occurrences during their residence | in London. | Illustrated with | an accurate map of their Over-hill Settlement, and a curious | secret journal, taken by the Indians out of the pocket | of a Frenchman they had killed. | *London:* | *Printed for the author; and sold by J. Ridley, in St.* | *James's-Street; W. Nicoll, in St. Paul's Church-Yard;* | *and C. Henderson, at the Royal-Exchange.* | *MDCCLXV.* [565]

viii, 160 p., folded frontispiece and folded map, 8vo. (22.2 x 13.8 cm.). Sabin 95836, De Renne I:175. GU-De, MH, MiU-C, NHi, NN, PHi, RPJCB, WHi.

Folded plate: *A curious secret journal taken by the Indians out of the pocket* | *of a French officer they had kill'd.* (22.2 x 13.8 cm.).

Folded map: *A draught of the* | *Cherokee Country,* | *on the West Side of the Twenty four Mountains,* | *commonly called Over the Hills;* | *Taken by Henry Timberlake, when he* | *was in that Country, in March 1762.* (38.8 x 23.8 cm.).

A German translation in J.T. Köhler's *Sammlung neuer Reise-Beschreibungen*, vol. 1, part 2, 1769, p. 397-544. BM, MH. French translation under 1706-7.

Important frontier work on the Cherokees and the French and Indian war in the southern colonies. Reprinted in *Johnson City, Tenn., 1927* and *Marietta, Ga., 1948*.

[WILLIAMSON, PETER]

Memorial for Peter Williamson . . . pursuer; against W. Fordyce . . . [and others], defenders. [By J. Maclaurin] *[Edinburgh. 1765].* [566]

4to. Sabin 104485. BM.

.   .   .   .   .

June 20, 1765. State of the process, Peter Williamson against W. Fordyce, and others. (Accompt Baillie W. Fordyce and Company to J. Smith.) *[Edinburgh. 1765].* [567]

2 parts, 4to. Sabin 104476. BM, F.C. Deering.

.   .   .   .   .

Proof and procedure before the arbiters on the submission. Peter William-

son against W. Fordyce and others. Printed in consequence of an inter-
locutor of the Court of Session, dated July 26, 1765. *[Edinburgh. 1765].*
[568]
4to. Sabin 100487. BM.

CLAP, ROGER

Memoirs of Capt. Roger Clap. . . . *Boston, in New England, printed,
1731. Reprinted by R. & S. Draper, 1766.*   [569]
[4], 33, 11 p., 8vo. Evans 10261, Sabin 13207. ICN, MB, MHi, PPL-R.

HENRY, WILLIAM

Account of the captivity of William Henry in 1755, and of his residence
among the Senneka Indians six years and seven months till he made his
escape from them. *Printed at Boston, 1766.*   [570]
160 p., 4to. No copy known.
Title from *The London Chronicle,* June 23, 1768, p. 601. MH, NHi, etc.
Extracts from this work appear in *The London Chronicle,* Vol. 23, no.
1798, June 23, 1768, p. 601 (2⅓ columns), and no. 1799, June 25, 1768,
p. 609-610 (3½ columns). Title of first installment: "Extract from an
Account of the Captivity of William Henry in 1755, and of his Residence
among the Senneka Indians six Years and seven Months till he made his
Escape from them. Printed at Boston, 1766. 4to, Pages 160." The extract
gives a brief summary of the author's life, tells an Oneida Indian creation
story as related to him by a Seneca warrior named Konnedohaga and a
Seneca account of the origin of the Five Nations as related by an old chief
named Canassetego. Henry (Seneca name: Coseagon) was an Englishman,
educated at an academy in Northampton, England, who came to America
and became a trader among the Ohio Indians where he was captured by
the Senecas. The Seneca creation myth appears in the second installment.
This extract is reprinted, from *The London Chronicle,* in the introduction
to the Boston, 1901 edition of Alexander Henry's *Travels,* p. vi-xvii, but
with no information about the mysterious book or its author.
    It is strange that this important narrative, filling 160 quarto pages, should
have completely disappeared and that there should be no known reference
to it other than that given above. The narrative, Indian names and legends
sound perfectly authentic, judging by the published extracts. Can anyone
discover this ghost book?

[ROGERS, ROBERT]

Ponteach: | or the | savages of America. | A | tragedy. | [rule, orn., rule] |
London: | *Printed for the author; and sold by J. Millan,* | *opposite the
Admiralty, Whitehall.* | [rule] | *M.DCC.LXVI.* | *(Price 2 s. 6 d.).*   [571]
110, [2] p., 8vo. (22.5 x 14 cm.). Sabin 72729. Copies in most large
libraries.

A tragedy in blank verse based on the author's experiences on the frontier.

[SMITH, PROVOST WILLIAM]

An historical account | of the expedition | against the Ohio Indians, | in the year MDCCLXIV. | Under the command of | Henry Bouquet, Esq. | Colonel of Foot, and now Brigadier General in America. | Including his transactions with the Indians, | relative to the delivery of their prisoners, | and the preliminaries of peace. | With an introductory account of the preceding campaign, | and battle at Bushy-Run. | To which are annexed | military papers, | containing | reflections on the war with the savages; a method of forming frontier | settlements; some account of the Indian country; with a list of | nations, fighting men, towns, distances, and different routs. | The whole illustrated with a map and copper-plates. | [rule] | Published, from authentic documents, by a lover of his country. | [double rule] | *Philadelphia, printed:* | *London, Re-printed for T. Jefferies, Geographer to his Majesty,* | *at Charing Cross. M DCC LXVI.* [572]

[2], xiii, 71 p., folded map, 4 plates, 4to. (28.5 x 22 cm.). Sabin 84617. CSmH, DLC, MB, MH, MWA, NHi, NjP, NN, PHi, WHi.

Maps and plates: *A map* | *of the country on the* | *Ohio & Muskingum Rivers* | *shewing the situation* | *of the Indian towns with* | *respect to the army under the command* | *of Colonel Bouquet* | *By* | *Thos. Hutchins Asst. Engineer.* [and below the main map:] *A survey* | *of that part of the* | *Indian country* | *through which* | *Colonel Bouquet* | *marched in 1764* | *By Thomas Hutchins* | *Assistant Engineer.* (40.5 x 33.5 cm.).; untitled plan showing *Camp, Disposition to receive the enemy, General attack* and *Line of march; Plan of the battle near Bushy-Run,* | *. . .* | *Survey'd by Thos. Hutchins, Assistant Engineer; The Indians giving a talk to Colonel Bouquet in a conference at a council* | *fire, near his camp on the banks of the Muskingum in North America, in 1764.* | *B. West invt. Grignion sculp.; The Indians delivering up the English captives to Colonel Bouquet,* | *near his camp at the forks of Muskingum in North America in Novr. 1764.* | *B. West invt. Canot sculp.* These two fine plates by Benjamin West have been frequently reproduced, for which see Sabin note. The maps and plans are from the first edition with changes noted by Sabin.

[STORCK, WILLIAM]

An | account | of | East-Florida. | With | remarks on its future importance | to trade and commerce. | . . . | *London:* | *Printed for G. Woodfall, near Charing-cross;* | *R. Dymont, opposite Somerset-house, in the Strand;* | *J. Almon, in Piccadilly; Richardson and Urqu-* | *hart, under the Royal-Exchange.* | *(Price two shillings.)* | *[1766].* [573]

[6], 90 p., 8vo., Sabin 92220. DLC, MH, MHi, RPJCB.

.   .   .   .   .

London: | *Printed for G. Woodfall, near Charing-cross; R. Dymont,*

opposite Somerset-house, in the Strand; | J. Almon, in Piccadilly; Richardson
and Ur- | quhart, under the Royal-Exchange. | (Price two shillings.) | [1766].
[574]
Same collation. Sabin 92220. CSmH, RPJCB.

. . . . .

Same imprint with last line omitted] [1766].   [575]
Same collation. Sabin 92220. CSmH.
Dedication signed: William Storck.

. . . . .

An account of | East-Florida, | with a | journal, | kept by | John Bartram
of Philadelphia, | Botanist to His Majesty | for | The Floridas; | upon | a
journey from St. Augustine up the | River St. John's. | London: | Sold by
W. Nicoll, at No. 51, St. Paul's Church-Yard | and G. Woodfall, Charing-
Cross. | (Price four shillings.) | [1766].   [576]
[6], 90, viii, 70 p., 8vo. Sabin 92221, De Renne I:181. CtY, GU-De,
MB, MBAt, MiU-C, NHi, NN, PHi, RPJCB.
A reissue of the sheets of the 1st ed. with the Bartram journal added.

. . . . .

An | extract | from the | account | of | East Florida, | published by Dr.
Stork [sic], | who resided a considerable time in Augustine, | the metropolis
of that Province. | With the observations | of | Denys Rolle, | who formed
a settlement on St. John's river, in the | same Province. | With | his pro-
posals | to | such persons as may be inclined to settle thereon. | London: |
Printed in the year MDCCLXVI.   [577]
[2], 39 p., 8vo. Sabin 92223, De Renne I:181. BM, DLC, GU-De,
RPJCB.
Promotion tract for Rolle's Florida colonization scheme.

WILLIAMSON, PETER

French and Indian cruelty, exemplified in the life, and various vicissitudes
of fortune, of Peter Williamson, . . . The seventh edition, with additions.
Dublin: Printed by Messrs. Adams and Ryder, for the author: . . . 1766 . . .
[578]
vi, 140 p., front., 12mo. (16.4 x 9.4 cm.). Sabin 104472, Ayer 319. ICN.

. . . . .

Edinburgh, 1766. N.   [579]

CAMPBELL, DONALD

The | case | of | Lieutenant Donald Campbell, | and the other children

of the deceased Capt. Lauchlin Campbell, of | the Province of New York. |
[Caption title] *[London? 1767?].*   [580]

   16 p., 4to. (25 x 18.5 cm.). BM, NHi.

   Sets forth the claim of the children of the late Captain Lauchlin Campbell
to a tract of land north of Saratoga, New York, and recites the latter's
attempts to promote a Scotch settlement of 93 families of 485 persons
brought over for that purpose. Includes two reprints of Colonial proclamations for the encouragement of settlers, here separately entered under 1734
and 1738.

HOLLISTER, ISAAC

   A brief narration | of the | captivity of Isaac Hollister, | who was taken
by the Indians, | Anno Domini, 1763. | [rule] | Written by himself. | [rule] |
Printed [by Timothy Green] and sold at the Printing-Office in | New-Lon-
don. | [1767].   [581]

   8 p., 8v. (17 cm.). Evans 10652, Trumbull 841. DLC.

   .   .   .   .   .

Hartford: Printed for, and sold by Knight and Sexton. [1767-1769?].
                                                                                 [582]

   8 p., 8vo. (17 cm.). Evans 10653 and 11684. Trumbull 842 and Supp.
2263. CtHi, F.C. Deering.

   Advertised by Sexton, with other books, in the Hartford *Courant,* April
17, 1769 but it may have been printed earlier. It is printed from the types
of the Hartford printing office, conducted by Thomas Green until April
18, 1768 when the firm became Green and Watson. Evans 10653, who
locates no copy and probably made up a supposititious imprint from an advertisement, gives the imprint as: "Hartford: Printed by Thomas Green.
[1767]." Evans 11684, dated [1770] has the Sexton imprint as above. He
described the CHi copy and doubtless dated it from the fact that an owner's
name and the date 1770 are written in that copy. Bates believes that Evans
was in error and that it should be dated 1769 or earlier. See: *Bibliographical*
essays. A tribute to Wilberforce Eames, 1924, p. 358. If printed at any date
up to April 18, 1768, the printer was Thomas Green, if between that date
and the end of 1770, the printers were Green and Watson.

   .   .   .   .   .

   A brief | narration | of the | captivity | of | Isaac Hollister, | who was
taken by the | Indians, | Anno Domini, 1763. | [double rule] | Written by
himself. | [double rule] | *Suffield: | Printed by Edward Gray, | -1803.-.* [583]

   10 p., 12mo. Sabin 32556. MWA.

   .   .   .   .   .

   A brief narration | of the | captivity | of | Isaac Hollister, | who was |

taken by the Indians, | Anno Domini, 1763. | [rule] | Written by himself. | [rule] | *Townsend [Mass.]:* | *Re-printed for Otis Seaver.* | *1855.* [584]
   8 p., 8vo. MWA, N, NN.

Same in William Henry Egle's *Contributions to Pennsylvania history.* *Harrisburg,* 1890, p. 39-47. DLC, NHi, NN.

Isaac Hollister was captured in the Wyoming Valley, Pennsylvania near the present town of Newbury, October 15, 1763, by a party of Delawares and Shawnees, his father (one of the original Connecticut settlers of the valley) and brother, both named Timothy, being killed. He was carried up the Susquehanna to the Indian villages. There he found a captive Dutchman and they planned an escape in the Spring of 1764. They got away, travelled many days until their food was gone and the Dutchman died of starvation. Four days later, Hollister was retaken and returned. He was soon sold to the Senecas who took him down the Allegheny and Ohio to the Seneca towns. In 1766 he was one of a number of captives surrendered by the Indians at Fort Pitt through the good offices of Sir William Johnson. He remained there eleven months and returned to his family at New London, Conn., April 14, 1767.

PENNINGTON, EDWARD

A description of Pennsbury Manor, which, as attorney for Ann Penn, he offers to sell. *[Philadelphia: 1767].* [585]
   Broadside, folio. Evans 10724, Hildeburn 2314. PHi.

"It sets forth Ann Penn's title to the estate and gives some descriptive and historical details concerning it."—Hildeburn.

WINKFIELD, MRS. UNCA ELIZA, *pseud.*

The female American; or, the adventures of Unca Eliza Winkfield. Compiled by herself. In two volumes. . . . *London: Printed for Francis Noble . . . and John Noble . . . MDCCLXVII.*   · [586]
   2 vols., [2], ii, 193, [2]; [2], 171, [9] p., 12mo. Sabin 104781. BM, NN.

Fictitious account of the Indian captivity of the heroine's father in Virginia in 1618 and his marriage to the Indian princess who rescued him. Most of the book is devoted to the adventures of their daughter Unca, named for her mother. Mr. H.F. De Puy said: "The statement has been made that it was written to satarize an old Virginia family with a slightly different name."

ALEXANDER, WILLIAM, REPUTED EARL OF STIRLING

A state of the Earl | of Stirling's title, to that part | of New-England, now commonly called | Sagadahook. | *[Woodbridge, N.J.? James Parker? 1768].* [587]
   Broadside, folio. Sabin 90611. M-Ar, photostat MWA.

. . . . .

To be sold, | a tract of land of one hundred thousand acres, situate on the | east side of Penobscot-River, in the eastern part of New-Eng- | land, on the following conditions, viz. | *[Woodbridge, N.J.? James Parker? 1768].* [588]

Broadside, folio, dated July 20, 1768. Sabin 90611. M-Ar, photostat MWA and NN.

The "Earl" had his office at Baskinridge, N.J., near Woodbridge. His title to nobility and to lands in America were apparently of equal value. At an earlier date he had claimed ownership of most of Canada (See Sabin 740 and 741) and as a result of his attempts to market his New England lands, Governor Bernard of Massachusetts issued a proclamation on Sept. 7, 1768, declaring that the "persons claiming under the said first Earl of Stirling have no right or title whatsoever to the said country or any part thereof . . ." See Sabin note.

BEATTY, REV. CHARLES

The journal of a two months tour; with a view of promoting religion among the frontier inhabitants of Pennsylvania, and of introducing Christianity among the Indians to the westward of the Alegh-geny Mountains. To which are added, remarks on the language and customs of some particular tribes among the Indians, with a brief account of the various attempts that have been made to civilize and convert them, from the first settlement of New England to this day; By Charles Beatty, A.M. . . . *London: William Davenhill and George Pearch, M DCC LXVIII.* [589]

110 p., 8vo. Title from Sabin 4149. Copies in many large libraries.

Excellent early account of the frontiers and of the Ohio and Pennsylvania Indians beyond the settlements, especially the Delawares.

Reprinted at the end of David Brainerd's *Journal, Edinburgh,* 1798, and as a separate from that volume, 56 p., 8vo. Copies of this or later editions in most large libraries.

WILLIAMSON, PETER

The | travels | of | Peter Williamson, | among the different nations and tribes of sa | -vage Indians in America; with | an account of their principles religious, civil, | and military; their genius, strength, ideas of a | Deity, and notions of the creation; with eve | -ry thing remarkable concerning their manners, | customs, employments, diversions, commerce, | agriculture, &c. &c. | Also, | a description of all the different serpents, and other | curious animals in America, delineated on copper- | plates, neatly engraven; | likewise, | an accurate description of the wonderful Falls of | Niagara, &c. &c. | Together with | a plate, description, use, advantage, manner of | making and handling the curious machine for reap | -ing of oats, barley, &c. | To which is added | a curious alphabetical view of the whole world. The |

length, breadth, produce, and capital cities of each | country; with an account of their inhabitants. | And, lastly, | some general observations on the nature of submis | -sions, and decreets-arbitral. | In three parts. | Written by himself. | *Edinburgh, Printed for the author, and sold | by him at his Coffee-room within the Parliament-house . . .* | *. . .* | *. . .* | *. . . 1768 . . .;*
[590]

viii, 184 p., 3 plates, one of which is folded, 12mo. Sabin 104492. F.C. Deering, N, NHi, NN, PHi.

Parts II and III have separate title pages.

An entirely different work than his *French and Indian cruelty*, his captivity being briefly mentioned in the preface only.

[CHETWOOD, W. R.]

The voyages, dangerous adventures and imminent escapes of Captain Richard Falconer . . . Sixth edition. *London: G. Keith and F. Blyth, 1769.* [6], 276, [5], viii, 46 p., front., 12mo. (17.6 x 10.5 cm.).   [591]

Ayer supp. 32, Sabin 23723. ICN, MiU, RPJCB.

DYER, ELIPHALET

Remarks on Dr. Gale's letter to J.W., Esq. [signed,] E.D. *[Hartford:] Printed Anno 1769.*   [592]

27 p., 8vo. Evans 11243. MHi, MWA, PPL.

An answer by the agent of the Susquehannah Company to Benjamin Gale's *Letter to J.W.*, 1769, which had attacked Connecticut's claim to the Wyoming Valley lands settled by that company.

GALE, BENJAMIN

Doct. Gale's letter to J.W. Esquire, containing a narrative of the principal matters, of a public and interesting nature, which were subjects of the debates and resolves of the General Assembly of the Colony of Connecticut, during their session in May, 1769. [3 lines quoted] *Hartford: Printed and sold by Green & Watson, near the Great-Bridge. 1769.*   [593]

34 p., 8vo. Sabin 26351, Evans 11269. CtHWatk, MBAt, MHi, RPJCB.

An attack on the Connecticut claim to lands in the Wyoming Valley, Pennsylvania, settled by the Susquehannah Company. Answered by Eliphalet Dyer's *Remarks on Dr. Gale's letter,* 1769, which was answered by Dr. Gale in:

.   .   .   .   .   .

Observations on a pamphlet, entitled Remarks on Dr. Gale's Letter to J.W. Esq.; signed E.D. Of which the Hon. Eliphalet Dyer is the reputed author. Shewing, from the matters therein contained, that such an imputation is highly injurious to the character of that worthy patriot. *Hartford: Printed by Green & Watson. [1769?].* [594]

40 p., 8vo. Sabin 26352, Evans 11270. MBAt, PPL, RPJCB.

ROGERS, ROBERT

A concise | account | of | North America: | containing | a description of the several British Colonies | on that Continent, including the Islands of | Newfoundland, Cape Breton, &c. | As to | their situation, extent, climate, soil, produce, | rise, government, religion, present boundaries, | and the number of inhabitants supposed to be in ! each. | Also of | the interior, or Westerly parts of the country, upon | the Rivers St. Laurence, the Mississippi, Chris- | tino, and the Great Lakes. | To which is subjoined, | an account of the several nations and tibes [sic] of | Indians residing in those parts, as to their customs, | manners, government, numbers, &c. | Containing many useful and entertaining facts, never before | treated of. | [rule] | By Major Robert Rogers. | [double rule] | *Dublin:* | *Printed for J. Milliken, in Skinner-Row.* | [rule] | *MDCCLXIX.* [595]

264 p., 12mo. (15.7 x 9.3 cm.). Sabin 72724. An-C-WlvA, CSmH, ICN, IHi, Nh, NHi, PPL-R.

. . . . .

1770. Sabin. 72724. [596]

. . . . .

Journals | of | Major Robert Rogers: | containing | an account of the several excursions he made | under the generals who commanded upon the | Continent of North America, during | the late War. | From which may be collected | the most material circumstances of every campaign upon | that Continent, from the commencement to the conclusion | of the War. | To which is added | An historical account of the expedition against the Ohio Indians | in the year 1764, under the command of Henry Bouquet, | Esq; Colonel of Foot, and now Brigadier General in America, | including his transactions with the Indians, relative to the | delivery of the prisoners, and the preliminaries of peace. | With an introductory account of the proceeding [sic] campaign, | and battle at Bushy-Run. [By William Smith] | *Dublin:* | *Printed by R. Acheson, at Horace's-Head, William-street,* | *for* | *J. Milliken, No. 10. in Skinner-row.* | *M,DCC,LX,IX.* [597]

x, 218, xx, 99 p., 12mo. Sabin 72726. DLC, MB, MiU-C, NN, RPJCB.

In the MB copy, *Horace's-Head* in the imprint is printed *Horaces's-Hbad.*

The *Historical account* has a separate title and was issued separately, for which see under William Smith.

[SMITH, PROVOST WILLIAM]

An | historical account | of the | expedition | against the | Ohio Indians,

| in the year MDCCLXIV, | under the command of | Henry Bouquet, Esq. | Colonel of Foot, and now Brigadier General | in America. Including his transactions with | the Indians, relative to the delivery of the | prisoners, and the preliminaries of peace. | With an introductory account of the preced- | ing campaign, and battle at Bushy-Run. | To which are annexed | military papers, | containing | reflections on the war with the savages; a | method of forming frontier settlements; some | account of the Indian country; with a list of | nations, fighting men, distances, and | different routes. | Published, from authentic documents, by a | lover of his country. | *Dublin.* | *Printed for John Milliken, at (No 10,) in Skinner-Row,* MDCCLXIX.   [598]

  xx, 99 p., 12mo. Sabin 84618. CSmH, DLC, MB, NN, PHi, WHi.

  For reprints, see Sabin note.

  Reprinted with preface by Francis Parkman, etc., Cincinnati, 1868. Sabin 84619.

.   .   .   .   .

Relation | historique | de | l'expédition, | contre | les Indiens de l'Ohio | en MDCCLXIV. | . . . Traduit de l'Anglois, | Par C.G.F. Dumas. | *A Amsterdam,* | *Chez Marc-Michel Rey,* | M.DCC.LXIX.   [599]

  xvi, 147, [10] p., 2 folded maps and 4 plates, 2 folded, 8vo. Sabin 84647. CSmH, DLC, MBAt, NN, PHi, RPJCB, WHi.

  Translation of London edition of the above with biographical sketch of Bouquet added by the translator. For English translations, see Sabin note.

[STORCK, WILLIAM]

  A | description | of | East-Florida, | with a | journal, | kept by | John Bartram of Philadelphia, | Botanist to his Majesty | for The Floridas; | upon | a journey from St. Augustine up the River St. John's, | as far as the lakes. | With explanatory botanical notes. | Illustrated with an accurate map of East-Florida, and two plans; one of | St. Augustine, and the other of the Bay of Espiritu Santo. | The third edition, much enlarged and improved. | [4 lines quoted] | *London:* | *Sold by W. Nicoll, at No. 51, St. Paul's Church Yard; and T. Jefferies,* | *at Charing-Cross, Geographer to His Majesty.* | MDCCLXIX.   [600]

  [4], viii, 40, [2], xii, 35, [1] p., folded front. map and 2 folded plans, 4to. (25.8 x 20.7 cm.). Sabin 92222, De Renne I:193. BM, CSmH, CtY, DLC, GU-De, MB, MH, MHi, NHi, NN, NNC, RPJCB, WHi.

  Maps and plans, each signed: *T. Jefferys Sculp.*: East Florida, | *from surveys | made since the last peace, | adapted to | Dr. Stork's* [sic] | *History of that Country. | By | Thomas Jefferys, Geographer | to the King.* (40.6 x 33.2 cm.); *St. Augustine | the capital of | East Florida.* (21.2 x 28.9 cm.); *The Bay of | Espiritu Santo, | in | East Florida.* 20 x 26.2 cm.).

[JOHNSTON, GEORGES MILLIGEN]

A | short description | of the | Province | of | South-Carolina, | with an account of | the air, weather, and diseases, | at | Charles-Town. | Written in the year 1763. | *London:* | *Printed for John Hinton, at the King's-Arms, in Pater-* | *Noster Row. MDCCLXX.* | *(Price one shilling.).* [601]

96 p., 8vo. Sabin 87948. DLC, DSG, MH, NN.

For attribution to Johnston, see Sabin note.

PITTMAN, PHILIP

The | present state | of the | European settlements | on the | Mississippi; | with | a geographical description of that river. | Illustrated by | plans and draughts. | By Captain Philip Pittman. | *London,* | *Printed for J. Nourse, Bookseller to His Majesty.* | *MDCCLXX.* [602]

viii, 99 p., 8 folded maps and plans, 4to. (28 x 21 cm.). Sabin 63103. DLC, ICU, InThE, MB, MiU-C, NHi, NjP, NN, OClWHi, PPL-R, RPJCB, WHi.

The author was an explorer and surveyor for several years in the part of the frontier he describes. His was the first English book on the region and describes the French settlements of the Illinois country before the coming of the Americans to the region.

Maps and plans: *Folded Plan of New Orleans. NB, No plan yet published like this, being its present state.* [signed:] *Thos Kitchin Sculp.; Draught of the | R. Ibbeville | Being a short communication | from the Sea to the first of the | English Settlements on the | Missisippi* | [signed:] *Thos. Kitchin Sculp.; Plan of Fort Rosalia.; A plan | of | Cascaskies* [signed:] *Thos. Kitchin Sculpsit; A draught of the | River Missisippi | from the Balise up to Fort Chartres. | 1.* | [signed:] *Thos. Kitchin Sculpsit.; A draught of the | River Missisippi | from the Balise up to Fort Chartres | 2* | ; *A draught of the | River Missisippi | from the Balise up to Fort Chartres. | 3; A plan | of | Mobile* | [signed:] *Thos. Kitchin Sculpsit.*

Same, ed. by F.H. Hodder, with maps and plans in facsimile. Cleveland, 1906.

ROGERS, ROBERT

Journals | of | Major Robert Rogers: | containing | an account of the several excursions he made | under the generals who commanded upon | the Continent of North America, during | the late War. | From which may be collected | the most material circumstances of every cam- | paign upon that Continent, from the commence- | ment to the conclusion of the War. | To which is added, | An historical account of the expedition against | the Ohio Indians in the year 1764, under the | command of Henry Bouquet, Esq; Colonel of | Foot, and now Brigadier General in America, | including his transactions with the Indians, re- | lative to the delivery of the prisoners, and the | preliminaries of peace. With an introductory | account of the

preceding campaign, and battle | at Bushy-Run. [By William Smith] |
Dublin: | *Printed by J. Potts, at Swift's Head in Dame-street.* | M,DCC,LXX.
[603]
    x, 218, xx, 99 p., 12mo. Sabin 72727. NN, etc.

The *Historical account,* with separate title page dated 1769, is identical
with that in the 1769 edition and the separate listed under William Smith.

For later editions and other works by Rogers, see Sabin. See also the special
two volume edition of Kenneth Roberts' *Northweast Passage* for the text of
the courtmartial of Robert Rogers and for certain of his journals.

ROWLANDSON, MARY

A narrative [sic] of the captivity, sufferings and removes, of Mrs. Mary
Rowlandson, who was taken prisoner by the Indians, with several others,
and treated in the most barbarous and cruel manner by those vile savages:
with many other remarkable events during her travels. Written by her own
hand, for her private use, and now made public at the earnest desire of
some friends and for the benefit of the afflicted. *Boston: Printed and sold by
Nathaniel Coverly, in Black-Horse Lane: North End. M,DCCLXX.*   [604]
    48 p., wdct. of adult and child on verso of title, 8vo. (16.5 cm.). DLC.
Title from DLC cat. and Brinley 486 (the DLC copy).

. . . . .

A | narrative | of the | captivity, | sufferings and removes | of | Mrs. Mary
Rowlandson, | who was taken prisoner by the Indians | with several others;
and treated in the | most barbarous and cruel manner by | those vile
savages: with many other | remarkable events during her travels. | Written
by her own hand, for her pri- | vate use, and now made public at the |
earnest desire of some friends and for | the benefit of the afflicted. | *Boston:*
| *Printed and sold by Nathaniel Coverly* | *in Black-Horse-Lane, North-End.*
| *M,DCCLXX.*   [605]
    60 p., wdct. of woman with musket on verso of title and wdct. of house on
fire on last page, 8vo. Sabin 73581, Evans 11841. Lancaster Town Library,
MB, MH (imperfect).

. . . . .

Printed and sold by Z. Fowle, | *at the Printing-Office in Back-Street,*
Boston. | *M,DCCLXX.*   [606]
    60 p., same wdct. on verso of title as in preceding ed., 8vo. Lancaster
Town Library.

Printed from the same type as the Coverly edition of same date, the only
difference being in the imprint. The woodcut on verso of title had been
previously used by Fowle in his *The new gift for children,* 1762. Advertised
by Fowle as "just published" in *Massachusetts Spy,* September 12, 1771.

The | state | of the | lands | said to be once within the | bounds of the charter | of the Colony of | Connecticut, | west of the Province of New-York, | considered. | By the publick's humble servant, *** | [rule, orn., rule] | *New York: Printed in the year 1770.* [607]

16 p., 8vo. (18 x 11.5 cm.). Sabin 15692, Evans 11869, Church 1079. CSmH, MBAt, MHi.

Tract opposing the claim of Connecticut to lands in the Wyoming Valley, Pennsylvania, claimed by both states under their colonial charters. The territory, settled by the Susquehannah Company of Connecticut in 1763, was opposed by the Indians (Wyoming Massacre) and Pennsylvanians (Pennamite Wars, with the Connecticut settlers aided by the Paxton Boys), with murder and arson on both sides, the affair being finally settled in 1803 when the Connecticut settlers in northeastern Pennsylvania had their titles confirmed. See cross references under Susquehannah Company for representative tracts on this controversy. See also J.P. Boyd's *The Susquehannah Company Papers*, and O.J. Harvey's *History of Wilkes-Barre*.

BEATTY, CHARLES

Tagebuch einer Zween Reise . . . herausgegeben aus dem Englischen von Carl Beatty A.M. und übersetzt . . . *Frankfurt und Leipzig, In Joh. Georg. Fleischers Buchhandlung, 1771.* [608]

157 p., 8vo. Title from Sabin 4150. MH, PHi, RPJCB.

Translation of his *Journal of a two months tour,* 1768.

ROWLANDSON, MARY

A | narrative | of the | captivity | sufferings and removes | of Mrs. | Mary Rowlandson, | [. . . etc., as in 1770 ed.] *Boston: | Printed and sold by N. Coverly, | near Liberty-Tree. M,DCCLXXI. | (Price six shillings.).* [609]

59 p., wdcts. on p. 4, 42 and verso of p. 59, 8vo. Sabin 73582, Evans 12217, Ayer 239. ICN (lacks last leaf), MWA, N.

[WHARTON, SAMUEL]

[Statement of the petitioners in the case of the Walpole Company]. Soon after the last European peace many of the King's subjects in the provinces of Virginia, Maryland, and Pennsylvania apprehended, that as the French were removed from the lands in the neighborhood of the Ohio, and the Indians were then in a pacific disposition, they might with propriety make settlements on the fertile country over the Allegany mountains . . . *[n.p., 1771?].* [610]

38, appendix 26 p., 4to. Sabin 101150 note. IU, MBAt, RPJCB.

Text begins, as above, with signature B, with title and signature A missing in all three located copies. Supplied title made up by Clarence W. Alvord in his: *Mississippi Valley in British politics,* 1917, vol. 2, which see for this and later promotion literature of the Grand Ohio, Vandalia or Walpole Company, probably all written by Samuel Wharton.

CHURCH, THOMAS

The | entertaining | history | of | King Philip's War, | which began in the month of June, 1675. | As also of | expeditions | more lately made | against the common enemy, and Indian | rebels, in the eastern parts of New-England: | with some account of the Divine| Providence towards | Col. Benjamin Church: | By Thomas Church, Esq. his son. | [rule] | The second edition. | [rule] | Boston: Printed, 1716. | *Newport, Rhode-Island: Reprinted and sold | by Solomon Southwick, in Queen-Street, 1772.*   [611]

198, [1] p., 2 ports., 8vo. (19 x 12.5 cm.). Evans 12352, Sabin 12997, Church 1091. Copies in most large libraries.

The portraits, engraved by Paul Revere, are not authentic. That of Church was copied from an English portrait of Charles Churchill, the English poet, published in 1768, with the powder horn added. See Mass. Hist. Soc. Proceedings, Feb., 1882, p. 245. Includes biography of Benjamin Church not in first edition.

DICKENSON, JONATHAN

God's protecting Providence, . . . [etc., as in 1720 ed.] The fifth edition. *London: Printed and sold by Mary Hinde at No 2, in George-yard, Lombard-Street. [1772].*   [612]

[14], 126, [4] p., 12mo. (16.7 x 9.4 cm.). Sabin 20015, Ayer 68. Copies in most large libraries.

Date assigned from publication date of one of the books advertised at end. This edition has been mistakenly dated [1759] and RPJCB dates in [1767-1774].

Invitation | serieuse | aux | habitants | des | Illinois. | [type orn.] | *Philadelphie | MDCCLXXII.*   [613]

15 p., 8vo. Sabin 34965, Evans 12421, Hildeburn 2784. PPL.

The place and date on title, not being centered, were probably printed in later. Evans supplies the printers as William and Thomas Bradford and describes this as the first work by an inhabitant of the western country printed in the colonies. It is signed: *Par un habitant des Kaskaskia* and Evans surmised that it might have been written by Phillipe François de Rastel, Chevalier de Rocheblave, the last British commandant of the Illinois but Clarence W. Alvord (*Mississippi Valley in British politics*, II:292), a better authority, suggests that the author was either Daniel Blöuin or William Clazon, both residents of the French colony at Kaskaskia. On the political and economic condition of the French settlers in Illinois.

It was reprinted in facsimile, with an introduction by Clarence W. Alvord and Clarence E. Carter as Club for Colonial Reprints, Pub. 4, Providence, 1908.

53 p., 8vo. Edition of 100 copies. CU, DLC, MB, MiU, MiU-C, NN, RPJCB, etc.

MORTON, NATHANIEL

New-England's | memorial: | or, | a brief relation of the most memorable and remarkable | passages of the providence of God, manifested to the | planters | of | New-England, in America: | With special reference to the first colony thereof, | called | New-Plymouth. | . . . | By Nathaniel Morton, | Secretary to the Court for the Jurisdiction of New-Plymouth. | [6 lines quoted] | *Boston: printed.* | *Newport : Reprinted, and sold by S. Southwick.* | *M,DCC,LXXII.* [614]

viii, 208, [8] p., 8vo., (18.5 x 11.5 cm.). Sabin 51014, Evans 12469. MB, MiU-C, MSaE, MWA, Nh, NHi, PPL-R, RHi, RNHi, RPJCB (2 variants).

For modern reprints, see Sabin and new John Carter Brown cat.

SPANGENBERG, AUGUST GOTTLIEB

Leben | des | Herrn | Nicholaus Ludwig | Grafen und Herrn | von | Zinzendorf | und | Pottendorf, | beschrieben | von | August Gottlieb Spangenberg. | . . . | *Zu finden* | *in den Bruder-Gemeinen.* | *[Barby? 1772-1775].* [615]

8 parts, [20], 5-176, [6], 179-393, [4], 395-766, [4], 767-1158, [4], 1159-1602, [4], 1603-1852, [4], 1853-2080, [4], 2081-2258, *Register* and *Errata,* [104] p., 8vo. Sabin 88931. DLC, NN (lacking parts 3 and 4).

Each part has a separate title page and table of contents. Includes accounts of Count Zinzendorf's missionary travels in New York and Pennsylvania. Translated by Samuel Jackson as: *The life of Nicholas Lewis Count Zinzendorf . . . With an introduction by Rev. P. La Trobe. . . . London: Samuel Holdsworth . . . 1838.*

xxxv, 511 p., port., 8vo. Sabin 88932. MBAt, MHi, NN, NNC.

To all | farmers and tradesmen, | who want good settlements for them- selves and families, especially | those lately arrived, or that may yet come, from Scotland or Ireland. | [etc., 38 lines] | [rule] | *Philadelphia: Printed by John Dunlap, at the Newest Printing-Office* | *in Market-Street, 1772.* | [Text within ornamental border]. [616]

Broadside, 4to. (24 x 19.7 cm.). Sabin 95884. PPL.

Describes the advantages of settlement in the counties of Albany, Tryon, Charlotte, Cumberland and Gloucester, New York, with statement of the prices of land, staple crops and means of reaching these tracts. Lands offered for sale by William Smith, Goldsborow Banyar, Thomas Smith and Mr. Kelly, "attorney at law in the street called Broadway," New York, "who

will shew any man the maps of said lands, and agree as to the price, which
if the stranger likes, upon viewing the land, he can instantly go to work
upon it." These lands were sold at six shillings per acre with six years given
in which to complete payment, or rented at sixpence per acre.

There are photostat copies at MH, MHi and MWA.

[WALKER, FOWLER]

The case of Mr. John Gordon, with respect to the title to certain lands
in East Florida, purchased of His Catholick Majesty's subjects by him and
Mr. Jesse Fish, for themselves and others his Britannick Majesty's subjects;
in conformity to the twentieth article of the last definitive treaty of peace.
With an appendix. *London: Printed in the year M.DCC.LXXII.*   [616A]

32, [42] p., folded plan, 4to. Sabin 101042. DLC, MH, NN. RPJCB.

Signed on p. 32: *Folwer Walker*. The folded plan: *A plan of the lands
of the estate called Palica* . . .

[WHARTON, SAMUEL]

Report | of the | Lords Commissioners for | Trade and Plantations | on
the | petition | of the | Honourable Thomas Walpole, Benjamin | Franklin,
John Sargent, and Samuel | Wharton, Esquires, and their associ- | ates; |
for | a grant of lands on the river Ohio, in North | America; for the purpose
of erecting a new | government. | With | observations and remarks. | [thick-
thin rule] | London: | Printed for J. Almon, opposite Burlington-House, in
| Piccadilly. | MDCCLXXII.   [617]

[2], 108, [1] p., folded table, 8vo. (21 x 13 cm.). Sabin 101150 note.
BM, DLC, MB, MH, NHi, NN, RPJCB, WHi.

The report was written by Lord Hillsborough, the Observations and Remarks by Samuel Wharton. Promotion tract of the Grand Ohio Company,
also known as the Vandalia Company and the Walpole Company.

[KIMBER, EDWARD]

The life, extraordinary adventures, voyages, and surprizing escapes of
Capt. Neville Frowde, of Cork . . . Written by himself, and now first
published from his own manuscript . . . *London, 1773.*   [618]

1 preliminary leaf, [5]-210 p., 12mo. (16.5 cm.). Title from DLC cat.
DLC.

For evidence of authorship, see F.G. Black: *Edward Kimber, in Harvard
Studies and Notes in Philology and Literature,* vol. 17, 1935, p. 27-42.

A novel including shipwreck, sojourn of six months with his crew on the
southeast coast of South America, an Indian attack, his captivity and release,
arrival at Rio Janeiro and voyage home. Based on the author's own American adventures. For his other works, see Black and DLC catalog.

The | right | of the | Governor and Company, | of the | Colony of | Con-necticut, | to claim and hold the lands | within the limits of their | charter, | lying west of the Province of New-York, | stated and considered: | in a letter to | J. H. Esquire. | To which is added, | An account of the purchase from the Indians, | of part of those lands, by the Susquehan- | nah and Delaware Companies, and their pro- | ceedings thereon. | [rule] | *Hartford:* | *Printed by Eben. Watson, near the Great- | Bridge. 1773.* [619]

47 p., 8vo. (19.3 x 13.5 cm.). Sabin 15689, Evans 12978, Church 1096. DLC, MB, MHi, NHi, NN.

Susquehannah Company promotion tract.

ROWLANDSON, MARY

A | narrative | of the | captivity, sufferings and removes | of | Mrs. Mary Rowlandson, | [wdct. of woman shooting at four men] | who was taken prisoner by the Indians with several others, | and treated in the most barbarous and cruel manner by those | vile savages: with many other remarkable events during her | travels. | Written by her own hand, for her private use, and now made | public at the earnest desire of some friends, and for the be- | nefit of the afflicted. | [double rule] | *Boston:* | *Printed and sold at John Boyle's Printing-Office, next door* | *to the Three Doves in Marlborough Street. 1773.* [620]

40 p., 12mo. (18.7 x 12 cm.). Sabin 73583, Evans 12988. DLC, Lancaster Town Library, MHi, MWA, RPJCB.

. . . . .

A | narrative | of the | captivity, sufferings and removes | of | Mrs. Mary Rowlandson, | [wdct.] | Who was taken prisoner by the Indians with several | others; and treated in the most barbarous and cruel | manner by those vile savages: with many other | remarkable events during her travels. | Written by her own hand, for her private use, and now made | public at the earnest desire of some friends, and for the benefit | of the afflicted. | [double rule] | *New-London:* | *Printed and sold by Timothy Green. 1773.* [621]

48 p., 12mo. (18.3 x 11.5 cm.). Sabin 73584, Evans 13589, Trumbull 1136. CSmH (title perfect but lacks last leaf), MWA (lacks title and last leaf imperfect), NHi (imprint date imperfect).

Advertised as "just published and for sale by the printer" in [Timothy Greene's] *New London Gazette,* November 12, 1773. The Brinley catalog, no. 488, described a copy with imprint date defective as *177[4]* which confused later bibliographers. The CSmH copy has the complete date *1773.* There was no 1774 edition, in the opinion of Dr. Wilberforce Eames.

SCOTUS AMERICANUS, *pseud.*

Information concerning the Province of North Carolina, addressed to emigrants from the Highlands and Western Isles of Scotland. By an impartial hand. *Glasgow: James Knox. MDCCLXXIII.*   [622]

32 p., 8vo. Sabin 34708, old John Carter Brown cat. 1873. RPJCB.

[SMITH, WILLIAM, historian of New York]

Information | to emigrants, | Being the copy of a letter from a | gentleman in North America: | containing | a full and particular account of the terms on which | settlers may procure lands in North-America, parti | cularly in the Provinces of New-York and Pensylvania. | As also, | the encouragement labourers, mechanics, and trades | men of every kind may find by going there to settle. | To which is added, | Observations on the causes of emigration. | *Glasgow:* | *Printed for, and sold by Morrison and M'Allum at their | Shop in Gibson's land Salt-market, and at J. Galbraith's Printing-Office. | (Price two pence.)* | *[1773].*   [623]

16 p., 16mo. Sabin 84574. DLC.

The author's name appears on p. 3.

[WHARTON, SAMUEL?]

The | advantages | of a | settlement | upon the | Ohio | in | North America. | *[London:] Printed for J. Ridley, Bookseller, St. James Street.* | *M DCC LXIII.* [i.e., 1773].   [624]

[4], 44 p., 8vo. (20.3 x 12.5 cm.). Sabin 56875, Thomson 7, old John Carter Brown cat. 1874. MH, NHi, OCHP, RPJCB.

"Refers to a proposed colony of Georgiana, or at least to a colony to be established west of Vandalia" (C.W. Alvord: *Mississippi Valley in British politics,* 1917, vol. 2, p. 266), on the Mississippi and Ohio rivers. Probably by Samuel Wharton, promoter of the Walpole Company.

WILLIAMS, JOHN

The redeemed captive returning to Zion. [. . . etc., as in 1758 ed.] The fourth edition. . . . *Boston: Printed. New-London: Re-printed by T. Green.* *[1773].*   [625]

79 p., 8vo. (18.5 x 12 cm.). Sabin 104265, Evans 13081, Trumbull 1670. CtHi, MWA (sermon only), NHi (lacks title and p. 79), NN (lacks p. 77-79).

Separate title of sermon has dated imprint: *New-London:* | *Re-printed and sold by T. Green. 1773.* Advertised as "just published" in *New London Gazette,* April 9, 1773.

[YOUNG, ARTHUR]

Observations | on the | present state | of the | waste lands | of | Great Britain. | Published on occasion of the establishment of | a new colony on the Ohio. | [rule] |. By the author of the Tours through England. | [thick-thin rule] | *London:* | *Printed for W. Nicoll, at No. 51, in St. Paul's* | *Church-yard. MDCCLXXIII.* [626]

83 p., 8vo. (20 x 12.5 cm.). Thomson 879, Sabin 106063. CSmH, DLC, MB, MBAt, MH, NHi, NN, PHi, RPJCB.

For other material on the Grand Ohio, Vandalia or Walpole Company, see under Samuel Wharton.

CLAP, ROGER

Memoirs | of | Capt. Roger Clap. | . . . | To which is annexed, | a | short account | of the | author and his family. | *Boston: Printed at Greenleaf's Printing-* | *Office, for Samuel Whiting, in Marshal's-* | *Lane, near the Boston-Stone, 1774.* [627]

48 p., 8vo. Evans 13199, Sabin 13208. MB, NHi.

. . . . .

Boston: Printed for William Tileston Clap | *1807.* [628]

39 p., 8vo. Sabin 13208. DLC, MB, MBAt, MH, MHi, NN, PMA.

For later editions, see Sabin.

CONNECTICUT, GENERAL ASSEMBLY

Report of the commissioners appointed by the General Assembly of this Colony to treat with the proprietaries of Pennsylvania respecting the boundaries of this Colony and that Province. *Norwich: Printed by Green & Spooner. 1774.* [629]

iv, 36 p., 4to. Evans 13214. DLC.

Has to do with the controversy between the two colonies over title to the lands of the Wyoming Valley, Pennsylvania, settled by the Susquehannah Company of Connecticut. The commissioners were Eliphalet Dyer, William Samuel Johnson and Jedidiah Strong. Their mission was entirely unsuccessful.

DICKENSON, JONATHAN

Jonathan Dickinsons erstaunliche Geschichte von dem Schiffbruche, den einige Personen in dem Meerbusen von Florida erlitten; als auch wie sie aus dem unmenschlichen Rachen der Cannibalen und Menschenfressern sind befrehet worden. Nebst einem Anhang von William Flemmings Trübsalen, die er nebst seiner Frau erlitten, wie sie beyde bey dem verwichenen Einfall der Indianer in dem grossen Wald (Grät-Grov) bey Canagodschick in Pensylvanien sind gefangen genommen worden. Nach dem Philadelphischen Original. *Frankfurt und Leipzig, bey Johann Georg Fleischer, 1774.* [630]

128 p., 8vo. (17.8 x 10.9 cm.). Sabin 20016, Ayer supp. 44. F.C. Deering, ICN, MH, NN, RPJCB.

Includes the captivity of William Fleming and his wife among the Pennsylvania Indians in 1755, for other editions of which, see under Fleming.

JONES, DAVID

A journal of two visits made to some nations of Indians on the West side of the River Ohio, in the years 1772 and 1773. By the Rev. David Jones, Minister of the Gospel at Freehold in New-Jersey. *Burlington: Printed and sold by Isaac Collins. M.DCC.LXXIV.*   [631]

95, [1] p., 8vo. Sabin 36487, Evans 13356. F.C. Deering, E.D. Graff, ICN, MH, MHi, MWA, PHC, PPiU, PPL-R, RPJCB, WHi.

Reprinted, New York, 1865, for which see Sabin 36488. Original MS owned by PHi.

The author was a missionary to the Delawares and Shawnees, 1772-1773 and gives an excellent account of their manners and customs. He travelled part of the way with George Rogers Clark and was an army chaplain under General Anthony Wayne from 1794 until peace was declared with the Indians.

PENNSYLVANIA, PROVINCE

[Arms] By the Honourable John Penn, Esquire, Governor and Commander in Chief of the Province of Pennsylvania, and Counties of New-Castle, Kent and Sussex, on Delaware, A Proclamation. [Directed against the Connecticut settlers in the Wyoming Valley. Dated, Feb. 28, 1774] John Penn. [Colophon;] *Philadelphia: Printed by Hall and Sellers. 1774.*   [632]

Broadside, folio. Evans 13518. PHi.

Part of the controversy involving the lands of the Susquehannah Company.

[SMITH, PROVOST WILLIAM]

an | examination | of the | Connecticut Claim | to | lands in Pennsylvania. | With | an appendix, containing extracts and | copies of original papers. | *Philadelphia:* | *Printed by Joseph Crukshank, in Market Street.* | *MDCCLXXIV.*   [633]

[2], 93, 32 p., folded map, 8vo. Sabin 84604, Evans 13629. DLC, RPJCB, WHi.

. . . . .

With same imprint and date but with added material. [2], 94, 32 p., folded map, 8vo. Sabin 84605. CSmH, DLC, ICN, MBAt, NN, PHi, PP, RPJCB.   [634]

For historical note, see Sabin.

[STORCK, WILLIAM]

A | description | of | East-Florida, | with a | journal, | kept by | John Bartram of Philadelphia, | Botanist to His Majesty | for | The Floridas; | upon | a journey from St. Augustine up the River St. John, | as far as the lakes. | With explanatory botanical notes. | Illustrated with an accurate map of East

Florida, and two plans; one of | St. Augustine, and the other of the Bay of Espiritu Santo. | The fourth edition, much enlarged and improved. | [4 lines quoted] | *London:* | *Printed for Faden and Jefferys, the corner of St. Martin's Lane, Charing-* | *Cross, Geographer to His Majesty; and W. Nicoll, at No. 51, St. Paul's* | *Church-Yard.* | *M DCC LXXIV.*   [635]

Same collation as 3d ed., 1769. Sabin 92222. MH, NN.

. . . . .

The | Susquehannah | Case. *[Norwich, 1774?]*   [636]
24 p., 4to. RPJCB.
Place and date supplied from Brinley 2127.

TRUMBULL, BENJAMIN

A | plea, | in | vindication | of the | Connecticut title | to the | contested lands, | lying west of the Province | of New-York, | addressed to the public, | by Benjamin Trumbull, A.M. | *New-Haven:* | *Printed by Thomas and Samuel Green.* | *M,DCC,LXXIV.*   [637]

102, [1] p., 8vo. Sabin 97189, Evans 13691. BM, NHi, NNUT, RPJCB, WHi.

. . . . .

Same title, imprint and date.   [638]

160, [1] p., 8vo. Sabin 97189, Evans 13692. BM, CSmH, DLC, MBAt, MH, MHi, MWA, NHi, NN, NNUT, PHi, RPJCB. One of these editions also at Cty and NBLiHi.

First published in *Connecticut Journal*, March 25, April 1 and 8, 1774. "To this, more than to any other single influence, is said to have been due the allowance of the claim of Connecticut to the Western-Reserve lands."— Dexter's *Yale Graduates*, vol. 2, p. 624.

[WHARTON, SAMUEL]

Considerations on the agreement of the Lords Commissioners of His Majesty's Treasury, with the Honourable Thomas Walpole and his associates, for lands upon the river Ohio, in North America. In a letter to a member of Parliament. *London, MDCCLXXIV.*   [639]

[4], 46 p., 8vo. Sabin 101150, note. NN, RPJCB, WHi.

Promotion tract for the Grand Ohio Company, also known as the Vandalia Company and the Walpole Company. Wharton's papers and those of the Company are at PHi. See K.P. Bailey: *The Ohio Company of Virginia and the westward movement. 1748-1792.* Glendale, 1939. 374 p., maps, 8vo.; and his: *The Ohio Company papers, 1753-1817, being primarily papers of the "suffering traders" of Pennsylvania.* Arcata, Calif., 1947. xi, 549 p., maps, 8vo.

. . . . .

To the King's most Excellent Majesty | in Council. | The memorial of the
Honourable Thomas Walpole, | in behalf of himself and the Earl of Hertford,
Earl | Temple, the Right Honourable Charles Lord Camden, | the Honour-
able Richard Walpole, the Honourable | Robert Walpole, Sir Harry Feather-
stonhaugh, Baronet, | Sir George Colebrooke, Baronet, Thomas Pitt, Esq. |
Richard Jackson, Esq. John Sargent, Esq. and Samuel | Wharton, Esq. and
their associates. | [Caption title] *[London, 1774].*   [640]

16 p., 4to (25 x 19 cm.). Sabin 101150. CSmH, NHi, RPJCB.

Signed and dated at end: *Thomas Walpole, London, August 1774* but
probably written, like the other Vandalia or Grand Ohio Company promotion
tracts, by Samuel Wharton.

WILLIAMS, JOHN

The redeemed captive returning to Zion. [. . . etc., as in 1758 ed.] The
fifth edition. . . . *Boston: Printed and sold by John Boyle next door to the
Three Doves in Marlborough Street. 1774.*   [641]

70, [1] p., 8vo. (19.3 x 12 cm.). Sabin 104266, Evans 13773, Ayer 309.
DLC, ICN, MB, MHi, MWA, MWiW-C, N, NN, RPJCB.

The sermon has a separate title page.

WOOLMAN, JOHN

The works of John Woolman. In two parts. *Philadelphia: Printed by
Joseph Crukshank, in Market-Street, between Second and Third Streets.
M.DCC.LXXIV.*   [642]

2 vols. in one, xiv, [2], 250, [2], 253-436 p., 8vo. Sabin 105211, Evans
13782. CtY, MWA, N, NN, PHi, RPJCB.

Separate titles for the two parts, imprints same as general title: *A journal
of the life, gospel labours, and Christian experiences of that faithful minister
of Jesus Christ, John Woolman, late of Mount-Holly, in the Province of
New Jersey . . . ; The works of John Woolman. Part the second. Containing
his last epistle and his other writings. . . .*

This famous Quaker preacher visited most of the frontiers and left an
interesting and very popular record of his travels. His works were reprinted
at London, and Philadelphia, 1775 and frequently thereafter, for which see
Sabin 105211. His journal was separately printed at *London, 1775* (3 eds.)
and frequently thereafter, for which see Sabin 105202.

ADAIR, JAMES

The history of the American Indians; particularly those nations adjoining
to the Mississippi, East and West Florida, Georgia, South and North Carolina
and Virginia: containing an account of their origin, language, manners, religious and civil customs, laws, form of government, punishments, conduct in

war and domestic life, their habits, diet, agriculture, manufactures, diseases and method of cure, and other particulars, sufficient to render it a complete Indian system. With observations on former historians, the conduct of our colony governors, superintendents, missionaries, &c. Also an appendix, containing a description of the Floridas and the Mississippi lands, with their productions—The benefits of colonizing Georgiana, and civilizing the Indians—And the way to make all the colonies more valuable to the mother country. By James Adair, Esq., a trader with the Indians and resident in their country for forty years. *London: Edward and Charles Dilly, MDCCLXXV.* [643]

[12], 464 p., folded map, 4to. Title from Sabin 155. Copies in most large libraries.

Standard work on the Southern Indians by a famous Indian trader and frontiersman who was one of the first to explore the Alleghanies.

Reprinted in various editions of Viscount Kingsborough's *Antiquities of Mexico.*

. . . . . .

Adair's history of the American Indians, . . . *Johnson City, Tenn.: The Watauga Press, 1930.* [644]

xxxviii, 508 p., folded map, 4to. (24.5 cm.).

Edited by S.C. Williams for the National Society of the Colonial Dames of America, in Tennessee.

GAGE, THOMAS

General Gage's instructions, of 22d February 1775, to Captain Brown and Ensign de Berniere, (of the army under his command) whom he ordered to take a sketch of the roads, passes, heights, &c., from Boston to Worcester, and to make other observations: With a curious narrative of occurrences during their mission. . . . Together with an account of their doings, in consequence of further orders . . . from General Gage, . . . to proceed to Concord, to reconnoitre and find out the state of the Provincial magazines, . . . Also, an account of the transactions of the British troops, from the time they marched out of Boston, on the evening of the 18th, 'till their confused retreat back, on the . . . nineteenth of April, 1775; and a return of the . . . killed, wounded . . . *Boston: J. Gill. MDCCLXXV.* [645]

20 p., 8vo. Sabin 26317. MBAt, MHi, MWA, NHi, RPJCB.

Same with notes, in Bostonian Soc. Pubs., vol. 9, 1912.

One of the very few Revolutionary War spy narratives. See also James Moody's *Narrative,* 1782; David Gray: *Gray's narrative* [of his services as a spy], *1776-82. [n.p.,n.d.].* 8 p., 8vo. Sabin 28379. Copy in N before the fire of 1911; and John Howe: *A journal kept by Mr. John Howe, while he was employed as a British spy, during the Revolutionary war; also, while he was engaged in the smuggling business, during the late war. Concord, N.H.*

Luther Roby, Printer, 1827. 44 p., 12mo. MWA, NHi, RPJCB. For the best contemporary account of the battles of Lexington and Concord, see Isaiah Thomas: *A narrative, of the excursion and ravages of the King's troops . . . Worcester: Isaiah Thomas, [1775].* MH, MWA, NN. The first book printed at Worcester. Evans 14269, Sabin 26318.

HUBBARD, WILLIAM

A narrative of the Indian wars of New-England, from the first planting thereof in the year 1607, to the year 1677. Containing a relation of the occasion, rise and progress of the war with the Indians, in the southern, western, eastern and northern parts of said country. By William Hubbard, A.M. Minister of Ipswich. [6 lines quoted] *Boston: Printed and sold by John Boyle in Marlborough-Street. 1775.*   [646]

viii, 288 p., 12mo. Sabin 33447, Evans 14120. ICN, MB, MH, MHi, MWA, NN, RPJCB, etc.

[POWNALL, THOMAS]

Speedily will be published, | (Sold by J. Almon, opposite Burlington-house, Piccadilly.) | A Map of the Middle British Colonies | in North-America. | First published by Mr. Lewis Evans, of | Philadelphia, in 1755; and since corrected and | improved, as also extended, with the addition of | New-England, &c. and bordering parts of Canada; | from actual surveys now lying at the Board of Trade. | By T. Pownall, M P. | [etc., 3 lines] | with | A topographical description of such parts | of North-America as are contained in the | map. | [Caption title] *[London, 1775].*   [647]

8 p., 8vo. (22.5 x 14 cm.). NHi, T.W. Streeter.

Prospectus of the above, p. [1]-4, advertisements of other Almon publications, p. 4-8. Issued separately and probably also to be bound at the end of other works of the publisher.

"Neither this improved map, nor analysis, are published with any view of profit to the Editor; if any should accrue, it will be given to Mr. Evan's daughter and her children."

[WHARTON, SAMUEL]

Facts and observations respecting the country granted to his Majesty by the Six United Nations of Indians, on the South-East side of the River Ohio, in North America; the establishment of a new colony there; and the causes of the Indian war, which, last year, desolated the frontier settlements of the provinces of Pennsylvania, Maryland, and Virginia. *London. 1775.*   [648]

170, [1] p., folded table, 8vo. (20.5 cm.). Sabin 103107. DLC (imp.), PHi, RPJCB.

[WHARTON, SAMUEL, AND EDWARD BANCROFT]

View | of the | title | to | Indiana, | a tract of country | on the | River Ohio,

| containing | Indian conferences at Johnson-Hall in May, | 1765; the deed of the Six Nations to the | proprietors of Indiana; the minutes of the | congress at Fort Stanwix, in October and | November, 1768; the deed of the Indians, | settling the boundary line between the Eng- | lish and Indian lands; and the opinion of | counsel on the title of the proprietors of | Indiana. | *[Philadelphia, 1775?]*. [649]

24 p., 8vo. (18 x 12.3 cm.). Sabin 25595, 34579-34580, 96769, 99584, entry following 101150, Church 1119, Evans 15219. CSmH, NjP, RPJCB, WHi.

Refers to a tract in northwestern West Virginia, not the present state of Indiana. See Sabin 99584 note, H.F. DePuy's *Colonial Indian treaties* 49, C.W. Alvord's *Mississippi Valley in British politics*. Later merged with the Grand Ohio, Vandalia or Walpole Company.

FISKE, NATHAN

Remarkable providences to be gratefully remembered, reli- | giously improved, and carefully transmitted to posterity. | [rule] | A | sermon | preached at | Brookfield | on the last day of the year 1775. | Together | with some marginal notes, &c. | Giving an account of the first settling of the town in the | year 1660; its desolations by the Indians in Philip's | war, in 1675; its distresses in Queen Anne's | War; and its increase and improvements to | the present time. | By Nathan Fiske, A.M. | Pastor of the Third Church in Brookfield. | [rule, 5 lines quoted, rule] | *Boston, New-England:* | *Printed by Thomas and John Fleet, 1776.* [650]

31, v p., 8vo. Sabin 24551, Evans 14754. MB, MBAt, MHi, MWA, etc.

Title from reprint, West Brookfield, 1860.

One of the first interesting historical frontier sermons. See also Thomas Wheeler's *A thankful remembrance*, 1676.

POWNALL, THOMAS

A | topographical description | of such parts of | North America | as are contained in | the (annexed) map | of the | Middle British Colonies, &c. | in | North America. | By T. Pownall, M.P. | late Governor, &c. &c. of his Majesty's Provinces of Massachusetts | Bay and South Carolina, and Lieutenant Governor of New | Jersey. | *London:* | *Printed for J. Almon, opposite Burlington House, in Piccadilly.* | *MDCCLXXVI.* [651]

vi, 46, 16 p., folded map, folio. (42.5 cm.). Sabin 64835. Copies in most large libraries.

A republication of Lewis Evans' map and extracts from the *Analysis* of 1755 with many additions to map and text.

Map: A map of the Middle British Colonies in North America. First published by Mr. Lewis Evans . . . in 1755; and since corrected and improved, as also extended, with the addition of New England, and bordering parts of Canada; from actual surveys . . . By T. Pownall . . .

The text, with numerous extracts from Evans, has the following appendices: I. The account of Capt. Anthony Van Schaick of the ground between the entrance of Lake Champlain at Crown Point, and the mouth of Otter Creek. II. Captain Anthony Van Schaick's journal. 1756. III. Captain [Humphrey] Hobbs's account of the way from No. 4, in New Hampshire, to the mouth of Otter Creek. IV. Extracts from the journal of Captain Harry Gordon, Chief Engineer in the Western Department in North America, who was sent from Fort Pitt on the River Ohio, down the said river, & to Illinois, in 1766. V. Extract from Mr. Lewis Evans's journal. 1743. VI. A journal, of Christopher Gist's journey, began from Col. Cresap's at the old town on Potomack river, Maryland, October 31, 1750, continued down the Ohio, within 15 miles of the falls thereof; and from thence to Roanoak river in North Carolina, where he arrived May 19, 1751; undertaken on the account of the Ohio company, and by the instructions of their committee.

For Gist's second journal, 1753, accompanying George Washington, see Mass. Hist. Soc. Coll., 3d ser., vol. 5, p. 101 and following.

Reprinted with the author's hitherto unpublished notes prepared in 1784 for a new edition, and edited by Lois Mulkearn from the author's copy in the Darlington Library, University of Pittsburgh. University of Pittsburgh Press, 1948 [i.e., 1949].

[Wharton, Samuel, and Edward Bancroft]

View | of the | title | to | Indiana, | a tract of country | on the | River Ohio. | Containing | Indian conferences at Johnson-Hall, in May, 1765—The | deed of the Six Nations to the proprietors of Indiana—The | minutes of the congress at Fort Stanwix, in October and | November, 1768—The deed of the Indians, settling the | boundary line between the English and Indian lands— | And the opinion of counsel on the title of the pro- | prietors of Indiana. | *Philadelphia:* | *Printed by Styner and Cist, in Second-* | *Street, near Arch-Street. MDCCLXXVI.*   [652]

46 p., 8vo. For references see under 1st ed., 1775. DLC, MBAt, MWA, PHi, PPL.

Williams, John

The redeemed captive returning to Zion. [. . . etc., as in 1758 ed.] The fifth [i.e., sixth] edition. . . . *Boston: Printed. New-London: Re-printed by T. Green. [1776].*   [653]

72 p., 8vo. (18.4 x 11.5 cm.). Sabin 104267, Evans 15221, Ayer 310, Trumbull supp. 2794-5. CtHi, Cty (imp.), DLC, ICN, MWA (imp.), NN, RPJCB.

Separate title of sermon dated 1776.

MBAt is said to have a fourth edition, Greenfield, 1789, which may be an error for the 1793 edition.

CARVER, JONATHAN

Travels | through the | interior parts | of | North-America, | in the | years 1766, 1767, and 1768. | By J. Carver, Esq. | Captain of a company of provincial | troops during the late | war with France. | Illustrated with copper plates. | *London:* | *Printed for the author;* | *and sold by J. Walter, at Charing-cross, and* | *S. Crowder, in Pater-noster Row.* | *M DCC LXXVIII.* [654]

[20], 543, [1] p., 2 folded maps, 4 plates, 8vo. (21.5 x 13 cm.). Copies in most large libraries. George Washington's copy in MWiW-C.

For more complete descriptions of this and later editions, see Sabin, Evans, DLC catalog and John Thomas Lee: *A bibliography of Carver's Travels,* in State Hist. Soc. of Wisconsin *Proceedings,* 1909, p. 143-183 and separate; and his: *Captain Jonathan Carver: additional data,* in same, 1912, p. 87-123, and separate.

Carver, one of the English soldiers wounded and captured at the massacre of Fort William Henry by the French and Indians in 1757, gives a vivid though short eye-witness account of the battle. Though a prisoner of the French and Indians for only three days, when he escaped to Fort Edward, his is one of the most spirited accounts of the famous massacre. His later frontier experiences in Minnesota and Wisconsin, though formerly discredited, have been accepted as one of the earliest and best accounts of pioneer days in this region.

HUTCHINS, THOMAS

A | topographical description | of | Virginia, Pennsylvania, | Maryland, and North Carolina, | comprehending the | Rivers Ohio, Kenhawa, Sioto, Cherokee, | Wabash, Illinois, Missisippi, &c. | The | climate, soil and produce, | whether | animal, vegetable, or mineral; | the | mountains, creeks, roads, distances, lati- | tudes, &c. and of every part, laid down in the an- | nexed map. | Published by Thomas Hutchins, | Captain ln [sic] the 60th Regiment of Foot. | With a | Plan of the rapids of the Ohio, a plan of the several | villages in the Illinois Country, a table of the | distances between Fort Pitt and the mouth of the | Ohio, all engraved upon copper. | And | an appendix, containing Mr. Patrick Kennedy's | journal up the Illinois River, and a correct list of the | different nations and tribes of Indians, with the | number of fighting men, &c. | [double rule] | *London:* | *Printed for the author, and sold by J. Almon,* | *opposite Burlington House, in Piccadilly.* | [rule] | *M DCC LXXVIII.* [655]

[2], ii, 67, [1] p., 2 folded plans, folded table, 8vo. (21 x 12.5 cm.). Sabin 34054. Copies in most large libraries.

First edition, first issue, with *in* spelled *ln* on title, as indicated, and with a final unnumbered page of errata on verso of p. 67. Second issue, with error on title and other errata corrected and without page of errata at end, leaving the verso of p. 67 blank.

Folded plans and table: *A plan of the* | *Rapids,* | *in the River Ohio,* | *by* |

Thos. Hutchins. | [signed:] *J. Cheevers sculpt.* (27 x 21 cm.); *A plan* | *of the several villages in the* | *Illinois Country,* | *with part of the* | *River Missisippi &c.* | *by* | *Thos. Hutchins.* (21 x 15.5 cm.); *A* | *table of distances,* | *between* | *Fort Pitt,* | *and the mouth* | *of the* | *River Ohio.*

Issued separately but intended to accompany this work: *A* | *new map* | *of the western parts of* | *Virginia, Pennsylvania,* | *Maryland and North Carolina; Comprehending the River Ohio, and all the rivers, which fall into it;* | *Part of the River Mississippi, the whole of the* | *Illinois River,* | *Lake Erie, part of the lakes Huron,* | *Michigan &c.* | *And all the country bordering on these* | *lakes and rivers.* | *By Thos. Hutchins.* | *Captain in the 60th Regiment of Foot.* | *London Published according to Act of Parliament Novembr. ye 1st. 1778 by T. Hutchins.* | [In lower right corner:] *Engrav'd by J. Cheevers.* (89.3 x 108.3 cm.).

Text reprinted in *Imlay's Topographical description,* 1797 ed.

One of the most important early descriptive and geographical works of the west.

KELLET, ALEXANDER

A | pocket | of | prose and verse: | being a | selection | from the | literary productions | of | Alexander Kellet, Esq. | *Bath: Printed for R. Cruttwell.* | *And sold by* | *E. and C. Dilly . . . London.* | MDCCLXXVIII.   [656]

[4], 283 p., 18mo. (15.3 x 9.2 cm.). Sabin 27253, Ayer 169. BM, ICN.

Sabin gives the imprint: *Bath: Printed by R. Crutwell.* | MDCCLXXVIII.

Contains: "A true relation of the unheard-of sufferings of David Menzies, surgeon, among the Cherokees, and of his surprising deliverance."

For second edition, see his: *Mental novelist,* 1783.

This curious narrative tells how David Menzies, a surgeon, was captured by a band of Cherokees about seventy miles from Augusta, Georgia "just before the breaking out of the Cherokee war." They took him to one of their towns and offered him for adoption to the mother of a lately deceased sachem but she refused to adopt him and ordered him tortured. Some of the Cherokees had tasted larded venison at the white settlements so they prepared to have him larded and roasted. They proceeded with the larding but by that time the Indians were too drunk to proceed with the roasting and by the time they had sobered up, Menzies had escaped. The author proposed the captivity as the subject for a tragedy to be called *Lardello* with Dr. Menzies playing the lead. The Cherokee war began in 1776.

[SMITH, PROVOST WILLIAM]

Voyage | historique | et politique, | dans l'Amérique, | du Chevalier Henry Bouquet, | Brigadier-Général, contenant ses détailles. | On y a joint des memoires militaires contenant des | réflexions sur la guerre avec les sauvages: une | méthode de former des établissemens sur la fron- | tiere: quelques détails concernant la contrée des | Indiens: avec une liste de nations, com-battans, | villes, distances, & diverses routes. | Le tout enrichi de cartes et tailles-douces. | Traduit de l'Anglois, | Séconde édition. | *A Paris,* | *Chez Merlin, Libraire, rue Poupée S. André* | *à Saint-Joseph.* | *MDCC.LXXVIII.* [657]

xvi, 147, [10] p., 2 folded maps, and 4 plates, 2 of which are folded, 8vo. Sabin 84676. NN, NNC.

Second French edition of *An historical account* from the sheets of the 1st French ed.: *Relation historique,* 1769.

CARVER, JONATHAN

Travels. *London, 1779.* Copies in most large libraries. [658]

. . . . .

Travels. *Dublin, 1779.* Copies in most large libraries. [659]
See note at end of 1798 edition.

DODGE, JOHN

A | narrative | of the | capture and treatment | of | John Dodge, | by the English at Detroit. | Written by himself. | *Philadelphia:* | *Printed by T. Brad-ford, at the Coffee-House.* | *MDCCLXXIX.* [660]

22 p., 12mo. Sabin 20501, Hildeburn 3871 and Evans 16262 locate only at PPL-R. Photostat copy NN.

Reprinted from first edition in: (Boston] *Continental Journal and Weekly Advertiser,* Dec. 30, 1799, Jan. 6 and 13, 1780; *Connecticut Gazette and Universal Intelligencer,* Feb. 2, 1780; *The Remembrancer.* London: J. Almon, 1779, p. 73-81.

John Dodge, an Indian trader at Sandusky, was captured at his house in January, 1776 by the British and Indians and taken to Detroit where Henry Hamilton, British commandant there, imprisoned him. He was released and continued as a trader in 1777 at which time he saved another prisoner from the stake but was rearrested by the British in January, 1778, sent to Quebec where he escaped and made his way to Boston and from thence to Philadelphia where he was interviewed by Washington and Congress.

EVANS, ISRAEL

A | discourse, | delivered | at Easton, | on the 17th of October, 1779, | to the | officers | and | soldiers | of the Western Army, | after their return from an expedition against | the Five Nations of hostile Indians. | By the Reverend Israel Evans, A.M. and | Chaplain to General Poor's Brigade. | Now pub-lished at the particular request of the Generals | and Field Officers of that Army. | And to be distributed among the soldiers.—Gratis. | *Philadelphia:* | *Printed by Thomas Bradford, at the Coffee-House.* | *M.DCC.LXXIX.* [661]

40 p., 8vo. Sabin 23160, Evans 16266, Hildeburn 3876. CSmH, DLC, MH, MHi, MWA, Nh, NHi, NN, PHi, PPAmP, PPL, PPL-R, RPJCB.

.   .   .   .   .

Lancaster, 1779. Sabin 23160; and *Germantown, 1914.*   [662]

A splendid frontier sermon delivered to the army on its return from the Sullivan Expedition against the Iroquois in Western New York. This patriot preacher published five other sermons, all but one while serving as chaplain in the Revolutionary army: a thanksgiving sermon, *Lancaster, 1778.* CHi, DLC, MH, NjP; funeral sermon for General Enoch Poor, *Newburyport, 1781.* DLC, MBAt, MH, MWA; sermon on the victory at Yorktown, *Phil., 1782.* DLC, MB, MBAt, MWA, NHi, NjP, NN, PHi, RPJCB; sermon of thanksgiving for peace, at New York, *N.Y., 1783.* MBAt, MH, MWA, NjP, NHi, RPJCB; New Hampshire election sermon, *Concord, 1791.* BM, DLC, MBAt, MHi, MWA, Nh.

[WHARTON, SAMUEL AND EDWARD BANCROFT]

View of the title to Indiana, a tract of country on the river Ohio . . . *Williamsburg: Printed by J. Dixon & T. Nicholson, M.DCC.LXXIX.* [663]

8 p., 4to. Sabin 99584 and other references under 1st ed., 1775. PP, RPJCB. Charles F. Heartman owned a copy in 1935.

The appendix of: *Case* [of William Trent and other traders, who were despoiled by the Indians near Fort Pitt in 1763. London? 1770?], 8, appendices 24 p., 4to. (Sabin 96769 NN) is, according to DePuy, the same as the *View of the title to Indiana,* without the legal opinions of Dagge and others.

CARVER, JONATHAN

Reisen. *Hamburg, 1780.* DLC, etc.   [664]

See note at end of 1798 edition.

DODGE, JOHN

An entertaining | narrative | of the cruel and barbarous treatment and | extreme sufferings of | Mr. John Dodge | during his | captivity | of many months among the | British, | at Detroit. | In which is also contained, | a particular detail of the sufferings of | a Virginian, who died in their hands. | [rule] | Written by himself; and now published to satisfy the cu- | riosity of every one throughout the United States. | [rule] | The second edition. | [double rule] | *Danvers, near Salem: Printed and sold by* | *E. Russell, next the Bell-Tavern. M,DCC LXXX.* | *At the same place may be had a number of new books,* | *etc. some of which are on the times:—Cash paid for rags.*

[665]

32 p., wdcts. on recto and verso of half title and two in text, 8vo. (16. x 10.5 cm.). Evans 16765. F.C. Deering, Mrs. Arthur M. Greenwood, ICN, MSaE, NN.

Half title: *Mr. Dodge's | narrative | of his sufferings among the | British |
at Detroit.* [wdct. of the author], the verso containing an advertisement for
Col. Ethan Allen's Captivity printed lengthwise of the page with a cut of a
British soldier at the left and a cut of an Indian at the right. There are two
wdcts. in text, pages 21 and 25.

. . . . .

*Narrative | of | Mr. John Dodge | during his captivity | at Detroit | Repro-
duced in facsimile from the | second edition of 1780 | With an introductory
note | by | Clarence Monroe Burton | [cut of torch] | Cedar Rapids, Iowa |
The Torch Press | Nineteen hundred nine.*   [666]

64 p., 4to. (26 x 20.5 cm.). Sixty-three copies printed, sixty being for sale.
Copies in most large libraries.

Introduction, p. [5]-23; facsimile reprint, p. 25-56; wdct. of Indian, p. 57;
Notes, p. [59]; Index, p. 61-64.

The half title leaf is not an exact facsimile. The lettering on the wdct. port.
on recto has been changed from *Letters to Congress* in one line to read:
Letters to | Congress in two lines. The verso omits the advertisement of Col.
Ethan Allen's Captivity and prints only the wdct. of the British soldier which
appeared at the left of the advertisement of the original edition. The wdct. of
the Indian at the right of the advertisement of the original edition appears on
page 57.

Hanson, Elizabeth

God's mercy surmounting man's cruelty. . . . *The third edition. Philadelphia: Printed; Danvers, near Salem: Re-printed and sold by E. Russell, near
the Bell-Tavern. M,DCC,LXXX. At the same place may be had, a number
of new books, &c. some of which are on the times—Cash paid for rags.*
                                                                             [667]

32 p., 8vo. Evans 16721, Sabin 30266. F.C. Deering, MHi, MWA, NN.

Text differs from that of the English editions, having been considerably
rewritten and "improved."

[Paine, Thomas]

*Public good, | being | an examination | into the claim of Virginia to the |
vacant Western Territory, | and | of the right of | the United States to the
same. | To which is added, | proposals for laying off a new state, | to be
applied as a fund for carrying on | the war, or redeeming the | national
debt. | By the author of Common Sense. | Philadelphia: | Printed by John
Dunlap, in Market-Street. | M,DCC,LXXX.*   [668]

38 p., 8vo. Sabin 58237, Evans 16920, Hildeburn 4035. DLC, MBAt,
NHi, PPL, RPJCB, etc.

Reprinted London, 1817 and 1819. Sabin 58238.

A defense of the government's claim to unsettled lands against that of the individual states, especially Virginia.

Reprinted with a separate title page, in 41 pages, in *The writings of Thomas Paine . . . Albany—State of New-York: Printed by Charles R. & George Webster.* [1792], various paging, totalling [517] p. Evans 24658, Sabin 58247; Same, with *Rights of Man*, part 2 and *Letter to Dundas* added, [1793?]. [617] p.; Same, rearranged in order of original publication, [1794]. [617] p. Evans 27466 with titles and collations of all parts and long note. Same in *Works, London,* 1792 (Sabin 58244), *Philadelphia,* 1797 (Sabin 58245, Evans 32633 with long note, and later editions. For a similar work, see under Columbus, pseud, 1795 and 1796.

Paine continued the discussion in his *Letter addressed to the Abbe Raynal . . . Philadelphia: Printed by Melchior Steiner . . . M,DCC,LXXXII* (Sabin 58222, Evans 17651) and later editions.

[VAN CAMPEN, MOSES]

A | narrative | of the capture | of certain Americans | at Westmorland, | by savages; | and the perilous escape which they effected, by | surprizing specimens of policy and heroism. | To which is subjoined, | some account of the religion, government, | customs and manners of the aborigines of | North-America. | *Hartford:* | *Printed and sold near the bridge.* [by Hudson and Goodwin] | *[1780?].*   [669]

24 p., 8vo. (19 cm.). Sabin 98426, Evans 18273, Trumbull supp., Ayer 212. DLC, ICN, NN.

The "certain Americans" of this narrative were Moses Van Campen, his nephew of the same name, Peter Pence, Abraham Pike and Jonah Rogers, a boy of 13. They were captured in March, 1780 near Wyoming, Pennsylvania. Van Campen was born in New Jersey in 1757, served in the Revolutionary army, part of the time as quartermaster during the Sullivan Expedition of 1779. At the time of his capture he was helping his father and younger brother on the home farm when the attack came. His father and brother were killed. He and Pence were taken westward and a few days later Pike was also captured. The group of five prisoners were guarded by ten Indians, nine of whom they killed and were soon back home.

After this narrative was written, Van Campen was captured again, in the spring of 1782. After a lively series of adventures they reached Fort Niagara where he was befriended by Colonel Butler. He was then sent to Montreal, Quebec and later to New York and home after eighteen months of captivity. Before reaching Niagara he had been helped by another captive, Horatio Jones who lived for some time with the Senecas and later became a government interpreter at the treaties with the Iroquois in the 1790s, under Colonel Israel Chapin, the Indian agent at Canandaigua. *The life of Horatio Jones,* by George H. Harris, including that of his wife, Sarah Whitmore, another captive, and Jasper Parrish, still another Seneca captive, was published in the Buffalo Historical Society Publications, vol. 6, 1903, p. 383-546, the latter based on a narrative dictated by Parrish himself. These three famous captives, Van Campen, Jones and Parrish, with Mary Jemison, "the White Woman of the Genesee," whose story was published in 1824 and has gone through some 35 editions and is still in print (the best collection of these editions is at the University of Rochester), all settled in Western New York. Jones and Parrish, who were adopted Indians, were given valuable tracts of land by the Indians, as was Mary Jemison. All of them lived in the Genesee Valley except Jasper Parrish who was sub-agent and interpreter under Colonel Israel Chapin at Canandaigua where he made his home. The Chapin papers are at the New York Historical Society and the Parrish papers at Vassar College. An oil portrait of Parrish hangs in the courthouse gallery at Canandaigua. Van Campen's gun and tomahawk are in the museum at Glen Iris, Letchworth Park where one may also see the grave of Mary Jemison, her daughter's log cabin and the last Iroquois council house of the Genesee Valley. The N copy of the Dansville edition contains an inserted photograph of an oil portrait of Van Campen.

Moses Van Campen served in the Ranging Companies, Northumberland County, Pennsylvania Militia during the Revolution in 1780, being promoted to Ensign in that year and Lieutenant the year following. After the war he became a Major of the local militia.

For second edition, see 707.

CARVER, JONATHAN

Travels. *London, 1781.* Copies in most large libraries.   [670]

Adds portrait and biographical sketch of Carver. See note at end of 1798 edition.

HUTCHINS, THOMAS

Description | topographique | de la Virginie, de la Pensylvanie, | du Maryland et de la Caroline | Septentrionale: | Contenant | les rivieres d'Ohio, Kenhawa, Sioto, | Cherokée, Wabash, des Illinois, du |Mississipi, &c.; | le climat, le sol, les productions, tant | animales que végétales ou minérales; | les montagnes, les rivieres, chemins, distances, | latitudes, et de toutes les parties représentées | dans les cartes ci-jointes; | Publiées par Thomas Hutchins, | Capitaine du soixantieme Régiment d'Infanterie: | Accompagnée d'un Plan des Sauts de l'Ohio, d'un autre | de tous les villages du Canton des Illinois; une table des | distances en milles entre le Fort-Pitt & l'embouchure de | l'Ohio dans le Mississipi; | Plus, un supplément, qui contient le journal de Patrice | Kennedy's, sur la Riviere des Illinois, & un etat véritable des | différentes nations & tribus des Indiens, avec le nombre des com- | battans. | Traduit de l'Anglois. | [orn.] | *A Paris,* | *Chez le Rouge, Géographe, rue des Grands-Augustins.* | [orn. rule] | M. DCC. LXXXI. | *Avec approbation, et privilége du Roi.*   [671]

68, [4] p., folded map, plan and table, 8vo. (19.5 x 12 cm.). Sabin 34055. DLC, ICN, MiU-C, NHi, OClWHi, RPJCB, ViU, etc.

Folded map, plans and table: *Carte | des environs du Fort Pitt | et | de la nouvelle Province | Indiana | dediée a M. Franklin* (36 x 24.5 cm.); [on same sheet:] *Plan | des villages | de la contrée | des Illinois | et partie de la Riviere | de Mississipi. | par Hutchins.* [and:] *Plan | des Rapides | de la Riviere | d'Ohio | par Hutchins.* (37.5 x 19.5 cm.); *Table | des distances en milles | entre | le Fort Pitt | et l'Embouchure | de l'Ohio.* (33.5 x 19.5 cm.).

[WHARTON, SAMUEL]

Plain facts: | being | an examination | into the | rights of the Indian nations of America, | to their respective countries; | and | a vindication of the grant, | from | the Six United Nations of Indians, | to | the proprietors of Indiana, | against | the decision | of the | legislature of Virginia; | together with | authentic documents, | proving | that the territory, Westward of the Allegany | Mountain, never belonged to Virginia, &c. | [double rule] | *Philadelphia: | Printed and sold by R. Aitken, Bookseller, in Market- | Street, three doors above the Coffee-House. | M.DCC.LXXXI.*   [672]

164, [1] p., 8vo. (20.5 x 12 cm.). Sabin 63221, Evans 17437. DLC, MB, MHi, MiU-C, NHi, NjP, NN, PHi, RPJCB, WHi.

ADAIR, JAMES

Geschichte der Amerikanischen Indianer; besonders der am Missisippi, an Ost-und Westflorida, Georgien, Süd-und Nord-Karolina und Virginien angrenzenden nationen, nebst einem anhange, von James Adair, Esquire. Aus dem Englischen übersetzt [von S.H. Ewald]. *Breslau, J.E. Meyer, 1782.*   [673]

[8], 419, [1] p., 8vo. (21.5 cm.). DLC, NN, PPL-R, RPJCB.

CRÈVECOEUR, MICHEL-GUILLAUME SAINT-JEAN DE

Letters | from an | American farmer; | describing | certain provincial situations, | manners, and customs, | not generally known; | and conveying | some idea of the late and present | interior circumstances | of the | British Colonies | in | North America. | [rule] | Written for the information of a friend | in England, | By J. Hector St. John, | a farmer in Pennsylvania. | [thick-thin rule] | *London, | Printed for Thomas Davies in Russell Street Covent- | Garden, and Lockyer Davis in Holborn. | M DCC LXXXII.*   [674]

[16], 318, [2] p., 2 folded maps, 8vo. (20 x 13 cm.). Sabin 17496. DLC, MB, MH, NHi, NN, RPJCB, etc.

Maps: *Map of | the | Island | of | Nantucket; Map | of the Island of | Martha's Vineyard | with | its dependencies.*

First edition, containing twelve letters. The author's farm was not in Pennsylvania but at Pine Hill, between Chester and Blooming Grove, Orange County, New York. This volume was more widely read in England and Europe and had a greater influence in attracting its readers to America than any other book of the period. Though not written for the promotion of American lands, it was frequently quoted by others for that purpose.

.   .   .   .   .

Letters | from an | American farmer; | . . . | *Dublin:* | *Printed by John Exshaw, in Grafton* | *Street, near Suffolk Street.* | *1782.*   [675]

[8], 256 p., 2 maps, 12mo. Sabin 17496. DLC, MB, RPJCB.

[GALE, BENJAMIN]

Brief, decent, but free remarks, and observations, on several laws passed by the Honorable Legislature of the State of Connecticut, since the year 1775. By a friend to his country. [2 lines quoted] *Hartford: Printed by Hudson & Goodwin. M,DCC,LXXXII.*   [676]

55 p., 8vo. Evans 17543. DLC, NN.

An anti-Susquehannah Company controversial tract.

HANSON, ELIZABETH

An account of the captivity of Elizabeth Hanson, . . . A new edition. . . . *London: Printed and sold by James Phillips, George-Yard, Lombard-Street, 1782.*   [677]

26, [2] p., 12mo. (15.8 x 9.5 cm.). Sabin 30265. CSmH, F.C. Deering, DLC, ICN, MWA, N, OClWHi, PBL, PHi, RPJCB.

[KIMBER, EDWARD]

The history of the life and adventures of Mr. Anderson. Containing his strange varieties of fortune in Europe and America. Compiled from his own papers . . . *Berwick, Printed for W. Phorson; and B. Law, London, 1782.*   [678]

243 p., 12mo. (17.5 cm.). Sabin 1380. DLC, MiU-C, NN, RPJCB.

Sabin mentions a frontispiece not in DLC cat. NN has an undated London edition, [1780?-1800?].

MOODY, JAMES

Lieutenant James Moody's narrative of his exertions and sufferings in the cause of government, since the year 1776. *London, Printed in the year 1782.*   [679]

59 p., 8vo. Sabin 50309. DLC, MWA, PBL, RPJCB.

Narrative of a New Jersey Tory farmer, officer of Skinner's New Jersey Tory Brigade, who served in the British army as spy, ranger and scout from 1776 to 1782. For other British spy narratives, see under Thomas Gage, 1775, no. 645.

For second edition, see under 1782.

[SPANGENBERG, AUGUST GOTTLIEB]

Von | der Arbeit | der | Evangelischen Brüder | unter | den Heiden. | *Barby,* | *bey Christian Friedrich Laur.* | *1782.*   [680]
168 p., 8vo. Sabin 88934. DLC.

For an English translation, see *An account of the manner,* 1788.

CRÈVECOEUR, MICHEL-GUILLAUME SAINT-JEAN DE

Letters | from an |American farmer: | . . . | A new edition, with an accurate index. | [thick-thin rule] | *Printed for Thomas Davies, in Russell-Street, Covent-* | *Garden; and Lockyer Davis, in Holborn.* | *M.DCC.-LXXXIII.*   [681]
[16], 326, [2] p., 2 folded maps as in 1st ed., 8vo. (21.5 x 13 cm.). DLC, MBAt, MH, NHi, NN, RPJCB, etc.

.   .   .   .   .

Letters | from an | American farmer; | . . . | *Belfast:* | *Printed by James Magee, at the Bible* | *and Crown, No 9, Bridge-Street.* | *M,DCC,LXXXIII.*
                                                                          [682]
[8], 208 p., 2 folded maps as in 1st ed., 12mo. (17.2 x 10 cm.). DLC, NHi.

KELLET, ALEXANDER

The | mental novelist, | and | amusing companion, | a collection of | histories, essays, & novels: | Containing | [contents in two columns] | With many other curious literary productions | of | Alexander Kellet, Esq. | *London:* | *Printed for W. Lane, Leadenhall-Street.* | *1783.*   [683]
[4], 283 p., 16mo. (16 x 9.5 cm.). Sabin 37252. BM, DLC, NHi, RPJCB.

Second edition of his: *A pocket of prose and verse,* 1778.

Contents includes: "Unheard of sufferings of David Menzies amongst the Cherokees, and his surprizing deliverance."

KNIGHT, JOHN, AND JOHN SLOVER

Narratives | of a late | expedition | against the | Indians; | with | an account of the barbarous | execution of Col. [William] Crawford; | and | the wonderful escape of Dr. [John] Knight and | John Slover from captivity, in 1782. | *Philadelphia:* | *Printed by Francis Bailey, in Market Street.* | *M,DCC,LXX[X]III.*   [684]
38 p., 12mo. (15 x 9.5 cm.). Sabin 38109, Evans 17993, Hildeburn 4262, Thomson's Ohio 682, Heartman: Brackenridge bibliography 12. Everett D. Graff (2d), MWA (title photostat), PPiU (1st), PU (2d).

There are two variants of this first edition, one with a figure X accidentally omitted from the imprint date, making the date read *M,DCC,LXXIII* (unique PPiU copy) and the other with the date corrected to read *M,DCC,LXXXIII*. (other recorded copies except MWA which has a photostat title and so cannot be identified as to state).

In his letter to the publisher, Hugh Henry Brackenridge, the editor, says of the two narratives: "That of Dr. Knight was written by himself at my request; that of Slover was taken by myself from his mouth as he related it . . . though perfectly sensible and intelligent, yet he cannot write."

These narratives were first published in the [Philadelphia] *Freeman's Journal*, Francis Bailey, editor, April 30-May 21, 1783, eleven files of which, containing these issues, are recorded by Brigham. The Knight journal (alone) appeared in the *New Haven Gazette* in 1788.

Dr. John Knight and John Slover were members of Colonel William Crawford's expedition against the Ohio Indians in the Spring of 1782. On June 5 while near the Indian town of Sandusky, Colonel Crawford decided to retreat, being heavily outnumbered. His men, fearing an immediate attack, broke and fled. Some were killed and a number captured, including Crawford, Knight and Slover. Knight saw and described Crawford's death at the stake and expected the same fate but escaped from his Indian guard and made his way to Fort McIntosh (present Beaver, Pa.). John Slover, captured the third day after the retreat began, was trying to reach Detroit when captured and taken to the chief town of the Shawnese. He was tied to a stake and a fire kindled but a rain storm put out the fire and his torture was postponed until the next day. In the night he untied himself, eluded his three guards, stole a horse and escaped and finally reached Wheeling. He had been previously captured at the age of eight and had lived twelve years among the Indians whose languages he understood. These two narratives are among the most interesting and important of the period.

MOODY, JAMES

Lieut. James Moody's narrative of his exertions and sufferings in the cause of the government, since the year 1776; authenticated by proper certificates. The second edition. *London: Richardson & Urquhart. MDCCLXXXIII.*
[685]
[2], 57, [7] p., 8vo. Sabin 50310. CSmH, DLC, MiU-C, RPJCB.

Second and best edition with new material of Revolutionary British spy narrative.

For modern reprints, see Sabin.

WILLIAMS, JOHN

Good fetch'd out of evil, | in | three short essays. | I. A pastoral letter, of | Mr. John Williams, | the faithful and worthy pastor of Deerfield; now detain'd a | captive in Canada; written to part of his flock, and some | others, returning out of their captivity. | II. The conduct and constancy of the New-

English captives, when | strongly tempted unto the Popish idolatries. And certain plain | poems, written by some of them, to fortify their children a- | gainst such temptations. | III. An account of most remarkable and memorable deliverances, | received by many of the captives; and great things done by | their Almighty deliverer for them. | [rule] | Collected and published, [by Cotton Mather] | that the glorious God may have the glory of his | power and goodness; and that his people may | reap some advantage from what has befallen | their brethren. | [double rule] | *[n.p.] Printed in the year M,DCC,LXXXIII.*   [686]

34 p., 4to. (19.5 x 13.5 cm.). Holmes: Bibliography of Cotton Mather 150 B, Sabin 104261. MWA (lacks half title). NHi (uncut but last leaf defective), ViU.

Second edition. For contents, see first edition, 1706.

CARVER, JONATHAN

Three years travels. *Philadelphia, 1784.* RPJCB, etc.   [687]

. . . . . .

Voyage. *Paris, 1784.* DLC, etc.   [688]

. . . . . .

Voyage. *Yverdon, 1784.*   [689]
See note at end of 1798 edition.

CRÈVECOEUR, MICHEL-GUILLAUME SAINT-JEAN DE

Sittliche Schilderungen | von | Amerika, | in Briefen | eines | Amerikanischen Guthsbesitzers | an | einen Freund in England. | Von | J. Hektor St. John. | . . . | Aus dem Englischen. | . . . | *Liegnitz und Leipzig,* | *bey David Siegert, 1784.*   [690]

10, 462 p., 2 maps, 12mo. Sabin 17500. DLC, NN, RPJCB.

. . . . . .

Brieven | van eenen | Amerikaenschen | Landman | van Carlisle in Pennsijlvaniën, | Geschreven aen eenen zijner vrienden in | Engeland; | behelzende | den toestand, zeden, landbouw, en ge- | woonten der inwoonders van eenige | der nu vereenigde dertien gewes- | ten van Noord Amerika, voor | en in den nu geëindigden | oorlog. | Uit het Engelsch. | . . . | *Te Leyden,* | *Bij L. Herdingh,* | *1784.*   [691]

xvi, 328 p. Translation attributed to Francis Adriaan Van der Kemp. Sabin 17499. DLC, RPJCB.

. . . . . .

Lettres | d'un | Cultivateur | Américain, | écrites à W.S. Ecuyer, | depuis l'année 1770, jusqu'à 1781. | Traduites de l'Anglois par ***. | Tome premier [second]. | [orn.] | *A Paris,* | *Chez Cuchet, Libraire, rue & hôtel Serpente.* | [thick-thin rule] | *M. DCC. LXXXIV.* [692]

2 vols., xxiv, iii, [iv], 422, [2]; [4], iv, 400, [2] p., 8vo. (19.5 x 13 cm.). Sabin 17494. Translated by the author. DLC, MB, MH, NHi, NN, RPJCB.

Contains much new material not in 1st ed.

. . . . .

Same imprint and date, xxiv, 422, [2]; iv, 392 p., 8vo. Ornaments differ. Howard C. Rice. [693]

FILSON, JOHN

The | discovery, settlement | and present state of | Kentucke: | and | an essay towards the topography, | and natural history of that im- | portant country: | To which is added, | an appendix, | containing, | I. The adventures of Col. Daniel Boon, one | of the first settlers, comprehending every im- | portant occurrence in the political history of | that province. | II. The minutes of the Piankashaw coun- | cil, held at Post St. Vincents, April 15, 1784. | III. An account of the Indian nations in- | habiting within the limits of the thirteen U- | nited States, their manners and customs, and | reflections on their origin. | IV. The stages and distances between | Philadelphia and the Falls of the Ohio; from | Pittsburg to Pensacola and several other places. | - The whole illustrated by a new and accu- | rate map of Kentucke and the country ad- | joining, drawn from actual surveys. | [rule] | By John Filson. | [rule] | *Wilmington, Printed by James Adams, 1784.* [694]

118 p., folded map, 8vo. (21.5 x 14 cm.). Sabin 24336, Church 1202, Evans 18467. Copies without the map in most large libraries.

Folded map: *This map | of | Kentucke, | drawn from actual observations, | is inscribed with the most perfect respect | to the Honorable the Congress of the | United States of America; and | to his Excellcy. George Washington | late Commander in Chief of their | army. By their | Humble Servant, | John Filson* | [Title in upper left corner within Chippendale border] [Imprint in lower margin below the map:] *Philada. Engrav'd by Henry D. Pursell, & Printed by T. Rook, for the Author 1784* [Date not on 1st issue] (51 x 44.5 cm.). See Stauffer I:216; Fielding 1239; P.L. Phillips: *The first map of Kentucky,* 1908, 22 p., folded map, 4to.; Lawrence Martin in W.R. Jillson's ed. of *Filson's Kentucke,* 1929, p. 169-178; same revised, in W.R. Jillson's *Kentuckie Country,* 1931, p. 45-59; Wroth and Adams: *American wood engraving,* 53; R.C.B. Thruston: *Filson's history and map of Kentucky,* in *Filson Club Historical Quarterly,* Jan., 1934, p. 1-38, illus., maps.

Thruston identifies six issues of the map. Copies of 1st ed. with map are located as follows, with issues of the map indicated when known: BM (3); CSmH (4); DLC (2); E.D. Graff (3); KyLoF (5 imp., 6); MBAt (no map but Filson's dedication copy to George Washington with the latter's signature on title); MH (6); MiU-C (4); MWA; NHi (6); PHi (4); PP (5 Presentation copy from Filson to Daniel Boone); RPJCB (6); Archivo Historico Nacional, Madrid (4); Colonial Office, London (4); F.C. Deering (only known copy of 1st state without date in imprint); A.S.W. Rosenbach (3).

See also separate editions of Boone's *Adventures,* 1786, etc.

The most famous and important frontier book of the period, by a frontiersman who was later killed by the Indians. Particularly important for its first map of Kentucky and its first published life of Daniel Boone. W.R. Jillson, in his reprint of the book, says of its author: "He saved Boone from an oblivion that has all but swallowed up Harrod and many others, and has left to posterity a priceless tale of early days in Kentucky, which, for stirring action and regional description, has rarely been equaled as a piece of frontier writing in any part of this country, and never surpassed." For an abbreviated plagiarized edition using the original Filson map, see under Alexander Fitzroy's *Discovery,* 1786.

Among his many adventures, Boone tells how he and John Stewart were captured by the Indians in 1769 while he was on his first exploration of Kentucky and how, a week later, they escaped while their captors slept. He tells of the capture of his daughter and the two daughters of Colonel Calaway near the fort at Boonsborough in 1776 and how he and eight men followed their captors and, two days later, recovered the girls and killed two of the Indians. Boone was again captured in 1778 near the Blue Licks, with his party of 27 men who were turned over to the British. But the Indians wished to adopt Boone whom they greatly admired and so took him to their town at Chelicothe where he remained for five months. Overhearing the Indians planning an attack on Boonsborough, he escaped at night, travelled the 160 miles to his home in five days with but one meal during the trip and got there in time to warn the settlement and help drive off the Indians.

[FRANKLIN, BENJAMIN]

[Type ornaments in double ruled frame] | Information | to those | who would remove | to America. | [Caption title] *[Passy: Benjamin Franklin, 1784].*   [695]

12 p., 12mo. (15.5 x 10.5 cm.). CtY.

Described from L.S. Livingston: *Franklin and his press at Passy,* 1914, p. 43.

"I am pestered continually with numbers of letters from people in different parts of Europe, who would go to settle in America, but who manifest very extravagant expectations, such as I can by no means encourage, and who appear otherwise to be very improper persons. To save myself trouble, I have just printed some copies of the enclosed little piece, which I purpose to send hereafter in answer to such letters." Franklin to Charles Thomson, President of Congress, March 9, 1784.

. . . . .

Avis | a ceux | qui voudraient s'en aller | en Amerique | [floral orn.] | [rule] | M, DCC, LXXXIV. | *[Passy: Benjamin Franklin, 1784].*   [696]
15 p., 12mo. (15.5 x 10.5 cm.). BM.
First French edition, described from Livingston, p. 44.

. . . . .

[Ornaments] | Remarks | concerning the savages | of North-America. | [rule] | [Caption title] *[Passy: Benjamin Franklin, 1784].*   [697]
8 p., 12mo. (15.5 x 10.5 cm.).
Described from Livingston, p. 49.

. . . . .

Remarques | sur la politesse | des sauvages | de l'Amerique Septentrionale. | *[Passy: Benjamin Franklin, 1784].*   [698]
16 p., 12mo. (15.5 x 10.5 cm.).
Described from Livingston, p. 49. The English editions of these two tracts were reprinted as:

. . . . .

Two tracts: | Information | to those | who would remove to | America | And, | Remarks | concerning the | savages of North America | By | Dr. Benjamin Franklin. | *London:* | *Printed for John Stockdale, opposite* | *Burlington-House,* | *Piccadilly.* | *MDCCLXXXIV.*   [699]
39, [1] p., 8vo. Sabin 25594. DLC, MB, NHi, PPAmP, RPJCB, etc.

. . . . .

Second edition, same imprint, date and collation. DLC, etc.   [700]

. . . . .

Third edition, same imprint, date and collation. DLC, etc.   [701]

. . . . .

Dublin: | *Printed for L. White, No. 86, Dame-street,* | *MDCCLXXXIV.*
[702]
40 p., 8vo. MWA, MWiW-C, etc. Same in Italian, 1775.

GATENBY, WILLIAM

A full and particular account, of the sufferings of William Gatenby; who is just arrived from America, With a true account of many circumstances relating to this unfortunate war, by which some hundreds of poor families are brought to utter ruin and destruction, to which himself and family have fallen victims. He gives an account of being attacked by the Indians from the back settlements, who took his wife and child by force away, and killed his two slaves. How he and others pursued them, retook his wife and child, and killed three of the savages. *[London] Printed in 1784.* [703]

8 p., 16mo. NN.

Mr. Julian Boyd believes that this is plagarized from the Peter Williamson captivity.

HILLIARD D'AUBERTEUIL, MICHEL RENÉ

Mis Mac Rea, | Roman | Historique, | Par M. Hilliard-D'Auberteuil. | *A Philadelphie.* [i.e., *Bruxelles].* | *M.DCC.LXXXIV.* [704]

xii, 146 p., 12mo. Sabin 31904, Hildeburn 4489. Bib. Nat., BM (imp.), CSmH, DLC, ICN, IU, MiU-C, MWiW-C, NN, RPJCB.

Hildeburn supplies [Paris] as place of publication.

A tale founded on the story of the Indian murder of Jane McCrea.

HUTCHINS, THOMAS

An | historical narrative | and | topographical description | of | Louisiana, | and | West-Florida, | comprehending the | River Mississippi with its principal branches | and settlements, and the Rivers Pearl, | Pascagoula, Mobille, Perdido, | Escambia, Chacta-Hatcha, &c. | The | climate, soil, and produce | whether | animal, vegetable, or mineral; | with | directions for sailing into all the bays, lakes, harbours and rivers on | the North side of the Gulf of Mexico, and for navigating between the | islands situated along that coast, and ascending the Mississippi River. | By Thomas Hutchins, | Geographer to the United States. | *Philadelphia:* | *Printed for the author,* *and sold by Robert* | *Aitken, near the Coffee-House, in* | *Market-street.* | *M,DCC,LXXXIV.* [705]

94, [1] p., 8vo. (21 x 13 cm.). Sabin 34056, Evans 18532. Copies in most large libraries.

Reprinted in the third edition of Imlay's *Topographical description,* 1797.

Bound with but not a part of the NHi copy is the following broadside:

．　．　．　．　．

Proposals | for publishing by subscription, | a map | of the coast of West-Florida, including its bays and lakes, | with the course of the Mississippi, from the junction of the Akansa | River, to it's entrance into the Gulf of Mexico. | . . . | By Thomas Hutchins, . . . has determined the author to fix the price of the map and pamphlet at three | Spanish dollars . . . | Mr. Robert Aitken, near the Coffee House in Market Street, is authorized to | receive the subscription money. | *Philadelphia, October 15th, 1781.* | [Signed with pen and ink: Tho: Hutchins] [706]

Broadside, folio (34 x 20.5 cm.). NHi.

This broadside shows that the author intended his *Historical narrative* to serve as explanatory text for *a map of the coast of West Florida,* the two to be sold together for $3.00, but we have located no such map and it is not mentioned with Hutchins' other works in the reprint of his *Topographical description of Virginia* . . . , edited by F.C. Hicks, Cleveland, 1904.

A clipping from an unidentified Philadelphia newspaper of May, 1784, advertises as "this day is published" the *Historical narrative* and says: "Such gentlemen who have subscribed for the map of West-Florida, are desired to call on Mr. Aitken, who will furnish the above pamphlet." This shows that the pamphlet was issued separately and not with the map as planned in the 1781 prospectus.

Mr. Burton W. Adkinson, Chief, Division of Maps, Library of Congress, reports that his collection does not contain this map though they have several copies of the pamphlet. He says further: "The only information we have that indicates such a map was published is from the Belknap Papers. On p. 53, Volume 2, he states, 'I also should be very glad to have Hutchin's map and description of Florida.' A bit farther on in the same volume (page 57) he notes, 'I have his [Hutchins] map and pamphlet containing a description of Florida.'"

[VAN CAMPEN, MOSES]

A narrative of the capture of certain Americans at Westmorland, by savages; and the perilous escape which they effected, by surprizing specimens of policy and heroism. To which is subjoined, some account of the religion, government, customs, and manners of the aborigines of North America. *New-London: Printed by T. Green. 1784.* [707]

16 p., 8vo. Evans 18850, Sabin 91798, Trumbull 1134. F.C. Deering, MHi.

Second edition. Title from Evans.

. . . . .

Same, as: *A narrative of the Pennsylvania frontier. The following narrative sent last winter to Congress, accompanied by a petition for a pension* . . . [for Van Campen] *Washington: Army and Navy Chronicle, 1838.* [708]

10 p., 16mo. Sabin 98428. DLC.

. . . . .

Same as above, in Waldie's Octavo Library, vol. VI. Phil., August 21, 1838, no. 8. [709]

4 p., 8vo., double column on salmon paper.

For Van Campen's application for a pension, see Senate and House reports and documents, 24th, 25th and 30th Congresses.

For a greatly enlarged narrative of Van Campen's adventures, see next four entries.

. . . . .

Sketches | of the | life and adventures | of | Moses Van Campen: | a surviving officer | of the | army of the Revolution. | [rule] | By his grand-son, | John Niles Hubbard, A.B. | [rule] | *Dansville, N.Y.* | *Printed by* | *George W. Stevens.* | *1841.*   [710]

310 p., 12mo. (20.5 x 12 cm.). Ayer 138. F.C. Deering, ICN, MWA, N, NRU.

First edition with copyright notice only on verso of title.

. . . . .

Sketches | of | border adventures, | in | the life and times of | Major Moses Van Campen, | a surviving soldier of the Revolution. | [rule] | By his grandson, | John N. Hubbard, A.B. | [rule] | *Bath, N.Y.:* | *R.L. Under-hill & Co.* | *1841.*   [711]

310 p., 12mo. F.C.Deering, MWA, N.

From the same setting of type as the first edition, with a new title leaf. Verso of title contains copyright notice and imprint: *Printed by George W. Stevens, Dansville, N.Y.* Underhill was a bookseller and publisher but had no press.

. . . . .

Same title and imprint, 1842.   [712]

310 p., 12mo. Sabin 33436, Ayer 139. DLC, F.C. Deering, ICN, MWA, N (both issues), NGH, NN, NRU, OClWHi, OFH, etc.

First issue: From the same setting of type as Dansville, 1841 edition, except for slight changes such as last word on p. 11: *benevo-* in Dansville edition, *benev-* in both issues of Bath, 1842 edition. This 1st issue, as well as the Dansville edition, has open face type in caption title on first page of text.

Second issue: Same title leaf as 1st issue but worn type. Preface and text reset, with many variations, including: different allignment on p. 1-23, 73-77. P. 191 has *Henlock* (for Hemlock Lake), whereas 1st issue has *Henlock's* as in Dansville edition. Last line of p. 72 of 2d issue inserted in error, this line being correctly placed in fourth line of p. 73, thus throwing allignment off for p. 73-77.

The NN copy, from the library of Dr. William Henry Egle, Anderson Auction Co. sale 607, Dec. 12, 1907, no. 157, has inserted the original manuscript petition of Moses Vancamp[en] to the Executive Council of Pennsylvania in 1780, reciting his story of captivity and escape from the Indians in that year and asking for the payment of a bounty on the two Indian scalps which he took at the time. It is endorsed by 20 of his friends who were familiar with the circumstances as recited in the petition.

Reprinted in: *The Rose, a Monthly Journal. Bath, N.Y., 1844.* F.C. Deering.

. . . . .

Sketches of border adventures in the life and times of Major Moses Vancampen. By his grandson J. Niles Hubbard, author of Red Jacket and His People. Edition of 1842 revised and enlarged by John S. Minard, who supplements Mr. Hubbard's work, with several chapters devoted to his later years; also treating of him as the surveyor, public official and prominent citizen. Concluding with a biographical sketch of the late Judge Phillip Church. Illustrated. *Published by Jno. S. Minard, Fillmore, N.Y. 1893.*
[713]

xxii, 337 p., 9 plates, 1 facsim., 12mo. (18.2 x 12 cm.). Ayer 140. Copies in most large libraries.

[VARLO, CHARLES]

Conditions for letting or selling, | Lord Earl Palatine of Albion's estate, New | Albion, in America. . . . *[London: Mr. Reynell's Printing-Office, No. 21, Piccadilly, near the Hay-Market, 1784?].*
[714]
Broadside, 8vo. (23 x 13 cm.). Sabin 98631 and 98637 note, Church 1209. CSmH.

The CSmH copy is bound with Varlo's *A true copy,* which see. Supposititious imprint from Varlo's broadside: *The finest part of America,* which see.

. . . . .

Earl of Albion's proclamation appointing Charles Varlo, Esq., his agent for New Albion. *[n.p., ca. 1784].*
[715]
1 leaf, folio. Title from Sabin 52434. DLC.

. . . . .

The finest part of America. | [rule] | To be sold, or lett, | from eight hundred to four thousand acres, in a farm, | all that entire estate, called | Long Island, in New Albion, | lying near New York: | belonging to the Earl Palatine of Albion, | granted to | his predecessor, Earl Palatine of Albion, | by King Charles the First. | [etc., 16 lines] | [hand] Letters (post paid) signed with real names, directed for F.P. at | Mr. Reynell's Printing-Office, No. 21, Piccadilly, near the Hay-Market, | will be answered, and the writer directed where he may be treated with, | relative to the conditions of sale, charter, title deeds, a map, with the | farms allotted thereon, &c. &c. | Just published, and may be had as above, (Price one shilling) | A true copy of the above charter, | with the conditions of letting, or selling the land, | and other articles relating thereto. | *[London: Mr. Reynell's Printing-Office, No. 21, Piccadilly, near the Hay-Market, 1784?].*
[716]
Broadside, 8vo. (23 x 13 cm.). Sabin 24365 and 98637 note, Church 1209. CSmH.

The CSmH copy is bound with Varlo's *A true copy*, which see.

.   .   .   .   .

. . . A true copy of the grant of King | Charles the First, to Sir Edmund Plowden, | Earl Palatine of Albion, of the Province | of New Albion, in America. | [Caption title with heading: *Chapter I.*] *[London: Mr. Reynell's Printing-Office, No. 21, Piccadilly, near the Hay-Market, 1784?].*   [717]

[3]-30 p., 8vo. (23 x 13 cm.). Sabin 98637, Church 1209. CSmH, DLC, MBAt, NN, PHi.

The CSmH copy has the two broadsides: *The finest part of America* and *Conditions for letting and selling* bound in preceding the *True copy*. The MBAt copy belonged to George Washington. The NN copy is in original bluish gray wrappers uncut. Suppositious imprint from Varlo's broadside: *The finest part of America*, which see.

See note under John Evelin's *A direction for adventurers*, no. 97, and in Church 1209.

[WALTON, WILLIAM]

A | narrative | of the | captivity | and | sufferings | of | Benjamin Gilbert | and his | family; | who were surprised by the Indians, and taken from | their farms, on the frontiers of Pennsylvania, | in the Spring, 1780. | [rule] | *Philadelphia:* | *Printed and sold by Joseph Crukshank, in Market-Street,* | *between Second and Third-Streets.* | [rule] | *M DCC LXXXIV.*   [718]

96 p., 8vo. (20 x 12.5 cm.). Sabin 27348, Evans 18497, Ayer 301. CSmH, DLC, F.C. Deering, ICN, MB, MH, MWA, MWiW-C, N, NHi, NN, PHi, RPJCB, etc.

First edition. Related by the Gilbert family to William Walton, Benjamin Gilbert's brother-in-law.

Benjamin Gilbert, a well-to-do Quaker farmer and miller, lived at Mahoning Creek, Penn township, Northampton County, Pennsylvania when, on June 25, 1780, a party of eleven Seneca Indians led by Rowland and John Montour, sons of the famous Catharine Montour, captured the Gilbert family of fourteen and a girl who happened to be at the mill. They were taken to Fort Niagara, divided among the Indians and scattered. Benjamin Gilbert, aged 69, and his wife were at once redeemed by Colonel Guy Johnson who, with Colonel Butler, Captain Powel and other British officers at the fort, were very kind to them. Jesse Gilbert, a son, and his wife were soon redeemed and with the parents sent to Montreal. Benjamin died in a boat while descending the St. Lawrence, was taken ashore and buried. The others were kindly treated at Montreal. The rest of the family was redeemed by degrees at Fort Niagara and sent to Montreal and finally returned to Pennsylvania November 28, 1782. Extremely valuable for its account of Indian life.

WASHINGTON, GEORGE

Mount-Vernon, April 2, 1784. The subscriber would lease about 30,000 acres of land on the Ohio and Great Kanhawa, for which he has had patents ten or twelve years [Caption title] [Colophon:] *Alexandria: Printed by G. Richards, and Company. [1784].*   [719]
    Folio broadside signed: *G. Washington.* Sabin 101745. NN.
    See Roy Bird Cook's *Washington's Western lands,* 1930, p. 123.

[CHETWOOD, W.R.]

The voyages, dangerous adventures and imminent escapes of Captain Richard Falconer . . . *Manchester: J. Imison, 1785.*   [720]
    Sabin 23723.

. . . . . .

London: S. Fisher, [1801].   [721]
    Ayer 95. ICN, ViU.

. . . . . .

1838.   [722]
    Sabin 23723 note.

[COLLES, CHRISTOPHER]

Proposals | for the speedy | settlement | of the | waste and unappropriated | lands | on the western frontiers of the State | of New-York, and for the im- | provement of the inland navigation | between Albany and Oswego. | [rule] | *New-York:* | *Printed by Samuel Loudon, at his Printing-* | *Office, No. 5, Water-Street, 1785.*   [723]
    14 p., 8vo. (19.5 x 12 cm.). Evans 18960, Sabin 14410. MWA, NHi.
    Signed at end: Christopher Colles. | New-York, Lower-Battery, No. 2.
    Colles was the first to propose what was later the Erie Canal.

CRÈVECOEUR, MICHEL-GUILLAUME SAINT-JEAN DE

Lettres | d'un | Cultivateur | . . . | *A Maestricht,* | *Chez J.E. Dufour & Phil. Roux,* | *Imprimeurs-Libraires associés.* | . . . | *1785.*   [724]
    2 vols., xxiv, 458; 432 p., 12mo. Sabin 17494. DLC, MH.

. . . . . .

Lettres d'un | Cultivateur | . . . | *[n.p.]* | *1785.*   [725]
    2 vols., xxiv, 422, [2]; 400, [2] p., 12mo. MB.

FILSON, JOHN

Histoire | de Kentucke, | nouvelle colonie | a l'ouest de la Virginie: |

contenant, | 1°. La découverte, l'acquisition, l'établissement, la | description topographique, l'histoire naturelle, &c. | du territoire: 2°. la Relation historique du Colonel | Boon, un des premiers colons, sur les guerres contre | les naturels: 3°. l'assemblée des Piankashaws au | Poste Saint Vincent: 4°. un exposé succinct des na- | tions Indiennes qui habitent dans les limites des | Treize États-Unis, de leurs moeurs & coutumes, & | des réflexions sur leur origine; & autres pièces: | Avec une carte. | Ouvrage pour servir de suite aux Lettres d'un | Cultivateur Américain. | Traduit de l'Anglois, de M. John Filson; | par M. Parraud, | de l'Académie des Arcades de Rome. | .[orn.] | *A Paris,* | *Chez Buisson, Libraire, Hôtel de Mesgrigny,* | *rue des Poitevins, No. 13.* | [double rule] | *M. DCC. LXXXV.* | *Avec approbation et permission.*   [726]

[4], xvj, 234 p., folded map and plate. 8vo. (21.3 x 13.8 cm.). Sabin 24338, Church 1212. BM, CSmH, MBAt, MH, NHi, NjP, NN, RPJCB, etc.

Folded map: *Carte de Kentucke,* | *d'après les observations actuelles;* | : . . | *André sculp.* (34.7 x 32 cm.).

First French edition of Filson's Kentucky.

Franklin, Benjamin

Observazione | a chiunque dersideri passare in | America; | e Riflessioni | circa i Salvaggi dell' America settentrionale | del Dre. Franklin | Dall' originale Inglese regate | in Lingua Italiano | da Pietro Antoricutti. | *In Padova MDCCLXXXV* | *Per Gio: Antonio Conzatti, A.S. Fermo.* | *Con Lic. de' Superiori.*   [727]

38, [1] p., 12mo. (19 cm.). Ford 371. DLC.

The *Advice* was published in German as: *Bericht für Diejenigen, Hamburg, 1786* (Ford 350); the *Remarks* in *Birmingham 1784* (Ford 365) DLC; and both separate tracts as well as *Two tracts* appeared separately and in other works during the 18th century and later, for which see Livingston, Ford's Franklin bibliography, Sabin, DLC catalog, etc.

[Jefferson, Thomas]

Notes on the state of Virginia; | written in the year 1781, somewhat cor- | rected and enlarged in the winter of 1782, | for the use of a Foreigner of distinction, in | answer to certain queries proposed by him | respecting | [contents, 23 lines] | [filet] | MDCCLXXXII. [Date of composition. *Printed at Paris, May 10, 1785*].   [728]

[2], 391 p., 1 illus., tables, 8vo. (19.5 x 12.5 cm.). Sabin 35894, Church 1189. CSmH, CtHWatk, DLC, ICN, MB, MH, MH-BA, MiU-C, MWiW-C, NHi, NjP, NN (2), PHi, PPAmP, RPJCB, J.H. Scheide, Vi, ViU, etc.

Folded table of locations of Indian tribes; plate of Madison's cave.

Some late copies have pp. 52-53 cancelled and new text substituted for

Jefferson's former theory on the formation of marine shells on mountain tops. Some copies have one, two or three appendices added at end, in the following order:

Draught | of a | fundamental constitution | for the | Commonwealth of Virginia. | [Caption title] [Paris, 1786]. 14 p. CSmH, DLC, NN, etc.

Notes | on the | establishment | of a | money unit, | and of a | coinage for the United States. | [Caption title] [Paris, 1786]. 14 p. DCL, NN, etc.

An act for establishing religious freedom, | passed in the assembly of Virginia in the beginning | of the year 1786. | [Caption title] [Paris, 1786]. 4 p. DLC, NN, etc.

Nearly all, if not all, copies of this privately printed first edition contain presentation inscriptions from the author.

The proof sheets with author's corrections were destroyed in the New York State Library fire in 1911.

KAYADEROSSERAS PATENT

1785. | Verkoop | van de onderstaande onbebouwde | Loten Landen | in de Patent van | Kayadarosseras, | in de County van Albany, New-York, viz. | [Caption title] [Colophon:] *Philadelphia: Gedrukt by F. Bailey, aan de Zuidy van Market-Straat, het Huis 6de Oostzy van de 4de Straat.* | *[1785]* [Title within ornamental border].   [729]

Broadside, folio (42.5 x 30 cm.). Sabin 98989. NHi.

In the NHi copy the date 1785 has been altered with a pen, in a contemporary hand, to read 1786 and the name of the agent, *Major George Turner,* has been crossed out and that of *Beriah Palmer, Ballston* substituted in ink.

An advertisement in Dutch for lands near Eava's Kill, Schenectady, Ballstown, Fort Edward, along the Hudson, Sacondago River, etc.

MARRANT, JOHN

A | narrative | of the | Lord's wonderful dealings | with | John Marrant, | a Black, | (Now going to preach the Gospel in Nova-Scotia) | Born in New-York, in North-America. | [rule] | Taken down from his own relation, | arranged, corrected, and published | by the Rev. Mr. [William] Aldridge. | [rule, 4 lines quoted, rule] | *London:* | *Printed by Gilbert and Plummer, No. 13, Cree-* | *Church-Lane, 1785;* | *and sold at the Chapel in Jewry-Street. - Price 6d.*   [730]

38 p., 8vo. (18.5 x 12 cm.). Ayer 7. F.C. Deering, ICN.

John Marrant was born in New York, June 15, 1755, his father died when he was four, his mother removed to St. Augustine, Florida, where they lived a year and a half and removed to Georgia. At the age of eleven, young Marrant was sent to Charleston, S.C. to learn a trade. He learned to play the violin and French horn and spent his time playing for dances, etc. When about fourteen, he was converted by George Whitefield, became a religious fanatic and his family believed him insane. In that mood he left home and strayed through the forest for some days, when he was captured (or rescued) by an Indian hunter who took him to a Cherokee village where he was about to be executed when he began to pray in the Cherokee language and as a result was taken before their "king" whom he converted. He remained with the Indians several months, then returned home until the outbreak of the Revolution when he was pressed into the British naval service and was at the surrender of Charleston where he again met his old friend the Creek chief. The book is mainly the story of a religious fanatic and says little about the Indians. It was one of the first American books by a Negro and was one of the three most popular stories of Indian captivity, the others being those of Peter Williamson, 1757 (our no. 521) and Mary Jemison, 1824.

. . . . .

The second edition, with notes explanatory, same imprint and collation, 1785. Sabin 44679, Porter 180. BM, DLC, MB, NN, RPJCB.   [731]

. . . . .

The third edition, with notes explanatory, same imprint and collation, 1785. Porter 181. NHi.   [732]

. . . . .

The fourth edition, with additions and notes explanatory, same imprint, 1785. 40 p. Porter 183. CtY, F.C. Deering, NN.   [733]

. . . . .

The fourth edition, enlarged by Mr. Marrant, and printed (with permission) for his sole benefit, with notes explanatory . . . London: Printed for the author, by R. Hawes . . . [1785].   [734]
40 p., 8vo. Porter 182. CtY, MB, NN.

. . . . .

The fifth edition, with additions and notes explanatory. [London? 1785?].
                                                                                      [735]
26 p., 4to. Porter 184. NN.

For these and some of the later editions, see Mrs. Dorothy B. Porter's Early American Negro writings; a bibliographical study, in Bibliographical Society of America Papers, vol. 39, 3d quarter, 1945, nos. 180-198.

ROACH, JOHN

The | surprizing | adventures | of | John Roach, | mariner, | of | Whitehaven. | Containing | a genuine account of his cruel treatment during | a long captivity amongst the Indians, | and | imprisonment by the Spaniards, in South America. | With | his miraculous preservation and delive- | rance by Divine Providence, | and | happy return to the place of his nativity, | after | being thirteen years amongst his inhuman enemies. | *Liverpool:* | *Printed by J. Schofield, in Prince's-Street.* | *M,DCC,LXXXV.* | *Price sixpence.* [736]

60 p., 12mo. Sabin 93907. F.C. Deering, NN, NNH.

Signed: *John Roach.* He was captured by Central American Indians which he calls the "Woolaways, or flat-headed tribe" in April, 1770 about fifty leagues west of Nombre de Dios. Escaping from these Indians, he was captured by a tribe which he calls "Assenwasses." Escaping again, he made his way to the Spanish town of Mataolpa, near Granada. Imprisoned in various Nicaraguan towns, he was finally sent to Jamaica and from thence to London. Probably fictitious.

· · · · ·

The | surprizing adventures | of | John Roach, | mariner, | of | Whitehaven. | Containing, | a genuine account of his cruel treatment | during a long captivity amongst the | savage Indians, and imprison- | ment by the Spaniards, | in South-America. | With, | his miraculous preservation and deliverance | by Divine Providence; and happy return | to the place of his nativity, after | being thirteen years amongst | his inhuman enemies. | [rule] | *Whitehaven:* | *Printed by F. Briscoe, in the Market-place.* | *Price sixpence.* | *[1785?]* [Title within fleur-de-lis border]. [737]

64 p., 8vo. Sabin 71709, Brinley 5567 to DLC. DLC, MWA (p. 17-18 in photostat).

Second edition according to cover title and statement on p. 64.

SCOTT, FRANCES

A narrative of the captivity and escape of Mrs. Frances Scott, an inhabitant of Washington County, Virginia. [738]

First published in the [Philadelphia] *Freeman's Journal*, December 14, 1785, p. [2], column 1-2. BM, DLC, MiU-C, MWA, NHi, PHi, PPiU, PPL.

Text begins: "On Wednesday the 29th of June, 1785, late in the evening . . . [and ends:] Mrs. Scott continues in a low state of health; and remains inconsolate for the loss of her family, particularly bewailing the cruel death of her little daughter."

The narrative was reprinted from the *Freeman's Journal* in the *New Haven Gazette*, December 29, 1785. CtHi, CtNhHi, CtY, MWA, NHi. It was reprinted, probably from the *New Haven Gazette*, in the [New London] *Connecticut Gazette*, January 13, 1786. BM, Ct, CtHi, CtY, MnHi, MWA. It was reprinted, probably from one of the above Connecticut newspapers, in John Filson's *The adventures of Col. Daniel Boon*, Norwich, 1786, p. 16-24, which see under the author. This may well be the first printing of the Scott narrative other than in a newspaper.

Mrs. Scott lived with her husband and four children in Washington County, Virginia. On June 29, 1785 their house was attacked by Indians and all but Mrs. Scott were killed. She was captured and, after eleven days, the Indians went hunting, leaving her with an old man from whom she escaped. She wandered through the forest from July 10 to August 11 when she reached a settlement on the Clinch River in a starving condition.

Swetland, Luke

A | very remarkable | narrative | of | Luke Swetland, | who was taken captive four times in the space of | fifteen months, in the time of the late contest be- | tween Great Britain and America; shewing how | and when taken, whether carried and how treated | until his return to his family; with a concise ac- | count of the exercise of his mind during his trials: | a short account of the manners of the Indians; | and a short sketch of the rarities of the Indian | country. | Written by himself. | [double rule] | Hartford: | Printed for the author. | [1785-1790?]. [739]

16 p., 8vo. (17.8 x 12 cm.). Trumbull supp. 2661. CtY, MWA (photostat).

.   .   .   .   .

A narrative | of the | captivity of | Luke Swetland, | in 1778 and 1779, | among the Seneca Indians. | Written by himself. | Waterville, N.Y.: | James J. Guernsey, Printer, Times Office. | 1875. [740]

38, [2] p., 8vo. (21 x 12 cm.). Sabin 94055, Ayer 289. F.C. Deering, ICN, MB, MH, MWA, NHi, NN.

In addition to the original text, this edition adds new material from the author's manuscripts owned by the family and genealogical notes by A.O. Osborn, the editor. This and the following work were privately printed for the author's descendants.

.   .   .   .   .

The story | of the captivity and rescue from the | Indians of | Luke Swetland | an early settler of the Wyoming Valley and a soldier of the | American Revolution | By Edward Merrifield | [rule] | Scranton, Pa., 1915. [741]

68 p., 12mo. (20 x 13.5 cm.). Sabin 94055 note. CtY, F.C. Deering, ICN, N, NN, R.W.G. Vail.

One of 100 copies privately printed for the descendants of the captive. Rewritten by one of his great-grandsons from the captive's own manuscript narrative owned by his family and from the somewhat different text in *A narrative*, above.

Luke Swetland, a pioneer settler of the Wyoming Valley, was born at Lebanon, Connecticut, June 16, 1729, O.S. At the age of 46 he enlisted in Captain Robert Durkee's Independent Company, also called the Wyoming

Valley Company, on September 17, 1776 and served at Valley Forge, Brandywine, etc. and was discharged January 8, 1778 so that he could go home and help defend the Wyoming Valley. He helped build Fort Forty and was stationed there at the time of the Wyoming Valley Massacre, July 3, 1778 and so was one of the few who escaped. On August 25th, he and a neighbor, Joseph Blanchard, started down the Susquehanna by canoe towards a mill at the mouth of Fishing Creek. As they stepped ashore, they were captured by a party of Seneca Indians, taken to their town Kendaia or Appletown, later in the town of Romulus, now in the town of Varick, Seneca County, New York where he lived until rescued by the American army when it destroyed this and other Iroquois towns during the Sullivan Expedition in 1779. He reached his family in Kent, Connecticut in October. He returned to the Wyoming Valley where he died June 30, 1823.

[WALTON, WILLIAM]

A | narrative | of the | captivity | and | sufferings | of | Benjamin Gilbert | and his | family; | who were surprised by the Indians, and | taken from their farms on the fron- | tiers of Pennsylvania. | In the Spring, 1780. | *Philadelphia, printed:* | *London: reprinted and sold by James Phillips,* *George-* | *Yard, Lombard-Street.* | *M.DCC.LXXXV.* [742]

123, [1] p., 12mo. (16.6 x 10.4 cm.). Sabin 27348, Ayer 302. F.C. Deering, ICN, MB, MBAt, NRU, PSC-Hi.

[FILSON, JOHN]

The | adventures | of | Colonel Daniel Boon, | one of the first settlers at Kentucke: | containing | The wars with the Indians on the Ohio, | from 1769 to 1783, and the first | establishment and progress of the set- | tlement on that river. | Written by the Colonel himself. | To which are added, | A | narrative | of the | captivity, | and extraordinary | escape | of | Mrs. Francis [sic] Scott, | an inhabitant of Washington-County Vir- | ginia; who after the murder of her | husband and children, by the Indians, was | taken prisoner by them; on the 29th of | June, 1785. | [rule] | *Norwich:* | *Printed* *by John Trumbull:* | *M,DCC,LXXXVI.* [743]

24 p., 8vo. (18 x 11 cm.). Evans 19514, Trumbull: *Connecticut imprints* 38, W.R. Jillson: *Rare Kentucky books,* p. 19. CSmH, T.W. Streeter, A.S.W. Rosenbach. Photostat copies at CtY, NHi, NN.

Taken down from Boone's dictation by Filson and "improved" by Humphrey Marshall (according to Josiah Collins who came to Kentucky in 1778, as quoted in Filson Club Quarterly, Jan., 1934, p. 4) and first printed as an appendix to Filson's *Kentucke,* 1784. Reprinted as above, abridged and somewhat rewritten by John Trumbull. The Scott narrative is here reprinted, perhaps for the first time as a separate, from the contemporary newspapers, for which see under Frances Scott.

. . . . .

Omitting the Scott narrative, in *The American Museum, or repository of ancient and modern fugitive pieces,* Phil., 1787, vol. 2, p. 321-328. In most large libraries.   [744]

FITZROY, ALEXANDER

The | discovery, purchase, and settlement | of the | Country of Kentuckie, | in | North America, | so famous for its | fertility of soil, produce, climate | minerals, quadrupedes, curiosities, trade, | rapid population, religion, &c. &c. | The whole illustrated by a | new and accurate map annexed. | [rule] | By Alexander Fitzroy. | [rule] | *London:* | *Printed by H. Goldney, No. 15, Pater-Noster Row.* | [rule] | *M.DCC.LXXXVI.*   [745]

15 p., folded map, 8vo. Sabin 24624. ICU, MH, NHi, PPAmP, RPJCB. Reprinted in facsimile, with notes, in W.R. Jillson's *Kentuckie Country,* 1931.

An abbreviated plagiarism of John Filson's *Kentucke,* 1784, using the original copperplate of Filson's map of the state, printed on English paper watermarked: *J Whatman.* In Jillson, above, Col. Lawrence Martin's "The association of Filson's map with Fitzroy's Kentuckie, 1789," p. 45-59, tends to prove that the final state of the Filson map was used in Fitzroy's book, though neither the MH or NHi copies of the map examined by him were in the book. However, both libraries have copies of the book from which the map was probably removed for preservation in their map collections. The other copies of the book have not been examined to see whether any of them contain the map. All copies of the map issued with the 1st ed. of Filson are on American watermarked paper.

JEFFERSON, THOMAS

Observations | sur | la Virginie, | Par M. J***. | Traduites de l'Anglois. | *A Paris,* | *Chez Barrois l'aîné, Libraire, rue du* | *Hurepoix, près le pont Saint-Michel.* | *1786.*   [746]

[4], viii, 290 [i.e., 390], [2], [3] p., folded map, folded table, 8vo. (21.5 x 14 cm.). DLC, MH, MWiW-C, NHi, RPJCB, etc.

First French edition of Jefferson's *Notes on Virginia,* translated by André Morellet.

McDONALD, PHILIP, AND ALEXANDER McLEOD

A | surprising account, | of the | captivity and escape | of | Philip M'Donald, | and | Alexander M'Leod, | of Virginia. | From the | Chick-kemogga Indians, | and of their | great discoveries | in the | western world. | From June 1779, to January 1786, when | they returned in health to their friends, | after an absence of six years and a half. | Written by themselves. | The second edition. | *Printed in Bennington: In the year* | *M,DCC,LXXXVI.* | *by Haswell & Russell.*   [747]

[16] p., 8vo. Evans 20472 (dates it incorrectly 1787), Spargo 24, Cooley: Vermont imprints 70. F.C. Deering (lacks title), NN (photostat).

Title from H.V. Jones cat., 1928, no. 186 with facsimile title.

Advertised as "just published" in *Vermont Gazette*, December 4, 1786. No copy of first edition located.

The two Virginians volunteered for service against the Indians in the Ohio country during the Revolution and their company met with disaster. With two wounded companions they were taken captive, witnessed the burning at the stake of their two friends, and in turn were prepared for the same treatment. At night they stealthily freed themselves, murdered a number of the Indians, and made good their escape to the westward. It is difficult to trace their exact route across the country but evidently they crossed Lake Michigan and pushed on until they reached a friendly tribe amongst whom they lived, later continuing their journey to the Pacific coast. A rather fanciful account of these adventures is given. They were ultimately picked up on the west coast by a Rusisan fur trading expedition and taken to St. Petersburg, whence they shipped on an English vessel for London, and finally home after six years absence. Summary from Eberstadt cat. 122, 1943, no. 242, which see under 1795. Probably fictitious.

[MILLER, JOHANN PETER]

Chronicon Ephratense. Enthaltend den Lebens-Lauf des ehrwürdigen Vaters in Christo, Friedsam Gottrecht, Weyland Stifters und Vorstehers des geistlichen Ordens der Einsamen in Ephrata in der Grafschafft Lancaster in Pennsylvania. Zusammen getragen von Br Lamech und Agrippa. *Ephrata: Gedruckt Anno MDCCLXXXVI.* [748]

[2], [4], 250, [2] p., 4to. Sabin 49044, Evans 19558. DLC, NjPlaSDB, P, PHi.

Foreword signed: *Bruder Agrippa*, the monastic name of Johann Peter Miller. According to Evans and Seidensticker, the secular name of Bruder Lamech, who began the chronicle, is Jacob Gass.

Account of the founding of the Ephrata Community and a biography of its founder, Johann Conrad Beissel. Written and printed at the Ephrata Cloister. An English translation was published at Lancaster in 1889.

THE OHIO COMPANY, 1786-1795

Articles | of an | association | by the | name | of the | Ohio Company. | *Printed at Worcester, Massachusetts, | by Isaiah Thomas, | M DCC LXXXVI.* [749]

12 p., the last six blank for "Subscribers' names," 12mo. (13.3 x 7.5 cm.). Sabin 56976, Evans 19877. DLC (blank pages filled in with names of subscribers), MWA, OCHP, RPJCB (blank pages filled in with names of subscribers).

First publication of the Ohio Company; others in 1787 and 1788. See also under Manasseh Cutler.

[ROACH] RHODES, JOHN

The surprising adventures and sufferings of John Rhodes, a seaman of Workington. Containing an account of his captivity and cruel treatment during eight years with the Indians, and five years in different prisons amongst the Spaniards in South America. By a gentleman perfectly acquainted with the unfortunate sufferer. *New York, 1786.*   [750]

16mo. Title from Cadmus Book Shop cat. 60, 1920, no. 726. $12.50. Perhaps an error for the New York, 1798 edition, since there is no bibliographical reference to this edition. A rewriting of the John Roach narrative.

SCOTT, FRANCES

A true and wonderful | narrative | of the surprising captivity and remarkable | deliverance of | Mrs. Frances Scott, | an inhabitant of Washington County, in the | State of Virginia; who was taken by the Indians | on the evening of the twenty-ninth of June, 1785. | Containing also, | a particular relation of her almost unparrelelled [sic] | sufferings, and the hardships she underwent during her | tedious and painful travels and perigrinations of thir- | ty-two days . . . | Likewise, a particular detail of the horrid, barbarous and cruel | massacre of her husband, Mr. Scott, and four chil- | dren, and a lad named Ball, who were most inhu- | manly murdered by the blood-thirsty savages, on | the fatal evening of the twenty-ninth of June. | . . . | *Boston: Printed by E. Russell, next Lib. Pole, 1786.* [Title on verso of half title].   [751]

24 p., woodcuts, 8vo. (18.5 cm.). Sabin 78263, Evans 19979. CSmH (lacks title and p. [7]-8), MHi Rosenbach Company (1945).

The preface calls this the third edition. Second title, p. 17: "A true and faithful narrative of the | surprizing captivity and remarkable | deliverance of Captain Isaac | Stewart . . ." which also appears in various editions of the Manheim captivity.

CRÈVECOEUR, MICHEL-GUILLAUME SAINT-JEAN DE

Lettres | d'un Cultivateur | Américain | addressées à Wm. S . . . on [Seaton] Esqr. | depuis l'année 1770 jusqu'en 1786. | Par M. St. John | de Creve Coeur, | Traduites de l'Anglois. | Keen feelings inspire resistless thoughts. | Tome I. [II., III.] | vignette, differing in each volume] | *A Paris. | Chez Cuchet Libraire, Rue et Hôtel Serpente. | 1787.*   [752]

3 vols., [2], xxxii, 478, [4] p., 3 plates, folded map; [2], 438, [6] p., 3 folded maps; [2], 592, [1] p., folded plate, folded map, 8vo., (19.5 x 12.5 cm.). Sabin 17495. DLC, MB, MH, NHi, NN, OClWHi, RPJCB, etc.

Maps: *Carte générale | des Etats-Unis . . . ; Carte générale des Etats | de Virginie, Maryland, Delaware, | Pensilvanie, Nouveau-Jersey, New-York, |*

Connecticut et Isle de Rhodes | . . . d'Après la carte Amériquaine | de Louis Evans | et la carte Anglaise | de Thomas-Jefferys, | . . . ; Carte | de l'Ile | de Nantucket, | . . . ; Carte | de l'Ie | de Martha's Vineyard | avec | ses dépendances, | . . . ; [3 on one:] Esquisse du | Muskinghum; Esquisse du | Sioto; Esquisse | de la Riviere | du Grand Castor, | . . .

Though so rewritten and "prettyfied" as to have lost much of its original charm, this edition is valuable as it is the most complete of all and uses much material in no earlier edition. Even this did not exhaust the author's trunk of writings, still preserved by his descendants, and a new selection of additional material appeared as: *Sketches of eighteenth century America,* New Haven, 1925. See also Howard C. Rice's *The American farmer's letters,* in the Colophon, Part 18, 1934.

[CUTLER, MANASSEH]

An | explanation | of the | map | which delineates that part of the | Federal Lands, | comprehended between Pennsylvania West Line, the Rivers Ohio | and Sioto, and Lake Erie; confirmed to the United States | by sundry tribes of Indians, in the treaties of 1784 and 1786, | and now ready for settlement. | [double rule] | *Salem: | Printed by Dabney and Cushing, |* MDCCLXXXVII.   [753]

24 p., 8vo. (19.5 x 12.5 cm.). Sabin 18174, Evans 20312, Thomson 299. DLC, MiD-B, MiU-C, MWA, N, NHi, NN, OClWHi, PHi, PPiU, PPL, PPL-R, RPJCB, WHi.

The first description of Ohio, published Nov. 27, 1787. The accompanying map was not published until May 27, 1788 and does not accompany any known copy of the pamphlet, though the copy burned in the New York State Library fire of 1911 was accompanied by the map according to Sabin 18175. There are separate copies of the map at DLC and MHi (somewhat defective). The pamphlet was reprinted in 1788.

The map: *A map | of the Federal Territory from the Western | boundary of Pennsylvania to the Scioto | River laid down from the latest informations | and divided into townships and fractional parts | of townships agreeably to the Ordinance of the | Honle. Congress passed in May 1785. |* [Inset:] *A plan | of the City to | be built on the | Muskingum | River |* [i.e., Marietta] (47 x 64.6 cm.). DLC, MHi. •

See: *The first map and description of Ohio, 1787, by Manasseh Cutler. A bibliographical account with reprint of the "Explanation"* [and the map]. Washington, 1918. 41 p., 4to., folded map.

DICKENSON, JONATHAN

God's protecting Providence, . . . The sixth edition. *London: Printed and sold by James Phillips, in George-Yard, Lombard-Street. M.DCC.LXXXVII.*
                    [754]

136 p., 8vo. (16.9 x 10 cm.). Sabin 20015, Ayer 69. BM, CtY, DLC, F.C. Deering, Friends Reference Library, London, ICN, NN, PHi, PSC-Hi.

GRAHAM, JOHN

John Graham's address | to the master and worthy family of this house; | shewing his sufferings among the Indians in West Florida. | Printed in November, 1787. for the benefit of John Graham and family and sold by no other | person; you will know him by sight when he calls again: he is about five feet five inches high, | short grey hair, aged forty seven, and his left hand cut off at the wrist. You are desired by him to | return this paper to none but himself, for this is all he will publish concerning these matters. | [Caption title] [Text in two columns with imprint at foot of second column:] *(W. Appleton, Printer, Darlington.)* | [County of Durham, England, 1787].   [755]

Broadside, folio (31.5 x 20.5 cm.). RPJCB Annual Report, 1939, p. 29-30. RPJCB. Photostat copy at NHi.

Distributed by Graham for begging purposes. Tells of his captivity, torture, rescue and later misfortunes.

Quoting from Dr. Wroth's annual report, we learn that: "Life had seemed fair enough to John Graham throughout his ten years of peaceful dealing with the Indians of West Florida. But on a day in 1785 a band with which he was about to do business turned upon his party and wiped it out with gun and hatchet. Graham was carried away and put to torture, but the unpleasant proceedings he describes were interrupted by the arrival of a detachment of British soldiers. For some time thereafter his life was a series of amputations of twisted limbs, of financial losses, shipwrecks, and other disasters which sent him back for refuge to his old home near Durham, and forced him to the practice of virtual mendicancy." Apparently the only known copy of a broadside captivity.

HANSON, ELIZABETH

An account of the captivity of Elizabeth Hanson, . . . A new edition. . . . *London: Printed and sold by James Phillips, George-Yard, Lombard-Street,* 1787.   [756]

28 p., 12mo. (16.1 x 9.3 cm.). Sabin 30265. An-C-OAr, DLC, F.C. Deering, ICN, MWA, NhHi, PSC-Hi, RPJCB.

HUBBARD, WILLIAM

History of the Indian wars, from the first settlement in New-England. *Philadelphia: Printed by William Young, the corner of Chestnut and Second-Streets. 1787.*   [757]

Title from Evans 20418 who gives no collation or location and probably took his entry from an advertisement for an edition which may never have been published.

HUTCHINS, THOMAS

A topographical description of Virginia, Pennsylvania, Maryland, and North-Carolina, comprehending the rivers Ohio, Kenhawa, Sioto, Cherokee, Wabash, Illinois, Mississippi, &c. The climate, soil and produce, whether animal, vegetable, or mineral; the mountains, creeks, roads, distances, latitudes, &c. and of every part, laid down in the annexed map. Published by Thomas Hutchins, Captain in the 60th Regiment of Foot. With a Plan of the Rapids of the Ohio, a Plan of the several villages in the Illinois Country, a Table of the distances between Fort Pitt and the mouth of the Ohio, all engraved upon copper. And an appendix, containing Mr. Patrick Kennedy's journal up the Illinois River, and a correct list of the different nations and tribes of Indians, with the number of fighting men, &c. *Boston: Printed and sold by John Norman, in Marshall's Lane near the Boston Stone. MDCCLXXXVII.*   [758]

[2], ii, 30, 2 p., 2 plans and table, 12mo. Sabin 34051, Evans 20424. MB, MBAt, MH, MWA, etc.

.   .   .   .   .

A topographical description of Virginia, Pennsylvania, Maryland, and North Carolina. Reprinted from the original edition of 1778. Edited by Frederick Charles Hicks. *Cleveland The Burrows Brothers Company 1904.*

143 p., 2 illus., 2 plans, table and facsimile of Hutchins' *A new map of the western parts of Virginia* . . . *1778,* from original in DLC. 245 copies printed.
                                                                              [759]

JEFFERSON, THOMAS

Notes | on the | State of Virginia. | Written by | Thomas Jefferson. | Illustrated with | a Map, including the States of Virginia, Mary- | land, Delaware and Pennsylvania. | *London:* | *Printed for John Stockdale, opposite* | *Burlington-House, Piccadilly.* | *M.DCC.LXXXVII.*   [760]

[4], 382 p., folded map, folded table, 8vo. (22.5 cm.). Sabin 35896. DLC, MWA, NHi, NjP, PPL, RPJCB, etc.

First London edition and second in English.

MARRANT, JOHN

A | narrative | of the | life | of | John Marrant, | of New-York, in North-America. | Giving an | account of his conversion | when only fourteen years of age. | He left his mother's house from religious motives, | wander'd several days in the desart without food, | and was at last taken by an Indian hunter among | the Cherokees, where he was condemned to die. | With his | conversion of the king of the Cherokees and his daugh- | ter, &c. &c. &c. | [rule] | The whole authenticated | by the Reverend W. Aldridge. | [double rule] | *[London?] Printed in the year 1787.*   [761]

iv, 22 p., 8vo. (20.5 x 13 cm.). Sabin 44679, Ayer 8, Porter 185. F.C. Deering, ICN, NHi.

For first edition, see under 1785.

THE OHIO COMPANY, 1786-1795.

Articles | of an | association | by the | name | of the | Ohio Company. | *New-York, Printed by | Samuel and John Loudon, Water Street,* | *MDCCLXXXVII.*   [762]
45 p., 8vo. (16.5 cm.). Sabin 56977, Evans 20605, Thomson 43. DLC, MH, MHi, OCHP, PPL, RPJCB, WHi.

Evans has variant title, perhaps a later issue, but with same imprint, date and collation, credited to MH, MHi, PPL: *Articles of an association, by the name of the Ohio Company. To which is added extracts from the letters of Mons. St. John de Creve Coeur, His Most Christian Majesty's Consul for New-York, &c.—Giving an elegant description of that truly fertile country; perhaps exceeded by none of this globe.*

.   .   .   .   .

At a meeting of the directors and agents of the Ohio Company, at Mr. Bracket's tavern, the 21st of November, and continued by adjournment to the twenty-second. . . . At a meeting of the directors of the Ohio Company at Mr. Bracket's tavern, in Boston, November 23, 1787—For the purpose of carrying into effect the surveys, and other business, of the Ohio Company; as agreed upon by the directors and agents, at their meeting of the 29th of August last, and the 21st instant. [Caption title] *[Worcester: Printed by Isaiah Thomas, 1787].*   [763]
4 p., 8vo. (16.5 cm.). Sabin 56978, Evans 20603. DLC, MWA, PPL.

.   .   .   .   .

August 29, 1787. | At a meeting of the directors and agents of the Ohio Company, | held at the Bunch of Grapes Tavern in Boston, the following report was | received from Rev. Manasseh Cutler. | [Caption title] *[Worcester: Printed by Isaiah Thomas, 1787].*   [764]
Broadside, folio. Evans 20602, Ford: Mass. Bdsds. 2497. MSaE, MWA.

.   .   .   .   .

The contract of the Ohio Company with the Honourable Board of | Treasury of the United States of America—Made by the Rev. Mr. Manasseh Cutler and Major Winthrop Sargent as agents for | the directors of said Company at New-York. October 27, 1787. | [Caption title] *[New York? 1787].*   [765]
4 p., 8vo. Sabin 18173, Evans 20604, Thomson 301. DLC, MWA, RPJCB.

PANTHER, ABRAHAM, *pseud.*

An account of a beautiful young lady, who was taken by the Indians and lived in the woods nine years, and then was providentially returned to her parent, &c. *[Middletown: Printed and sold by Woodward and Green?]* 1787.
[766]

Advertised in the [Middletown] *Middlesex Gazette,* printed by Woodward and Green, May 21, 1787, as "To be had at this office." Evans 20615, Sabin 93891.

. . . . .

A surprising account of the discovery of a lady who was taken by the Indians in the year 1777, and after making her escape, she retired to a lonely cave, where she lived nine years. [767]

In Benjamin West's *Bickerstaff's almanack, for . . . 1788, Norwich: Printed by J. Trumbull, [1787],* p. [19-24]. Sabin 93891 note, Evans 20875, Ayer supp. 13. CtHi, ICN, MWA, NHi, NN. Probably printed in October, 1787. This edition reprinted, with a bibliographical introduction by R.W.G. Vail, in the *American Book Collector,* vol. 2, 1932, p. 165-172.

. . . . .

A surprising narrative of a young woman, discovered in a rocky cave, after having been taken by the savage Indians of the wilderness in the year 1777. *New-York: [1787].* [768]

9 p., 12mo. Title from Evans 20616 who gives no collation or location, Sabin 93891.

The anonymous heroine was supposed to have been born in Albany, New York in 1760 and captured four or five days' journey from her home in 1777, to have lived alone for nine years in the Iroquois country without ever having been discovered by red man or white, a surprising adventure which is altogether too surprising to be credited. This then, is a simple and somewhat crude, though interesting, bit of early American fiction which became a best seller in the day when it was legitimate to read a true story but considered improper to read fiction. If she was captured in 1777 and lived alone for nine years, the narrative was, presumably written in 1786 or 1787, the year the three above editions were printed. There is nothing to show which is the first edition.

The | returned captive. | A | poem. | Founded on a late fact. | [rule, 6 lines quoted, rule] | *Hudson:* | *Printed by Ashbel Stoddard.* | *M.DCC.- LXXXVII.* [769]

60 p., 12m. (19.5 x 12 cm.). Sabin 70149, Evans 20676. CSmH, DLC, NHi, NN, RPB.

A fictitious Indian captivity in verse in which John, with his daughter Nelly, returns from nine years of captivity among the Indians, presumably in

Canada, during and after the Revolutionary War, finds his wife Phebe married to his old friend Charles who sadly gives her back to John. No surnames or geographical names appear. Reprinted 1790 and 1800.

[SYMMES, JOHN CLEVES]

To the | respectable public. | *[Trenton? 1787?]*.   [770]
30 p., 24mo. Sabin 94102, Evans 20738. DLC, MWA.

Caption title. On p. 28: "Signed at Trenton, the 26th day of November, A.D. 1787. John Cleves Symmes."

First publication relating to the Miami Purchase in Ohio, by its founder.

. . . . .

To the | respectable | public. | *[Trenton? 1787?]*.   [771]
16 p., 16mo. Sabin 94103, Evans 20739. CtY, OCHP.

Same signature and date as above appear on p. 15 of this edition. See Thomson's Ohio bibliography for long note, and Beverly W. Bond, Jr.'s *The correspondence of John Cleves Symmes. Founder of the Miami Purchase.* New York, 1926. 312 p. Also the founder of Cincinnati, Ohio.

WILLIAMSON, PETER

French and Indian cruelty exemplified, in the life, and various vicissitudes of fortune, of Peter Williamson . . . *Edinburgh: Printed for, and sold by J. Stewart, Bookseller, Lawn-Market. 1787*.   [772]
vi, 150 p., front. port., 12mo. (16.2 x 9.3 cm.). Sabin 104473, Ayer 320. DLC, F.C. Deering, ICN, MBAt, NN.

CRÈVECOEUR, MICHEL-GUILLAUME SAINT-JEAN DE

Briefe | eines | Amerikanischen Landmanns | an | den Ritter W.S. | in den Jahren 1770 bis 1781. | . . . | Ais dem | Englischen ins Französische von *** | und jetzt | aus dem Französischen übersetzt und mit einigen | Anmerkungen begleitet | von | Johann August Ephraim Götze, | erstem Hofdiaconus der St. Servatii-Kirche zu Quedlinburg. | . . . | *Leipzig, 1788.* [-1789] | *Bey Siegfried Lebrecht Crusius.*   [773]
3 vols., viii, 512; vi, 512; 668 p., plate, 8vo. DLC.

[CUTLER, MANASSEH]

An explanation of the map which delineates that part of the Federal Lands, comprehended between Pennsylvania West Line, the Rivers Ohio and Sioto, and Lake Erie; confirmed to the United States by sundry tribes of Indians in the treaties of 1784 and 1786, and now ready for settlement. With extracts from the writings of Mr. St. John de Creve-Coeur, on the passage of the Ohio River. *Newport, Rhode-Island. Printed by Peter Edes. MDCCLXXXVIII.*   [774]

24 p., 12mo. Evans 21037. CSmH, NBLiHi, RHi, RNHi.

Issued without the map, as in 1st ed., 1787, but probably planned to accompany it. Evans says that the map was printed at Boston by Adams and Nourse, 1788, but the map as reproduced by Phillips (see note to 1st ed.) has no imprint or name of author or engraver.

[DECALVES, DON ALONSO, *pseud.*]

New travels to the Westward, or, Unknown parts of America. Being a tour of almost fourteen months. Containing, an account of the country, upwards of two thousand miles west of the Christian parts of North-America; with an account of white Indians, their manners, habits, and many other particulars. By Don Alonso Decalves. Confirmed by three other persons. *Boston: Printed and sold by John W. Folsom, No. 30, Union-Street. Sold also by Benjamin Larkin, No. 46, Cornhill. [1788].*   [775]

[2], vi, [1], 7-44 (misnumbered 45) p., 8vo. Sabin 98445, Evans 21044 and (incorrectly under 1796) 30321. CSmH, DLC, F.C. Deering, MB, MHi, MWA, NN, OClWHi.

Advertised in *Boston Gazette* on May 19, 1788 as "An entire new work. Just published."

Fictitious narrative which, however, includes the true story of the Indian captivity of John Vandeleur, (a Dutch member of the crew of a ship commanded by Captain James Van Leason), who was captured on the Pacific Northwest Coast in 1784, married a native wife and continued to live with his Indian family. Frequently reprinted. A fuller separate account of his adventures appeared in 1812 and later and the story is also included in the voyage of Van Leason, 1801 and later, for which see elsewhere in this bibliography.

. . . . . .

New | travels | to the | Westward, | or, | Unknown parts of America. | Being a tour of almost fourteen months. | Containing, | An account of the country, upwards of two | thousand miles West of the Christian parts | of North-America; with an account of white | Indians, their manners, habits, and many | other particulars. | [rule] | By Don Alonso Decalves. | Confirmed by thee [sic] other persons. | [rule] | *Norwich: Printed and sold by John* | *Trumbull, M,DCC,LXXXVIII.*   [776]

34 p. (copy described has 32 p. and lacks last leaf), 12mo. Trumbull supp. 2456; Edward Eberstadt & Sons cat. 122, 1943, no. 106, lacking last leaf. $250. Above title from facsimile in Eberstadt cat. MWA (30 p. only).

Evans 21786, copied by Trumbull supp. 2457, lists a Norwich edition of 1789. Since he gives no collation or location, his entry was probably taken from an advertisement for unsold copies of the 1788 edition.

Eastern lands for sale. The public are notified of tracts of land for sale, situated between the Highlands and the Atlantic Ocean, from North to South; and between the River St. Croix, and the State of New-Hampshire, from East to West . . . June 18, 1788. [Colophon:] *Boston:—Printed by Adams & Nourse, Printers to the Honourable General Court. [1788].*   [777]

Broadside, folio. Evans 21244, Ford's Mass. Bdsds. 2507. MWA.

Refers to lands in York, Cumberland and Lincoln counties, District of Maine.

HUMPHREYS, DAVID

An | essay | on the | life | of the | Honorable Major-General | Israel Putnam: | addressed to the State Society of the Cincinnati, | in Connecticut. | By Col. David Humphreys. | *Hartford: | Printed by Hudson & Goodwin.* | *M.DCC.LXXXVIII.*   [778]

187 p., 12mo. Sabin 33804, Evans 21160. BM, CtY, DLC, MBAt, MH, MWA, NBLiHi, NHi, NN, etc.

Frontier adventures and Indian captivity of a famous soldier in two wars.

JEFFERSON, THOMAS

Notes | on the | State | of Virginia. | Written by | Thomas Jefferson. | *Philadelphia: | Printed and sold by Prichard and Hall, ın Market | Street, between Front and Second Streets. | M.DCC.LXXXVIII.*   [779]

[2], [ii], 244, [4] p., 1 illus., folded table, 8vo. (20 cm.). Sabin 35897, Evans 21176. CtHWatk, DLC, MWiW-C, NHi, PPL, RPJCB, etc.

First American edition.

Sabin 35909 notes a German translation: *Beschreibung von Virginien* . . . Leipzig, 1789 but does not give full title, collation or location.

McDONALD, PHILIP, AND ALEXANDER McLEOD

A surprising account of the captivity and escape of Philip M'Donald and Alexander M'Leod of Virginia, from the Chickkemogga Indians, and of their great discoveries in the western world. From June 1779 to February 1786, when they returned in health to their friends after an absence of six years and a half. Written by themselves. The third edition. *Pittsfield: Printed by Roger Storrs, near the Meeting-House. 1788.*   [780]

14 p., 16mo. Evans 21210. MiU-C.

MARRANT, JOHN

A | narrative | of the | Lord's wonderful dealings | with | John Marrant, | a Black, | (Now gone to preach the gospel in Nova-Scotia) | Born in New-York, in North-America, | [rule] | Taken down from his own relation, | arranged, corrected and published, | By the Rev. Mr. Aldridge. | [rule] | The sixth edition, | with additions and notes explanatory. | [rule, 4 lines quoted, rule] | *London: | Printed and sold by Gilbert and Plummer, No. 13,* |

Cree-Church-Lane, Leadenhall-Street, 1788; | *and sold at the Chapel in Jewry-Street; and by all | booksellers and newscarriers in town and country.* [781]

40 p., 8vo. (22 x 14 cm.). Sabin 44679, Ayer 9, Porter 186. F.C. Deering, ICN, NHi.

MINOT, GEORGE RICHARDS

The history of the insurrections, in Massachusetts, in the year MDCC-LXXXVI, and the rebellion consequent thereon. By George Richards Minot, A.M. *Printed at Worcester, Massachusetts, by Isaiah Thomas. MDCC-LXXXVIII.* [782]

192 p., 8vo. Sabin 49324, Evans 21259. Copies in most large libraries.

Second edition, *Boston, 1810,* third edition, *Boston, 1840.*

History of "Shays' Rebellion," a Massachusetts frontier insurrection against the severe laws regarding debt and the heavy taxation during the economic depression following the Revolutionary War. Though the rebellion failed, the state government was ousted at the next election and less severe laws regarding debt were enacted. The affair showed the need for a stronger central government and, indirectly, aided in the enactment of a strong federal constitution. The resultant unrest stimulated rapid migration from central and western Massachusetts and Connecticut to the new, fertile and tax free lands of Western New York, Pennsylvania and the Ohio Country.

THE OHIO COMPANY, 1786-1795

Articles of agreement entered into by the subscribers, for constituting an association, by the name of the Ohio Company. *[Newport: Printed by Peter Edes, 1788].* [783]

4 p., 12mo. Title from Evans 21348 who does not locate a copy.

Hammett says, "prefixed to a Description of the map of the Federal lands, [by Manasseh Cutler] and was intended for the use of Newport subscribers, a list of seventy-four of which appears in that work."

. . . . .

At a meeting of the directors and | agents of the Ohio Company, at | Mr. Rice's Tavern, in Providence, State of Rhode-Island, Wednesday | March 5, 1788. [Caption title] *[Providence: Printed by John Carter? 1788].* [784]

4 p., 8vo. (16.5 cm.). Sabin 56979, Evans 21349. DLC, RPJCB.

See also: *The records of the original proceedings of the Ohio Company.* Edited by Archer Butler Hulbert. (Marietta College Hist. Coll. Vols. 1-2.) Marietta, 1917. 2 vols., illus., ports., map, 8vo.

PHELPS AND GORHAM PURCHASE, 1788.

The promotion for this Western New York land company was carried on mainly by newspaper advertising and resident agents. Since large sections of the original purchase were sold en bloc to foreign companies (The English Associates and the Holland Land Company), no pamphlet literature was issued by Phelps and Gorham but they did issue a very fine separate map of their purchase, which see under Augustus Porter, [1794], which was copied by the English Associates, which see. A few of the fundamental documents of the purchase are in NCanHi, the large bulk of the Oliver Phelps papers dealing with this purchase are in N. The Israel Chapin papers, also dealing with the purchase, are at NHi, and the papers of William Walker, resident agent of the purchase at Canandaigua, N.Y. are owned by a descendant. Transcripts of the more important Walker Papers, made by George S. Conover in 1889, are owned by R.W.G. Vail. A selection of them, edited by Conover, appeared in five chapters in the *Geneva* [N.Y.] *Gazette* in 1889; and another selection in the [Canandaigua] *Ontario County Times* in seven chapters about 1889-1890. [785]

ROACH, JOHN

The surprising adventures | of | John Roach, | mariner, | of | Whitehaven. | Containing | a genuine account of his cruel treatment during | a long captivity amongst the savage Indians, and | imprisonment by the Spaniards in South America. | With | his miraculous preservation and deliverance by | Divine Providence; and happy return to the place | of his nativity, after being thirteen years amongst | his inhuman enemies. | *Dumfries: Printed by Robert Jackson, 1788.* | *(Price six-pence.)* [786]

62 p., 8vo. Sabin 93908. CSmH, NHi, RPJCB.

SCOTT, FRANCES

A true and wonderful narrative of the surprising captivity and remarkable deliverance of Mrs. Frances Scott, . . . The third edition. *Boston, 1788.*
[787]

Not seen. Copy at MHi.

SPANGENBERG, AUGUST GOTTLIEB

An | account | of the manner in which the | Protestant Church | of the | Unitas Fratrum, | or | United Brethren, | preach | the Gospel, and carry on their missions | among the heathen. | Translated from the German of the | Rev. August Gottlieb Spangenberg. | . . . | *London:* | *Printed and sold by H. Trapp, No. I. Pater-noster Row, for the | Brethren's Society for the Furtherance of the Gospel; also sold at | all the Brethren's Settlements and Chapels in Great Britain and | Ireland.* | M.DCC.LXXXVIII. [788]

[4], vii, [1], 127, [1] p., 8vo. Sabin 88925. MBAt, NHi, NN.

Translation of his *Von der Arbeit,* 1782.

An account of their work among the Indians of Pennsylvania, New York, Georgia, etc.

VARNUM, JAMES MITCHELL

An | oration, | delivered at Marietta, July 4, 1788, | By the Hon. James M. Varnum, Esq. | one of the Judges of the Western Territory; | the | speech | of His Excellency | Arthur St. Clair, Esquire, | upon the proclamation of the commission appointing him | Governor of said Territory; | and the | proceedings of the inhabitants | of the city of | Marietta. | *Newport (Rhode-Island)* | *Printed by Peter Edes, MDCCLXXXVIII.* [789]

14 p., 4to. Sabin 98639, Evans 21538. DLC, MBAt, MHi, MWA, RPJCB, WHi.

Account of the first Fourth of July celebration west of the Alleghany Mountains. Published by the Ohio Land Company.

CARVER, JONATHAN

Three years travels. *Philadelphia, 1789.* DLC, etc. [790]

See note at end of 1798 edition.

CLINTON, GENERAL J[AMES]

To be sold, | Fine wheat, hemp and grass lands in the State of New-York, Paten- | ted and free from taxes for 5 or 6 years to come. | [Caption title] *[New York? 1789].* [791]

Broadside, folio. (42 x 25 cm.). NHi.

Included 7,040 acres in Onochquaga, Montgomery County (later Oquaga or Ouaquaga, Broome County, near Binghamton); 10,030 acres at Chenango; 1,280 acres at Unadilla; and 1,860 acres in Washington County. "For terms apply to General J. Clinton, New-York, to Messrs. Muhlenberg and L. Swyler, or Isaac Melcher, Philadelphia." One of the accompanying letters of endorsement is dated February 12, 1789.

COMPAGNIE DU KENTUCKY

[Ornamental rule] | Notice sur Kentucke, | contrée de l'Ohio, | envoyée au Comte de Hillsborough (à Londres) | en 1770, lorsqu'il avoit le département de l' Amérique | Septentrionale, en qualité de Secrétaire d'Etat. [Caption title] [Second title:] Plan d'un établissement | qu'une compagnie pourroit former à Kentucky, Province des | Etats-Unis d'Amérique. | [Caption title] *[Paris, 1789].* [792]

4; 14 p., folded map, 4to. (24 x 17 cm.). Title from Mass. Hist. Soc. Photostat Americana, 2d ser., 1936, no. 51 from original in RPJCB.

Folded map, without title, of a tract northwest of the Ohio, showing four unnamed streams with caption: *Loutre Briques* [i.e., *Criques*] *ou petites*

Rivieres. [Otter creeks or little rivers]. *La Riviere Ohio* is also named. (36.5 x 24 cm.).

Contains unsigned inscription: "Jadresse au Colonel Blackden Américain, Hotel d'Angleterre rue Traversiere a Paris 1789."

English text of the *Notice sur Kentucke* appears in Thomas Hutchins's *A topographical description of Virginia . . . London, 1778,* p. 15-18, showing that the French company used as their introduction an English text published some years earlier.

Prospectus for a 50,000 acre tract, 12 by 6 miles square, northwest of the Ohio in Jefferson County, Kentucky, which the promoters called "Necker." They hoped to encourage Scotch and Irish settlers and a few French and Flemish.

[Cutler, Manasseh]

Description du sol, des productions, &c. &c. de cette portion des Etats-Unis, située entre la Pensylvania, les rivières de l'Ohio & du Scioto, & le lac Erie. Traduit d'une brochure imprimée à Salem, en Amérique en 1787. *Paris.* 1789.   [793]

30 p., 8vo. (22 cm.). Sabin 18176, Thomson 300. Bib. Nat., DLC, MH, NN, OClWHi, PHi, RPJCB.

Translation of his: *An explanation of the map,* 1787.

Probably issued without the map but perhaps intended to accompany the French map, obviously based on Cutler's map described under 1st ed.: *Plan | des achats des | Compagnies de | l'Ohio et du Scioto. | [in margin:] Gravé par P.F. Tardieu. | [Paris, 1789?] (54 x 38.5 cm. over all, 45.5 x 35.5 cm. within plate mark). Colored map, originally folded. Shows V. [ille] de Mariana* [Marietta], founded April 7 and named Marietta July 2, 1788, not on original Cutler map of May 27, 1788. The French map is at NHi. The map is reproduced from another copy in: *Ohio in the time of the Confederation,* ed. by A.B. Hulbert. (Marietta College Hist. Coll., vol. 3), Marietta, 1918, p. 100. This map may also have appeared with the Scioto Land Company Prospectus, which see.

Drown, Solomon

An | oration, | delivered | at Marietta, | April 7, 1789, | in commemoration of the commencement of the settlement formed by the | Ohio Company. | [orn.] | By Solomon Drown, Esq. M.B. | [orn.] | [double rule, orn., double rule] | *Printed at Worcester, Massachusetts, | by Isaiah Thomas. | Sold at his bookstore in Worcester, and by him and Company in Boston.* | [double rule] | MDCCLXXXIX.   [794]

[2], 17 p., 4to. (28.5 x 22.5 cm.). Sabin 20966, Evans 21802. BM, DLC, MHi, MWA, NHi, NN, OC, OClWHi, OMC, RPJCB.

LOSKIEL, GEORGE HENRY

Geschichte | der | mission der evangelischen Brüder | unter | den Indianern in Nordamerika | durch | Georg Heinrich Loskiel. | [orn.] | [rule] | *Barby,* | *zu finden in den Brüdergemeinen, und in Leipzig in Com-* | *mission bey* *Paul Gotthelf Kummer.* | *1789.* [795]

[16], 783, [1] p., 8vo. (19 cm.). Sabin 42109. BM, DLC, MB, NHi, NN, RPJCB, etc.

The official history of the missionary work of the United Brethren among the North American Indians in Georgia, Pennsylvania, New York and the Middle West, 1735-1787, based on the journals and letters of the missionaries, particularly those of David Zeisberger and Gottlieb Spangenberg, the latter having examined and approved the work for publication. The best contemporary account of the Iroquois, Delawares, Shawanese, etc., including a narrative of the travels of the missionaries and of the massacre of the peaceful Indians of Gnadenhutten and Salem. Unlike most contemporary accounts of the Indians, this work is friendly to them and is honest and accurate. Published in Swedish in 1792 and in English in 1794.

MERCER, JAMES

Lands. | For sale, | [Caption title] [Lands in Hampshire County and lots in Romney, Hampshire County and in Winchester, Virginia. signed:] James Mercer. | Fredericksburg, July 2, 1789. | [Colophon:] *Fredericksburg:* *Printed by Timothy Green, near the Post-Office.* | [1789]. [796]

Broadside, folio. (33 x 20 cm.). Evans 21957. NHi, NN.

SCIOTO LAND COMPANY

Édit du Congrès des États-Unis de l'Amérique. Traduit de l'Anglois. Pour les terres dépendantes des dits États, situées au Nord Ouest de la Rivière de l'Ohio, dans lesquelles se trouvent celles de la Compagnie du Scioto. *[Paris:]* *De l'Imprimerie de Prault, Imprimeur du Roi, quai des Augustins, 1789.* [797]

16 p., 12mo. Sabin 78124, Thomson 365, old John Carter Brown cat. 3332. Bib. Nat., MH, RPJCB.

Translation of the Northwestern Ordinance of July 13, 1787.

.   .   .   .   .

Prospectus pour l'établissement sur les rivieres d'Ohio et de Scioto, en Amérique. *[Paris: De l'Imprimerie de Prault. 1789].* [798]

[2], 16, Avis 14, Supplement 3 p., map, table, 4to. Sabin 66090, Thomson 956, with long historical note. Bib. Nat.

.   .   .   .   .

Avis. Le Compagnie du Scioto, établie à Paris pour l'exploitation & la vente de trois millions d'acres anglois de terres, situés dans l'Amérique Sep-

tentrionale, entre l'Ohio, dite la Belle Rivière, & le Scioto . . . annonce [. . .
Caption title] *[Paris, De l'imprimerie de Prault, imprimeur du roi, 1789].*

[799]

15 p., map, 4to. (24 cm.). Sabin 78123, DLC cat. CSmH, DLC (lacks map).

Perhaps part of or reprinted from the above Prospectus.

. . . . .

Supplement. [Same imprint as above? 1789].   [800]

3 p. Perhaps part of or reprint from above Prospectus. CSmH.

. . . . .

Avis aux citoyens. Précis justificatif en faveur de la Compagnie du Scioto.
[Paris?] Imprimerie de la Becq [1789?].   [801]

3 p., 4to. (21 cm.). Title from DLC cat. for copy at OClWHi.

In 1787 William Duer, Royal Flint, Andrew Craigie, Richard Platt and other New York speculators contracted for the purchase of nearly five million acres on the Scioto River, northwest of the Ohio Company's purchase. The poet Joel Barlow was sent to France as their agent in 1789 where, with a crooked Englishman inappropriately named Playfair, he organized the Compagnie du Scioto and issued a lying prospectus with a false map which sold much stock and brought some 500 prospective settlers to America. Playfair embezzled the company's funds, the owners failed in the panic of 1792, the lands were never paid for but about 100 of the Frenchmen found their way to the tract and founded Gallipolis, Ohio in 1790 and were given titles to their lands in Scioto County by Congress in 1795. The Duer papers in the New-York Historical Society and the Craigie papers in the American Antiquarian Society include material on the purchase. See also Frank Moneghan's *Scioto madness*, in: *Legion d'Honneur*, vol. 4, no. 2, 1933, p. 114-120. Also Bernard Faÿ's *Bibliographie critique des ouvrages français relatifs aux États-Unis, 1770-1800.* Paris, 1925. [4], 108, [4] p.;.and Bib. Nat. *Catalogue de l'histoire de l'Amerique*, vol. III, p. 85-87. There are said to be 40 Scioto pamphlets in the Public Record Office, London, class mark F.O. 4.10.

SCOTT, FRANCES

A remarkable narrative of the captivity and escape of Mrs. Frances Scott, . . . *Newburyport*, 1789.   [802]
Not seen. F. C. Deering.

Perhaps same as the *Newburyport, [ca. 1799]* edition below.

SPANGENBERG, AUGUST GOTTLIEB

An account of the manner in which the Protestant Church of the Unitas Fratrum, or, United Brethren, preach the Gospel, and carry on their missions among the heathens. Translated from the German of the Rev'd August Gottlieb Spangenberg. [2 lines quoted] *Philadelphia: Printed for Thomas Dobson, at the Stone House, in Second-Street, between Market and Chestnut-Streets. 1789.* [803]

Sabin 88926 who quotes Evans 22155 who gives no collation or location.

Address | to the | inhabitants of Alexandria, | and | other sea-ports | in the | United States of America. | [double rule] | From | a proprietor of lands on the Sioto. | [double rule] | [New York?] *Printed in the year 1790.* [804]

15 p., 16mo. (15.5 x 9.5 cm.). Evans 22298. NHi.

A remonstrance against the policy of the people of Alexandria and other American sea ports who had attempted to discourage French emigrants from proceeding west to the Scioto lands, thus damaging the business of the "proprietor of lands on the Sioto."

Probably written by or for Colonel William Duer of New York City, American agent of the Scioto Land Company.

ALLEMAGNE, ——d'

Nouvelles | du Scioto, | ou | relation fidèle | du voyage | et des infortunes | d'un Parisien, | qui arrive de ces pays-là. où il etait allé | pour s'établir. | Vive la France et Paris! | *A Paris,* | *Chez Lenoir et Leboucher,* | *Imprimeurs, rue des Mauvais-Garçons,* | *Faubourg S. Germain, au Café la Fayette.* | *Août 1790.* [805]

16 p., 8vo. BM, NN (photo).

BARTH, —— DE, AND —— THIÉBAUD

Lettre à MM. de la Société des Vingt-quatre. *[Paris? 1790].* [805A]

8 p., 8vo. Title from Bib. Nat. cat. Bib. Nat.

By two members of the society, de Barth and Thiébaud, on the Scioto Company, dated from New York, May 20, 1790. Favorable report.

BUÉ, ——, AND —— VONSCHRITZ

Compagnie de Scioto. *[Paris? 1790].* [805B]

4 p. Bib. Nat.

Extracts from letters regarding the French colonists who have set out for the Scioto lands, the first from M. Bué to M. Farmain, Notary at Paris, dated from New York, May 21, 1790, and the second from M. Vonschritz, passenger on *The Recovery,* dated from Amboy [Perth Amboy, N.J.], May 15, 1790.

[CAREY, MATHEW]

Information for Europeans who are disposed to migrate to the United States. In a letter from a citizen of Pennsylvania, to his friend in Great-

Britain. *Philadelphia: Carey Stewart & Co. (Price one eighth of a dollar.)* *[1790].* [806]

16 p., 16mo. Evans 22390, Sabin 34702. DLC, MHi, RPJCB.

Decalves, Alonso, *pseud.*

New | travels | to the | westward, | or, | unknown parts of America. | Being a tour of almost fourteen months, | containing | an account of the country, upwards of twc | thousand miles west of the Christian parts | of North-America; with an account of white | Indians, their manners, habits, and many | other particulars. | By Don Alonso Decalves. | Confirmed by three other persons. | The third edition. | *Norwich: Printed and sold by John* | *Trumbull, M,DCC,XC.* [807]

34 p., 12mo. (16.5 cm.). OClWHi.

Dickenson, Jonathan

God's protecting Providence, . . . The seventh edition. *London: Printed and sold by James Phillips, George-Yard, Lombard-Street. M,DCC,XC.* [808]

136 p., 8vo. (15.9 x 9.5 cm.). Sabin 20015, Ayer 70. Copies in most large libraries.

Filson, John

Reise nach Kentucke und Nachrichten von dieser neu angebaueten Landschaft in Nordamerika: von John Filson. Aus dem Englischen übersetzt. *Leipzig: C. Weigel und Schneider, 1790.* [809]

124 p., 8vo. (20 cm.). (Bibliothek der neuesten Reisebeschreibungen). DLC, RPJCB.

Issued with Claude E. Savary's *Reise nach Griechenland.* Nürnberg, 1789.

Title from DLC card. W.R. Jillson's reprint of *Filson's Kentucke,* 1929, p. 154, calls this the 3d. German edition and says: "The first German translation was made by Ludwig Heinrich Bronner, octavo, 254 pages, and was published in Frankfort, 1785; a second was published in Nürnberg in 1789, together with a description of Greenland [sic] by Claude E. Savary."

Lettre écrite par un Français émigrant sur les terres de la Compagnie du Scioto, à son ami à Paris. *[Paris? 1790].* [809A]

27 p., 8vo. Bib. Nat.

"The division of emigrants, of which I am one, is under the care of M. Boulogne, a young Parisian lawyer." He speaks of "the imposture of the Scioto Company." Dated from New York, May 23, 1790.

Marrant, John

A narrative of the Lord's wonderful dealings with John Marrant, a Black, born in New-York, in North-America. Taken down from his own relation, arranged, corrected, and published by the Rev. Mr. Aldridge. The sixth

edition, with additions and notes explanatory . . . *Dublin: Printed by B. Dugdale, 1790.*   [810]
31, [1] p., 12mo. Porter 187. MWA, NN.
Title from NN catalog.

. . . . .

London, 1790. MB, A.B. Spingarn.   [811]

. . . . .

The seventh edition, *London, 1802.*   [812]
40 p., 8vo. (20.5 cm.). Porter 188. A.B. Spingarn.

. . . . .

Halifax: | Printed at the office of J. Nicholson | 1808.   [813]
iv, 22 p., 8vo. (21.3 x 12.9 cm.). Ayer supp. 2. F.C. Deering, ICN.

. . . . .

Leeds: | Printed by Davies and Co. at the Stanhope Press, Vicar-Lane. | 1810.   [814]
24 p., 8vo. (20.7 x 13 cm.). Sabin 44678, Ayer supp. 3, Porter 189. DLC, F.C. Deering, ICN, MH, NN.

. . . . .

Leeds: | Printed by Preston and Co., at the Stanhope Press, Vicar-Lane. | 1810.   [815]
24 p., 8vo. (20.5 cm.). Porter 190. A.B. Spingarn.

. . . . .

Halifax: | Printed at the office of J. Nicholson. | 1812.   [816]
48 p., 12mo. (17 x 10.5 cm.). Ayer 10, Porter 191. ICN, NHi.

. . . . .

York: Printed by R. and J. Richardson, 1812. F.C. Deering.   [817]

. . . . .

An interesting narrative, of the life of John Marrant (a man of color). Containing an account of his birth, extraordinary conversion, and remarkable success among the Cherokee Indians, his arrival in England, and departure as a missionary to America. Compiled originally by the Rev. J. [sic] Aldridge . . . A new edition. *Brighton: T. Sharp. 1813.*   [818]
27, [1] p., 12mo. (18.5 cm.). Sabin 44677, Porter 192. NN.

. . . . .

A narrative . . . *Halifax: Printed at the office of J. Nicholson & Co., 1813.*   [819]

48 p., illus., 8vo. (17 cm.). Porter 193. BM, DLC, F.C. Deering, MB, MWA, MWH, NN.

. . . . .

Newry: *Printed for Alexander Wilkinson. 1813.* F.C. Deering.   [820]

. . . . .

Halifax: *Printed at the office of J. Nicholson & Co., 1815.*   [821]
48 p., 8vo. Porter 194. F.C. Deering, MiU, NN.

. . . . .

Leeds: | *Printed by Davies and Co. at the Stanhope Press, Vicar-Lane.* |
1815.   [822]
24 p., 8vo. (22 x 13.3 cm.). Ayer supp. 4, Porter 195. F.C. Deering, ICN, MB, MH, NHi, NN, A.B. Spingarn.

. . . . .

Carmarthen: | *Printed at the Gomerian Office, by Z.B. Morris.* | *1817.*
                                                                      [823]
35, [1] p., 12mo. (17.3 x 10.7 cm.). Ayer supp. 5. ICN.

. . . . .

In Welch: Adroddiad | am | ymdriniaethau rhyfeddol | yr | Arglwydd | a | Ioan Marrant, | dyn du, | a aned yn New-York, yn Ngogledd Americ, | yr hwn a aeth i bregethu'r efengyl yn Nova-Scotia, [yn yflwyddyn 1785. | A ysgrifenwyd ganddo ei hun, | ac a gyhoeddwyd gan | gan y Parch. Mr. Aldridge, | *Caerdydd: Argraffwyd gan Richard Lloyd.* | *1818.*   [824]
iii, 21 p., 12mo. (17 x 9.2 cm.). Ayer 13. ICN.

. . . . .

A narrative . . . *Middletown, 1820.* F.C. Deering.   [825]

. . . . .

The third edition . . . *Yarmouth: Printed by J. Barnes, 11, Regent-Street,* *1824. Price sixpence.*   [826]
iv, [7]-38 p.,   Porter 196. NHi.

. . . . .

Halifax: | *Printed and sold by J. Nicholson.* | *1825.*   [827]
26 p., front., 8vo. (21.9 x 13.2 cm.). Ayer 11. F.C. Deering. ICN.

. . . . .

An interesting narrative . . . *Brighton, 1829.*   [828]
27 p., 12mo. (17 cm.). Porter 197. CtY, MB.

. . . . . .

London, 1829. CtY, MB.   [829]

. . . . . .

London, 1835. DHU.   [830]

. . . . . .

A narrative . . . Manchester: | *Re-printed by John Gadsby, Newall's-buildings.* | *London:* | *E. Fowler* . . . | . . . | *1835* . . . | . . . | [831]
27 p., 12mo. (17.8 x 10.4 cm.). Ayer 12, Porter 198. F.C. Deering, ICN, MH.

. . . . . .

Third edition, *London: R. Groombridge; Manchester: J. Gadsby, 1838.*
                                                                      [832]
22 p., 12mo. F.C. Deering, NN.

. . . . . .

London, Printed by request. [n.d.] F.C. Deering.   [833]

MOUSTIER, ÉLÉONORE-FRANÇOIS-ÉLIE, COMTE DE

Lettre | de M. de Moustier, | Ministre du Roi | auprès des Etats-Unis, | à l'Assemblée Nationale. | Séance du 2 Août 1790. | Imprimée par Ordre de l'Assemblée. *[Paris] Impr. Nationale.* [1790].   [833A]
3 p., 8vo. Title from Bib. Nat. cat. Bib. Nat.
Same, in *Procès-verbal de l'Assemblée Nationale,* tome XXVI, no. 368. 4 p. Bib. Nat.
Violent attack on the Scioto Company.

Observations générales et impartiales sur l'Affaire du Scioto. *A Paris: Didot le jeune. 1790.*   [834]
25 p., 8vo. Sabin 56476, old John Carter Brown cat. 3400. RPJCB.

. . . . . .

Observations relatives au plan de l'Établissement d'une Colonie sur les bords de l'Ohio et du Scioto dans l'Amerique Septentrionale. *Paris. 1790.*
                                                                      [834A]
13 p., map, 8vo. Sabin 56575. Bib. Nat.
Against the Scioto Company. Reprinted from the *Spectateur National.*

PANTHER, ABRAHAM, *pseud.*

A very | surprising narrative, | of a | young woman, | discovered in a | rocky-cave, | after having been taken by the | savage Indians of the wilderness, | in the year 1777, | and seeing no human being for the space of nine years. | In a letter from a gentleman to his friend. | (Fifth edition.) | *New-York.* | *Printed for the purchasers.* | *[1790?].* [835]

11 p., 12mo. Sabin 93892. DLC, WHi.

Le Parlement de Paris etabli au Scioto. Sur les bords de l'Oyo. *Et se trouve á Paris, chez tous les Marchands de Nouveautes, 1790.* [836]

60 p., 8vo. Thomson 708.

PLAYFAIR, WILLIAM

Lettre et observations adressées à M. l'Abbé Aubert, au sujet de l'extrait d'un écrit intitulé: Le Nouveau Mississippi ou les dangers d'habiter les bords du Scioto, inséré dans les affiches, annonces et avis divers, no. 102, du lundi 12 avril 1790. *[Paris, 1790].* [836A]

4 p., 16mo. Bib. Nat.

Signed: William Playfair, Directeur de la Compagnie du Scioto.

An answer to our no. 838.

The returned captive. A poem. Founded on a late fact. *Reprinted Norwich: John Trumbull. 1790.* [837]

12mo. Evans 22834, Trumbull 1296, H.V. Jones checklist 614. F.C. Deering. The H.V. Jones copy offered by the Rosenbach Co. cat. 1942, no. 137. $585. Same in their 1947 cat. no. 242, same price, described as "Believed to be the only perfect copy known. . . . The poem is said to have been written by Major Wood."

[Roux, ———]

Le Nouveau | Mississipi, | ou | les dangers | d'habiter | les bords du Scioto, | par un Patriote Voyageur. | [orn.] | *A Paris,* | *De l'Imprimerie de Jacob-Sion, rue* | *St. Jacques. No. 251.* | *Et se vend chez les Libraires du Palais-Royal.* | [filet] | *1790.* [838]

44 p., 12mo. (20.2 x 12.3 cm.). Sabin 73511 and 35512, old John Carter Brown cat. 3381. DLC, MH, NHi, NN, RPJCB.

The author's name: "M. Roux" appears in the Advertisement. Edited with a preface by N. F. Jacquemart. For a reply, see no. 836A above.

SCIOTO LAND COMPANY

Nouveau prospectus de la Compagnie du Scioto, avec plusieurs extraits de lettres, écrites du Scioto même, en date du 12 octobre 1790. *[Paris, De l'imprimerie de Clousier, imprimeur du roi] 1790.* [839]

[2], 20 p., 8vo. (19.5 cm.). Sabin 78125, DLC cat. Bib. Nat., DLC.

See also under Lezay-Marnezia; Roux; *Address to the inhabitants;* d'Allemagne: *Nouvelles du Scioto; Observations générales; Observations relatives* and *Le parlement de Paris*. See also Frank Monoghan: *Scioto madness*, in: *Legion d'Honneur*, vol. 4, no. 2, 1933, p. 114-120.

[WALTON, WILLIAM]

A | narrative | of the | captivity | and | sufferings | of | Benjamin Gilbert | and his | family; | who were surprised by the Indians, and | taken from their farms, on the fron- | tiers of Pennsylvania. | In the Spring, 1780. | *Philadelphia, Printed:* | London: | *Reprinted and sold by James Phillips, George-* | *Yard, Lombard-street.* | M.DCC.XC. [840]

124 p., 12m. (18.4 x 10.7 cm.). Sabin 27348, Ayer 303. BM, CSmH, DLC, F.C. Deering, ICN, MH, MiU-C, MnHi, MWA, N, NN, PSC-Hi, RPJCB.

.   .   .   .   .

On the | captivity | of | Benjamin Gilbert & family. | By the Indians in 1780. | Composed by the late Paul Preston | *Doylestown, 1808.* Printed by Asher Miner. [841]

5 p., 12mo. (16.5 x 11.4 cm.).

Title from bibliography of the 1904 edition. Abbreviated from the Walton narrative.

.   .   .   .   .

A | narrative | of the | captivity and sufferings | of | Benjamin Gilbert and family; | who were surprised by the Indians, and taken | from their farms, on the frontiers | of Pennsylvania. | [double rule] | *Philadelphia:* | *Printed for the publisher.* | [dotted rule] | *1813.* [842]

[2], vii-viii, 9-45, 48-82, [2], 89-96 p., front., 12mo. (15.2 x 8.3 cm.). Sabin 101219. CaT, DLC, N.

.   .   .   .   .

A narrative | of the | captivity and sufferings | of | Benjamin Gilbert | and his family, | who were taken by the Indians | in the Spring of 1780. | Third edition, | revised and enlarged. | To which is prefixed | a short account of the Gilbert family | who settled at Byberry. | An appendix, | giving some account of the captives | after their return. | *Philadelphia:* | *Printed by John Richards, No. 299 Market Street.* | *1848.* [843]

240 p., 16mo. (15.1 x 8.9 cm.). Ayer 304, Sabin 27348. DLC, F.C. Deering, ICN, N, NHi, NN, NRU, PSC-Hi.

Rewritten and enlarged by John Comly, a teacher at Byberry, for the benefit of Elizabeth Webster, the last survivor of the captives.

.   .   .   .   .

A narrative | of the | captivity and sufferings | of | Benjamin Gilbert | and | his family. | Who were surprised by the Indians and taken from | their farm, on Mahoning Creek, in Penn township, | Northampton County, not far from where Fort Allen was built, on the frontier of Penn- | sylvania, in the Spring of 1780. | Only 150 copies—privately printed. | *Lancaster, Pa.* | *1890.*   [844]

[2], 38 p., 8vo. (23 x 14.3 cm.). Ayer 305. DLC, F.C. Deering, ICN, MBAt, MH, N, NHi, NRU.

Abridged and rewritten.

.   .   .   .   .

Narratives of captivities | The captivity and sufferings of | Benjamin Gilbert and | his family, 1780-83 | Reprinted from the original edition of 1784 | with introduction and notes by | Frank H. Severance | [publisher's device] | *Cleveland: The Burrows Brothers Company* | *1904.*   [845]

204 p., illus., folded map, 8vo. (20.5 x 14 cm.). Ayer 306. Copies in most ·large libraries.

There were 27 copies on Japan paper, 267 copies on book paper.

For reprints in other works, see Sabin 101219 and the bibliography in the 1904 edition.

WINTHROP, JOHN

A journal of the transactions and occurrences in the settlement of Massachusetts and the other New-England colonies, from the year 1630 to 1644: written by John Winthrop, Esq. First Governor of Massachusetts: and now first published from a correct copy of the original manuscript. [2 lines quoted] [publisher's monogram] *Hartford: Printed by Elisha Babcock.* M,DCC,XC.
                                                                                    [846]

[6], 364, [4] p., 8vo. Sabin 104847, Evans 23086. Copies in most large libraries.

The original manuscript journal in 3 vols. was owned by Thomas Prince before the Revolution. The first two volumes were discovered in the hands of the Winthrop family after the war and published as above, edited, not too well, by Noah Webster. The third volume was discovered in Prince's library in Boston in 1816 and a complete edition was planned but while in preparation, the second volume was burned, so the text for that volume had to be taken from that of the 1790 edition. The complete work was published as: *The history of New England from 1630 to 1649. . . . With notes . . . by James Savage . . . Boston: Printed by Phelps and Farnham* [vol. 2 by *Thomas B. Wait and Son* . . .] . . . 1825 [-1826]. 2 vols., port., folded facsim., 8vo. Sabin 104845; same, reprinted, 1853. Another ed., 1908.

This, with William Bradford's *History of Plymouth Plantation, Boston, 1856* and later editions, is the foundation of our knowledge of the first years of the history of Massachusetts.

ASPLUND, JOHN

The annual register of the Baptist Denomination, in North-America; to the first of November, 1790. Containing an account of the churches and their constitutions, ministers, members, associations, their plan and sentiments, rule and order, proceedings and correspondence. Also remarks upon practical religion. Humbly offered to the public by John Asplund. *[Norfolk: Printed by Prentis and Baxter? 1791].* [847]

70 [i.e. 60] p., including index, 4to. Evans 23132, De Renne I:249. BM, DLC, GU-De, MWA, NHi, NN, RPJCB.

. . . . .

70 p., no index. It is not certain which of the above libraries has which issue, except that GU-De and NHi have both. [847A]

. . . . .

The annual register of the Baptist denomination in North America, to the first of December 1790, containing an account of the churches and their constitutions, ministers, members, associations, their plan and sentiments, rule and order, proceedings and correspondence . . . *[n.p., 1791].* [848]

72 p., 4to. Title from Sabin 2222.

Frequently reprinted with additions, presumably at Norfolk or Richmond in 1791 and 1792 and at Philadelphia in 1792. See Evans 26579-83. One or more editions in the following libraries: GSDe, MiUW, MWA, NCU, NHi, OCl, RPJCB, ScCoT, Vi, WHi.

Report of social and religious conditions on the frontiers.

BARTRAM, WILLIAM

Travels through North and South Carolina, Georgia, East & West Florida, the Cherokee country, the extensive territories of the Muscogulges, or Creek Confederacy, and the country of the Choctaws; containing an account of the soil and natural productions of those regions, together with observations of the manners of the Indians. Embellished with copper-plates. By William Bartram. *Philadelphia, Printed by James & Johnson, M,DCC,XCI.* [849]

[2], xxxiv, 522 p., port., map and 7 plates, 8vo.

Title from Sabin 3870, Evans 23159-60, 2 variant issues. Copies in most large libraries.

. . . . .

London, 1792. In most large libraries. [850]

. . . . .

Dublin, 1793. In most large libraries. [851]

. . . . .

London, 1794. In most large libraries.   [852]

. . . . .

In German, *Berlin,* 1793. MIU-C, PHi, PPAmP, PW-B, RPJCB.   [853]

. . . . .

In German, *Wien,* 1793. MH-A.   [854]

. . . . .

In Dutch, *Haarlem,* 1794. GSDe, MH-A, NN, PPAmP, PU-B, RPJCB.
                                                                          [855]

. . . . .

In French, *Paris,* an VII [1798-1799]. MH-A and others.   [856]

. . . . .

In French, *Paris,* an IX [1801] NN and others.   [857]

. . . . .

In French, *Paris,* 1800. RPJCB.   [858]

[BOWLES, WILLIAM AUGUSTUS ?]

Authentic memoirs of William Augustus Bowles, Esquire, Ambassador from the United Nations of Creeks and Cherokees, to the court of London. *London: R. Faulder. M. DCC. XCI.*   [859]
[4], vi, 79 p. Title from Sabin 7082. DLC, GSDe, MH, PPL-R, RPJCB. Reprinted in Mag. of Hist., extra no. 46, 1916.

A native of Maryland, lived as an adopted Indian. See also: *The life of General W.A. Bowles . . . New York,* 1803. Sabin 7083, and sketch in Haywood's *Tennessee.*

BRADMAN, ARTHUR

A narrative of the extraordinary sufferings of Mr. Robert Forbes, his wife, and five children, during an unfortunate journey through the wilderness, from Canada to Kennebeck River in the year 1784: in which three of their children were starved to death. (Taken partly from their own mouths and partly from an imperfect journal; and published at their request.) By Arthur Bradman. *Portland: Printed at Thomas Baker Wait's Office. MDCCXCI. Price nine pence.*   [860]
13 p., 16mo. Evans 23221. MWA.

. . . . .

Same title, imprint and date.   [861]

23 p., including half title and postscript, 8vo. NN. Title from Rosenbach Company catalog: *Monuments of wit and learning,* 1946, no. 167. $750.00. Note suggests that MWA copy may be imperfect but, since Evans describes the MWA copy as a 16mo and this copy is described as an 8vo, they may be different editions.

While this story of frontier tragedy is generally listed as an Indian captivity, the Forbes family were never captives, though the editions from 1794 on include the separate captivity of Mrs. Frances Scott, which see. The Forbes family started in March, 1784, to go overland from Canada to the settlements on the Kennebec River under the guidance of three Indians who, however, deserted them midway in their journey, taking most of their food. They continued alone, met an Indian who gave them some moose meat and when that was gone, the father and eldest son pushed on ahead in search of help. After ten days they reached the settlement, sent out a relief party which failed to find them and returned. A second party then set out and, fifty days after the father and son had left them, the rest of the family was found. The mother and one child were alive but the other three children had starved.

BRISSOT DE WARVILLE, JEAN PIERRE

Nouveau voyage | dans | les États-Unis | de | l'Amérique Septentrionale, | fait en 1788; | Par J.P. Brissot (Warville), | Citoyen François. | [rule, 3 lines quoted, rule] | Tome Premier [Second, Troisième] | [rule] | *A Paris,* | *Chez Buisson, Imprimeur et Libraire, rue* | *Haute-Feuille, No. 20.* | [double rule] | *Avril 1791.* [862]

3 vols., [4], lij, 395; [4], 460; iv, xxiij, 448 p., folded table, 8vo. (19.5 x 12.5 cm.). Sabin 8035. Copies in most large libraries.

First edition of first two volumes (the travels), second edition of vol. 3: *De la France et des États-Unis . . . Par Étienne Clavière, et J.P. Brissot (Warville).*

Brissot de Warville came to America before the French Revolution to find an asylum for French refugees and to secure all possible information about America. His book was widely read in English, German and Dutch as well as French, and had great influence in bringing European emigrants to our cities and our frontiers.

The | Columbian tragedy. | Containing a particular and official | account | of the brave and unfortunate officers and soldiers, who were | slain and wounded in the ever-memorable and | bloody Indian battle, | . . . on Friday morning, Nov. 4, 1791 . . . *America: Boston; Printed by E. Russell,* | *for Thomas Bassett, of Dun-* | *barton, (New-Hamp.) . . . [1791].* [863]

Broadside, folio (55 x 42 cm.). Evans 23268, Ford's Mass Bdsds. 2612. MB, MHi, MiU-C, MWA, NHi, NN.

At top of the broadside are two rows of 39 coffins bearing the names of the officers killed in the battle, and two crude woodcuts. As later news reached Boston, the number of coffins was increased. A copy of this later issue, possibly issued in 1792, is at MWA. There is also an issue later than the first, at NN. The first issue is reproduced in Ola E. Winslow's *American broadside verse*, 1930, no. 29.

. . . . .

Same, reprinted. *[Boston, 1822].* Ford 2613. CtY, MB, MWA, NN.

[864]

A similar broadside: Boston, December 19. | Melancholy account | respecting the | western army. | [Boston:] Printed by B. Edes and Son, | State-Street. [1791].

Broadside, folio. Evans 23214, Ford 2615. MWA.

See also under Matthew Bunn, 1792.

[DAVIS, DANIEL]

An | address | to the | inhabitants of the District | of Maine, | upon the subject of their | separation | from the present | government of Massachusetts. | By one of their fellow citizens. | [rule] | *Printed at Portland, by Thomas B. Wait.—April, 1791.*   [865]

54 p., 4to. Evans 33313. Copies in most large libraries.

Early agitation for the separation of the District of Maine from Massachusetts. The new state was not erected until 1820.

DICKENSON, JONATHAN

God's protecting Providence, . . . The seventh edition. *Philadelphia: Printed by Joseph Crukshank, in Market-Street, between Second and Third-Streets. M DCC XCI.*   [866]

123 p., 12mo. (13.5 cm.). H.V. Jones catalog 617. CtY (H.V. Jones-Rosenbach Company copy), PSC-Hi.

[FRANKLIN, WILLIAM TEMPLE?]

An | account | of the | soil, growing timber, and other productions, | of the | lands in the countries situated in the back parts of | the State of New-York and Pensylvania, | in | North America. | And | particularly the lands in the County of Ontario, | known by the name of | The Genesee Tract, | lately located, | and now in the progress of being settled. | [rule] | *[London:] Printed in the year 1791.*   [867]

[2], 37, 4, [39]-45 p., 2 folded maps, small folio (25.5 cm.). Sabin 26926. BM, DLC, MBAt, MWA, NHi, NN. The DLC copy lacks title and that and the MWA copy have only 37 p.

Two folded maps: *A map of the Genesee Tract, in the County of Ontario, & State of New York:* | . . . (36 x 25.5 cm.). NHi copy partly colored; *A* map of the Genesee Lands in the County of Ontario and State of New York | . . . 1790. (37 x 26 cm.). NHi copy colored. The first map shows the territory from Lake Ontario to Cape Henry, the second shows the Phelps and Gorham Purchase. The first was copied, with French titles, for use in Van Pradelles: *Réflections offertes*, 1792.

This work was issued in the interest of Robert Morris and was printed in London, probably by his agent, William Temple Franklin, grandson of Benjamin Franklin, who was in England at the time, attempting to sell Morris's Genesee lands to English investors. He succeeded in selling the remaining unsold portions of the tract to the English Associates (Pulteney, Hornby and Colquhoun). It was reprinted in Imlay's *Topographical description*, 1797, and was translated into German in the interest of the English associates, for which see the following title.

. . . . .

Berichte | über den | Genesee-Distrikt | in dem | Staate von Neu-York | der | vereinigten Staaten von Nord-Amerika | nach der | im Jahr 1791 | Englischen [sic] herausgegebenen Ausgabe | übersetzt. | [rule] | *[n.p.]* *Gedruckt im December 1791.* [868]

32, 8, 8 p., 8vo. (19.5 x 12 cm.). MH (2 copies, one with additional text inserted), photostat copies at NHi and NN.

Second title: *Betrachtungen über Auswanderung der Völker.* [Caption title] 8 p. Third title: *Auszug der Anmerkungen zum Unterricht derjenigen Europäer, die sich in Amerika niederzulassen gesonnen sind, von dem letztlich verstorbenen berühmten Dr. Franklin.* [Caption title] 8 p.

Second copy at MH has following additions inserted after p. 8 of first supplement: *A map of the Genesse Tract* (from 1st ed.); text without title, beginning: "Da es der erstlichste Wunsch der Genesee Association ist, . . . Hamburg, April, 1792" 16 p.; text without title, beginning: "Es gehen jährlich viele Hundert gute . . ." 16 p.; at end, folded broadside redemptioner contract, left half in English, right half in German, filled out and signed by William Berczy.

This translation was made for and probably by William Berczy, agent of the English Associates for bringing German emigrants to the Company's New York lands. In the above work he is styled "Agent of the Genesee-Association of London" and the last document is dated at Hamburg, April 17, 1792. See A.C. Parker's *Charles Williamson*, Miss H.I. Cowan's *Charles Williamson* in Rochester Hist. Soc. Pubs., 19, 1941 and William Berczy's *Journal* in Buffalo Hist. Soc. Pubs. The scheme for bringing German emigrants to the Association's tract in Western New York was a failure since the emigrants from German cities were totally unsuited to pioneer life. Berczy and his German colony finally removed to Canada. For a further account of Morris's unfortunate land speculations, see: "Brief of the titles of Robert Morris, Esquire, to a tract of country in the County of Ontario, in the State of New-York, one of the United States of America. Extracted from authentic documents, by Miers Fisher, Counsellor at Law, in the Supreme Court of the United States. To which is added a schedule, containing authentic copies of the principal acts and resolves of the general Congress of the United States, and of the Legislatures of the States of Massachusetts and New-York, and of other deeds and evidences of title, cited in the brief, for the satisfaction of those who may wish to see them at full length. *Philadelphia: Printed by Benj. Franklin Bache, . . . 1791."* [2], 45 p., 4to. Title from Evans 23376. MBAt, NN.

For a further account of Robert Morris's Western New York lands, see the following title, prepared for the use of the judges of the United States Supreme Court in the bankruptcy proceedings against Morris who was in jail for debt in Philadelphia at the time: "Account of Robert Morris' property. *[n.p., n.d.]."* 74 p., 8vo. NN.

For the sheriff's sale of part of his Philadelphia real estate, see Jonathan Penrose, no. 1207.

HANSON, ELIZABETH

An account of the captivity of Elizabeth Hanson, . . . A new edition. Taken in substance from her own mouth. By Samuel Bownas. To which is added, The great audit; or, good steward . . . Taken out of the writings of . . . Sir Matthew Hale . . . *Cork: Printed by Jones and Co., 1791.*   [869]

21 p., 12mo. Title from NN catalog card. NN.

Follows the text of the 1787 edition.

. . . . .

God's mercy surmounting man's cruelty, . . . The third edition. *Stanford (State of New-York): Printed and sold by Daniel Lawrence, and Henry & John F. Hull. 1803.*   [870]

22, [1] p., 16mo. Title from DLC card. DLC, F.C. Deering, N, NN.

Title and probably the text follows the 2d. Amer. ed., Phil., 1754.

. . . . .

An account . . . *Leeds, 1810.* Rosenbach Company cat., 1911. Not seen.   [871]

. . . . .

An account . . . *Leeds, 1815.* F.C. Deering. Not seen.   [872]

. . . . .

An account . . . *[Leeds? 1815?]*   [873]

16 p. Caption title only. CSmH, ICN.

Not seen. Probably same edition or from same type as [1830?] ed., which see below.

. . . . . .

The remarkable captivity and surprising deliverance of Elizabeth Hanson, wife of John Hanson, of Knoxmarsh, at Kecheachy, in Dover Township, who was taken captive with her children and maid-servant, by the Indians in New-England, in the year 1724, in which are inserted sundry remarkable preservations, providences, and marks of the care and kindness of Providence over her and her children, worthy to be remembered, the substance of which was taken from her own mouth. *Dover. Re-printed [by J. Mann] from a copy of the third edition, printed, M,DCC,LXXX. 1824.* [874]

24 p., 12mo. (17.5 cm.). Sabin 69376. F.C. Deering, DLC (the A.A. Tufts-John Farmer-S.G. Drake-George Brinley 479 copy with presentation inscription from Tufts to Farmer and notes by Farmer and Drake), MH, Nh, NhDo, NhHi.

Reprinted from third American edition, Phil., 1780.

. . . . . .

Same title, *Dover. Re-printed from a copy of the fourth edition 1824. [ca. 1896].* [875]

[15] p., text in double columns, light blue wrappers with title repeated on front cover, 8vo. (23.5 x 15.5 cm.). NHi. Nh.

Copy owned 1935 by two sisters, 8th generation descendants of Elizabeth Hanson, Ossipee, NH., lent by them to Edward A. Preble of Washington, D.C. who then planned to reprint it.

NHi copy received Oct. 9, 1896. Type and woodpulp paper seem to be of that period. Reprinted from Dover, 1824 ed., above.

. . . . . .

An account of the remarkable captivity of Elizabeth Hanson, her four children and servant-maid, who were taken by the Indians. *[n.p., n.d.]* [876]

16 p., 8vo. (21.4 x 12.7 cm.). Perhaps same as [Leeds?, 1815?] ed. OCl (according to Union Cat., dates a copy [1741?]). ICN (dates their copy [London? ca. 1820]. NN and PCDHi (date their copies [London? 1830?]. The Late Wilberforce Eames considered [ca. 1830] the correct date for the NN copy. Whether printed in London or Leeds has not been determined. The Leeds, 1810-1815 editions and the London?, 1820-30 edition, with same pagination, are doubtless related.

Reprinted from the Dover, 1824 ed. in Samuel G. Drake: *Indian captivities,* Bost., 1839; *Auburn,* 1850, 1851, 1852, 1853, 1854; *New York,* 1855; *Boston,* 1856; *New York and Auburn,* 1856; *New York,* 1857, 1859, 1870, 1872; same issued under title: *Tragedies of the wilderness, Boston,* 1841, 1844, 1846.

Reprinted in [Wimer, James, ed.] *Events in Indian history, Lancaster,* 1841; *Phil.,* 1842; *Lancaster,* 1843.

JOHONNOT, JACKSON

The remarkable adventures of Jackson Johonnet of Massachusetts. Who served as a soldier in the Western Army, in the Massachusetts Line, in the expedition under General Harmar, and the unfortunate General St. Clair. Containing an account of his captivity, sufferings, and escape from the Kickapoo Indians. Written by himself, and published at the earnest importunity of his friends, for the benefit of American youth. *Printed at Lexington, (Kentucky) by John Bradford. 1791.*   [877]

Title from Evans 33474 who gives no collation or location and who probably took the title from an advertisement, from the copyright entry or from the imprint of the Providence, 1793 edition which reads: *Printed at Lexington (Kentucky) 1791. Re-printed at Providence. M,DCC,XCIII.* McMurtrie's *Check list of Kentucky imprints,* no. 4, copies Evans and locates no copy.

Jackson Johonnot, a native of Falmouth, Maine, left home at the age of seventeen, went to Boston, enlisted and was sent to join the Western Army at Fort Washington, Cincinnati, Ohio. On August 4, 1791, with several others, he was captured by a band of Kickapoos on the banks of the Wabash and carried to their village on the Upper Miami, five of his companions having been killed and scalped in the fight. Four others, whom he also names, all from Massachusetts, were captured but separated from him, his only remaining companion being Richard Sackville. On the night of August 30, they killed the small squad of Indians with them and started to escape to Fort Jefferson, near the present Greenville, Ohio. On their way, they discovered four Indians with two prisoners, shot two of the Indians, reloaded and killed one more but the last Indian killed Sackville and one of the prisoners before he too was killed. Johonnot and the other prisoner, Gregory Saxton of Newport, Rhode Island, then made their way to Fort Jefferson where they arrived on September 18. He ends his narrative with his first-hand account of St. Clair's defeat at the site of Fort Recovery on November 4, 1791 in which battle he took part and escaped unscratched to Fort Jefferson the following day. This is one of the best true stories of adventure and captivity of this period, if it *is* a true story and not a later fabrication made from contemporary evidence.

It has been argued that, since St. Clair's defeat took place at present-day Fort Recovery, Ohio on Nov. 4, 1791, there was not time for this narrative to have reached Lexington, Kentucky in time to be printed in 1791, and that, therefore, there was no Lexington edition of that year and the statement in the imprint of the Providence edition was a deliberate falsehood. This reasoning, however, does not seem conclusive for the author reached Fort Jefferson, six miles below present-day Greenville, the day after the St. Clair defeat and it is only about 140 miles as the crow flies from there to Lexington. The remaining 56 days of the year 1791 would have given Johonnot ample time to write his 15 page narrative, take or send it to Lexington and have it printed before the end of the year, especially as his story was spot news and its publication would be rushed. From Fort Jefferson to Frankfort, down the Ohio and Kentucky rivers, was a quick and easy water route and there was a good road for the 25 miles from Frankfort to Lexington, so the entire journey would take only a few days. And, of course, the fact that no copy of the pamphlet is now known is no proof that it was never printed. We do not hold with the man who claimed there was no such animal as a camel just because he had never seen one.

However, Mr. Ernest J. Wessen, a careful student of the history of this region, states that there is no announcement of the supposed Lexington edition in the *Kentucky Gazette,* the only Lexington newspaper for the years 1791-92. He further maintains that the narrative is completely fraudulent; an account drawn from eastern newspapers by someone unfamiliar with the details of the campaign. The hero was supposed to have been captured on an expedition with Harmar at a time when Harmar was under suspension and preparing his defense and so not on active duty. The narrator arrived at Fort Jefferson a month before it was located and named. If this is true, the Beers's Almanac edition of 1792 (our no. 914) is probably the first edition, reprinted at Providence in 1793 with a misleading imprint (our no. 950), and the Lexington, 1791 edition never existed. In this case, the Johonnot narrative is probably not a true story but an interesting example of early American historical fiction.

LONG, J[OHN]

Voyages and travels | of an | Indian interpreter and trader, | describing | the manners and customs | of the | North American Indians; | with | an account of the posts | situated on | the river Saint Laurence, Lake Ontario, &c. | To which is added, | a vocabulary | of | the Chippeway language. | Names of furs and skins, in English and French. | A list of words | in the | Iroquois, Mohegan, Shawanee, and Esquimeaux tongues, | and a table, shewing | the analogy between the Algonkin and Chippeway languages. | By J. Long. | [thin-thick rule] | *London:* | *Printed for the author; and sold by Robson, Bond-Street; Debrett,* | *Piccadilly; T. and J. Egerton, Charing-Cross; White and Son, Fleet-* | *Street; Sewell, Cornhill; Edwards, Pall-Mall; and Messrs. Tay-* | *lors, Holborn, London; Fletcher, Oxford; and Bull, Bath.* | M,DCC,XCI. [878]

[2], x, [2], 295 p., folded map, 4to. (29 x 22.5 cm.). Sabin 41878. Copies in most large libraries.

The most valuable record of Indian life and the fur trade of the period, by a fur trader who lived 19 years in the old Northwest. The vocabularies occupy pp. 183-295 and are of great value. The map, showing the territory from the Great Lakes north to James's Bay and from the Mississippi east to the St. Lawrence, is entitled: *Sketch | of the | Western countries | of | Canada | 1791.* (28 x 37 cm.).

. . . . .

J. Long's Westindischen Dollmetchers und Kaufmanns See- und Land-

Reisen, enthaltend: eine Beschreibung der Sitten und Gewohnheiten der Nordamerikanischen Wilden; der Englischen Forts oder Schanzen längs dem St. Lorenz-Flusse, dem See Ontario u.s.w.; ferner ein umständliches Wörterbuch der Chippewäischen und anderer Nordamerikanischen Sprachen. Aus dem Englischen. Hrsg. und mit einer kurzen Einleitung über Kanada und einer erbesserten Karte versehen von E.A.W. Zimmermann . . . *Hamburg: B. Gottlob Hoffmann. 1791.*   [879]

xxiv, 334, [2] p., map, 8vo. (21.5 cm.). Sabin 41881. DLC, RPJCB, etc.

Translation of his: *Voyages and travels,* above.

MORRIS, CAPTAIN THOMAS

Miscellanies | in | prose and verse. | [thick-thin rule] | By | Captain Thomas Morris. | [thin-thick rule] | *London:* | *Printed for James Ridgway, No. 1, York-Street,* | *St. James's-Square.* | [short double rule] | *1791.*   [880]

[2], 181, [4] p., front. (oval stipple port. of author), 20.5 x 12.5 cm. Sabin 50876. An-C-T, F.C. Deering, ICN (imperfect, lacking all after p. 39), MIU-C, NHi, NN, OCU, PPiU (J.B. Shea copy), RPB, RPJCB, ViU, WHi.

The journal is reprinted in: Thwaites: *Early western travels,* vol. I, 1904; *Magazine of history,* Extra no. 76, 1922, p. 5-29.

Journal of Captain Thomas Morris, of His Majesty's XVII Regiment of Infantry, p. [1]-39, dated at end: *Detroit, September 25, 1764.* The author served under General Bradstreet in the campaign against Pontiac in the Ohio Country, was captured by the Indians but released by Pontiac.

The Journal is followed by: *Letter to a friend on the poetical elocution of the theatre and the manner of acting tragedy,* p. [43]-64; and poems, p. 68-181, [4].

The NHi copy has the following contemporary manuscript note following the name of the author on the title page: *Died in London 10 Feb 1818.* [aged] 74.

ROWLANDSON, MARY

A | narrative | of the | captivity, sufferings and removes | of | Mrs. Mary Rowlandson, | who was taken prisoner by the Indians; with several | others, and treated in the most barbarous and cruel | manner by those vile savages; with many other | remarkable events during her travels. | Written by her own hand for her private use, and since | made public at the earnest desire of some friends, and for | the benefit of the afflicted. | *Boston:* | *Reprinted and sold by Thomas and John Fleet, at the | Bible and Heart, Cornhill, 1791.*   [881]

40 p., 8vo. Sabin 73585, Evans 23745. F.C. Deering, MBAt.

SOUTH CAROLINA YAZOO COMPANY

An | extract | from the | proceedings | of the | South Carolina | Yazoo Company. | *Charleston:* | *Printed for A. Timothy, Printer to the State.* | *MDCCLXXXXI.*   [882]

[6]; [2]; [2], 44; [2], 11; [2], 27, 13, [1] p., 8vo. Sabin 88054, De Renne I:253. DLC, GU-De, MBAt, MH, ScC.

The GU-De copy contains an autograph inscription signed: *Axr. Moultrie Presidt. Bd Proprs. S.C.Y.C.* The ScC copy contains a ms. note: *Said to be drawn up by R.G. Harper.* [Robert Goodloe Harper].

TENNESSEE COMPANY

Notice is hereby given, to those who may become adventurers to the Tennessee Purchase, that the subscriber intends to set out from Sanville, on the tenth of March next for the settlement of Muscle Shoals . . . *[n.p., 1791].*
[883]

Broadside, folio. Sabin 94806. CU-B.

Signed: John Gordon. Terms of agreement between the company and colonists signed by: Zachariah Cox, Thomas Gilbert, John Strother.

ASBURY, FRANCIS

An extract from the journal of Francis Asbury, Bishop of the Methodist Episcopal Church in America, from August 7, 1771, to December, 29, 1778. Volume I. *Philadelphia: Printed by Joseph Crukshank, No. 87, High-Street: Sold by John Dickins, No. 182, in Race-Street, near Sixth-Street. 1792.* [884]
[4], 356 p., 12mo. Sabin 2162, Evans 24060. MWA, NN, PHi, PPL, PPL-R, etc.

. . . . .

Continued. *Philadelphia*, 1802, 136 p. Sabin 2163. MWA, etc.   [885]

. . . . .

Continued, from 1771 to 1815. *New York*, 1821. 3 vols., 8vo. Frequently reprinted.   [886]
Bishop Asbury travelled far and was a close observer of life on the frontier.

BAYARD, STEPHEN N.

Mohawk General Land-Office, | held at Schenectady, in Washington-Street, | fronting Nestigeuna-Street, west of the Dutch Church, by | Stephen N. Bayard. | Office rules, | relative to proprietors of land. | [second page:] Rules relative to purchasers of land. . . . Rules, | relative to surveys made by persons employed by this office. . . . [Colophon at foot of second page:] *Printed by Barber & Southwick, Albany. [1792-1800].*   [887]
Broadsheet, folio. (33.5 x 21 cm.). NHi.

BRADMAN, ARTHUR

A | narrative | of the | extraordinary sufferings | of | Mr. Robert Forbes, | his wife and five children: | during | an unfortunate journey through the wil- | derness—from | Canada to Kennebeck River, | in the year 1784: | in which three of their children were | starved to death. | Taken partly from their own mouths, and | partly from an imperfect journal, and | compiled at their request. | [double rule] | By Arthur Bradman. | [double rule] | *Portland Printed:* | *Re-Printed at Exeter,* | *by Henry Ranlet, and sold at his office,* | *MDCCXCII.*   [888]

23 p., 8vo. (17.6 x 11.1 cm.). NHi.

Another copy, described as an unrecorded edition, in the Rosenbach Company catalog: *Monuments of wit and learning,* 1946, no. 168. $450.00. (The NHi copy was bought in 1903 for $5.00.)

In this edition, the three unfaithful guides who deserted them were not Indians but Dutchmen named Midstaff, Pancake and Christian.

·   ·   ·   ·   ·

Printed at Windsor, 1792, by Alden Spooner, and sold at his office.   [889]
15 p., 16mo. Evans 24144. F.C. Deering, ICN, NhHi.

BRISSOT DE WARVILLE, JEAN PIERRE

New travels in the United States of America. Performed in 1788. By J.P. Brissot de Warville. Translated from the French. *London: J.S. Jordan. MDCCXCII.*   [890]
[4], 483, [4] p., 8vo. Title from Sabin 8025. Copies in most large libraries.

·   ·   ·   ·   ·

Dublin: Printed by W. Corbet, for P. Byrne, A. Gueber . . . 1792.   [891]
[8], 483 p., 8vo. (21.5 cm.). Sabin 8025. DLC.

·   ·   ·   ·   ·

New-York: Printed by T. & J. Swords, for Berry & Rogers, Booksellers and Stationers, No. 35, Hanover-Square.—1792.—   [892]
264, [8] p., folded table, 12mo. (17.5 cm.). Sabin 8025, Evans 24146. Copies in most large libraries. Reprints the travels only.

·   ·   ·   ·   ·

Neue Reise durch die Nord-Amerikanischen Freistaaten im Jahre 1788, mit Anmerkungen von J.R. Foster, aus dem Französischen. *Berlin. 1792.*
                                                                      [893]
8vo. Title from Sabin 8033.

·   ·   ·   ·   ·

J.P. Brissot's von Warwille Reise durch die Vereinigten Staaten von Nord-America, im Jahr 1788. Aus dem Französischen . . . von Theophil Friedrich

Ehrmann. *Dürkheim an der Haard: F.L. Pfähler. 1792.* [894]
  lxviii, 625, [3] p., table, 8vo. Title from Sabin 8038. DLC.

. . . . .

  Heidelberg. 1792. [895]
  8vo. Sabin 8038. DLC.

[BUNN, MATTHEW]

  St. Clair's defeat. | A poem. | A tale, which strongly claims the pitying
tear, | And ev'ry feeling heart, must bleed to hear. | *Harrisburgh:* | *Printed
by John W. Allen and John Wyeth.* | *MDCCXCII.* [896]
  [2], 14 p., 16mo. (15.5 cm.). Evans 24474, Wegelin's Poetry 239. CSmH.
  The ballad is included in the 1828 edition of Bunn's *Narrative.*

. . . . .

  A tragical account of the defeat of Gen. St. Clair by the savages. [and]
Battle of Bunker's Hill. [Boston? ca. 1792]. [897]
  Broadside, folio (33.5 x 26 cm.). Ford 2614. NHi.
  Attributed to Matthew Bunn by E.B. O'Callaghan in: *The author of the
ballad entitled: "St. Clair's Defeat"* in *Historical Magazine*, Dec., 1868, p.
261-263, with reprint of the ballad. It has also been attributed to Eli Lewis.
  Probably another version of the same: "Bloody Indian battle, fought at the
Miami village, November 4, 1791. A mournful elegy on the occasion. And
Jemmy and Nancy: a tragical garland. [orn.] *New-Haven: Printed by Moses
H. Woodward. [1798]."*
  12 p., 12mo. Evans 33432.
  See also under *Columbian tragedy, 1791.*
  The defeat of General Arthur St. Clair at the site of present day Fort
Recovery, Ohio, on November 4, 1791 with the loss of 900 men (two-thirds
of his army) killed and wounded, caused consternation throughout the coun-
try and especially on the frontier. The above ballad, the *Columbian Tragedy*
and other broadsides reflect the contemporary concern which was only
relieved by Mad Anthony Wayne's smashing victory over the Indians at the
Battle of Fallen Timbers on August 20, 1794, which quieted the uneasiness
of the frontier.

CARVER, JONATHAN

  Three years travels. *Philadelphia, 1792.* MWA, NHi, NN, etc. [898]
  See note at end of 1798 edition.

[CHASSANIS, PIERRE?]

  Description | topographique | de six cents mille acres de terres | dans
l'Amérique Septentrionale, | mises en vente par actions, suivant le Plan

d'Association | ci-joint. | [rule] | Prospectus. | [rule] | [orn.] | Le Bureau de la Compagnie est à Paris, rue de la | Jussienne, n°. 20. | [rule] | 1792. | [Colophon:] *[Paris:] De l'Imprimerie de Froullé, Quai des Augustins.* [899]

[2], 14, 8 p., 4to. (27 x 21 cm.). Sabin 19728. MH, MHi, MWiW-C, N, NHi, NN, RPJCB, R.W.G. Vail.

Caption title of second part: *Association | Pour la possession & exploitation de six cents mille acres de | terre concédées par l'État de New-Yorck, & situées dans cet | État entre les 43e. & 44e. degrés de latitude sur le Lac Ontario. | à 35 lieues de la Ville & Port d'Albany, où abordent les | vaisseaux de l'Europe.*

This tract was bought from William Constable by Pierre Chassanis of Paris in 1792 who sold it to 41 Frenchmen, many of them titled French Revolution refugees and none of them suited to the rigors of pioneer life. They were organized as *Le Compagnie de New-York* and called their tract *Castorland;* also known as *The Chassanis Purchase.* It was located in Lewis and Jefferson Counties, N. Y.

Translated in F.B. Hough's *History of Jefferson County, N. Y.* and his *History of St. Lawrence and Franklin Counties, N.Y.* See also *Le Compagnie de New York* and under Rodolphe Tillier.

CURRIE, WILLIAM

An | historical account | of | the climates and diseases | of | the United States of America; | and of | the remedies and methods of treatment, which | have been found most useful and efficaci | -ous, particularly in those diseases which | depend upon climate and situation. | Collected principally from | personal observation, | and | the communications of physicians of talents and | experience, residing in the several states. | [double rule]· | By William Currie, | Fellow of the College of Physicians of Philadelphia. | [double rule, line quoted, rule] | *Philadelphia: | Printed by T. Dobson, at the Stone-House, No. 41, | South Second-Street. | M,DCC,XCII.* [900]

[4], 4, 409, v p., 8vo. Sabin 17999, Evans 24239. BM, DLC, DSG, MBAt, MH, NHi, RPJCB.

One of the first important contributions to American medicine, showing health conditions on the frontier as well as in the towns.

DICKENSON, JONATHAN

The remarkable deliverance of Robert Barrow, with divers other persons, from the devouring waves of the sea, among which they suffered shipwreck; and also from the cruel devouring jaws of the inhuman cannibals of Florida: God's protecting Providence, man's surest help and defence, in times of greatest difficulty, and most eminent danger. Faithfully related by Jonathan Dickenson, one of the persons concerned therein. [five lines quoted from the Psalms] *Dover [N.H.]: Printed by Eliphalet Ladd M,DCC,XCII.* [901]

xii, 111, [1] p., 8vo. (20 x 12.5 cm.). Evans 25393. DLC, MWiW-C, NHi, PHC.

Title from reproduced title in Fabyan sale cat., Amer. Art Ass'n, Feb. 17, 1920, no. 33, sold to F.E. Heald for $15.00.

. . . . .

Narrative of a shipwreck in the Gulph of Florida; shewing, God's protecting Providence, man's surest help and defence, in times of greatest difficulty, and most eminent danger. Faithfully related by one of the persons concerned therein, Jonathan Dickenson. [five lines quoted from the Psalms] The sixth edition. *Stanford (State of New-York) Printed by Daniel Lawrence, for Henry and John F. Hull. M.DCCC.III.* [902]

96 p., 12mo. (16 x 10.4 cm.). Sabin 20015, Ayer supp. 45. CSmH, DLC, F.C. Deering, FHi, FTaSC, ICN, N, NN.

Stanford is now Stanfordville, Dutchess County, New York.

. . . . .

God's protecting Providence . . . 1807. [903]

In PPFr, according to Union Catalog, DLC, but no such edition is now in that library.

. . . . .

Narrative of a shipwreck . . . *Burlington, N.J. Printed at The Lexicon Press of D. Allinson & Co. 1811.* [904]

107 p., 12mo. (16 x 10 cm.). Sabin 20015, Ayer 71. CSmH, ICN, NN, PHC, PPFr, PPPr-Hi, PSC-Hi.

. . . . .

The shipwreck and dreadful sufferings of Robert Barrow, with divers other persons, amongst the inhuman cannibals of Florida; faithfully related by Jonathan Dickenson, who was concerned therein. To which are added some remarks & observations, made by a person who renounced Deism: also, the dying expressions of some persons of eminence & learning, who had embraced the same principles. *Salem, (O.) Re-published by Joshua Shinn. Robert Fee, Printer. 1826.* [905]

120 p., 12mo. (16.2 x 9.5 cm.). Copies in most large libraries.

. . . . .

God's protecting Providence, . . . *Philadelphia: Printed by Ezra Townsend Cresson, at No. 518 South Thirteenth Street. 1868.* [906]

[14], 126, iv p., 8vo. (16.4 x 11.6 cm.). Copies in most large libraries.

Privately printed in an edition of 250 copies by and for the Cresson family, descended from one of the captives, 25 copies in presentation leather bindings, the rest in wrappers.

There are two issues, the second with an eight page signature bound in at the end with the separate title: "Testimony concerning that faithful servant of the Lord Robert Barrow. Extracted from Dickenson's Narrative. First edition. Printed at Philadelphia in 1699 by Reinier-Jansen (and) printed for C.C.C. Philadelphia. Printed by Ezra T. Cresson. 1869."

.   .   .   .   .

Jonathan Dickinson's journal or, God's protecting Providence. Being the narrative of a journey from Port Royal in Jamaica to Philadelphia between August 23, 1696 and April 1, 1697. Edited by Evangeline Andrews and Charles McLean Andrews, Farnam Professor of American History in Yale University, Emeritus. *New Haven, Connecticut Printed for the Yale University Press. London: for sale by Humphrey Milford at the Oxford University Press. M D CCCC XLV.*   [907]

x, 252 p., illus., maps, 8vo. (20 x 13.5 cm.). Copies in most large libraries. The most scholarly edition of any story of Indian captivity.

GOOKIN, DANIEL

Historical collections of the Indians in New England. Of their several nations, numbers, customs, manners, religion, and government, before the English planted there. Also a true and faithful account of the present state and condition of the Praying Indians, (or those who have visibly received the Gospel in New England:) declaring the number of that people, the situation and place of their towns and churches, and their manner of worshipping God . . . Together with a brief mention of the instruments and means, that God hath pleased to use for their civilizing and conversion, briefly declaring the prudent and faithful endeavors of the Right Honorable the Corporation of London, for promoting that affair; also suggesting some expedients for their further civilizing and propagating the Christian faith among them. By Daniel Gookin . . . Now first printed from the original manuscript . . . *Printed at the Apollo Press, in Boston, by Belknap and Hall. MDCCXCII.*   [908]

89 p., 8vo. (20 cm.). Sabin 27959, Evans 24362. Copies in most large libraries.

Reprinted from Mass. Hist. Soc. Coll., I, 1792. Same, reprinted 1806. The original manuscript is in the library of F.C. Deering.

.   .   .   .   .

An historical account of the doings and sufferings of the Christian Indians in New England, in the years 1675, 1676, 1677. Impartially drawn by one well acquainted with that affair, and presented unto the Right Honourable the Corporation residing in London, appointed by the King's most excellent Majesty for promoting the Gospel among the Indians in America. (In American Antiquarian Society. *Archaeologia Americana. Transactions and collections.* Cambridge, 1836, vol. 2, p. 423-534).   [909]

Howe, Mrs. Jemima

A genuine and correct account | of the | captivity, sufferings & deliverance | of | Mrs. Jemima Howe, | of | Hinsdale, | in | New-Hampshire. | [rule] | Taken from her own mouth, and written, by the Rev. | Bunker Gray [sic], A.M. Minister of Hinsdale, in a letter to | the author of the *History of New-Hampshire*, extracted | from the third volume of said history, by consent of the | author. | In this account the mistakes of Col. Humphreys, relating to | Mrs. Howe, in his "Life of General Putnam," are rectified. | [double rule] | *Printed at the Apollo Press, in Boston,* | *by Belknap and Young,* | *North side of the State-House* | *State-Street MDCCXCII.* [910]

20 p., 8vo. (20.3 x 13.2 cm.). Sabin 26777 and 28377, Evans 24343, Ayer 105. DLC, F.C. Deering, ICN, MHi, MWA.

First separate edition, reprinted from Jeremy Belknap's *History of New Hampshire*, Boston, 1792, vol. 3, p. 370-388. This account was prepared especially for Belknap by the captive, Rev. Bunker Gay acting as amanuensis. For an earlier and less complete and accurate account, see David Humphreys: *An essay on the life of . . . Israel Putnam*, 1788. The Bunker Gay version was reprinted in Caleb Bingham's *American preceptor*, Boston, 1794 and in many later editions; in Noah Webster's *An American selection*, many editions, and in numerous other compilations, for which see Ayer. Also in John Hancock's *E Pluribus Unum. British cruelty, oppression, and murder. Two orations*, *[n.p.]* P.M. Davis, Publisher . . . 1824. 23 p., 12mo. Sabin 30178.

. . . . . .

The | affecting history | of | Mrs. Howe, | the wife of a British officer | in America; | who | after seeing her husband murdered, | was, | with her seven children, | siezed by | the Indians, | and carried by them many hundred miles to the country | of their tribe; | and, | after enduring shocking hardships, by the intervention of | Providence, was restored to her country. | Interspersed with | an exact account of the brutal manners, | horrid customs, | and monstrous barbarities, | of | the savages of America. | *London:* | *Printed and sold by J. Bailey, 116, Chancery-Lane,* | *and may be had of most Booksellers.* | *Price sixpence* | *[1815].* [911]

28 p., folded colored frontispiece, 12mo. (18.5 x 10.5 cm.). F.C. Deering, MH, NHi, NN.

Issued in printed wrappers with a folded colored frontispiece by George Cruikshank in which the Indians wear Roman helmets. Reprinted in *Magazine of History*, extra no. 190, 1933, p. 5-35, front. This version is largely rewritten and the heroine's frontiersman husband made a British officer for the benefit of the English chapbook trade.

. . . . . .

Narrative | of the | captivity | of | Mrs. Jemima Howe, | taken by the Indians, at Hins- | dale N.H. July 27, 1755. | [eagle cut] | *Watertown:* | *Published by Knowlton & Rice.* | *1830.* | [Cover title only]. [912]

16 p., yellow printed wrappers, 16mo. F.C. Deering, NhD.

The Bunker Gay version, reprinted from Caleb Bingham's *American preceptor*. Also reprinted in Frank D. Rogers: *Folk stories of the Northern border*, 1897, and rewritten in verse in Angela Marco [pseud. for Mrs. Annie L. Mearkle]: *Fair captive . . .* Brattleboro, 1937. DLC.

Jemima Howe was the wife of Caleb Howe of Hinsdale, N.H. On July 27, 1755, Caleb Howe, Hillkiah Grout and Benjamin Gaffield were returning from work to a place called Bridgman's Fort when they were attacked by a party of twelve Abenaki Indians of the St. Francis tribe. Howe was killed, Grout escaped and Gaffield was drowned while trying to swim the river. The Indians then went on to the fort and captured the families (three women and eleven children) of the three men, taking them to Crown Point and thence to Canada where the Indians tried with little success to sell them to the French. In the autumn, Mrs. Howe was taken by the family to which she had been assigned to the lower end of Lake Champlain where they spent the winter. After nearly a year with the Indians she was sold to a French family named Saccapee at St. Johns. There she met Col. Schuyler, also a prisoner, who later ransomed her and three of her children and took them back with him to Albany where she met Israel Putnam and told him her story, as related in Humphreys' life of Putnam. Two of her daughters were put in a convent at Montreal (partly to protect them from the Frenchmen) and one of them was sent to France where she married a French gentleman named Cron. Lewis [sic] who eventually came to Boston with the French fleet under Count d'Estaing in 1779. The St. Francis Indians were punished for this and other similar border depredations when, in 1759, Major Robert Rogers and his Rangers wiped out the Indian town, killed 200 Indians and released five white captives, for which see the original documents in volume 2 of the Special Edition of Kenneth Roberts' *Northwest Passage*.

IMLAY, GILBERT

A topographical description of the Western Territory of North America; containing a succinct account of its climate, natural history, population, agriculture, manners and customs; with an ample description of the several divisions into which that country is partitioned. And an accurate statement of the various tribes of Indians that inhabit the Frontier Country. To which is annexed, a delineation of the laws and government of the State of Kentucky. Tending to shew the probable rise and grandeur of the American Empire. In a series of letters to a friend in England. By G. Imlay, a Captain in the American Army during the late War, and a Commissioner for laying out land in the Back Settlements. *London: J. Debrett. 1792.*   [913]

[4], xv, 247 p., 8vo. (20.5 cm.). Sabin 34354. Copies in most large libraries.

First edition of the most important volume on the topography of the American frontier of the late eighteenth century. Title from DLC cat.

JOHONNOT, JACKSON

The remarkable adventures of Jackson Johonnet, of Massachusetts. Who served as a soldier in the Western Army, in the Massachusetts Line, in the expedition under General Harmar, and the unfortunate General St. Clair. Containing an account of his captivity, sufferings, and escape from the Kickapoo Indians. Written by himself, and published at the earnest importunity of his friends, for the benefit of American youth. [occupies 8 p. of:] Beers's Almanac and Ephemeris . . . for the year of our Lord, 1793 . . . *Hartford: Printed by Hudson and Goodwin. [1792].*   [914]

36 p., 12mo. Evans 24083. CtHi, MWA, RPJCB, etc.

Probably the first edition. See notes under no. 877.

[KIMBER, EDWARD]

The | life, | extraordinary | adventures, voyages, | and | surprising escapes | of Capt. Neville Frowde, | of | Cork. | In four parts. | Written by himself. | [4 lines quoted] | *Berwick:* | *Printed for W. Phorson; B. Law and son,* *Ave-* | *Maria-Lane, London.* | [rule] | M DCC XCII.   [915]

iv, [6], 218, [2] p., 12mo. NHi.

LONG, J[OHN]

Reisen eines Amerikanischen Dolmetschers und Pelzhändlers, welche eine Beschreibung der Sitten und Gebräuche der Nordamerikanischen Eingebornen, und einige Nachrichten von dem Posten am St. Lorenz-Flusse, dem See Ontario u.s.w. enthalten. Hrsg. von J. Long. Aus dem Englischen übersetzt. Nebst einer vorläufingen Schilderung des Nordens von Amerika von Georg Forster. Mit einer neuen Karte und einem Kupfer. *Berlin: In der Vossischen Buchhandlung. 1792.*   [916]

vi. [2], 88, 176 p., plate, folded map, 8vo. (21 cm.). Sabin 41880. DLC, RPJCB, etc.

LOSKIEL, GEORGE HENRY

Georg Hinrich Loskiels historiske Beskrifning öfwer Evangeliska Brödernes Missions-Arbete ibland Indianerne uti Norra America. Utgifwen i Barby 1789. Ofwersättning. *Stockholm, Tryckt hos J.C. Holmberg, 1792.*   [917]

[22], 872, [2] p., 8vo. (18 cm.). Title from DLC cat. DLC.

Swedish translation of his: *Geschichte der mission,* 1789, which see.

Observations | on | the present situation of landed property in America. | [Caption title] *[London:* dated at end of p. 3:] *January, 1792.*   [918]

3, [1] p., folio (39 x 23.5 cm.). MiU-C, NHi, NN, R.W.G. Vail.

The fourth page has the docketed title: *Observations | on the | present state of landed property | in | America. | [rule] | 1792. | (2.)*

The first two pages contain general arguments for English speculators to invest in American lands, especially in an 800,000 acre tract "situated on the eastern boundary of Lake Ontario, and on the South Side of St. Lawrence River." The third page contains a *Prospectus* showing the profits to be realized from the purchase and settlement of this tract. The exact location of the tract is not stated and the late Henry F. DePuy believed that it was Tract no. 1 of the Macomb Purchase, for the history of which see F.B. Hough's histories of Lewis and Jefferson counties. This tract contained 821,819 acres. It is more probable, however, that the prospectus refers to Thomas Boylston's Tract which contained 817,155 acres and was bounded on the west by Lake Ontario, while Macomb's Purchase was considerably farther east and did not approach Lake Ontario. Both tracts were "on the south side of St. Lawrence River" but only the Boylston Tract was "on the eastern boundary of Lake Ontario."

Reprinted in Gilbert Imlay's *Topographical description,* 1797.

PASTORIUS, FRANCIS DANIEL

Geographisch-statistische Beschreibung der Provinz Pensylvanien Von Fr. Dan. Pastorius. Im Auszug mit Anmerkungen. *Memmingen: A. Seyler, 1792.*
[919]
44 p., 12mo. (17.5 cm.). DLC, RPJCB.

Abridgement of his *Umständige Geographische Beschreibung,* 1700. Title from E.F. Robacker's *Pennsylvania German literature,* 1943.

POPE, JOHN

A | tour | through the | Southern and Western territories | of the | United States | of | North-America; | the | Spanish dominions | on the river Mississippi, | and the | Floridas; | the countries of the | Creek nations; | and many | uninhabited parts. | [rule] | By John Pope. | [thick-thin rule, one line quoted, thin-thick rule] | *Richmond: Printed by John Dixon. | For the author and his three children, Alexander D. | Pope, Lucinda C. Pope, and Anne Pope.* | [double rule] | M,DCC,XCII.   [920]
105, [1] p., 8vo. (18.5 x 12 cm.). Sabin 64109, Evans 24705. E.D. Graff, ICN (104 p.), MoSM (104 p.), NjR, RPJCB (104 p.), ViU (the A. Norton 1922-H.V. Jones-Rosenbach Co. copy), WHi.

An important frontier narrative which was reprinted in New York in 1888 from the imperfect copy now at ICN.

STADNITSKI, PIETER

Voorafgaand | Bericht, | wegens eene | Negotiatie, | op landen in | America; | door | Pieter Stadnitski. | [orn.] | *Amsterdam,* | 1792.   [921]
37 p., small 8vo. (18.5 x 11.5 cm.). Sabin 90061. DLC, MWA, N (lacks title), NCanHi, NIC, NN, U. Amsterdam, R.W.G. Vail.

This preliminary report regarding a negotiation of lands in America was written by one of the principal Dutch stockholders of the Holland Land Company of Western New York. Though no map accompanied it, a map of the Holland Purchase, without title but signed: *C. van Baarsel, sculpsit, Amsterdam.* [ca. 1792], 71.5 x 53 cm., was published, presumably by the Company, for use in promoting sales in Holland. There is a copy at N. It is earlier than the Joseph Ellicott map of the Purchase published in this country in 1800. Van Baarsel also engraved the map in Van Pradelles's *Réflections offertes,* Amsterdam, 1792.

TONTINES ET LOTERIES-IMMOBILIAIRES

Terres dans l'Amérique | Septentrionale. | [filet] | 135,000 acres de terres a vendre présentement, en totalité ou en partie. | Et environs un million d'acres de pareilles terres, a vendre, à la charge de délivrer | les titres sous six mois. | Ces terres, situées dans la Caroline du nord, . . . S'adresser au Bureau d'Agence de l'Administration des Tontines & Loteries-Immobiliaires, rue Montmarte, No. 184, où sont déposés les titres, plans & | descriptions, & où l'on donnera les instructions les plus détaillées sur ces possessions. | [thickthin rule] | [Paris:] *De l'Imprimerie des Tontines-Immobiliaires, rue Favart, No. 5, 1792.* [922]

Broadside, oblong folio (26 x 39 cm.). Sabin 96173. NN.

[TOULMIN, HARRY?]

A description of Kentucky, in North America: to which are prefixed miscellaneous observations respecting the United States. *[London:] Printed in November, 1792.* [923]

121, [3] p., map, with descriptive leaf, 8vo. Sabin 96327. CSmH, DLC, MH, NHi, NN, RPJCB, WHi.

A letter received "since the preceding account was printed," dated Feb. 2, 1793, p. 117-119. Part of *Thoughts on emigration,* below, but also issued separately.

. . . . .

Thoughts | on | emigration. | [orn rule] | To which are added. | miscellaneous observations | relating to | The United States of America: | and | a short account | of the | State of Kentucky. | [filet, one line quoted, filet] | *[London:] Printed in October [-November],* | *1792.* [924]

24, 121, [3] p., map with descriptive leaf, 8vo. Sabin 96328, Church 1258. BM, CSmH, DLC, ICN, MB, MH, NN, RPJCB, WHi.

Map: *Kentucky* | *Baines, sculp.*

The latest edition, in Kentucky Reprints No. 3, *Univ. of Kentucky Press, 1945,* suggests this imprint for the first edition: *[Lexington: Kentucky Gazette? 1793?].*

Reprinted in Jillson's *Transylvanian trilogy,* 1932. An anthology of frontier literature, the last item signed *H.T.* but Miss Tinling doubts that this work should be attributed to Toulmin, though Jillson credits him with it. See: *The Western Country in 1793. Reports on Kentucky and Virginia by Harry Toulmin. Edited by Marion Tinling and Godfrey Davies*, 1948. xx, 141 p., 8vo.

VALINIÈRE, PIERRE HUET DE LA

Vraie histoire ou simple précis des infortunes, pour ne pas dire, des persécutions qu'a souffert & souffre encore la Reverend Pierre Huet de la Valinière. Mis en vers par lui-même, en Juillet 1792. [Quotations] *A Albany; Imprimé par Charles R. & George Webster, No. 46, Rue des Etats, aux dépens de l'Auteur, 1792.*   [925]

50 p., 8vo. (20 x 12 cm.). Sabin 98366, Evans 24462, McMurtrie's Albany imprints 65. An-C-M, An-C-MS, MWA, NN (photostat).

Autobiography in verse, in French and English, of a priest in the Illinois country in 1786 and later in a parish on Lake Champlain, 1790-1791, also near Albany. He also travelled in the East and South and was always in civil, military and ecclesiastical hot water, mainly because he was sympathetic with the people of the United States. He was also the author of a *Curious and interesting dialogue . . .* New York, 1790. Sabin 98365, Evans 22607. NN. His important unpublished manuscript narrative, in English and French, partly in verse: *True and single* [simple] *account of the conduct of the Revd Peter Huet de la Valinièr, since he is arrived at the Illinois Country the 20th Jany 1786*, 250 p., 16mo., is at MHi. There are also a few letters regarding his difficulties in the Illinois Country in DLC.

[VAN PRADELLES, CAPTAIN BENJAMIN]

Réflections | offertes aux | capitalistes | de | l'Europe, | sur les bénéfices immences, | que présente l'achat de | terres incultes, situées | dans les | États-Unis | de | l'Amérique. | [orn.] | *A Amsterdam.* | [thick-thin rule] | *1792.*   [926]

42 p., folded map, folded table, 8vo. (21.8 x 13.2 cm.). Sabin 98538. DLC, MB, NHi, NIC, RPJCB, R.W.G. Vail.

Engraved folded map: *Carte servant à faire connaitre les distances et la situation du pays de la Genesee | relativement aux navigations et aux villes principales de l'Amerique.* | [signed:] *Gravé à Amsterdam, par C. van Baarsel* (39.5 x 26 cm.). Map shows territory from Lake Ontario to Cape Henry and from Lake Champlain to Pittsburg, *Genesee Lands* (Phelps and Gorham Purchase) and routes leading to this tract. Folded table: *Appercu des progrès probables dans la valeur (a) & dans les prix de vente de 400,000 acres de terres incultes de la Genesée . . .*

According to A.A. Barbier's *Dictionnaire des ouvrages anonymes*, Paris, 1879, vol. 4, p. 134, this work was written by Captain [Benjamin] van Pradelles, an infantry captain born in French Flanders who emigrated to

America, became a citizen, and spent the greater part of twelve years there. See also Van Winter, II:235, 241 and following. Perhaps he was the same as a "B. Van Predelles, Baltimore," whose name appears in a list of subscribers to Oliver Evans's *Young millwright and miller's guide*, Phil., 1795; or the "B. Van Pradelles, Justice of Peace," before whom a deposition was made in New Orleans in 1808, according to Edward Livingston's *Address*, New Orleans, 1808, p. 67-68. MWA.

Promotion tract written to interest European investors in the Genesee lands offered by Robert Morris and described in William Temple Franklin's *An account of the . . . Genesee Tract*, 1791, which lands were sold by him to the English Associates and to the Holland Land Company. The map in the Van Pradelles pamphlet is a copy, with titles in French, of the map in the Morris pamphlet above. The Van Pradelles pamphlet may have been used by Robert Morris, by the English Associates (Pulteney Tract) or by the Holland Land Company or by all three but it was probably initiated by Morris.

WILLIAMSON, PETER

French and Indian cruelty exemplified, in the life, and various vicissitudes of fortune, of Peter Williamson . . . *Edinburgh: Printed for and sold by the booksellers. M.DCC.XCII.*   [927]

156 p., front., 12 mo. (16.3 x 9.7 cm.). Sabin 104474, Ayer 321. BM, CSmH, F.C. Deering, ICN, N, NN, PHi, WHi.

Affecting history | of the | dreadful distresses | of | Frederick Manheim's family. | To which are added, the | sufferings of John Corbly's family. | An encounter between a white man and | two savages. | Extraordinary bravery of a woman. | Adventures of Capt. Isaac Stewart. | Deposition of Massey Herbeson. | Adventures and sufferings of Peter | Wilkinson. | Remarkable adventures of Jackson | Johonnet. | Account of the destruction of the set- | tlements at Wyoming. | [vignette] | *Printed and sold by H. Ranlet, Exeter—1793.*

[928]

[2], [5]-66 p., 12mo. (17.2 x 11.3 cm.). Evans 25080, Ayer 4, Sabin 105687. F.C. Deering, ICN, MWA, NN, The Rosenbach Company (1945).

First edition. Frederick Manheim was captured with his twin daughters, aged 16, at his farm 8 miles west of Johnstown, N.Y. on Oct. 9, 1779. The two girls were burned at the stake before their father's eyes. The story is included in most of the collected editions of Indian captivities.

BLEECKER, ANN ELIZA (SCHUYLER)

The posthumous works of Ann Eliza Bleecker, in prose and verse. To which is added, a collection of essays, prose and poetical, by Margaretta V. Faugeres. *New-York: Printed by T. and J. Swords, No. 27, William-Street. 1793.*   [929]

[12], xviii, [19]-375 p., port., 12mo. (16 x 10 cm.). Sabin 5896, Evans 25208. Copies in most large libraries.

The author was the daughter of Brandt Schuyler of New York and the wife of John J. Bleecker of New Rochelle. The work includes a memoir of the author by her daughter, Mrs. Margaretta V. Faugeres.

The history of Maria Kittle. In a letter to Miss Ten Eyck, p. 19-87. First published in *The New York Magazine*, September, 1790. Reprinted as a separate in 1797. Though described as *A pathetic story, founded on fact*, this fictionized story of the captivity of Maria Kittlehuyne and the massacre of her family during King George's War (1744-8) is included in Lyle Wright's *Early American fiction*; though the DLC catalog treats it as fact.

BRADMAN, ARTHUR

A narrative of the extraordinary sufferings of Mr. Robert Forbes, his wife and five children, during an unfortunate journey through the wilderness, from Canada to Kennebec-River, in the year 1784. In which three of their children were starved to death. Taken partly from their own mouths, and partly from a journal, and published at their request. By Arthur Bradman. *Norwich.—Printed by John Trumbull, 1793.*   [930]

16 p., 8vo. Evans 25226. F.C. Deering, NN.

.   .   .   .   .

Printed at Windsor, 1793, by Alden Spooner, and sold at his office. [931]
15 p., 16mo. F.C. Deering.

.   .   .   .   .

Printed at Worcester [by Leonard Worcester] *MDCCXCIII.*   [932]
24 p., 12mo. F.C. Deering (imperfect), MWA, Hamilton B. Wood.

CAMPBELL, PATRICK

Travels | in the interior inhabited parts | of | North America. | In the years 1791 and 1792. | In which is given an account of the manners and customs | of the Indians, and the present war between them and the | Foederal States, the mode of life and system of farming a- | mong the new settlers of both Canadas, New York, New | England, New Brunswick, and Nova Scotia; interspersed | with anecdotes of people, observations on the soil, natural | productions, and political situation of these countries. | Illustrated with copper-plates. | By P. Campbell. | [filet] | *Edinburgh:* | *Printed for the author, and sold by John* | *Guthrie No. 2 Nicholson Street Edinburgh.* | [rule] | *MDCCXCIII.*   [933]

x, 387, [1] p., front. (port), folded plate, small plate, folded table, 8vo. (21 x 12.5 cm.). Sabin 10264. An-C-OAr, An-C-T, DLC, MWA, N, NHi, NN, RPJCB.

This fascinating volume, though not written by a frontiersman, is included because of *The story of David Ramsay,* a frontier and Indian captivity narrative largely written for Campbell by Ramsay himself, p. 226-247.

The Ramsay narrative is reprinted, with notes, in Buffalo Hist. Soc. Pubs., 7, 1904, p. 441-451. Campbell's *Travels* are reprinted entire in Champlain Soc. Pubs., vol. 23, 1937.

LA COMPAGNIE DE NEW-YORK

Constitution | de La Compagnie | de New-York. | [Caption title] [Colophon: *Paris:] De l'Imprimerie de Froullé, Quai des Augustins, N°. 39.* | *[1793].*   [934]

32 p., 4to. (23.5 x 18 cm.). Sabin 95825 note. N, NHi.

Dated at end at Paris, June 28, 1793.

Original manuscript of the constitution and Journal of Castorland, 1793-1796, in MHi. Translation in F.B. Hough's *History of Lewis County, N.Y.*

This tract was bought from William Constable by Pierre Chassanis of Paris in 1792 who sold it to 41 Frenchmen, many of them titled French Revolution refugees and none of them suited to the rigors of pioneer life. They were organized as *Le Compagnie de New-York* and called their tract *Castorland;* also known as *The Chassanis Purchase.* It was located in Lewis and Jefferson Counties, N.Y. See F.B. Hough's *History of Jefferson County, N.Y.* and his *History of St. Lawrence and Franklin Counties, N.Y.* See also under Pierre Chassanis and Rodolphe Tillier. See also W. Hudson Stephens: *Notes of the voyage, in '93, towards "Castorland," and operations therein, in Lewis Co.,* N.Y. [Lowville: Lewis County Democrat, 1868]. 8 p., 4to. Sabin 95825 states that only 65 copies were printed. MWA, N, R.W.G. Vail. Original certificates of stock in the company are in N and NN. See also John Appleton, ed.: *Journal de Castorland,* reprinted from Mass. Hist. Soc. Proceed., Boston, 1864. 15 p., 8vo. Sabin 1809. MH.

CONGREGATIONAL CHURCH IN CONNECTICUT

An address to the inhabitants of the new settlements in the northern and western parts of the United States. *New Haven: Printed by T. and S. Green.* *[July 2, 1793].*   [935]

6 p., 8vo. Evans 25329, Trumbull 36., Sabin 420. NNUT.

Signed by Ezra Stiles and four others of a committee of the General Association.

CRÈVECOEUR, MICHEL-GUILLAUME SAINT-JEAN DE

Letters | from an | American farmer, | describing | certain provincial situations, | manners, and customs, | and conveying | some idea of the state | of the people of | North America. | [rule] | Written to a friend in England, | By J. Hector St. John, | a farmer in Pennsylvania. | [rule] | *Philadelphia:* | *From the press of Mathew Carey.* | *March 4,—M,DCC,XCIII.*   [936]

240 p., 12mo. (17 x 10 cm.). Sabin 17496, Evans 25357. DLC, MB, MH, MWA, NHi, NN, RPJCB, etc.

First American edition. Sabin describes an edition, Philadelphia, M,DCC,-XCVIII. 260 p., 12mo. and his note is reprinted by Evans but we have located no copy. The work was reprinted N.Y., 1904; same plates, London, 1908; London and New York (Everyman), 1912; New York, 1925.

The author also wrote a rather dull work, but with many details not found elsewhere, including the best account of an Iroquois council, of which there are copies in most large libraries but an author's presentation copy in original boards, paper labels, uncut, at NHi. It appeared in 3 vols., 8vo. as: *Voyage | dans | la Haute Pensylvanie | et dans l'État de New-York, | par un membre adoptif de la Nation Onéida. | . . . | Pąris, 1801.* It was published in abridged translation as: *Reise | in | Ober-Pensylvanien | und | im Staate Neu-York, | . . . Berlin, 1802.* Sabin 17501-2. DLC, NHi, NN.

[FILSON, JOHN]

The adventures of Col. Daniel Boon, one of the original settlers of Kentucky. *Windsor: Printed by Alden Spooner. 1793.*   [937]

Advertised as "For sale by George Hough, Concord." "Travelling traders are desired to call at Osborne's Printing-Office, Newburyport." Entry from Evans 25480, reprinted in Cooley's *Vermont imprints* 212, neither of which was able to locate a copy.

. . . . .

In [Andrew] *Beers's almanac . . . for the year of our Lord 1795 . . . Hartford: Printed by Hudson and Goodwin.* [1794].   [938]

[36] p., 12mo. (16.6 x 11 cm.). Evans 26632, Ayer Supp. 55. CtHi. MWA, NN, RPJCB, etc.

The Boone narrative, with caption title, occupies 8 pages.

For later editions, see Ayer 99, DLC cat., W.R. Jillson: *Boone narrative,* 1932.

. . . . .

The | discovery, settlement, | and | present state | of | Kentucky. | And | an introduction | to the topography and natural history | of that rich and important country; | also, | Colonel Daniel Boon's | narrative of the wars of Kentucky: | with | an account of the Indian nations within the limits of the United States, | their manners, customs, religion, and their origin; | and | the stages and distances between Philadelphia and the Falls of the Ohio, | from Pittsburgh to Pensacola, and several other places. | By John Filson. | Illustrated with a large whole sheet map of Kentucky from actual sur- | veys, and a plan with a description of the rapids of the river Ohio. | By Capt. Thomas Hutchins, Geographer to the Congress. | [rule] | *London:* | *Printed for John Stockdale, Piccadilly,* | *1793.* | (*Price two shillings.*).   [939]

67, advs. 68 [wrongly numbered 57]-[72], folded map, 8vo. (22.4 x 13.5 cm.). Sabin 24337, Church 1261. Copies in most large libraries, some lacking the catalog of books for sale following p. 67.

Folded map: *A map | of | Kentucky | drawn from | actual observations. | . . . | Published Novr. 23, 1793, by John Stockdale, Piccadilly. |* (49 x 44.8 cm.).

First English edition.

Reprinted in following, and later, editions of George Imlay's *A topographical description of the western territory of North America, London, 1793, Dublin, 1793, New York, 1793, London, 1797* and, in German, *Berlin, 1793.*

IMLAY, GILBERT

The emigrants, &c., or the history of an expatriated family, being a delineation of English manners, drawn from real characters. Written in America, by G. Imlay, Esq. . . . *London: A. Hamilton. 1793.* [940]

3 vols., xii, 221; 222; 192 p., 12mo. Sabin 34353.

A frontier novel by an author long familiar with the frontier, in the form of letters written chiefly from Pennsylvania. Reprinted in Dublin, 1794.

. . . . .

A topographical description of the Western Territory of North America: Containing a succinct account of its soil, climate, natural history, population, agriculture, manners, and customs. With an ample description of the several divisions into which that country is partitioned; to which are added, The discovery, settlement, and present state of Kentucky. And an essay towards the topography, and natural history of that important country. By John Filson. To which is added I. The adventures of Col. Daniel Boon, one of the first settlers, comprehending every important occurrence in the political history of that Province. II. The minutes of the Piankashaw Council, held at Post St. Vincent's April 15, 1784. III. An account of the Indian nations inhabiting within the limits of the Thirteen United States; their manners and customs; and reflections on their origin. By George [sic] Imlay, a Captain in the American Army during the War, and Commissioner for laying out lands in the Back Settlements. Illustrated with correct maps of the Western Territory of North America; of the State of Kentucky, as divided into counties, from the latent [sic] surveys; and a plan of the Rapids of the Ohio. The second edition, with considerable additions. *London: J. Debrett. MDCCXCIII.* [941]

[2], xvi, [2], 433, [20] p., 2 folded maps, folded plan, folded table, 8vo. (22 cm.). Sabin 34355. Copies in most large libraries.

Second edition with addition of Filson's *Kentucky*, an index, maps, etc. Title from DLC cat.

. . . . .

A topographical description of the Western Territory of North America;

containing a succinct account of its climate, natural history, population, agriculture, manners and customs, with an ample description of the several divisions into which that country is divided. And an accurate statement of the various tribes of Indians that inhabit the Frontier Country. To which is annexed a delineation of the laws and government of the State of Kentucky. Tending to shew the probable rise and grandeur of the American empire. In a series of letters to a friend in England. By G. Imlay, a Captain in the American Army during the late War, and a Commissioner for laying out land in the Back Settlements. *New-York: Printed by Samuel Campbell, No. 37, Hanover Square. M,DCC,XCIII.* [942]

2 vols., 260; 204 p., 2 folded maps, folded plan, 12mo. (16.7 x 10 cm.). Sabin 34356, Evans 25648. Copies in most large libraries.

Filson's Kentucky, which occupies vol. 2, has a separate title.

Maps and plan: *New map of the States of Georgia, South and North Carolina, Virginia and Maryland, including the Spanish Provinces of West and East Florida from the latest surveys. Cornelius Tiebout sculp. N. York; A map of the State of Kentucky, drawn from the best authorities. 1793.; A plan of the Rapids of the Ohio.*

. . . . .

A description of the Western Territory of North America; containing a succinct account of its climate, natural history, population, agriculture, manners and customs, with an ample description of the several divisions into which that country is partitioned, and an accurate statement of the various tribes of Indians that inhabit the Frontier Country. To which is annexed. A delineation of the laws and government of the State of Kentucky. Tending to shew the probable rise and Grandeur of the American Empire. In a series of letters to a friend in England. By G. Imlay, a Captain in the American Army during the late War, and a Commissioner for laying out land in the Back Settlements. *Dublin: William Jones. 1793.* [943]

[4], xx, 249 p., 12mo. (17 cm.). Sabin 34357. Copies in most large libraries.

. . . . .

Nachrichten von dem westlichen Lande der Nord-Amerikanischen Freistaaten, von dem Klima, den Naturprodukten, der Volksmenge, den Sitten und Gebräuchen desselben, nebst einer Angabe der Indianischen Völkerstämme, die an den Gränzen wohnen, und einer Schilderung von den Gesetzen und der Rigierung des Staates Kentucky. In Briefen an einen Freund in England. Aus dem Englischen übersetzt mit vielen Anmerkungen und Bestimmungen der natürlichen Produkte, von E.A.W. Zimmermann . . . *Berlin, In der Vossischen Buchhandlung, 1793.* [944]

xv, [1], 168 p., 8vo. (21 cm.). Sabin 34359. DLC, RPJCB, etc.

JOHONNOT, JACKSON

The | remarkable adventures | of | Jackson Johonnet, | of | Massachusetts, | who served as a soldier in the Western Army, in the Massa- | chusetts Line, in the expedition under | General Harmar, | and the unfortunate | General St. Clair. | Containing | an account of his captivity, sufferings, | and escape from the | Kickapoo Indians. | Written by himself, | and published at the earnest importunity of his friends, | for the benefit of | American youth. | *Printed at Boston, | For Samuel Hall, No. 53, Cornhill. | MDCCXCIII.*

[945]

16 p., 8vo. (18.7 x 11.5 cm.). Evans 25665, Ayer 167. BM, CSmH, F.C. Deering, ICN, MHi, NN, RPJCB, F.T. Siebert.

This has been called the first edition but there is no known priority of the 1793 editions and it was certainly published previously in Beers's Almanac and perhaps at Lexington, as above, no. 877.

. . . . .

Same title, *Concord: Printed and sold by George Hough. 1793.*   [946]

Title from Evans 25666 who gives no collation or location and probably took the title from an advertisement or copyright entry.

. . . . .

Same title, *Printed by Henry Blake, & Co. Keene, New-Hampshire. M, DCC, XCIII.*   [947]

12 p., 12mo. Evans 25667. MWA.

. . . . .

Same title, *Printed at Newburyport, by George Jerry Osborne, Guttemberg's [sic] Head, MDCCXCIII.*   [948]

12 p., 12mo. Evans 25668. DLC.

. . . . .

Same title, *Printed at Newburyport by George Jerry Osborne, Guttemburg's [sic] Head. MDCCXCIII.*   [949]

30 p., 8vo. Evans 25669. DLC.

. . . . .

Same title, *Printed at Lexington (Kentucky) 1791. Re-printed at Providence. M,DCC,XCIII.*   [950]

15 p., 8vo. (21.5 cm.). Sabin 69374, Evans 25670. DLC, F.C. Deering, RPJCB.

. . . . .

Same title, *Windsor: Re-printed by Alden Spooner. M,DCC,XCIII.* [951]

16 p., 8vo. Evans 25671. CtY, MWA, NN (photostat).

[LINCOLN, BENJAMIN?]

[double rule] | A | description | of the | situation, climate, soil and pro-
ductions | of | certain tracts of land | in the | District of Maine, | and | Com-
monwealth of Massachusetts. | [double rule] | *[n.p., 1793].*   [952]

44 p., map, 4to. (19.5 x 15.5 cm.). Evans 25720. MBAt, NHi (lacks
map), NN, PPAmP, RPJCB.

Includes letter of B. Lincoln, Hingham, February 26, 1793, to William
Bingham.

"Attributed also to William Bingham, to whose purchase of over two
million acres of land, in Hancock and Washington Counties, for an eighth of
a dollar per acre, it refers; but, probably, based on Lincoln's 'Observations on
the climate, soil and value of the Eastern counties in the District of Maine,'
published in the Collections of the Massachusetts Historical Society. 4: 14."
—Evans.

RYER, JOHN

Narrative | of the life, | and | dying speech, | of | John Ryer: | who was
executed at White-plains, | in the County of Westchester, state of | New-
York, on the second day of oc- | tober, 1793, for the murder of | Dr. Isaac
Smith, Deputy-Sheriff | of that county. | [cut of coffin] | *Printed at Danbury,*
by Nathan Douglas, | *for the publisher.—1793.* | Copy-right secured ac-
cording to law. | [Title within mourning border].   [953]

15 p., 8vo. (20.5 x 13.5 cm.). MWA, NHi.

.   .   .   .   .

Narrative | of the | life | and | dying speech | of | John Ryer, | who was
executed at White-Plains, in the | county of Westchester, state of New-York,
| October 2d, 1793, | for the murder | of Dr. Isaac Smith, Deputy-Sheriff | of
that county. | [3 skulls] *[Poughkeepsie?] Printed for, and sold by, the Flying-*
stationers. [1793].   [954]

24 p., 12mo. (17 x 10 cm.). Sabin 74542, Evans 26118. NHi. RPJCB.

John Ryer was a rascally Tory who lived in Fordham, now a part of New
York City. While a soldier in Colonel De Lancy's Tory regiment in the
Revolution, he was given, as he says, to "excess of drinking, card-playing,
cock-fighting, cursing, swearing, together with almost every kind of vice,
wickedness and debauchery." He was a quarrelsome, shiftless and shifty
individual much like his Patriot contemporaries Henry Tufts and Stephen
Burroughs, both of whom published their autobiographies. Ryer, overhauled
by the deputy sheriff in a tavern, killed him, was tried and hung, to the
satisfaction of the community and the widow of the deputy sheriff. He is
introduced here as a pioneer underworld type whose narrative is interesting
and a great rarity.

[SMITH, DANIEL]

A | short description | of the | Tennassee government, | or the | territory of the | United States | south of the River Ohio, | to accompany and explain a | map of that country. | *Philadelphia:* | *Printed by Mathew Carey, Book-seller,* | *No. 118, High-street.* | *-1793.-* [955]

20 p., 8vo. (23.5 cm.). Sabin 82420, Evans 26168. BM, DLC, MBAt, MH, MWA, MWiW-C, NHi, NN, PHi, RPJCB, ViU, WHi.

The map was not published with the pamphlet but the latter sometimes (as in MH) appears with the following folded map, "Engraved for Carey's American edition of Guthrie's Geography improved" which was published shortly after the pamphlet: *A map of the Tennessee government formerly part of North Carolina, taken chiefly from surveys by General D. Smith and others. J.T. Scott sculp.* (52 x 24 cm.). The DLC copy has inserted a copy of the reprint of this map which appeared in Imlay's *Topographical description*, London, 1797, the map being dated 1795.

.   .   .   .   .

Description abrégée du territoire & gouvernement des États-Unis de l'Amérique au Sud de l'Ohio. [Colophon:] *[Paris:] De l'Imprimerie de L. Potier.* [1793-1796?]. [956]

28 p., 8vo. Sabin 56908.

Translation of the above title. Could not have been printed later than 1796 for in that year Tennessee became a state.

WILLIAMS, JOHN

The redeemed captive returning to Zion . . . The fourth edition with additions. *Printed at Greenfield, Massachusetts. By Thomas Dickman. MDCC-XCIII.* [957]

[2], iii, 154 p., 12mo. Sabin 104268, Evans 26485. CtHWatk, F.C. Deering, MBAt, MHi, MWA, NN, RPJCB.

Affecting history | of the | dreadful distresses | of | Frederic Manheim's family. | To which are added, the | sufferings of John Corbly's family. | An encounter between a white man | and two savages. | Extraordinary bravery of a woman. | Adventures of Capt. Isaac Stewart. | Deposition of Massey Herbeson. | Adventures and sufferings of Peter | Wilkinson. | Remarkable adventures of Jackson | Johonnot. | Account of the destruction of the | settlements at Wyoming. | *Philadelphia:* | *Printed (for Mathew Carey) by* D. Humphreys, No. 48, | Spruce-Street. 1794. | (Price a quarter dollar.). [958]

48 p., front. by S. Folwell, engraved by P. Maverick, 8vo. (23 x 14.3 cm.). Sabin 44258 and note following 105687, Evans 26540, Ayer supp. 1. DLC, ICN (lacks front.), MHi, MWA, N (lacks front.), NHi, NN, PHi, PPAmP, PPL-R, RPJCB.

Reprinted in Benjamin West's *The town and country almanack, for the year of* our Lord, 1797. . . . *Norwich: John Trumbull, [1796].* CtHi, CtY, F.C. Deering, MWA, NN, PHi; and in *Der neue Hoch-Deutsche Americanische Calender, auf das Jahr* Christi, 1798 . . . *Baltimore: Samuel Saur, [1797]*, with plate of a burning at the stake; and in *A dish of all sorts . . . [Norwich: John Trumbull]*, 1797. NHi.

ASPLUND, JOHN

The | universal register | of the | Baptist denomination | in | North America, | for 1790-1-2-3 and part | of 1794. | Containing | [etc, 13 lines of contents] | [filet] | By John Asplund. | [filet] | Boston: Printed by John W. Folsom, for the author. | M,DCC,XCIV.   [959]

86, [7] p., 12mo. (17.5 x 12.4 cm.). Sabin 2223, Evans 26585. NN (photostat); Boston or Richmond editions at MWA, NN, RPB, ScCoT, Vi; Hanover, 1796 ed. at ScCot, Vi.

There has been much confusion over the various editions of Asplund's works. See entries in the card catalog at NN and D.C. McMurtrie's *Key to the bibliographical puzzle presented by the Baptist Association Minutes.* Evanston, 1943. Reproduction of typed copy in DLC.

THE ASYLUM COMPANY

Articles of agreement, made and | entered into this twenty-second day of April, one thousand seven hundred and ninety-four, | by and between Robert Morris, Esquire, . . . and others his associates, of the one part; and John Nicholson, Esquire, . . . and others his associates, of the other part: Witnesseth, that the said parties have entered into an association or company, for the purpose of settling and improving one or more tracts of country within the state of Pennsylvania, having already acquired the title to a number of valuable tracts of land situated in Luzerne, Northumberland and Northampton counties, which they are ready to dispose of to actual settlers, and to such others as will send settlers upon the lands they purchase. . . . This association shall be stiled "The Asylum Company." . . . this twenty-second day of April, one thousand seven hundred and ninety-four. . . . Robt. Morris. [seal] Jno. Nicholson. [seal] [Followed by the stock certificate of the company, filled in and signed in ink:] . . . [ninth] day of [October] 17[94] [Rob Morris] President. [James Duncan] Secretary. *Philadelphia: Printed by Zachariah Poulson, Junior, number eighty, Chestnut-Street. [1794].*   [960]

4 p., folio. (40.5 x 24.5 cm.). Evans 26586. CSmH, MWA, NHi.

The company was so named since the land was to serve as an asylum for a colony of French refugees who lived there, at *Asylum,* for some years and, for the most part, returned to France on the restoration of the monarchy. For their *Plan of association,* see under 1795.

.   .   .   .   .

[Philadelphia? 1801?] 15 p., PHi.   [961]

. . . . .

Aux | émigrés | de | toutes les contrées | de l'Europe. | [rule] | [3 lines quoted] | [two rules] | *A Philadelphie [Paris?] 1794.* [962]

[2], 31, 8 p., 4to. (23.5 x 18.5 cm.). Sabin 60086. Bib. Nat., NHi.

Caption title, p. 2: *Une société | de citoyens des États-unis de l'Amérique | a tous ceux | des différentes contrées de l'Europe, que les dangers d'une | révolution, et les troubles des guerres ont obligès d'a- | bandonner leurs foyers.* Caption, p. 13: *Plan de vente | de 300 mille acres de terres situées dans les comtés de Northumberland, | et de Huntingdon dans l'état de la Pensylvanie, divisés en | 750 lots de 400 acres, et formant 750 actions, proposées par | souscription.* Appendix caption, p. [1]: *Observations;* caption, p. 3: *Notes instructives.*

General agents: "Couderc-Brants et Changuion, et Cuny et compagnie à Amsterdam, qui le transporteront à Hambourg, ville neutre." Appendix, p. 7, quotes a paragraph descriptive of these lands from [Thomas] Cooper's *Some information respecting America,* which was about to be published. This work was probably printed in French in the interest of the Asylum Company as: *Renseignemens sur l'Amérique,* Hambourg, 1795, which see under author.

. . . . .

Plan de vente de trois cent mille acres de terres situées dans les Comtés de Northumberland et de Huntingdon dans l'Etat de Pensylvanie. *A Philadelphie [Paris?]: 1794.* [963]

Title from Evans 27527. MH.

Addressed especially to the refugees from the French Revolution, showing the advantages of emigration to the Company's lands in Pennsylvania. The refugee town of Azilum on the Susquehannah was the result.

BRADMAN, ARTHUR

A | narrative | of the | extraordinary sufferings | of | Mr. Robert Forbes, his wife, and | five children; | during | an unfortunate journey through the wilderness, | from Canada to Kennebeck River, | in the year 1784: | in which three of their children were starved to | death. | Taken partly from their own mouths, and partly from an | imperfect journal; and published at their request. | By Arthur Bradman. | *Philadelphia— | Printed for M. Carey—1794.* | *Price, six pence.* [964]

16 p., 8vo. (18.6 x 11.2 cm.). Sabin 7288, Evans 26698, Ayer 31. Copies in most large libraries.

This is the first edition to include: "A narrative of the captivity and escape of Mrs. Frances Scott, an inhabitant of Washington County, Virginia." For other editions, see under her name.

There were two settings of type of the title page. In one: *Printed for M. Carey* is in large capitals, in the other: *Printed for* has the *P* in large capital, the rest in small capitals, according to Mr. Lindley Eberstadt.

BRISSOT DE WARVILLE, JEAN PIERRE

New travels in the United States of America, including the Commerce of America with Europe; particularly with France and Great Britain. In two volumes. To which is prefixed a sketch of the life of Brissot, with an elegant portrait. *London: J.S. Jordan. MDCCXCIV.*   [965]
lxiv, 348 p., port., 8vo. Sabin 8026. Same with new title and an added volume:

. . . . .

New travels in the United States of America, . . . Second edition, corrected. *London: J.S. Jordan. M DCC XCIV.*   [966]
2 vols., xii, 416; [2], lxiv, 348 p., port., folded table, 8vo. Sabin 8027. DLC, MH, etc.

. . . . .

With general title and separate title for each volume, same imprint and date.   [967]
2 vols., [2], xii, 416; [2], lxiv, 348 p., port., folded table, 8vo. Sabin 8028-8030.

. . . . .

Nieuwe Reize in de Vereenigde Staaten van Noord-Amerika, door J.P. Brissot (Warville), uit het Fransch vertaald, en met eenige Ophelderingen en bijvoegselen vermeerderd. *Amsterdam, M. de Bruijn [1794].*   [968]
3 vols. (23 cm.). Sabin 8034, title from DLC cat. DLC.

CARVER, JONATHAN

Three years travels. *Portsmouth, 1794.* DLC, etc.   [969]
See note at end of 1798 edition.

CONGREGATIONAL CHURCH IN CONNECTICUT

A narrative of the missions to the new settlements according to the appointment of the General Association of the State of Connecticut: together with an account of the receipts and expenditures of the money contributed by the people of Connecticut, in May, 1793, for the support of the missionaries, according to an act of the General Assembly of the State. *New-Haven—Printed by T. & S. Green. 1794*   [970]
[2], 16, [1] p., 8vo. Evans 26803, Sabin 15789 and 15807, Trumbull 1137. DLC, MBAt, MH, MWA, NN, NNUT, RPJCB.

. . . . .

A continuation of the narrative . . . [as above] 1795.   [971]

21, [2] p., 8vo. Evans 28464, Sabin 15809, Trumbull 1138. BM. DLC, MHi, NN, NNUT.

. . . . .

A continuation of the narrative | . . . [as above] 1796.   [972]
Evans 30259, Trumbull 1139.

. . . . .

A continuation of the narrative . . . [as above] 1797.   [973]
15 p., 8vo. Evans 31968, Sabin 15790 and 15810, Trumbull 1140.
MHi, MWA, NN, NNUT, RPJCB.

. . . . .

A continuation of the narrative . . . [as above] 1798.   [974]
Trumbull 1141.

. . . . .

A continuation of the narrative . . . [as above] 1799.   [975]
Trumbull 1142.

. . . . .

A continuation of the narrative . . .[as above] 1800.   [976]
Trumbull 1143.
Continued annually until 1830.

COOPER, THOMAS

Some information | respecting | America, | collected by | Thomas Cooper, | late of Manchester. | *London:* | *Printed for J. Johnson, in St. Paul's Church yard.* | *MDCCXCIV.*   [977]
iv, 240 p., folded map, 8vo. Sabin 16615. BM, DLC, NN, RPJCB, etc.

Map: *A map of the | Middle States | of | America, | drawn from the latest and | best authorities; | by Thos. Conder. London. Published Augt. 12th 1794, by J. Johnson, St Pauls Church Yard.*

Includes Tench Coxe's *View of the United States of America* and Benjamin Franklin's *Information to those who would remove to America.* Written to promote the sale of some hundred acres of land in Northumberland County, Pa., owned by Cooper and Joseph Priestly, son of Dr. Joseph Priestly.

Reprinted Dublin, 1794, London, 1795, in French as: *Renseignemens,* Hambourg, 1795. The first letter reprinted as: *Thoughts on emigration,* London, 1794 and as *Extract of a letter,* [London? 1798]. Cooper also wrote:

A ride to Niagara, in *Portfolio,* July-October, 1810, reprinted Rochester, 1915. 2 p.l., [9]-49 p., folded map, 8vo. (23.5 cm.). DLC, etc.

.   .   .   .   .

Thoughts | on | emigration, | in | a letter | from a | gentleman in Philadelphia, | to | his friend in England. | *London:* | *1794.*   [978]
[2], 17 p., 8vo. (20.5 x 12.5 cm.). Sabin 22509. DLC, NHi, NN, RPJCB, WHi.

Originally published as letter I, p. 1-29 of his: *Some information respecting America,* 1794, which see. Same, as:

.   .   .   .   .

Extract of a letter from a gentleman in America to a friend in England, on the subject of emigration. [n.p., 1794], "in the library of the late Judge Wilson of Lexington, Kentucky"; same, another edition, [n.p.,n.d.] 16 p., 8 vo.; same, another edition, [London? 1798].   [979]
29 p., 8vo. (20.5 cm.). Sabin 16611. DLC, NN.

DECALVES, ALONSO, *pseud.*

Travels | to the | Westward, | or the unknown parts of | America: | In the years 1786 and 1787. | Containing an account of the country to the Westward | of the river Missisippi [sic], its productions, animals, | inhabitants, curiosities, &c. &c. | [rule] | By Alonso Decalves. | [rule, orn. rule] | *Keene —(Newhampshire:)* | *Printed and sold by Henry Blake & Co.* | *M,DCC,-XCIV.*   [980]
35 p., 12mo. Sabin 98446, Evans 26860. RPJCB.

.   .   .   .   .

Travels to the Westward, or the unknown parts of America: in the years 1786 and 1787. Containing an account of the country to the Westward of the River Missisippi [sic], together with its productions, animals, inhabitants, vegitables [sic], curiosities, &c. &c. By Alonso Decavles [sic]. *Printed by Alden Spooner, at Windsor, (Vermont) M,DCC,XCIV.*   [981]
36 p., 12mo. (16.8 cm.). *Gazette of the Grolier Club,* October, 1944, p. 99. T. W. Streeter.

DRAYTON, JOHN

Letters written during a tour through the northern and eastern states of America; By John Drayton. [Two lines from:] Young's Night Thoughts. [Printer's mark] *Charleston: South-Carolina, Printed by Harrison and Bowen. M,DCC,XCIV.*   [982]
[4], iv, [8], [3]-138 p., 3 plates, 8vo. Entry from Evans 26912, Sabin 20913. DLC, MB, MH, NN, RPB, RPJCB, ScC, etc.

Author was a district judge and later Governor of South Carolina. For his later works, see Sabin 20914-20915.

[HODGKINSON, ——]

Letters on emigration. By a gentleman, lately returned from America. *London: Printed for C. and G. Kearsley. MDCCXCIV.* [983]

[2], 76 p., 8vo. Title from Sabin 22502. CtY, ICN, MBAt, NHi, NN (lacks title).

A warning against emigration to America.

[HOLLAND LAND COMPANY]

[Map of the Holland Purchase] C. van Baarset, sculpsit, *Amsterdam. [1794-1800].* [984]

Folio map. (71.5 x 53 cm. over all, 63.5 x 44 cm. within the plate mark). N.

Shows territory from border of Western Territory west of Presque Isle [Erie, Pa.] east to Seneca Lake; from lower shore of Lake Ontario south to northern Pennsylvania.

Main captions within map: *Part of the State of New York; The State of Pennsylvania; Robert Morris's Purchase.* Shows lakes, rivers, forts, portages, *Rijckman's Reservation;* towns of *Romulus, Ovid, Hector.* Phelps and Gorham Purchase is shown without name or towns; Morris's Purchase shown as partly surveyed, with forts and Indian towns named but no white settlements. Trails from Genesee to Niagara river and to Lake Ontario are indicated.

Probably the earliest map of Western New York prepared for the use of the Holland Land Company. Engraved with English titles but issued in Holland for use of the Dutch investors. Precedes the Ellicott map of the purchase published in 1800.

The original manuscript *Map of Holland Land Company's Preliminary Survey, 1797,* is in the Grosvenor Library, Buffalo, New York and is published in the Livingston County Historical Society's *A History of the Treaty of Big Tree,* 1897, p. 91.

The records of the Holland Land Company (Hollandsche Land Compagnie) are owned by their business descendant, Van Eeghen & Co. of Amsterdam, Holland. Most of the papers of the local Western New York agent, Joseph Ellicott, not sent to the archives of the company in Holland, are at NBuHi, one volume of his letters in the Henry O'Rielly collection at NHi, some of the old ledgers, etc. in the original land office of the company, now a museum, at Batavia, N.Y. See Orsamus Turner: *History of the Holland Purchase,* Buffalo, 1849, P.D. Evans: *The Holland Land Company,* 1924 and P.J. Van Winter's *Het aandeel van den Amsterdamschen handel aan den opbouw van het Amerikaansche Gemeenebest.* Gravenhage, 1927. 2 v., especially Vol. II, chapters 7 and 8. See also under Jean Louis Bridel, Joseph Ellicott, Pieter Stadnitski and Captain Van Pradelles.

Evans found the following promotion material among the company's papers at Amsterdam: a folder issued in 1792 for distribution in Europe; their New York agent Jan Lincklaen's Albany handbill, April 23, 1793, announcing the formation of a settlement at Cazenovia, N.Y.; his handbills and engraved maps for use in New England in 1798; "posters and fliers" advertising the company's lands northwest of the Alleghany River, 1797; and their agent in India, Bon Albert Briois de Beaumetz: *900,000 acres of land offered for sale* [in Western New York]. Calcutta, 1797.

HUMPHREYS, DAVID

An essay on the life of the Honorable Major-General Israel Putnam: addressed to the State Society of the Cincinnati in Connecticut. By Col. David Humphreys. *Middletown: Printed by Moses H. Woodward, for Hudson and Goodwin, Hartford. M,DCC,XCIV.*   [985]

v, 7-168 p., 12mo. Sabin 33804, Evans 27144. MH, MWA, NN, RPJCB, etc.

IMLAY, GILBERT

The emigrants, &c., or, the history of an expatriated family, being a delineation of English manners, drawn from real characters, written in America, by G. Imlay, Esq. . . . *Dublin, Printed for C. Brown, 1794.*   [986]

[2], vii, 325 p., 12mo. (17 cm.). MdBP.

JEFFERSON, THOMAS

Notes | on the | State | of | Virginia. | By Thomas Jefferson. | Second American edition. | *Philadelphia:* | Printed for Mathew Carey, | No. 118, Market-street, | November 12, 1794.   [987]

[4], 336 p., illus., folded map, folded table, 8vo. (20.5 cm.). Sabin 35898, Evans 27162. BM, DLC, ICN, MH, MHi, MWA, NHi, NN (2), RPJCB, etc.

Printed on thick and also on ordinary book paper. Both in NN.

LE BEAU, C[LAUDE]

Karl [sic] le Beau's Begebenheiten und merkwürdige Reise. Begebenheiten und merkwürdige Reise zu den Nord-Amerikanischen Wilden. Mit einer genauen Beschreibung von Kanada und den alten Gebräuchen, Sitten und Lebensart der Kanadier. Aus dem Französischen . . . In zwei theilen. *Leipzig, Weygand. 1794.*   [988]

[10], [3]-430 p., 8vo. (17 cm.). Sabin 39585, DLC cat. DLC.

Sabin gives abbreviated title without collation or location and dates it 1793.

Translation of his: *Avantures . . . Amsterdam, 1738,* which see.

LONG, J[OHN]

Voyages | chez | différentes nations sauvages | de l'Amérique | Septentrionale; | renfermant des détails curieux sur les moeurs, usages, | cérémonies religieuses, le systeme militaire, &c. des | Cahnuagas, des Indiens des Cinq & Six Nations, | Mohawks, Connecedagas, Iroquois, &c. des Indiens | Chippeways, & autres sauvages de divers tribus; sur | leurs langues, les pays qu'ils habitent, ainsi que sur | le commerce de pelletries & fourrures qui se fait | chez ces peuples; | avec | un état exact des postes situés sur le Fleuve S. Laurent, | le Lac Ontario, &c. &c. | Par J. Long, trafiquant, | & interprète de langues Indiennes; | traduits de l'Anglois, | avec des notes & additions intéressantes, | par J.B.L.J. Billecocq, Citoyen Français. | [orn.] | A Paris, | Chez [bracket] *Prault l'aîné, Imprimeur, quai des Augustins,* | *à l'Im-* | *mortalité, No. 44.* | *Fuchs, Libraire, même Quai, au coin de la rue* | *Gît-le-* | *Coeur, No. 28.* | [rule] | *II. année de l'Ère Républicaine.* | *[1794].* [989]

[4], xxxvi, 320 p., folded map, 8vo. (20 cm.). Sabin 41879. MBAt, NHi, etc.

Reissued with new title page dated Paris, 1810.

Folded map: *Carte* | *des pays situes à l'Ouest du* | *Canada* | *1791.* | (24 x 35 cm.), copied from that of the first English edition.

Translation of his: *Voyages and travels*, 1791, which see.

The English edition was reprinted in Thwaites' *Early Western Travels,* vol. II, Cleveland, 1904 and, edited by M.M. Quaife, in the Lakeside Classics, Chicago, 1922.

LOSKIEL, GEORGE HENRY

History | of the | mission | of the | United Brethren | among the | Indians of North America. | [rule] | In three parts. | [rule] | By | George Henry Loskiel. | [rule] | Translated from the German | by Christian Ignatius La Trobe. | [thin-thick rule] | London: | Printed for the Brethren's Society for the | Furtherance of the Gospel: | Sold at No. 10, Nevil's Court, Fetter Lane; | and by John Stockdale, opposite Burlington House, | Piccadilly. | [rule] | 1794. [990]

xii, 159, 234, 233, [22] p., 8vo. (21 x 13.5 cm.). Sabin 42110. Copies in most large libraries.

Folded map: *Part* | *of the* | *United States* | *of* | *North America.* From the Great Lakes south to South Carolina and from Kentucky east to Maine. (44 x 52 cm.).

. . . . .

Abridged as: *The history of the Moravian mission among the Indians in North America.* London, 1838. DLC, etc. [991]

McDONALD, PHILIP, AND ALEXANDER McLEOD

A | surprising account | of the | captivity and escape | of | Philip M'Donald & Alexander M'Leod | of Virginia, | from the | Chickkemogga |

Indians. | And of their great discoveries in | the western world, | from June 1779, to January 1786, when they return- | ed in health to their friends, after the absence of six | years and a half. | [rule] | Written by themselves. | [rule, orn. rule] | *Printed by Henry Blake, & Co.* | *Keene, New Hampshire:* | *M,DCC,XCIV.*   [992]

11 p., 8vo. (17.3 x 9.8 cm.). Sabin 43167, Evans 27248, Ayer 193. CSmH (photostat), F.C. Deering, ICN, MWA, NN (photostat).

New York Society for the Information and Assistance of Persons Emigrating from Foreign Countries.   [993]

> Constitution of the . . . *New York. 1794.*

> 1 leaf, folio. Sabin 54538.

> Perhaps the same as:

.   .   .   .   .

New-York Society for the Information and Assistance of | Persons Emigrating | from Foreign Countries. | [Caption title] From reviewing the great inconveniences that frequently attend emigration, . . . Names of the Committee. Melancton Smith [and six others] By order of the committee, L. Wayland, Secretary. | New-York, 30th June, 1794. | *[New-York, 1794].*
                                                                        [994]

Broadside, folio. Evans 27408. RPJCB.

PANTHER, ABRAHAM, *pseud.*

A very | surprising narrative | of a | young woman, | who was | discovered in a rocky cave; | after having been taken by the | savage Indians of the wilderness, | in the year 1777, | and seeing no human being for the space of | nine long years. | In a letter from a gentleman to his friend. | *Printed by Alden Spooner* | *—at his office in Windsor—* | *M.DCC.XCIV.*   [995]

11 p., 12 mo. Sabin 93893, Evans 27471. WHi (lacks last leaf).

.   .   .   .   .   .

Second Windsor edition. *[Windsor:] Printed by Alden Spooner . . . 1794.*
                                                                        [996]

12 p., 16mo. Sabin 93894. F.C. Deering, MWA.

.   .   .   .   .   .

Third edition. *Springfield, 1794.*   [997]

Edition reported by Edward Eberstadt and Sons.

Plan of a society for the sale of lands in America, for which a subscription is opened, containing a very beneficial speculation, whereby both large and small sums of money may be improved to very great advantage, without any hazard of loss. [filet] *[London:] Instituted 25 February, 1794.*   [998]

12 p., plan, 4to. Sabin 63284, old John Carter Brown cat. 3680. MH, RPJCB.

Tract of 15,000 acres of land in Kentucky owned by Henry Peckitt, William Mee and Richard Farmer.

PORTER, A[UGUSTUS]

A | map | of | Messrs. Gorham & Phelps's | Purchase; | now the County of | Ontario, | in the State of | New York; | From actual Survey | By A Porter | *Engraved by A. Doolittle N Haven* | *[ca 1794].* [999]

Folio map (69.5 x 48 cm. over all, 62.4 x 40 cm. within the plate mark). Evans 29341, Bates supp. to Trumbull's Conn. Imprints, p. 43. DLC, NCanHi, NHi.

Used for promotion of the Phelps and Gorham Purchase, which see.

RISLER, JEREMIAS

Leben August Gottlieb Spangenbergs Bischofs der Evangelischen Brüder-Kirche. . . . *Barby: In den Brüdergemeinen. 1794.* [1000]

516 p., 12mo. Sabin 71550. RPJCB.

Includes Bishop Spangenberg's missionary travels among the Indians and frontiersmen in Georgia, North Carolina and Pennsylvania. Same in French:

.   .   .   .   .

Spangenberg, Évêque de l'Église des Frères. Sa vie, par Jeremie Risler. Traduite de l'Allemand. *Neuchatel. 1835.* [1001]

8vo. Sabin 71551.

ROWLANDSON, MARY

A | narrative | of the | captivity, sufferings and removes, | of | Mrs. Mary Rowlandson, | who was taken prisoner by the Indians, with | several others; and treated in the most | barbarous and cruel manner by those vile | savages:—With many other remarkable | events during her travels. | [thick-thin rule] | Written by her own hand, for her private use, and afterwards made | public at the earnest desire of some friends, and for the bene- | fit of the afflicted. | [thin-thick rule] | [orn.] | [thick-thin rule] | *Printed and sold by S. Hall, in Cornhill, Boston.* | *M,DCC,XCIV.* [1002]

57 p., 12mo. (17.3 x 10.7 cm.). Sabin 73587, Evans 27646. DLC, F.C. Deering, Lancaster Town Library, MWA (imperfect), NHi, RPJCB (lacks title), The Rosenbach Company (1945).

.   .   .   .   .

A | narrative | of the | captivity, sufferings, and re- | moves, | of | Mrs. Mary Rowlandson, | who was taken by the Indians, with several | others; and treated in the most barbarous and cruel | manner by those vile savages;— With many other | remarkable events during her travels. | Written by her own hand, for her private use, and after- | wards made public at the earnest

desire of some friends, | and for the benefit of the afflicted. *[Leominster, Mass.:] Printed [by Charles Prentiss] for Chapman Whitcomb. [1794].*
[1003]

54 p., 12mo. (18.2 x 10.8 cm.). Sabin 73588, Ayer supp. 109. F.C. Deering, ICN, Lancaster Town Library, Leominster Public Library, MWA, N (imperfect), NN, RPJCB.

The preface of the Clinton edition of 1853 says: "Two or three copies of the edition of 1794, published in Leominster, and now in the hands of old residents of Lancaster, are the only ones known to the publishers." The librarian of the Lancaster Town Library states that "it is known" that this was printed in 1794. The late J.C.L. Clark, leading authority on Leominster printing and on Chapman Whitcomb, said in the *Clinton Daily Item,* August 2, 1910, that this edition was printed in 1794, the year that Charles Prentiss set up his press in Leominster. He began publishing the *Rural Repository* there on October 22, 1795 but ran a job press a few months earlier. He left Leominster at the end of 1799, after which the local press was continued by Daniel Adams and Salmon Wilder, by Salmon and James Wilder and by Salmon Wilder until 1810.

SCUDDER, WILLIAM

The | journal | of | William Scudder, | an officer in the late New-York Line, | who was taken captive by the Indians at | Fort Stanwix, | on the 23d of July, 1779, and was holden a pri- | soner in Canada until October, 1782, and then | sent to New-York and admitted on parole: | with | a small sketch of his life, | and some | occurrences of the war, | which chiefly happened under his notice previous | to his captivity. | Containing also, some | extracts from history, novels, &c. | [ornamental rule] | *[New York?] Printed for the author.* | *M DCC XCIV.*   [1004]

250 p., 12mo. (16 x 10 cm.). Sabin 78533, Evans 27681. NHi.

Lieutenant William Scudder was born at Westfield, N.J., July 25, 1747 and, while an officer of the First Regiment of the New York Line in the Revolution, was captured by the Indians near Fort Stanwix (Rome), N.Y., July 23, 1779, was taken to Montreal and thence to Quebec where he was a prisoner until October 10, 1782 when he returned by ship to New York, thence to American headquarters at Newburgh and so home where he arrived November 25th. He tells of attending the funeral of Jane McCrea in 1777, gives his adventures in detail, mentioning numerous other Indian captives, including Lieutenant Moses Van Camp[en]. He dates his note *To the printer* from *New-York, May 10, 1794,* from which we assume that the book was printed there. The first part of the journal was written while the author was still a prisoner at Quebec in September, 1779, the remainder finished in 1784. Though simply written, it is fresh, detailed and accurate and it is surprising that it has never been reprinted and that, so far as we can discover, only a single copy has survived. A contemporary MS copy of that part of the journal covering August 4, 1779 to February 1, 1780 is at NHi, the gift of a direct descendant of the author.

WILLIAMSON, PETER

French and Indian cruelty exemplified in the adventurous life, and various vicissitudes of fortune, of Peter Williamson . . . *[n.p.] Printed in the year 1794.* [1005]

24 p., 12mo. (16.2 x 8.7 cm.). Sabin 104475, Ayer 322. ICN.

THE ASYLUM COMPANY

Plan of association of the Asylum Company. *Philadelphia: Printed by Zachariah Poulson, junior? 1795.* [1006]

24 p., 12mo. Evans 28215. MH-BA, NN, PPL-R.

. . . . .

Catalogue of the lands and stock of the Asylum Company. *Philadelphia, 1819.* [1007]

17 p. PHi, PPL.

BOWNAS, SAMUEL

An account of the life, travels, and Christian experiences of . . . [Title as in 1st ed., 1756] *London, Printed and sold by James Phillips, George Yard, Lombard Street, 1795.* [1008]

vii, 196 p., 8vo. (17 x 10 cm.). Sabin 7097. CP, CtY, InU, IU, NHi, NN, NNUT, PHC, PSC, PSC-Hi.

Includes the Hanson captivity.

. . . . .

Stanford, Re-printed: By Daniel Lawrence, for Henry and John F. Hull, M.DCCC.V. [1009]

306, [2] p., 8vo. (16 cm.). Sabin 7097. Copies in many large libraries.

Includes the Hanson captivity. Printed at Stanford, now Stanfordville, Dutchess County, New York.

. . . . .

New edition. *London: Charles Gilpin, 1846.* [1010]

288 p., 8vo. Title from Sabin 7097.

Reprinted in *Friends Library*, vol. 12, *London, 1836*, and same, *Philadelphia, 1839.*

BRACKENRIDGE, HUGH HENRY

Incidents of the insurrection in the western parts of Pennsylvania, in the year 1794. By Hugh H. Brackenridge. *Philadelphia: Printed and sold by John M'Culloch, No. 1 North Third-Street. - 1795.* [1011]

[2], [5]-124; [5]-84; [5]-154 p., 8vo. Sabin 7189, Evans 28332. Copies in most large libraries.

The author's explanation of his sympathies with the insurgents in the Whiskey Rebellion of Pennsylvania frontiersmen against the excise tax. Reprinted, with an introduction by the author's son, Henry M. Brackenridge, defending his father, as: *History of the Western Insurrection in Western Pennsylvania, commonly called the Whiskey Insurrection. 1794. . . . Pittsburgh: Printed by W.S. Haven. 1859.* 336 p., 8vo. Sabin 7166. Copies in most large libraries.

CARVER, JONATHAN

Three years travels. *Philadelphia, 1795.*   [1012]

Sabin 11185. Not in Lee. Doubtful. See note at end of 1798 edition.

COLUMBUS, *pseud.*

Cautionary hints to Congress, respecting the sale of the western lands, belonging to the United States. *Philadelphia: William W. Woodward, Printer, Franklin's Head, green sign, No. 36, Chestnut-Street, South Side. 1795.*   [1013]

15 p., 8vo. (22.5 cm.). Evans 28459. CSmH, MWA, NHi, RPJCB.

Reprinted the following year.

For a similar work, see Thomas Paine's *Public good,* 1780.

CONGREGATIONAL CHURCH IN CONNECTICUT

An address to the inhabitants of the new settlements in the northern and western parts of the United States. *New-Haven: Printed by T. & S. Green. [1795].*   [1014]

6 p., 8vo. Evans 28463, Bates supp. to Trumbull 1748. DLC, NN.

Signed at New Haven, June 27, 1795.

CONNECTICUT GORE LAND COMPANY

Articles of agreement. *[n.p., 1795].*   [1015]

Broadside, folio. (45 x 26.5 cm.). CtY, MH, PPiU.

.   .   .   .   .

Brief articles of agreement. [Dated at Hartford, Sept. 17, 1795] *[Hartford, 1795?]*   [1016]

[8] p., 12mo. MWA.

Concerning the Gore in Southern New York, according to A.C. Bates.

CONNECTICUT LAND COMPANY

Articles of association and agreement constituting the Connecticut Land Company. [Dated September 5, 1795] *[Hartford: Printed by Hudson and Goodwin? 1795]* [1017]

7 p., 16mo. Evans 28475, Sabin 15712, Trumbull 513. DLC, NHi.

The beginnings of the Western Reserve in Ohio.

. . . . .

Votes of the Connecticut Land Company. Hartford, September 5, 1795. *[Hartford, 1795]*. [1018]

Broadside? Four hundred copies printed. Original MS in OclWHi. Title from Bates supp. to Trumbull 2002.

COOPER, THOMAS

Renseignemens sur l'Amérique. Rassemblés par Thomas Cooper, ci-devant de Manchester. Traduit de l'Anglois; avec une carte. *Paris: An III [1795].* [1019]

Title from Sabin 16616.

. . . . .

A Hambourg: Chez Pierre Francois Fauche. 1795. [1020]

xx, 218, 74 p., folded map, 8vo. (22 cm.). Sabin 16616. DLC.

DECALVES, ALONSO, *pseud.*

Travels to the Westward . . . [as in 1st Keene ed., 1794] Second Keene edition. *Keene—(Newhampshire:) Printed and sold by Henry Blake & Co. M,DCC,XCV.* [1021]

35 p., 12mo. Sabin 98449, Evans 28547. MWA, RPJCB.

. . . . .

The second edition. *Printed in Keene, Newhampshire; for the purchaser [by Cornelius Sturtevant, Jr. & Co., successors to Henry Blake who died in March, 1795], 1795.* [1022]

35 p., 12mo. Sabin 98448, Evans 28548. MWA, RPJCB.

. . . . .

New travels | to the Westward, | or unknown parts of America: | Being a tour of almost fourteen months. | Containing, | An account of the country, upwards of | two thousand miles west of the Chri- | stian parts of North-America; with an | account of the white Indians, their man- | ners, habits, and many other particulars. | By Don Alonso Decalves. | Confirmed by three other persons. | *[N.p.] Printed in the year 1795.* [1023]

[2], 58 p., 18mo. (12.1 x 7.7 cm.). Sabin 98447. NHi.

GEORGIA MISSISSIPPI COMPANY

Grant | to the | Georgia Mississippi Company, | the | constitution | thereof, | and | extracts relative to the situation, soil, | climate, and navigation of the Western | territory of the State of Georgia; | and particularly of that part | thereof in which the Compa- | ny's lands are situated. | [filet] | Published by order of the directors. | [filet, thick-thin rule] | *Augusta:* | *Printed by John Erdman Smith.* | *MDCCXCV.* [1024]

28 p., 8vo. (21.5 x 12.5 cm.). Evans 28742. DLC, GA, GMW, GU-De, MB, MBAt, MH, MWA, NHi, NN, RPJCB.

Issued with *State of facts,* below. It is not certain which of the Augusta editions should be credited to the above locations.

This and the following entries under this heading have to do with the Yazoo Frauds, for which, see C.S. Haskins: *The Yazoo Land Companies.* No attempt is made to record the many controversial publications which appeared in later years.

.　.　.　.　.　.

Augusta: Printed by John Erdman Smith, MDCCXCV. And reprinted with an appendix, by desire of the purchasers in Connecticut. [1025]

39 p., 8vo. Evans 28743, Sabin 27054 note, De Renne I:269. GU-De, MBAt, MH, MWA, NHi, NN, RPJCB.

.　.　.　.　.　.

. . . Published by order of the directo [sic] *Augusta: Printed by John Erdman Smith. MDCCXCV.* [1026]

40 p., 8vo. Sabin 27054, Evans 28744. DLC, MB, MBAt, MWA, etc. (See note to 1st ed.)

.　.　.　.　.　.

State of facts. | Shewing the | right | of | certain companies | to the | lands | lately purchased by them | from the | State of Georgia. | *[Phila-delphia:] United States,* | *Printed in the year 1795.* [1027]

64 p., 8vo. Sabin 27112, Evans 28745, De Renne I:270. BM, DLC, GA, GMW, GU-De, MBAt, MH, MWA, NHi, NN, RPJCB.

Generally found bound with *Grant,* above. The GU-De copy has inserted: *Map of the grants of the Georgia Western Territory, based on a map in Dr. Morse's American Gazetteer,* 1797. (17.7 x 14.6 cm.). For some of the more important controversial tracts on this company and the Yazoo frauds, see under John E. Anderson, Abraham Bishop, Robert Goodloe Harper and James Jackson.

[JACKSON, JAMES]

The | letters of Sicilius, | to the | citizens of the State of Georgia, | on the | constitutionality, the policy, | and the legality of the | late sale of Western lands, | in the | State of Georgia, | considered in a | series of numbers, | By a Citizen of that State. | August, 1795. *[Augusta: Printed by John E. Smith? 1795].* [1028]

66 p., 8vo. (21.3 x 13.5 cm.). Sabin 27067, Evans 28889, De Renne I:269. GU-De, etc.

This first edition has only ten letters.

. . . . .

With twelve letters. 94 p. Evans 28889. MBAt, etc. [1029]

An attack on the Georgia Mississippi Company and the Yazoo Frauds.

JOHONNOT, JACKSON

The remarkable adventures of Jackson Johonnet, of Massachusetts. Who served as a soldier in the Western Army, in the Massachusetts Line, in the expedition under General Harmar, and the unfortunate General St. Clair. Containing an account of his captivity, sufferings and escape from the Kickapoo Indians. Written by himself, and published at the earnest importunity of his friends, for the benefit of American youth. *Exeter: Printed by and for J. Lamson. [1795].* [1030]

Title, not seen, from the library of F.C. Deering.

John Lamson published *Lamson's Weekly Visitor* at Exeter, New Hampshire, May 5-December 26, 1795.

. . . . .

The remarkable adventures of Jackson Johonnet of Massachusetts, who served as a soldier in the Western Army, in the expedition under Gen. Harmar and Gen. St. Clair. Containing an account of his captivity, sufferings, and escape from the Kickapoo Indians. Written by himself, and published at the earnest request and importunity of his friends for the benefit of American youth. *Printed at Walpole, Newhampshire by I. Thomas and D. Carlisle, jun. MDCCXCV.* [1031]

12 p., 12mo. Sabin 36403, Evans 28907. MH, MWA.

KINNAN, MARY

A | true narrative | of the | sufferings | of | Mary Kinnan, | who was taken prisoner by the Shawanee Na- | tion of Indians on the thirteenth day of | May, 1791, and remained with them till | the sixteenth of August, 1794. | [rule] | *Elizabethtown:* | *Printed by Shepard Kollock.* | *M.DCC.XCV.* [1032]

15 p., 12mo. (18 x 10.6 cm.). Evans 28931, Sabin under title, Ayer 174. F.C. Deering, ICN. Photostats of ICN copy in NHi, NN.

Mary Kinnan was taken by the Shawnees from her Virginia home in 1791 and, after having been sold into several other tribes, was rescued by her brother, Jacob Lewis, near Detroit in 1794. According to O.M. Voorhees, the captive's grand-niece told him that this narrative was taken down, and "improved" by Shepard Kollock, the printer. She was present at St. Clair's defeat and rescued by General Wayne's army.

. . . . .

A | true narrative | of the | sufferings | of | Mary Kinnan, | who was taken prisoner by the Shawanee | Nation of Indians on the thirteenth | day of May, 1791, and remain- | ed with them till the | sixteenth of Aug. | 1794. | [orn. rule] | *New Haven:* | *Printed by William W. Morse.* | [rule] | 1801.   [1033]

12 p., 8vo. Sabin 97131, Herschel V. Jones checklist 680. Frank T. Siebert.

The Siebert copy, in contemporary wrappers, edges cut, was sold in Anderson Galleries sale 1831, April 2, 1924, lot 298 for $100. to H.V. Jones whose library was bought by the Rosenbach Co. who sold this item to Dr. Siebert for $450. Another copy, sewed, uncut, was offered by Cadmus Book Shop, Miniature List 18, for $250.

Same, in Andrew Beers's *Washington Almanac* for 1805 [Monmouth Co., N.J., 1804]. MWA, NjHi. Same, in Randolph Co., W.Va. Hist. Soc. *Magazine of History-Biography*, 1926., with introd. by Boyd B. Stutler. Same, with introd. and notes by Rev. Oscar M. Voorhees, as: *A New Jersey woman's captivity among the Indians,* in N.J. Hist. Soc. Proceed., April, 1928, p. 152-165. Includes Mary Kinnan's letter of July 29, 1793 to her brother, asking him to come to her rescue. See also Oscar M. Voorhees: *"Aunt Polly" Kinnan; an Indian tragedy of the eighteenth century,* in Somerset Co. (N.J.) Hist. Quar., July, 1912, p. 179-190; and his first publication of Mary Kinnan's letter in: *The pension secured for "Aunt Polly" Kinnan,* in Somerset Co. Hist. Quar., April, 1916, p. 106-108. For Jacob Lewis's own account of his rescue of his sister, see *A history and biographical cyclopaedia of Butler County, Ohio,* 1882, p. 180-182. See also Oscar McMurtry's *A short history of the capture by Indians of Mrs. Mary Kinnan, and subsequent rescue from captivity by her brother, 1791-94.* [n.p., Regimental Press, Eighth U.S. Cavalry (on back wrapper), n.d. but ca. 1903, the date of the watermark]. [19] p., 8vo. CtY, DLC. *Oscar McMurtry* was a pseudonym for Oscar McMurtrie Voorhees. This narrative was secured from the accounts of surviving friends and relatives of the captive. The Fred W. Alsopp copy (sold at Parke-Bernet Galleries, April 1, 1947, lot 175) was inscribed: "Compliments of Geo. G. Anderson, Col. 8th Cav." and brought $100. There are two other recent auction records. There is also an inaccurate account of this captivity in Ludwig Schumacher's *The Somerset Hills,* p. 103-110.

McDONALD, PHILIP, AND ALEXANDER McLEOD

A | surprising account | of the | captivity and escape | of | Philip MacDonald, | and | Alexander M'Leod, | both of Virginia, | from the |

Chickkemogga Indians: | and of their great discoveries in the west- | ern world—from Jene [sic] 1779, to January | 1786; when they returned to their friends in | health, after an absence of six years and a half. | [double rule] | Written by themselves. | [double rule] | *Windsor:* | *Re-printed by Alden Spooner, and sold to* | *the peddlers, cheap for cash, by the* | *gross, hundred, or dozen.* | *[1795].*   [1034]

12 p., 12mo. Title from the only known copy, described, with facsimile of the title, in Edward Eberstadt & Sons cat. 122, 1943, no. 242 (where it is dated [c. 1786]), $400.00. Present location unknown.

Advertised as "Just published" in the Windsor *Vermont Journal,* June 15, 1795, published by Alden Spooner. No other reference to a Windsor edition in the files of this paper.

NORTH AMERICAN LAND COMPANY

Plan | of | association | of the | North American | Land Company. | Established February, 1795. | [filet] | *Philadelphia:* | *Printed by R. Aitken and Son, Market Street.* | [rule] | *M,DCC,XCV.*   [1035]

25 p., 1 folded leaf, 8vo. (20 x 12 cm.). Sabin 55548, Evans 29220, De Renne I:270. DLC, GU-De, MB, MBAt, MH, MHi, MiU-C, MWA, MWiW-C, NHi, NN, PP, PPL-R, RPJCB.

Their holdings included over six million acres of lar.d in Kentucky, Georgia, North and South Carolina, Pennsylvania and Virginia. RPJCB has three variants, each differing on p. 21 and two of them have added, on the folded leaf, the notarial seal and signature of Clement Biddle.

· · · · ·

Philadelphia, printed. London, Reprinted for C. Barrell, and H. Servante, 1795.   [1036]

[2], 35, [1] p., folded facsim., 8vo. (18.5 cm.). Title from catalog of DLC. DLC, MH-BA.

· · · · ·

[Alterations proposed to be made in the original articles of agreement and association of the North American Land Company, dated 20th February, 1795, as unanimously agreed to by the shareholders of said company, assembled at their annual meeting in Philadelphia on the 31st December, 1805. *Philadelphia? 1805?*]   [1037]

4 p., 4to. (21 cm.). Title from catalog of DLC.

Title taken from note at end, signed: James Greenleaf, Secretary of the North American Land Company.

PANTHER, ABRAHAM, *pseud.*

A surprising narrative of a young woman who was discovered in a cave. After having been taken from her companions by the savage Indians. Second Windsor edition. *Windsor: Printed by Alden Spooner. 1795.*   [1038]

Title from Evans 29276, copied by Sabin 93895, and perhaps same as the 1794 edition above. Entry probably taken from an advertisement published in 1795 for an unsold remainder of the 1794 edition or for a reprint of it with the 1795 date.

.   .   .   .   .

A | surprising narrative | of a | young woman | discovered | in | a cave | in the | wilderness, | after having been taken | by the | savage Indians, | and seeing no human being for the | space of nine years. | In a | letter. | [wavy rule] | By a gentleman to his friend. | [wavy rule] | [double rule] | *Leominster:* | *Printed for Chapman Whitcomb,* | *By Charles Prentiss.* | *[1795-1799].*   [1039]

12 p., 12mo. (18 x 10.5 cm.). Sabin 93900. F.C. Deering, MWA.

Charles Prentiss was printing in Leominster from October, 1795 to December, 1799, when he was succeeded by Adams and Wilder.

Description from photostat at NHi of a copy owned by Rosenbach Co. in 1925.

PRICE, JONATHAN

A description of Occacock Inlet, and of its coasts, islands, shoals, and anchorages, with the courses and distances, to and from the most remarkable places, and directions to sail over the bar and through the channels. *Newbern: Printed by Francois-X. Martin. 1795.*   [1040]

8 p. (16.5 x 12.5 cm.). Evans 29351, McMurtrie: North Carolina imprints, 214. NHi.

"North Carolina District Copyright, issued to Jonathan Price, William Johnston, and Francois Xavier Martin, on a Map, and Pamphlet, as Proprietors, 12 December, 1795."—Evans.

The NHi copy evidently never had a title page and consists of a single sheet folded to form a quarto of eight pages with the first page beginning with a row of type ornaments and the caption title: *A | description | of | Occacick Inlet.* | There is no accompanying map. Evans, who gives neither collation nor location, evidently took his title from the copyright description and not from an actual title page. There is no imprint or indication of printer in the NHi copy.

Probably issued to accompany a 1795 edition of the following map in DLC: *To navigators this chart, being an actual survey of the sea coast and inland navigation, from cape Henry to cape Roman is most respectfully inscribed by Price and Strother. Published agreeable to act of Congress. Engraved by W. Johnston, New-Bern, North Carolina, 1798.* (35 x 96.3 cm.). (Title from Phillips).

Tract issued for purposes of topographical description and promotion for Occacock Peninsula (formerly Island), off the coast of North Carolina.

ROWLANDSON, MARY

A | narrative, | of the | captivity, | sufferings and removes, | of Mrs. | Mary Rowlandson, | who was taken prisoner by the Indians, with | several others, and treated in the most | barbarous and cruel manner by those vile | savages. With many other remarkable events | during her travels. | Written by her own hand, for her private use, | and now made public, at the earnest desire of | some friends, and for the benefit of the afflicted. | *Amherst, (New-Hampshire)* | *Printed and sold, by Nathaniel* | *Coverly and Son, near the Court-* | *House.* | *[1795].* [1041]

64 p., 12 mo. Sabin 73586, Evans 29436, Brinley 489 to DLC. DLC, Lancaster Town Library, MH, MWA.

Following Brinley, most bibliographers have dated this edition [1792], at which time Coverly was still in Boston. He began publishing the *Amherst Journal* on January 16, 1795 and on April 24th of that year took his son into partnership. The paper was discontinued on January 9, 1796 and the Coverlys moved to Haverhill.

SOUTH-CAROLINA SOCIETY

Information, | to those who are disposed to migrate to South-Carolina. | . . . | Charleston, South-Carolina, | March 26, 1795. | Published by order of the South-Carolina Society, for the information | and assistance of persons emigrating from other countries. | *[Charleston, 1795].* [1042]

Broadside, folio. Sabin 87854. MWA.

Signed by John Rutledge, President, other officers, and the Committee of Correspon`ence.

TERRITORIAL COMPANY

Plan of association of the Territorial Company. Established April, 1795. *Philadelphia: Printed by R. Aitken and Son, Market Street. M,DCC,XCV.* [1043]

21 p., 8vo. Sabin 63287 and 94879, Evans 29550. DLC.

Company organized to sell 310,904 acres of land in Hawkins, Knox and Washington counties, South Western Territory (Tennessee).

WILLIAMS, JOHN

The redeemed captive returning to Zion . . . The sixth edition. *Printed by Samuel Hall, No. 53, Cornhill, Boston. 1795.* [1044]

132 p., 12mo. (17.6 x 10.5 cm.). Sabin 104269, Evans 29893, Ayer supp. 136, Church 1267. CSmH, DLC, F.C. Deering, ICN, MB, MHi, MWA, N, NHi, NN, RPJCB.

.   .   .   .   .   .

. . . Subjoined to this is, a sermon, delivered in the First Parish in Springfield, on the 16th of October, 1775. just one hundred years from the burning of the town by the Indians. By Robert Breck, A.M. Pastor of the church there. The sixth edition, with additions. *Printed and sold at Greenfield, Mass. by Thomas Dickman. MDCCC.* [i.e., 1802].   [1045]

248 p., 12mo. Sabin 104270, Ayer supp. 137. BM, DLC, F.C. Deering, ICN, MH, MWA, MWiW-C, N, NN, OO, PHi, RPJCB.

Date supplied from letter of John Taylor, p. 197-198, dated, Deerfield, Jan. 1st, 1802. He adds to this edition a sketch of Deerfield, p. 198-220.

. . . . .

New-Haven: Printed by William W. Morse. 1802.   [1046]

188 p., 12mo. Sabin 104271, Ayer 311. CtY, DLC, F.C. Deering, ICN, MB, MH, MHi, MWA, MWiW-C, N, NHi, NN, WHi.

. . . . .

The captivity and deliverance of Mr. John Williams, Pastor of the Church in Deerfield, and Mrs. Mary Rowlandson, of Lancaster, who were taken, together with their families and neighbors, by the French and Indians, and carried into Canada. Written by themselves. *Brookfield, Printed by Hori Brown, from the press of E. Merriam & Co. September—1811.*   [1047]

116, 80 p., 12mo. (16.6 x 9.8 cm.). Sabin 104272, Ayer 313. An-C-OAr, BM, DLC, F.C. Deering, ICN, Lancaster Town Library, MWA, N, NN.

Omits the appendices of earlier editions. Mrs. Rowlandson's narrative has a separate title page and separate pagination but the signatures are continuous.

Second title: *The captivity and deliverance of Mrs. Mary Rowlandson, of Lancaster, who was taken by the French and Indians. Written by herself.* [Imprint as above]. For other editions, see under her name.

. . . . .

The | redeemed captive: | a narrative | of the | captivity, sufferings, and return | of the | Rev. John Williams, | who was taken prisoner by the Indians | on the destruction of the | town, A.D. 1700. | [rule] | For Sabbath schools. | [rule] | *New-York: | Published by S.W. Benedict & Co. | Evangelist Office, No. 20, Ann st. | 1833.*   [1048]

116 p., 2 plates, 24mo. (12.5 x 9 cm.). Sabin 104273, Ayer 234. DLC, F.C. Deering, ICN, MWA, NHi, NN.

Condensed narrative in form of letters by Rev. Joshua Leavitt, reprinted from the *New York Evangelist*, February-March, 1833.

. . . . .

The redeemed captive returning to Zion . . . To which is added, A biographical memoir of the Reverend author, with an appendix and notes, by Stephen W. Williams, A.M., M.D., Honorary Member of The New York Historical Society, Corresponding Member of the National Institute, etc., etc. *Northampton: Hopkins, Bridgman, and Company. 1853.*   [1049]

192 p., frontispiece and portrait of the author, 12mo. (17.5 x 11 cm.). Sabin 104274, Ayer 312. Copies in most large libraries.

The *Biographical memoir* is a reprint of: "A biographical memoir of the Rev. John Williams, first Minister of Deerfield, Massachusetts. With a slight sketch of ancient Deerfield, and an account of the Indian wars in that place and vicinity. With an appendix, containing the journal of the Rev. Doctor Stephen Williams, of Longmeadow, during his captivity, and other papers relating to the early Indian wars in Deerfield. By Stephen W. Williams . . . Greenfield, Mass. Published and printed by C.J.J. Ingersoll. 1837." 127 p., 12mo. Same, reissued with a cover title dated 1841. NN. Sabin 104378. See also: "What befell Stephen Williams in his captivity. With an appendix. Printed from the original by the Pocumtuck Valley Memorial Association. . . . Edited by George Sheldon. Deerfield, Mass. 1889." 35 p., 8vo. Reprints the original manuscript journal of Stephen Williams who was captured with his father, Rev. John Williams in 1703-4, with other historical manuscripts from his papers, including the captivities of Daniel Belding and Mahuman Hinsdale. His journal also appears in the 1837 *Biographical memoir* but with the spelling modernized. See also "The Deerfield captive, an Indian story; being a narrative of facts, for the instruction of the young. A Phelps, *Greenfield, Mass. 1832.*" 68 p., front., 18mo. Same, Second edition, 1834; Third edition, 1837; Fourth edition, 1842; *Greenfield,* 1884. Sabin 93077 for locations. There are later children's stories based on this narrative. See also: "Half century at the Bay 1636-1686. Heredity and early environment of John Williams 'The Redeemed Captive' by George Sheldon. *Boston,* 1905." 149, x p., 8vo. See also: "New tracks in an old trail." By George Sheldon. [*n.p.,* 1899]. 11 p., 8vo. Analysis of the narratives of John and Stephen Williams.

. . . . .

The redeemed captive returning to Zion or the captivity and deliverance of Rev. John Williams of Deerfield. Reprinted from the sixth edition. *The H.R. Huntting Company, Springfield, Massachusetts, MCMVIII.* [1049A] xxiv, 212 p., front., 12mo.

An edition of 526 copies of which 26 are large paper, edited by George Sheldon, with a bibliography by Wilberforce Eames.

See also Rev. Solomon Williams: "The power and efficacy of the prayers of the people of God, when rightly offered to him; and the obligation and encouragement thence arising to be much in prayer. A sermon preach'd at Mansfield, Aug. 4, 1741. At a time set apart for prayer for the revival of religion; and on the behalf of Mrs. Eunice, the daughter of the Reverend Mr. John Williams, (formerly pastor of Deerfield) who was then on a visit there, from Canada; where she had been in a long captivity. . . . Published at the desire, and expence of many that heard it. *Boston: Printed by S. Kneeland and T. Green, in Queenstreet. 1742.*" [2], 28 p., 12mo. Evans 5094, Sabin 104364. CtHi, MB, MBAt, MWA, RPJCB.

See also Rev. John Fessenden: "Sermon preached to the First Congregational Society in Deerfield, Mass. in the hearing of several Indians of both sexes supposed to be descendants of Eunice Williams, daughter of Rev. John Williams, first minister of Deerfield. *Greenfield, Mass., Printed by Phelps and Ingersoll, 1837.*" 15 p., 8vo. (21 cm.). DLC, etc. See also Rev. Isaac Chauncy: "A blessed manumission of Christ's faithful ministers. A sermon at the funeral of the Reverend Mr. John Williams, pastor of the church in Deerfield, who deceased June 12, 1729. *Boston: Printed for D. Henchman. 1729.*" 32 p., 8vo. Evans 3145, Sabin 12335 note. MWA. See also Rev. Robert Breck: "The departure of Elijah lamented. A sermon, preached at the funeral of the Rev. Stephen Williams, D.D. pastor of a church in Springfield. Who departed this life, June 10th, 1782, in the ninetieth year of his age. [one line quoted] *Springfield: Printed by Babcock & Haswell. M,DCC,LXXXII.*" 27 p., 8vo. Sabin 7658, Evans 17483. BM, DLC, MHi.

[BIDWELL, BARNABAS]

The | Susquehannah title | stated and examined, | in a series of | numbers, | first published in the | Western Star [Stockbridge, Mass.], | and now republished, in this form, for the | benefit of the public in general, and | all persons concerned in | particular. | [orn. rule] | *Printed in Catskill, by Mackay Croswell.* | *1796.*   [1050]

115 p., 8vo. (17 x 10.5 cm.). Evans 30091. CSmH, CtY, DLC, MiU-C, MWA, NHi, NNUT, P, PPL, RPJCB.

NHi copy has inserted a folded printed page with the caption: *Copy of a letter,* | *from the Honorable Cyrus Griffin . . . September 15, 1796.*

First four chapters reprinted from the Stockbridge *Western Star* in Mackay Croswell's *Catskill Packet*, August 22-29, 1796. CtY, MWA, NHi.

Reprinted, edited by J.P. Boyd, in Wyoming Hist. and Geol. Soc. Proceedings, vol. 20, 1929, and as a separate.

BRISSOT DE WARVILLE, JEAN PIERRE

Neue Reise durch die Vereinigten Staaten von Nord Amerika im Jahre 1788. . . . Neue unveränderte Auflage. . . . *Hof: Gottfried Adolph Grau. 1796.*   [1051]

3 vols., 8vo. Sabin 8032.

BUNN, MATTHEW

A journal of the adventures of Matthew Bunn, a native of Brookfield, Massachusetts, who enlisted with Ensign John Tillinghast, of Providence, in the year 1791, on an expedition into the Western Country;— was taken by the savages, and made his escape into Detroit the 30th of April, 1792. Containing a very circumstantial account of the cruel treatment he suffered while in captivity, and many of the customs of the savages, which have never before appeared in print. Published by the particular request of a number of persons who have seen the manuscript. *Providence: Printed for the author, and sold by him; also at Mr. Todd's Book-Store near the Baptist-Meeting-House, and at the Printing-Office [of Bennett Wheeler] in the Market-House. [1796].* [1052]

24 p., 8vo. (22.5 x 13 cm.). Evans 30135 who gives incorrect description from a Bennett Wheeler advertisement. E.D. Graff.

. . . . .

Providence printed: Litchfield, re-printed by Thomas Collier, -D,DCC,- XCVI [1796]. [1053]

24 p., 8vo. (21.5 x 12 cm.). Evans 30136, Trumbull 421. CtY, MiD-B, RPJCB, Lemuel A. Welles. Photostat copies of Welles copy at NHi, NN.

. . . . .

Printed at Walpole, New Hampshire, by David Carlisle, Jun. 1796. [1054]

22+ p., 8vo. (22.5 x 13.5 cm.). OClWHi.

Title from imperfect copy at OClWHi.

Matthew Bunn was an Ensign with General St. Clair, was captured in the Ohio Country in 1792, escaped and was recaptured by George Girty, gave him the slip and surrendered to the British garrison at Detroit the following year. For damning King George and all the royal family he was thrown into jail and sent to Fort Niagara and, to save his hide, joined the Queen's Rangers, escaped, got caught and was given 500 lashes, escaped again and, after still more adventures along the Niagara Frontier, returned to his native Massachusetts in 1795. A stout fellow!

CARVER, JONATHAN

Three years travels. *Philadelphia, 1796.* DLC, etc. [1055]

. . . . .

Reize. *Leyden, 1796.* DLC, etc. [1056]

See note at end of 1798 edition.

COLUMBUS, *pseud.*

Cautionary hints to Congress respecting the sale of the Western Lands, belonging to the United States. Second edition. *Philadelphia: Printed for Mathew Carey, by Lang and Ustick. Feb. 24, 1796.* [1057]

13, [2] p., 8vo. (20.5 cm.). Sabin 11587, Evans 30254. DLC, MHi, MWA.

The first edition appeared the previous year.

LA COMPAGNIE DE NEW-YORK

Faits et calculus | sur la population et le territoire | des États-Unis d'Améri-que. | [wavy rule] | Traduit de l'Anglois. | [wavy rule] | *[Paris, 1796?]*.
[1058]

12 p., 4to. (24 x 19 cm.). Title from photostat at N.

Probably by Pierre Chassanis. Compiled from American sources and issued for the promotion of the Castorland tract of La Compagnie de New-York though the pamphlet contains nothing specifically on that tract. The latest information in the text is dated 1796.

[CONDY, JONATHAN WILLIAMS?]

A | description | of the | River Susquehanna, | with | observations | on the | present state of its trade and navigation, | and their | practicable and probable improvement. | [rule] | Illustrated with a map and an appendix. | [rule] | *Philadelphia:* | *Printed by Zachariah Poulson, Junior,* | *Number eighty, Chesnut-Street.* | [rule] | *1796.*
[1059]

[4], 60 p., folded map, 8vo. (21 x 12.5 cm.). Sabin 93935, Evans 30338. DLC, MBAt, MH, MHi, MiU-C (no map), MWA, NHi, NN, PPAmP, PPL-R, RPJCB, ScC.

The untitled map, engraved by W. Barker, shows the territory from the City of Washington north to Lake Ontario and from Fort Pitt east to New York, including towns, roads and rivers.

A general promotion tract on Northeastern Pennsylvania and South-western New York with emphasis on the importance of the Susquehanna as a means of reaching the back country and the desirability of improving its navigation. Probably issued in the interest of the Schuylkill and Susquehanna Navigation Company or one of Robert Morris's other companies.

CONNECTICUT, GENERAL ASSEMBLY

Act of the General Assembly of Connecticut, incorporating the Proprietors of the Sufferers' Land, so called. *New-Haven: Printed by Thomas and Samuel Green. 1796.*
[1060]

4to. Evans 30265, locates no copy and probably copies Brinley 2127 which was sold to W.M. Darlington, probably now PPiU.

Has to do with the lands of the Susquehannah Company in the Wyoming Valley, Pennsylvania, claimed both by Connecticut and Pennsylvania.

CONNECTICUT GORE LAND COMPANY

Articles of agreement for conducting the business of the Connecticut Gore Land Company. *Hartford, 1796.*
[1061]

16mo. Title from Evans 30272. MH.

.   .   .   .   .

Supplementary articles of agreement. [Dated at Hartford, April 8, 1796] *[Hartford, 1796].*
[1062]

7 p., 16mo. Bates supp. to Trumbull 2001. MWA, PPiU.
Concerning the Gore in Southern New York, according to A.C. Bates.

CONNECTICUT LAND COMPANY

Mode of partition of the Western Reserve. [Determined by the Connecticut Land Company, at their meeting held at Hartford, by adjournment, on the first Tuesday of April (April 5), 1796] *[Hartford, 1796].*   [1063]
    [8] p., 16mo. Evans 30273, Bates supp. to Trumbull 2401. DLC, MWA.

DECALVÉS, ALONSO, *pseud.*

Eine ganz neue und sehr merkwürdige Reisebeschreibung, oder, zuverlässige und glaubwürdige Nachrichten von den Westlichen bisjetzt noch unbekannten Theilen von America. Enthaltend: Eine Beschreibung derjenigen Länder, welche auf einige tausend Meilen gegen Westen und oberhalb den Christlichen Staaten von Nord-America liegen; wie auch eine Schilderung der Weissen Indianer, ihrer Sitten, Gebräuche und Kleidertrachten. Von Don Alonzo Decalves. *Philadelphia, Gedruckt und zu haben bey den Herren Buchhändlern. 1796.*   [1064]
    82, [2] p., 8vo. Sabin 98450, Evans 30324, Seidensticker p. 145. DLC, MH, MIU, MWA, NN, PPG.
First German edition of the Vandeleur captivity. The last leaf contains an advertisement of the booksellers, Neale and Kämmerer, jun., for whom the German edition was presumably published.

.   .   .   .   .

New travels to the Westward, or Unknown parts of America; Being a tour of almost fourteen months. Containing, An account of the country, upwards of two thousand miles west of the Christian parts of North-America; with an account of white Indians, their manners, habits, and many other particulars. By Don Alonso Decalves. Confirmed by three other persons. *[Dover, N.H.] Printed [by Samuel Bragg, jun.] in the year 1796.*   [1065]
    34 p., 8vo. Sabin 98451, imprint from Evans 30319. MWA.

.   .   .   .   .

New travels to the Westward, or, Unknown parts of America. Being a tour of almost fourteen months. Containing, An account of the country, upwards of two thousand miles west of the Christian parts of North-America; with an account of white Indians, their manners, habits, and many other particulars. By Don Alonso Decalves. Confirmed by three other persons. The fourth edition. *New-London: Printed and sold by James Springer, opposite the market. 1796.*   [1066]
    35, [1] p., 12mo. Sabin 98452, Evans 30322, Trumbull 1157. DLC.

.   .   .   .   .

Norwich: Printed by John Trumbull. [1796].   [1067]

Sabin 98453, Trumbull supp. 2458, both taken from Evans 30323 who probably took his entry from an advertisement since he gives no collation. Copy in F.C. Deering library where it is erroneously dated [1788].

.   .   .   .   .

Printed at Portland. [by Benjamin Titcomb, jun. May 16.] MDCCXCVI.
[1068]
28 p., 12mo. (18 cm.). Sabin 98454, Evans 30320, Noyes Maine imprints 84. DLC, F.C. Deering, MWA, RPJCB.

DERKINDEREN, JAMES

A | narrative | of the | sufferings | of | James Derkinderen, | who was taken prisoner by the Halifax Indians, | on the 10th of the 6th mo. (commonly | called June) 1759. | [rule] | *Philadelphia:* | *Printed for the purchaser.* | *MDCCXCVI.*   [1069]
8 p., 12mo. Sabin 19674, Evans 30336. MHi, MWA.

A brief but very interesting journal "printed verbatim et literatim from the author's manuscript," with all its quaint phraseology and mistakes in spelling.

FINDLEY, WILLIAM

History | of the | insurrection, | in the | four Western counties | of | Pennsylvania: | in the year M.DCC.XCIV. | With a recital of the circumstances speci- | ally connected therewith: | and an | historical review of the previous situation of the country. | [double rule] | By William Findley, | Member of the House of Representatives of the United States. | [double rule] | *Philadelphia:* | *Printed by Samuel Harrison Smith,* | *No. 118, Chesnut-Street.* | [rule] | *M.DCC.XCVI.*   [1070]
328 p., 8vo. (20.5 x 12.5 cm.). Sabin 24360, Evans 30419. Copies in most large libraries.

Contemporary history of the Whiskey Rebellion, touched off by the 1791 excise law taxing whiskey, the chief exportable product of the frontier, but based on numerous other infringements on the freedoms of the democratic frontiersmen of western Pennsylvania.

HARPER, ROBERT GOODLOE

Observations on the North American Land Company, lately instituted in Philadelphia; containing an illustration of the object of the Company's Plan, the Articles of Association, with a succinct account of the states wherein their lands lie; to which are added, Remarks on American lands in general, more particularly the pine lands of the Southern and Western states, in two letters from Robert G. Harper, Esq. of South Carolina, to a gentleman in Philadelphia. *London: H.L. Galabin. MDCCXCVI.*   [1071]
149 p., 8vo. Sabin 30437. MHi, etc.

. . . . .

H.L. Galabin. 1796. [1072]
xviii, 145 p., 8vo. Sabin 30438. RPJCB, etc.

. . . . .

London: Printed by H.L. Galabin, Ingram-Court, for C. Barrell and H. Servanté, American Agents, No. 6, Ingram-Court, Fenchurch-Street: sold also by J. Debrett, Piccadilly; J. Johnson, No. 72, St. Paul's Church-Yard; and W. Richardson, under the Royal Exchange. M.DCC.XCVI.
[1073]
[4], 149 p., 1 leaf, 8vo. Sabin 30439, De Renne I:274. DLC, GU-De, RPJCB, etc.

One of the editions is also at ICN, MWA, NN, PPL-R, PU.

Promotion tract for the North American Land Company.

HASTINGS, SUSANNAH WILLARD (JOHNSON)

A | narrative | of the | captivity | of | Mrs. Johnson. | Containing | an account of her sufferings, | during four years with the Indians | and French. | [rule] | Published according to act of Congress. | [rule] | [double rule] | *Printed at Walpole, Newhampshire,* | *By David Carlisle, jun.* | [rule] | *1796.*
[1074]
144 p., 12mo. (16 x 10 cm.). Sabin 36324, Evans 30180 and 30641, Ayer 117. DLC, F.C. Deering, IaU, ICN, MeB, MH, MHi, MWA, N, Nh, NHi, NN, RPJCB.

The RPJCB copy contains the interesting Indian book label, within a diamond of type ornaments: *The | property | of the | Independent Confederacy.*

Note on verso of title: "Part of the following pages were dictated [to John C. Chamberlain] by Mrs. Johnson, now Mrs. Hastings, herself, and part were taken from minutes, made by Mr. Johnson and herself, during their imprisonment. She is much indebted to her fellow prisoner, Mr. Labarree, by whose assistance many incidents are mentioned, which had escaped her recollection."

Mrs. Johnson was the wife of James Johnson who lived on Township No. 4 (Charlestown) in New Hampshire, having moved there from Lunen-burgh, Massachusetts in 1750. On August 30, 1754 his house was attacked by a party of Abeneki Indians from St. Francis village in Canada. All in the house were made prisoners, including Johnson, his wife and three children, Peter Labarree, Ebenezer Farnsworth and Miriam Willard, a sister of Mrs. Johnson. The party started at once for Lake Champlain but before reaching there, Mrs. Johnson gave birth to a daughter whom she named Captive. From there they were taken to Crown Point where they were well treated. On September 16th they reached St. Johns where again they were shown every kindness. The Indians, too, had shown them every attention along the trail. They stopped for a day and built a "booth" for Mrs. Johnson for her confinement and carried her on a litter as long as they could and allowed her sister and husband to render her all necessary assistance. Such a proceeding is almost without precedent in stories of Indian captivity. On reaching St. Francis they were divided among the several Indian families and before the end of November had been taken to Montreal and sold to the French.

From Montreal, Mr. Johnson was allowed to go to Boston on parole to secure funds for their ransom. There he was detained by Governor Shirley for several months beyond his parole and so, on his return, was imprisoned for breaking his parole and the money he brought back was taken by a Frenchman and never used for their ransom. From then until 1757 they spent most of their time in jail. In July of that year Mrs. Johnson was exchanged and sent to England, thence to New York and home. Her husband returned January 1, 1758. He joined the army being sent to attack Ticonderoga and was killed in battle July 8, 1758. All of the captives, including the baby, Captive, were finally returned. Mrs. Johnson also tells of the captivity of her brother-in-law Joseph Willard and his family and of the return of Colonel Robert Rogers from his attack on the Indian village of St. Francis.

Look before you leap; | or, | a few hints | to such | artizans, mechanics, labourers, | farmers and husbandmen, | as are desirous of emigrating to | America, | being a genuine | collection of letters, | from | persons who have emigrated; | containing remarks, notes and anecdotes, political, | philosophical, biographical and literary, of the present | state, situation, population, prospects and advantages, | of America, together with the reception, success, mode | of life, opinions and situation, of many characters | who have emigrated, | particularly to | the Federal City of Washington. | Illustrative of the prevailing practice of indent- | ing, and demonstrative of the nature, | effects and consequences, of that | public delusion. | *[London] Printed for W. Row, Great Marlborough Street; Walker, | Paternoster Row, and J. Barker, Russell Court, Drury Lane. | 1796.* | [double rule] | *Entered at Stationers Hall.* [1075]

144 p., 8vo. (22 cm.). Sabin 41943. DLC, MH, MiU-C, MnU, RPJCB.

. . . . . .

Second edition. [Same imprint, date and collation]. NHi. [1076]

. . . . .

Second edition. To which is added an appendix containing some animadversions and remarks on the conduct of popular societies, and American emissaries relative to this very interesting performance. [Same imprint and date]. [1077]

144, 24 p., 3vo. Sabin 41943.

. . . . .

Third edition. [Same imprint, date and collation]. Sabin 41943. RPJCB.
[1078]

Violently against British emigration to America, the letters supposedly forged but interesting as showing the crooked methods of agents working in England.

MCDONALD, PHILIP, AND ALEXANDER MCLEOD

A surprising account of the captivity and escape of Philip M'Donald and Alexander M'Leod, of Virginia, from the Chickkemogga Indians, and of their great discoveries in the western world, from June 1779, to January 1786, when they returned in health to their friends, after an absence of six years and a half. Written by themselves. *Haverhill, (New-Hampshire): Printed and sold by Nathaniel Coverly. 1796.* [1079]

14 p., 12mo. Evans 30713. RPJCB.

Copy offered in Goodspeed's *Month*, October, 1948, p. 7-9 at $200.00.

[NORTH AMERICAN LAND COMPANY]

Plan | for the settlement of 552,500 acres of land in the district of | Morgan, County of Wilkes, in the State of North Carolina, | North America, between 36 and 37 degrees North Latitude, | and 80 and 82 degrees West Longitude. [Caption title] *[London, 1796?]*. [1080]

39 p., double column, 4to. (29 x 22.5 cm.). Sabin 63279. MHi.

Title from Mass. Hist. Soc. Photostat Americana, 2d ser., 1936, no. 127.

NORTHWEST TERRITORY

Plat of the Seven Ranges of Townships, being part of the Territory of the United States N. W. of the River Ohio, which by a late act of Congress are directed to be sold. *[Philadelphia: Printed for Mathew Carey, 1796]*. [1081]

Title from Evans 30918, taken from a copyright entry, Sept. 30, 1796, and copied from Evans by Sabin 94884.

The first land surveyed in the Northwest Territory under the Ordinance of 1785. This tract was laid out south of the Geographer's Line, a line from the intersection of the Pennsylvania boundary with the Ohio River and running due west. The tract consisted of a triangle with a 91 mile western boundary, a 42 mile northern boundary and with the Ohio River forming the third side of the triangle. Settlement began in 1787 before the survey, which had begun in 1785, was completed. The survey was made by Thomas Hutchins, Geographer of the United States.

PANTHER, ABRAHAM, *pseud.*

A very | surprising narrative | of a | young woman, | who was | discovered in a rocky cave; | after having been taken by the | savage Indians of the wilderness, | in the year 1777, | and seeing no human being for the space of nine years. | [rule] | In a letter from a gentleman to his friend | [rule] | [double rule] | *Printed and sold [by Thomas Dickman] at Greenfield* | *Massachusetts.* | [double rule] | *MDCCXCVI.*   [1082]

10 p., 12mo. (17.5 x 10 cm.). Sabin 93897, copied from Evans 30956, probably taken from an advertisement since the entry is incomplete and no copy located by Evans. C.G. Littell, MWA.

. . . . .

A very | surprising narrative | of a | young woman, | who was discovered in the gloomy mansion of a | rocky cave! | [cut] | After having been taken from her companions by the | savage Indians of the wilderness, | in the year 1787, | and seeing no human being for the space of 9 years. | (In a letter from a gentleman to his friend.) | Third Windsor edition. | *[Windsor, Vt.]* *Printed by Alden Spooner, 1796, and for sale at his office.* | ([hand] *Price—* *four cents.*)   [1083]

11 p., 12mo. (16.5 x 10.8 cm.). Evans 30957, Sabin 93896. CSmH (H.F. De Puy copy), DLC.

Papers | respecting | intrusions | by | Connecticut claimants. | [Caption title] [Colophon:] *[Philadelphia:] Printed by Hall & Sellers, 1796.*   [1084]

24 p., 8vo. Evans 30958, Sabin 15684. NN, NNC, RPJCB.

For another attack on the Connecticut claim to lands in Pennsylvania, see Provost William Smith's *An examination,* 1774.

Pennsylvania Land Company

The subscribers, proprietors of lands in the State of Pennsylvania, finding it necessary to protect their property from unlawful intrusions, have agreed to form themselves into an Association of the following terms and principles. *[Philadelphia:] June 7, 1796.*   [1085]

Broadside. Evans 30988 does not locate a copy.

Rowlandson, Mary

A | narrative, | of the | captivity, | sufferings and removes, | of Mrs. | Mary Rowlandson, | who was taken prisoner by the Indians, with | several others, and treated in the most | barbarous and cruel manner by those vile | savages. With many other remarkable events | during her travels. | [double rule] | Written by her own hand, for her private use, | and now made public, at the earnest desire of | some friends, and for the benefit of the afflicted. | [double rule] | *Haverhill, (New-Hampshire)* | *Printed and sold,* *by Nathaniel* | *Coverly and Son, near the Court-* | *House. (Price one shilling.)* | [Hand] *Great allowance by the gross or dozen.* | *[1796].*   [1086]

64 p., 12mo. Evans 31127. DLC, F.C. Deering, Lancaster Town Library.

Other bibliographers have dated this edition [1770?] and [1792]. at which dates Coverly was still in Boston. He appeared in Amherst, N.H. in 1795, in which year he to(k his son into partnership and moved to Haverhill where they began publishing *The Grafton Minerva, and Haverhill Weekly Bud* on March 3, 1796 and continued it at least until January 23, 1797. At some time between April 7 and May 12, 1796, the son, Nathaniel Coverly Jr., departed to establish *The Orange Nightingale* at Newbury, Vermont on May 12th of that year, according to C.S. Brigham's Newspaper Bibliography.

SMITH, DANIEL

A | short description | of the | State of Tennassee, | lately called | The Territory of the United States, | South of the River Ohio; | to accompany and explain a map of | that country. | [thick-thin rule] | *Philadelphia:* | *Printed for Mathew Carey,* | *No. 118, Market-street,* | *by Lang and Ustick,* | *March 9, 1796.* [1087]

36 p., 12mo. (17 x 10 cm.). Sabin 82421, Evans 31199. DLC, MHi, MWA, NHi, PHi, PPiU.

The map does not accompany the pamphlet. See note under 1st ed., 1793.

Described from Mass. Hist. Soc. Photostat Americana, 2d ser., 1936, no. 68. Reprinted in Gilbert Imlay's *Topographical description*, London, 1797.

. . . . .

A short description of the State of Tennessee, lately called The Territory of the United States, South of the River Ohio. To which is prefixed, the constitution of that state. *Philadelphia: Printed for Mathew Carey, No. 118, Market-Street, by Lang and Ustick, Sept. 20. 1796.* [1088]

44 p., 12mo. (16.5 cm.). Sabin 82422, Evans 31200. DLC, MBAt, NHi, WHi.

[SMITH, PROVOST WILLIAM]

An | account | of the | proceedings | of the | Ilinois and Ouabache | Land Companies, | in pursuance of their purchases ¦ made of the independent natives, | July 5th, 1773, and 18th October, 1775. | [filet] | *Philadelphia:* | *Printed by William Young, No. 52. Second-* | *Street, the corner of Chesnut-Street.* | [rule] | *1796.* [1089]

[15], 55 p., 8vo. (20.5 x 13 cm.). Evans 30618. DLC, MBAt, MWA, NHi, A.S.W. Rosenbach, RPJCB, ScC.

Contains *Introduction, Indian deeds, State of facts* and documents *In support of the facts. Illinois* in title spelled with one l. For later editions, see under 1797.

The Illinois Company bought lands from the Illinois Indians on the East side of the Mississippi River in 1773 and the Wabash Company bought from the Piankashaw Indians on both sides of the Wabash River in 1775. The two companies merged in 1780 as the United Illinois and Ouabache Land Companies. Provost William Smith was their principal Congressional lobbyist.

Original MS contract with the Indians, from the Ward sale in 1913, in Cyrus H. McCormick collection at NjP, with privately printed edition edited by C.W. Alvord and published by McCormick in 1915.

SYMMES, JOHN CLEVES

(A true copy) of Judge Symme's [sic] pamphlet. On the first settlement of this country. *[Cincinnati: Office of the Centinel of the North-Western Territory. 1796].* [1090]

Sabin 94104.

Note from Sabin: Title from Rusk's "Literature of the Middle Western Frontier," vol. 2, 1925, p. 224, according to which this was from the March 12 and 26, 1796, issues of the *Centinel.* William Maxwell was the printer of that paper at the time, and the above is probably the same as Evans no. 31261, taken from a reference to "Judge Symmes' pamphlet" in a Letter of the Attorney General, dated March 11, 1796.

A reprint of his *To the respectable public,* [1787?], which see.

TIMBERLAKE, HENRY

Voyages | du Lieutenant | Henri Timberlake, | qui fut chargé, dans l'année 1760, | de conduire en Angleterre trois | sauvages, de la tribu des | Cherokees; | Renfermant des détails intéressans sur | cette peuplade d'habitans du Nord | de l'Amerique, sur leurs moeurs, | leurs usages, leur forme de gouver- | nement, leurs principes religieux et | politiques; | Traduits de l'Anglais | par | J.B.L.J. Billecocq, Citoyen Français. | [orn.] | A Paris, | de l'Imprimerie de Hautbout l'ainé. | [filet] | L' an V. | [1796-97]. [1091]

[2], viii, 187, [1] p., front., 8vo. (13.1 x 8 cm.). Sabin 95837, De Renne I:275. DLC, GU-De, NHi.

Copperplate: *Ma femme et mon troupeau partageoient tour à tour | mes occupations et varioient mes plaisirs.*

[WEST, MRS. JANE]

The history of Ned Evans; a tale of the times. *London, 1796.* [1092]

4 vols., 12mo. Title from Henry Stevens, Son and Stiles cat. 6, 1934, no. 147, $50.00; and cat. 8, 1935, no. 138, $50.00, with the following note:

"Ned Evans served with the British in South Carolina and while wandering in the woods was captured by a party of Cherokee Indians, after an engagement in which the British were defeated. He was adopted into the tribe with whom he remained for about eighteen months. Leaving the Indians by consent he endeavored to find his way back to Charlestown, where he arrived to find that peace had been declared and his regiment ordered home. His experiences while a captive among the Cherokees occupy nearly 100 pages of volume three. We have not seen this edition before and it is probably the first." It is, of course, entirely fictitious.

. . . . .

Dublin, [1796]. 2 vols. Title from Halkett and Laing.   [1093]

WILLIAMSON, PETER

Sufferings of Peter Williamson, one of the settlers in the back parts of Pennsylvania. *Stockbridge. 1796.*   [1094]
Sabin 104489.
Title from a clipping from an unidentified bookseller's catalog.

BISHOP, ABRAHAM

Georgia | speculation | unveiled; | in two numbers. | [double rule] | By Abraham Bishop. | [double rule] | *Hartford: | Printed by Elisha Babcock.* | *(Copy-right secured.)* | 1797.   [1095]
39 p., 8vo. (21 x 12 cm.). Sabin 5593, Evans, 31830, De Renne I:278. BM, CtY, DLC, GU-De, MBAt, MH, MHi, MWA, NHi, NN, RHi, RPJCB.
Exposure of the Yazoo Frauds. An answer to the Georgia Mississippi Company's *State of facts.* For a second part, see under 1798.

BLEECKER, ANN ELIZA (SCHUYLER)

The history of Maria Kittle. By Ann Eliza Bleecker. In a letter to Miss Ten Eyck. *Hartford: Printed by Elisha Babcock. 1797.*   [1096]
70 p., 12mo. (16.3 x 9.8 cm.). Evans 31837, Ayer supp. 18. CSmH, CtY, DLC, F.C. Deering, ICN, MWA, NHi, RPB, RPJCB.

. . . . .

Hartford: John Babcock, 1802. DLC, MH.   [1097]
For first edition, see her *Posthumous works,* 1793.

BRADMAN, ARTHUR

A narrative of the extraordinary sufferings of Mr. Robert Forbes, his wife and five children; during an unfortunate journey through the wilderness from Canada to Kennebeck River, in which three of their children were starved to death. To which is added, a narrative of the captivity and escape of Mrs. Frances Scott, an inhabitant of Washington County, Virginia. *Elizabeth (Hager's) Town: Printed by Thomas Grieves, near the Court-House. 1797.*   [1098]
Title from Evans 31864 who evidently copied the title from a copyright entry or advertisement, since he gives no collation or location.

. . . . .

Narrative of the sufferings of Mr. Robert Forbes, and family, in a journey

from Canada to the Kennebec River in which three of their children were starved to death. *Portland: Printed by A.W. Thayer. 1823.*
    19 p., 12mo. MWA. A rewritten and abridged edition edited by Ebenezer Greenleaf (1781-1851), of Williamsburg, Maine. In the MWA copy, the Preface, which is signed: *The writer,* has these words crossed out and: *Uncle Eben* written in by the former owner, Charlotte K. Greenleaf whose autograph appears in this copy. Her *Uncle Eben* was Ebenezer Greenleaf.
                                                                              [1099]

· · · · ·

    Abby Forbes: | a tale of | unparalleled sufferings. | Founded on facts. | [double rule] | Written by W.H. Guy, Esq. | [double rule] | *Boston:* | *Published by the author.* | *1846.*   [1100]
    36 p., 12mo. F.C. Deering, MWA (2 variants). Portrait of heroine on verso of title and on printed front wrapper. Wdcts. in text, p. 19 and 27, repeated on back wrapper. Copyright 1845 by Isaac H. Welton. Cover titles of MWA copies vary. Guy took considerable liberty with the facts of the original narrative.

· · · · ·

    Abbe Forbes: | or the | unfortunate family. | A tale | of | sea and land. | Founded on facts. | By W.H. Guy. | Second edition of five thousand. | *Boston:* | *Published for the author.* | *1846.*   [1101]
    64 p., illus., yellow wrappers, 16mo. (15.5 x 9 cm.). The author states that the first edition sold in less than three months and that this edition is "much improved from the former." It sold for 12½ cents. The H.F. De Puy copy sold at Anderson Galleries sale 1458, Jan. 26, 1920, no. 999 to George D. Smith for $10.50.
    The 1794 edition of the original Bradman narrative was reprinted in the *Magazine of History,* Extra No. 56, 1917.

BRISSOT DE WARVILLE, JEAN PIERRE

    New travels | in the | United States | of | America. | Performed in 1788, | by J.P. Brissot de Warville. | Translated from the French. | [5 lines quoted] | *From the Press of Joseph Bumstead,* | *Union-Street—Boston.* | *1797.*
                                                                              [1102]
    276, [3] p., folded table, 12mo. (17.5 cm.). Sabin 8031, Evans 31871. Copies in most large libraries.
    First 2 vols. only.

BUNN, MATTHEW

    A short narrative of the life and sufferings of Matthew Bunn, after his arrival at the British garrison at Detroit, at which place he arrived the 30th

of April, 1792, from his Indian captivity; an account whereof was lately published, entitled, "A journal of the adventures of Matthew Bunn, a native of Brookfield, Massachusetts." &c. *Printed in the year 1797.* [1103]
36 p., 12mo. (19 x 12 cm.). Sabin 9185, Evans 31890, Thomson's Ohio 137, Church 1272. CSmH, F.C. Deering, MWA.

. . . . .

A narrative, of the life and sufferings of Matthew Bunn; who was taken by the Indians, in 1791, and afterwards made his escape, to the British; together with an account of his treatment, while with them. *Peacham: Printed by Samuel Goss, 1806.* [1104]
55 p., 8vo. (23.4 x 13.5 cm.). Ayer 39. F.C. Deering (lacks p. 55), ICN (lacks p. 55).

. . . . .

Boston, 1806. MiD-B. [1105]

. . . . .

A narrative of the life and adventures of Matthew Bunn of Providence, Rhode Island. In an expedition against the North Western Indians, in the years 1791, 2, 3, 4, and 5. *Batavia: Reprinted by B. Blodgett. 1826.* [1106]
44 p., 8vo. (20.5 x 12.5 cm.). Ayer 40. F.C. Deering, ICN, OClWHi.

. . . . .

Batavia: Printed for the author, by Adams & Thorp. 1827. [1107]
71 p., 12mo. (17.5 x 10.5 cm.). Sabin 9186. F.C. Deering, ICN, N, NHi (photostat), NN (photostat), OClWHi, RP.

. . . . .

[7th edition, revised—4000 copies.] *Batavia: Printed for the author, by Adams and Thorp. 1828.* [1108]
59 p., 12mo. (20 x 12 cm.). Ayer 41. Copies in most large libraries.
This edition was reprinted from the DLC copy in Buffalo Hist. Soc. Pubs., vol. 7, 1904, p. 377-436.

CARVER, JONATHAN
Three years travels. *Boston, 1797.* DLC, etc. [1109]
See note at end of 1798 edition.

COLDEN, CADWALLADER
History of the Six Nations. *Troy: Luther Pratt, 1797.* [1110]
Title from Evans 31952 who says that proposals for printing this edition were published in 1797. It was probably never printed.

COMPAGNIE DE WILMINGTON

Prospectus. | [rule] | Compagnie de Wilmington, | dans la Caroline du Nord, sur la Riviere de Cape-Fear, | aux États-Unis de l'Amerique. | [Caption title] *[Paris, 1797]*.   [1111]
4 p., folded map, 4to. (26 x 19 cm.). Sabin 104584. DLC, NHi, RPJCB.
Map: *Partie* | *de la* | *Province* | *de la* | *Caroline du Nord.*

DECALVES, ALONSO, *pseud.*

Travels | to the | westward; | or | unknown parts of America. | Being a tour of almost fourteen months. | Containing | an account of the country, upwards of two thou- | sand miles west of the Christian parts of North | America; with an account of white In- | dians, their manners, habits, and ma- | ny other particulars. | By Don Alonso Decalves. | Confirmed by three other persons. | The second Dover edition. | *[Dover, N.H.:] Printed and sold [by Samuel Bragg, jun.], at the Sun Office. [1797].*   [1112]
39 p., 8vo. (18.5 x 10.5 cm.). Sabin 98457, Evans 32022, Ayer 59. F.C. Deering, ICN.

.   .   .   .   .

The third Dover edition. *[Dover, N.H.:] Printed at the Sun-office, for J. Asplund [1797?].*   [1113]
41 p., 12mo. Sabin 98458, Evans 33616, CSmH, DLC.

.   .   .   .   .

Travels to the Westward, | or the unknown parts of | America: | In the years | 1786, and 1787. | Containing an account of the | country to the | westward of the river | Missisippi, | its productions, animals, inhabitants, | curiosities, &c. &c. | By | Alonso Decalves. | *From the Herald-Office, Rutland.* | *Printed by Josiah Fay.* | *M.DCC.XCVII.*   [1114]
48 p., 12mo. Sabin 98459, Evans 32023, Cooley Vermont imprints 370. CSmH (lacks title), F.C. Deering, ICU.
Title from facsimile in Heartman sale cat., April 2, 1927, no. 107, sold for $132.50 to Mr. Deering.

.   .   .   .   .

Travels to the Westward, or the unknown parts of America in the years 1786 and 1787. Containing an account of the country to the westward of the Mississippi, together with its productions, animals, inhabitants, vegetables, curiosities, &c. By Don Alonso Decalves. *Windsor: Printed by Alden Spooner. 1797.*   [1115]
36 p., 12mo. Sabin 98460, Evans 32025, Cooley: Vermont imprints 368.

.   .   .   .   .

Second impression. Sabin 98460, Evans 32026, Cooley 369.   [1116]

· · · · · ·

New travels to the Westward, or unknown parts of America: being a tour of almost fourteen months. Containing an account of the country, upwards of two thousand miles West of the Christian parts of North America; with an account of white Indians, their manners, habits, and many other particulars. By Don Alonso Decalves. Confirmed by three other persons. To which is added, The interesting history of Charles Mortimer. An American tale. *[n.p.] Printed in the year 1797.* [1117]

81 p., 18mo. Sabin 98455, Evans 33615, listed under 1798. F.C. Deering. The history of Charles Mortimer, p. 51-81.

· · · · · ·

New travels to the Westward, or Unknown parts of America: being a tour of almost fourteen months. Containing, an account of the country, upwards of two thousand miles West of the Christian parts of North America; with an account of white Indians, their manners, habits, and many other particulars. The whole forming an agreeable, instructive, and entertaining narrative. *Schenectady: Printed by Cornelius P. Wyckoff. 1797.* [1118]

Title from Sabin 98456, copied from Evans 32024 who probably took the title from an advertisement since he gives neither collation nor location.

HARPER, ROBERT GOODLOE

Case of the Georgia sales on the Mississippi, considered; with an appendix of records, etc. *Philadelphia, Printed for Benjamin Davies . . . 1797.* [1119]

[4], 109 p., 8vo. Title (probably abbreviated) from Brinley 3930 for a copy now at CtY, MH.

HASTINGS, SUSANNAH WILLARD (JOHNSON)

A | narrative | of the | captivity | of | Mrs. Johnson. | Containing an account of her sufferings, | during four years | with the Indians and French. | Glasgow: | Printed by R. Chapman, | for Stewart & Meikle, | . . . | 1797. [1120]

71, [1] p., 12mo. (17 x 10.5 cm.). Ayer 118. ICN, MB, NN.

· · · · · ·

The | captive American, | or a | narrative | of the | sufferings of Mrs. Johnson, | during | four years captivity | with the | Indians and French | Written by herself. | [7 lines quoted] | *Newcastle | Printed and sold by M. Angus. | Sold also by the Booksellers, Newsmen and Distributors | of Numbers in Town and Country | [1797].* [1121]

72 p., 12mo. (17 x 9.2 cm.). Sabin 36325. CSmH, NN.

· · · · · ·

The | captive | American; | containing an | account of the sufferings | of

Mrs. Johnson, | during four years | with the Indians and French. | The author, Mrs. Johnson, now Mrs. Hast- | ings, is still living in Charlestown, | Newhampshire, and first published her | narrative at Walpole in New- hampshire, | in the year 1796.—The sufferings she met | with during her captivity, she bore with | a degree of magnanimity that will astonish | the reader while he peruses the following | pages. | *Air, Printed by J. & P. Wilson, 1802.* | . . .   [1122]

24 p., 12mo. (16.5 x 8.8 cm.). Sabin 36326, Ayer 119. DLC, ICN.

. . . . .

A | narrative | of the | captivity | of | Mrs. Johnson. | Containing | an account of her sufferings, | during four years, with the Indians | and French. | [rule] | Published according to act of Congress. | [rule] | Second edition, corrected and enlarged. | [double rule] | *Windsor, (Vt.)* | *Printed by Alden Spooner.* | [orn. rule] | *1807.*   [1123]

144 p., 12mo. (15 x 9.2 cm.). Sabin 36327, Ayer 120. DLC, F.C. Deer- ing, ICN, MWA, N, Nh, NHi, NN, ViU.

. . . . .

A | narrative | of the | captivity of Mrs. Johnson. | Containing | an account of her sufferings, during | four years, with the In- | dians and French. | Together with an | appendix ; | containing the sermons, preached at her funeral, and that of | her mother; with sundry other interesting articles. | [filet] | Third edition corrected, and considerably enlarged. | [filet] | *Windsor, (Vt.)* | *Printed by Thomas M. Pomroy.* |*1814.*   [1124]

178 p., 12mo. (17.2 x 10 cm.). Sabin 36327, Ayer 121. DLC, F.C. Deering, ICN, MWA, N, NN, OClWHi.

. . . . .

A | narrative | of the | captivity of Mrs. Johnson, | containing | an account of her sufferings during | four years with the | Indians and French. | Together with | an appendix, | containing the sermons preached at her funeral, | and that of her mother, with sundry | other interesting articles. | [rule] | Fourth edition. | [rule] | *Lowell:* | *Published by Daniel Bixby,* | *No. 11 Merrimac Street.* | [rule] | *MDCCCXXXIV.*   [1125]

150 p., 18mo. (14.7 x 9.4 cm.). Sabin 36327, Ayer 122. DLC, F.C. Deering, ICN, MBAt, MWA, Nh, NHi, NN.

Verso of title: *John Emmes Dill, Printer,* | *Cornhill, Boston.*

. . . . .

A | narrative | of the | captivity | of | Mrs. Johnson, | containing | an account of her sufferings, during | four years, with the Indians | and French. | [filet] | *New York:* | *1841.*   [1126]

111 p., 16mo. (13.6 x 9 cm.). Sabin 36327, Ayer 123. DLC, F.C. Deering, ICN, MWA, N, NhHi, NHi, NN.

Dated at end: *Charlestown, June 20, 1798.*

. . . . . .

A | narrative | of the | captivity of Mrs. Johnson | Reprinted from the third edition, published | at Windsor, Vermont, 1814 | with all corrections and additions | The H.R. *Huntting Company* | *Springfield, Massachusetts* | *MCMVII.* [1127]

xiii, 194 p., facsim. title, 12mo. (15.5 x 11 cm.). Ayer 124. Copies in most large libraries.

. . . . . .

A New England pioneer | "The captivity of Mrs. Johnson" | The story of her life with an account of her | capture and experiences during four years | with the French and Indians, 1746-1750; | in part as written by her and in part | as condensed by | [Mrs.] Mary M. Billings French | Illustrated with photographs by | Clara E. Sipprell. | [cut of an elm tree] | *The Elm Tree Press Woodstock Vermont* | *[1926].* [1128]

x, [2], 44 p., 8 illus. and map, 8vo. (23 x 15.5 cm.). Issued at $5.00. MWA, N.

Retold with original narrative abridged by the captive's great-great-great-granddaughter.

ILLINOIS AND WABASH LAND COMPANIES

Memorial | of the | Illinois and Wabash | Land Company. | 13th January, 1797. | Referred to Mr. Jeremiah Smith, | Mr. Kittera, and | Mr. Baldwin. | Published by order of the House of | Representatives. | *Philadelphia:* | *Printed by Richard Folwell.* | *[1797].* [1129]

8, 8, 7, 7 p., 8vo. Sabin 84577. MBAt (another issue without imprint), NN, PHi, A.S.W. Rosenbach, RPJCB.

Issued both separately and bound with William Smith's *An account of the proceedings, 1796* [i.e., 1797], for which see long note under Sabin 84577.

There were other memorials of the company to Congress in 1802 (Sabin 34295), 1810 (Sabin 34296) NHi, etc. and in 1816. NHi. See also the *Report of the Committee* [of Congress on] *the Memorial of the Illinois and Wabash Land Company. 3d February, 1797.* [Philadelphia, 1797]. 4 p., 8vo. MBAt, NHi, RPJCB, etc.

For Provost William Smith's *An account of the proceedings,* see nos. 1089, 1141-1143.

IMLAY, GILBERT

A topographical description of the Western Territory of North America: containing a succinct account of its soil, climate, natural history, population, agriculture, manners, and customs. With an ample description of the several divisions into which that country is partitioned. To which are added, I. The discovery . . . of Kentucky . . . by J. Filson. . . . II. An account of the Indian nations . . . III. The culture of Indian corn . . . IV. Observations on the ancient works . . . by Major Jonathan Heart. V. Historical narrative and topographical description of Louisiana and West-Florida . . . by Mr. Thomas Hutchins. VI. Account of the soil . . . the Genesee Tract . . . VII. Remarks . . . by Dr. Franklin. VIII. Topographical description of Virginia, Pennsylvania, Maryland, and North-Carolina, by Mr. Tho. Hutchins. IX. Mr. Patrick Kennedy's journal up the Illinois River, &c. X. Description of the State of Tenasee . . . XI. An act for establishing Knoxville. XII. Treaty concluded between the United States of America and the Crown of Spain, for the free navigation of the Mississippi. XIII. Plan of association of the North American Land Company, &c. By Gilbert Imlay, a Captain in the American Army during the War, and Commissioner for laying out lands in the Back Settlements. Illustrated with correct maps of the Western Territory of North America; of the State of Kentucky, as divided into counties, from actual surveys by Elihu Barker; a map of the Tenasee Government; and a plan of the Rapids of the Ohio. The third edition, with great additions. *London: Printed for J. Debrett, opposite Burlington House, Piccadilly.* 1797. [1130]

xii, 598, [28], [2] p., 3 folded maps, folded plan, 8vo. (22 cm.). Copies in most large libraries.

Third and best English edition. Maps and plan: *A map of the Western part of the territories belonging to the United States of America. Drawn from the best authorities. Engraved for Imlay's Topographical Description of that Country.* [dated in lower margin:] 1795. (39 x 25.5 cm.); *A map of the State of Kentucky, from actual survey by Elihu Barker of Philadelphia.* [in lower margin:] 1795. (76 x 37.5 cm.); *A map of the Tennessee Government, formerly part of North Carolina, taken chiefly from surveys by Genel. D. Smith & others.* [in lower margin:] 1795. (46 x 20.5 cm.); *A plan of the Rapids of the Ohio.* [in lower margin:] 1793. (23.5 x 19.7 cm.).

JOHONNOT, JACKSON

The remarkable adventures of Jackson Johonnet, of Massachusetts. Who served as a soldier in the Western Expedition, under General Harmar. Containing an account of his captivity, sufferings, and escape from the Kickapoo Indians. *Schenectady: Printed by Cornelius P. Wyckoff.* 1797. [1131]

Title from Evans 32322 who gives no collation nor location and probably took the title from an advertisement or copyright entry.

McDONALD, PHILIP, AND ALEXANDER McLEOD

A surprising account of the captivity and escape of Philip M'Donald and Alex M'Cloud, of Virginia, from the Chickkemogga Indians, and of the great discoveries in the western world, from June 1779, to January 1786, when they returned in health to their friends, after an absence of six years and a half. Written by themselves. *Printed at Rutland, Vermont, by Josiah Fay, for S. Williams & C. MDCCXCVII.* [1132]

14 p., 8vo. Evans 32401. Cooley Vermont imprints 383, Gilman Vermont bibliography, p. 271. BM.

MIGNARD, JACQUES

Quelques escrocs Anglais démasqués, ou les Déserts de l'Amérique du Nord présentés tels qu'ils sont, par Jacques Mignard, . . . *Paris, au bureau de la "Gazette Historique et Politique," An VI.* [1797-98]. [1132A]

52 p., 8vo. Title from Bib. Nat. cat. Bib. Nat.

Against the land agents in Paris. The author was in Philadelphia in 1791 where he met a Frenchman who owned Scioto lands. For his other attacks on the Americans and English, see Bib. Nat. cat.

MORSE, JEDEDIAH

A | description | of the | soil, productions, commercial, agri- | cultural and local advantages | of the | Georgia Western Territory: | together with | a summary and impartial view of the claims of Geor- | gia and of the United States to this Territory, | and of the principal arguments ad- | duced by the purchasers | against these claims. | Collected and stated from various authentic | documents. | Extracted, and published in this form, (by per- | mission) | from | Rev. Dr. Morse's American Gazetteer, | a new work. | [rule] | Illustrated with a new and correct map. | [rule] | [thick-thin rule] | *Boston:* | *Printed by Thomas & Andrews.* | [rule] | *1797.* [1133]

24 p., folded map, 12mo. (17 x 11 cm.). Evans 32510, De Renne I:281. MBAt, MHi, MWA, NHi, NN.

Map: *A correct map of the | Georgia | Western Territory.* | [Below the map:] *Engraved for Morse's American Gazetteer. Callender Sc.* (24 x 19.5 cm.).

Reprinted from Jedediah Morse's *American Gazetteer. Boston, 1797.* viii, 619 p., 7 maps, 8vo. Copies in most large libraries. Probably reprinted in the interest of the New England Mississippi Land Company, which see.

NEW ENGLAND MISSISSIPPI LAND COMPANY

Articles of association and agreement, constituting the New-England Mississippi Land Company. | *[Boston, ca. 1797].* [1134]

7 p., 8vo. De Renne I:281. GU-De.

For second edition, see under 1798.

PANTHER, ABRAHAM, *pseud.*

A very surprising narrative of a young woman discovered in a rocky cave; after having been taken by the Indians, in the year 1777, and seeing no human being for the space of nine years. In a letter from a gentleman to his friend. *Putney, (Vermont): Printed [by Cornelius Sturtevant jun. & Co.] for the purchaser. M,DCC,XCVII.*   [1135]

12 p.´, 12mo. Evans 32637, Sabin 93898.

Advertised in Sturtevant's Putney *Argus*, February 19, 1798.

.   .   .   .   .

A very surprising narrative of a young woman who was discovered in a cave, after having been taken by the Indians in the year 1777, and seeing no human being for the space of nine years. *Rutland, Printed by Josiah Fay, 1797.*   [1136]

12 p., 12mo. (16.6 x 10.2 cm.). Evans 32638, Sabin 93906.

Title from Dawson's Book Shop cat. 177, 1943, no. 143. $85.00

Advertised as "just from the press, and for sale at this office," in Fay's *Rutland Herald*, June 12, 1797.

PENNSYLVANIA LAND COMPANY

Plan of Association of the Pennsylvania Land Company, established March 1797. *Philadelphia: Printed by R. Aitken, Market Street. M,DCC,-XCVII.*   [1137]

15, 12, 3 p., 8vo. Evans 32660. DLC, Pennsylvania Department of Archives.

Robert Morris's own copy, owned by Colonel Robert Morris, is deposited with other Robert Morris family papers, with the Pennsylvania Department of Archives at Harrisburg.

.   .   .   .   .

Statement of the incumbrances at present on the property of the Pennsylvania Land Company. *[n.p., 1797].*   [1138]

3 p., 12mo. Sabin 60341 locates no copy.

PENNSYLVANIA PROPERTY COMPANY

Plan of Association of the Pennsylvania Property Company. *Philadelphia: 1797.*   [1139]

16 p., 8vo. Evans 32661 locates no copy.

SMITH, DANIEL

A short description of the State of Tennessee, lately called The Territory of the United States, south of the River Ohio. To which is prefixed, the constitution of that state. *New-York: Printed by J.S. Mott, no. 70 Vesey-street, 1797.* [1140]

47 p., 12mo. (17.5 cm.). CSmH.

Described from DLC card.

[SMITH, PROVOST WILLIAM]

An | account | of the | proceedings | of the | Illinois and Oubache | Land Companies, | in pursuance of their purchases | made of the independent natives, | July 5th, 1773, and 18th October, 1775. | *Philadelphia: Printed by William Young, No. 52. Second- | street, the corner of Chesnut-street. | 1796. | [i.e., 1797].* [1141]

[16], 55, 8, 8, 7, 7 p., 8vo. Sabin 84577. InHi, MBAt, NN, PHi, RPJCB.

Text as in 1st ed., 1796, with addition of following separately printed tracts bound with original *Account: Memorial | of the | Illinois and Wabash | Land Company. | 13th January, 1797. | Referred to Mr. Jeremiah Smith, | Mr. Kittera, and | Mr. Baldwin. | Published by order of the House of | Representatives. | Philadelphia: Printed by Richard Folwell. | [1797].* 8 p.; *No. I. | To the | committees | of the | Senate & House of Representatives, | on the | Ilinois and Wabash Memorial. | [n.p., n.d.].* 8 p.; *No. II. | Additional statements | by the | agents of the | Illinois and Wabash Land Companies. | [n.p., n.d.).* 7 p.; *No. III. | To the | honorable committees | of the | Senate & House of Representatives | of the United States, | on the | Illinois and Wabash Land Purchases. | [n.p., n.d.].* 7 p.

. . . . .

Same text through p. 55 but with remainder reprinted with continuous pagination. [16], 55, 26 p., 8vo. (20.5 x 12 cm.). Sabin 84577. Evans 30618. CSmH, NHi, WHi. [1142]

. . . . .

1803, for which see Sabin 84578. NHi, etc. See also under the name of the company. [1143]

[WEST, MRS. JANE]

The history of Ned Evans; a tale of the times. Second edition. *London, 1797.* [1144]

4 vols., 12mo. BM.

A copy sold at the James Stillman sale, American Art Galleries, Nov. 18, 1918, no. 1940, $12.00.

. . . . .

History of Ned Evans. Interspersed with remarks, anecdotes and characters of many persons well known in the polite world, and incidental strictures on the present state of Ireland. *Dublin, 1805.* [1145]

2 vols., 12mo. Title from Henry Stevens, Son and Stiles cat. 40, 1943, no. 154. $32.50.

His experiences in America occupy about 90 pages in the second volume.

.   .   .   .   .

Affecting history of the dreadful distresses of Frederic Manheim's family. To which are added, the sufferings of John Corbly's family. An encounter between a white man and two savages. Extraordinary bravery of a woman and the adventures of Capt. Isaac Stewart. *Newport: Printed by H. & O. Farnsworth. [1798-1799].*   [1146]

12mo. Sabin 105688. Title from catalogue of the Roderick Terry sale, part 3, American Art Ass'n-Anderson Galleries, sale no. 4154, Feb. 15, 1935, lot 180.

Bishop, Abraham

Georgia speculation | unveiled. | Second part. | Containing | the third and fourth numbers; | with a | conclusion, | addressed to the Northern purchasers. | [double rule] | By Abraham Bishop. | [double rule] | [double rule] | *Hartford:* | *Printed by Hudson & Goodwin.* | [rule] | *M,DCC,XCVIII.*
                                                                   [1147]

[2]. [43]-144 p., 8vo. (18 x 11.4 cm.). Sabin 5594, Evans 33425, De Renne I:278. BM, CtHi, CtY, DLC, GU-De, MBAt, MHi, MWA, NHi.

For first part, see under 1797.

Burroughs, Stephen

Memoirs | of | Stephen Burroughs. | [rule] | When such sad scenes the bosom pain, | What eye from weeping can refrain. | [rule] | Copy right secured. | [rule] | [orn.] | *Printed at Hanover, Newhampshire,* | *by Benjamin True.* | *MDCCXCVIII.*   [1148]

[4], [8]-296 p., 8vo. (21 cm.). Evans 33478, Sabin 9466. BM, DLC, MB, MBAt, MH, MiU-C, MWA, Nh, NHi, NN, RPJCB.

Vol. II, Boston, 1804. MH, MWA, RPJCB.

Many reprints, complete or abridged, the latest N.Y., 1924. Best collection at MWA.

One of the two great eighteenth century American criminal autobiographies, the other being that of Henry Tufts: *A narrative of the life of* . . . Dover, 1807. MWA, NHi, etc. and as: *The autobiography of a criminal,* N.Y., 1930. Sabin 97416.

Carver, Jonathan

Three years travels. *Edinburgh, 1798.* DLC.   [1149]

.   .   .   .   .

Charlestown, 1802. DLC.   [1150]

. . . . .

Voyage. *Paris, 1802.*   [1151]

. . . . .

Three years travels. *Glasgow, 1805.*   [1152]

. . . . .

Edinburgh, 1807.   [1153]

. . . . .

Edinburgh, 1808.   [1154]

. . . . .

Walpole, 1813. DLC, etc.   [1155]

. . . . .

J. Carver's Reisen. *Braunschweig, 1830* and later reprints.   [1156]

. . . . .

Carver's travels in Wisconsin. *New York, 1838.* DLC, etc.   [1157]

. . . . .

Three years travels. *Walpole, 1838.* Sabin 11185. Not in Lee.   [1158]

. . . . .

Aventures. [abridged] *Tours,* 1845, 1846, 1849, 1850, 1852 DLC, 1858,
1861, 1865, 1870.   [1159]

For more complete descriptions of the various editions, see Sabin, Evans,
DLC catalog and John Thomas Lee: *A bibliography of Carver's Travels,* in
State Hist. Soc. of Wisconsin *Proceedings,* 1909, p. 143-183, and separate;
and his: *Captain Jonathan Carver: additional data,* same, 1912, p. 87-123,
and separate.

CONNECTICUT LAND COMPANY

Lands in New-Connecticut, that part of the Connecticut Reserve, or New-
Connecticut, to which the Indian title has been extinguished, lying west of
Pennsylvania, and south of Lake Erie, having been surveyed and divided.
[26 lines of description] Simon Perkins. Agent for the Erie Company. [Colo-
phon:] *Printed at J. Trumbull's Press, Norwich. [1798].*   [1160]

Broadside, folio. Evans 33565. MWA.

DECALVES, ALONSO, *pseud.*

Travels to the Westward . . . [as in 2d Dover ed.] The third Dover edition.
[Dover, N.H.:] Printed at the Sun-Office for J. Asplund. [1798].   [1161]
41 p., 12mo. Evans 33616. DLC.

FLETCHER, EBENEZER

A narrative of the captivity and sufferings of Mr. Ebenezer Fletcher, of
Newipswich, who was wounded at Hubbarston [sic], in the year 1777, and
taken prisoner by the British, and, after recovering a little from his wounds,
made his excape [sic] from them, and returned back to Newipswich. Written
by himself. *Printed by Samuel Preston, Amherst. 1798.*   [1162]
26 p., 12mo. Title from Evans 33740. F.C. Deering, NhHi, NN.

. . . . . .

A | narrative | of the | captivity & sufferings | of | Ebenezer Fletcher | of
New-Ipswich | who was severely wounded in the battle of Hubbardston | at
the retreat from Ticonderoga, in the year 1777 and | taken prisoner by the
British at the age of 16 years | and who after recovering in part from his
wound | made his escape and returned home | Written by himself and pub-
lished at the | request of his friends | *Windsor Vt.* | *Printed by Charles*
Kendall | *1813.*   [1163]
22 p., 12mo. (18.5 x 11.7 cm.). DLC, F.C. Deering, MH, MWA.

. . . . . .

Narrative | of the | captivity & sufferings | of | Ebenezer Fletcher, | of
New-Ipswich, | who was severely wounded and taken prisoner at the battle
of | Hubbardston, Vt. in the year 1777, by the British and | Indians, at the
age of 16 years, after recovering in | part, made his escape from the enemy,
and | travelling through a dreary wilderness, fol- | lowed by wolves, and
beset by tories on | his way, who threatened to take him | back to the enemy,
but made his es- | cape from them all, and arrived | safe home. | [rule] |
Written by himself, and published at the request of his | friends. | [rule]
Fourth Edition, | revised and enlarged. | [rule] | *New-Ipswich, N.H.* |
Printed by S. Wilder, | *-1827-.*   [1164]
24 p., 12mo. (17.2 x 9.8 cm.). Sabin 24718, Ayer 100. DLC, F.C. Deering, ICN, MWA.

. . . . . .

A | narrative | of the | captivity & sufferings | of | Ebenezer Fletcher, |
of New-Ipswich, | who was severely wounded and taken prisoner at the
battle | of Hubbardston, Vt. in the year 1777, by the British | and Indians
at the age of 16 years, after recover- | ing in part, made his escape from the
enemy | and travelling through a dreary wilder- | ness, followed by wolves

and beset | by Tories, and by the assist- | ance of a friend arrived | safe home. | [rule] | Written by himself, and published at the request of his friends. | [rule] | *New-Ipswich, N.H.* | *Printed by S. Wilder.* | *[ca. 1827-8].* [1165] 24 p., 12mo. F.C. Deering, MWA.

. . . . .

The narrative of Ebenezer Fletcher, a soldier of the Revolution, written by himself, With an introduction and notes, by Charles I. Bushnell. *New York: Privately printed, 1866.* [1166] 86 p., 2 ports., 8vo. Copies in many large libraries.

. . . . .

Same sheets bound with three other narratives with the general title page: *Crumbs for antiquarians By Charles I. Bushnell Vol. 2. New-York Privately printed. 1866.* [1167]

Also reprinted in Fitchburg, Massachusetts *Sentinel,* Jan. 30, 1863; and in *Magazine of History with Notes and Queries,* Extra no. 151, 1929, p. 5-23. There was an edition of this narrative in verse according to C.H. Chandler's *History of New Ipswich,* 1914, p. 414.

Ebenezer Fletcher, a sixteen-year-old fifer in Captain James Carr's Company of the Second New Hampshire regiment opposed to Burgoyne in 1777 was wounded and captured by the Indians at the Battle of Hubbardston. A few weeks later, his wound having partially healed, he managed to escape and after an exciting series of adventures with wolves and Tories, returned to his regiment and served in the Sullivan Expedition against the Iroquois two years later.

HUMPHREYS, DAVID

An essay on the life of the Honorable Major-General Israel Putnam: addressed to the State Society of the Cincinnati in Connecticut. By Col. David Humphreys. *Philadelphia: Printed for Robert Campbell & Co. 1798.* [1168] 125 p., 18mo. Evans 33914. CtY, CtHWatk, NHi, NN.

. . . . .

Same, as: Life of . . . *New York, 1810.* DLC, NHi; Life of . . . *Phil., 1811.* DLC; An essay . . . *Brattleboro', 1812.* DLC; An essay . . . *Bost., 1818.* DLC, MB, MBAt, NHi, etc. and many later editions, for which see Sabin under Humphreys and Putnam. Abridged as: [1169]

. . . . .

The interesting life and adventures of General Israel Putnam, an officer in the British Army, and afterwards a General in the Army of the United States of America; Giving an account of his uncommon bravery and atchievements [sic] in many battles during the American War; together with a description of the manners and customs of the American Indians, by whom he was taken prisoner, and their cruelty towards him; also, of his following a desperate wolf, the terror of the country, into a cavern, 41 feet long, in the fissure of a rock, where he could not stand upright, and killing it: To which is added, the singular case of Dr. Menzies, also taken prisoner by the Cherokee Indians, who nearly roasted him alive, and his miraculous escape from them. *London: Printed and sold by J. Bailey . . . [ca. 1800].* [1170]

24 p., 12mo. Sabin 66804. ICN.

. . . . .

Same as: The life and adventures . . . *Falkirk: Printed by T. Johnston.* *1817* [1171]

24 p., 12mo. Sabin 66805.

JOHONNET, JACKSON

The | remarkable adventures | of | Jackson Johonnet, | of Massachusetts, | who served as a soldier in the Western Army, in the Massa- | chusetts Line. in the expedition under | Gen. Harmar, | and the unfortunate | Gen. St. Clair. | Containing, | an account of his captivity, sufferings, | and escape from the | Kickapoo Indians. | Written by himself, | and published at the earnest importunity of his friends, | for the benefit of | American youth. | [double rule] | *Salem, (Massa.)* | *Printed by Nathaniel Coverly, jun'r* | 1802.
[1172]

20 p., 8vo. Tapley: Salem imprints, p. 384. OClWHi.

Title from facsimile title in catalog of the Fabyan sale, Amer. Art. Gal., Feb. 17, 1920, no. 34. Five copies, including some duplication, have been sold at auction since 1920.

. . . . .

Second Salem edition. *[Salem: Printed by Nathaniel Coverly, Jun'r.* *1802?].* [1173]

20 p., 8vo. (21 x 13.5 cm.). MWA.

. . . . .

The remarkable adventures of Jackson Johonnet . . . [published in:] Stewart's Washington Almanac for . . . 1808. By Andrew Beers. *Philadelphia. [1807].* [1174]

Title from C.F. Heartman: *New Jersey Almanacs,* 112, who located a copy in the library of L.W. Smith.

. . . . .

The | remarkable adventures | of | Jackson Johonnot, | of Massachusetts, | who served as a soldier in the Western Army, | in the expedition under | Gen.

Harmar and Gen. St. Clair. | Containing | an account of his captivity, suffer- | ings, and escape from the | Kickappo [sic] Indians. | [filet] | Written by himself, and published at the earn- | est request and importunity of his friends, | for the benefit of American youth. | [filet] | *Greenfield, Mass.* | *Printed by Ansel Phelps.* | *1816.* [1175]
24 p., 12mo. (21 x 14 cm.). Sabin 36403, Ayer 168. DLC, I, ICN, MiU-C, MB, MWA, NHi, NN, PPiU.

Also published in at least eight editions of: *Affecting history of the dreadful distresses of Frederick Manheim's family,* which see, and in several of the collections of frontier narratives.

In spite of the fact that the title page of every edition but the last spells the author's name *Johonnet,* the Library of Congress catalog spells it Johonnot which we assume to be correct.

KNOX, HENRY

For sale, lots or tracts of land, of any size, as may best suit the purchasers, from 100 acres to 1000 acres and upwards. *[n.p., 1798].* [1176]
Broadside. Evans 33967. MB.

The former bookseller and Secretary of War was evidently a land speculator, as well, probably in New England.

NEW ENGLAND MISSISSIPPI LAND COMPANY

XXIII Articles of association and agreement, constituting the New-England Mississippi Land Company, as amended March 12, 1798. *[Boston, 1798].* [1177]
9 p., 8vo. Evans 34178, Sabin 52708. CtY, GU-De, MWA.

. . . . .

Memorial. [to the President of the United States] *[Boston, 1798].* [1178]
19 p., 8vo. Evans 34179. GU-De, MBAt, RPJCB.

For publications after 1800 see Sabin 52708 note. See also Georgia Mississippi Company, with which the above was allied. All part of the Yazoo Frauds.

PANTHER, ABRAHAM, *pseud.*

A very surprising | narrative | of [a] | young woman | who was discovered in a rocky cave, | after having been taken by | the savage Indians of the wilderness, | in the year 1777, | and seeing no human being for the space of | nine years. | In a letter from a gentleman to his friend. | *Printed and sold [by Peter Edes] at the Printing Office in | Augusta. | [1798?].* [1179]
12 p., 12mo. Evans 34305, Sabin 93899. F.C. Deering (the Braislin copy).

Peter Edes, printer of the *Kennebeck Intelligencer,* published his paper with the imprint *Hallowell* from 1795 to March 18, 1797. At about this time, the town was divided and the northern part called Harrington. In June of the same year the name was changed to Augusta, which name appears in the imprint of the *Intelligencer* beginning with the issue of June 30. In July, 1799, the place of publication is again called Hallowell. Information from Brigham.

[RICKMAN, THOMAS CLIO]

Emigration | to | America, | candidly considered. | In a series of letters, | from a | a [sic] gentleman, resident there, | to his | friend, in England. | [rule] | *London* | *Printed and sold by Thomas Clio Rickman,* | *'Upper Mary-le-bone street.* | *1798.*   [1180]

viii, 62, [2] p., 8vo. Sabin 22496 and 71241. MH, NN, PPL, RPJCB, WHi.

A tract against emigration to America based on the experience of a man who lived for a year in Pennsylvania, New York and the Jerseys.

[ROACH] RHODES, JOHN

The | surprising adventures | and | sufferings | of | John Rhodes, | a | seaman of Workington. | Containing | an account of his captivity and cruel treatment dur- | ing eight years with the Indians, and five years in | different prisons amongst the Spaniards in South- | America. | By a gentleman per- fectly acquainted with the unfortunate | sufferer. | *New-York:* | *Printed for R. Cotton, by G. Forman, No. 64,* | *Water-street.—1798.*   [1181]

250 [i.e., 252] p., 16mo. (17 x 10.4 cm.). Sabin 70763, Evans 34461, Ayer supp. 123. CSmH, DLC, F.C. Deering, ICN (imp.), MWA (imp.), NHi, NN, PU, RPJCB.

A rewriting of the John Roach narrative.

[WILLIAMSON, CHARLES]

Description | of the | Genesee Country, | its rapidly progressive | popula- tion and improvements: | in a series of letters | from a gentleman to his friend. | [double rule] | *Albany:* | *Printed by Loring Andrews & Co.* | [double rule] | *1798.*   [1182]

37 p., folded front, 2 folded maps, 4to. (18 x 16 cm.). Sabin 104441, Evans 35033. CSmH, CtHWatk, DLC, ICN, MH, MHi, MWA, N, NBLiHi, NGH, NHi, NN, NRHi, PHi, PPAmP, PPL, PPL-R, A.S.W. Rosenbach, RPJCB, R.W.G. Vail.

Front: *A view of Fort Oswego on the shore of L Ontario Lat: 43°, 28, 05* | [signed around base of oval view:] *De Witt S.G. del. Fairman Sc.* (21 x 18 cm.).

Folded maps: *Map* | *of* | *Ontario* | *and* | *Steuben* | *Counties* | [signed:] *Heslop Del. Fairman sculp.* [Map of the Phelps and Gorham Purchase] (45 x 38 cm.).; *A | map of the middle | states, shewing the | situation of the Genesee | Lands & their connection | with the Atlantic coast | 1798 |* [title within a scroll supported by a cupid]. (30.5 x 29 cm.). The map of Ontario and Steuben counties appears on both thin and thick paper (NHi and R.W.G. Vail copies) and also as an unfolded separate (NRHi and R.W.G. Vail copies).

First edition with five letters, written by the resident agent of the English Associates (Sir William Pulteney, Governor William Hornby and Patrick Colquhoun) for the promotion of their Western New York lands, also known as the Pulteney Estate. The second edition: *Description of the settlement,* N.Y., 1799.

ANDERSON, JOHN E., AND WILLIAM J. HOBBY

The | contract | for the purchase of | Western Territory, | made with the | Legislature of Georgia, | in the year 1795; | considered with a reference to the subsequent attempts of | the State, to impair its obligation. | [double rule] | By John E. Anderson & William J. Hobby, Esq'rs. | [double rule] | (Published at the instance of the purchasers.) | [thick-thin rule] | *Augusta: | Printed by Randolph & Bunce.* | [thick-thin rule] | *1799.*   [1183]
[6], [3]-93 p., 4to. (21.2 x 16.5 cm.). Evans 35111, De Renne I:286. DLC, GU-De, MBAt, NHi, NN (2 copies), RPJCB.

In one of the NN copies p. 17-24, 74-90, relating to the Yazoo land companies, have been cancelled. GU-De formerly had another issue with comma omitted after *Georgia* on the title and with pages 88-91 corresponding to pages 90-93 of their present copy. They have photos of these variant pages.

BRISSOT DE WARVILLE, JEAN PIERRE

J.P. Brissot's Nya resa genom Nord-Americanska Fristaterna år 1788. Från franska originalet sammandragen . . . af Johan Forster . . . Öfwersatt från tyskan. *Stockholm, A.J. Nordston, 1799.*   [1184]
[4], 328 p., 12mo. Title from DLC cat. DLC.

BROWN, CHARLES BROCKDEN

Edgar Huntly; or, memoirs of a sleep-walker. By the author of Arthur Mervyn, Wieland,—Ormond, &c. Vol. I. [II, III.] *Philadelphia: Printed by H. Maxwell, No. 3 Letitia Court, and sold by Thomas Dobson, Asbury Dickins, and the principal booksellers. 1799.*   [1185]
3 vols., 250; 252; 193, 48 p., 12mo. Evans 35244. Copies in most large libraries.

Charles Brockden Brown, the first American professional man of letters, attempts to use native American material in the writing of a tale of adventure and horror. The hero, in a cave full of Indians with a girl captive, kills the Indian guard and escapes with the girl, runs into more Indians and kills them, then another, gets lost (and no wonder for he and the author are not very familiar with frontier ways), is chased by hunters who think he is an Indian, and finally gets back home only to find that his uncle, with whom he had lived, had been killed by some other Indians in his absence. This may not be a great novel but it is the first to use the American frontier and an Indian captivity for its theme, other than the numerous brief yarns which purported to be true stories but were fiction nevertheless. Collectors can never get enough editions of the Abraham Panther captivity, which is pure fiction and was far more popular than *Edgar Huntly*, but we have never seen a copy of Brown's novel included in a captivity collection though it has as good a right to be there as some other fictitious captivities.

CONNECTICUT GORE LAND COMPANY

The Connecticut Gore title, | stated and considered, | showing | the rights of the proprietors, | to the | lands lately purchased by them, | from the | State of Connecticut: | lying west of the Delaware River. | [ornament] | *Hartford:* | *Printed by Hudson & Goodwin.* | *1799.* [1186]

80 p., 8vo. (22 x 13.5 cm.). Sabin 15681, Evans 35345, Trumbull 512. DLC, MBAt, MWA, NHi, NN, NNUT, P, RPJCB.

Concerning a strip of land along the southwestern border of New York State. The controversy over title continued for many years and included: *Memorials to the Governor and Legislature of New York, by the claimants of the lands purchased of Connecticut, commonly called the Gore, dated Connecticut, March 9, 1801.* Sabin 15683; *The rise, progress, and effect of the claim of the Connecticut Gore stated and considered, 1802.* NNC; and: *An enquiry concerning the grant of the Legislature of Connecticut, to Andrew Ward and Jeremiah Halsey; and the rights and obligations of the parties under the same. Hartford, 1829.* 26, [1] p., 8vo. Sabin 15682. MWA, NHi.

CONNECTICUT LAND COMPANY

For sale and settlement in Connecticut Reserve. [Dated at New Haven County, Connecticut, March 27, 1799] *[New Haven?] 1799.* [1187]

Broadside, folio. (32.5 x 20.5 cm.). CtY.

DECALVES, ALONSO, *pseud.*

New travels to the Westward; or, Unknown parts of America. Being a tour of almost fourteen months. Containing, an account of the country, upwards of two thousand miles West of the Christian parts of North-America; with an account of white Indians, their manners, habits, and many other particulars. By Don Alonso Decalves. Confirmed by three other persons. The fifth edition. *Hudson: Printed and sold by A. Stoddard, M,DCC,XCIX.* [1188]

44 p., 12mo. Sabin 98461, Evans 35391. CSmH, MHi, OClWHi.

Later versions of the Vandeleur captivity: *New travels*, 6th ed., Hudson: A. Stoddard, 1801. Sabin 98463. F.C. Deering; *A narrative of a voyage taken by James Van Leason,* Windsor, for the Purchaser, 1801. Sabin 98462.; *New travels,* Hartford, 1801. CtY; *New travels,* Danbury, 1802. PSC-Hi; *New travels,* Lexington, 1802. WHi; *New travels,* Cooperstown, 1803. DLC; Same, Lexington, 1804. Recorded by Union Cat., DLC but no copy located; *New Travels,* Greenwich, Mass., 1805. Sabin 98465. DLC, ICN, MWA, OCHP, RPJCB; *A history of the voyages and adventures of John Van Delure,* Montpelier, 1812. Sabin 98466. CSmH, ICN, MWA, T.W. Streeter, VtHi; *A history . . . John Van Delure,* Northampton, 1816. Sabin 98467. Perhaps in CCP; *A narrative of a voyage, taken by Capt. James Vanleason,* Ballston Spa, 1816. Sabin 98468. WHi. (A note from the Deering library stated that he had a Phil., 1796 ed. but this has not been verified); *A narrative of the travels of John Vandeluer,* Hallowell, 1817. Sabin 98469. BM, CSmH, DLC, MWA; Josiah Wheet, Jr.: *History of John Vandelure,* Andover, N.H. [1819?]. Sabin 103225. NN; *A history of the voyages . . . of John Van Delure,* Vergennes, 1827. Sabin 98470. DLC, NHi, NN.

FULLER, SYLVESTER

New Ohio lands, and title indisputable. The subscriber having lately purchased a tract of 21,401 acres of land, lying on the waters of Elk River, one of the sources of the Great Kanhaway and Ohio River, in the County of Randolph, State of Virginia. [Two columns] Sylvester Fuller. *Providence, [Printed by John Carter, junior] May 11, 1799.* [1189]

Broadside, folio. Evans 35526. MWA, RHi, RPJCB.

HARPER, ROBERT GOODLOE

The case of the Georgia sales on the Mississippi considered: with a reference to law authorities and public acts; with an appendix, containing certain extracts, records, and official papers. *Philadelphia: Printed by Richard Folwell, No. 33, Carter's-Alley. 1799.* [1190]

91 p., 4to. Evans 35587, De Renne I:288. CtY, DLC, GU-De, NN, RPJCB, ViU.

. . . . .

Philadelphia: Printed [by Richard Folwell] for Benjamin Davies. 1799.

[1191]

[4], 109 p., 8vo. Evans 35588. MH.

Horrid Indian cruelties! Affecting history of the dreadful distresses of Frederic Manheim's family. To which are added, An encounter between a white man and two savages. Remarkable bravery of a woman. Sufferings of John Corbly's family. *Boston: Printed by James White, near Charles River Bridge. 1799.* [1192]

12 p., 12mo. (18 cm.). Evans 35639, Sabin 105689. DLC.

Reprints only four of the nine narratives of the 1st ed.: *Affecting history*, 1793.

HUBBARD, WILLIAM

A narrative of the Indian wars, in New England . . . [as in 1775 ed.] [1799?].   [1193]
Entry from Evans 35646 who says that "Proposals for printing the above, in a volume of over 300 pages, were issued by Moses Davis, Concord, New Hampshire, in 1799" but there is no evidence that the book ever appeared.

· · · · ·

Printed at Worcester, (Massachusetts) by Daniel Greenleaf, for Joseph Wilder. 1801.   [1194]
410 p., 12mo. Sabin 33448.

· · · · ·

Norwich: Printed by John Trumbull. [1802].   [1195]
228 p., 12mo. Sabin 33449.

· · · · ·

Printed at Stockbridge, (Massachusetts) by Heman Hilliard May 1803.
                                                                               [1196]
375, 6 p., 8vo. Sabin 33450.

· · · · ·

Danbury: Printed by Stiles Nichols. 1803.   [1197]
274 p., 12mo. Sabin 33451.

· · · · ·

Fourth edition. *Brattleborough: William Fessenden. 1814.*   [1198]
359 p., 12mo. Sabin 33452. MH.

· · · · ·

Edited by Samuel G. Drake. *Roxbury, Mass.: W. Elliot Woodward. MDCCCLXV.*   [1199]
2 vols., [2], xxxi, [1], 292, map; 303 p., 4to. Sabin 33453. MB, MBAt. 50 copies 4to and 350 copies 8vo.

[KIMBER, EDWARD]

The history of the life and surprising adventures of Mr. Anderson. Containing his strange varieties of fortunes in Europe and America. Compiled from his own papers . . . *Glasgow, W. Neilson, 1799.*   [1200]
243 p., 12mo. (17 cm.). Title from DLC cat. DLC.

KNIGHT, JOHN, AND JOHN SLOVER

Narrative | of a late | expedition | against the | Indians; | with an | account | of the | barbarous execution | of | Col. Crawford; | and the | wonderful escape | of | Dr. Knight & John Slover | from | captivity in | 1782. | To which is added, | a narrative | of the | captivity & escape | of | Mrs. Frances Scott, | an inhabitant of Washington County, Virginia. | [double rule] | *Andover:* | *Printed by Ames & Parker.* | *[1799?].* [1201]

46 p., 12mo. (15 cm.). Sabin 38109, Evans 35689. DLC, F.C. Deering, MWA, NN, PPL, WHi.

Ames & Parker began printing in Andover in 1798 and continued for a short time. Wilberforce Eames, in the H. V. Jones catalog, dates this title [1799].

. . . . .

A remarkable narrative of an expedition against the Indians with an account of the barbarous execution of Col. Crawford and Dr. Knight's escape from captivity. *[Leominster, Mass.] Printed for Chapman Whitcomb.* *[1799?]* [1202]

There was printing at Leominster between 1796 and 1813.

23, [1] p., 12mo. Sabin 38110. Leominster Public Library, MWA.

. . . . .

Indian atrocities. | Narratives | of the | perils and sufferings | of | Dr. Knight and John Slover, | among the | Indians, | during the | Revolutionary War. | *Nashville:* | *W.F. Bang & Co. Printers . . .* |1843. [1203]

96 p., 12mo. (15.4 x 8.6 cm.). Sabin 38111, Ayer 176. CSmH, ICN.

Sabin adds to title, after the word *War: With short memoirs of Col. Crawford & John Slover. And a letter from H. Brackinridge, on the rights of the Indians, etc.*

. . . . .

Indian atrocities. | [rule] | Narratives | of the | perils and sufferings | of | Dr. Knight and John Slover, | among the Indians, | during the | Revolutionary War, | with short memoirs of | Col. Crawford & John Slover. | And a letter from H. Brackinridge, on the rights of | the Indians, etc. | [rule] | *Cincinnati:* | *U.P. James, Publisher.* | (Reprinted from the Nashville edition of 1843.) | *1867.* [1204]

72 p., 8vo. (20 x 12.5 cm.). Sabin 38111. Copies in most large libraries.

Though the edition was supposed to have been limited to 500 copies, including 75 on thick paper, it must have multiplied like the loaves and fishes for this is one of the commonest of all captivities. The fact that it is so plentiful and that nearly all copies are fresh, unworn and in their original yellow printed wrappers, would seem to indicate that an unsold remainder came to light in recent years.

Evans 17993 says there was a London edition but we have never heard of a copy. The narrative was reprinted from the Andover edition in J.G.E. Heckewelder's *Narrative of the mission of the United Brethren* and in most of the collections of frontier narratives. An extended account also appears in Butterfield's *History of the Girtys,* chapters 17-20.

PANTHER, ABRAHAM, *pseud.*

A | surprising narrative | of a | young woman, | who was discovered in the gloomy mansion of a | rocky cave! | After having been taken from her companion by | the savage Indians of the wilderness, | in the year 1787, | and seeing no human being for the space of 9 | years. | [rule] | (In a letter from a gentleman to his friend.) | [rule] | [2 orn. rules] | *Printed at Fryeburgh [by Elijah Russell].* | *1799.*   [1205]

8 p., 12mo. (17.5 x 11 cm.). MWA.

Title supplied by M.J. Walsh for a copy in Goodspeed's Book Shop cat. 385, 1945, no. 220. $175.00, now in MWA.

.   .   .   .   .

Amherst, 1799. From notes of Charles Evans for use in a forthcoming volume of his *American bibliography,* at MWA.   [1206]

PENROSE, JONATHAN

Philadelphia, March 4, 1799. | By virtue of a Writ of Levari Facias to me directed, will be sold by | public vendue, at the Merchants Coffee-house, (by adjournment) | on Tuesday, the 26th of March inst. | at six o'clock in the evening, all the lots that remained unsold on | the 15th inst. | [Caption title] [Colophon:] *Printed by D. Humphreys, No. 48, Spruce-street. [Philadelphia, 1799].*   [1207]

Broadside, folio. (49 x 19.5 cm.). NHi.

Sheriff's sale of part of Robert Morris's lands in Philadelphia city and county, in various lots described in the handbill, totalling over 140 acres.

For the liquidation of other Robert Morris properties, see under William Temple Franklin.

[ROACH] RHODES, JOHN

The | surprising adventures | and | sufferings | of | John Rhodes, | a | seaman of Workington. | -Containing- | An account of his captivity and cruel treatment dur- | ing eight years with the Indians, and five years in | different prisons amongst the Spaniards in South- | America. | By a gentleman perfectly acquainted with | the unfortunate sufferer. | [filet] | *Newark:* | *Printed by Pennington and Dodge,* | *for R. Cotton, New-York*—*1799.*   [1208]

268 p., 12mo. (16.5 x 10 cm.). Sabin 70764, Ayer 287. DLC, F.C. Deering, ICN, MBAt, MWA, N, NHi, NN, OFH, PPL, PPL-R, RPJCB.

. . . . .

The | powow. | Being a complete and an exact | description of an | Indian banquet, | held betwixt two friendly tribes of | Indians, in the southerly part of | North-America, A.D. 1777. | By John Rhodes, | a seaman of Workington, | who was a prisoner among the most | uncultivated savages, in different | tribes, thirteen years; and five years | in different prisons amongst the | Spaniards, in South-America, and | is now alive, tho' much crippled, | in the 54th year of his age. | [thick-thin rule] | *Otsego,* | *Printed by E. Phinney.* | *1808.*   [1209]

144 p., 24mo. Sabin 70765, Brinley 5438 to DLC.

An excerpt from *The surprising adventures,* with his captivity summarized in the appendix.

. . . . .

A | narrative | of the | surprising adventures and sufferings | of | John Roach, | mariner, | of | Whitehaven: | containing | an accurate detail of his long captivity | by the | Indians & Spaniards | in South America; | and including a | curious account of the manners of some of the tribes | on the | Isthmus of Darien, | &c. &c. | [orn. rule] | *Workington:* | *Printed by Edmund Bowness.* | *[rule]* | *1810.*   [1210]

83 p., 12mo. (17 x 11.5 cm.). CSmH.

Described from a photostat copy of the Wilberforce Eames-CSmH copy at NHi.

Publisher stated that it is rewritten and enlarged from earlier editions.

"The internal evidence is not sufficient to settle the question of its veracity."—Field 1299. If his story is true, he was born at Workington in 1755 and became a sailor. In 1774 he was sent ashore with others for wood and water on the coast of Central America where he was captured by an Indian tribe which he calls Woolaways. He spent two years with them, escaped and was recaptured by the Buckeraws and after thirteen months again escaped and was captured by another tribe and so he went from one captivity to another and finally fell into the hands of the Spaniards. He spent a total of thirteen years in captivity and, at last, escaped on an English ship. Perhaps inspired by the Spanish captivities related by the Gentleman of Elvas and Alvar Nuñez Cabeza de Vaca, which see.

SCOTT, FRANCES

A remarkable narrative of the captivity and escape of Mrs. Frances Scott, an inhabitant of Washington County, Virginia. *Newburyport: Printed and sold by Parker & Robinson. [ca. 1799].*   [1211]

16mo. (9.5 x 7.5 cm.). Not seen. Title from facsimile of title page in

Goodspeed Book Shop catalog 283, 1937, no. 131. $125.00, of a copy now at MWA.

. . . . .

A remarkable narrative of the captivity and escape of Mrs. Frances Scott, an inhabitant of Washington County, Virginia. *[Leominster:] Printed for Chapman Whitcomb. [ca. 1799-1810].*   [1212]
16 p., 12mo. (11 x 7.5 cm.). F.C. Deering, MWA.

. . . . .

A remarkable narrative of the captivity and escape of Mrs. Frances Scott, an inhabitant of Washington County, Vir. *Leominster: Printed by Salmon Wilder. 1811.*   [1213]
15 p., wdct. front. (paged in), wdct. in text on p. 7, wdct. on verso of p. 15. 16mo. (10.5 x 7 cm.). F.C. Deering, photostat copy of original owned 1933 by L.C. Harper, at NHi.

Has long sentence added at end of original text, ending: ". . . sending the birds to direct her course."

The H.V. Jones catalog, no 593, describes as "Probably first edition," a copy lacking title and front. but having 15 p. and a cut on verso of p. 15, with the supplied imprint: *[Boston: E. Russell, 1785?].* However, NN has a photostat of this imperfect copy which shows that it is probably a copy of the 1811 edition.

. . . . .

2d ed., *Leominster: James Wilder, 1811.*   [1214]
NN has an imperfect copy, lacking title and perhaps a final leaf, which may be this edition. It has 14 p. and is a 16mo. (10 x 8.5 cm.). Its caption title and text, on p. [3], are same as those on p. [5] of the 1811 edition.

The H.V. Jones catalog, no 594, describes a copy as "Perhaps the second edition" with the title: "A remarkable narrative of the captivity and escape of Mrs. Frances Scott from the Indians. [1785?] 16mo." which is probably this second 1811 edition.

. . . . .

Reprinted in: Beers's almanac . . . for . . . 1796. *Hartford, [1795].* Evans 28248; Bradman, Arthur. A narrative of the extraordinary sufferings of Mr. Robert Forbes . . . *Phil., 1794;* same, *Elizabeth (Hager's) Town, 1797.* Evans 31864; Knight, John. Narrative of a late expedition against the Indians . . . *Andover, [1799].* Evans 35689; Loudon, Archibald. A selection . . . Vol. 1. *Carlisle, 1808;* Pritts, Joseph. Incidents of border life . . . *Chambersburg, 1859;* De Hass, Wills. History of the early settlement . . . western Virginia . . . *Wheeling, 1851;* Frost, John. Thrilling adventures. *Phil., 1851;* Schoolcraft, H.R. The American Indians . . . *Buffalo, 1851;* Heckewelder, J.G.E. A narrative of the mission of the United Brethren . . . *Cleveland, 1907.*

[1215]

SMITH, JAMES

An account | of the | remarkable occurrences | in the life and travels of | Col. James Smith, | (Now a citizen of Bourbon County, Kentucky,) | during his captivity with the Indians, | in the years 1755, '56, '57, '58, & '59, | in which the customs, manners, traditions, theological sen- | timents, mode of warfare, military tactics, discipline and | encampments, treatment of prisoners, &c. are better ex- | plained, and more minutely related, than has been heretofore | done, by any author on that subject. Together with a de- | scription of the soil, timber and waters, where he travel- | led with the Indians, during his captivity. | To which is added, | a brief account of some very uncommon occurrences, which | transpired after his return from captivity; as well as of the | different campaigns carried on against the Indians to the | westward of Fort Pitt, since the year 1755, to the present | date. | [double rule] | Written by himself. | [double rule] | *Lexington:* | *Printed by John Bradford, on Main Street,* | [filet] | *1799.* [1216]

88 p., 8vo. (20.5 x 12.3 cm.). Sabin 82763, Ayer 266, Church 1287, Thompson 1055, McMurtrie Kentucky imprints 122. CSmH, F.C. Deering, E.D. Graff, ICN, NHi, PPiU, WHi (imperfect).

First edition of one of the most historically valuable of captivities. He was a captive at Fort Duquesne in 1755 and witnessed the Indians' preparations for and celebration after the Braddock defeat. He was a captive and adopted Indian on the Ohio until 1759 when he escaped while at Montreal and spent a useful life as frontiersman in Pennsylvania and Kentucky. His oil portrait by Chester Harding is reproduced in W.R. Jillson's *A bibliography of the life and writings of Col. James Smith.* Frankfort: Kentucky Historical Society, 1947. 51 p., port., 8vo.

The Joseph B. Shea copy, sold at American Art-Anderson sale 1453, Dec. 2, 1937, no. 580, was sold for $1,000. to F.C. Deering; the H.V. Jones copy, described in his *Adventures in Americana* 193, and in his library catalog 672, was sold to the Rosenbach Company and by them sold for $1,650. to Mr. E.D. Graff.

Other editions: *Philadelphia, 1831.* 162 p., 18mo. Four copies located; *Philadelphia, 1834.* 162 p., 18mo. Same sheets, new title. Four copies located; Life of. *Philadelphia, 1838.* No copy located; *Cincinnati, 1870.* Regular edition and 50 on large paper. Many copies; *Cincinnati, 1907.* Same plates as preceding edition. Many copies; In *Magazine of History,* Extra no. 7, 1914. Many copies; Reprinted in whole or in part in at least 16 other western histories.

. . . . . .

A treatise, | on the mode and manner of Indian war, | their tactics, discipline and encampments, | the various methods they practise, in | order to obtain the advantage, by | ambush, surprise, surrounding, &c. | Ways and means proposed to prevent the | Indians from obtaining the advantage. | A chart, or plan of marching, and encamping, laid down, | whereby we may undoubtedly surround | them, if we have men sufficient. | Also—a brief account of twen- | ty-three campaigns, carried on | against the Indians with | the events, since the | year 1755; Gov. Harri- | son's included. | [thick-thin rule] | By Col. James Smith. | [rule] | Likewise—some abstracts selected from his | Journal, while in captivity with the In- | dians, relative to the wars: which | was published many years ago, but | few of them now to be found. | [rule] | *Paris Kentucky,* | [type ornaments] *Printed by Joel R. Lyle* [type ornaments] | -1812.-   [1217]

[1], 59 p., 8vo. (21.1 x 12.3 cm.). Sabin 82771, Ayer 269, McMurtrie's Kentucky imprints, 1811-1820, no. 438, Jillson's Bibliog. of Col. James Smith, p. 29. CSmH (imperfect), E.D. Graff (imperfect), ICU, ICN, MHi, NN, WHi (imperfect).

Written as a guide for fighting the Indians in the War of 1812. Largely taken from his *Account* but *To the reader,* p. [2]-3 and *On Indian treaties,* p. 52-59, are entirely new.

SYMMES, THOMAS

The | history | of the | fight | of the intrepid | Captain John Lovell, | which took place | on the eighth day of May, 1725, | on the beach of Lovell's Pond, in | Fryeburgh, | in the District of Maine. | Together with the | commemoration sermon, | delivered | by the Rev. Mr. T. Symmes. | Published according to act of Congress. | *Printed at Fryeburg, by and for* | *Elijah Russell.* | *1799.*   [1218]

60 p., 12mo. Sabin 94109, Church 897 note, Noyes: Maine imprints 162. MWA.

Third edition of *Lovewell lamented,* 1725, with a new preface and changes by the publisher.

. . . . .

Same, as: *A brief history . . . Portland, 1818.*   [1219]

19 p., 12mo. Sabin 94110, Noyes: Maine imprints 835. DLC, NHi, NN.

For other reprints, see Sabin 94112. For a contemporary ballad on this event, see under *Voluntier's* march, 1725, no. 348.

WALLWILLE, MARIA OWLIAM, GRÄFIN VON, *pseud?*

Die wilde Europäerinn oder Geschichte der Frau von Walwille von A.C., einem alten Seeofficier. Aus dem Französischen. *Meissen: Bey Erbstein, 1799.*   [1220]

Sabin 101130, quoting title from Heinsius: *Allgemeines Bücher-Lexicon,* 1700-1810, vol. 4, 1813, col. 65; and from review in *Neue allgemeinen deutsche Bibliothek,* 1800, p. 327-329.

. . . Merkwürdige und interessante Lebensgeschichte der Frau von Wallwille, welche vier Jahre lang an eined Irokesen verheyrathet war. Kein Roman. Meissen, bey Friedrich Wilhelm G[ödsche]. [Colophon:] *Sulzbach, Gedruckt mit Kommerzienrath Seidlischen Schriften [1809].*

284, [1] p., 16mo. Sabin 101129. F.C. Deering.

The Deering copy lacks part of the imprint. This and the date are supplied from Heinsius, as above, col. 225.

The probably fictitious story of the captivity and marriage of an English woman among the Iroquois, from about 1755 to 1759, her escape, later experiences among the Indians, and marriage to a certain "Walwille." Told after the death of the latter for the information of officers from a ship who encountered her while she was living near St. John, Newfoundland in 1778. After the introduction, the story is told in the first person. Heinsius included the title in a list of novels. Entries and note from Sabin.

[WILLIAMSON, CHARLES]

Description | of the | settlement | of the | Genesee Country, | in the | State of New-York. | In a | series of letters | from a | gentleman to his friend. | [orn.] | [thin-thick rule] | *New-York:* | *Printed by T. & J. Swords, No. 99 Pearl-street.* | [rule] | *1799.*   [1221]

63 p., folded map, 8vo. (22 x 14 cm.). Sabin 104442. Copies in most large libraries.

Folded map: *Map | of the | middle states of North America. | Shewing the position of the Geneseo | Country comprehending the Counties of | Ontario & Steuben as laid off in Town- | ships of Six Miles square Each. |* [Scale of miles] | *Maverick Sculpt.- 65 Liberty Street, N.Y.* There are three states of the map: 1. Unsigned, lacks *References* and many geographical details and has only first three lines of title. (NHi, NN, R.W.G. Vail); 2. Unsigned, has *References,* some geographical details added and has only first three lines of title (NHi); 3. Signed, has *References,* a large number of additional geographical details and title complete in seven lines. Some copies (NN and R.W.G. Vail) have the *Map of Ontario and Steuben Counties* of 1st ed. added and at least one copy has the view of Fort Oswego of 1st ed. added (NHi).

Some copies of the pamphlet were printed on thin white paper, others on thick brownish paper (R.W.G. Vail copies, the former containing the 1st state of the map).

Second edition containing eight letters and list of taverns.

Reprinted as supplement to John Payne's Geography, N.Y., 1799, vol. 4, 11 p., view of Fort Oswego, reengraved from 1st ed. by T. Clarke.

For Williamson's *A view of the present situation of . . . Genesee Country,* 1804, and its three later editions: *A description of the Genesee Country,* 1804, see R.W.G. Vail's *A Western New York land prospectus* in: *Bookmen's holiday,* N.Y., 1943, p. 112-126.

See Miss H.I. Cowan's *Charles Williamson* in Rochester Hist. Soc. Pubs.,
19, 1941. His papers are owned by ICN.

[WILLIS, HANNAH?]

Surprizing account of the captivity of Miss Hannah Willis, who was
taken by the Indians, on the 30th of July 1791, . . . To which is added An
Affecting history, of the dreadful distresses of Frederic Manheim's family,
who was [sic] taken prisoners by the Indians in 1779. *Stonington-Port,
Printed by S. Trumbull. 1799.*   [1222]

15, [1] p., 12mo. Title from Trumbull supp. 2658. MWA.

For other editions of the Manheim captivity, see *Affecting history,* 1793,
no. 928.

Affecting history | of the | dreadful distresses | of | Frederick Manheim's
family. | To which are added, | an encounter between a white man | and
two savages. | Adventures of Capt. Isaac Stewart. | Deposition of Mercy
Herbeson. | Adventures and sufferings of Pe- | ter Williamson. | Remarkable
adventures of Jackson | Johonnot. | Account of the destruction of the |
settlements at Wyoming. | [rule] | *[Leominster:] Printed for Chapman
Whitcomb.* | *[1800?].*   [1223]

39 p., 12mo. Sabin 105690, Ayer 3. ICN, Leominster Pub. Lib., MWA,
NN (photostat), PHi.

See Sabin note as to date. See also note to the Chapman Whitcomb,
[1794] edition of the Mary Rowlandson captivity.

. . . . . .

Affecting | history | of the | dreadful distresses | of | Frederic Manheim's |
family: | To which are added, the | sufferings of John Corbly's family.—An
encounter | between a white man and two savages.—Extraor- | dinary
bravery of a woman—Adventures of | Capt. Isaac Stewart.—Deposition of
Massy | Herbeson.—Adventures and sufferings of | Peter Wilkinson.—Re-
markable adventures of Jackson Johonnot. | With an account | of the
destruction of the settle- | ments at Wyoming. | *Philadelphia:* | *Printed by
Henry Switzer,* | *for Mathew Carey, No. 118 High-Street.* | *1800.* | *Price
a quarter-dollar.*   [1223A] ·

48 p., front. as in 1794 ed., 8vo. (22.9 x 14.3 cm.). Sabin note following
105689, Ayer 5. DLC, F.C. Deering, ICN, MBAt, MWA, NN.

. . . . . .

Bennington: Printed by Collins & Stockwell. 1802.   [1224]

33 p., 8vo. Sabin note following 105690; Magazine of History extra no.
152, 1929, p. 5-32, plate, and in many collections of Indian narratives.

BARRY, THOMAS

Narrative | of the | singular adventures and captivity | of | Mr. Thomas Barry, | among the | Monsipi Indians, | in the unexplored regions of | North America, | during the | years 1797, 1798, & 1799: | including | the manners, customs, &c. of that tribe; | also | a particular account of his escape, accompanied by an | Indian female; | the extraordinary hardships they encountered; and | their safe arrival in London. | Written by himself. | *Sommers Town:* | *Printed and published by A. Neil,* | *No. 30, Chalton Street;* | *and sold by all other booksellers.* | *1800.* | *(Price one shilling.).* [1225]

60 p., front., 12mo. (15.2 x 9 cm.). Church 1288. CSmH.

Supposed to have been captured while on an Indian trading expedition out of Charlestown in April, 1797. Probably fictitious.

. . . . .

Same title, *Somers Town:* | *Printed and published by A. Neil,* | . . . | *sold also by T. Hurst . . . London.* | *1800.* | *(Price one shilling.).* [1226]

60 p., front., 12mo. (17.1 x 9.9 cm.). Sabin 3690, Ayer 20. DLC, ICN, RPJCB.

. . . . .

The singular | adventures and captivity | of | Thos. Barry, | among the | Monsipi Indians, | in the | unexplored regions of North America; | including the | manners, customs, &c. of that tribe; | also, | a particular account of his escape, accompanied by an | Indian female; | the extraordinary hardships they encountered in their | flight; | and their safe arrival in London, | December the 6th, 1799. | Written by himself. | *Printed and published by A. Neil,* | *at the Sommers-Town Printing Office, Charlton-Street;* | *and may be had of all the other booksellers.* | *1802.* | *(Price one shilling.).* [1227]

[2], [v]-vii, [1], [9]-62 p., colored front., 12mo. (18.3 x 10.3 cm.). Ayer 21. DLC, ICN, MWiW-C.

Brinley 5482 sold to Elisha Turner, founder of the Torrington, Conn. Public Library where this copy may now be.

. . . . .

Narrative of the singular adventures and captivity of Thomas Barry, among the Monsipi Indians, in the unexplored regions of North America, during the years 1797, 1798, & 1799: Including the manners, customs, religion, &c. of that tribe; Also a particular account of his escape, accompanied by an Indian female; the extraordinary hardships they encountered; and their safe arrival in London. *Manchester: A. Swindells. [180–?].* [1228]

48 p., 16mo. NN.

CHASSANIS, PIERRE

Réponse au mémoire de Mr. Tillier. [Caption title] [Signed at end:] Pierre Chassanis. [Docketed on back:] Réponse | de | Pierre Chassanis | à | Rodolphe Tillier. | [n.p., ca 1800]. [1229] 3 p., 4to. (23 x 18 cm.). DLC, N.

For the *Memoire* to which this is an answer, see under Rodolphe Tillier.

ELLICOTT, JOSEPH

Holland Land Company West Geneseo Lands—Information. The Holland Land Company will open a land office in the ensuing month of September, for the sale of a portion of their valuable lands in the Genesee country . . . [By Joseph Ellicott, Agent. Albany: November 25, 1800] [Albany, 1800]. [1230]

Small broadside. NBuHi (Ellicott letter book, 1814-1821).

Described from partial reprint in Orsamus Turner's *Pioneer history of the Holland Purchase*. Buffalo, 1849, p. 424; in L.R. Doty's *History of the Genesee Country*, Chicago, 1925, vol. 1, p. 399; and in P.D. Evans: *Holland Land Company*, 1924, p. 224, 299.

Joseph Ellicott was appointed local agent of the Holland Land Company Oct. 1, 1800 with temporary headquarters at Asa Ransom's house in Ransom's Hollow, Erie County. One of his first official acts was the publication of this prospectus. Headquarters of the company were later removed to Batavia, N.Y. where their original building is still preserved as a local museum, still containing some of the original local records of the company. One volume of his Holland Land Company letters is in the Henry O'Rielly Collection at NHi, the rest at NBuHi.

ELLICOTT, JOSEPH, AND B[ENJAMIN]

Map | of two million acres of land | West Genesee | in the State of New York | recorded in the names of Wilhem Willink; | Nics van Staphorst; | Pieter van Eeghen; | Hendrik Vollenhaven; | Rutger Jan Schimmelpenninck. | To the | Society in Holland | this map | is respectfully inscribed | bij | Joseph & B. Ellicott. | 1800. | [Amsterdam? 1800]. [1231]

Title of a folio map described by William H. Samson from an original owned in 1904 by Howard L. Osgood of Rochester who bought it about 1894 in Holland for $8.00. Mr. Samson says (MS notes owned by the compiler): "This looks to me like a map made from partial surveys, because some parts of the territory are left absolutely blank. . . . The names of the proprietors are given on this map and though dated 1800, was probably made before all the surveys were completed, and possibly before the company [Holland Land Company] was really organized in Holland." It is probable that this map is now with the other Osgood papers in the Rochester Historical Society, Rochester Public Library, Rochester, New York, though it may be with a portion of the Osgood papers at the Ontario County Historical Society, Canandaigua, New York.

Since this map was secured in Holland and since the Dutch word *bij* is used in the English title instead of *by*, it is probable that this map was engraved in Amsterdam, the home of the Company, from an original map supplied by the Ellicotts. Its rarity is probably explained by its being superseded by the following map which was made after the surveys were completed.

. . . . . .

Map | of | Morris's Purchase | or | West Geneseo | In the State of New York: | Exhibiting | Part of the Lakes Erie and Ontario, the | Straights of Niagara, Chautauque Lake | and all the principal Waters, the Boundary | lines of the several Tracts of Land purchased | by the | Holland Land Company | William and John Willink | and others. | Boundary lines of Townships: | Boundary lines of New York and | Indian Reservations: | Laid down from actual Survey: | Also | A Sketch of part of Upper Canada | by | Joseph & B: Ellicott | 1800. | [rule] | To the | Holland Land Company | their General Agents | Theophilus Cazenove & Paul Busti Esquires | This Map | Is respectfully inscribed | by the | Authors. | Explanation. | [6 lines] *[New York? 1800].* [1232]

Folio map (76 x 54.5 cm. over all, 67.5 x 52.3 cm. within the plate mark.). NHi, etc.

Most important map of the Holland Land Company, published for the promotion of sales of their Western New York lands.

. . . . . .

With date *1804* added after dedication. Same size. NHi, etc. [1233]

Town of Batavia and numerous roads and other geographical features added.

For earlier map of the purchase, see under Holland Land Company, [1794-1800].

JEFFERSON, THOMAS

An | appendix | to the | Notes on Virginia | relative to the murder of Logan's family. | By Thomas Jefferson. | *Philadelphia:* | *Printed by Samuel H. Smith.* | *M.D.CCC.* [1234]

51 p., map on verso of p. 51, 8vo. (22.5 cm.). Sabin 35880. NHi, etc.

. . . . . .

Same sheets with pp. 53-58, material "received after the publication of the preceding Appendix," added. DLC, NHi, etc. [1235]

Evidence to prove that Michael Cresap and his party murdered Logan's family and other peaceful Indians.

. . . . .

Jefferson's | notes, | on the | State of Virginia; | with the | appendixes—complete. | *Baltimore:* | *Printed by W. Pechin, corner of Water & Gaystreets.* | *1800.*   [1236]
194, 53 p., map and plan in text, folded table, 8vo. (21.5 cm.). Sabin 35899. MB, NHi, etc.

. . . . .

With addition of: *A vindication of the religion of Mr. Jefferson,* with separate title page, 21 p., DLC.   [1237]

. . . . .

To which is subjoined, | a sublime and argumentative | dissertation, | on | Mr. Jefferson's | religious principles. | [Same imprint and date].   [1238]
194, 53, 21 p., map and plan in text, folded table, 8vo. (22 cm.). Sabin 35900. DLC, NHi, etc.

Final supplement on Jefferson's religion has separate title page.

For many later editions, see Sabin and DLC catalog.

Outline of a plan for an establishment to be formed on the left bank of the Mobile River, in Georgia, one of the United States of North America. *London: Printed by Wm. Phillips, George Yard, Lombard Street. 1800.*
                                                                            [1239]
15 p., 8vo. De Renne I:293. GU-De.

PANTHER, ABRAHAM, *pseud.*

A very surprising narrative of a young woman who was discovered in a cave, after having been taken by the Indians in the year 1777, and seeing no human being for the space of nine years. In a letter from a gentleman to his friend. Misfortunes constantly await the human race. *Bennington, (Vermont) Printed by Collier & Stockwell, 1800.*   [1240]
12 p., 12mo. Sabin 93901. Title supplied by Harold G. Rugg.

. . . . .

A very | surprising narrative | of a | young woman, | discovered in a | rocky cave. | After having been taken by the | savage Indians of the wilderness, | in the year 1777. | And seeing no human being for the space of nine years. | [rule] | In a letter from a gentleman to his friend. | [rule] | [rule] | *Brookfield [Mass.: Printed by Ebenezer Merriam & Co.],* | *December,* *1800.*   [1241]
12 p., 12mo. Sabin 93902. DLC, F.C. Deering, MWA.

. . . . .

A very surprising narrative . . . *New-Haven: Printed for every purchaser.* *1802.*   [1242]

10 p., 12mo. Sabin 93903, Ayer 220. DLC, F.C. Deering, ICN (lacks title).

. . . . . .

A very surprising narrative . . . *Troy, N.Y., Printed for Amos Taylor, by Wright, Goodenow, & Stockwell, 1806.* [1243]

8 p., 16mo. Title from Goodspeed's Book Shop cat. 377, 1944, no. 399. $75.00, for a copy now at MWA.

. . . . . .

A very surprising narrative . . . *[n.p.] Printed in the year 1812.* [1244]

11 p., 12mo. Sabin 93904, Ayer supp. 95. F.C. Deering, ICN.

. . . . . .

A very surprising narrative . . . *New Haven, 1812.* F.C. Deering. [1245]

. . . . . .

A very surprising narrative . . . *Printed at Jaffrey, N.H. [by Salmon Wilder]. [1814?].* [1246]

12 p., 12mo. Sabin 93905, Ayer supp. 94. CSmH, F.C. Deering, ICN.

Salmon Wilder was Jaffrey's only printer. He went there from Leominster, Massachusetts in 1814 and operated a job press there until 1816 when he removed to New Ipswich, New Hampshire.

The | returned captive, | a | poem. | Founded on a late fact. | [rule] | [6 lines quoted] | [double rule] | *Northampton: | Printed by Andrew Wright. | Sold by him, wholesale and retail.—1800.* [1247]

50 p., 12mo. (20 x 12 cm.). MWA, Forbes Library Northampton.

ROUSO D'ERES, CHARLES DENNIS

Memoirs | of | Charles Dennis Rusoe d'Eres, | a native of Canada; | who was with the Scanyawtauragahrooote | Indians eleven years, with a particular | account of his sufferings, &c. during | his tarry with them, and his safe | return to his family connec- | tions in Canada; | To which is added | an appendix, | containing | a brief account of their persons, dress, | manners, reckoning time, mode of govern- | ment, &c. Feasts, dances, hunting, wea- | pons of war, &c. Making peace, diversions, | courtship, marriage, religious tenets, | mode of worship, diseases, method of | cure, burying their dead, character | of the Scanyawtauragahrooote Indians, | particular description of the quadru- | peds, birds, fishes, reptiles and insects, | which are to be met with on and in the | vicinity of Scanyawtauragahrooote | Island. | [rule] | Copy right secured. | [thick-thin rule] | *Printed for, and sold by Henry Ranlet, Exeter.* | [double rule] | *1800.* [1248]

176 p., 12mo. (18 cm.). Sabin 22731, Ayer 236. DLC, F.C. Deering, ICN, MBAt, MH, MiD-B, MWA, N, Nh, NHi, RPJCB.

This story has generally been considered fictitious, mainly because of the unfamiliar name of the Indian tribe mentioned in the title and because of a certain amount of embroidery of the tale. However, it has been accepted by the Library of Congress as true to a considerable extent and there is no doubt that the author did exist, was an Indian captive and later married and settled as a blacksmith in Spencer, Massachusetts where he was known as Charles Rouso. As to the name of the tribe, the American Antiquarian Society has a letter from F.W. Hodge, Ethnologist-in-Charge of the Bureau of American Ethnology of the Smithsonian Institution, written December 11, 1916 to the late Henry F. DePuy in which he says: "Scanyawtauragah-rooote is evidently a white man's attempt to pronounce *Skaniadaradihronon*, the Iroquois name for the Nanticokes." DePuy, in the accompanying notes, refers to Sir William Johnson's spelling of the word as published in his: *An account of conferences held and treaties made between* . . . [himself] *and the chief sachems* . . . London, 1756, which is *Skan-ia-da-ra-di-ghro-nos*, which is obviously the same name as that quoted by Rouso. DePuy translates this Iroquois name as *Those who dwell on the other side of the river*, that is, across the Niagara.

The author's father was a blacksmith near Quebec who, with his elder son, joined the Americans under Montgomery in 1775. They and the younger son Charles were captured at their farm six miles from Quebec, the two older men imprisoned and Charles, then fourteen years of age, was given to the Indians who carried him west. On reaching their village, he found there some abandoned blacksmith's tools and set to work to repair their tools and weapons and make new ones for them which gave him considerable influence with them. After eleven years with the Indians, he returned to New England, married and continued his work as a blacksmith. DePuy believed all of the story except the author's account of a purely imaginary visit to the Spanish settlements in the southwest.

ROWLANDSON, MARY

A | narrative | of the | captivity, sufferings, and removes, | of | Mrs. Mary Rowlandson, | [etc., 7 lines] | Boston: | *Re-printed and sold by John and Thomas Fleet, at the Bible and Heart, Cornhill, 1800.*   [1249]
36 p., 12mo. (17.1 x 10 cm.). Ayer 240. ICN, Lancaster Town Library. Title from Ayer.

. . . . .

New Haven, 1802. F.C. Deering.   [1250]

. . . . .

A | narrative | of the | captivity, sufferings and removes | of | Mrs. Mary

Rowlandson, | [wdct. of woman shooting at four men] | [etc., 7 lines] | [rule] | *Boston: Printed & sold by Thomas Fleet, 1805.* [1251]

36 p., 12mo. Sabin 73589. F.C. Deering, MH, MSaE, MWA.

. . . . .

The | captivity and deliverance | of | Mrs. Mary Rowlandson, | of Lancaster, | who was taken by the French and Indians. | Written by herself. | *Brookfield,* | *Printed by Hori Brown,* | *from the Press of E. Merriam &* *Co.* | *September, 1811.* [1252]

80 p., 12mo. (17 x 9.5 cm.).

Has separate title and pagination but is really part of John Williams: *The captivity and deliverance* . . . *Brookfield, 1811,* which see for references and locations.

. . . . .

Narrative | of | the captivity and removes | of | Mrs. Mary Rowlandson, | . . . | Fifth edition. | [rule] | *Lancaster: Published by Carter, Andrews, and* *Co.* | *1828.* _ [1253]

xii, 81 p., 12m. Sabin 73590. Lancaster Town Library, MBAt, MWA.

Edited by Joseph Willard.

. . . . .

Sixth edition. | Second Lancaster edition. | *Lancaster:* | *Published by* *Carter, Andrews, and Co.* | *1828.* [1254]

100 p., front., 18mo. (14.6 x 8.5 cm.). Sabin 73590, Ayer 241. DLC, F.C. Deering, ICN, Lancaster Town Library, MWA, N, NHi.

. . . . .

Narrative | of the | captivity, sufferings and removes | of | Mrs. Mary Rowlandson, | . . . | To which is appended | a century sermon, | preached at the | First Parish in Lancaster, May 28, 1753, | by Rev. Timothy Harrington. | [rule] | A reprint from an old edition. [Boston, 1753. Evans 7020] | [rule] | *Clinton:* | *Published by Ballard & Bynner.* | *1853.* [1255]

73 p., 12mo. Sabin 73591. DLC, F.C. Deering, Lancaster Town Library, MBAt, MWA, NHi, etc.

. . . . .

A | narrative | of the | captivity, sufferings, and removes, | of | Mrs. Mary Rowlandson, | [etc., 7 lines] | *Boston:* | *Re-printed and sold by Thomas* *and John Fleet, at the* | *Bible and Heart, Cornhill, 1791.* | *By the Mass.* *Sabbath School Society, 13 Cornhill,* | *1856.* [1256]

122 p., 8vo. (17.5 x 10.5 cm.). Sabin 73592, Ayer 242. DLC, F.C. Deering, ICN, Lancaster Town Library, MH, MWA, N (variant), NN, etc.
On verso of title: *Riverside, Cambridge, Printed by H.O. Houghton & Co.*

.   .   .   .   .

Concord, N.H. Reprinted by the Republican Press Association for Eleanor S. Eastman, 1883.   [1257]
53 p., 12mo. (17.7 x 11.4 cm.). Lancaster Town Library.

.   .   .   .   .

The narrative | of the | captivity and restoration | of | Mrs. Mary Rowlandson | First printed in 1682 at Cambridge [sic], | Massachusetts, & London, England. | Now reprinted in fac-simile | Whereunto are annexed | a map of her removes, biographical & historical | notes, and the last sermon of her husband | Rev. Joseph Rowlandson | *Lancaster, Massachusetts* | *MDCCCC-III* | *[Cambridge: J. Wilson and Son, 1903].*   [1258]
vii, [6], 158 p., illus., map, facsim., 4to. (27 x 20.5 cm.). Ayer 243. DLC, F.C. Deering, ICN, Lancaster Town Library, MWA, NHi, NN, RPJCB, etc.
Edited by Henry S. Nourse. An edition of 250 copies privately printed for Colonel John E. Thayer as a gift to the citizens of the town of Lancaster.

.   .   .   .   .

The narrative of the | captivity | and | restoration | of | Mrs. Mary Rowlandson | . . . | The Lancaster edition | [seal of the town of Lancaster] | *Boston* | *Printed and sold by Houghton Mifflin* | *Company in Park Street opposite the Common, 1930.*   [1259]
vi, [2], 86 p., illus., map, 12mo. (18.5 x 12 cm.). Copies in most large libraries.
Reprinted in an edition of 1500 copies from the MB copy of the second edition, Cambridge, 1682, as reprinted in the Lancaster, 1903 edition.

.   .   .   .   .

[Cut of Redemption Rock] | Redemption Rock | A brief outline of how Mary Rowlandson, | the preacher's wife, of Lancaster, was captured by | Indians—their wanderings in the wilderness— | her sufferings—her redemption | [rule] | Refreshments served at "Redemption Rock Rest" | (on route 64) by Joseph Mason, Proprietor | *[n.p., 193-?]* [Cover title].   [1260]
8 p., 12mo. MWA.

.   .   .   .   .

Mary Rowlandson's narrative. By John Nelson. Reprinted from "Americana," Vol. XXVII, No. 1 By special permission of the publishers. Sixty copies printed for C.S. Yowell. *Somerville, N.J., 1933.*   [1261]
16 p., 4to. MWA.

Preprinted in *Americana* from John Nelson's "Worcester County, a narrative history." *N.Y., 1934,* vol. I, p. 86-105. Extracts from Mary Rowlandson's narrative.

TENNESSEE COMPANY

The Tennessee Company | to | Messrs. Strawbridge | Jackson and Dexter | [bracket] Deed of trusts. | Dated 20th of June, 1800. | *[Philadelphia, 1800].*
[1262]
23, [1] p., 8vo. (20.5 x 13.5 cm.). Sabin 94807, De Renne I:294. GU-De, MWA, NHi, NN, RPJCB.

On last page: Recorded in the Office for Recording of | Deeds, &c. for the City and County of Philadel- | phia . . .

TILLIER, RODOLPHE

Memoire pour Rodolphe Tillier, Commissaire-Gérant de la Compagnie de New-York. | [Caption title] [Colophon:] *De l'Imprimerie de J.C. Parisot [New York, 1800].* [1263]
18 p., 8vo. Sabin 95824. RPJCB.

Signed and dated at end: *Rodolphe Tillier. New-York, le 15 Mai 1800.* Title from Sabin. For translation, see:

. . . . . .

Translation | of a | memorial | of | Rodolphe Tillier's | justification | of the | administration | of | Castorland, | County of Oneida, State of New-York. | [double rule] | *Rome:* | *Printed by Thomas Walker.* | [thick-thin rule] | *October—1800.* [1264]
16 p., 8vo. (19.5 x 11.5 cm.). DLC, NHi (photostat).

Signed and dated at end: *R. Tillier. Rome, Oct. 30, 1800.* Described from photostat of DLC copy at NHi. The author conducted a store in Philadelphia in 1783 according to an advertisement in the *Pennsylvania Packet* of Nov. 18, 1783. He was resident agent of the Compagnie de New-York until removed from office in 1800.

See also under Le Compagnie de New-York and under Pierre Chassanis.

[WILLIAMSON, CHARLES]

Observations | on the | proposed | state road, | from | Hudson's River, near the City of Hudson, to Lake Erie, | by the Oleout, Catharine's, Bath, and Gray's | Settlement, on the Western Bounds | of | Steuben County. | [thin-thick rule] | *New-York:* | *Printed by T. & J. Swords, No. 99 Pearlstreet,* | [rule] | *1800.* [1265]
18 p., folded map, 8vo. (21 x 13 cm.). Sabin 104444. N, NHi, NN, T.W. Streeter, R.W.G. Vail, WHi, WiW-C.

Same map as in his *Description of the settlement,* 1799: Map | of the | *middle states of North America,* | . . .

The old Genesee Road did not reach most of the lands of the English Associates in Western New York of which Williamson was agent. He therefore wrote this pamphlet as part of his eventually successful campaign to build a second road across Western New York some fifty miles south of the old road, thus reaching the principal towns in the tract of the English Associates. He had previously issued a printed broadside subscription paper in promotion of this road: *The Legislature at their last session, having granted considerable aid to improve the Great Road leading from Fort-Schuyler . . . to the county of Ontario* . . . [Albany, 1797]. Broadside, folio. Sabin 104443. NN.

WILLIAMSON, PETER

The life and curious adventures of Peter Williamson . . . *Aberdeen, [ca 1800?].*   [1266]

Title from Anderson Art Galleries auction, February 26, 1901.

. . . . . .

The life and curious adventures of Peter Williamson . . . *Aberdeen: Printed by John Burnett . . . 1801 . . .*   [1267]

144 p., 12mo. (16 x 9.8 cm.). Sabin 104480, Ayer 324. BM, DLC, F.C. Deering, ICN, NN.

. . . . . .

The surprising history of Mr. Peter Williamson . . . *Stirling Printed and sold by C. Randal, 1803.*   [1268]

24 p., 12mo. (16.4 x 9 cm.). Sabin 104490, Ayer 325. BM, ICN.

. . . . . .

The life and curious adventures of Peter Williamson . . . *Edinburgh: Printed by J. Tod & Son, Forrester's Wynd, for W. Coke, bookseller, Leith. 1805. . . .*   [1269]

vi, 138 p., front. port., 12mo. (16.5 x 9.9 cm.). Sabin 104481, Ayer 326. F.C. Deering, ICN, NN.

. . . . . .

Authentic narrative of the life and surprising adventures of Peter Williamson . . . *London: Printed for T. Hughes, Stationers'-Court, by Dewick and Clarke Aldersgate-street. 1806.*   [1270]

[2], [5]-38 p., 12mo. (17.5 x 10.5 cm.). Sabin 104463, Ayer 327. ICN, NHi, NN.

．．．．．

The life and adventures of Peter Williamson, . . . *Liverpool: Printed for T. Troughton, at the Minerva Library, Ranelagh-street. 1807.* [Colophon:] *S. and T. Dodd, Printers, Tythebarn-Street, Liverpool.* [1271]
34 p., front., 12mo. (16.7 x 10.2 cm.). Sabin 104477, Ayer 328. BM, F.C. Deering, ICN, NN, PHi.

．．．．．

Liverpool: Printed by T. Dodd, No. 10, Vernon-street. 1807. [1272]
34 p., 12mo. Sabin 104477. Cover title dated 1808. NN.

．．．．．

Authentic narrative of the life and surprising adventures of Peter Williamson, . . . *New-York, Printed by James Oram, No. 114, Water-Street. 1807.* [1273]
[2], [5]-38 p., front., 12mo. (18.5 x 12 cm.). NHi, PHi.

Frontispiece: *The author discovers Miss Long | bound* [nude] *to a tree.* | [signed:] *Scoles sculp.*

．．．．．

The | life, travels, voyages, | and daring | engagements | of | Paul Jones: | Containing | numerous anecdotes of undaunted | courage. | [filet] | To which is prefixed, | the life and adventures | of | Peter Williamson, | who was kidnapped when an infant from his | native place, Aberdeen, | and | sold for a slave in America. | [thick-thin rule] | *Albany:* | *Printed by E. & E. Hosford.* | [filet] | *1809.* [1274]
96 p., 24mo. (15 x 7.5 cm.). Sabin 36555. F.C. Deering, MH, N, NN, PP.

The Williamson narrative, abridged, occupies p. [47]-96.

．．．．．

Authentic narrative of the life and surprising adventures of Peter Williamson, . . . *London: Printed for the Booksellers, Price six-pence. [1810?].*
[1275]
[2], [5]-34 p., 8vo. Sabin 104463. NN.

Mr. Julian P. Boyd dates this edition [1800?].

．．．．．

The life and astonishing adventures of Peter Williamson, . . . *Glasgow: Printed for the Booksellers. [n.d.]* [Title within a border of type ornaments].
[1275A]
24 p., 12mo. Sabin 104478, Ayer 323. CSmH, ICN, MiU-C.

．．．．．

Same title, without title page border. Sabin 104479. CSmH. [1276]

This and preceding edition have been dated all the way from [ca. 1800 to 1830].

. . . . .

The life and curious adventures of Peter Williamson, . . . *Aberdeen: Printed for the Booksellers. 1812.* [1277]
.144 p., 16mo. (17.4 x 10 cm.). Sabin 104482, Ayer 329. CSmH, DLC, F.C. Deering, ICN, MBAt, MnHi, MWA.

. . . . .

Edinburgh: Printed by John Orphoot, Blackfriars Wynd, for W. Coke, Bookseller, Leith. 1812. (Price one shilling and sixpence.). [1278]
135 p., front. port., 12mo. (18 x 10.5 cm.). Sabin 104481, Ayer 330. ICN, NHi.

. . . . .

The life, travels, voyages, and daring engagements of Paul Jones: . . . [as in 1809 ed.] *Albany: Printed by H.C. Southwick. 1813.* [1279]
108 p., 18mo. Sabin 104464. DLC, F.C. Deering, MWA, NN.
The Williamson narrative has a separate title and occupies p. [43]-103.

. . . . .

Same title. *Hartford: Printed by John Russell, Jr., State Street. And for sale, wholesale and retail. 1813.* [1280]
106 p., 16mo. DLC, F.C. Deering, MH, NN.

. . . . .

Philadelphia, 1817. Title from Mr. Julian P. Boyd. [1281]

. . . . .

Hartford, 1818. Title from Mr. Julian P. Boyd. [1282]

. . . . .

The surprising life and sufferings of Peter Williamson . . . *Falkirk. [1820?].* [1283]
12mo. Sabin 104491. BM.

. . . . .

The eventful life and curious adventures of Peter Williamson, . . . *Glasgow: Published by J. Lumsden & Son. 1821.* [Colophon:] *J. Neilson, printer, Paisley.* [1284]
24 p., 16mo. (16.2 x 9.8 cm.). Sabin 104466, Ayer supp. 140. BM, CSmH, ICN.

Also included in *Wonderful characters* . . . London, 1821. 3 vols., 50 ports., vol. 2, p. 431-449, port. NN.

. . . . . .

The surprising life and sufferings of Peter Williamson . . . *Glasgow.*
1822. [1285]
12mo. Sabin 104491. BM.

. . . . . .

The life and curious adventures of Peter Williamson . . . A new edition.
Aberdeen: Printed for the Booksellers. 1826. [verso of title:] *Aberdeen:*
Printed by R. Cobban & Co. [1286]
[12], 7-155 p., 18mo. (14.9 x 8.3 cm.). Sabin 104483, Ayer 331. DLC.
ICN, NN.
Cover title of NN copy dated 1828.

. . . . . .

Same title. *Aberdeen: Lewis Smith, 66, Broad street. 1841.* [1287]
108 p., 18mo. (14.8 x 9.2 cm.). Sabin 104484, Ayer supp. 141. BM,
ICN, NN-Sc.

. . . . . .

Edinburgh, 1850. Sabin 104484 note. F.C. Deering. [1288]

. . . . . .

The curious adventures of Peter Williamson, . . . *Aberdeen: J. Clark,*
1865. [1289]
120 p., 16mo. NN.

. . . . . .

The life and curious adventures of Peter Williamson, . . . *Aberdeen:*
J. Daniel & Son. 1878. [1290]
108 p. Sabin 104484 note. NN.

. . . . . .

Same title. *Aberdeen: Lewis Smith, and all booksellers. 1878.* [1291]
107 p., 16mo. (15.7 x 9.8 cm.). Sabin 104484 note, Ayer 332. ICN.

. . . . . .

Same title. *Aberdeen: Lewis Smith & Son, and all booksellers. 1885.*
[1292]
107 p., 16mo. (16.3 x 10.2 cm.). Sabin 104484 note, Ayer 333. CSmH,
F.C. Deering, ICN, NN.
Included with the Manheim captivity, 1793 and later, and in many
periodicals and collections.

WINKFIELD, MRS. UNCA ELIZA, *pseud.*

The female American, | or, the | extraordinary adventures | of | Unca Eliza Winkfield. | Compiled by herself | *Newburyport:* | *Printed for & sold by Angier March,* | *North-Corner of Market-Square.* | *[1800?].*   [1293]
213 p., front., 12mo. (17.2 x 10.2 cm.). Sabin 104781. DLC, MeB, MWA, MH, NN.

.   .   .   .   .

The | female American | or the | extraordinary adventures | of | Unca Eliza Winkfield. | Compiled by herself. | *Vergennes, Vt.* | *Published by Jepthah Shedd and Co.* | *Wright & Sibley, printers.* | *1814.*   [1294]
270 p., 18mo. Sabin 104781. MWA, NHi, NN, RPB.

LEZAY-MARNEZIA, CLAUD FRANCOIS ADRIEN, MARQUIS DE

Lettres écrites des rives de l'Ohio, Par Cl. Fr. Ad. de Lezay-Marnezia, Citoyen de Pensylvanie. *Au Fort-Pitt, et se trouvent a Paris, Chez Prault, Imprimeur, rue Taranne, No. 749, à l'Immortalite.* [double rule] *An IX de la République. [1801].*   [1295]
viii, 144 p., 8vo. Sabin 40912, Thomson 718. Bib. Nat., DLC, InHi, MH, MiU-C, NN, OCHP, PPiU, The Rosenbach Company (1945), RPJCB.
The volume was suppressed by the French police.

BRIDEL, REV. [JEAN] LOUIS

Le | pour et le contre | ou | avis | à ceux qui se proposent de passer dans les | États-Unis d'Amérique. | Suivi | d'une description du Kentucky et du Genesy, deux | des nouveaux établissemens les plus considérables | de cette partie du nouveau monde. | Avec une carte typométrique. | Par | Louis Bridel, | Pasteur de l'eglise française à Basle. | [line quoted] | *À Paris | chez Levrault, Schoell & Comp.* | *quay Malaquay.* | *Imprimé à Basle chez Guillaume Haas,* | *an XII. 1803.* | [1296]
[4], 162 p., folded map, 8vo. (18.5 x 11.5 cm.). Map of the Holland Land Company in Western New York, title and text in French, composed with movable type (not engraved), (29.5 x 23 cm.). Issued uncut in red marbled wrappers, dark red paper back. (NHi copy). Bib. Nat., CSmH, DLC, Franco-American Library of Hugh C. Wallace, American Embassy, Paris, 1933, NHi, NN, NRHi, PHi (Amsterdam dealer—H.F. De Puy-Rosenbach copy), R.W.G. Vail.

.   .   .   .

Wie's halt ist, mit dem Reisen | nach | Amerika | besonders in | Kentucky und Genesy. | Nach dem Französischen | des Herrn L. Bridel; | frey übersetzt | von | Christoph Winckelblech. | *Basel,* | *bey Wilhelm Haas und Christoph Winckelblech* | *1804.*   [1297]
88 p., folded map, 8vo. (18 cm.). DLC, NHi, NN.

A translation of original French edition above, with preface paraphrased with additions. Same typometric map used but with text in German.

French original was translated into English by Henry F. De Puy and published in Buffalo Hist. Soc. Pub. 18, 1914, p. 257-312, map slightly reduced; and as a separate, 1914. 56 p., map, in an edition of 25 copies. DLC, N, NN, R.W.G. Vail.

The author, according to Frank Monaghan: *French travellers in the United States,* lived for nearly 20 years in America.

"A new invention of printing has lately been put in practice at Basil in Switzerland. It is a mode of printing maps of countries with type, in the usual manner of letter press. The types consist of an infinite variety of forms, by which the turnings and windings of road, rivers &c. are expressed with a very considerable degree of beauty and accuracy." (From *The Diary,* N.Y., Feb. 23, 1797, p. 3, col. 1.).

The descriptions of Kentucky and the Genesee country in the following work, especially p. 174-243, were largely taken from the French edition of Bridel, with additions from the French, 1785, edition of Filson's *Kentucky* and other contemporary French works on America:

. . . . .

Voyage au Kentoukey, et sur les bords du Genesée, précédé de conseils aux libéraux, et à tous ceux qui se proposent de passer aux États-Unis. Par M *******. [quotation] Ouvrage accompagné d'une carte géographique, levée sur les lieux par l'auteur, en 1820. *Paris, M. Sollier, Editeur, rue Beaujolais, no 7, Palais-Royal; Germain-Mathiot, Libraire, rue du Cimitière Saint-André-des-Arts, no 4. 7bre 1821.* [at foot of last page:] *Imprimerie de P. Gueffier, rue Guénégaud, no. 31.*   [1298]

iv, 243, [1] p., folded map. (21.5 cm.). Though the title page states that the map: *Carte de la partie du Genesée, ou l'on envoie des habitans pour le mettre en culture* (30.5 x 23 cm.) was drawn on the spot by the author, in 1820, the editor states, on p. 204, that he copied it from the Holland Purchase map of 1804, which is obvious by comparison and since Rochester, founded in 1812 and a village of 1500 inhabitants in 1820, does not appear on the map. Sabin 42898 BM, DLC, MB, MH, MiU-C, N, NHi, NN, R.W.G. Vail, WHi.

CHURCH, JOHN B.

A map | shewing the relative situation of a | tract of land belonging to | I.B. Church Esqr. [Caption title within lower border of map] | Jos. Fr. Mangin del. [in left corner] | Peter Maverick sculp. | 20 Nassau Street, N-York [in lower right corner] | New-York, July 1st 1803 [center lower margin] [Text in lower right corner of map:] This | tract of land | contains 100,000 acres, | and is situated on the | Geneseo River; | 22 miles South of | Williamsburg, 100 East of Presque-Isle, | 8 North of the Pennsylvania line, and 16 West of | the navigable waters of the Susquehannah. | [filet] |

[Text continues for 37 lines, describing location, town of Angelica in center of the tract, terms of sale of the lands, etc., signed by the local agent:] | Evert Van Wickle. *[New York, 1803].*   [1299]

The map shows in outline the territory from the Connecticut River west to Presque Isle [Erie, Pa.] and from Baltimore North to Lake Ontario, showing lakes and rivers, roads and tracts, including the location of the Church tract. An inset map (22.5 x 8 cm.) shows the Church tract on a scale of three miles to the inch, as divided into numbered lots. The over-all measurement of the map is 51.5 x 40.5 cm. N, NHi.

The John B. and Philip Church business and family papers were owned some years ago by Mr. R.J. Faust, Jr., Vice President of the Bank of the Manhattan Company of New York. The principal town in the tract was Angelica (named for Angelica Schuyler Church, wife of the founder of the town, Philip Church, son of John B. Church. Angelica Church was the eldest daughter of General Philip Schuyler), county seat of Allegany County, New York.

COOPER, [WILLIAM]

A | guide | in the | wilderness; | or, the | history of the first settlements | in | the western counties | of | New York, | with | useful instructions to future settlers. | In | a series of letters | addressed by | Judge Cooper, | of Coopers-Town, | to | William Sampson, barrister, | of New York. | [rule] | Dublin: | Printed by Gilbert and Hodges, | 27, Dame-Street. | [rule] | 1810.
[1300]

[2], 71 p., 8vo. (23.2 x 14.2 cm.). Church 1304. J.F. Cooper, CSmH, MH, NHi, NN, OClWHi, OO. Mr. H.F. De Puy bought his copy in 1908 from Dodd, Mead & Co. for $100. At his sale on Nov. 18, 1919, no. 642, it was sold to George D. Smith for $190. from whom it went to Dr. William C. Braislin, at whose sale on March 21, 1927, it was sold to Dr. A.S.W. Rosenbach for $275. Next owner unknown, but probably sold to Herschel V. Jones in whose checklist it appears as no. 738. The Jones library was bought by Dr. Rosenbach and, again, the present owner is unknown.

It was reprinted in an edition of 300 copies, with an introduction by James Fenimore Cooper of Albany, N.Y., for George P. Humphrey, *Rochester, N.Y.: The Genesee Press, 1897.* viii, 41 p., 8vo.; and again, same text, with port. of author added, printed at *Cooperstown: The Freeman's Journal Company, April, 1936.* [2], ix, 49 p., port., 8vo.

By a great up-state New York land speculator and pioneer, founder of Cooperstown and father of James Fenimore Cooper. Though a bit late for this bibliography, we could not resist including it because of its interest, importance and rarity.

Index to the Appendix

This index includes the names of authors and their books, titles of anonymous books, biographical references, and a few series and subject entries. *All references are to numbers, not to pages.*

As the chief reference value of the work is in its Bibliography, no index to the lectures has been included, especially as a combination of numbers and page references would make the index more confusing to the user.

A

Abstract, or abbreviation . . . New-Jersey, 194
Account of . . . Carolina, 216, 217
Account of East-Florida, 573-576
Account of Robert Morris' property, 868
Account of the foundation . . . Golden Islands, 329
Account of the proceedings of the Illinois and Ouabache Land Companies, 1089, 1141-1143
Account of the soil, 867
Account shewing the progress . . . Georgia, 411, 418
Account shewing what money . . . Georgia, 420
Acrelius, Israel, *Beskrifning om de Swenska,* 528
Adair, James, *Geschichte der Amerikanischen Indianer,* 673; *History of the American Indians,* 643-644
Address to the inhabitants of Alexandria, 804
Address to the inhabitants of . . . Maine, 865
Advantages of a settlement upon the Ohio, 624
Adventures of Colonel Daniel Boon, 743, 744, 937, 938
Advertisement. [land in New Jersey], 385
Advertisement. At a meeting of the Proprietors of the Town of Brunswick, 454
Advertisement concerning . . . East-New-Jersey, 217 A, 237
Advertisement. The Proprietors of the Kennebeck Purchase, 547, 552
Advertisement, to all trades-men, 226
Advertisement. Whereas, the lands of Narragansett, 190
Affecting history of . . . Frederick Manheim's family, 928, 958, 1146, 1192, 1223, 1224
Alabama, promotion, 1024-1029, 1119, 1133, 1134, 1147, 1177, 1178, 1183
Albion, Earl of, 714-717
Alexander, William, *State of the Earl of Stirling's title,* 587; *To be sold, a tract of land,* 588
Allemagne, ———— d', *Nouvelles du Scioto,* 805

Allen, Mrs. I. *Short narrative of the claim*, 354
Alsop, George, *Character of the Province of Mary-land*, 153
America painted to the life, 143
Amsterdam, Holland, Burgomasters of, *Conditien*, 244, 245
Anderson, ————, 678, 1200
Anderson, Hugh, 413-415
Anderson, John E., and William J. Hobby, *Contract for the purchase of Western Territory . . . Georgia*, 1183
Answer to the remarks of the Plymouth Company, 462
Archdale, John, *New description of . . . Carolina*, 299
Argonautica Gustaviana, 85
Articles of an association by the name of the Ohio Company, 749, 762
Asbury, Francis, *Extract from the journal*, 884-886
Ash, Thomas, *Carolina*, 200
Asplund, John, *Annual register of the Baptist denomination*, 847, 848; *Universal register of the Baptist denomination*, 959
Asylum Company, *Articles of agreement*, 960, 961; *Aux émigrés de . . . Europe*, 962; *Catalogue of the lands and stock*, 1007; *Plan of association*, 1006; *Plan de vente de trois cent mille acres de terres*, 963
Aussführlich und umständlicher Bericht, 309, 310
Authentic memoirs of William Augustus Bowles, 859
Aux émigrés . . . Europe, 962
Avis a ceux qui voudraient s'en aller en Amerique, 696
Azilia, 322, 323
Azilum, 960-963, 1006, 1007

B

Baltimore, Cecil Calvert, Lord, 84, 86, 88, 106
Bancroft, Edward, 649, 652, 663
Banners of grace and love, 141
Banyar, Goldsborow, 616
Bard, John, *Letter to the proprietors of the Great-Nine-Partners-Tract*, 448
Barrow, Robert, 281
Barry, Thomas, *Narrative of the singular adventures*, 1225, 1226, 1228; *Singular adventures*, 1227
Barth, ———— de, *Lettre*, 805 A
Bartram, John, 576, 600; *Observations on the inhabitants . . . Pensilvania to Onondago*, 449
Bartram, William, *Travels through North and South Carolina*, 849-858
Bateman, Edmund, *Sermon . . . Georgia*, 407
Bayard, Nicholas, and Charles Lodowick, *A journal of the late actions of the French in Canada*, 267; *Narrative of an attempt made by the French of Canada upon the Mohaques country*, 266
Bayard, Stephen N., *Mohawk General Land-Office. . . . Office rules*, 887
Bearcroft, Philip, *Sermon . . . Georgia*, 401
Beatty, Charles, *Journal of a two months tour*, 589; *Tagebuch einer zween Reise*, 608
Beaumetz, Bon Albert Briois de, *900,000 acres of land offered for sale*, 984
Beissel, Johann Conrad, *Vorspiel der Neuen-Welt*, 361
Berczy, William, 868
Bericht für Diejenigen, 727

Berichte über den Genesee-Distrikt, 868

Berkeley, William, *Discourse and view of Virginia,* 147

Berriman, William, *Sermon . . . Georgia,* 404

Beschrijvinge van Nieuw-Nederlant, 136

Beverley, Robert, *Histoire de la Virginie,* 300-303; *History and present state of Virginia,* 297, 337-339

Bidwell, Barnabas, *Susquehannah title stated and examined,* 1050

Bingham, William, 952

Bishop, Abraham, *Georgia speculation unveiled,* 1095, 1147

Bland, Edward, *Discovery of New Brittaine,* 123

Bleecker, Ann Eliza (Schuyler), *History of Maria Kittle,* 1096, 1097; *Posthumous works,* 929

Blodget, Samuel, *Prospective plan of the battle near Lake George,* 473

Blome, Richard, *Amerique angloise,* 253; *Description des isles et terres,* 254; *Englischem America,* 255; *Present state of His Majesties isles and territories in America,* 252

Bloody Indian battle, 897

Bloüin, Daniel, 613

Board of General Proprietors of the Eastern Division of New Jersey. [Scottish Proprietors' Tracts], 173, 194, 201, 210, 217 A, 218, 223, 226, 237

Boehme, Anton Wilhelm, *Das verlangte, nicht erlangte Canaan,* 314, 315

Bolzius, Johann Martin, 382

Bom, Cornelius, 236; *Missive van . . . geschreven uit de Stadt Philadelphia,* 238

Bonoeil, John, *His Maiesties gracious letter,* 53; *Observations to be followed . . . silk-wormes,* 43

Boone, Daniel, 694, 726, 743, 744, 809, 937, 938, 939

Bouquet, Henry, 564, 572, 598, 657

Bowles, William Augustus, *Authentic memoirs,* 859

Bownas, Samuel, 355; *Account of the life, travels,* 496, 529, 546, 1008, 1010; *Journals,* 530

Brackenridge, Hugh Henry, *Incidents of the insurrection,* 1011

Bradford, William, 60; *History of Plymouth Plantation,* 846

Bradley, Hannah Heath, 307

Bradman, Arthur, *Narrative of . . . sufferings of Mr. Robert Forbes,* 860, 861, 888, 889, 930-932, 964, 1098, 1099

Bradstreet, Simon, *An advertisement,* 190

Brainerd, David, *Mirabilia Dei inter Indicos,* 432

Breck, Robert, *Departure of Elijah lamented . . . funeral of the Rev. Stephen Williams,* 1049 A

Breeden-Raedt, 112

Brereton, John, *Briefe and true relation,* 9, 10

Bridel, Jean Louis, *Le Pour et le contre,* 1296; *Voyage au Kentoukey,* 1298; *Wie's halt ist,* 1297

Brief account of . . . East: New: Jersey, 218

Brief account of . . . Georgia, 426

Brief account of . . . Pennsylvania, 198, 206, 207

Brief account of the Province of East-Jersey, 201, 202

Brief and true narration of the late wars risen in New-England, 163

Brief, decent, but free remarks, 676

Brief description of Carolina, 154

Brief history of the rise and progress of the charitable scheme, 491

Briefe declaration, 41

Briefe eines Amerikanischen Landmanns, 773
Briefe relation of . . . New England, 57
Brieven van eenen Amerikaenschen Landman, 691
Brissot de Warville, Jean Pierre, J. P. *Brissot's Nya resa*, 1184; J. P. *Brissot's von Warwille Reise*, 894, 895; *Neue Reise*, 893, 1051; *New travels*, 890-892, 965-967, 1102; *Nieuwe Reize*, 968; *Nouveau voyage*, 862
Brooke, Christopher, *A poem on the late massacre in Virginia*, 54
Brown, Charles Brockden, *Edgar Huntly*, 1185
Brown, Thomas, *Plain narrative of the uncommon sufferings*, 537-540
Bruce, Lewis, *Happiness of man the glory of God. A sermon . . . Georgia*, 427
Brunswick Township, Maine, Proprietors, 447, 454, 461-464, 547, 552
Budd, Thomas, *Good order established in Pennsilvania & New-Jersey*, 239
Bué, ————, *Compagnie de Scioto*, 805 B
Bullock, William, *Virginia impartially examined*, 113
Bunn, Matthew, *Bloody Indian battle*, 897; *Journal of the adventures*, 1052-1054; *Narrative*, 1104-1108; *St. Clair's defeat. A poem*, 896; *Short narrative*, 1103; *Tragical account*, 897
Bushnell, Charles I., *Crumbs for antiquarians*, 1167
By his Maiesties Counsell of Virginea, 34

C

Cabeza de Vaca, Alvar Nuñez, 1, 2
Calvert, Cecil, Baron Baltimore, *Moderate and safe expedient*, 106; *Relation of Maryland*, 88
Campanius Holm, Tomas, *Kort beskrifning om . . . Nya Swerige*, 291
Campbell, Donald, *Case of*, 580
Campbell, Lauchlin, 580
Campbell, Patrick, *Travels*, 933
Carew, Bampfylde-Moore, *Life and adventures*, 430, 431
Carey, Matthew, *Information for Europeans*, 806
Carolana (Ala., Fla., Ga., La., Miss.), promotion, 340, 350, 353, 409, 410
Carolina (see also under N. C. and S. C.), promotion, 151, 154, 200, 203, 204, 216, 217, 219, 227, 246, 251, 299, 309-311, 316, 319, 324, 344, 345, 379, 381
Carolina, Lords Proprietors of, *Carolina described more fully*, 227; *True description of Carolina*, 203
Carolina described more fully, 227
Carolina; or a description, 200
Carver, Jonathan, *Aventures*, 1159; *Carver's travels in Wisconsin*, 1157; *J. Carver's Reisen*, 1156; *Reisen*, 664; *Reize*, 1056; *Three years travels*, 687, 790, 898, 1012, 1055, 1109, 1149, 1150, 1152-1155, 1158; *Travels*, 654, 658, 659, 670; *Voyage*, 688, 689, 1151
Case of Mr. John Gordon, 616 A
Case of the Georgia sales, 1119, 1190-1191
Castorland, 934, 1058, 1229, 1263, 1264
Cautionary hints to Congress, 1013, 1057
Chalkley, Thomas, *Collection of the works*, 441, 450, 466; *Journal*, 451
Chassanis, Pierre, 934, 1058, 1229, 1263, 1264; *Description topographique*, 899; *Réponse au mémoire de Mr. Tillier*, 1229
Chauncy, Charles, *Letter to a friend*, 474-476; *Second letter to a friend*, 477; *Two letters to a friend*, 478

Chauncy, Isaac, *Blessed manumission . . . funeral of Reverend Mr. John Williams,* 1049 A

Chetwood, W. R., *Voyages . . . of Captain Richard Falconer,* 326, 349, 374, 375, 555, 591, 720-722

Christie, Thomas, *Description of Georgia,* 408

Chronicon Ephratense, 748

Church, Benjamin, 321

Church, John B. *Map shewing . . . a tract of land belonging to I. B. Church,* 1299

Church, Thomas, *Entertaining history of King Philip's War,* 611; *Entertaining passages relating to Philip's War,* 321

Clap, Roger, *Memoirs,* 358, 569, 627, 628

Clazon, William, 613

Clement, Timothy, *Plan of Hudson's River,* 473

Clinton, James, *To be sold . . . lands in . . . New-York,* 791

Colden, Cadwallader, *History of the Five Indian Nations,* 352, 435, 444, 479, 480; *History of the Six Nations,* 1110; *Papers relating to . . . encouragement of the Indian trade,* 342

Collection of voyages and travels, in three parts, 410

Colles, Christopher, *Proposals for the speedy settlement of . . . lands,* 723

Colonization tract, first, 5

Columbian tragedy, 863, 864

Columbus, *Cautionary hints to Congress,* 1013, 1057

Comly, John, *Narrative of the captivity . . . of Benjamin Gilbert,* 843

Compagnie du Kentucky, *Notice sur Kentucke,* 792

Compagnie de New-York, 1229, 1263, 1264; *Constitution,* 934; *Faits et calculus,* 1058

Compagnie de l'Occident, 328

Compagnie de Wilmington, *Prospectus,* 1111

Company of Mississippi, 328

Company of the Indies, 328

Conditions for letting or selling . . . New Albion, 714

Condy, Jonathan Williams, *Description of the River Susquehanna,* 1059

Congregational Church in Connecticut, *Address to the inhabitants of the new settlements,* 935, 1014; *Continuation of the narrative,* 971-976; *Narrative of the missions,* 970

Connecticut, promotion, 138, 485, 486

Connecticut, General Assembly, *Act . . . incorporating the proprietors of the Sufferers' Land,* 1060; *Report of the Commissioners appointed . . . to treat with Pennsylvania,* 629

Connecticut Gore Land Company, *Articles of agreement,* 1015, 1061; *Brief articles of agreement,* 1016; *Connecticut Gore title stated and considered,* 1186; *Supplementary articles of agreement,* 1062

Connecticut Land Company, *Articles of association,* 1017; *For sale and settlement in Connecticut Reserve,* 1187; *Lands in New-Connecticut,* 1160; *Mode of partition of the Western Reserve,* 1063; *Votes,* 1018

Considerations on the agreement . . . Thomas Walpole . . . lands upon the river Ohio, 639

Considering there is no publicke action, 20

Contest in America between Great Britain and France, 520

Continuation of the state of New-England, 171

Cooper, Thomas, *Extract of a letter . . . on . . . emigration,* 979; *Renseignemens sur l'Amérique,* 1019, 1020; *Some information respecting America,* 977; *Thoughts on emigration,* 978
Cooper, William, *Guide in the wilderness,* 1300
Copia eines Send-Schreibens, 271
Copland, Patrick, *A declaration how the monies,* 55; *Virginia's God be thanked,* 56
Council for New England, 71; *Briefe relation of . . . New England,* 57
Coxe, Daniel, *Collection of voyages,* 410; *Description of . . . Carolana,* 340, 350, 353, 409
Coxe, Tench, *View of the United States,* 977
Crafford, John, *New and most exact account of . . . Carolina,* 219
Crashaw, William, *Sermon preached in London,* 22
Crawford, William, 684, 1201-1204
Crèvecoeur, Michel-Guillaume Saint-Jean de, *Briefe eines Amerikanischen Landsmanns,* 773; *Brieven van eenen Amerikaenschen Landman,* 691; *Letters from an American farmer,* 674, 675, 681, 682, 936; *Lettres d'un cultivateur Américain,* 692, 693, 724, 725, 752; *Sittliche Schilderung von Amerika,* 690
Crime and criminals, 357, 430, 431, 953, 954, 1148
Crosbie, Andrew, 548
Crowe, William, *Duty of public spirit . . . sermon . . . Georgia,* 405
Crozat, Anthony, *Letter to a member,* 318
Currie, William, *Historical account of the climate and diseases,* 900
Cushman, Robert, *Sermon preached at Plimmoth,* 58
Cutler, Manasseh, *Description du sol . . . Ohio,* 793; *Explanation of the map . . . Ohio,* 753, 774

D

Dalton, James, *Life and actions,* 357
Davis, Daniel, *Address to the inhabitants of . . . Maine,* 865
Day breaking, if not the sun-rising, 108
Decalves, Alonso, *Ganz neue und sehr merkwürdige Reisebeschreibung,* 1064; *New travels to the westward,* 775, 776, 807, 1023, 1065-1068, 1117, 1118, 1188; *Travels to the westward,* 980, 981, 1021, 1022, 1112-1116, 1161
Decennium luctuosum, 282
Declaration for . . . drawing the . . . lottery, 39
Declaration how the monies, 55
Declaration of former passages . . . Narrowgansets, 105
Declaration of the Lord Baltimore's plantation in Mary-land, 85 A
Declaration of the state of the Colonie . . . Virginia, 45-49
Declaration of the state of . . . Virginia, 66
Defense of the remarks of the Plymouth Company, 463, 464
Delaware, promotion, 85 A, 97, 110, 118, 149, 291, 528, 714-717, 1111
De La Warr, Thomas West, 3d Baron, 31
Denton, Daniel, *Brief description of New-York,* 157
Derkinderen, James, *Narrative of the sufferings,* 1069
Description abrégée de . . . Caroline, 359, 367
Description abrégée du territoire . . . sud de l'Ohio, 956
Description du sol . . . Ohio, 793
Description of East-Florida, 600
Description of Georgia, 408
Description of Kentucky, 923

Description of New England, 40
Description of Occacock Inlet, 1040
Description of the Genesee Country, 1182, 1221
Description of the Golden Islands, 330
Description of the Province of New Albion, 110, 118
Description of the Province of West-Jersey, 178
Description of the River Susquehanna, 1059
Description of the settlement of the Genesee Country, 1221
Description of the situation . . . land in . . . Maine, 952
Description topographique de six cents mille acres de terres, 899
De Soto, Hernando de, 3
Dickenson, Jonathan, *God's protecting Providence,* 281, 284, 285, 288, 327, 376, 386, 452, 531, 612, 754, 808, 866, 903, 906; *Göttliche Beschützung,* 497, 498; *Jonathan Dickinson's erstaunliche Geschichte,* 630; *Jonathan Dickinson's journal,* 907; *Narrative of a shipwreck,* 902, 904; *Ongelukkige schipbreuk,* 304, 305; *Remarkable deliverance of Robert Barrow,* 901
Direction for adventurers, 97
Discourse and view of Virginia, 147
Discovery of New Brittaine, 123
Dodge, John, *Entertaining narrative,* 665-666; *Narrative of the capture,* 660, 665, 666
Donck, Adriaen van der, *Beschrijvinge van Nieuw-Nederlant,* 133, 136; *Vertoogh van Nieu-Neder-Land,* 117
Donne, John, *Sermon,* 59
Doolittle, Thomas, *Short narrative of mischief done by the French and Indian enemy,* 445
Douglas, Da., 413-415
Douglass, William, *Summary, historical and political,* 442, 455
Drayton, John *Letters written during a tour,* 982
Drown, Solomon, *Oration delivered at Marietta,* 794
Duodecennium luctuosum, 320
Durand, ————, *Voyage d'un Francois . . . Virgine & Marilan,* 256
Durans, ————, 256
Dustan, Hannah, 275, 282, 294
Dutch West India Company, 79, 82, 83, 139, 140
Dyer, Eliphalet, *Remarks on Dr. Gale's letter,* 592

E

Earl of Albion's proclamation, 715
Eastburn, Robert, *Faithful narrative,* 522, 523
Eastern lands for sale, 777
Edgar Huntly, 1185
Egmont, John Perceval, Second Earl of, *Faction detected,* 424
Eliot, John, *Brief narrative of the progress,* 158; *Further accompt of the progresse of the Gospel,* 142, 145; *Late and further manifestation,* 134; (with Thomas Mayhew) *Glorious progress,* 114; *Tears of repentance,* 131
Eliot Indian Tracts, 98, 108, 111, 114, 124, 127, 131, 134, 142, 145, 158
Ellicott, Benjamin, 1231-1233
Ellicott, Joseph, *Holland Land Company West Geneseo Lands,* 1230; (with Benjamin Ellicott) *Map of Morris's Purchase or West Geneseo,* 1232, 1233; *Map of two million acres of land West Genesee,* 1231

Elvas, Gentleman of, *Relaçam verdadeira*, 3; *Virginia richly valued*, 13; *Worthye and famous history* . . . *Florida*, 29
Emigration to America, 1180
Enquiry into the causes of the alienation of the Delaware and Shawanese Indians, 535
Entertaining passages relating to Philip's War, 321
Ephrata Community, 361, 748
Erzehlung von den Trübsalen . . . *William Flemming*, 507-509
Erzehlungen von Maria le Roy, 532
Evans, Israel, *Discourse delivered at Easton*, 661-662
Evans, Lewis, *Geographical, historical*, . . . *essays* . . . *map of the Middle British Colonies*, 481-484; Same, *Number II*, 499, 500
Evans, Ned, 1092, 1093, 1144, 1145
Evelin or Evelyn, John, *A direction for adventurers*, 97
Examination of the Connecticut claim, 633, 634
Explanation of the map which delineates . . . *Ohio*, 753, 774
Extract from the account of East Florida, 577
Extract of a letter . . . *on* . . . *emigration*, 979

F

F., R., *Present state of Carolina*, 204
Faction detected, 424
Faits et calculus sur la population . . . *des États-Unis*, 1058
Falckner, Daniel, 295; *Curieuse Nachricht von Pensylvania*, 292
Falckner, Justus, *Abdruck eines Schreibens* . . . *aus Germanton in* . . . *Pensylvania*, 293
Falconer, Richard, 326, 349, 374, 375, 555, 591, 720-722
Farther brief and true narrative of the late wars risen in New-England, 172
Female American, 1293, 1294
Fenwick, John, *Friends, these are to satisfie you*, 164; *Testimony against*, 165; *True state of the case*, 183, 560.
Fessenden, John, *Sermon preached* . . . *in Deerfield*, 1049 A
Filson, John, 745; *Adventures of Colonel Daniel Boon*, 743, 744, 937, 938; *Discovery, settlement and present state of Kentucke*, 694, 939; *Histoire de Kentucke*, 726; *Reise nach Kentucke*, 809
Findley, William, *History of the insurrection* . . . *Pennsylvania*, 1070
Finest part of America, 716
Fish, Jesse, 616 A
Fisher, Miers, *Brief of the titles of Robert Morris*, 868
Fiske, Nathan, *Remarkable providences*, 650
Fitzroy, Alexander, *Discovery* . . . *of Kentuckie*, 745
Fleming, William and Elizabeth, 630; *Erzehlung von den Trübsalen* . . . *William Flemming*, 507-509; *Narrative of the sufferings*, 501-506
Fletcher, Ebenezer, *Narrative of the captivity*, 1162-1167
Flores, Bartolomé de, *Obra nvevamente compvesta*, 5
Florida, promotion, 5, 13, 29, 573-577, 600, 616 A, 635
For the planting in Virginia, 21
Forasmuch and notwithstanding . . . *lotteries*, 34
Forbes, Abby, 1100, 1101
Forbes, Robert, 860, 861, 888, 889, 930-932, 964, 1098, 1099, 1100, 1101
Ford, Philip, *Vindication of William Penn*, 220, 221

Four Kings of Canada, 312

Frame, Richard, *Short description of Pennsilvania,* 263

Frame of the government of . . . Pennsilvania, 208, 261

Francklin, Thomas, *Sermon . . . Georgia,* 446

Franklin, Benjamin, 617; *Avis a ceux qui voudraient s'en aller en Amerique,* 696; *Bericht für Diejenigen,* 727; *Information to those who would remove to America,* 695, 977; *Narrative of the late massacres,* 556; *Observazione a chiunque dersideri passare in America,* 727; *Remarks concerning the savages of North-America,* 697; *Remarques sur la politesse des sauvages de l'Amerique Septentrionale,* 698; *Two tracts,* 699-702

Franklin, William Temple, *Account of the soil,* 867; *Berichte über den Genesee-Distrikt,* 868

Free Society of Traders in Pennsylvania, *Articles, settlement and offices of,* 205

French East India Company, 328

Frontiers well defended, 306

Frowde, Neville, 618, 915

Full and authentic narrative of the sufferings . . . of William and Elizabeth Fleming, 505

Full and impartial account of the Company of Mississipi, 328

Fuller, Sylvester, *New Ohio lands,* 1189

Further accompt of the progresse of the Gospel, 142

Further account of East-New-Jersey, 223

Further account of New Jersey, 173

Further account of . . . Pennsylvania, 240, 241

G

Gage, Thomas, *General Gage's instructions,* 645

Gale, Benjamin, *Brief, decent, but free remarks,* 676; *Doct. Gale's letter to J. W.,* 593; *Observations on a pamphlet,* 594

Gatenby, William, *Full and particular account of the sufferings,* 703

Gay, Bunker, 910

General Gage's instructions, 645

Georgia (in New England), proposed Province, *Abstract of the scheme,* 334; *Doctor [Charles] Pinfold's state of the case,* 335; *Memorial, humbly shewing,* 333

Georgia, promotion, 363-365, 368-373, 377, 378, 382, 383, 387, 389, 393, 394, 396, 397, 399, 400, 401, 404-408, 411-415, 417-428, 433, 434, 440, 443, 446, 470, 1024-1029, 1035-1037, 1095, 1119, 1133, 1134, 1147, 1177, 1178, 1183, 1239

Georgia, a poem, 397

Georgia, oder: kurtze Nachricht, 368

Georgia, Trustees for establishing the Colony of, in America, 363-366, 369-372, 411, 412, 418, 433; promotion sermons: 373, 377, 383, 396, 400, 401, 404, 405, 407, 425, 427, 434, 440, 443, 446; *Resolutions,* 417

Georgia Mississippi Company, *Grant,* 1024-1026; *State of facts,* 1027

Georgiana, proposed colony west of Vandalia, on the Mississippi near Natchez, 624

Gilbert, Benjamin, 718, 742, 840-845

God's mercy surmounting man's cruelty, 467

Golden Islands, 329, 330

Good fetch'd out of evil, 686

Good newes from New-England, 69, 109

Good newes from Virginia, 37, 67
Good speed to Virginia, 14
Gookin, Daniel, *Historical account of the doings . . . of the Christian Indians*, 909; *Historical collections*, 908; *To all persons*, 137
Gordon, John, 616 A
Gorges, Ferdinando, *America painted to the life*, 143
Grace, Henry, *History of the life and sufferings*, 557, 561
Graham, John, *John Graham's address*, 755
Grand Ohio Company, 610, 617, 624, 626, 639, 640, 648, 649-652, 663, 672
Gray, Bunker, 910
Gray, Robert, *Good speed to Virginia*, 14
Great examples of judgment and mercy, 272
Greevous grones for the poore, 51
Grondel, Jean-Philippe Goujon de, *Lettre d'un officier de la Louisiane*, 558
Guy, W. H., *Abby Forbes*, 1100, 1101
Gyles, John, *Memoirs of odd adventures*, 391

H

Hales, Stephen, *Sermon . . . Georgia*, 377
Hammon, Briton, *Narrative of the uncommon sufferings*, 541
Hammond, John, *Leah and Rachel*, 137 A
Hamor, Ralph, *True discourse of . . . Virginia*, 38
Hanson, Elizabeth, *Abstract of an account*, 551; *Account of the captivity*, 542, 543, 677, 756, 869, 871-873; *Account of the remarkable captivity*, 876; *God's mercy surmounting man's cruelty*, 355, 467, 667, 870; *Remarkable captivity*, 874, 875
Hariot, Thomas, *A briefe and true report*, 6, 7
Harper, Robert Goodloe, *Case of the Georgia sales*, 1119, 1190, 1191; *Observations on the North American Land Company*, 1071-1073
Hartshorne, Richard, *Further account of New Jersey*, 173
Harvest, George, *Sermon . . . Georgia*, 443
Hastings, Susannah Willard (Johnson), *Captive American*, 1121, 1122; *Narrative of the captivity*, 1074, 1120, 1123-1127; *New England pioneer*, 1128
Hazard, Samuel, *Scheme for the settlement of a new colony*, 485, 486
Hennepin, Louis, *Description de la Louisiane*, 222; *New discovery*, 278, 279; *Nouveau voyage, Nouvelle decouverte*, 274
Henry, William, *Account of the captivity*, 570
Het groote Tafereel, 328
Higginson, Francis, *New Englands plantation*, 72-74
Hilliard d'Auberteuil, Michel René, *Mis Mac Rea, roman historique*, 704
Hillsborough, Lord, 617
Hilton, William, *Relation of a discovery . . . Florida*, 151
Historical account of the expedition against the Ohio Indians, 564, 572
History and present state of Virginia, 297
History of . . . Mr. Anderson, 468, 469, 678, 1200
History of Ned Evans, 1092, 1093, 1144, 1145
History of the Five Indian Nations, 352
Hobby, William J., 1183
Hodgkinson, ———, *Letters on emigration*, 983
Holland Land Company, 1230-1233; *Map of the Holland Purchase*, 984
Hollandsche Land Compagnie, 984, 1230-1233

Hollister, Isaac, *Brief narrative of the captivity*, 581-584
Hopkins, Samuel, *Abridgment of Mr. Hopkins's historical memoirs . . . Housatun-nuk or Stockbridge Indians*, 517; *Address to the people of New-England*, 518; *Historical memoirs relating to the Housatunnuk Indians*, 460
Horrid Indian cruelties! Affecting history . . . Frederic Manheim's family, 1192
Hortop, Job, *Travailes of an Englishman*, 8
How, Nehemiah, *Narrative of the captivity*, 437, 438
Howe, Jemima, *Affecting history*, 911; *Genuine and correct account of the captivity*, 910; *Narrative of the captivity*, 912
Hubbard, John Niles, *sketches of . . . Moses Van Campen*, 710-713
Hubbard, William, *History of the Indian wars*, 757; *Narrative of the Indian wars of New-England*, 646, 1193-1199; *Narrative of the troubles with the Indians*, 184; *Present state of New England*, 185
Humble request, 76
Humiliation follow'd with deliverances, 275
Humphreys, David, *Essay on the life of . . . Israel Putnam*, 778, 985, 1168; *Interesting life . . . Israel Putnam*, 1170; *Life and adventures of Israel Putnam*, 1171; *Life of Israel Putnam*, 1169
Hutchins, Thomas, *Description topographique de la Virginie,.*671; *Historical narrative . . . Louisiana*, 705; *Proposals for publishing . . . a map of the coast of West Florida*, 706; *Topographical description of Virginia*, 655, 758, 759

I

Illinois and Wabash Land Companies, 1089, 1141-1143; *Memorial*, 1129
Imlay, Gilbert, *Description of the Western territory*, 943; *Emigrants*, 940, 986; *Nachrichten von dem Westlichen Lande*, 944; *Topographical description*, 913, 941, 942, 1130
Impartial enquiry . . . Georgia, 412
Inconveniences that have happened, 62
Indian atrocities. Narratives of . . . Dr. Knight and John Slover, 1203, 1204
Indiana, proposed colony in present West Virginia, 649, 652, 663, 672
Indians, Captives (first editions, arranged by subject), Anderson, Mr. ————, 468; Barrow, Robert, 281; Barry, Thomas, 1225; Boone, Daniel, 694; Bradley, Hannah (Heath), 307; Brown, Thomas, 537; Bunn, Matthew, 1052; Carver, Jonathan, 654; Crawford, William, 684; Derkinderen, James, 1069; Dickenson, Jonathan, 281; Dodge, John, 660; Dustan, Hannah, 275; Eastburn, Robert, 522; Evans, Ned, 1092; Falconer, Richard, 326; Fleming, William and Elizabeth, 501; Fletcher, Ebenezer, 1162; Frowde, Neville, 618; Gatenby, William, 703; Gilbert, Benjamin, 718; Grace, Henry, 557; Graham, John, 755; Gyles, John, 391; Hammon, Briton, 541; Hanson, Elizabeth, 355; Hastings, Susannah Willard (Johnson), 1074; Hennepin, Louis, 222; Henry, William, 570; Hollister, Isaac, 581; Hortop, Job, 8; How, Nehemiah, 437; Howe, Jemima, 910; Huntley, Edgar, 1185; Johnson, Susannah Willard, *see* Hastings, Susannah Willard (Johnson); Johonnot, Jackson, 877; Kinnan, Mary, 1032; Kittle (or Kittlehuyne), Maria, 929; Knight, John, 684; [Lady in a Cave, Abraham Panther's], 766; Leininger, Barbara and Regina, 532; Le Roy, Marie, 532; Lowry, Jean, 544; McCrea, Jane, 704; McDonald, Philip, 747; McLeod, Alexander, 747; Manheim, Frederick, 928; Marrant, John, 730; Maylem, John, 524; Menzies, David, 656; Morris, Isaac, 453; Morris, Thomas, 880; Norton, John, 439; Nuñez Cabeza de Vaca, Alvar, 1; Oritz, Juan, 3; Putnam, Israel, 778; Ramsay, David, 933;

[Returned captive "John ————"], 769; Rhodes, John, 750; Roach, John, 736; Rouso d'Eres, Charles Dennis, 1248; Rowlandson, Mary, 211; Saunders, Charles, 553; Scott, Frances, 738; Scudder, William, 1004; Slover, John, 684; Smith, James, 1216; Smith, Captain John, 68; Staden, Hans, 4; Stockwell, Quentin, 228; Swarton, Hannah, 275; Swetland, Luke, 739; Van Campen, Moses, 669; Vandeleur (various spellings), John, 775; Wallwille, Maria Owliam, Gräfin von, 1220; Williams, John, 308; Williamson, Peter, 521; Willis, Hannah, 1222; Winkfield, ———— (father of Unca Eliza Winkfield), 586
Indians, first captive among, 1
Indians, first English captive among, 8
Indians (North American), first pictures of, 7
Indians, Connecticut, Wars, 92, 93, 392
Indians, New England, 58, 102, 108, 111, 114, 124, 127, 131, 134, 142, 145, 158, 160, 269, 460, 518, 650
Indians, New England, Wars, 91, 92, 105, 132, 163, 168, 170, 171, 172, 174, 176, 177, 179-182, 184, 186, 189, 191, 192, 228, 258, 264, 268, 272, 282, 298, 306, 307, 320, 321, 346, 348, 351, 356, 445
Indians, New Jersey, 432
Indians, New York, 104, 157, 312, 342, 352, 402, 449, 513, 554
Indians, New York, Wars, 266, 286
Indians, Pennsylvania, 432, 556, 615, 680, 788, 795, 917, 990, 991, 1000, 1001
Indians, Southern and Western, 222, 274, 277, 429, 535, 562, 563, 565, 571, 589, 631, 643, 795, 849, 859, 878, 879, 917, 920, 989, 990, 991, 1000, 1001, 1091
Indians, Southern and Western, Wars, 562-564, 571, 863, 864, 880, 896, 897
Indians, Virginia, 7, 68, 343
Indians, Virginia, Wars, 54, 64, 67, 68
Information and direction to such persons as are inclined to America, 230, 247
Information concerning . . . North Carolina, 622
Information for Europeans, 806
Information to emigrants . . . New York and Pensylvania, 623
Information to those who would remove to America, 695
Insinuatie, Protestatie, ende Presentatie, 99
Instruction très-exacte, 248
Invitation serieuse aux habitants des Illinois, 613

J

Jackson, James, Letters of Sicilius, 1028, 1029
Jamestown, first account of, 12
Jefferson, Thomas, Appendix to the Notes on Virginia, 1234, 1235; Jefferson's notes on the State of Virginia, 1236-1238; Notes on the State of Virginia, 728, 760, 779, 987; Observations sur la Virginie, 746
Johnson, Edward, History of New-England, 132
Johnson, Robert, New life of Virginia, 32; Nova Britannia, 15
Johnson, Susannah Willard, 1074
Johnson, William, Camp at Lake George, Sept. 9. 1755, 487-490; Relação de huma batalha . . . Lake Giorge, 519
Johnston, Georges Milligen, Short description of . . . South-Carolina, 601
Johnston, William, 1040
Johonnot, Jackson, Remarkable adventures, 877, 914, 945-951, 1030, 1031, 1172-1175

Jones, David, *Journal of two visits*, 631
Jones, Hugh, *Present state of Virginia*, 343
Jones, [Captain John] Paul, 1274, 1279-1282
Josselyn, John, *Account of two voyages to New-England*, 162, 166; *New-Englands rarities*, 160, 167
Jourdain, Silvester, *Discovery of the Bermudas*, 23; *Plaine description of the Barmvdas*, 35

K

Kayadarosseras Patent Verkoop . . . Patent van, 729
Kellet, Alexander, *Mental novelist*, 683; *Pocket of prose and verse*, 656
Kennebeck Purchase, 447, 454, 461-464, 547, 552
Kentucky, description and promotion, 694, 745, 792, 923, 924, 998, 1035-1037, 1298
Kimber, Edward, *History of . . . Mr. Anderson*, 468, 469, 678, 1200; *Life . . . of Capt. Neville Frowde*, 618, 915
King, James, *Sermon . . . Georgia*, 425
King Philip's War Narratives (Folios), 168, 169, 171, 176, 181, 189; (Quartos), 163, 170, 172, 174, 177, 179, 180, 182, 184, 186, 321, 611
Kinnan, Mary, 1032-1033
Kittle, Maria, 929, 1096, 1097
Kleinknecht, Conrad Daniel, *Conrad Daniel Kleinknechts . . . Zuverlässige Nachricht*, 406
Knight, John, and John Slover, *Indian atrocities*, 1203, 1204; *Narrative of a late expedition*, 1201; *Narratives of a late expedition*, 684; *Remarkable narrative of an expedition*, 1202
Kocherthal, Joshua von, *Ausführlich und umständlicher Bericht*, 309, 310
Kollock, Shepard, 1032, 1033
Kort Bericht van Penn-Sylvania, 196
Kort Verhael van Nieuw-Nederlants, 148
Kurtze Nachricht von der Christlichen . . . Anstalt, 492
Kurtze Nachricht von . . . Pennsilvania, 199
Kurtze Relation . . . Georgien, 378

L

Laet, Joannes de, *Beschrijvinghe van West-Indien*, 75; *Histoire du Nouveau Monde*, 96; *Historie ofte Iaerlijck Verhael*, 103; *Nieuw Wereldt*, 70; *Novvs Orbis seu Descriptionis*, 84
Lampe, Barend, and Nicholaas van Wassenaer, *Historisch Verhael*, 65
Lands in New-Connecticut, 1160
Law, John, *Full and impartial account of the Company of Mississipi*, 328
Lawson, John, *Allerneueste Beschreibung . . . Carolina*, 316; *History of Carolina*, 319, 324; *New voyage to Carolina*, 311
Le Beau, Claude, *Avantures*, 402; *Geschichte des Herrn C. Le Beau*, 456-458: *Karl le Beau's Begebenheiten . . . Reise*, 988
Lederer, John, *Discoveries of*, 161
Leininger, Barbara and Regina, 532, 533
Le Roy, Marie, *Erzehlungen*, 532; *Narrative*, 533

Lescarbot, Marc, *Nova Francia*, 16, 17
Letter from New-England, 215
Letter from a Romish priest, 356
Letter from South Carolina, 313, 325, 362
Letter to a friend . . . Ohio defeat, 474-476
Letter to a member of the P————t, 318
Letters from an American farmer, 674, 675, 681, 682, 936
Letters of Sicilius, 1028, 1029
Letters on emigration, 983
Lettre d'un officier de la Louisiane, 558
Lettre écrit par un Français, 809 A
Lettres d'un cultivateur Américaine, 692, 693, 724, 725, 752
Levett, Christopher, *A voyage into New-England*, 71
Lezay-Marnezia, Claud François Adrien, Marquis de, *Lettres écrites des rives de l'Ohio*, 1295
Life . . . of Capt. Neville Frowde, 618, 915
Lincoln, Benjamin, *Description of the situation . . . land in . . . Maine*, 952
Lockhart, George, *Further account of East-New-Jersey*, 223
Lodowick, Charles, 266, 267
Long, John, *J. Long's Westindischen . . . See—und Land-Reisen*, 879; *Reisen*, 916; *Voyages*, 989; *Voyages and travels*, 878
Look before you leap, 1075-1078
Loskiel, George Henry, *Georg Hinrich Loskiels historiske Beskrifning*, 917; *Geschichte der Mission der evangelischen Brüder*, 795; *History of the mission of the United Brethren*, 990; *History of the Moravian mission*, 991
Louisiana, promotion, 318, 328, 429, 558, 602
Lovewell, John, 346-348, 1218, 1219
Lowry, Jean, *Journal of the captivity*, 544

M

Mc Donald, Philip, and Alexander Mc Leod, *Surprising account of the captivity*, 747, 780, 992, 1034, 1079, 1132
Maclaurin, J., 566
Mc Leod, Alexander, 747
Mc Murtry, Oscar, 1033
Maine, promotion, 11, 143, 447, 454, 461-464, 547, 552, 777, 952
Manheim, Frederick, 928, 958, 1146, 1192, 1223, 1224
A map of Virginia, 33
Marrant, John, *Adroddiad am ymdriniaethau*, 824; *Interesting narrative*, 818, 828-830; *Narrative*, 730-735, 761, 781, 810-817, 819-823, 825-827, 831-833
Martin, Francois Xavier, 1040
Martyn, Benjamin, *Account shewing the progress . . . Georgia*, 411, 418; *Impartial enquiry . . . Georgia*, 412; *Neueste und richtigste Nachricht . . . Georgia*, 433; *New and accurate account of . . . South-Carolina and Georgia*, 363, 369; *Reasons for establishing . . . Georgia*, 370-372; *Select tracts relating to colonies*, 364; *Some account of the designs of the trustees . . . Georgia*, 365, 366
Maryland, promotion, 84, 86, 88, 106, 153, 156, 256, 398, 510
Mason, John, 186; *Brief history of the Pequot War*, 392
Mason, Joseph, *Redemption Rock*, 1260

Massachusetts Bay Colony, 76, 80, 90, 132, 270, 273, 276, 283, 358, 445, 460, 517, 518, 569, 627, 628, 846
Massachusetts or the first planters of New-England, 273
Mather, Cotton, 686; *Decennium luctuosum*, 282; *Duodecennium luctuosum*, 320; *Fair weather*, 264; *Frontiers well defended*, 306; *Great examples of judgment and mercy*, 272; *Humiliations follow'd with deliverances*, 275; *Magnalia Christi Americana*, 294; *Memorial of the present deplorable state of New-England*, 307; *Present state of New-England*, 258; *Short history of New-England*, 268
Mather, Increase, *Brief history of the warr with the Indians*, 174, 175; *Essay for the recording of illustrious providences*, 228; *Relation of the troubles . . . in New-England*, 186
Mayhew, Matthew, *Brief narrative . . . Indians, of Martha's Vineyard*, 269
Mayhew, Thomas, 131
Maylem, John, *Gallic perfidy*, 524
Medicine, 78, 160, 448, 900
Megapolensis, Johannes, Jr., *Kort Ontwerp*, 104
Melancholy account, 864 A
Memorial for Peter Williamson, 566
Memorial for poor Peter Williamson, 548
Mercer, James, *Lands, For sale*, 796
Merrifield, Edward, *Story of the captivity . . . of Luke Swetland*, 741
Miami Purchase, 770, 771, 1090
Mignard, Jacques, *Quelques escrocs Anglais*, 1132 A
Miller, Johann Peter, *Chronicon Ephratense*, 748
Minard, John S., 713
Minot, George Richards, *History of the insurrections, in Massachusetts*, 782
Mirabilia Dei inter Indicos, 432
Mis Mac Rea, roman historique, 704
Mississippi, promotion, 1024-1029, 1119, 1133, 1134, 1147, 1177, 1178, 1183
Mississippi Bubble, 328
Mississippi Company, 328
Missive van William Penn, 231, 232
Mitchell, John, *Contest in America*, 520
Mittelberger, Gottlieb, *Gottlieb Mittelberger's Reise nach Pennsylvanien*, 511, 512
Model of the government of . . . East-New-Jersey, 243
Moderate and safe expedient, 106
Montgomery, Robert, *Account of the foundation . . . Golden Islands*, 329; *Description of the Golden Islands*, 330; *Discourse concerning . . . a new colony*, 322; *Proposals for raising a stock . . . colony of Azilia*, 323
Moody, James, *Lieutenant James Moody's narrative*, 679, 685
Moore, Francis, *Voyage to Georgia*, 428
More, Nicholas, *Letter from Doctor More*, 257
More news from Virginia, 187
Morris, Isaac, *Narrative of the dangers and distresses*, 453, 459
Morris, Thomas, *Miscellanies in prose and verse*, 880
Morse, Jedediah, *Description of the soil . . . Georgia Western Territory*, 1133
Morton, Nathaniel, *New-Englands memorial*, 155, 336, 614
Morton, Thomas, *New English Canaan*, 90
Mo[u]rning Virginia, 64
Mourt (or Morton), George, *Relation or journall*, 60
Moustier, Éleonore François Élie, Comte de, *Lettre*, 833 A

N

Nachricht wegen . . . Pennsilvania, 197

Nader Informatie . . . Pensylvania, 249, 250

Nairne, Thomas, *Letter from South Carolina,* 313, 325, 362

Narrative of an attempt made by the French . . . upon the Mohaques Country, 266

Narrative of a late expedition against the Indians, 1201

Narrative of Marie Le Roy, 533

Narrative of the capture of certain Americans, 669, 707

Narrative of the late massacres, 556

Narrative of the Pennsylvania frontier, 708, 709

Narrative of the planting of the Massachusets Colony, 270

Narrative of the sufferings of William and Elizabeth Fleming, 501-506

Narratives of a late expedition, 684

Narvaez, Pamfilio de, 3

Necker Tract, 792

Negroes, 541, 730-735, 761, 781, 810-833

Nelson, John, *Mary Rowlandson's narrative,* 1261

Neu-Gefundenes Eden, . . . Carolina, 398

Neue Nachricht . . . Carolina, 379

Neueste und richtigste Nachricht . . . Georgia, 433

New Albion, 97, 110, 118, 714-717

New and accurate account of South-Carolina and Georgia, 363, 369

New and further narrative of the state of New-England, 176

New and most exact account of . . . Carolina, 219

New England, description and promotion, 9, 10, 40, 44, 57, 61, 69, 71-74, 80, 81, 87, 89, 95, 109, 119, 155, 160, 162, 166, 185, 187, 190, 193, 215, 268, 269, 294, 336, 351, 384, 390, 395, 555, 587, 588, 614, 646, 846, 908, 909, 1134, 1176, 1177, 1178

New England, Council for, 57, 71

New England Mississippi Land Company, *Articles of association,* 1134, 1177; *Memorial,* 1178

New England's crisis, 179

New Englands first fruits, 98

New Englands plantation, 72-74

New-England's present sufferings, 170

New-England's prospect, 559

New Englands tears, 180

New Englands trials, 44, 61

New Hampshire, promotion, 354

New Haven Colony, promotion, 138

New-Haven's settling in New-England, 138

New Jersey, promotion, 97, 110, 118, 164, 165, 173, 178, 183, 194, 200, 201, 210, 217 A, 218, 223, 226, 237, 239, 243, 385, 560, 714-717

New Jersey, Scottish Proprietors' tracts, *See* Board of General Proprietors of the Eastern Division of New Jersey

New life of Virginia, 32

New Netherland, 57, 65, 70, 75, 79, 82, 83, 85, 92, 96, 97, 99-101, 103, 104, 110, 112, 117, 118, 133, 135, 136, 139, 140, 144, 146, 148, 150, 159, 244, 245

New Sweden, promotion, *See* Delaware, promotion

New voyage to Georgia, 387, 399

New York, description and promotion, 152, 157, 266, 267, 286, 289, 290, 312, 342, 352, 380, 403, 435, 444, 448, 449, 473, 477-480, 487-490, 513, 514, 519, 554, 580, 616, 623, 674, 675, 714-717, 723, 729, 785, 791, 867, 868, 887, 899, 918, 921, 926, 934, 984, 993, 994, 999, 1058, 1059, 1061, 1062, 1182, 1186, 1221, 1229-1232, 1263, 1264, 1265, 1296-1300

New York Province, *At a council held at Fort George . . . tracts of land . . . still remain uncultivated,* 380; *Encouragement given . . . to . . . settle in . . . New-York,* 403; House of Representatives, *Some queries sent up to his Excellency . . . fort for the defense of the Five Nations,* 286

New York Society for the Information and Assistance of Persons Emigrating from Foreign Countries, *Constitution,* 993; *From reviewing the great inconveniences,* 994

New York under the Dutch, *See* New Netherland

News from New-England, 177

Nicolls, Richard, *Conditions for new-planters,* 152

Norris, John, *Profitable advice for rich and poor,* 317

North American Land Company, 1071-1073; *Alterations proposed,* 1037; *Plan of association,* 1035, 1036; *Plan for the settlement of 552,500 acres of land,* 1080

North Carolina (see also under Carolina and S. C.), promotion, 398, 622, 922, 1035-1037, 1040, 1080

Northwest Territory, *Plat of the Seven Ranges of Townships,* 1081

Norton, John, *Redeemed captive,* 439

Note of the shipping . . . Virginia, 50, 52, 63

Notes on the State of Virginia, 728

Notice is hereby given . . . Tennessee Purchase, 883

Notice sur Kentucke, 792

Nouveau Mississipi, ou les dangers . . . Scioto, 838

Nouvelle relation de la Caroline, 246

Nouvelles du Scioto, 805

Nova Britannia, 15

Nova Francia, 16, 17

Nummehro in dem Neuen Welt, 381

Nuñez Cabeza de Vaca, Alvar, *Relacion,* 1, 2

O

Observations générales et impartiales sur l'affaire du Scioto, 834

Observations on a pamphlet, entitled Remarks on Dr. Gale's letter, 594

Observations on the present situation of landed property in America, 918

Observations on the present state of the waste lands, 626

Observations on the proposed state road, 1265

Observations relatives au . . . Scioto, 834 A

Observations sur la Virginie, 746

Observations to be followed . . . silk-wormes, 43

Observazione a chiunque dersideri passare in America, 727

Oglethorpe, James Edward. *See under his agent,* Benjamin Martyn

Ohio, promotion, 749, 753, 762-765, 770, 771, 774, 783, 784, 789, 793, 794, 797-801, 804, 805, 834, 834 A, 836, 838, 839, 1017, 1018, 1063, 1081, 1090, 1160, 1187, 1189

Ohio Company, *Articles of agreement,* 783; *Articles of an association,* 749, 762;
    At a meeting of the directors, 763, 764; *At a meeting of the directors and
    agents,* 784; *Contract,* 765
Oritz, Juan, 3
Outline of a plan for an establishment . . . Georgia, 1239

                                           P

Paine, Thomas, *Public good,* 668
Panther, Abraham, *Account of a beautiful young lady,* 766; *Surprising account of
    the discovery of a lady,* 767; *Surprising narrative of a young lady,* 768, 1038,
    1039, 1205, 1206; *Very surprising narrative,* 835, 995-997, 1082, 1083, 1135,
    1136, 1179, 1240-1246
Papers respecting intrusions by Connecticut claimants, 1084
Parlement de Paris etabli au Scioto, 836
Paskell, Thomas, *Abstract of a letter . . . Pennsylvania,* 224
Pastorius, Francis Daniel, 265; *Copia, eines, von einem Sohn,* 229; *Geographisch-
    statistische Beschreibung . . . Pensylvanien,* 919; *Sichere Nachricht auss
    America,* 229 A; *Umständige geographische Beschreibung . . . Pennsylvaniae,*
    287, 296; *Vier kleine . . . Tractätlein,* 259; (with Gabriel Thomas and
    Daniel Falckner), *Continuatio der Beschreibung,* 295
Pastorius, Melchior Adam, *Kurtze Beschreibung,* 265
Penhallow, Samuel, *History of the wars of New-England,* 351
Penn, William, *Briefe account of . . . Pennsylvania,* 198, 206, 207; *Description
    of the Province of West-Jersey,* 178; *Frame of the government of . . . Penn-
    silvania,* 208, 261; *A further account of . . . Pennsylvania,* 240, 241; *Infor-
    mation and direction,* 230, 247; *Instruction très-exacte,* 248; *Kort Bericht van
    Penn-Sylvania,* 196; *Kurtze Nachricht von . . . Pennsilvania,* 199; *A letter
    from, . . . to the . . . Free Society of Traders,* 225; *Missive van,* 231, 232;
    Nachricht wegen . . . Pennsilvania, 197; *Nader Informatie,* 249, 250; *Plan-
    tation work,* 209; *Present state of the Colony of West-Jersey,* 198; *Recüeil de
    diverses pieces,* 233; *Some account of the Province of Pennsilvania,* 195; *Some
    letters . . . from Pennsylvania,* 262; *Some proposals for a second settlement,*
    260; *Tweede Bericht,* 242
Pennington, Edward, *Description of Pennsbury Manor,* 585
Pennsylvania, promotion, 97, 110, 118, 195-199, 205-209, 220, 221, 224, 225,
    229-236, 238, 239, 240-242, 247-250, 257, 259-263, 265, 271, 280, 287, 292,
    293, 295, 296, 314, 315, 361, 398, 491-495, 511, 512, 515, 516, 585, 623,
    714-717, 748, 919, 960-963, 1006, 1007, 1035-1037, 1059, 1071-1073, 1085,
    1137-1139, 1207
Pennsylvania, Province, *By the Honourable John Penn* [against the Connecticut
    settlers], 632
Pennsylvania Land Company, *Plan of association,* 1137; *Proprietors . . . form . . .
    an association,* 1085; *Statement of the incumbrances,* 1138
Pennsylvania Property Company, *Plan of association,* 1139
Penrose, Jonathan, *Philadelphia, March 4, 1799. By virtue of a writ,* 1207
Pequot War, 92-94, 392
Perfect description of Virginia, 115
Perth Amboy, New Jersey, 210
Phelps and Gorham Purchase, 785, 999
Phillips, George, *Humble request,* 76
Pinfold, Charles, 335
Pittman, Philip, *Present state of the European settlements on the Missisippi,* 602

Plain facts, 672
Plaine description of the Barmudas, 35
Plan de vente de trois cent mille acres de terres, 963
Plan for the settlement of 552,500 acres of land, 1080
Plan of a society for the sale of lands, 998
Plan pour former un establissement en Caroline, 251
Plantaganet, Beauchamp, *Description of the Province of New Albion,* 110, 118
Plantation work, 209
Planters plea, 80
Plat of the Seven Ranges of Townships, 1080
Playfair, William, *Lettre et observations,* 836 A
Plockhoy, Pieter Corneliszoon, *Kort en klaer ontwerp,* 149
Plowden, Sir Edmund, grant, New Albion, 97, 110, 118, 714-717
Plymouth Colony, 58, 60, 90, 107, 116, 336
Plymouth Company (The Kennebeck Purchase), 447, 454, 462; *Advertisement . . . 1761,* 547; *Advertisement . . . 1763,* 552; *Defense of the remarks,* 463, 464; *Remarks on the plan,* 461
A poem on the late massacre in Virginia, 54
Ponteach: or the savages of America, 571
Pope, John, *Tour through the southern and western territories,* 920
Porter, Augustus, *Map of Messrs. Gorham & Phelps's Purchase,* 999
Post, Christian Frederick, *Second journal,* 534
Pownall, Thomas, *Considerations towards a general plan . . . for the English provinces,* 514; *Proposals for securing the friendship of the Five Nations,* 513; *Speedily will be published . . . A Map of the Middle British Colonies,* 647; *Topographical description of such parts of North America,* 651
Present state of Carolina, 204
Present state of His Majesties isles and territories in America, 252
Present state of New-England . . . Indian war, 168, 169
Present state of the Colony of West-Jersey, 198
Present state of the country . . . Louisiana, 429
Preston, Paul, *On the captivity of Benjamin Gilbert,* 841
Price, Daniel, *Saul's prohibition staide,* 18
Price, Jonathan, *Description of Occacock Inlet,* 1040
Profitable advice for rich and poor, 317
Proof and procedure . . . Peter Williamson, 568
Proposal for the speedy settlement of . . . lands, 723
Proposals by the proprietors of East-Jersey, 210
Proposals for raising a stock . . . colony in Azilia, 323
Proprietors of Brunswick Township, Maine, 461, 463, 464, 547, 552; *Advertisement,* 447, 454; *Answer to the remarks,* 462
Public good, 668
A publication by the Counsell of Virginia, 26
Purry, Jean Pierre, *Description abrégée de . . . Caroline,* 359, 367; *Description of . . . South Carolina,* 360; *Memoire presenté,* 344; *Memorial presented,* 345
Putnam, Israel, 778, 985, 1168-1171

R

Ramsay, David, 933
Rastel, Phillipe François de, 613
Rawson, Edward, 172
Reasons for establishing . . . Georgia, 370-372

Reck, Georg Philipp Friedrich, and Johann Martin Bolzius, Extract of the journals, 382
Recüeil de diverses pieces, concernant la Pensylvanie, 233
Redeemed captive, 439
Redres van de Abuysen, 100
Réflections offertes aux capitalistes de l'Europe, 926
Relaçam verdadeira, 3
Relaçõa de huma batalha . . . Lake Giorge, 519
Relation historique de l'expédition contre les Indiens de l'Ohio, 599
Relation of Maryland, 88
Relation of the Right Honourable the Lord De-La-Warre, 31
Relation of the successfull beginnings of . . . Mary-land, 86
Relation or journall of . . . Plimoth in New England, 60
Remarkable narrative of an expedition against the Indians, 1202
Remarks concerning the savages of North-America, 697
Remarks on the plan . . . proprietors of the Township of Brunswick, 461
Remarques sur la politesse des sauvages de l'Amerique Septentrionale, 698
Returned captive. A poem, 769, 837, 1247
Rhodes, John, 750, 1181, 1208, 1209
Rich, Robert, Newes from Virginia, 24
Rickman, Thomas Clio, Emigration to America, 1180
Ridley, Glocester, Sermon . . . Georgia, 434
Right of the Governor and Company of . . . Connecticut to claim and hold the
    lands . . . west of . . . New-York, 619
Risler, Jeremias, Leben August Gottlieb Spangenbergs, 1000; Spangenberg . . .
    Sa vie, 1001
Roach, John, Narrative of the surprising adventures, 1210; [Rhodes] Powow,
    1209; Surprizing adventures, 736-737, 750, 786, 1181, 1208
Rogers, Robert, Concise account of North America, 562, 595, 596; Journals, 563,
    597, 603; Ponteach: or the savages of America, 571
Rosier, James, True relation, 11
Rouso d'Eres, Charles Dennis, Memoirs, 1248
Roux, ———, Nouveau Mississipi, ou les dangers . . . Scioto, 838
Rowlandson, Mary, 1260, 1261; Captivity and deliverance, 1252; Narrative of
    the captivity, 604-606, 609, 620, 621, 881, 1002, 1003, 1041, 1086, 1249-
    1251, 1253-1259; Soveraignty & goodness of God . . . captivity, 211-213, 331;
    True history of the captivity, 214
Rundle, Thomas, Sermon . . . Georgia, 383
Ryer, John, Narrative, 953, 954

                                       S

St. Clair, Arthur, 863, 864, 896, 897
St. Clair's defeat. A poem, 896
St. John, J. Hector, 674
Salzburgers in Georgia, 378, 382, 393, 394, 406, 470
Sargent, John, 617
Saunders, Charles, Horrid cruelty of the Indians, 553
Scheme for the settlement of a new colony, 485, 486
Scioto Land Company, 793, 804, 805, 805 A, 805 B, 809 A, 833 A, 834, 834 A,
    836, 836 A, 838, 1132 A; Avis. Le Compagnie du Scioto, 799; Avis aux
    citoyens, 801; Édit du Congrès, 797; Nouveau prospectus, 839; Prospectus,
    798; Supplement, 800

Scot, George, *Model of the government of* . . . *East-New-Jersey,* 243
Scott, Frances, 964; *Narrative of the captivity,* 738; *Remarkable narrative,* 802, 964, 1098, 1211-1215; *True and wonderful narrative,* 751, 787
Scottow, Joshua, *Massachusetts or the first planters of New-England,* 273; *Nar-rative of the planting of the Massachusets Colony,* 270
Scotus Americanus, *Information concerning* . . . *North Carolina,* 622
Scudder, William, *Journal,* 1004
Seccombe, Joseph, 391
Second letter to a friend . . . *defeat of the French army at Lake George,* 477
Seeing it hath pleased God, 30
Seelig, Johann Gottfried, *Copia eines Send-Schreibens,* 271
Seguenot, Father François, *Letter from a Romish priest,* 356
Select tracts relating to colonies, 364
Seller, John, *A description of New-England,* 193
Sermon preached at Plimmoth in New-England December 9. 1621, 58
Sewall, Samuel, *Phaenomena quaedam Apocalyptica,* 276
Shakespeare, William, *Tempest,* origin of, 23, 28
Shepard, Thomas, *Clear sun-shine,* 111; *Day-breaking, if not the sun-rising,* 108
Short account of . . . *Virginia,* 388
Short collection of the most remarkable passages, 126
Short description of . . . *South-Carolina,* 601
Short description of the State of Tennassee, 1087, 1088, 1140
Short description of the Tennassee government, 955
Short narrative of the claim, 354
Shrigley, Nathaniel, *True relation of Virginia and Mary-land,* 156
Sicilius, 1028, 1029
Sittliche Schilderung von Amerika, 690
Slover, John, 684, 1201-1204
Smith, Daniel, *Description abrégée du territoire* . . . *sud de l'Ohio,* 956; *Short description of the State of Tennassee,* 1087, 1088, 1140; *Short description of the Tennassee government,* 955
Smith, James, *Account of the remarkable occurrences,* 1216; *Treatise, on the mode and manner of Indian war,* 1217
Smith, John, *Advertisements for the unexperienced planters,* 81; *Description of New England,* 40; *Generall historie of Virginia,* 68; *New Englands trials,* 44, 61; *True relation,* 12; *True travels,* 77; (with William Symonds), *A map of Virginia,* 33
Smith, Samuel, *Sermon* . . . *Georgia,* 373
Smith, Thomas, 616
Smith, William (historian of New York), *Information to emigrants,* 623
Smith, William (of New York), 616
Smith, Provost William, *Account of the* . . . *Illinois and Ouabache Land Companies,* 1089, 1141-1143; *Brief history of the rise and progress of the charitable scheme,* 491; *Brief state of* . . . *Pennsylvania,* 493-495, 515; *Brief view of the conduct of Pennsylvania,* 516; *Examination of the Connecticut claim,* 633, 634; *Historical account of the expedition against the Ohio Indians,* 564, 572, 598; *Kurtze Nachricht, von der Christlichen* . . . *Anstalt,* 492; *Relation historique de l'expédition contre les Indiens de l'Ohio,* 599; *Voyage historique et politique, dans l'Amérique, du Chevalier Henry Bouquet,* 657
Some account of the designs of the trustees . . . *Georgia,* 365, 366
Some account of the Province of Pennsilvania, 195
Some information respecting America, 977

Some letters . . . from Pennsylvania, 262
Some proposals for a second settlement in . . . Pennsylvania, 260
Soon after the last European peace, 610
South Carolina (see also under Carolina and N. C.), promotion, 313, 317, 325,
    359, 360, 362, 363, 367, 369, 398, 601, 882, 1035-1037, 1042
South-Carolina Society, Information, 1042
South Carolina Yazoo Company, Extract from the proceedings, 882
Spangenberg, August Gottlieb, Account of the manner in which the . . . United
    Brethren, preach the Gospel, 788, 803; Leben . . . Nicholaus Ludwig . . . von
    Zinzendorf, 615; Von der Arbeit der Evangelischen Brüder, 680
Sparke, Michael, Greevous grones, 51
Spies, British, in Revolutionary War, 645, 679, 685
Staden, Hans, Warhaftige Historia, 4
Stadnitski, Pieter, Voorafgaand Bericht, 921
State of facts. Shewing the right of certain companies, 1027
State of the lands said to be . . . within . . . Connecticut, 607
State of the process, Peter Williamson, 567
Statement of the petitioners in the case of the Walpole Company, 610
Steendam, Jacob, Klacht van Nieuw-Amsterdam, 144; 't Lof van Nuw-Nederland,
    146; Zeede-sangen, 159
Stephens, Thomas, Account shewing . . . Georgia, 420; Brief account . . . Georgia,
    426; Hard case of the distressed people of Georgia, 419
Stephens, William, Journal . . . Georgia, beginning October 20, 1737, 421; Jour-
    nal received February 7, 1741, 422; State of the Province of Georgia, 423
Stith, William, History of . . . Virginia, 436, 465
Stockwell, Quentin, 228
Stoddard, Anthony, At a council held at Boston . . . 1678, 192; Report of the
    trustees . . . for the ransom of the captives, 191
Storck, William, Account of East-Florida, 573-576, 600; Description of East-
    Florida, 600, 635; Extract from the account of East Florida, 577
Strange news from Virginia, 188
Summary, historical and political, 442, 455
Surprizing account of the captivity of Miss Hannah Willis, 1222
Susquehannah Case, 636
Susquehannah Company, 556, 592, 593, 594, 607, 619, 629, 632, 633, 634, 636,
    637, 638, 676, 1050, 1060, 1084
Susquehannah River, 1059
Susquehannah title stated and examined, 1050
Swarton, Hannah, 275, 294
Swetland, Luke, Narrative of the captivity, 740; Very remarkable narrative, 739
Symmes, John Cleves, To the respectable public, 770, 771; A true copy of Judge
    Symme's [sic] pamphlet, 1090
Symmes, Thomas, History of the fight of the intrepid Captain John Lovell, 1218;
    Lovewell lamented, 346; Historical memoirs of the late fight at Piggwacket,
    347
Symonds, William, Virginia, 19; (with John Smith), A map of Virginia, 33

T

Tailfer, Patrick, True and historical narrative . . . Georgia, 413-415
Tennessee, promotion, 883, 955, 956, 1043, 1087, 1088, 1140, 1262
Tennessee Company, Notice is hereby given, 883; Tennessee Company to Messrs.
    Strawbridge, Jackson and Dexter, 1262

Terres dans l'Amérique, 922
Territorial Company, *Plan of association*, 1043
Thomas, Gabriel, 295; *Historical and geographical account of . . . Pensilvania*, 280
Thomson, Charles *Enquiry into the causes of the alienation of the Delaware and Shawanese Indians*, 535
Thomson, John, *Travels and surprising adventures*, 549
Thoresby, Ralph, *Excellency and advantage of doing good*, 440
Thoughts on emigration, 924, 978
Tillier, Rodolphe, *Memoire*, 1263; *Translation of a memorial*, 1264
Timberlake, Henry, *Memoirs*, 565; *Voyage*, 1091
To all farmers and tradesmen, 616
To the King's most Excellent Majesty . . . memorial of . . . Thomas Walpole, 640
To the respectable public, 770, 771
Tompson, Benjamin, *New Englands crisis*, 179; *New Englands tears*, 180
Tontines et Loteries—Immobiliaires, *Terres dans l'Amérique*, 922
Toulmin, Harry, *Description of Kentucky*, 923; *Thoughts on emigration*, 924
Trauailes of an Englishman, 8
Travels and surprising adventures of John Thomson, 549
Treatise of New England, 119
A trip to New-England, 283
True account of the most considerable occurrences, 181
True and sincere declaration . . . of Virginia, 27
True copy of the grant . . . New Albion, 717
True declaration of . . . Virginia, 28
True description of Carolina, 203
True discourse of . . . Virginia, 38
True relation of the late battell, 91
True relation of . . . Virginia, 12
Trumbull, Benjamin, *Plea in vindication of the Connecticut title*, 637, 638
Tryon, Thomas, *Country-man's companion*, 234; *Planter's speech to his neighbours*, 235
Twee Missiven geschreven uyt Pensilvania, 236
Tweede Bericht ofte Relaas van William Penn, 242
Two letters to a friend, 478
Two years journal in New-York, 289, 290

U

Underhill, John, *Newes from America*, 92
Urlsperger, Samuel, *Americanisches Ackerwerk Gottes*, 470; *Ausführlichen Nachrichten*, 389; *Send-Schreiben*, 393; *Zuverläsziges Sendschreiben*, 394
Usselinx, Willem, *Argonautica Gustaviana*, 85

V

Valinière, Pierre Huet de la, *Vraie histoire*, 925
Van Campen, Moses, 710-713; *Narrative of the capture of certain Americans*, 669, 707; *Narrative of the Pennsylvania frontier*, 708, 709
Vandalia Company, 610, 617, 624, 626, 639, 640, 648, 649-652, 663, 672
Vandelure, John, *History of*, 1188; *Narrative of the travels*, 1188; Van Delure, *History of the voyages and adventures*, 1188
Van Leason, James, *Narrative of a voyage*, 1188
Van Pradelles, Benjamin, *Réflections offertes*, 926

Van Rensselaer, Kiliaen, *Insinuatie*, 99; *Redres*, 100; *Waerschovwinge*, 101
Varlo, Charles, *Conditions for letting or selling* . . . *New Albion*, 714; *Earl of Albion's proclamation*, 715; *Finest part of America*, 716; *True copy of the grant*, 717
Varnum, James Mitchell, *Oration, delivered at Marietta*, 789
Vaughan, William, *Newlanders cure*, 78
Verkoop van de . . . *Patent van Kayadarosseras*, 729
Verlangte, nicht erlangte Canaan, 314, 315
Vertoogh van Nieu-Neder-Land, 117
View of the present situation of . . . *Genesee Country*, 1221
View of the title of Indiana, 649, 652, 663
Vincent, Philip, *True relation of the late battell*, 91, 93, 94
Virginia, promotion, 156, 161, 188, 256, 297, 300-303, 337-339, 343, 398, 510, 719, 728, 796, 1035-1037, See also under Virginia Company.
Virginia Company, 12-16, 18, 19, 22-24, 31-33, 37, 38, 43, 51, 53-56, 59, 66, 67; *A briefe declaration*, 41; *Considering there is no publicke action*, 20; *Declaration for* . . . *drawing the* . . . *lottery*, 39; *Declaration of the state of the colonie*, 45-49; *For the planting in Virginia*, 21; *Forasmuch as notwithstanding* . . . *lotteries*, 34; *Inconveniences that have happened*, 62; *Mo[u]rning Virginia*, 64; *Note of the shipping*, 50, 52, 63; *A publication by the Counsell of Virginea*, 26; *Seeing it hath pleased God*, 30; *A true and sincere declaration*, 27; *A true declaration*, 28; *Whereas sundrie the adventurers to Virginia*, 36; *Whereas the good Shippe* . . . *Hercules*, 25; *Whereas upon the return of Sir Thomas Dale*, 42
Virginia richly valued, 13
Voluntier's march, 348
Voorhees, Oscar McMurtrie, *New Jersey woman's captivity*, 1033; *Short history of the capture* . . . *of Mrs. Mary Kinnan*, 1033
Vorspiel der Neuen-Welt, 361
Voyage historique et politique, dans l'Amérique, du Chevalier Henry Bouquet, 657
Voyages . . . *of Captain Richard Falconer*, 326, 341, 349, 374, 375, 555, 591, 720-722
Vries, David Pietersz. de, *Korte historiael ende Journaels*, 135
Vryheden by de Vergaderinghe, 79
Vryheden ende Exemptien, 82

W

W., J., *Letter from New-England*, 215
Waerschovwinge, Verboth, ende Toe-latinghe, 101
Waldo, Samuel, *Boston, May 22d. 1735*. . . . *St. George's River*, 390; *Defence of the title*, 395; *Samuel Waldo of Boston, Merchant* . . . *settle towns* . . . *St. George's River*, 384
Walker, Fowler, *Case of Mr. John Gordon*, 616 A
Wallwille, Maria Owliam, *Wilde Europäerinn*, 1220
Walpole Company, 610, 617, 624, 626, 639, 640, 648, 649, 652, 663, 672
Walpole, Thomas, 617
Walton, William, *Narrative of the captivity* . . . *Benjamin Gilbert*, 718, 742, 840, 842-845
Ward, Edward ("Ned"), *A trip to New-England*, 283
Warr in New-England visibly ended, 189
Warren, Robert, *Industry and diligence* . . . *sermon* . . . *Georgia*, 400

Warville, Jean Pierre Brissot de, 862
Washington, George, *Journal of Major George Washington*, 471, 472; *Mount Vernon . . . The subscriber would lease about 30,000 acres of land*, 719
Washington, D. C., description and anti-promotion, 1075-1078
Wassenaer, Nicholaas van, 65
Waterhouse, Edward, *Declaration of the state of . . . Virginia*, 66
Watts, George, *Sermon . . . Georgia*, 396
Weiser, Conrad, *Translation of a German letter*, 554; *Wohl-gemeindter und ernstlicher Rath*, 416
Wertmuller, Joris, and Cornelius Bom, *Twee Missiven geschreven uyt Pensilvania*, 236
Wesley, Samuel, *Georgia, a poem*, 397
West, Jane, *History of Ned Evans*, 1092, 1093, 1144, 1145
West, Thomas, third Lord De La Warr, *Relation of*, 31
West-Indische Compagnie, *Articulen*, 83; *Conditien*, 139, 140; *Vryheden by de Vergaderinghe*, 79; *Vryheden ende Exemptien*, 82
Western Reserve in Ohio, 1017, 1018, 1063, 1160, 1187
Wharton, Edward, *New-England's present sufferings*, 170
Wharton, Samuel, *Advantages of a settlement upon the Ohio*, 624; *Conditions on the agreement . . . Thomas Walpole*, 639; *Facts and observations respecting the country*, 648; *Plain facts*, 672; *Report of the Lords Commissioners . . . on the petition of . . . Thomas Walpole, Benjamin Franklin, John Sargent, and Samuel Wharton*, 617; *Statement of the petitioners in the case of the Walpole Company*, 610; *To the King's most Excellent Majesty . . . memorial of . . . Thomas Walpole*, 640; (with Edward Bancroft), *View of the title to Indiana*, 649, 652, 663
Wheeler, Thomas, *Thankfull remembrance*, 182
Whereas sundrie the aduenturers to Virginia, 36
Whereas the good Shippe . . . Hercules, 25
Whereas upon the return of Sir Thomas Dale, 42
Whitaker, Alexander, *Good newes from Virginia*, 37
White, Andrew, *Declaration of the Lord Baltimore's plantation*, 85 A; *Relation of the successful beginnings*, 86
White, John (of New England), 76; *Planters plea*, 80
White, John (of Virginia), drawings by, 7
Whitfield, Henry, *Banners of grace and love*, 141; *Light appearing more and more*, 124; *Strength out of weaknesse*, 127-130
Wilde Europäerinn, 1220
Williams, Edward, *Virginia in America*, 125; *Virginia's discovery of silke-wormes*, 122; *Virgo triumphans: or, Virginia richly and truly valued*, 120, 121
Williams, John, *Captivity and deliverance*, 1047; *Good fetch'd out of evil*, 298, 686; *Redeemed captive*, 308, 332, 525, 625, 641, 653, 957, 1044-1046, 1048-1049 A
Williams, Roger, *Key into the language of America*, 102
Williams, Solomon, *Power and efficacy of the prayers of the people*, 1049 A
Williams, Stephen, 1049 A
Williams, Stephen W., *Biographical memoir of Rev. John Williams*, 1049
Williamson, Charles, *Description of the Genesee Country*, 1182, 1221; *Description of the settlement of the Genesee Country*, 1221; *Observations on the proposed state road*, 1265; *View of the present situation of . . . Genesee Country*, 1221

Williamson, Peter, 703; *Authentic narrative,* 1270, 1273, 1275, 1276; *Brief account of the war in N. America,* 545; *Curious adventures,* 1289; *Eventful life,* 1284; *French and Indian cruelty,* 521, 526, 526 A, 536, 550, 578, 579, 772, 927, 1005; *June 20,* 1765. *State of the process,* 567; *Life and adventures,* 1271, 1272; *Life and curious adventures,* 1266, 1267, 1269, 1277, 1278, 1286-1288, 1290-1292; *Life, travels, voyages, . . . Paul Jones,* 1274, 1279-1282; *Memorial for,* 566; *Memorial for poor,* 548; *Proof and procedure,* 568; *Some considerations on the present state of affairs,* 527; *Sufferings,* 1094; *Surprising history,* 1268; *Surprising life and sufferings,* 1283, 1285; *Travels,* 590; *Travels and surprising adventures of John Thomson,* 549

Willis, Hannah, *Surprizing account of the captivity,* 1222

Wilson, Samuel, *Account of . . . Carolina,* 216, 217

Winkfield, Unca Eliza, *Female American,* 586, 1293, 1294

Winslow, Edward, 60; *Dangers of tolerating levellers,* 116; *Good newes from New-England,* 69; *Hypocrisie unmasked,* 107

Winthrop, John, 76; *Declaration of former passages,* 105; *Journal,* 846

Wolley, Charles, *A two years journal in New-York,* 289, 290

Wood, William, *New Englands prospect,* 87, 89, 95, 559

Woodnoth, Arthur, *Short collection,* 126

Woolman, John, *Works,* 642

Worthye and famous history of . . . Terra Florida, 29

Y, Z

Yazoo Frauds, 1024-1027, 1097, 1119, 1133, 1134, 1147, 1177, 1178, 1183, 1190, 1191

Young, Arthur, *Observations on the present state of the waste lands,* 626

Zeekere Vrye-Voorlagen, 150

Zinzendorf, Nicholaus Ludwig von, 615

LAUS DEO